About the Editors

Thillai Rajan A is a Professor in the Department of Management Studies, Indian Institute of Technology Madras. He is also an associate at the Mossavar Rahmani Center for Business and Government, Harvard Kennedy School, Harvard University. His research interests encompass start-ups, ventures and SMEs. During 2009–18, he edited the annual India Venture Capital and Private Equity Report. In 2020, he played a key role in the formation of the Innovation, Venturing and Entrepreneurship in India Network (iVEIN), a multi-institutional consortium to research on innovation and venturing in India. He is also a co-founder of YNOS Venture Engine, a start-up set up to address the pain points of early-stage entrepreneurs.

Srivardhini K Jha is an Associate Professor in the Entrepreneurship area at the Indian Institute of Management Bangalore. Her research has been published in several leading international journals such as MIS Quarterly, MIT Sloan Management Review, Annals of the New York Academy of Sciences and others. She teaches MBA, PhD and executive education courses on Entrepreneurship, Corporate Innovation and Strategic Partnerships. A firm believer in experiential learning, she has developed simulations and in-class exercises to bring theoretical concepts to life in the classroom. Prior to moving into academia, she held several senior managerial positions at Microsoft, Sun Microsystems and Infosys.

Joffi Thomas is an Associate Professor in the Marketing area at the Indian Institute of Management Kozhikode. He has a rich blend of teaching, research, consulting and training as well as industry experience with focus on aligning customer management and business strategy, for over two decades. He has been engaged in outcome-focussed organisational interventions, including consulting and training for several leading public and private corporations. He has been instrumental in enhancing their effectiveness in managing customers.

Rohan Chinchwadkar is an Assistant Professor (Finance) at the Shailesh J Mehta School of Management, Indian Institute of Technology Bombay. He has been an Assistant Professor at the Indian Institute of Management Tiruchirappalli and a Visiting Professor at the Indian Institute of Management Calcutta. He holds a PhD (Finance) from the Indian Institute of Management Calcutta and a BTech (Electronics) from the Veermata Jijabai Technological Institute, Mumbai, and has worked with the prestigious consulting firm McKinsey & Company. His research and teaching interests lie in entrepreneurial finance, money and banking, and practice theory. He has written opinion pieces for national newspapers like *The Economic Times, Mint, The Hindu Business Line, The Financial Express* and *Bloomberg Quint.* He is also a national-level silver medallist in table tennis.

TESTIMONIALS

It is very heartening to see contemporary work on entrepreneurship from academic experts in the Indian context. It is timely with the start-up ecosystem taking centre stage due to all stars aligning together in India – the emergence of accelerators/ incubators, active mentoring and angel investing momentum, disruptive companies building scale and valuation, potential IPO of tech giants in India and a lot of risk capital funding flowing in. The inter-institutional effort involving multiple IIMs and IITs, a first of its kind is worthy of emulation as Indian case studies and published research on entrepreneurship are very much needed especially covering emerging new age sectors like deep tech start-ups, socio-tech ventures, Fin-tech and Agri-tech.

K Ganesh, Serial Entrepreneur, Promoter – BigBasket Portea Medical, HomeLane, GrowthStory.in

Having been a keen observer of the Indian innovation and start-up scenario for over fifteen years, I had long wondered why a book on the evolution of the Indian ecosystem had not been published. Now it is here – what a great compilation of deep insights. Every innovation and start-up ecosystem is idiosyncratic. This book will advance the cause of bringing enterprise in India into the sweet spot of nation-building.

R Gopalakrishnan, Author and Corporate Advisor, former Vice Chairman, Hindustan Unilever and Director, Tata Sons

Indian capitalism is changing – from being dominated by family-run businesses to one being driven by first-generation entrepreneurs. This book provides a comprehensive overview of different elements of the start-up ecosystem, and will help inform readers about the change that lies in the decade ahead.

Gautam Mago, General Partner at A91 Partners; former Managing Director at Sequoia Capital

Entrepreneurs are now looking forward to building India-based consumer internet and software start-ups with high focus on deep-tech for global delivery, while retaining the omni-channel delivery models for local needs. This book brings together a sharp link between the early evolution of the Indian start-up ecosystem, the regulatory evolution and the wide venture financing options created for entrepreneurs. Particularly, the pictorial narration of the book was innovative.

Abhijeet Muzumdar, Head of Amazon Smbhav Venture Fund

Shifting Orbits outlines the period from our independence to the present day while also touching upon essential enabling factors such as corporate-start-up collaboration thesis, patenting, funding, incubation, and the various key players across the start-up ecosystem. It is a commendable interdisciplinary effort from academicians, researchers, and operators – to provide a holistic view on 'what was' to 'what is' to 'what it should be' through in-depth research and analysis. This book stands out because of how it takes a "systems approach" to acknowledge the current state while also laying out what we should do to unlock value. The book's narrative is all-encompassing and comprehensive. Whether you're an entrepreneur, an investor or a start-up enthusiast, there's something for everyone to learn.

Pari Natarajan, CEO, Zinnov

Very few publications have attempted to capture all the building blocks of the entrepreneurial ecosystem – and this publication does a fantastic job of covering all the complicated nuances of constructing such ecosystems!

Madan Padaki, President, TiE Bangalore, and Co-founder GAME (Global Alliance for Mass Entrepreneurship)

This book explains the key building blocks making this innovation happen, the various policies by the government, the initiatives by our higher education institutions and corporates and the tremendous work done by various leaders across the social, political and business spectrum. A must read for all who have an interest in innovation and in making a positive impact on society.

TV Mohandas Pai, Chairman, Aarin Capital Partners

This book distills what the experts think about the start-up world. It documents how start-ups participate and connect to the innovation ecosystem, and how they impact key sectors like education, healthcare and financial services. It is a good resource for people to understand the Indian start-up world deeply.

Hari Pulakkat, Editor, Shaastra, and Former Senior Editor *The Economic Times*

This book is a must read for anyone seeking to understand the Indian start-up ecosystem. The trajectory from a fledgling stature to become the third largest start-up ecosystem in the world is well brought out by researchers from reputed institutions across India. The book also provides a number of useful recommendations for policymakers, like creating innovative funding mechanisms such as Social Stock Exchange for social sector start-ups.

NS Raghavan, Co-founder of Infosys Technologies and Philanthropist

The rapid increase in the number of homegrown unicorns in recent years shows how the Indian start-up ecosystem has come into its own. This book is brimming with insights from scholars as well as entrepreneurs on how the start-up ecosystem can be deepened, covering key issues on innovation, incubators and funding. It deserves to be read by policymakers, practitioners, researchers and students.

Dr. Niranjan Rajadhyaksha, Research Director and Senior Fellow, IDFC Institute and former Executive Editor, *Mint*

Shifting Orbits vividly captures the vibrancy and potency of the start-up ecosystem in India. It blends perspectives from the lens of academia as also from that of practitioners to present a comprehensive view of the hot-bed of global entrepreneurship. In addition to covering innovation, incubation and funding, the book also provides clear insights on specific thematics – agritech, edtech, healthtech and fintech. Shifting Orbits is a must read to gain meaningful understanding of the metamorphosis happening in the Indian start-up landscape.

K Ramakrishnan, Senior Managing Director Spark Capital Advisors (India) and Veteran Investment Banker

Continued on page iv

Shifting Orbits

Decoding the Trajectory of the Indian Start-up Ecosystem

Shifting Orbits paints a complete picture and provides an in-depth understanding of the country's start-up ecosystem. It is a must read for anyone interested in innovation and start-ups. The four section of this book trace the developments over the years, put issues in perspective, draw upon lessons learnt and prescribe policy formulations to make India a start-up powerhouse. Given my long years of association with the ecosystem, I would venture to say that this is probably the most comprehensive publication on the subject.

R Ramaraj, Senior Advisor, Elevar Equity, and Co-Founder and Former CEO, Sify

Shifting Orbits has brought a fresh outlook to the Indian start-up ecosystem. Today, students graduating from IITs, IIMs and NITs as well as those from small town-based tier 2 and tier 3 colleges, think about joining a start-up or starting one of their own. Also the acceptability of parents for such risk taking has turned around. This is reflected in this book about the changing trajectory.

Dr Anil Sahasrabudhe, Chairman All India Council for Technical Education

The Indian start-up ecosystem is the most exciting in the world given the combination of visionary leaders, exceptional engineering talent, an underserved domestic market and a young workforce striving to create a better future. This book brings together leading entrepreneurs, investors and academics to intelligently unpack this market and analyse the key opportunities and obstacles. This is a must read book for anyone interested in the world's most innovative and promising market.

Eric Savage, Co-founder and CEO, Unitus Capital

In the midst of the gloom and doom of Coronavirus, 21 more Indian start-ups became Unicorns in 2020 and Q1 2021. At this juncture, it is important to ask: how can we strengthen the foundations in order to ensure that the start-up ecosystem can continue to grow in breadth and depth? How can we broad base the catalytic role played by angel investors, family offices and VCs?

This timely book presents a balanced view of the Indian start-up and venturing ecosystem: celebrating the wonderful growth over the last decade but, at the same time, highlighting various aspects that deserve attention from the ecosystem participants. The book provides foundations for identifying solutions that can guide us towards a more start-up friendly policy regime, a more broad based venture investment ecosystem, and a society that derives more benefit from the inherent enterprising zeal of the Indian entrepreneurs.

Dr. Ajay Sethi, Venture Capitalist, Accel

This book shines a light on the contours of the emerging innovation architecture of start-ups in India. Our start-ups are becoming bolder ... they are leveraging digital public infrastructure like India Stack aggressively. A new India is slowly taking shape in front of our eyes.

Sharad Sharma, Co-founder, iSPIRT Foundation

Shifting Orbits is an insightful collection of articles based on original research and in-depth analysis. A first of its kind, this book is an inter-institutional effort involving multiple IIMs and IITs with contributions from experts in the area. Through analytical articles, roundtable articles and case studies, the rapid evolution of the start-up ecosystem in India is covered across innovation, incubation, financing and in-depth study of various sectors. The book is the outcome of a commendable effort in capturing one of the largest start-up ecosystems, provides important insights to a range of ecosystem actors – deeptech start-ups, socio-tech ventures, large corporates, venture capitalists and policymakers.

Dr Devi Shetty, Founder and Chairman, Narayana Health

A lot has happened in the innovation and entrepreneurship ecosystem in India in the last 20 years. Shifting Orbits attempts to bring it all together - so we see the "whole elephant" taking shape – and also shows us the enormity of what is happening in each part of this ecosystem. The combination of insightful analysis of the limited data available, and easy to understand frameworks to guide future action is a big value add for entrepreneurs, investors and just anyone interested in this space.

Rajan Srikanth, Chairman and Managing Director SmartKapital, and Co-President, Keiretsu Forum, Chennai and Singapore

I am very glad to read this book on Entrepreneurship. It is the true celebration of the spirit of New India, Young India and the enormous opportunities available for them to seize the moment!

It would be wonderful to see all stakeholders specifically focussing on inclusive entrepreneurship, making the ecosystem equally available to people who are not privileged to have studied in storied institutions or coming from metros. And it would also be wonderful to see more entrepreneurs creating innovative solutions for the real-life problems of the underprivileged and low-income population of the country, especially rural.

This would ensure that we can savour the taste of success without the guilt of creating a divided society. May entrepreneurship march on and be the bridge between the haves and the have-nots!

Vasudevan PN, Managing Director & CEO Equitas Small Finance Bank

The essays in this book provide a terrific perspective on ecosystem actors including VCs, lenders, policymakers, companies and incubators and also the most promising sectors for mass entrepreneurship. I recommend it highly.

Ravi Venkatesan, Founder and Chairman of GAME (Global Alliance for Mass Entrepreneurship)

Shifting Orbits

Decoding the Trajectory of the Indian Start-up Ecosystem

Edited by

Thillai Rajan A
Professor, Department of Management Studies
Centre for Research on Start-ups and Risk Financing
Indian Institute of Technology Madras

Srivardhini K Jha
Associate Professor, Entrepreneurship
Indian Institute of Management Bangalore

Joffi Thomas
Associate Professor
Indian Institute of Management Kozhikode

Rohan Chinchwadkar
Assistant Professor, Shailesh J Mehta School of Management
Indian Institute of Technology Bombay

Universities Press

SHIFTING ORBITS: DECODING THE TRAJECTORY OF THE INDIAN START-UP ECOSYSTEM

UNIVERSITIES PRESS (INDIA) PRIVATE LIMITED

Registered Office
3-6-747/1/A & 3-6-754/1, Himayatnagar, Hyderabad 500 029, Telangana, India
info@universitiespress.com; www.universitiespress.com

Distributed by
Orient Blackswan Private Limited

Registered Office
3-6-752 Himayatnagar, Hyderabad 500 029 Telangana, India

Other Offices
Bengaluru / Chennai / Guwahati / Hyderabad / Kolkata / Mumbai / New Delhi / Noida / Patna

Reprinted 2022, 2023, 2024

Cover and book design:

ISBN : 978-93-89211-95-5
e-ISBN : 978-93-89211-96-2

502071

Typeset in IBM Plex Sans 9.5/14 points

Printed in India at
Ratna Offset, Chennai 600 014

Published by
Universities Press (India) Private Limited
3-6-747/1/A & 3-6-754/1, Himayatnagar, Hyderabad 500 029, Telangana, India

Editorial Advisory Board

Consulting Editor
N Ramakrishnan

Assistant Research Editors
Akshay Natteri Mangadu
Rashmi Dyondi
Sumelika Bhattacharyya

Research Assistance
Arushi Gupta
Ramesh Kuruva

Practice Editor
Dinesh Tiwari

Illustrations
Florina Soren
Manvi Vakharia
Puneeth R
K Raja
KG Rangarajan

Foreword

Building an ecosystem for innovation excellence

The Indian economy is at an inflection point. The COVID-19 pandemic–induced lockdown took a toll on all types of economic activity for the major part of 2020. Happily, there are now indications that the economy is bouncing back into positive territory earlier than expected. Projections for GDP growth are being revised upwards and the BSE SENSEX keeps touching new peaks.

However, we are not yet out of the woods, especially with a second surge staring us in the face. While large and established businesses have found ways to move past the COVID-19 period, a large number of start-ups and small and medium enterprises (SMEs) have suffered, not to mention workers who had left their homes to find employment in different parts of the country. It is more important than ever for the country to get back on its feet, particularly to generate employment to meet the needs and aspirations of our ever-growing youthful population. If ever there was a time for us to innovate ourselves out of our problems, it is now. The most wonderful silver lining to the darkness of the last year is that the pandemic has served as a catalyst to innovation, particularly among start-ups.

Our entrepreneurs, young and old alike, have mitigated the effects of the pandemic by using technology to solve the difficulties thrown up by the pandemic, be it in the financial services sector or in healthcare or in education or in the door delivery of food, medicines and groceries. Each of these start-ups is unique and harnesses technology and increased Internet penetration to serve a growing population hungry for better services and products. The strides made by ventures in the financial inclusion space or in online education, where there is a lack of proper classroom infrastructure or inadequate teachers, are tremendous. In the course of tackling the pandemic, they have mapped the face of the future.

I am very happy that this publication covers so many aspects of this evolving scenario. I think it is a wonderful development that graduates from elite engineering and management institutions are no longer looking in such large numbers to go abroad in search of greener pastures. There is increasing scope for them to start their own ventures here, for both domestic and for global markets. Over the years, the ecosystem has matured. Almost all technical, scientific and management institutions have in-house incubators that help and encourage entrepreneurs to develop their idea into a viable business. Faculty members with years of theoretical experience are willing to spare their time and effort in helping these budding entrepreneurs go to market, most often picking up equity stakes in the ventures for their efforts. The pandemic could well be the turning point in the battle for our best brains. The success of an institution should no longer be measured just by the number of graduate or postgraduate students or doctoral candidates it churns out, but by the number of entrepreneurs that come out of its portals.

Another significant development that is aiding the growth of entrepreneurship is the return to India of those who had stints in the corporate world or in start-ups abroad, especially in Silicon Valley, who are either setting up ventures themselves here or helping out other start-ups. We are also seeing the trend of entrepreneurs who have made money by selling their business to larger companies taking fresh guard for a second innings or backing start-ups with money and their experience. The much-maligned public sector too is actively engaging with start-ups, helping them in pilot tests or building a proof of concept or getting their product ready for the market. All this augurs well for the start-up ecosystem in the country. With a greater emphasis now on a self-reliant India, an Atmanirbhar Bharat, the start-ups have an even greater role to play as opportunities abound.

The third, largely unsung, development is that accelerators aimed at specific sectors have been set up across the country. Ventures are no longer concentrated in just the metros; numerous initiatives have come up in tier two and three towns. There are enterprises that are solving problems for the bottom of the pyramid population in a commercial way. Enterprising founders are using technology to address the various issues in agriculture, looking at the complete value chain – from the farm to the fork.

We are also seeing a gradual increase in the number of mentors – individuals with years of experience who are willing to help the entrepreneurs in their initial years, which greatly increases the chances of success of the venture. Entrepreneurs too are much better networked now than before, always willing to tap into whatever resource that is available to help build their business.

And finally, there is the issue of funding, which is one of the most critical parts of the ecosystem. I think this is growing satisfactorily, although it can always do with more participants. Angel investors, seed funds, venture capital and private equity funds are beginning to burgeon. Quite a few start-ups backed by venture capital and private equity funds have recently been listed on the stock exchanges. May their tribe increase as our innovation ecosystem grows. I find it very exciting to be an active investor in my personal capacity in start-ups because I believe they are doing wonderful work and have great potential, not just for commercial success, but also for impacting lives.

Another potential source of funding is family offices – wealthy individuals belonging to industrial houses or who have made money by selling their business – investing their time and money in backing start-ups and their founders. In the western world, family offices commit nearly a fifth of their wealth to the start-up ecosystem; this number is still in single digits in India, but is bound to grow as it provides an alternate investment avenue for family businesses.

Finally, a brief mention on the role being played by the Government to foster entrepreneurship. India's ranking in the Ease of Doing Business is improving, thanks to Government initiatives. However, a lot more needs to be done. Success for an entrepreneur means playing hopscotch on the investment landscape minefield. Though there has been solid progress in improving the ease of doing business, the urgency of reviving investment post–COVID-19 requires that we sweep away these landmines. In particular, the Government should make it much easier to close down a venture or a business. At present, this is a protracted process that saps the time and energy of the entrepreneur and prevents the start of new ventures. Making it easier to shut down a business for genuine reasons will go a long way in improving the ease of doing business.

I am happy to note that the Innovation, Venturing & Entrepreneurship in India Network (iVEIN), a consortium of leading academic institutions, is bringing out its first biennial publication, titled *Shifting Orbits: Decoding the Trajectory of the Indian Start-up Ecosystem*. The publication has an excellent mix of articles by reputed writers from academia and industry and addresses all the myriad issues pertaining to the entrepreneurship ecosystem under one umbrella. I am sure, it will become a 'must-read' for all those interested in entrepreneurship in the country and abroad.

I believe that the various pieces of the start-up ecosystem jigsaw puzzle are slowly but surely falling into place. With the right actions to ensure that the whole ecosystem takes off, we can make India the start-up capital of the world.

Anand G Mahindra
Chairman, Mahindra Group

Foreword

Fostering scientific innovation for impact and profit

Integrating scientific innovation with our lives creates both impact and profit. The COVID-19 pandemic has provided us a cue that science must have a strong societal purpose and our strength lies in maximising opportunities to continuously innovate and evolve. There is enormous untapped potential in harnessing the power of science and technology, across the entire developing world. India is favourably positioned, due to its unique strengths and challenges, for a broad-based, science-centric effort to transform society. Careful and consistent investments have created a large and capable base of skilled human capital and extensive physical resources across universities, government organisations and the private sector.

For centuries, scientists have been working towards advancing human development, by developing new technologies and innovations. Over the years, we have built a strong set of research and development institutions through our national and state laboratories and universities. The pressing need is to add the direction towards connecting science with need-driven technology innovation. A combination of forces of higher investments in science, globalisation of indigenous scientific talent, prioritisation of goals for science and technology, and deeper interaction among different stakeholders domestically and internationally will drive the way forward for India to become a scientific power and lead the world's mega science projects.

Several institutes of excellence in higher learning are doing cutting edge research in various areas of science and technology. Traditionally, a dominant route for commercialization of technologies from research has been through the process of licensing, either to public sector undertakings and research laboratories or to private corporations. However, the winds of change have been sweeping the campuses and research laboratories in recent years. With several entrepreneurs becoming tremendously successful by becoming start-up founders, the university and research community, comprising faculty members, research scholars, research scientists and students, started showing interest in becoming entrepreneurs. Start-up seemed to be an idea whose time had come, so to speak.

At the same time, policymaking at the highest levels geared up to support entrepreneurship in scientific and academic institutions. This convergence of policy support and interest in creating start-ups meant that commercialization of research did not need to depend on licensing out to external organisations. Researchers, scientists, and faculty members who were involved in developing the technology could actually use the start-up route to explore commercialization of the technologies. Indian scientific and higher education institutions with the best minds from the academic field would be best positioned to provide the expertise to build products that help solve complex problems. This would be the way forward if India is to become a scientific superpower and become a hub of product development. For its part, the Government of India is keen to develop entrepreneurship and foster an ecosystem that helps entrepreneurs. The Prime Minister announced the StartUp India initiative in August 2015 to build a robust ecosystem to nurture innovation and start-ups to drive sustainable economic growth and generate enormous employment opportunities. Simultaneously, the government also implemented the Atal Innovation Mission, the Government's flagship initiative to create and promote a culture of innovation and entrepreneurship in educational institutions.

The Union Budget for 2021–22 had a few specific points pertaining to innovation and research and development. It had allocated ₹500 billion over five years for the National Research Foundation, which was announced in 2019. The budget also announced a new initiative on National Language Translation Mission. The Government recently liberalised the mapping policy, allowing free access to geospatial data. As the next generation of mapping technologies develop, these guidelines will enable Indian innovators to make advanced maps at highest resolution and also empower small businesses. Start-ups can innovate and take advantage of the latest map-making technologies. The Indian Space Research Organisation is gearing up to provide technical support to Indian academia, industries and start-ups to achieve broader participation and self-reliance in the Indian space sector. Various ministries of the Government are actively engaging with start-ups, throwing them real-world challenges to solve and engaging with them productively. A number of public sector units provide vital investment to the start-ups and also help them with pilot projects for their technology. Recently, corporates have also been active in engaging with start-ups in the form of hackathons and innovation challenges.

Over the years, we have seen start-ups not just duplicating models and businesses that are already prevalent in other countries, but coming up with ideas and innovations to solve problems peculiar to our country. Thanks to start-ups, tremendous progress has been made in financial inclusion, while those in the educational technology space are striving to fill the gap in physical infrastructure in schools. India's models and ideas in financial technology, educational technology and digital lending are setting examples for even the developed countries to follow.

In the last one year, when the COVID-19 pandemic affected normal life in the country and across the world, start-ups in the online education space and digital lending helped consumers in a big way. COVID-19 changed the way we do science, develop technology-based solutions and innovate. There is now greater academic–industry partnership. When the pandemic was raging, a textile company used its technological know-how to make better fabrics for frontline workers who were at a higher risk of getting infected. From a shortage of masks and personal protection equipment, we quickly became surplus and were even able to export them to countries that needed these.

Science and technology is the fulcrum for the levers of the Government to effect social and economic change. For this, scientists and society must connect closely, build stronger foundations in education, fundamental research, applications in agriculture, health, environment and energy.

I am happy to note that four eminent institutions – IIT Madras, IIT Bombay, IIM Bangalore and IIM Kozhikode – have come together to form the Innovation, Venturing & Entrepreneurship in India Network (iVEIN). Convergence of the triumvirate, viz., academia and research, policy and practice is important for sustained leadership in any sector. I am confident that the creation of iVEIN will provide a thrust to thought leadership and knowledge creation on innovation and new venture creation. Such an academic initiative will go a long way to help the entrepreneurial ecosystem in the country.

One of the activities of the iVEIN network is the biennial publication on Innovation and Venturing in India that provides analytical narratives and traces the contours of the Indian entrepreneurial and innovation ecosystem. This first edition has articles that focus on different stages of the start-up life cycle: innovation, incubation, funding and impact. Efforts such as iVEIN's bring together India's finest minds and contribute significantly to India's intellectual bank. The articles emphasize science management as a skill, in addition to high-quality science research. The real-world insights help to create an ecosystem that allows leveraging science and technology for regional problem-solving and positioning India on the global map for cutting-edge scientific research-driven innovation. Such multi-disciplinary and multi-institutional national efforts will help to transform the overall public perception towards science. I am also sure that this publication will help policymakers in framing better policies that go a long way in helping start-ups and their founders.

I would urge iVEIN to not restrict itself to a biennial publication, but come out with regular well-researched publications that will help those involved in policymaking. It is important to note that increasing spend in R&D alone will not lead to better technology outcomes, as anticipated in a linear approach to science, technology and innovation. Instead, India is seeing a shift in mindset, with a special emphasis on creating enabling structures, and building a culture that rewards risk-taking in cutting-edge science research and development. It is time we look at science both as a public good and as a profitable business opportunity for scientists.

Professor K VijayRaghavan
Principal Scientific Advisor to the Government of India
New Delhi

Preface

"You must be the change you wish to see in this world."

"The future depends on what you do today."
—MK Gandhi

Traditionally, India has been a very vibrant entrepreneurial economy. However, the contours of entrepreneurship have changed significantly since the millennium, if not in numbers, most definitely in impact. If India is to emerge as a global powerhouse economy, it can only happen by riding on technology and innovation.

Today, India has become one of the largest start-up and innovation hubs in the world. The Indian start-up ecosystem has rapidly scaled new heights and has become an important contributor in the journey to become a $5 trillion economy. In the last decade, policymakers have looked to start-ups as a policy prescription that can achieve multiple objectives: promote innovation, generate employment and transform society. This has resulted in a great swathe of programmes to strengthen the start-up ecosystem in India. Some examples include the formulation of state and national start-up policies, the setting up of incubation centres across the nation, heightened investments in domestically grown start-ups and the increased focus on entrepreneurship in academic curricula.

Shifting Orbits consists of four sections: innovation, incubation, funding and industry perspectives.

Innovation

Innovation is the engine that can catapult nations into the league of superpowers. Innovation-led entrepreneurship will not only strengthen India's position in the global economy but also address some of our most pressing social and environmental challenges. The section on 'Innovation' dives deeper into understanding how India is faring on innovation-led entrepreneurship and what are the challenges, that needs to be overcome in order to become a hub of innovation.

Chapter 1 provides a historical account of India's innovation system since the time of independence and the different phases of its evolution. It critically analyses the policy interventions that have shaped the system over the years and identifies gaps that remain to be addressed. Chapter 2 analyses the patenting activity of Indian start-ups, since patents are an important indicator of innovation. The authors find that patenting activity is on the rise, but the absolute numbers are still quite small. This prompts a stronger regulatory framework. Chapter 3 engages with experts from deep technologies (Space, AI and ML and Biomedical Sciences) to understand the ecosystem for these technologies. Chapter 4 explores how large corporates and start-ups can partner to create a robust platform for open innovation. Chapter 5 examines the potential and challenges of social start-ups that aspire to create social impact using market mechanism. Overall, this section provides a well-rounded view of the role of innovation in powering Indian start-ups.

Incubation

Incubators provide a safe harbour for start-ups so that they can survive and flourish as viable businesses. According to the National Science and Technology Development Board, Department of Science and Technology, Government of India, incubators help in improving the survival rate of start-ups substantially, from 30 per cent to over 70 per cent. Over time, incubators in India have grown and evolved significantly, creating a diverse and vibrant incubation ecosystem. The five chapters in the 'Incubation' section help us shed light on the history, current landscape and future of incubation in India, learn from the practices of successful public and private incubators, understand the role of government and policymakers and build a dialogue between incubators, entrepreneurs, policymakers, academics and corporations.

Chapter 6 examines the past, present and future of start-up incubation in India, identifying gaps in the policy landscape and opportunities for better regulations. Chapter 7 discusses the framework and practices associated with technology incubation and the creation of MedTech start-ups at Biomedical Engineering & Technology Innovation Centre, IIT Bombay. Chapter 8 looks at the virtual incubation programme of NASSCOM (10,000 Start-ups), and traces its evolution, strategy and benefits. Chapter 9 highlights the role and impact of government programmes by studying Atal Incubation Centres. Chapter 10 presents edited excerpts from a first-of-its-kind roundtable discussion with the heads and managers of leading academic incubators in India, giving us a peek into incubation practices, how they differ across university incubators, criteria used for start-up evaluation and funding, virtual incubation and the impact of the COVID-19 pandemic.

Funding

For start-ups to be able to grow and create an impact, funding is critical. Most start-ups would be unable to generate the cash flows that would meet their investment requirements. The need for external investment is, therefore, inevitable. Private equity capital such as angel investments and venture capital (VC) are some of the dominant sources that fund start-ups. This section provides perspectives on the role of funding in creating and sustaining ventures.

Three major themes of articles are explored under this broad edifice. The first theme reflects on the past trajectory in venture financing. It explores trends in angel and VC investing in India, simultaneously signposting some of the major advances made in the Indian funding ecosystem in the past decade, while identifying bottlenecks and pain points that need to be addressed (Chapters 11, 12, 13 and 17).

The second theme illuminates the present role of the venture capital ecosystem in India. It details the contribution of VC firms to the growth and expansion of start-ups, and their impact on the broader economy. India's VC firms have played a remarkable role in supporting start-ups that have provided the much-needed solutions to India-centric problems, specifically in the time of the COVID-19 pandemic. During the pandemic, VC-backed start-ups enabled several organisations to seamlessly transition into a fully digital platform. Going a step further, VCs firms have provided Indian entrepreneurs with the necessary capital to break into well-established markets (dominated by multinational firms), while generating quality jobs in India (Chapter 16).

The third theme is future-looking, exploring potential avenues for VCs to help galvanise the growth in start-ups, specifically in frontier technology sectors such as Brain Science and Artificial Intelligence (Chapter 15). Further, it draws the attention of start-ups to new entrants in the venture financing ecosystem such as the family offices of high-net-worth individuals (HNIs). Family offices can be a crucial source for start-ups looking for both patient capital and strong mentorship (Chapter 14).

Overall, the funding section captures the past, present and future of the venture financing ecosystem in India.

Industry Perspectives

The section on 'Industry Perspectives' takes an analytical, practice-centred view of the growth of the Indian innovation ecosystem. By the end of 2020, India had found its place among the top four countries in the world, with a vibrant start-up ecosystem with 36 Unicorns.

Chapter 18 examines the enablers contributing to the growth of the Indian innovation ecosystem in three five-year phases, from 2006 to 2020; it further offers directions for accelerating the innovation-led economic growth. Authors with a ringside view of practice developments analyse the evolution and growth of four vibrant start-up sectors – AgriTech, EdTech, HealthTech and FinTech – in chapters 19–22. The potential and possible growth directions for the technology-enabled transformation of Indian agriculture is analysed in Chapter 19. In Chapter 20, the strategic significance of EdTech in transforming learning in different markets segments and the potential in domestic as well as the global markets is discussed. The growth of the FinTech sector, especially over the last 15 years, developments and trends is explored in Chapter 21. It underscores the huge growth potential, given the relatively low levels of financial assets in India, and highlights emerging opportunities in segments like Lending, apart from the Payment vertical. In the chapter on the HealthTech sector, the author discusses the immense possibilities of the sector in domestic as well as international markets, the broadening of growth into newer segments like chronic disease management, e-pharmacies and health-data–based start-ups, and offers suggestions for leveraging the potential.

Taken together, *Shifting Orbits* is a comprehensive narrative on innovation and venturing in India. We really enjoyed working on this publication, and we hope that you will find it insightful as well as thought-provoking.

Thillai Rajan A
Srivardhini K Jha
Joffi Thomas
Rohan Chinchwadkar

Acknowledgements

"And, when you want something, all the universe conspires in helping you to achieve it."

—Paulo Coelho, *The Alchemist*

This publication is a testament to what can be achieved with the support and encouragement of well-wishers, even during times of great global distress such as the COVID-19 pandemic. At the outset, we would like to thank our respective institutions, namely, Indian Institute of Technology Madras, Indian Institute of Management Bangalore, Indian Institute of Management Kozhikode and Indian Institute of Technology Bombay, for supporting this cross-institutional collaboration and giving us the full freedom to give form and structure to our vision. The recognition provided by our institutions has enabled us to galvanise broader support for academic research in the start-up ecosystem.

We would also like to express our heartfelt gratitude to the contributors who have written the different chapters. We thank them for devoting their time and effort, despite their busy schedules and commitments.

Several leaders in the start-up ecosystem have participated in the in-depth roundtable discussions featured in the publication. Their profound insights and opinions have greatly enriched this work. We are very grateful to all the roundtable panellists for participating in the discussions and for sharing their valuable insights.

On behalf of the iVEIN consortium, we would like to extend our deepest gratitude to Kris Gopalakrishnan, Chiratae Ventures, SIDBI and NSRCEL for their generosity in extending financial support to this publication.

Many thanks to Madhavi Sethupathi, the editor, for painstakingly reviewing the report to ensure its accuracy and consistency in a very cheerful manner. By bringing in a lot of organisation to our disorganised way of working, she gave much-needed momentum during the production phase of this publication. Special thanks to Madhu Reddy, our publisher, for his impeccable support and leadership in the publication process.

We are very grateful to the members of the advisory board for their sage advice and guidance. They have been a strong pillar of support for this effort and no amount of words can express our gratitude and appreciation for their support. We were fortunate to have a dedicated team of Assistant Research Editors, Akshay Natteri Mangadu, Rashmi Dyondi and Sumelika Bhattacharyya, who went beyond their call of duty in supporting us and took complete ownership in all the tasks they were involved in. We would also like to acknowledge the contributions of N Ramakrishnan and Dinesh Tiwari, which helped us to integrate the perspectives of practice and policymaking. They reviewed all the chapters and their suggestions played an important role in enhancing the final output.

It is indeed a matter of great privilege and honour to have received the foreword from Indian luminaries, Anand G Mahindra (Chairman, Mahindra & Mahindra) and Professor K VijayRaghavan (Principal Scientific Advisor to the Government of India). We are deeply indebted to them for supporting and highlighting the role of innovation and start-ups in building a modern India.

Last but not least, we would like to thank our families for their unwavering encouragement, love and support. We have tried our very best to recollect and register our gratitude to all those who have helped this publication. We sincerely apologise to those whom we may have missed due to our oversight.

Thillai Rajan A

Srivardhini K Jha

Joffi Thomas

Rohan Chinchwadkar

Contents

List of Contributors

Abha Rishi, CEO, Atal Incubation Centre-BIMTECH, is one of the few Indians to hold both a Chevening Scholarship (CRISP 2014, University of Oxford) and a Fulbright Scholarship (Rutgers University, USA). With 27 years of experience, and an EEC Honors from STVP, Stanford University, she has mentored more than 1000 women and student entrepreneurs.

Ajith Chandran, Managing Director, Development Interlinks International, is a Chevening scholar (Bradford), a Governing Council member of Chevening Alumni India and IET India's Water Working Group. With over 30 years in environment and development, he is a graduate of PGIMER (Chandigarh), a post-graduate from IIFM (Bhopal) and a doctorate from UBC (Vancouver).

Akshay Natteri Mangadu is an econometrician with experience in research and consulting. He is an alumnus of the University of Chicago (Harris) and the Chinese University of Hong Kong.

Arjun Mohan, CEO of upGrad, is focussed on scaling the company to dominate the higher education space globally. A gold medalist for all-round performance from Indian Institute of Management Kozhikode, Arjun has diverse experience, having worked in the Sales, Marketing and Product Development domains across various industries: EdTech (upGrad and BYJU'S), Fashion (Titan), Automotive (Tata Motors), Realty (TRIL) and Electronics (Mentor Graphics).

Atit Danak is Principal and Head – CoNXT at Zinnov. A former entrepreneur, with 12+ years of technical and general management experience, at Zinnov, he has helped global Fortune-500 companies design, build and implement customised start-up collaboration strategies. He holds a BE in Electrical and Electronics Engineering from Manipal Institute of Technology, India.

Bhallamudi Ravi is an Institute Chair Professor of Mechanical Engineering at IIT Bombay. He heads BETIC (Biomedical Engineering & Technology Innovation Centre) as well as the Desai Sethi School of Entrepreneurship. The BETIC team developed 50 novel medical devices, incubated 15 start-up companies, licensed 5 products to industry and won many awards.

Dinesh Tiwari, Managing Director, Broad Peak Capital Advisors LLP, is a seasoned private equity professional with over 25 years of investing experience in emerging markets. Dinesh has a bachelor's degree in Physics and an MBA from Indian Institute of Management Bangalore.

Joffi Thomas is an Associate Professor in the Marketing Management area at the Indian Institute of Management Kozhikode. He has a rich blend of teaching, research, consulting and training as well as industry experience for over two decades, broadly in the business strategy and customer management areas. He has BE in Computer Engineering, an MBA and a Fellow in Management from the Management Development Institute, Gurgaon.

Krishnan Naryanan is Co-Founder and President of itihaasa Research and Digital. He brings over two decades of experience in digital consulting and technology commercialisation. He founded a water start-up in India. Krishnan has a BTech degree from Indian Institute of Technology Madras and a management degree from XLRI, Jamshedpur.

Kritika Murugesan currently leads the NASSCOM 10,000 Start-ups programme. She also works closely with various state governments to build the ecosystem for tech entrepreneurs. In her previous roles, Kritika has worked closely with CEOs and CXOs of major IT companies for overall engagement programmes ranging from technology, societal impact, diversity and inclusion, value proposition for GICs, education, growth of SMEs and development of states.

Madan Dhanora is a doctorate in Economics from the Indian Institute of Technology Indore and MA in

Economics from the University of Hyderabad. He is currently Assistant Professor of Economics, Government Mahaveer College, Petlawad (Higher Education Department, Government of Madhya Pradesh).

N Dayasindhu is Co-Founder and CEO of itihaasa Research and Digital. With over two decades of experience in research and consulting, his research interests are competitiveness, national R&D and innovation ecosystems. Daysindhu holds a PhD in Management from Indian Institute of Management Bangalore, and a master's in Physics from Indian Institute of Technology Madras. He has two US patents.

Neha Singh is the CEO and Co-Founder of Tracxn, a leading market intelligence platform for tracking start-ups and private companies. An alumnus of Indian Institute of Technology Bombay and Stanford GSB, Neha featured among Forbes 40 under 40 in 2018 and 2019. Prior to starting Tracxn, she was a venture capitalist with Sequoia Capital India.

Neharika Vohra is currently serving as a Vice-Chancellor of Delhi Skill and Entrepreneurship University, Delhi. She is a psychologist who teaches organisational behaviour at Indian Institute of Management Ahmedabad as a full-time faculty. Her research interests are in leadership, gender, governance, entrepreneurship and incubation. She is currently on the board of CIIE Initiatives.

Priya Nair Rajeev is Associate Professor, OB & HR Area, Indian Institute of Management Kozhikode. Trained in Participant Centred Learning from Harvard Business School, Priya (PhD in Management Studies, Indian Institute of Technology Madras) is a recipient of the Highly Commended Emerald/EFMD Outstanding Doctoral Research Award 2011.

Qambar Abidi obtained his PhD from Indian Institute of Management Ahmedabad and is currently working as an Assistant Professor in the Finance area at Indian Institute of Management Kozhikode. Prior to his PhD, he worked in the financial services industry for seven years, mostly providing advisory to buy side firms based on proprietary quant asset allocation models.

Rahul Singh is Professor of Strategy and Globalisation and Chair of Strategy and Innovation Area at Birla Institute of Management Technology, India, and Chair of the Executive Education Programme. He works in the Strategy, Globalisation, Emerging Markets and Digital Transformation disciplines.

Rajesh Ranjan is the CEO of NABVENTURES, a NABARD-anchored VC fund focussed on investments in early-to-mid-stage start-ups in AgriTech, FoodTech, agri/rural FinTech, rural HealthTech and rural EdTech. He has an MBA from Indian Institute of Management Calcutta and a BA (Honors) in Economics from St. Stephen's College (Delhi University).

N Ramakrishnan, an independent journalist, has over three decades of experience in mainstream and business journalism. He has a BSc in Physics, a postgraduate diploma in Journalism & Mass Communication, and an MSc in Media Management from the University of Stirling, UK, on a Chevening/FCO scholarship. He has written extensively on the start-up ecosystem.

Rashmi Dyondi received her PhD from Shailesh J Mehta School of Management, Indian Institute of Technology Bombay. With her comprehensive knowledge and experience in the Hindi motion picture industry, she has also been a visiting faculty at Flame University and Symbiosis Centre of Media and Communication. Her research interest is in content distribution and risk in the film industry.

Rishikesha T Krishnan is Director and Professor of Strategy at the Indian Institute of Management Bangalore. An alumnus of Indian Institute of Technology Kanpur, Stanford University and Indian Institute of Management Ahmedabad, he has been listed in the Thinkers50 India list of most influential management thinkers and is currently also on the advisory board of YourNest Investment Advisors

Rohan Chinchwadkar is an Assistant Professor (Finance) at the Shailesh J Mehta School of Management, Indian Institute of Technology Bombay. He has been an Assistant Professor at Indian Institute of Management Tiruchirappalli, and a Visiting Professor at Indian Institute of Management Calcutta. He holds a PhD (Finance) from IIM Calcutta, BTech (Electronics) from Veermata Jijabai Technological Institute, Mumbai, and has worked with the prestigious consulting firm McKinsey & Company. His research and teaching interests lie in entrepreneurial finance, money and banking, and practice theory.

Ruchi Sharma is an Associate Professor of Economics at Indian Institute of Technology Indore. Ruchi obtained her PhD from Indian Institute of Technology Kanpur, and MPhil and MA (Economics) from Punjab University, Chandigarh. Ruchi's research area is Economics of Innovation with specific focus on R&D, patenting and other innovation-related aspects of firms, start-ups, universities and academic institutions. She was awarded the Kusuma Young Faculty Incentive Fellowship at Indian Institute of Technology Delhi.

Sameer Wagle has 26 years of private equity and operating experience in Asia and is currently the Managing Director at Asian Healthcare Fund, a healthcare-focussed private equity firm. Sameer has been part of organisations such as Nomura, Vertex, IL&FS, GVFL and Crompton Greaves. Sameer is also involved with the Takshashila Institution and Aavishkaar Microventure Fund.

Shailaja Shukla is an Associate at CIIE.CO. Her research interests and her most recent endeavours have been in financial services and inclusion, crafts and civic tech. Having been a part of the University of Tampa, Florida, Shailaja has a global outlook and has undertaken specialised courses in Data Analytics and Finance.

Simy Joy currently holds the position of a Faculty Fellow at the Indian Institute of Management Kozhikode, India. A PhD from Case Western Reserve University, USA, Simy's research focusses on social innovation, social enterprises, socio-tech enterprises and micro-enterprises that target the inclusion and empowerment of marginalised and under-served groups.

Srivardhini K Jha is Associate Professor of Entrepreneurship at the Indian Institute of Management Bangalore. Her research interest is in Innovation and Entrepreneurship in the emerging country context. She has published her work in several peer-reviewed international journals. Prior to entering academia, she held senior management positions at Microsoft and Sun Microsystems.

Sumelika Bhattacharyya is Assistant Professor at OB-HRM, Goa Institute of Management, India. She has a PhD in Organisational Behaviour from IESE Business School, Barcelona (FT'21 MBA Rank 4), sponsored by the Shanghai-based China Europe International Business School (FT'21 Rank 7). She is currently researching organisational behaviour in Indian social and deep tech start-ups.

Supriya Sharma leads research at CIIE.CO. She is an academia–industry translator. She also teaches courses in entrepreneurship and organisational behaviour. Supriya is a Fellow of the Indian Institute of Management Ahmedabad and an alumni of the International Visitor Leadership Programme, USA.

Thillai Rajan A is a Professor in the Department of Management Studies and the Centre for Research on Start-ups and Risk Financing at Indian Institute of Technology Madras. He is also an associate at the Harvard Kennedy School's Mossavar Center for Business and Government and has co-founded a start-up called YNOS Venture Engine, an AI-driven business intelligence and analytics platform for early-stage start-ups and investors.

About iVEIN and the Publication Series

Innovation, Venturing and Entrepreneurship in India Network (iVEIN) is a consortium of academic institutions aimed at building a cross-institutional network to bridge the different stakeholders in the start-up ecosystem and create new knowledge by engaging in high-quality research on topics pertaining to innovation and venturing.

iVEIN leverages the strengths of the partner institutions and partners with other stakeholders such as incubators, government and investors in generating and disseminating knowledge. The research ensures that the various activities such as incubation, policymaking and investing are not seen in isolation, but as a part of the bigger ecosystem with interdependencies.

iVEIN Innovation and Start-up Economy Publication Series is a biennial publication focussed on Indian Innovation, Venturing and Entrepreneurship. The publication series aims to develop a comprehensive narrative on the contours of innovation, venturing and entrepreneurship in India, while creating thought leadership for practice. For more details about iVEIN, please visit: https://doms.iitm.ac.in/iVEIN/

Financial support from the following is gratefully acknowledged:

Kris Gopalakrishan
Chairman of Axilor Ventures

chiratae
VENTURES

Small Industries Development Bank of India (SIDBI)

Over the years, as a DFI for the MSME sector, SIDBI has been at the forefront of initiatives to develop the VC ecosystem for MSMEs/start-ups. Beginning with contributions to state-level venture capital funds in the early 1990s, followed by participation in the All India VCFs set up by public as well as private sector entities, the initiatives have aimed to cover the entire journey of an innovation-driven enterprise. These have included setting up a dedicated VC funding arm for MSMEs, support for incubation centres in early days, fund of funds contributing in MSME/start-up-focussed VCFs/AIFs funding various stages of venture growth, innovative products in equity/quasi-equity domain, besides ecosystem level interventions for growth of technology and innovation-driven MSMEs/start-ups.

SIDBI is the operating agency for the Fund of Funds for Start-ups (FFS), a programme of the Department for Promotion of Industry and Internal Trade (DPIIT), Ministry of Commerce and Industry, Government of India (GoI), under the Startup India Action Plan, which has a corpus of ₹10,000 crore for contribution to AIFs. It is heartening to mention that the FFS has been catalysing significant investments in start-ups (through partner/supported AIFs) and several start-ups in turn are emerging as forerunners for economic growth, employment generation and wealth creation. As of March 31, 2021, commitments stood at ₹5,409 crore to 71 AIFs whereas draw downs of ₹1,485 crore had catalysed investments of ₹5,648 crore in start-ups. SIDBI is also operating the "ASPIRE" Fund of Fund of the Ministry of MSME, GoI for supporting rural and agro sector MSMEs/start-ups as well as the UP Startup Fund of the Government of Uttar Pradesh (UP) for start-ups registered in UP.

Sustained developmental measures have similarly been taken with the equally important objective of developing the entrepreneurial ecosystem at grassroot level. SIDBI's umbrella programme, "Mission Swavalamban", has been undertaking a range of activities to bring about a radical shift in the outlook and approach of being a Swavalambi (self-reliant). With the target "**Har Ghar Ek Swavalambi**", the programme touches base with three influencers in every person's life, that is, parents [especially mother], teachers and peers to inculcate a culture of entrepreneurship; resulting in transformation of youth from "job seekers" to "job creators", thereby promoting sustainable livelihood opportunities at the base of the pyramid, unserved/underserved segments and micro and small enterprises and restricting rural migration to urban areas.

Implementation of the initiatives in association with prestigious partners such as DFID-UK (now FCDO), USHA Social Services, IIM Lucknow, IIT Kanpur, CRISIL, CIBIL, PSB Loanin59Minutes, ET, GeMS, Invest India and NITI Aayog has helped touch 0.6 million+ aspirants/entrepreneurs in FY 2021. Through promotion and developmental initiatives, SIDBI has conducted 55+ thematic and programmatic engagements and reached out to around 1.4 million people.

To passionate entrepreneurs and innovators
driving economic and social progress

Section I

INNOVATION

IN BRIEF

- In recent years, a slew of policy measures by the central and state governments has signalled a strong intention to encourage innovation-led start-ups and has created a framework to spur innovation-led growth.
- The government's efforts need to be complemented by the private sector, both in terms of expanding the pool of patient capital available and by becoming customers of start-up products and services.
- The incentive system in academia needs to be redesigned to enable research translation so that more breakthrough academic work can find commercial application.

1

India's Innovation System and Start-ups: Achievements and Opportunities

Rishikesha T Krishnan, Srivardhini K Jha and Sumelika Bhattacharyya

Krishnan, RT, Jha, SK and Bhattacharyya, S. 2021. "India's Innovation System and Start-ups: Achievements and Opportunities". In *Shifting Orbits: Decoding the Trajectory of the Indian Start-up Ecosystem*, edited by Thillai Rajan A, Srivardhini K Jha, Joffi Thomas and Rohan Chinchwadkar, 2–11. Hyderabad: Universities Press (India) Private Limited.

The Evolution of India's Innovation System

Among the newly independent nations of the mid-twentieth century, India was distinctive in making significant investments in science and technology as a means of development. Policymakers were convinced that creating domestic capabilities in science and technology was key to building a modern nation. This belief was manifested primarily in the form of creating government-owned, -funded and -managed research institutions and networks devoted to what was considered strategic (Atomic Energy, Space and Defence) and basic or key areas (discipline-based laboratories for Scientific and Industrial Research, Agriculture and Medicine). By the early 1990s, India had an impressive base of Science and Technology (S&T) manpower and had built and demonstrated technological capabilities in some of the strategic areas, but had had limited success in creating and diffusing technologies for industrial use.[1] From an innovation system standpoint, this period from 1950 to 1990 can be counted as Phase 1. The absence of diffusion and adoption of technologies was attributed to two main reasons – the structure of the model adopted (standalone research and development [R&D] institutions with no organic links to industry) and industrial and trade policies which offered limited incentive for firms to seek technological advancement.

Phase 2 of India's innovation system can be closely linked to the deregulation and opening up of the Indian economy, which began in the early 1990s. One of the objectives set out in India's Industrial Policy Statement of July 1991 was the strengthening of technological capabilities in Indian industry. Yet, what manifested in Phase 2 of the evolution of independent India's innovation system was the emergence of India as a hub of R&D centres of multinational enterprises (MNEs). These MNEs took advantage of the availability of a large, relatively low-cost talent pool to shift a part of their R&D and related activities to India. By 2019, there were around 1,250 global capability centres (GCCs)[2] set up by MNEs in India, accounting for a business value of $15.7 billion from engineering services and R&D (out of a total GCC business value of $28.3 billion). The growth in importance of MNE R&D was also reflected in the average number of US patents awarded annually to Indian inventors, increasing from 62 (1976–1994) to 375 (1995–2008) to 3,498 (2009–2016) – 79 per cent of these patents in the last period were assigned to multinational enterprises.[3] However, the focus of R&D in these MNE R&D centres in India was on using India's technical talent pool to support the global innovation efforts of their parent companies, and there were limited spill-overs to the Indian economy. In Phase 2, the R&D capabilities available within the country deepened, but the objective of using India's S&T prowess for the country's development remained largely elusive.

India has recently embarked on what could be called Phase 3 in its efforts to orient innovation activities towards local needs, as well as building innovation capacity in the ecosystem to compete in global markets. A key vehicle for accomplishing this has been through a slew of policies and programmes to support start-ups. In this paper, we explore the challenges and prospects of this start-up–focussed innovation policy to achieve the objective of linking India's large talent base of technically trained manpower to innovation that can drive India's economic growth and development.

Exhibit 1.1: Indian government policies over the years as relevant for technology innovation

	PHASE I 1950	PHASE II 1990	PHASE III 2015
POLICY RATIONALE	Nation-building and enhancing India's status as a modern nation through investment in science and technology	Strengthen technological capabilities of Industry. India's Industrial Policy Statement, 1991	Make innovation central to the economy, through innovation-based, entrepreneurship-led growth – Startup India, 2016
POLICY FOCUS	Government funding of research institutions in geo-strategic and development-related sectors	Deregulation and privatisation; promoting MNE entry	Government programmes to fund and support numerous innovative start-ups
EDUCATION FOCUS	Establish and standardise high-quality higher education institutes (HEI) such as IITs and IIMs	Standardise systems nationally to equalise skill development opportunities for all	NEP 2020, engender innovative mindset, inter-disciplinary educational tinkering labs in schools, incubators in HEIs
INDUSTRY FOCUS	Limited attention to industry application	Focus on enabling technology entry (Foreign Technology Agreement)	Focus on start-ups; policy framework created for enabling research translation
OUTCOME	Creating solid R&D foundation but limited research translation, considerable success in some fields such as space, nuclear energy and agriculture (green revolution)	India becomes a GCC hub with its low-cost talent pool supporting global innovation; limited spill-overs to local economy	Early signs show an increase in patenting activity and an interest in innovation-led entrepreneurship

Innovation and the Government's Start-up Policy

While the government recognised the potential of start-ups early, it took some time for start-ups to become a focus of the policy framework. Early discussions focussed largely on funding issues and easing the availability and flow of venture capital. Proposals to set up government-supported start-up funds go back to at least 2010, but did not translate into any significant investment. Possibly because the Indian economy was growing at a robust pace compared to the rest of the world, and because of a focus on large companies, there was no concerted policy attention on start-ups.

Start-up activity in India finally received policy support because of the need to create employment. The new government came to power in mid-2014 on a plank of creating "achhe din" – better days. With India being a large economy with a young population, better days meant that the challenge of creating economic opportunities for millions of people entering the workforce loomed large. Entrepreneurship was seen as a way to create more jobs – the government exhorted young people to become job creators rather than job seekers. This became the foundation of the Government of India's start-up policy that culminated in the Startup India Initiative in 2016.

Startup India was formally launched in January 2016, though many of the ideas contained in the policy were already a part of public discourse. According to the central government, *"Startup India is a flagship initiative of the Government of India, intended to build a strong ecosystem that is conducive for the growth of startup businesses, to drive sustainable economic growth and generate large scale employment opportunities."* The initiative is intended to *"empower startups to grow through innovation and design."* The principal architect of the start-up policy, Prime Minister Narendra Modi, said, *"I see startups, technology and innovation as exciting and effective instruments for India's transformation."*[4]

Innovation has figured as one of the pillars of the start-up policy. The registration process with the Department for Promotion of Industry and Internal Trade (DPIIT) emphasises innovation. As per the original policy announced in 2016, for an entity to be considered as a start-up, it should be working towards *"innovation, development, deployment or commercialisation of new products, processes or services"* driven by technology or intellectual property. The guidelines stated that *"an entity shall be considered a startup only if it aims to develop and commercialise a new product, service or a process or significantly improves on a product or service or process, which will add significant value for customers or workflow."*[5]

With the recognition of start-ups as the primary vehicle for innovation-led growth, several policies and initiatives have been put in place to create a supportive environment. Some of these are aimed at addressing the immediate issues faced by the start-ups (for example, funding, intellectual property) and increase their chances of survival and growth, while others are aimed at building an ecosystem that would support them over the long run (such as education reforms). We will highlight some important initiatives in the following sections.

Financing and Intellectual Property (IP) Protection

Start-ups registered with the DPIIT are entitled to receive equity investment from government-supported venture funds. The government is supporting these funds indirectly – it has committed to provide ₹100 billion to the Small Industries Development Bank of India (SIDBI), which will in turn contribute to the capital of schemes of SEBI-approved[6] venture funds. Start-ups can self-certify themselves for compliance to nine environmental laws and three labour laws, allowing them to become operational quickly. Their profits will be exempt from income tax for three of the first seven years of operation. They will be exempt from "angel tax" – a tax that is levied on the company if it receives an investment at a price higher than the "fair market value" according to the Income Tax Act. These last two benefits need additional approval from an Inter-Ministerial Board.

To support late-stage start-ups to raise capital from public capital markets, a start-up exchange platform called BSE Startups Platform was started on the Bombay Stock Exchange (one of the two stock exchanges of India) in December 2018.[7] The first company was listed in August 2019.[8]

Another undertaking under the Startup India Action Plan to promote innovation was the introduction of the National Intellectual Property Rights (IPR) Policy

(NIPR Policy) in 2016.[9] The DPIIT created the Cell for IPR Promotion and Management (CIPAM) to administer and manage the seven objectives set out by the policy, including awareness generation, legal protection, administration and commercialisation of IPR. Under the policy, the Patent Rules, 2003 was amended to make IPR filing and granting streamlined and easier. For example, a business process reengineering was introduced that imposed timelines for speedy disposal and allowed expedited examination of filed patents (on certain grounds). As per CIPAM statistics, IP registrations have increased significantly post 2016. For example, patent grants increased 294 per cent in FY 2019–20 as compared with FY 2015–16.[10] Trademark Rules were also amended. Specifically, with respect to start-ups, a scheme called Start-ups Intellectual Property Protection (SIPP)[11] was launched. Administered by DPIIT's Controller General of Patents, Designs and Trade Marks (CGPDTM), the scheme has now been twice extended in periods of three years each from 2017 till 2023, post the initial one-year period. Under the scheme, the government will bear the start-up's patent agent and facilitator costs for any number of patents, trademarks or designs (prior to registration) and patent filing fees are discounted by 80 per cent (50 per cent for MSMEs or micro, small and medium enterprises). Start-ups and MSMEs have also been given a 50 per cent rebate in trademark fees. Reports state that there has been faster and increased grant of patents to start-ups due to the scheme – a record 120 start-ups were granted patents in FY 2016–17 alone, with one receiving it in as few as 101 days (compared with the average of 6 years in 2015).[12]

Education Reforms

The Indian education system is often criticised for its rigidity, focus on examinations, rote learning and failure to promote innovation and creativity. The government, through the Atal Innovation Mission (AIM), sought to change this by building 5,000 tinkering laboratories to promote experimentation in schools across the country. Challenge contests and hackathons have been the means to identify creative ideas and support them through small grants of up to ₹10,000. At the college level, the programme envisaged creating new incubation centres and strengthening existing ones. Ministries sought to provide seed money to these centres to support start-ups in their respective sectors.

The government has committed to setting up research parks in top engineering institutions to facilitate the transfer of ideas between researchers at these institutions and small and large companies. The objective here has been to emulate the success of the IIT Madras Research Park.[13] There have also been other policy-level innovation grant initiatives such as the Ucchatar Aavishkar Yojana (UAY), as formulated by the Ministry of Human Resource Development (MHRD), which sought to promote industry–academia collaboration by disbursing project-based grants of ₹2.5 billion per year to the 16 IITs (in the field of manufacturing and design).[14] In 2019, for the first time, the government ranked educational institutions on their efforts to promote innovation and entrepreneurship, complementing the National Institutional Ranking Framework (NIRF), which has been acknowledged as a comprehensive assessment based on different academic parameters. This was in addition to rolling out the National Innovation and Startup Policy (NISP) in September 2019 for students and faculty of higher education institutions (HEIs).[15] Under this policy framework, guidelines were provided to bring uniformity across HEIs in terms of Intellectual Property (IP) ownership management, technology licensing and institutional start-up policy. This was done to enable the creation of a robust innovation and start-up ecosystem across all HEIs by helping the institutes to actively engage students, faculty and staff in innovation and entrepreneurship-related activities. The guidelines pertain to detailed recommendations on institutional support, funding, shareholding, faculty and student entrepreneurship engagement guidelines (such as the number of hours spent, shareholding, and so on), incubation, technology commercialisation, innovation events, industry partnership and effecting mindset change, among others.

The above efforts were given additional impetus in 2020 through the approval of the National Education Policy (NEP) by the Union Cabinet. Apart from directly encouraging innovation activities through efforts such as the tinkering labs mentioned above, the NEP aimed to boost innovation in India by effecting a new learning model and creating a culture of research. At the school level, the policy framework aimed to introduce critical and holistic thinking in students by focussing on application-oriented (especially in the STEM[16] disciplines) rather than exam-based rote learning and breaking the rigid barriers between subject areas. It also envisioned the establishment of a National Research Foundation (NRF) that would coordinate between departments of the government supporting research, fund promising research in universities and enable industry–university collaboration. Further activities of the NRF to promote innovation at the HEIs include *"setting up startup incubation centres; technology development centres; centres in frontier areas of research; greater industry–academic linkages; and interdisciplinary research including humanities and social sciences research."*[17]

Innovation Platforms

Several government ministries and departments are working to promote start-up–led innovation in India through platforms and challenges. These include the Ministry of Electronics and Information Technology (MeitY), the National Institute for Transforming India (NITI Aayog, the premier government think-tank that initiated AIM), Department of Science and Technology (DST), DPIIT (and its initiatives Startup India and Invest India).

Recent initiatives include:

- *Aatmanirbhar Bharat:* One key initiative launched in the wake of the COVID-19 pandemic has been the economic package under the Aatmanirbhar Bharat Abhiyaan, or self-reliant India programme. Two focussed programmes conducted under the aegis of this initiative so far include the Digital Indian Aatmanirbhar Bharat App Innovation Challenge and the Aatmanirbhar Bharat ARISE–Atal New India Challenge (ANIC). The MeitY launched the app innovation challenge in partnership with AIM and the government think-tank NITI Aayog to make Indian apps world-class. The ARISE–ANIC programme has been launched in partnership with the ministries of Defence, Food Processing Industries, Health and Family Welfare, Housing and Family Affairs and ISRO under the Department of Space. The ministries and ISRO have outlined three pressing challenges to be addressed by start-ups and MSMEs, which stand to gain up to ₹5 million in grants if successful.

  Under Aatmanirbhar Bharat, the government has also launched public–private partnerships and consortia to orchestrate the indigenous

Exhibit 1.2: Key initiatives by the Government of India for promoting innovation

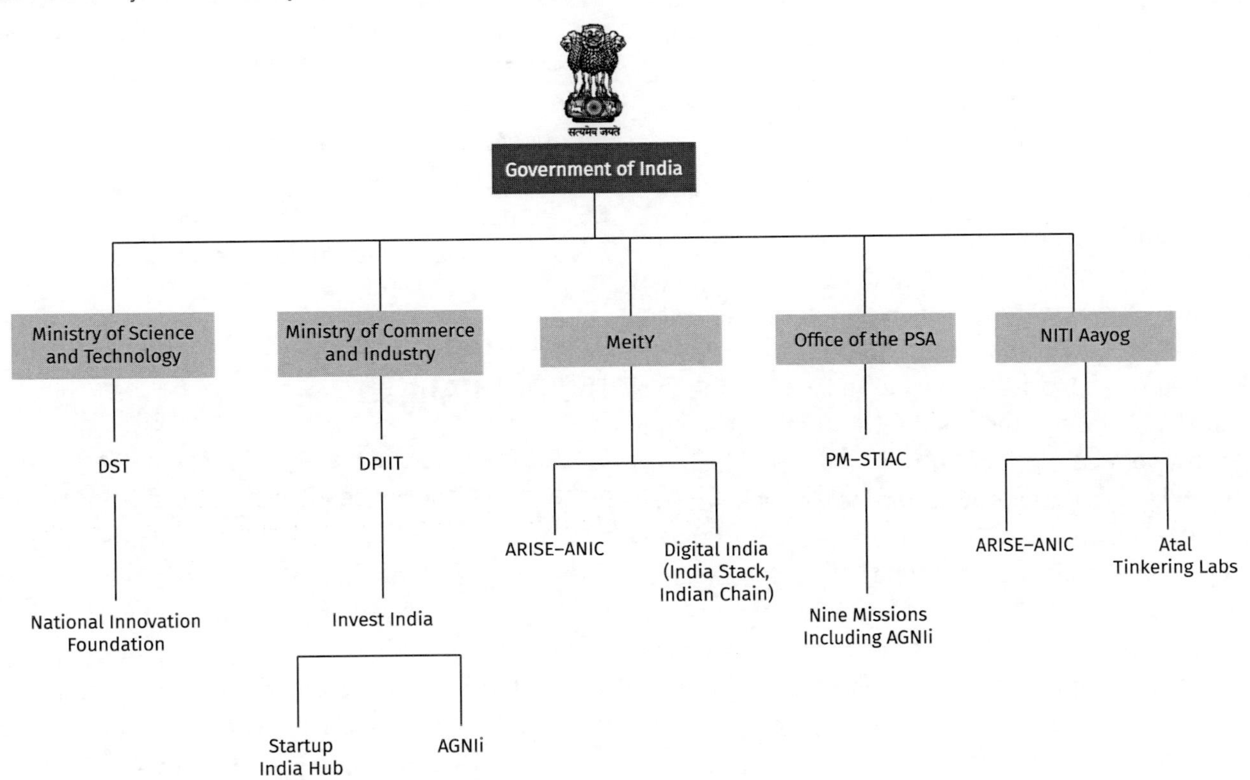

response to COVID-19. For instance, the National Biomedical Resource Indigenisation Consortium (NBRIC) was created to foster innovations for reagents, diagnostics, vaccines and therapeutics for COVID-19. While these initiatives have worked effectively in a crisis situation, it remains to be seen whether the momentum carries over into a post-COVID world.

- *Platforms to commercialise innovation*: To facilitate solutions for indigenous problems, the government has set up innovation platforms to connect creators and users of innovation. The Office of the Principal Scientific Advisor (PSA) launched the programme AGNIi or Accelerating Growth of New India's Innovations,[18] which is also a Mission under the Prime Minister's Science, Technology and Innovation Advisory Council (PM-STIAC). AGNIi, housed in the Invest India offices, aims to commercialise Indian technological innovations and provides a platform for innovators to submit their technologies. Another platform that not only connects innovation creators and users but also conducts regular innovation generating activities such as hackathons and science summits is Innovate India,[19] launched by NITI Aayog–AIM in collaboration with the government's citizen's platform, mygov.in. Other platforms that showcase ready-to-commercialise innovations include the DST-run National Innovation Foundation (which also accepts submission of innovations online) and Agrinnovate India, a Department of Agricultural Research and Education (Ministry of Agriculture and Farmers' Welfare)-run programme.
- *Digital India*: Launched in July 2015, this flagship programme of the government aims to digitise various aspects of governance and public services through ICT and other IT-enabled technologies. It has been a supporter of Startup India, engendering start-ups under the initiative that take the government as their customer. Initiatives such as the India Stack (open APIs for the FinTech sector) and the National Health Stack are seeking to make deep-rooted changes that connect different sections of the population, and thus stimulate innovation through policy for public good. The services of different sectors of governance are scheduled to be digitised with the help of start-ups, including certain key public service challenges. For example, the MeitY conducted a Grand Challenge in October 2020 to scout for start-ups that could develop innovative solutions for a *"smart water supply measurement and monitoring system"*.[20]

The Role of State Governments

An important development to be noted in the case of start-up policies is that state governments are also stepping in to promote innovation-led entrepreneurship. While state governments did earlier come up with policies centred on tax concessions and quick ("single window") clearances to attract investment, most such policies were focussed on attracting big ticket investments to the state. However, now 30 states and union territories (out of a total of 36; 29 states + 7 union territories) have their own start-up policies, which supplement those of the central government. These policies now extend not only to start-ups but also, in various cases, to incubators, academia and investors. Apart from concessions, clearances and certifications, the policies pertain to funding, incubating, marketing and, in some cases, even to land allotment.[21] For example, the Karnataka Startup Policy 2015–20 envisages fostering partnerships between R&D institutions and industry; providing early-stage proof-of-concept funding; encouraging entrepreneurship education; creating incubation infrastructure through public–private partnerships; channellising innovation for social impact through five grand challenges to be conducted every year; start-up funding through fund-of-funds; promoting capacity building through exposure visits and workshops; and financial incentives (VAT or CST reimbursement; patent spends including foreign filings; and support for marketing expenditure).[22]

The Outcome of Policy Initiatives and the Path Ahead

Startup India has achieved progress in the three years since it was started (see Exhibit 1.3).

While it is clear that the start-up policy has caught the imagination of India, we now return to the question we had posed at the beginning of this study: is the growth of the start-up ecosystem achieving the objective of linking India's large talent base of technically trained manpower to innovation that can drive India's economic growth and development? Are we now able to create

Exhibit 1.3: Startup India – plans and achievements

	Activity	Target/Goal	Achievement
1	Start-ups registered with DPIIT (as on 18/12/2020)		40,812
2	Start-ups receiving tax exemptions		221[23]
3	Facilitators for patent and design applications under SIPP		March 2020: 516[24]
4	Facilitators for trademarks under SIPP		March 2020: 392[25]
5	Start-ups applied for patents, 2015–2020		3,204
6	Patents granted to start-ups, 2015–2020		309
7	Start-ups applied for trademarks, 2015–2020		6,090[26]
8	Atal Tinkering Labs	5,000 (date not specified)	2,071 received ₹1.2 million each by November 2018
9	Research Parks in top institutions	7 costing ₹1 billion each	₹1.91 billion to 4 institutions by November 2018
10	Ucchatar Aavishkar Yojana	₹2.5 billion/year	₹1.62 billion disbursed by November 2018

and commercialise technologies that can address India's needs? Will Phase 3 of the evolution of the Indian innovation system be different from the first two phases in this respect?

To address these questions, we conducted in-depth interviews with six experts who interact closely with start-ups: venture capitalists (VCs), venture advisors and intellectual property attorneys. The interviews revealed the following trends and challenges.

Technology versus Application Orientation

Very few Indian start-ups are innovative in the sense of developing new technology or advancing technological frontiers. This is because the academic incentive system supports patenting and publication but not commercialisation of technology. As a consequence, technological breakthroughs in universities and research labs do not find commercial application and often remain as prototypes. Further, there is inadequate funding available at the lab stage, which means even the few companies that come out of the university system do not have technology that is mature enough to seek venture funding.

However, Indian start-ups are innovative in the sense of solving Indian problems or "gaps" using available technology. If one uses the terminology of software stacks, then Indian firms have been working on the top layers of the stack (application level) and not the more technologically complex layers below (such as the network stack or the security stack). In this, they have been pushed by affordability constraints.

Prevalent Business Models and the Role of IP

In the consumer space, the majority of Indian start-ups tend to be similar to the corresponding ones abroad, with a focus on adaptation to the local market, particularly through processes and business models. Quality of execution and ability to raise funding tend to determine who are the winners (one or two firms in each space). In the B2B space, Indian start-ups typically follow the Software as a Service (SaaS) model. The challenge here is that Indian customers (that is, businesses) are quite conservative when it comes to technology investments, demand a high level of customisation and tend to give out smaller orders. This makes it difficult to scale purely on the back of the domestic market. Hence, scaling involves addressing an international market, which poses a new set of challenges for fledgling firms.

The above models are reflected in the start-ups' approach to intellectual property. While some start-ups do have IP in the form of patents, typically the firms' advantage comes from faster and better execution, which is not reflected in IP. Firms prefer not to patent process innovations so as to avoid disclosure to other firms. Some firms in the B2B space have an advantage in a complex or unique code they have written, but again do not seek formal IP protection for this (it should also be noted that by Indian law, software protection is provided by copyright and not patents). In any case, patenting at the application level is tough because business method patents are more complex to obtain and considerable sophistication is required to get such patents.

Source and Focus of Funding

The funding ecosystem plays an important role in influencing the nature of innovation. In developed countries, foundations and philanthropy play a key role in supporting breakthrough technologies through their long gestation period. Such support is limited in India – large Indian business houses and family wealth funds have not participated in funding in a big way. The absence of patient capital from philanthropic foundations is one of the reasons deep tech start-ups have been slow to take off. The government's initiative for a fund-of-funds to support investment in early-stage ventures is new and may have a positive impact in the years ahead. But so far, the bulk of investments have come from mainstream VCs with a 10–12-year fund cycle, who have placed their bets on companies deploying proven technologies towards solving well-defined problems.

In summary, India has taken giant strides forward in creating a conducive policy framework for innovation-led entrepreneurship. This has borne some results as is evident by the steady rise in patenting activities, improvement in the ease of doing business and a general buzz around innovation-led entrepreneurship. However, there are still several gaps to be addressed to make India an innovation hub. Alignment of incentives to promote the commercialisation of technologies coming out of universities and research labs, availability of patient capital and promotion of domestic consumption, both by the government and by large corporates, will be key.

Endnotes

[1]Krishnan, RT. 2003. The Evolution of a Developing Country Innovation System during Economic Liberalization: The Case of India. *The First Globelics Conference*.

[2]Global capability centres are facilities that were started to handle operations and IT support tasks. For many MNEs, they have gradually evolved to become centres of innovation, automation, research and analytics as well.

[3]Krishnan, RT and Prashantham, S. 2019. Innovation in and from India: The who, where, what, and when. *Global Strategy Journal* 9(3): 357–377.

[4]Quoted in *Startup India Action Plan 2016*, Government of India, https://www.startupindia.gov.in/content/dam/invest-india/Templates/public/Action_Plan.pdf
Accessed on March 17, 2021

[5]Agarwal, M. 2017. Government revises startup definition: increases startup age limit from five to seven. *Inc42*, 26 May 2017. https://inc42.com/buzz/government-revises-startup-definition/
Accessed on March 17, 2021

[6]Securities and Exchange Board of India, the regulator of Indian stock markets

[7]https://www.bseindia.com/markets/MarketInfo/DispNewNoticesCirculars.aspx?page=20181127-23
Accessed on March 17, 2021

[8]https://inc42.com/buzz/8-months-after-launch-bses-startup-platform-gets-its-first-listing/
Accessed on March 17, 2021

[9]Policy document available at https://dipp.gov.in/sites/default/files/national-IPR-Policy2016-14October2020.pdf
Accessed on May 21, 2021

[10]http://cipam.gov.in/index.php/iptrends/
Accessed on March 17, 2021

[11]http://cipam.gov.in/index.php/about/national-ipr-policy/
Accessed on March 17, 2021

[12]https://economictimes.indiatimes.com/small-biz/startups/newsbuzz/startup-action-plan-120-ventures-get-patents-1-granted-in-just-101-days/articleshow/68724356.cms
Accessed on March 17, 2021

[13]See the Incubation section for more on the IIT Madras Research Park.

[14]https://uay.iitm.ac.in
Accessed on March 17, 2021

[15]Policy document available at https://www.aicte-india.org/sites/default/files/AICTE%20Brochure_10.09.19.pdf Accessed on March 17, 2021

[16]Science, technology, engineering, mathematics

[17]National Education Policy, 2020, policy document, p 38. Accessed through https://www.mhrd.gov.in/sites/upload_files/mhrd/files/NEP_Final_English_0.pdf Accessed on March 17, 2021

[18]https://www.agnii.gov.in
Accessed on March 17, 2021

[19]https://innovate.mygov.in
Accessed on March 17, 2021

[20]https://app.thebizplanner.com/public/application/inc/5f6095637ab12a895ed4a38b
Accessed on March 17, 2021

[21]https://www.startupindia.gov.in/content/sih/en/startup-scheme/state-startup-policies/Bihar-state-policy.html
Accessed on March 17, 2021

[22]http://startup.karnataka.gov.in/startup-policy/
Accessed on March 17, 2021

[23]*Source:* Startup India, direct communication

[24]http://www.ipindia.nic.in/SIPP.htm
Accessed on March 17, 2021

[25]Ibid.

[26]http://www.ipindia.nic.in/writereaddata/Portal/Images/pdf/18-8-2020_Achievements_of__CGPDTM_during_2014-15_to_2019-2020_and_Impact_of_steps_taken-converted.pdf
Accessed on March 17, 2021

IN BRIEF

- Start-ups in India with technological innovations have taken advantage of the formal means of intellectual property (IP) protection such as patenting. Numbers are small but are on the upswing.
- Most patents to start-ups have been granted in the fields of electrical and mechanical engineering. These pertain to innovations in developing AI-based applications and products for consumers.
- Medical technology has been another productive area on the patent landscape of Indian start-ups.
- Such technology-driven start-ups are likely to generate higher value and, in turn, strengthen the entrepreneurial ecosystem of India.

ANALYTICAL ARTICLE

2

Patenting by Indian Start-ups: Moving Forward

Ruchi Sharma and Madan Dhanora

Sharma, R and Dhanora, M. 2021. "Patenting by Indian Start-ups: Moving Forward". In *Shifting Orbits: Decoding the Trajectory of the Indian Start-up Ecosystem*, edited by Thillai Rajan A, Srivardhini K Jha, Joffi Thomas and Rohan Chinchwadkar, 12–21. Hyderabad: Universities Press (India) Private Limited.

The Context

Start-ups play a crucial role in shaping market economies through innovation, which involves knowledge creation activities, identifying and creating new market opportunities and disrupting the status quo. Such creative activities involve introducing novel products, configuring better ways of doing business, identifying hitherto unexplored markets and pioneering marketing techniques that are uncertain, risky and expensive. These endeavours necessitate the existence of a strong and well-enforced intellectual property (IP) regime in an economy. A good IP regime incentivises businesses to engage in knowledge creation activities.

Companies employ both formal mechanisms (such as intellectual property rights) and informal ones (such as secrecy, lead time, access to complementary assets) to protect their innovations from imitation and earn profits. Such innovations are classified as technological – including product and process innovation – and non-technological – comprising marketing, organisational and business model changes. Technological innovations (product and process) are best captured and protected through patenting.

Start-ups often target technologically advanced economies like the US to patent and market their knowledge-intensive products due to easy acceptance of such products in these markets.[1] A thriving and supportive start-up ecosystem in those economies further helps such companies by attracting investors for funding. Hence, we find that many Indian start-ups file patents at the United States Patent and Trademark Office (USPTO). According to a NASSCOM (2020) report, over 280 technology patents were filed by Indian start-ups during 2015–2019 at the USPTO, showing a growth of over 40 per cent in the four-year span.[2]

Since Indian patent laws mandate foreign filing permission,[3] we capture the patenting activity of start-ups at the Indian Patent Office (IPO) in this chapter. This automatically includes all the patents filed with the USPTO and those filed only with IPO. We begin by stating the advantages of patenting as learnt from international experiences. We then elaborate upon the patents granted to Indian start-ups and highlight the technological and geographical aspects of these patents. A few cases of start-ups that have received awards for patenting from IPO or have relatively large numbers of patents will be discussed in the third section.

Why Patent?

Patenting – the formal means of intellectual property protection – has gained popularity in India since the start of the twenty-first century. Companies have become aware of the availability of such appropriability (ways to capture gains from innovation) tools and employ them strategically to increase their market share and deal with competitors. Patents allow businesses to:

- Build a competitive advantage, especially against established incumbents
- Prevent competitors from using their technology
- Obtain equity finance by signalling to investors about the appropriability of their technology
- Protect themselves while negotiating business deals
- License and have a bargaining chip while cross-licensing
- Defend themselves against patent lawsuits by others
- Own a sellable asset that increases the company's value

For a start-up, patents are often an important signal of its innovativeness and a vital precursor to the commercialisation of invention. The grant of patent increases the probability of venture funding as the granted patents signal the technological innovativeness of the new venture to investors. For instance, Berkeley Patent Survey found that start-ups predominantly patent in order to secure financing.[4] A study based on Israeli technology start-ups showed that patents help in attracting new investors as opposed to old investors, and patents are used by start-ups as a signal and not simply as an input in their value function.[5] Zhang and colleagues[6] highlight that start-ups can convey three types of signals – technological, commercial and legal – to the investor through patents. Further, based on the Chinese biopharmaceutical industry, the results of the study show that legal signals have compelling influence over venture capital funding levels, closely followed by technological signals. Further, prompt patent approvals were found to be associated with greater job and sales growth and higher investor returns among the US start-up firms.[7]

Helmers and Rogers[8] studied the growth between 2001 and 2005 of British start-ups that patented in 2000. Their work shows that start-ups that owned patents had a lower likelihood of failure and such firms also experienced higher asset growth. Patenting also positively influences the productivity and profitability of firms.[9] Thus, the involvement of start-ups in patenting is likely to create firms that survive longer with better probability to grow into large firms. The growth of such firms, apart from generating employment and income, contributes to the start-up ecosystem of a country.

The growth story of Amazon with "single-action ordering" patents filed in 1997 is a case in point. "1-Click" was path-breaking in the e-commerce business. With the help of this technology, customers needed to enter billing, shipping and payment information just once, and afterwards they could buy their products and services with one click. This innovation helped Amazon to create a monopolistic position in the e-commerce business.[10] This patent also helped Amazon to expand its business to the Amazon Marketplace, where third parties could buy and sell their products online. This technology also increased the customer base for Amazon as they had information about customer payment and their preferences. Today, Amazon has 1.1 million employees and a market valuation of more than $1.6 trillion.[11] Amazon's "1-Click" patent expired in 2017 and other retailers adopted it as the knowledge became part of the public domain.

Patenting by Start-ups: The Aggregates

Studies on start-ups in developed economies may also guide the behaviour of Indian start-ups. With this motivation, we look at the patent statistics of start-ups at Indian Patent Office (IPO), initially at aggregate level and then in detail. Exhibit 2.1 shows the increasing trend in the applications filed by start-ups since 2016–17 while garnering a larger share of total applications. Interestingly, within two years, the share of patent applications by start-ups grew from 0.35 per cent to 1.6 per cent. There has been an overall growth in filing of requests by start-ups for expedited examination every year, from 161 in 2017–18 to 293 in 2018–19. In the same period, the patents granted to start-ups increased from 10 to 110 (See Exhibit 2.2). The applications in the expedited examination category are examined and processed for granting of patent quickly, and the average time taken for the decision is less than a year from the date of receipt of the request for expedited examination.

Exhibit 2.1: Patent applications filed at Indian Patent Office

Year	Applications by start-ups*	Total applications
2016–17	160 (0.35%)	45,444
2017–18	511 (1.07%)	47,854
2018–19	801 (1.58%)	50,659

*The number in the parentheses is the percentage share of start-up applications in the total applications.

Source: Annual Reports, Indian Patent Office, various issues. The numbers are reported for financial year April–March.

Our analysis of patents granted to start-ups shows that the grant lag duration between application and grant is rather encouraging, as, on an average, start-ups received patents in 2.10 years. The policy of expedited examination seems to be reducing the waiting period for start-ups to receive patents, though they need not wait for the grant to commercialise the technology, as application filing establishes the priority date.

In the year 2017–2018, 10 patents were granted and 8 patents were rejected by the Indian Patent Office. Similarly, in the year 2018–19, around 110 patents were granted and 34 were rejected. The patent office ensures that the invention for which the patent is sought does not belong to a list of non-patentable inventions before examining it for patentability criteria. These criteria entail novelty, inventive step and industrial applicability.

Methodology and Data

We used the list of 14,476 entities recognised by DIPP as “start-ups” as on 17 December, 2018 and searched for those that had received patents using PatSeer, a private patent database owned by Gridlogics Technologies Pvt Ltd. Using patent statistics as a measure of innovation entails making a choice between application and grant data. Nagoka et al.[12] argue that patent grant is a poor indicator of innovative activity, particularly for cross-country analysis, since not all patent applications are requested for examination and only a part of them result in granted patents. However, while considering the data for a single country, using granted patent data strongly establishes the novelty of the technology as it ensures that the application has gone through the requisite examination process. Accordingly, we used the data on granted patents for further analysis, which has rendered the patent numbers a bit on the conservative side.

Exhibit 2.2: Patent applications filed and granted by IPO under expedited examination scheme

	Request for expedited examination filed	First Examination Report issued	Patent granted	Refused
2017–18	161	137	10	8
2018–19	293	263	110	34

Source: Annual Reports, Indian Patent Office, various issues

Second, there is a possibility that some entrepreneurs patent as individual inventors instead of with the start-up as an applicant. Inclusion of entrepreneur-based search may increase the total number of patents granted to start-ups but may not significantly affect the trends we observed. For technology classification, we used Schmoch's (2008)[13] report to the World Intellectual Property Organisation (WIPO) that collates different International Patent Classification Codes (IPC) into different technology areas.

Patenting by Start-ups: The Details

How Many Are Patenting?

Our data search has shown that 147 entities have been granted 219 patents by the IPO. Thus, around 1 per cent of DPIIT-recognised start-ups have been involved in technological innovations that they aim to protect using formal means. Comparatively, around 4 per cent of start-ups patented in the UK.[14] This can be attributed to the lack of understanding of IP systems in India, particularly among small companies. Patents as a tool to appropriate new ideas are predominantly used by high and medium technology manufacturing industries including pharmaceutical, chemical, electrical machinery and equipment, motor vehicles, medical instruments, aircraft and spacecraft, office, accounting and computing machinery, and so on. Among the different high and medium technology industries, research further highlights that companies use other informal ways (like lead time to market – first mover advantage) to protect their creative ideas. Thus, it is mostly patent-sensitive industries that give prominence to protection by patenting. In the case of the service sector, copyrights and trademarks are significant tools that help companies to protect and commercially exploit their ideas. Accordingly, the patenting activity of the Indian start-ups (dominated by service sector ventures)[15] should be located in the specific industrial milieu. Thus, the involvement of a small number of start-ups in patenting needs to be viewed considering the limited reach of patents as an appropriation means for service-oriented businesses. Other potential explanations could be the financial constraints, long grant lags, lack of infrastructure support and lack of awareness, which current IP regime policies have begun to address.

Indian start-ups represent a satisfactory picture of the growth rate of patenting activities. For example, there was an annual growth of 56.75 per cent in patent filing by start-ups in the year 2018–2019. Companies like String Bio (biotechnology-based start-up), which works towards the production of animal feed, and Log 9 Materials (nanotechnology start-up), which specialises in the energy sector, are actively patenting their technologies and raising funds from various sources.[16] We have also explored patenting activities by Indian Unicorns that have a valuation of more than $1 billion. Among the 23 Unicorns that we identified,[17] 17 per cent are actively filing patent applications, greater than the proportion of start-ups patenting in the whole sample.[18] However, most of these patents are held by a handful of Unicorns, and those that operate service-oriented businesses have limited patenting activity. For instance, InMobi, with more than 15 patent applications, received funds from Google and Mithril Capital. The majority of start-ups that are active in patenting activities belong to the mechanical engineering, electrical engineering, chemical and instruments domains. Consequently, we discuss this aspect in detail.

What Is Being Patented?

The technological area classification based on the International Patent Classification codes of these patents is given in Exhibit 2.3. The technological classification reveals that 28.8 per cent of patents are granted in the fields of mechanical engineering, followed by electrical engineering (26.5 per cent) and chemistry (19.9 per cent). These ratios for patenting by start-ups are different from the overall India trends in total patenting (all companies), where the majority of patents are granted in the chemical (35 per cent) sector. Start-ups have been focussing on the electrical and mechanical sectors with inventions based in the subdomains of computer technology (electrical) and transportation (mechanical). These sectors are characterised by technology advancement and robust market growth along with a supportive ecosystem. Start-ups like SigTuple Technology and Twenty Two Motors have been developing AI-based solutions for the health and transportation sectors, respectively.

Exhibit 2.3: Percentage share of different technological domains

Mechanical Engineering: **29.7%**
Electrical Engineering: **27.4%**
Chemistry: **20.5%**
Instruments: **14.6%**
Other Fields: **7.8%**

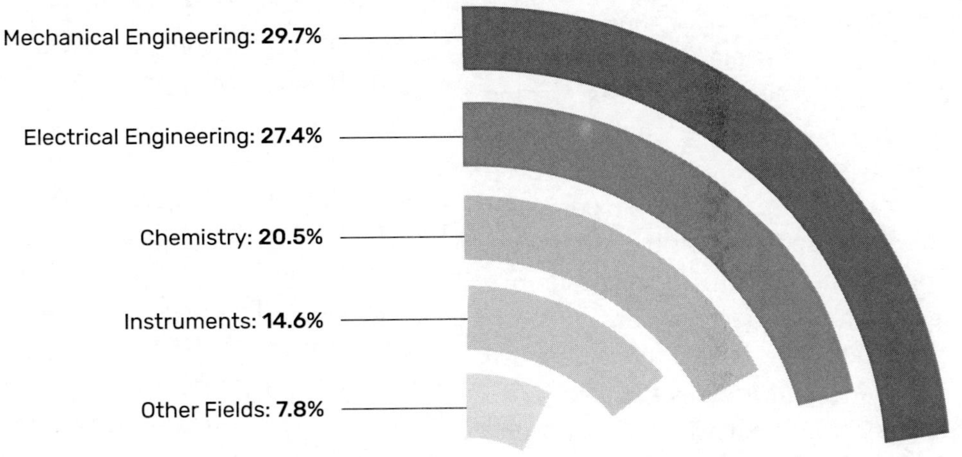

Exhibit 2.4: Percentage share of different technological subdomains

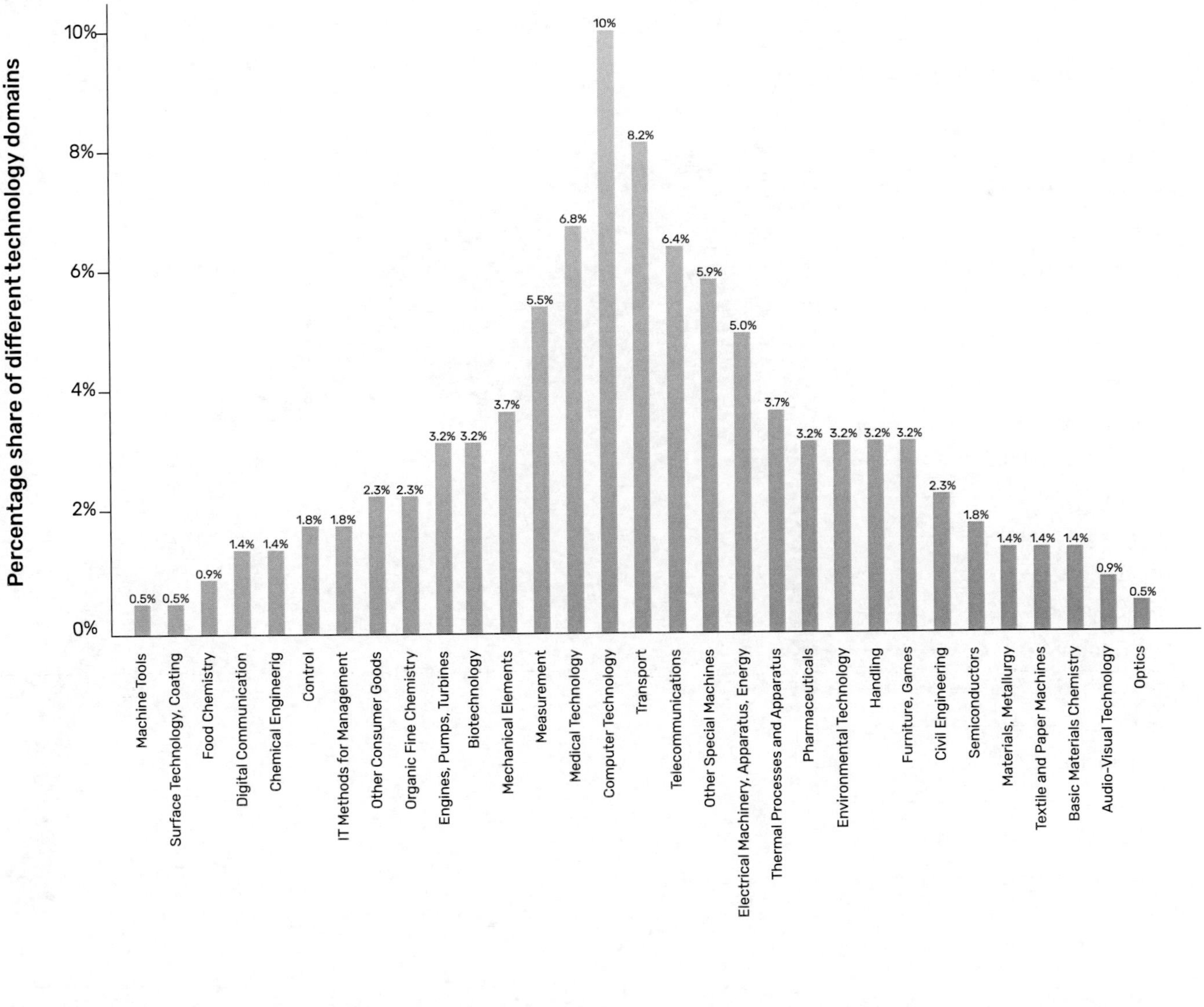

Percentage share of different technology domains
10%
8%
6%
4%
2%
0%
Machine Tools 0.5%
Surface Technology, Coating 0.5%
Food Chemistry 0.9%
Digital Communication 1.4%
Chemical Engineerig 1.4%
Control 1.8%
IT Methods for Management 1.8%
Other Consumer Goods 2.3%
Organic Fine Chemistry 2.3%
Engines, Pumps, Turbines 3.2%
Biotechnology 3.2%
Mechanical Elements 3.7%
Measurement 5.5%
Medical Technology 6.8%
Computer Technology 10%
Transport 8.2%
Telecommunications 6.4%
Other Special Machines 5.9%
Electrical Machinery, Apparatus, Energy 5.0%
Thermal Processes and Apparatus 3.7%
Pharmaceuticals 3.2%
Environmental Technology 3.2%
Handling 3.2%
Furniture, Games 3.2%
Civil Engineering 2.3%
Semiconductors 1.8%
Materials, Metallurgy 1.4%
Textile and Paper Machines 1.4%
Basic Materials Chemistry 1.4%
Audio-Visual Technology 0.9%
Optics 0.5%

Who Is Patenting?

It is important to understand the epicentre of innovation activity to design appropriate policies. The state-wise distribution of patents granted to start-ups (Exhibit 2.5) shows that the majority of patents have been granted to start-ups from Karnataka (24.2 per cent), followed by Maharashtra (18.3 per cent). This is no surprise as the majority of patents are granted in computer technology, and the geographical distribution reflects the concentration of granted patents at the country's IT hubs due to agglomeration effects. Locating a start-up in such an area helps an entrepreneur because of a favourable innovation environment, potential to collaborate and gains through knowledge spill-overs. National Capital Region (NCR), including Delhi, parts of Haryana and Uttar Pradesh, accounts for about 15 per cent of patents. No regional difference was observed in the technology or the nature of businesses patenting between Karnataka, Maharashtra and NCR, with almost similar spread of patents among different technology domains. That more than 70 per cent of the patents have been from just five states represents a concentration of innovation activities within the country. The remaining states that have identified start-ups and patenting as a core area for policymaking need to design policies accordingly.

The 219 patents granted involved 574 inventors in total, with an average of three inventors per patent. The gender diversity of innovation by start-ups is rather dismal as these inventions involved only 49 women, highlighting the lack of gender diversity in the innovation process of start-ups. The top five start-ups hold 16 per cent of the total patents granted and the top 10, around 24 per cent. The concentration of patents with few companies is evident in Exhibit 2.6, where the graph tapers to a long tail on the right.

The international research discussed earlier indicates that the entrepreneurial ecosystem in India is likely to generate more value as start-ups start patenting actively. The patenting start-ups with higher likelihood

Exhibit 2.5: Percentage share of different states

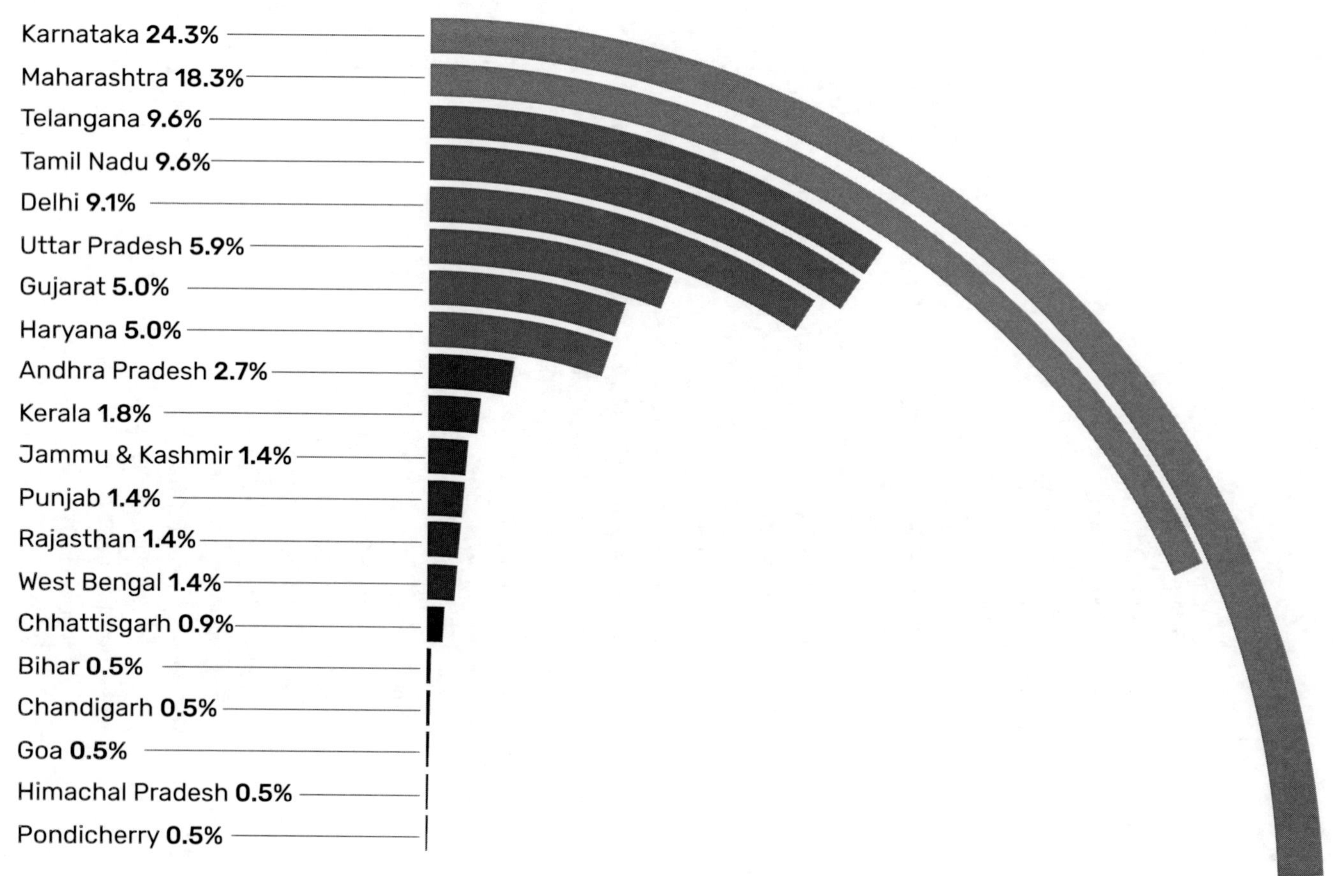

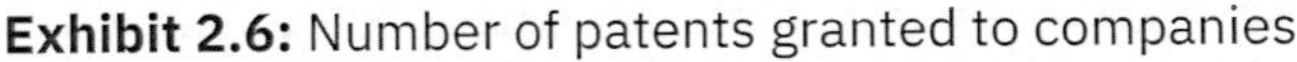

Exhibit 2.6: Number of patents granted to companies

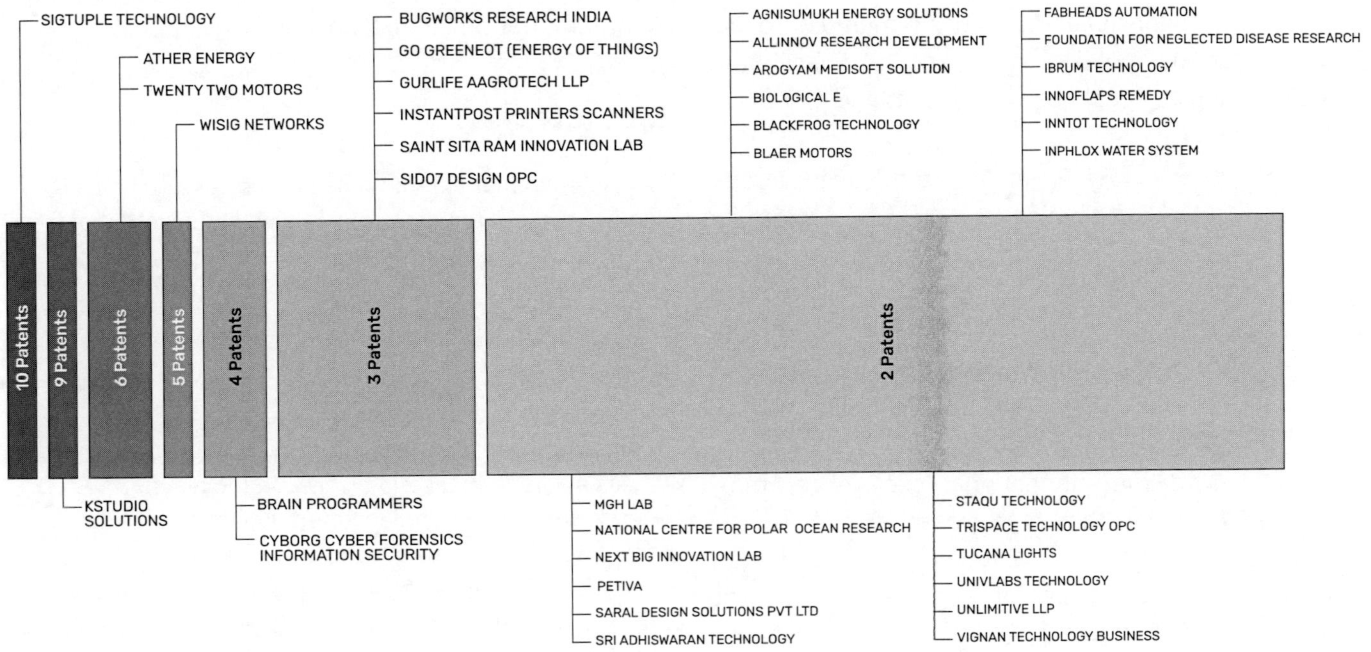

of survival will contribute to the growth of the local ecosystem. Innovative firms further the technological frontiers of a country and help in attaining international competitiveness. It is interesting to note that Indian start-ups are patenting in the general-purpose technology (computer technology and transport) sectors that are likely to boost economy-wide efficiency and productivity growth. These sectors are also major drivers of Industry 4.0 based on digital transformation. The patenting trend by start-ups in India, still at an incipient stage, is likely to pick up, considering the spurt witnessed in the past five years and the positive policy framework created by the government.

Illustrative Case Studies

An analysis of those start-ups that have been granted more than five patents by the IPO and two other start-ups that have been granted awards for their IP commercialisation provides interesting insights.

Allinnov Research and Development Private Limited was recognised by the IPO as the Top Startup for IP Commercialisation in 2017. The start-up was incorporated in October 2015 and is involved in business and management consultancy. The key focus of the start-up has been on indigenous product research and innovation training to organisations on research activities in diverse fields of engineering and science. It supports innovators from the product conceptualisation stage to final launch.

Kstudio Solutions Private Limited was awarded the Top Startup by the IPO for IP Commercialisation in 2019. It was founded in 2016 by Viraj Kalyani in Pune and had filed 49 patents, designs and trademarks till April 2019. The company focussed on delivering engineering insights through mechanical technology products. It has an IoT-based product line called Magic Measure, which enables high reliability, accuracy and precision in OEM assembly lines. The start-up also creates new inventions and patents to license or sell to third parties.

Ather Energy Private Limited[19] designs and sells electric two-wheelers for the Indian market and has its academic roots in IIT Madras. The main objective of the company was to create high-performing smart electric vehicles with low maintenance. The company had received funding from the Technology Development Board under the Department of Science and Technology and a handful of angel investors, followed by investment from Hero MotoCorp. It signed an MoU with the Tamil Nadu Government in December 2019 to set up a 400,000 sq. ft manufacturing plant for electrical vehicles in Hosur.

SigTuple Technologies Private Limited is a Health-Tech organisation focussed on healthcare delivery while innovating in diagnostic tools. This start-up employed AI-powered tools to create intelligent screening solutions that aid in diagnosis. It has raised multiple rounds of funding from angel investors and leading venture investors such as Accel Partners, Chiratae Ventures and pi Ventures.

Twenty Two Motors Private Limited,[20] incorporated in 2016, works on technologies such as AI, lithium-ion storage, Internet of Things (IoT) and advanced electric power trains. KYMCO India, a sports motorbikes brand, holds a 25 per cent stake in Twenty Two Motors, and invested $15 million, with a plan to invest another $50 million in the next three years. The company has also raised ₹102 million from a leading angel investor.

In line with the international experience, these examples highlight that start-ups that are actively patenting have been successful in attracting venture investors. Securing a patent successfully not only signals the commercial potential of the inventions, but also gives strong protection to the invention in the competitive marketplace. The investment thus received helps to commercialise the patents, as start-ups rarely have sufficient internal resources to finance their downstream activities following an invention. The start-ups illustrated here have been engaged in AI-based solutions for the transportation and healthcare sectors. These young innovative companies are building capabilities with their novel products and using formal means to protect those capabilities. Though the impact of patents on the growth and survival of start-ups is yet to be conclusively established, what has clearly emerged has been the interest of investors to invest in start-ups that have patents.

Summary

Patenting of technology-driven innovations by Indian start-ups is in a nascent phase. It is important to increase awareness among small companies about IP, reduce the financial burden of patenting and hasten the pace of grants. As awareness among start-ups about the IP regime increases, and grants are received faster, the growth in patenting would increase. Various central government and state-level organisations along with industry partners are involved in organising workshops on educating start-ups about IP rights, their benefits and strategic use. While the effort taken by the government to intensify patenting by start-ups has been laudable and is a step in the right direction, success needs sustained commitment from all the stakeholders.

Endnotes

[1] Considering that patent rights are territorial in nature, separate patent applications are filed in the patent offices of the respective countries to seek protection.

[2] NASSCOM. 2020. *IoT: Driving the Patent Growth Story In India*. https://nasscom.in/knowledge-center/publications/iot-driving-patent-growth-story-india

[3] According to Indian patent law, the filing of patent applications outside the territory of India is not permitted unless a patent application is filed in India first. Under Section 39(1) of the Indian Patent Act, such a foreign patent application can be filed only after six weeks from the Indian filing, provided no secrecy directions are imposed by the Patent Office within that period. An exception in the form of applying and receiving Foreign Filing Licence is also provided in the act.

[4] Graham, SJ and Sichelman, T. 2008. Why do start-ups patent? *Berkeley Technology Law Journal* 23 (3): 1063–1097; Graham SJ, Merges, RP, Samuelson, P and Sichelman, TM. 2009. High Technology Entrepreneurs and the Patent System: Results of the 2008 Berkeley Patent Survey (June 30, 2009). *Berkeley Technology Law Journal* 24(4): 255–327.

[5] Conti, A, Thursby, J and Thursby, M. 2013. Patents as signals for start-up financing. *The Journal of Industrial Economics* 61(3): 592–622.

[6] Zhang, L, Guo, Y and Sun, G. 2019. How patent signals affect venture capital: The evidence of bio-pharmaceutical start-ups in China. *Technological Forecasting and Social Change* 145: 93–104.

[7] Farre-Mensa, J, Hegde, D and Ljungqvist, A. 2016. The bright side of patents (No. w21959). *National Bureau of Economic Research*.

[8] Helmers, C and Rogers, M. 2011. Does patenting help high-tech start-ups?. *Research Policy* 40(7): 1016–1027.

[9] Ambrammal, SK and Sharma, R. 2016. Impact of patenting on firms' performance: An empirical investigation based on manufacturing firms in India. *Economics of Innovation and New Technology* 25(1): 14–32.

[10] https://knowledge.wharton.upenn.edu/article/amazons-1-click-goes-off-patent/

[11]https://www.wsj.com/articles/amazon-competition-shopify-wayfair-allbirds-antitrust-11608235127
Accessed on May 21, 2021

[12]Nagaoka, S, Motohashi, K and Goto, A. 2010. "Patent statistics as an innovation indicator". In *Handbook of the Economics of Innovation* 2:1083–1127, North-Holland.

[13]Schmoch, U. 2008. Concept of a technology classification for country comparisons. *Final Report to the World Intellectual Property Organisation, WIPO.*

[14]Helmers, C and Rogers, M. 2011. Does patenting help high-tech start-ups? *Research Policy* 40(7): 1016–1027.

[15]https://www.financialexpress.com/industry/sme/cafe-sme/india-gearing-up-for-next-wave-of-saas-start-ups-perfecting-their-business-models-expanding-globally/2164530/

[16]https://yourstory.com/2019/12/india-top-50-disruptive-startups-yourstory/amp
Accessed on May 21, 2021

[17]These are Paytm, OYO Rooms, BYJU'S, Ola Cabs, Swiggy, Zomato, Paytm Mall, ReNew Power, Zerodha, BigBasket, Udaan, BillDesk, Delhivery, Mu Sigma, Lenskart, PolicyBazaar, FirstCry, Dream11, Hike, Ola Electric, Rivigo, InMobi and Druva.

[18]These Unicorn start-ups are Mu Sigma, Rivigo, InMobi and Druva.

[19]https://www.wikiwand.com/en/Ather_Energy#/History

[20]https://yourstory.com/2019/04/electric-vehicles-start-up-twenty-two-motors

IN BRIEF

- Deep technology start-ups do not fit squarely into the existing funding stages and lean start-up model of the software-led entrepreneurial ecosystem. Product development from idea to market can take years, requiring a long-haul mindset. Those interested in investing with patient capital may need to develop a template that is different from the venture capital (VC) growth model that currently exists.
- Clarity of vision and goal behind the product innovation helps in decision-making when facing a fork in the road, such as commercialisation of sub-scale prototype versus development of full-scale product. Finding investors who agree with the initial vision helps start-ups stay the course and being viable for the long haul.
- It is essential to be mindful from the beginning about regulations (which the new products may be contravening), customers and the nature of the industry sector in which market entry would occur.
  The business aspect is as important in the pre-market technology development phase as well.
- The steps required to take the Indian innovation ecosystem to the next level requires targeted efforts to build a risk funding ecosystem. Building a mindset of risk funding requires incentives and subsidies for investors in the initial years.
- Innovation requires individuals from diverse backgrounds and collaboration; therefore, building porous systems such as the IIT Madras Research Park with a focus on research translation is essential.

ROUNDTABLE

3

GOING DEEP: THE DYNAMICS OF FOUNDING RADICALLY INNOVATIVE START-UPS

Srivardhini K Jha

Jha, SK. 2021. "Going Deep: The Dynamics of Founding Radically Innovative Start-ups". In *Shifting Orbits: Decoding the Trajectory of the Indian Start-up Ecosystem*, edited by Thillai Rajan A, Srivardhini K Jha, Joffi Thomas and Rohan Chinchwadkar, 22–29. Hyderabad: Universities Press (India) Private Limited.

Deep science and technology start-ups (deep tech for short) are companies whose products and services are based on substantial scientific and/or engineering breakthroughs. Deep science encompasses fundamental inventions and discoveries in pure science fields such as physics and chemistry. Examples of deep tech include artificial intelligence (AI), Internet of Things (IoT), Machine Learning (ML), Natural Language Processing (NLP), quantum computing, blockchain, robotics, data analytics and others. These find application in a wide variety of industrial sectors, ranging from agriculture and automotive to energy production, healthcare and textiles. However, certain industrial sectors such as life sciences and space technology are more reliant on deep tech than others.

Deep tech is being heralded as the foundation of the fourth industrial revolution, as steam engine, transport and communication, and computing were for the first, second and third. Deep science and technology innovations are extremely essential, especially for a developing country such as India, as they can better people's lives and can fuel rapid economic growth. However, companies based on deep tech face a unique set of challenges in developing and commercialising their products. They require an ecosystem that supports the journey from scientific breakthrough to market success.

To help us understand the Indian deep tech ecosystem better, Srivardhini K Jha, Associate Professor of Entrepreneurship at IIM Bangalore, conducted a roundtable discussion with a panel of distinguished speakers: Satyanarayanan R Chakravarthy, Taslimarif Saiyed and Umakant Soni from the fields of aerospace, life sciences, AI and ML.

This chapter is an excerpt from the conversation pertaining to the dynamics of the Indian deep tech ecosystem.

Uniqueness of the Deep Tech Sector

***Srivardhini:* What are the unique challenges that one would face as a deep tech entrepreneur and how do you tackle these challenges?**

Umakant: I would say there were three challenges at the time I was starting up in 2009–10. The first was the lack of a start-up orientation in academic and research institutes. The second was finding early customers who were willing to take a bet on you. And the third was the funding ecosystem for deep tech, as proof of concept could easily take four years, which is much longer than usual in a start-up scenario. The ecosystem is getting better with respect to all these aspects.

Satya: The single biggest problem in deep tech is the long time it takes to go from ideation to market entry. This also means that it takes a while before ecosystem stakeholders start having confidence in the product. However, there are several ways by which one can make them believe in one's endeavours, such as by showing sub-scale prototypes or early proofs of concepts. This might require bootstrap funding. The next challenge is to decide if one wants to commercialise the prototype or engage in building the full-scale product, as one may not have the resources to do both. There does not exist a template for this kind of decision-making. It really depends on the entrepreneur's aims and the ability to focus on that. The third challenge is speaking to ecosystem stakeholders such as investors who are used to the software start-up model. They tend to slot a deep

Exhibit 3.1: Understanding the differences between proof of concept, prototype and minimum viable product

THREE STAGES OF PRODUCT DEVELOPMENT

PROOF OF CONCEPT

Test the practical feasibility of a hitherto theoretical concept.

Example: The theoretical idea that microwave radiation can be used to heat food is tested out.

PROTOTYPE

Develop a working model of the product replete with many functional features, in addition to the core concept. The objective is to check feasibility and fix errors.

Example: A working model of a microwave oven is developed, fitted with internal light and other features. Product design, colour and style are considered.

MINIMUM VIABLE PRODUCT

Minimum Viable Product (MVP): This is derived from Silicon Valley's lean start-up model. Release the bare minimum marketable (error-free and design-ready) product in the market to get customer feedback. Future changes are largely due to customer needs rather than technological feasibility.

Example: A "beta" model of the microwave oven is released to a focus group of customers. MVPs work best for software products. For deep tech and science, it is largely the final market-ready product that is developed, due to the R&D, investment and production model of such products, vis-à-vis an app or software release.

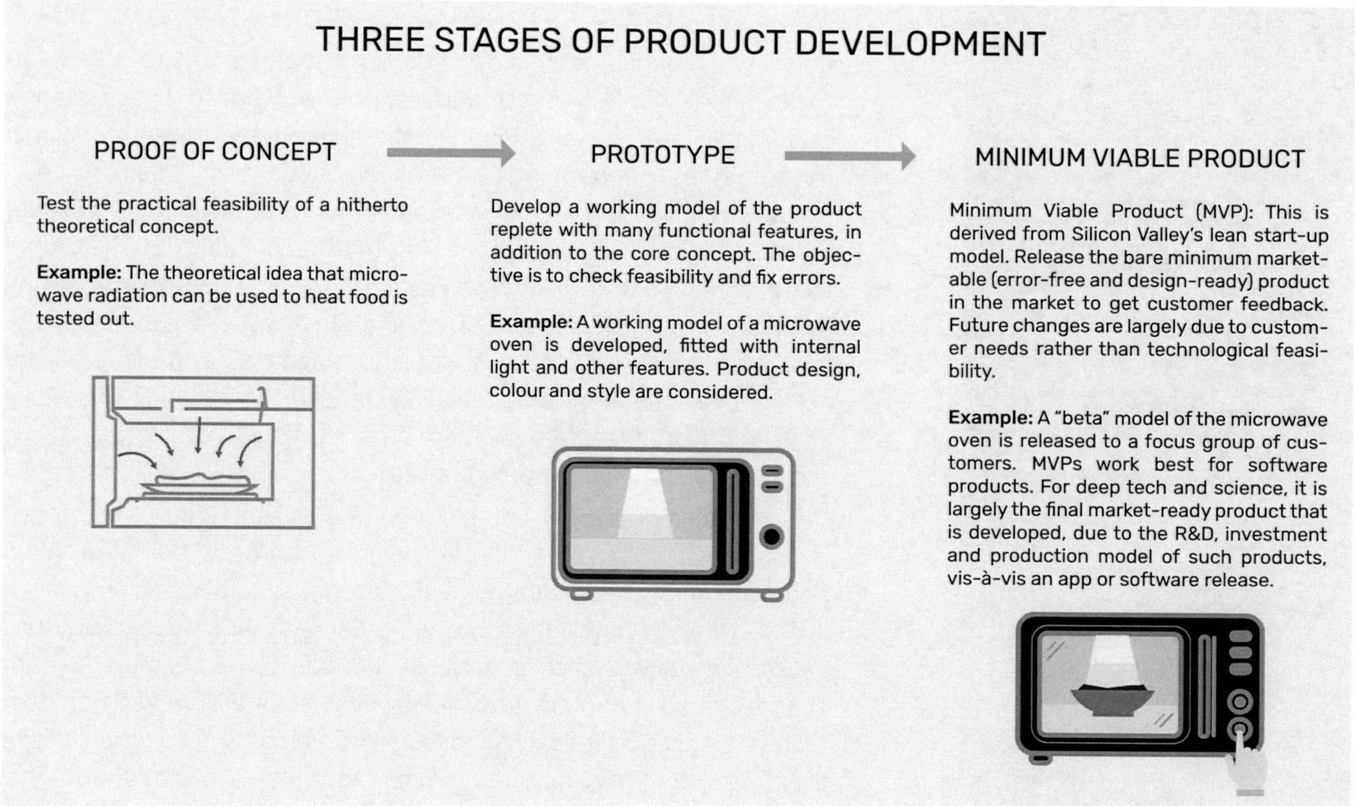

tech enterprise into the typical VC funding stages such as series A, series B, and so on.[1] Given the different nature of product innovation when compared to software, this template naturally does not work for deep tech.

Srivardhini: **How does one snap out of the tension between commercialising a sub-scale prototype and building the full-scale product? What has been your experience?**

Satya: There are two factors to the decision: the kind of product the entrepreneur has and the entrepreneur's vision. I will elaborate on the first factor with the example of rockets. I mentioned earlier about going from sub-scale prototype to full-scale product. However, in the case of rockets, product specificity dictates that the starting prototype itself has to have a minimum largeness to it. Therefore, we may not actually scale up but scale down. In Agnikul, for example, we have a 100-kg rocket prototype and are trying to scale it down to a 30-kg one. The second factor is the founders' vision in terms of the kind of impact they want to have. Let me take the example of ePlanes.[2] We have sub-scale prototypes which can ferry cargo, but we wish to ferry passengers. It may even be possible that the cargo market is actually bigger than the passenger market. How do we decide between building the full-scale ePlane or commercialising the sub-scale prototype for the cargo market? It is about the vision and the dream, about the impact that we are trying to make in people's lives. And we need to find that particular investor who is as passionate about that dream as we are. We need to find someone who would be able to see the vision of passenger planes and not opt for the low hanging fruit, be it cargo or whatever else.

Umakant: That is actually a real challenge because this whole lean start-up methodology does not work in deep tech start-ups. So many entrepreneurs end up harming their start-ups because they try to fit into the perspective of MVP (minimum viable product). This is a challenge if we want to develop the ecosystem for deep

Exhibit 3.2: Technology commercialisation versus prototype development

Technology Commercialisation

The process of transferring the intellectual property right (licence) for a technology by its inventor. Enables technology to be taken from the laboratory for practical use.

Example: A cancer screening method is developed and patented by students and faculty in a university.

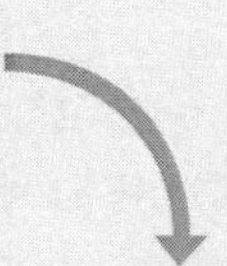

Licensing Out to Corporates

When licensing out from labs to other parties, full-scale marketable product development is not required.

Example: Licensing the method to a big medical devices company like GE who develops the final device. This expedites and optimises the product-to-market cycle, while bringing in significant income for the inventors.

Starting Up

When innovators form their own start-ups, they need to go the long haul and develop the market-ready product.

Example: Develop the method to create a cancer screening device for underserved markets. Inventors think they can best develop the device as per the customer's needs.

tech innovation. The frank answer, in a nutshell, is that we don't have one.

Satya: I just want to quickly add that unlike the software sector, in deep tech, at least in rockets and planes, we do not have a choice of failure. So, for example, the Zoom call that we are doing or the Google Meet or Microsoft Teams software that we use these days have gone through multiple iterations. These kinds of products can develop errors and the consequences are not severe. Due to the immense resources we use, and at times the danger to human lives, many deep science sectors cannot afford to fail. Especially when they are one of the few, initial, small start-ups pioneering entrepreneurship in the sector.

***Srivardhini:* Fair point and I think it is applicable to the life sciences sector as well, right?**

Taslimarif: There is no doubt in my mind that tech (software) and healthcare have phenomenal convergence potential, and India needs it. Thirty per cent of our population is underserved in terms of healthcare and, therefore, we need to urgently tap into that potential. But one of the core challenges of the healthcare sector, as compared to say software, is that the industry itself is complex. Healthcare is a state subject and we have different kinds of players influencing the narrative. Different aspects such as reimbursement, government, primary healthcare, prevention – all have their own dynamics. On top of it, there is the regulatory aspect. You are actually sitting on top of one black box after another. To bring in and position a new technology in this kind of a system has been difficult for start-ups. That's where I think one requires a clear long-term approach and not look at a HealthTech company as another software tech company.

We should look at a HealthTech company as a long-term haul. It is not a sector where start-ups can scale up in a short term with high valuations. Rather than valuations, we should look at the revenue potential of the products when they enter the market. We should look at commercialisation and entrepreneurship from a market and greater good point of view. Can the same technology be useful for other established players through licensing? We need to understand that we should treat this baby differently than the baby that we have taken care of for the last few years.

Positives and Challenges of the Indian Deep Tech Ecosystem

***Srivardhini:* Given that we have established that this is different, what has been going well and what are the catalytic factors that we still need from an ecosystem perspective? If one looks at Israel, Silicon Valley or Boston, not to compare ourselves with them – I know we are different – but what does it take for us to become a vibrant deep tech ecosystem?**

Umakant: I think one of the fantastic things that is actually happening out there is the roll-out of NM-ICPS (National Mission on Interdisciplinary Cyber-Physical Systems) by the Department of Science and Technology for setting up research parks, with close to $0.5 billion of investment.

Satya: In the space sector, what has been positive is that the tide has turned completely in our favour because of the Aatmanirbhar Bharat programme. With programmes such as IN-SPACe[3] and SEED[4], the government is trying to support the sector in many ways. For example, launching is now permitted. A lot of these aspects have changed for the positive in the last six months. And we look forward to benefitting from the numerous opportunities created through these programmes for the private sector due to the vast breadth of the industry, from commercial, space-related airspace to drone-related airspace.

Taslimarif: What is going well for us is that there is a belief in the products that our people are building. Indian innovators are actually challenging devices made by Baxter, Philips, Bosch, J&J and many other big names.

In terms of building a real solid ecosystem, what we need is a critical mass of deep tech stakeholders in one place and such clusters across India. Bengaluru is definitely emerging as one. Even within Bengaluru, we need a solid critical mass of deep tech work happening around an epicentre, which can possibly even be academic institutes like the Indian Institute of Science. It is the top-most priority to have a phenomenally porous system wherein we have new start-ups talking to professors of science and tech institutes on a daily basis. They should be sharing the same cafeteria, the same corridor and bumping into each other regularly. That has happened possibly a little bit with the IIT Madras Research Park, if I am not wrong.

The second thing that we need to build is a large ecosystem of risk funding for product development. In the last few years, there has been good support from the government for early proof-of-concept studies. However, in deep tech and science, it is a long journey where risk remains till one reaches the product stage. If there is no risk funding, start-ups stagnate after proof of concept, struggle and then pivot. There has to be some subsidy for investors to come in and actually invest in the risk, as we see in the case of Israel.

Umakant: I feel that we need to build ideas to impact innovation engines. The Indian Institutes of Technology and other similar institutes were set up mainly for teaching and a bit of research, but the research translation element was missing in our universities. They were not really hiring people who could translate research into prototypes or products into companies. We need to build that layer. We are trying to build a prototype of that layer in ARTPARK, to be associated with the Indian Institute of Science. ARTPARK stands for AI and Robotics Technology Park and is purpose-built for research translation. We are also building an associated venture studio. The model is that you have research universities developing prototypes in deep association with research parks and venture studios which take those prototypes and convert them into products. Even then, to really build these companies and sustain them over a long period of time, one needs venture funds with a timeline of 12 to 15 years. One of the main reasons behind the low number of deep life sciences start-ups is the long duration of 15 years required from the proof-of-concept stage. There are 15-year funds in the US and Europe. For example, in just tiny nations like Switzerland and Sweden, you see these interesting companies sprouting up. Innovation is systemic and, therefore, you have to build the system for innovation. Failing that, we will be only talking about Aatmanirbhar, but we will never possess autonomy in terms of having access to deep tech. And I think that in some small pockets there have been positive developments, such as IIT Madras, Kanpur and now IISc. So, I think that in the next 3 to 4 years we should start to see an alternative model emerge.

Satya: I would answer you with the example of NCCRD,[5] which is doing reasonably well. NCCRD was originally conceived as an R&D centre for combustion but in the last few years it has actually been transformed into a hub of deep tech start-ups. That solid R&D base needs to be available where products and new IP can be developed. Incubators and accelerators alone are not sufficient for fostering deep tech. Tinkering labs are a step in the right direction, but not as solid. Second, we need to also make sure that the product is commercially viable. We need to compare the cost of production with the price potential customers are willing to pay for the pain point we are trying to solve. The third requirement is conducive regulations. Do the current regulations permit you to do whatever you are trying to do? This is often a question for innovative products. Fourth, apart from the physical infrastructure including high-tech machines, we also need business infrastructure and the requisite human talent – a chief business officer, chief technology officer, a CEO, COO. We have all these individuals taking care of running the show at the Centre, including looking at the legalities and advising on regulatory changes. Finally, if you were to talk about funding, give me a cheque for ₹750 million to ₹1 billion and I can show exactly how to do it – we are already doing all of the above with much less money.

Funding Deep Tech

***Srivardhini:* Picking up on what you all are saying about funding being a major bottleneck, what could be some innovative funding models?**

Taslimarif: The one thing that we keep mentioning is the need to take failures into account in this space, as they are inevitable. We have to work with investors and give them some cushioning. We can do that by bringing in both state-level and federal machinery. There is no dedicated risk fund yet for deep tech. We need that in addition to subsidised capital for the tech aspect that the government can bring in. We will have to do it for possibly 5 to 10 years. Many geographies have implemented a 5-to-10-year subsidy model, by the end of which the investors have gotten used to this style of funding, risk, and so on. Once investors are given time to get used to it, then such subsidy relaxations can be tapered off.

***Srivardhini:* In some ways, it is almost a public–private partnership towards funding deep tech start-ups.**

Taslimarif: As for me, the simple definition of the government's role is to intervene when private players do not come.

Satya: I do not believe in free money. Some government funding for developing prototypes is fine, but there needs to be an equity stake, as otherwise there is no accountability. I think there are three approaches. First, we need to get out of this software template "Series A, B" mould. Second, instead of raising small chunks of funds repeatedly, we need bigger chunks for longer periods as the founders can then focus on developing the tech. Third, we need to start having confidence in our people, our tech, which will lead to longer term funding. We find it easier to believe in Western tech. One way to solve this is to get the prototype out there, which in itself requires a few years. This is the kind of hump we have to go through, unfortunately, but we have to start instilling confidence and change this over the next few years.

Umakant: If there are areas wherein the government is looking to encourage the development of certain strategic products, they would have to think about an evergreen venture fund similar to In-Q-Tel in the US. In-Q-Tel is the $150-million evergreen fund established by the CIA. Such a fund can be managed professionally and can co-invest along with venture funds. That will also ensure that the government gets access to technology. One critical thing in all of this is the role of the government as a customer. I am looking at the US government, which has a buying capacity of $500 billion. It is difficult unless we turn on the buying power of the government, which is probably in the region of $50 to $70 billion per year in India. The government buying process is currently set up on the lowest cost model. With lowest cost, you can never buy innovation, which always comes at a premium.

Talent Pipeline

***Srivardhini:* You already touched upon the talent pipeline. Can you tell us a bit about the talent pipeline that we have in this country and how it actually supports the deep tech ecosystem and if we are lacking in some form.**

Umakant: I think the talent pipeline is phenomenal, given the work that IITs have done. They have nurtured the talent pipeline for the whole world – 15,000 fellow IITians are driving Silicon Valley. Additionally, I think that in business model innovation, Indians are way more creative. I have interacted with start-ups in other countries such as the US, Europe and Canada and I felt that they are no match for Indian entrepreneurs. If we can give such entrepreneurs a sound deep tech innovation engine or ecosystem, we would really leapfrog into what we are supposed to be. There is a report that says that India and China will be the centre of the tech revolution by 2035, but it won't happen by itself. We would have to take concrete steps.

Taslimarif: We have a very smart talent pool consisting of individuals who have the curiosity to address the problems around them. These are mostly people coming from fields such as design engineering or mechanical engineering and putting together medical devices. On the other hand, in the biological sciences, namely, molecular biology and so on, we will require more people to actually take the plunge into biotech. What we are seeing is the largest front of real smart engineers building biotech tools in MedTech. What we are not seeing in the same ratio is the pure biological sciences actually taking that plunge.

Satya: In March 2018, I travelled to France as part of a FICCI delegation, representing Agnikul as a space sector start-up at the Paris Space Week. One of things that I immediately realised was that there was a huge amount of credibility associated with India in the space sector. ISRO has established that kind of a reputation for us outside India and that is something that we definitely benefit from. SpaceTech start-ups can ride on the ISRO bandwagon and go outside to win laurels for ourselves. When we came back, we could actually tap into lot of ex-ISRO scientists and start talking to ISRO players again.

Open Innovation: The Role of Established Large Firms

Srivardhini: What is the role of the larger players in nurturing the ecosystem, similar to what an ISRO is doing for Agnikul? Even in the life sciences, we have lot of biotech and pharmaceutical companies. What role do you see them playing in this deep tech ecosystem?

Taslimarif: I always see long gestation sectors such as the life sciences as a baton race where you have different players having complementary expertise.

And if you see the life sciences as including medical devices – which actually leads to digital HealthTech – there is a relay run that happens where expertise, risk checkers, risk mitigators and clinical trials are part of a very good pipeline. They co-exist and at times co-reside in the same spatial locations. I think that is the role that the Indian pharmaceutical industry or the larger MedTech device industry needs to play as well – R&D. The incoming technology doesn't need to come from headquarters in Europe or happen in one part of Bengaluru – it can happen outside and then be taken in and forward. I would be honest and say that this has not happened in large numbers. I think we need it more. I will conclude by what this means in terms of software-driven health area deep tech – a lot of drug discovery is going to happen more on a software data–driven basis. There will be a combination of tech capabilities of software firms with pharmaceutical companies or even medical device companies. This is happening in many parts of the world and could also happen right here.

Umakant: For AI too, large companies are crucial. For this reason, we are adopting the triple helix model at ARTPARK, where global industry, academia and government can come together.

***Srivardhini:* That sounds very promising. All the best and thank you very much for joining us today and sharing your valuable insights. I wish you the very best for all your endeavours.**

Panel Members

Satyanarayan R Chakravarthy is an accomplished rocket scientist and combustion expert with over 25 years of experience and is the co-founder of three IIT Madras start-ups. Prof. Chakravarthy has been coordinating the National Centre for Combustion Research and Development (NCCRD), established by the Department of Science and Technology, Government of India, since 2011.

Taslimarif Saiyed received his PhD from the Max-Planck Institute for Brain Research, Germany, and followed it up with postdoctoral training at the University of California San Francisco (UCSF). He heads the Discovery to Innovation Accelerator programme at the Centre for Cellular and Molecular Platforms (C-CAMP).

Umakant Soni is an IIT Kanpur alumnus and is the co-founder of AI Foundry and ARTPARK, which aims to build an "AI mothership" for six billion users. He co-founded India's first AI fund (pi Ventures) and backed some of the most well-known AI companies in India. He was the CEO and co-founder of AI BOT start-up Vimagino (2009) and has also served as a consultant in the Strategy For Advanced Technology & Innovation Arm at Wipro.

Endnotes

[1]Refer to Funding section for models of funding.

[2]Electric planes, touted as the "next big thing" in the aviation sector.

[3]Indian National Space Promotion and Authorisation Centre (IN-SPACe) is a new organisation set up by the Government of India to coordinate private sector commercial activities in the space sector.

[4]Space Enterprise Encouragement & Development (SEED) is a programme set up by the Indian Space Research Organization (ISRO), the main space activity body of the Government of India, to encourage start-ups and micro, small and medium enterprises (MSMEs) in the space sector.

[5]National Centre for Combustion Research and Development (NCCRD), IIT Madras.

IN BRIEF

- Corporates are increasingly building start-up collaboration programmes to capture extrinsic value through commercial partnerships. Structured collaboration programmes that gradually build up the corporate–start-up engagement have become the preferred choice for corporates, given the flexibility they provide.
- Corporate start-up programmes are two-sided platforms. Designing and operating a successful programme requires both the corporate business units (that is, the sponsor) and the start-ups to be viewed as "customers".
- A copy–paste approach to designing collaboration programmes does not work. Customisation significantly improves the odds of success of the programme.
- Designing a programme blueprint anchored on 12 critical success elements is vital to improve the short- and long-term odds of success of the programme. These critical success elements allow a corporate to proactively identify and resolve challenges. Importantly, they allow for informed decisions and trade-offs – an essential pre-requisite to review and iterate the programme with time.

ANALYTICAL ARTICLE

4

Corporate–Start-up Collaboration Programmes: Improving the Odds of Success

Atit Danak

Danak, A. 2021. "Corporate–Start-up Collaboration Programmes: Improving the Odds of Success". In *Shifting Orbits: Decoding the Trajectory of the Indian Start-up Ecosystem*, edited by Thillai Rajan A, Srivardhini K Jha, Joffi Thomas and Rohan Chinchwadkar, 30–45. Hyderabad: Universities Press (India) Private Limited.

Changes in Corporate Innovation

Open innovation proposes that established firms use external sources as pathways to new ideas, technologies, business models and markets. At the core, the concept is that successful ideas can originate from both within and outside the company.

In contrast to traditional settings, where the companies only conducted internal R&D and the innovation process was closely guarded, companies today are leveraging external partners to successfully achieve the desired innovation and business outcome. The intent is to drive business outcome rapidly (reduce time-to-market), frugally (de-risk investments) and through a fail-fast (increase the pace of experimentation) approach.

The new-age innovation fabric of a large established firm is globalised, with multiple R&D centres worldwide and a highly decentralised operating model, with each centre deeply embedded in the local innovation ecosystem (Exhibit 4.1). The eventual goal is to combine internal and external expertise from across the world.

Exhibit 4.1: The new-age innovation fabric is decentralised and distributed

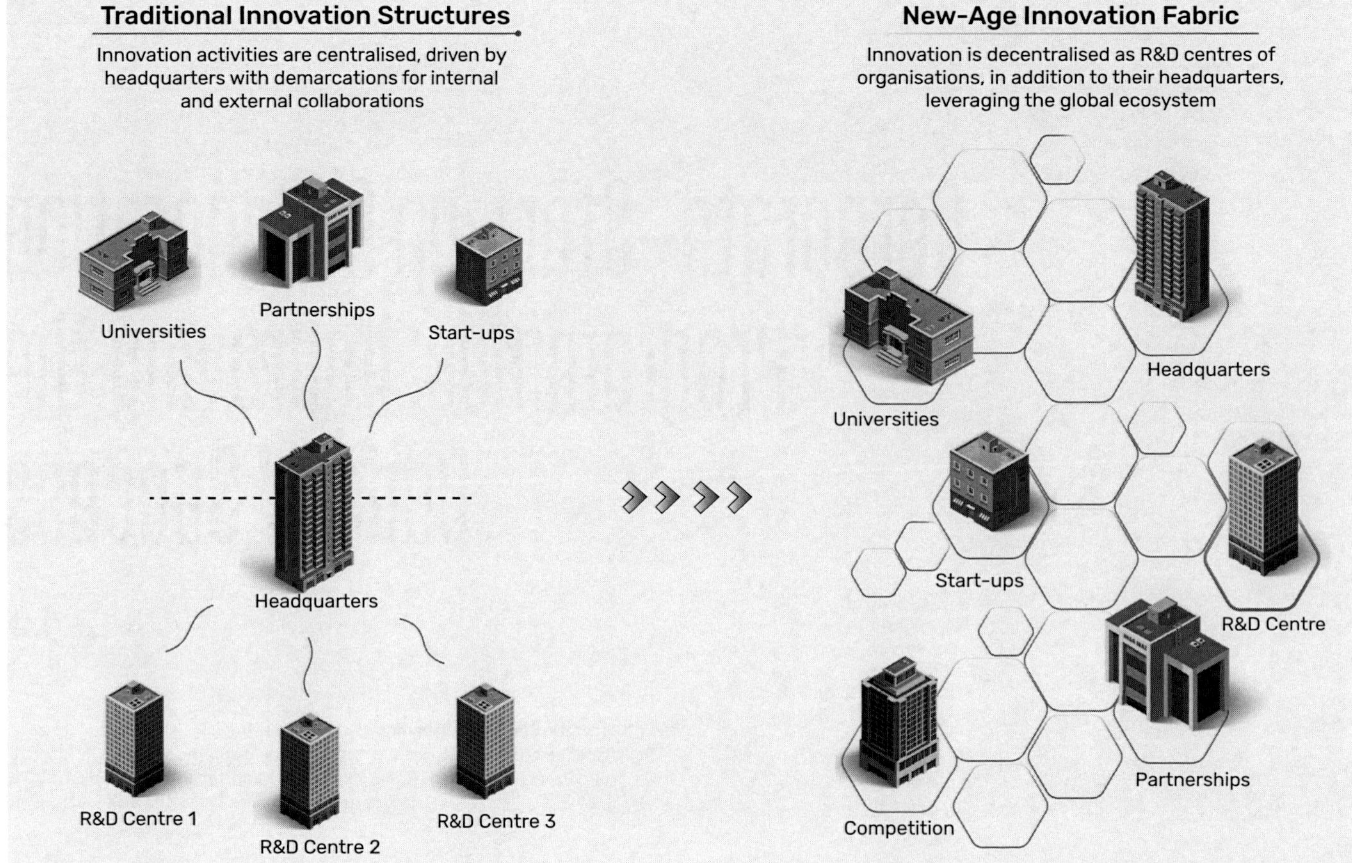

Collaborating with Start-ups

Under growing market pressure and in the face of disruption, an increasing number of corporates are acquiring, investing in, outsourcing to and partnering with start-ups to profit from their knowledge and innovation capacity.

Start-ups can provide early recognition of threats and competition, introduce an entrepreneurial spirit and provide specialised talent and resources. The corporate can focus on its core business while simultaneously increasing the pace of experimentation (that is, discovering new opportunities) with fewer resources. Collaborations reduce risk by limiting escalation of commitment and simplifying project close-down when necessary. In summary, collaborating with start-ups provides the freedom required to nurture innovation while minimising the risks. Beyond the need for radical or breakthrough innovation, corporates are also building relationships with future suppliers and partners and importing a sense of dynamism and entrepreneurial impulses.

Corporates have been leveraging a combination of collaboration models, which are derivatives of the classical build, buy and partner approach for intrinsic and extrinsic value capture.

a) Corporate Development

The classical approach to capture the intrinsic value of a business – merge or acquire the business; that is, its its team, intellectual property, product, users and revenue.

b) Corporate Venture Capital

Designed on venture capital fund lines, corporate venture capital divisions are usually independent entities created to make equity investments in start-ups with or without high synergies with the core business.

c) Partner Programmes

Modelled on the lines of classic partnership programmes, these are rolling and highly flexible

Exhibit 4.2: A variety of approaches used by corporates to drive different collaboration models with start-ups

Collaboration models		Collaboration approaches				
Type	**Definition**	**Corporate Development**	**Corporate Venture Capital**	**Partner Programme**	**Accelerator/ Incubator**	**Ecosystem Outreach**
Platform Evangelization	Corporates enable start-ups to adopt their technology platform with a promise to improve the odds of success via better data, tools and market access.			👍	👍	👍
Licence/ Vendor Agreement	Corporates seek to leverage the start-up's product as part of a new or existing solution. Alternatively, this is a commercial agreement for soving an internal requirement/problem for the corporate.			👍	👍	
Joint Go-to-Market	The corporate integrates its existing products with the start-up's offering to cross-sell solutions to each other's customers. Typically, this is driven by the need to expand revenue from existing accounts or deliver a certain customer experience.			👍	👍	
Co-Innovation	The corporate offers its domain experiences, and non-financial capabilities, to leverage a start-up's technology prowess to create new products and solutions for internal or customer-facing applications.				👍	
Acqui-hire	The corporate acquires a start-up primarily for its talent and/ or intellectual property. No premium is paid for the product, customers or revenue from the start-up's existing offerings.	👍				
Investments	The corporate buys a minority stake in a start-up to capture intrinsic value in a business outside its core, possibly, a disruptor to its existing business.		👍		👍	
Acquisitions	The corporate acquires a start-up for its team, intellectual property, product, customers and revenues.	👍			👍	

programmes for growth-to-late-stage start-ups, typically for licence or vendor or joint go-to-market (GTM) opportunities.

d) Accelerators and Incubators

Inspired by the success of Y-Combinator, these are fixed-duration structured programmes for early-to-growth-stage start-ups to explore a variety of collaboration models.

e) Ecosystem Outreach

Corporates host events for start-ups in the form of showcase days, hackathons or challenges. By nature, these are short-duration engagements.

Corporates use a variety of approaches to drive these collaboration models (Exhibit 4.2).

An increasingly popular approach is the use of an accelerator, incubator or partner programme. The immense flexibility they provide – in terms of the variety of collaboration that can be driven – is the primary reason behind their rapidly growing prevalence.

Accelerator, incubator and partner programmes can vary significantly in their design. For example, programmes can be

a) Managed internally or outsourced to another organisation
b) Organised into cohorts or in a rolling model
c) With or without an equity commitment from the start-ups
d) Hosted at a particular location or operated in a remote-work environment

Yet these programmes are structurally quite similar.

Each of them has three key phases:

a) Pre-Programme

The selection phase focusses on identifying internal needs and relevant stakeholders, marketing the programme, sourcing applications and selecting relevant start-ups.

b) During-Programme

Using a combination of methodologies, the corporate and selected start-ups work towards building the

Exhibit 4.3: The three phases of a corporate–start-up collaboration programme

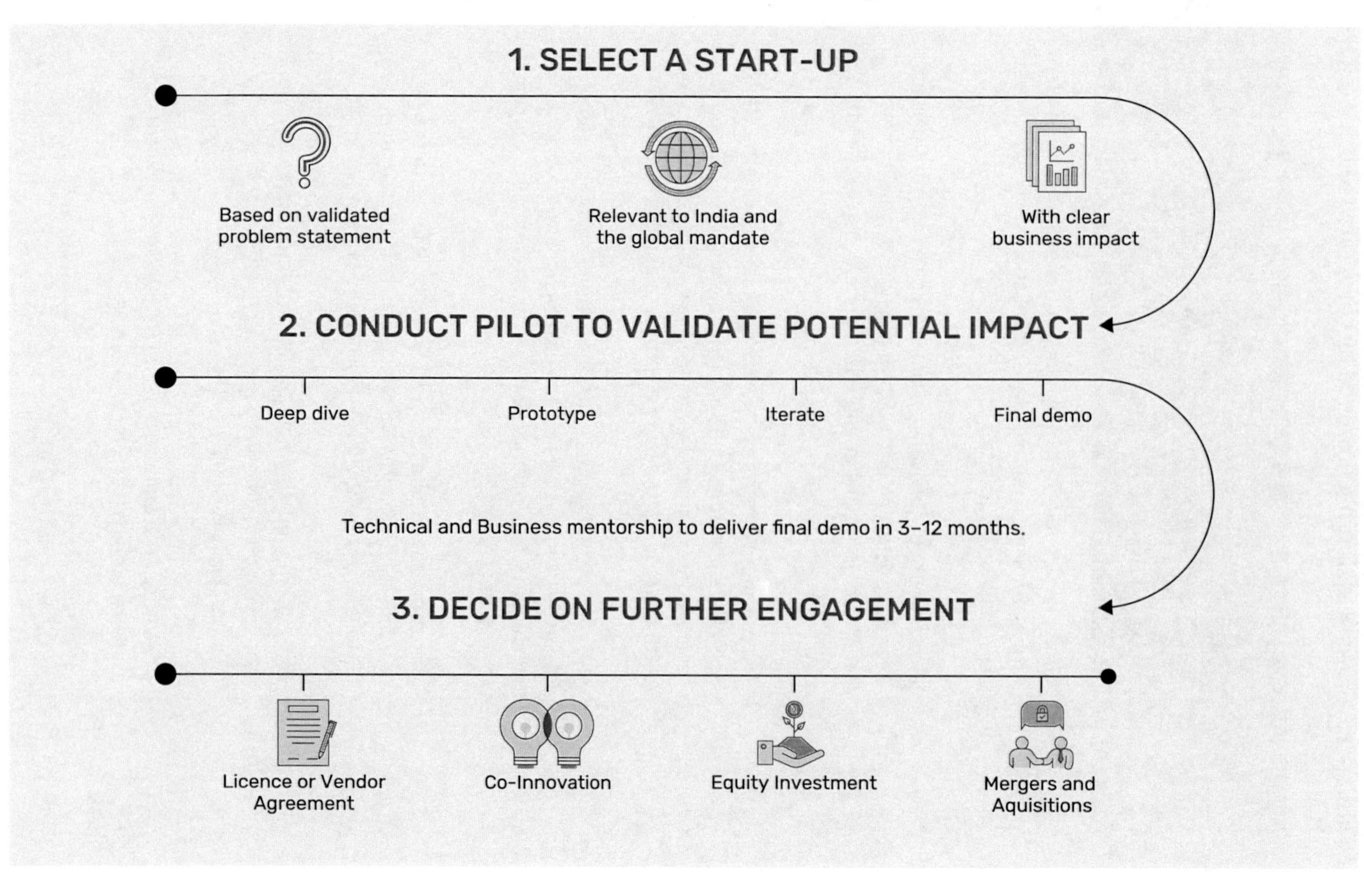

proof of concept. That is, applying a start-up's solution to a corporate's problem in a controlled environment. It is the most intensive phase, with rapid experimentation and mentoring, and can be an equity-free or an equity-linked programme.

c) Post-Programme

The focus is only on start-ups that successfully meet the qualification criteria defined for the initial engagement. These shortlisted start-ups are then provided additional support by the corporate till a collaboration model is finalised and deployed. The rest of the start-ups are typically engaged as alumni, but with limited time and resource commitment.

Based on this commonality and for the sake of simplicity, we will be referring to accelerators, incubators and partner programmes interchangeably as "structured corporate–start-up collaboration programme" or "collaboration programme" in short.

Designing an Effective Collaboration Programme

This section provides an overview of the different types of corporate–start-up collaboration programmes and highlights the critical success factors of effective programmes based on the experience of running several of these programmes. The intent is to identify drivers that can improve the odds of success of a corporate–start-up collaboration programme.

The pool includes a programme established as far back as 2007 to the most recent launches in 2020 – providing a spectrum to understand the structural shift in the industry and study the typical evolution of a programme. Notably, 46 per cent of all programmes were set up in the last three years. In terms of sponsor organisation, more than 80 per cent of the programmes were operated by global MNCs – primarily through their R&D centres in India.

Exhibit 4.4: Distribution of programmes

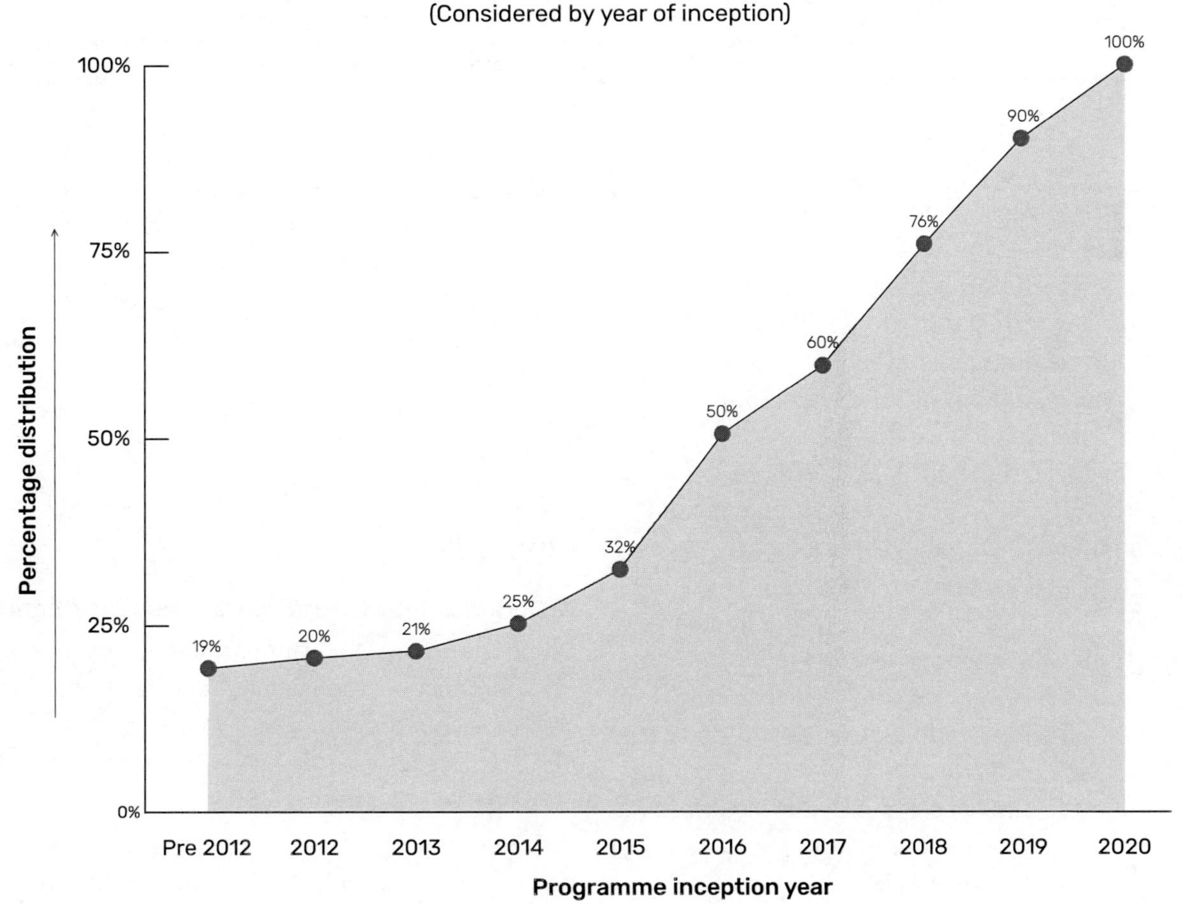

Exhibit 4.4: Distribution of programmes (contd.)

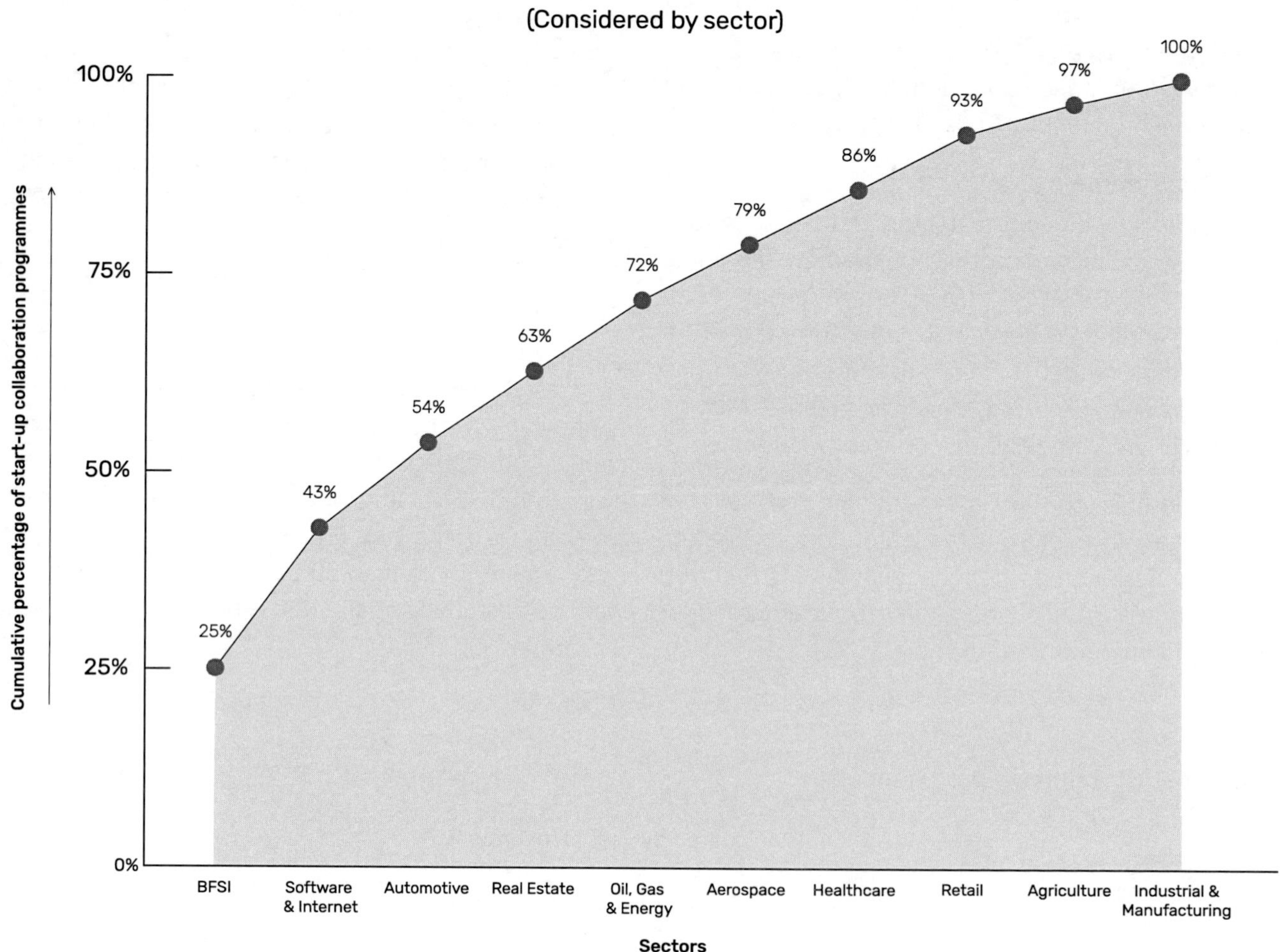

For this article, we studied 75+ corporate–start-up collaboration programmes across 15+ industry sectors, incepted since 2007, in the form of accelerators or incubators or partner programmes, operated by Indian or global MNCs.[5,6] Notably, we considered only active programmes, that is, programmes operational as of June 2020. Furthermore, we will be commenting primarily on programmes focussed on extrinsic value capture, that is, commercial partnerships. We have, intentionally, not commented on programmes seeking equity in start-ups.

We limited ourselves to initiatives with a dedicated team and clearly defined structures and processes. Tactical or one-off initiatives and programmes were not considered.

Data collection took the form of extensive secondary research, primary surveys and semi-structured interviews with the key stakeholders involved in the corporate programmes – start-ups, corporate leadership, investors and the programme management team. Bound by non-disclosure agreements, we are unable to comment on the actual success rates or achieved outcomes.

Findings

A. Corporate–Start-up Programmes Vary Significantly

Corporates consider various factors and use a variety of approaches in designing and implementing their collaboration programmes. Variation was visible, not just across sectors, but also within different corporates in the same industry.

Interestingly, it also highlighted a fundamental nomenclature challenge for corporate programmes,

Exhibit 4.5: Key findings from the study

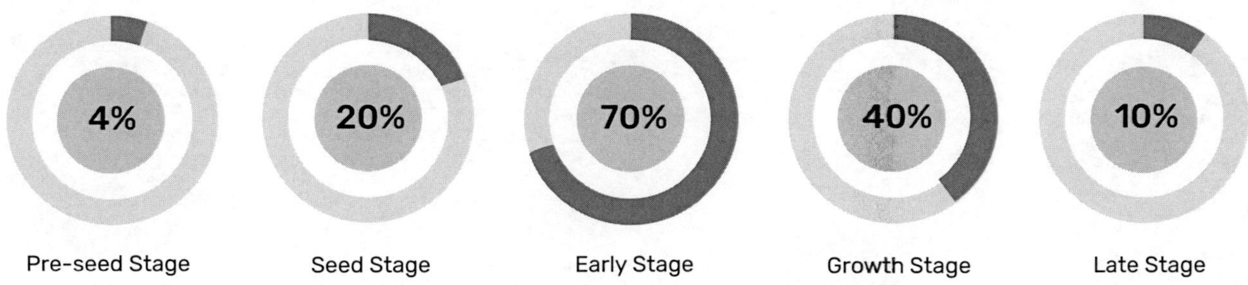

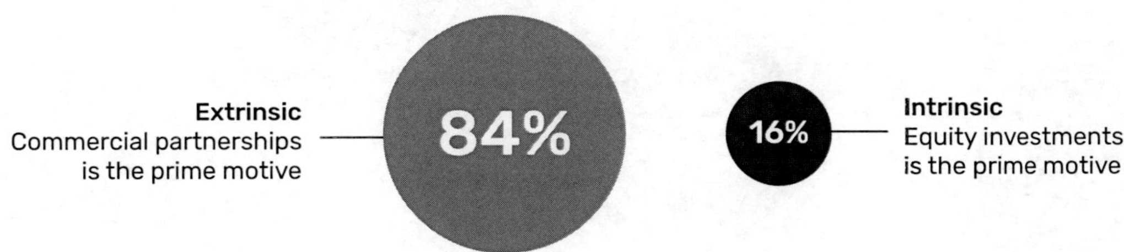

and its impact on the programme's success. For example, most corporations choose to call their start-up programmes accelerators, even though a high majority of the corporate programmes do not seek any equity in the start-up. In contrast, most accelerators (like Y-Combinator) seek equity from start-ups. We will restrict our observations to programmes focussed on extrinsic value capture, that is, commercial partnerships. Programmes seeking equity in start-ups have not been the focus of this study, since they are like traditional venture investments.

Furthermore, a typical accelerator in the start-up ecosystem engages with pre-seed or seed-stage start-ups, while a significantly high majority of corporate programmes engage with early-stage, or relatively more mature, start-ups.

This observation is further evident in the key performance indicators (KPIs) monitored by corporate–start-up programmes. The primary KPIs monitored can be classified into two buckets:

a) For Use in Marketing the Programme

These would typically include metrics like the number of start-ups engaged, number of active start-ups, funding raised post-programme and exits.

b) For Monitoring Business Impact

These would typically include the number of technical integrations, revenue and cost savings enabled, the number of active partnerships and the start-ups' current valuation.

Commonality, across all the programmes, was limited to the value proposition offered to start-ups and in the broader structure. These included:

a) Technical and Business Expertise

To build an initial proof of concept and early validation of the solution from a market and scalability perspective.

b) Financial Support

Predominantly in the form of zero-equity cash grants to fund the start-ups for the duration of the programme.

c) Tools, Data and Technology

To build a compelling product, closer to the corporate's requirements, with possibly better results and in a short period.

d) Revenue Opportunity

Either from the corporate itself or from its partners.

Exhibit 4.6: Most common KPIs tracked by programmes

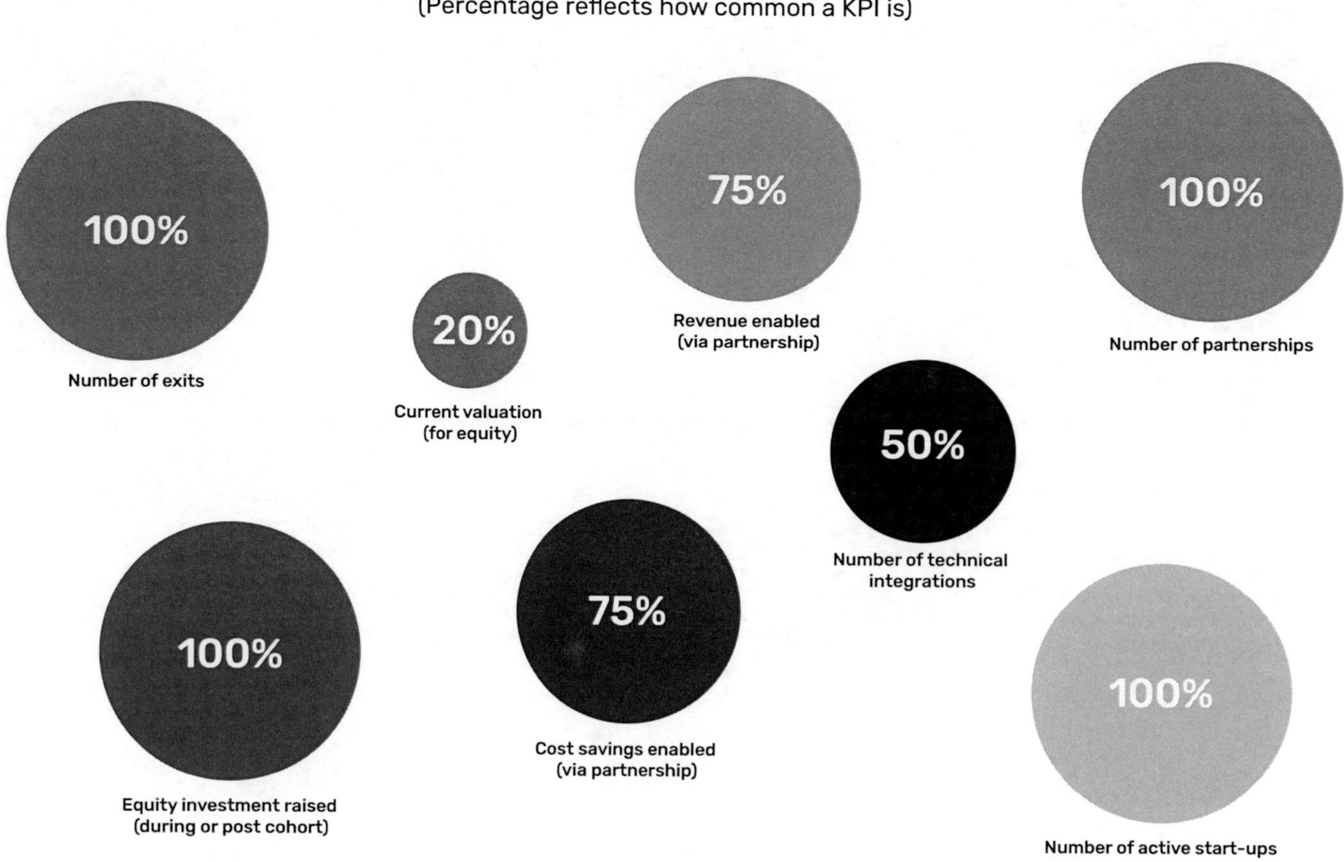

Corporate–start-up collaboration is still a relatively nascent phenomenon. The varied approaches taken by corporates to build their programmes pose challenges for both practitioners and academicians.

Benchmarking the efficacy of each programme is difficult due to fundamental variations within objectives and goals. This variation makes it challenging to identify an ideal model for abstracting knowledge on best practices. This lack of an ideal model in turn leads to slower transfer of knowledge on actionable insights between actors and sub-optimal application of the knowledge, a situation exacerbated by the difference in terminologies used by corporates, given the nascency of the sector.

These challenges compound and translate into two fundamental problems:

a) It slows down the pace for corporate participation in the ecosystem – despite overwhelming evidence on the advantages of collaboration and inclination to participate.

b) It becomes difficult for innovation managers and leaders at ongoing and active programmes to clearly distinguish themselves from their peers – both internally and externally.

B. Typology of Corporate–Start-up Collaboration Programmes

The differences in the operating model of a corporate–start-up collaboration programme can be attributed to the differences in corporate goals and objectives, availability of resources and operating entity.

Literature reviews reflect different classifications of programmes based on their strategic goals and objectives,[1] by operating entity[2,3] and by the process.[4] While a collaboration programme can have multiple objectives and goals, our emphasis is on the business impact it can generate. Respondents in our interviews indicated that successful programmes invariably start with a very sharp focus and then expand scope based on tangible outcomes delivered.

Exhibit 4.7: Most common value propositions articulated by programmes

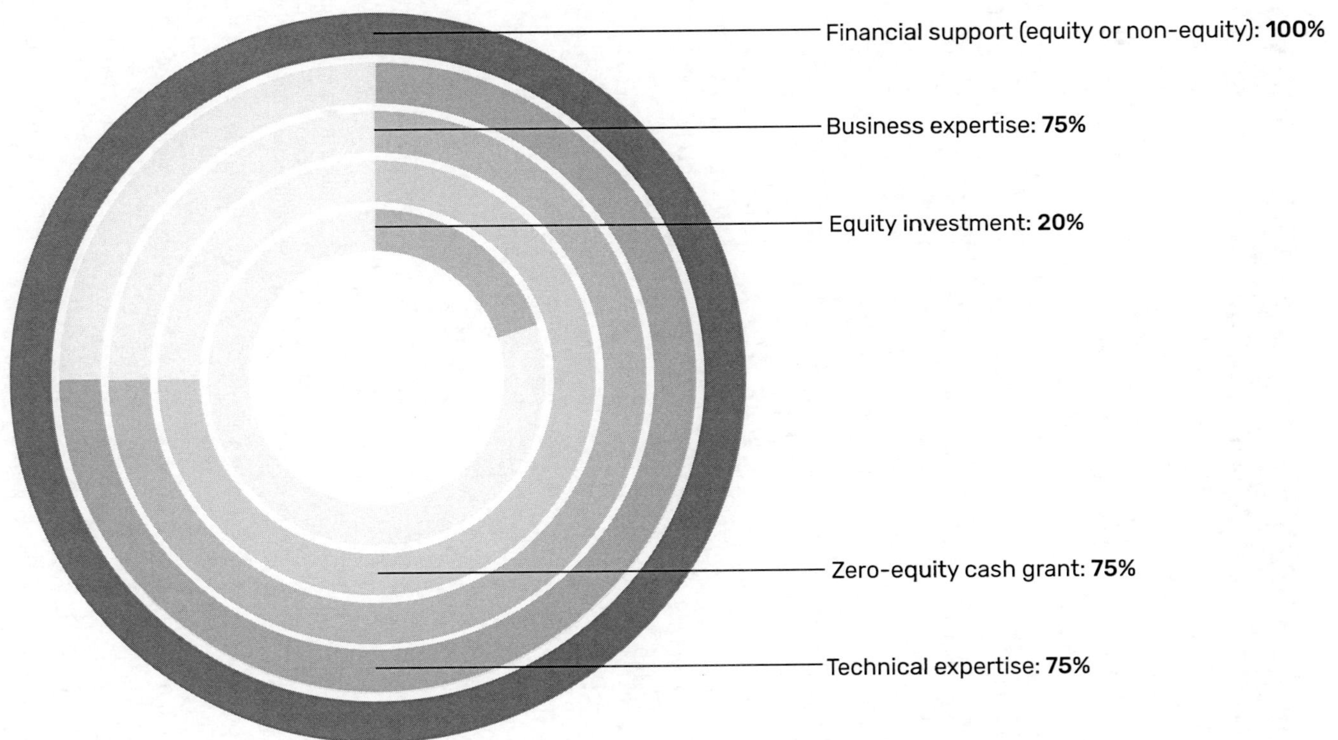

We have layered academic frameworks in a practitioner's perspective to propose a typology based on the strategic intent – in terms of the type of outcome expected, primary motive or logic to leverage start-ups, and the organisational charter. We have identified four archetypes in this article on the basis of 16 unique programme attributes clustered into four success factors.

These archetypes are as follows:

a) Enabler

Designed to drive the operational objectives of the corporate – these are typically leveraged by firms building a platform business. The platform could be software-based or hardware- or licence-based. Examples include GE Healthcare Edison Accelerator, NVIDIA Inception and YES FinTech.

b) Orchestrator

Typically preferred by technology creators, these programmes are leveraged for either accelerating product development or for building new products and services on top of the existing product portfolio. Examples include Cisco Launchpad and NetApp Excellerator.

c) Transformer

Typically preferred by non-digital natives, that is, industries like retail and financial services, these programmes help accelerate the digital transformation journey of a corporate. Examples include Société Générale Catalyst, Essel's Esselerator and Falabella Exceed.

d) Explorer

These are invariably an extended form of the Orchestrator and Transformer archetypes. However, we have found examples like Swiss Re InsurTech Accelerator that are set up to drive product and service expansion into adjacent and new business areas. A good example is the Jio GenNext programme.

The typology proposed should enable a corporation to identify the right peers to benchmark itself and allow a new entrant into the ecosystem to make trade-offs efficiently and effectively. Additionally, it would help an existing programme to identify additional opportunities within the firm and define the approach to expand the programme's scope.

Exhibit 4.8: Typology of corporate–start-up collaboration programmes

Programme type: Success Factor	Programme type: Attributes	Enabler	Orchestrator	Transformer	Explorer
Objective	Intent	Operational	Strategic	Operational	Strategic
	Charter	Accelerate adoption and evolution of existing product portfolio	Identify, develop and integrate new products and services	Accelerate digital transformation across the value chain to drive business objectives	Expand product and services portfolio in adjacent and new business areas
	Collaboration Model (Preferred)	Platform Partnership	Licence Agreement Joint Go-To-Market		Co-Innovation / Licence Agreement / Joint Ownership
Programme Governance	Structure	Part of Sponsor Organisation	Part of Sponsor Organisation	Part of Sponsor Organisation	Separate Legal Entity / Part of Sponsor Organisation
	Intensity of Internal Participation	Medium	High	High	Medium
	Funding Source(s)	Sales & Marketing Budget Business Unit	Business Unit / Innovation Budget	Business Unit / Innovation Budget	Innovation Budget / Business Unit
	Typical KPIs	1. No. of integrations. 2. No. of products launched. 3. No. of features added / prioritised 4. No. of active integrations	1. No. of PoCs executed. 2. No. of commercial agreements signed. 3. No. of impact of partnership	1. No. of PoCs executed. 2. No. of deployment to production. 3. No. of impact of deployments	1. No. of PoCs executed. 2. No. of experiments completed. 3. No. of deployments to production. 4. No. of impact of deployments
Programme Focus	Thematic Focus	Tightly aligned to sponsor's sectors of interest	Tightly aligned to sector of interest of sponsor's clients	Agnostic – is driven by technology or functional themes	Agnostic – is driven by technology, industry and functional themes
	Start-up Maturity (Seed, Early, Growth, Late)	Seed to Growth Stage	Early to Growth Stage	Early to Growth Stage	Seed to Growth Stage
Value Proposition	Financial Grant	Cash + In kind (for tools, products, data)	Cash, amounts can vary by start-up	Cash, amounts can vary by start-up	Cash, amounts can vary by start-up
	Structured Mentorship (Internal + External)	Medium to High (Equal emphasis on product adoption and strengthening of start-up's business and technical maturity)	Low to Medium (Limited to providing inputs for executing effective PoCs; primarily internal)	Low to Medium (Limited to providing inputs for executing effective PoCs; primarily internal)	Medium to High (Equal emphasis on solution and strengthening start-up's maturity)
	Data, Toolkits and Sandbox Environment	Yes, this is a core value proposition	Yes, this is a core value proposition	Selective, Case-by-Case Decision	Selective, Case-by-Case Decision
	Revenue from Sponsor	Nil to Low	Low to Medium	Medium to High	Medium to High
	Access to Sponsor's Customers / Suppliers	Medium to High	Medium to High	Nil to Low	Low to Medium
	Cohort Based	Initially cohort-based and then rolling model	Usually start as cohort-based and then shift to rolling format	Invariably rolling model	Initially cohort-based and then rolling model
	Geographical Coverage	Local / Regional	Regional / Global	Regional / Global	Local / Regional

Exhibit 4.9: Typology concerning corporate and start-up objectives

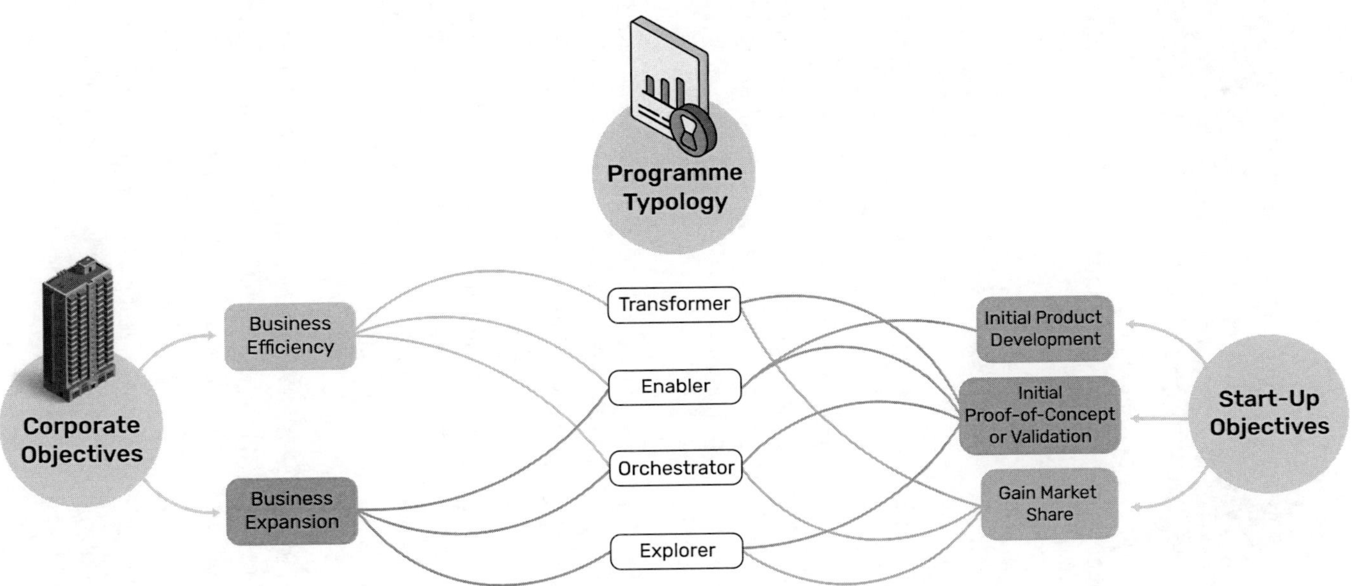

More critically, the typology enables a corporation to align programmes to the start-up's objectives and make better design and implementation decisions. Analysing a few corporate–start-up programmes across the four archetypes helps in understanding this better.

C. Critical Success Elements of an Effective Collaboration Programme

Our first-hand experience, as well as interview findings, confirm that structured collaboration programmes act as a filter that increases the pace of experimentation, reduces blind spots, weeds out failures early on and enables a data-and-insights–led selection of start-ups for deeper engagement. Risk is easier to manage without sacrificing scale and repeatability. They help reduce the uncertainty associated with innovation by applying well-defined processes, assessment criteria, allocation of appropriate resources and decision points, thereby allowing corporations to match a start-up's pace and creativity without deviating from the core corporate strategy.

The next step, then, is to identify the essential and non-essential elements of a collaboration programme. Combining the results from secondary research and primary interviews, we took an abductive process to define 12 critical success elements that we believe each innovation manager or leader should incorporate in their programme design.

Each of these critical success elements has been selected to enable proactive action and holds particular importance from a programme design and implementation perspective.

All the 12 critical success elements have high interdependencies. The design process often requires a trade-off depending on the larger organisational strategy, access to resources, the expected time-to-impact and peer activity. More importantly, the programmes act as an interface between the internal stakeholders and the external ecosystem in a dynamic environment.

Under such circumstances, it is more than likely that a dominant model for the collaboration programme will take more time to evolve, and hence, so will the specifics of each critical success element. Innovation programmes, much like start-ups, need to undergo continuous experimentation and iteration. That said, the 12 critical success elements should enable an organisation to proactively identify risks and assumptions during the design phase and provide a reference point for future iterations.

Summary

Corporate start-up collaboration programmes is an evolving area. However, the growing number of programmes reflects a conviction on the benefits of implementing an effective collaboration programme.

Exhibit 4.10: Illustrative examples of corporate–start-up collaboration programs

Programme name	Sponsor organisation	Type	Incepted in	No. of start-ups	Key attributes	Impact
Edison Accelerator	GE Healthcare	Enabler	2019	11	A 6-month cohort-based programme for early-stage deep tech start-ups in healthcare to integrate products on the Edison platform followed by joint Go-To-Market	Programme is now being replicated in Europe and China, following success in India
Microsoft ScaleUp	Microsoft	Enabler	2012	135	Highly customised rolling programme for growth-stage B2B start-ups to refine their business model before co-selling with Microsoft globally	Only programme in India to count a Unicorn in its portfolio. The programme was scaled to 8 countries after initial success in India and the US
Cisco Launchpad	Cisco	Orchestrator	2016	47	A 6-month cohort-based programme for early- stage deep tech start-ups to accelerate technology development using Cisco mentorship and explore licence/joint GTM agreement	Only engineering-led programme in Cisco; globally, the programme now engages with global start-ups to build global products from India
Exceed	Falabella	Transformer	2019	6	Highly customised rolling programme for early- to-growth-stage B2B start-ups to secure licence/vendor agreement with Falabella Group of companies	Latin America market–focussed programme, it is being built from India given the initial success of PoCs with Indian start-ups
Catalyst	Societe Generale	Transformer	2019	69	A 4-month intense programme wherein use-cases are collected from across the world and then PoC is executed with internal technology teams for licence / vendor agreements	Flagship start-up programme of Societe Generale, it recently expanded into the Africa market to support the company's global transformation mandates
Construct	Lowe's	Explorer	2014	7	A 4–6-month programme, customised to a start-up, for seed-to-growth-stage start-ups to co-innovate with Lowe's for licence/ vendor/ joint Go-To-Market mandates	Programme is already on expansion mode, within 12 months of inception, on account of tangible business outcomes from the initial cohort
Jio GenNext	Jio	Explorer	2020	137	A 3–4-month intense programme with multiple thematic tracks each year, designed to explore co-innovation/licence/joint Go-To-Market opportunity with Jio	Second largest corporate programme in India with multiple licence agreements, and post-programme investments in start-ups

Exhibit 4.11: Twelve critical success elements to build effective collaboration programmes

Sustenance Model
Estimate programme budget and revenue model for building revenue-neutral programme

Growth Strategy
Chart programme's evolution and maturity map to build world-class programme from India

Charter & Focus Areas with KPIs
Define programme charter and focus based on organisation roadmap and lay down the vision

Ecosystem Collaboration
Identify and build partnerships with stakeholders who add value to the programme

Curriculum and Mentorship Activity Map
Design curriculum and identify relevant trainers, facilitators - internal and external

Marketing and Communication Strategy
Define objectives, channels (internal and external), and publish calendar in line with MarCom protocols

Programme Governance Structure
Design the governance and organisation structure and define KRA

Post-Programme Support
Define the role of the start-up programme in supporting successful outcomes and alumni

Value Proposition for Start-ups
Propose robust and competitive programme offerings to attract quality start-ups

Use-case and Opportunity Index
Build approach for collecting use-cases and opportunities from organisation and prioritise

Evaluation Framework and Process
Define the staged evalution process, criteria and framework for each stage

On-Boarding Documentation
Recommendation on nature of contract and nature of clauses; drafting support

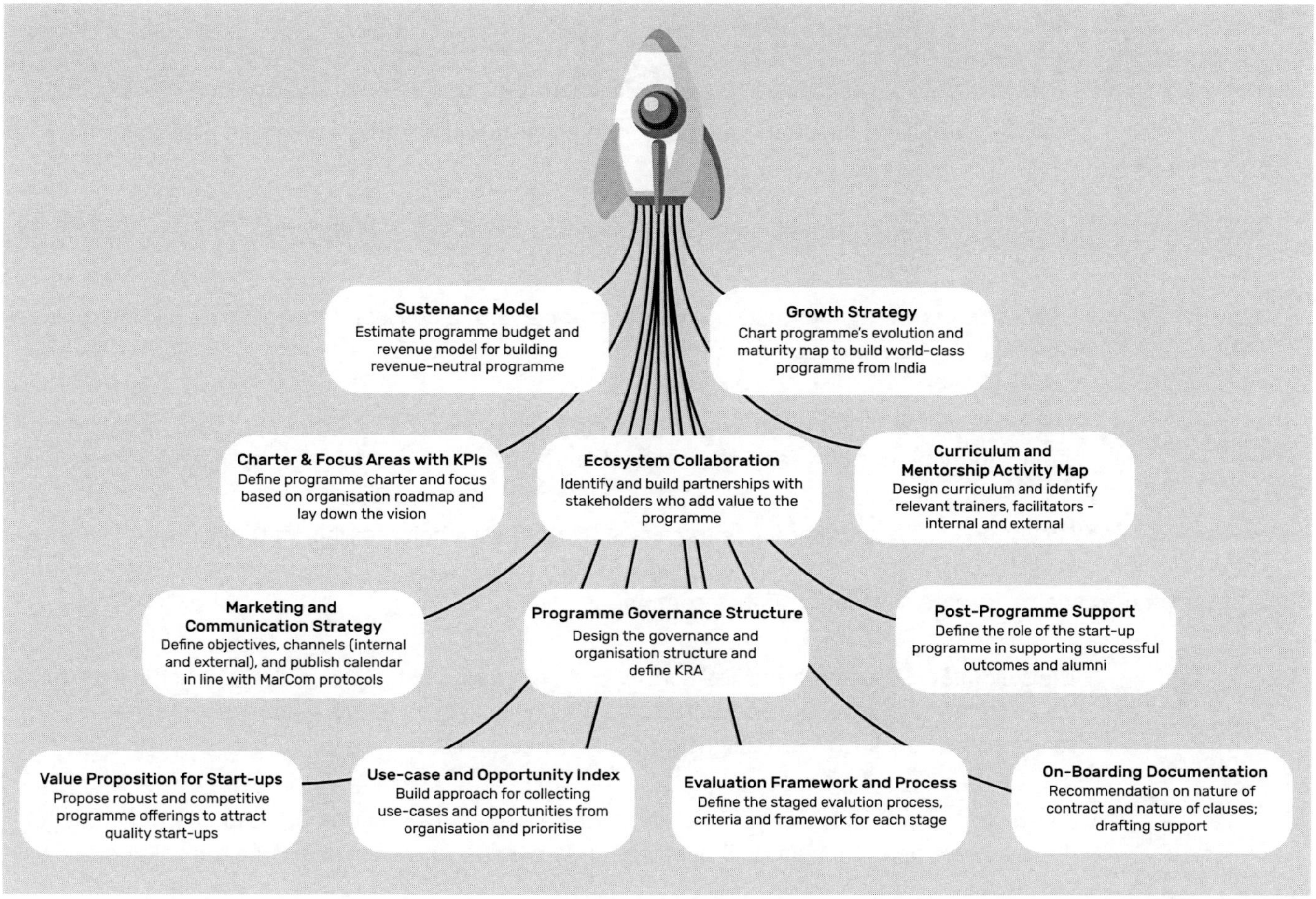

No other approach allows a corporate to engage with start-ups more deeply and efficiently at a lower risk. The concept by itself is simple, namely, to identify a relevant start-up to test a hypothesis in a controlled environment before deciding on a long-term collaboration.

Nevertheless, as with many simple concepts, the devil is in the details. The key to success is building a customised programme with a singular view that programmes are two-sided platforms. The programme has two customers, the corporate business units and the start-ups, and without both, it fails in its role. The programme operates in a highly dynamic environment, and iterations are not just a feature but a necessary ingredient for a successful programme.

We argue that corporates, to improve their odds of success, should consider the 12 critical success factors while designing and implementing a start-up collaboration programme. These critical success factors provide practitioners with a structured approach to develop a new programme and run diagnostics on an existing programme to improve the impact.

Lastly, the success of a collaboration programme is heavily dependent on its customisation. Not all corporates are at equal maturity or operate in similar conditions or have similar strategies. The design and operational decisions are highly contextual to a corporate and are a function of its corporate goals and objectives.

Lastly, we believe that the time has come to develop a tool which would help innovation practitioners to design, launch and build scale for new-age global start-up collaboration programmes from India.

Exhibit 4.12: How critical success elements help

Critical success element	Why is it important?
Charter and focus area with KPI	Provides clarity and direction to the programme team while setting up correct expectations internally.
Sustenance model	Enables the corporate to allocate enough resources for the corporate programme to deliver on its mandate and bring accountability within the organisation.
Governance structure	Ensures the corporate operates in an agile manner with a quick and proactive resolution to challenges while enabling a smooth flow of information.
The value proposition for start-ups	Sets expectations with the external ecosystem and enables the corporate programme to become the programme of choice for high-potential start-ups vis-a-vis other peer programmes.
Problem statement or opportunity index	Allows the corporate programme to engage internal stakeholders while setting clear expectations. Transparent processes enable scalability. Importantly, it enables the programme team to create new opportunities continuously.
Evaluation framework and stage-gated process	The stage-gated process brings objectivity to an otherwise subjective process. It helps not just in selecting the most promising start-ups but also in closing the loop with start-ups that are not selected, by providing clear reasons for a no-go decision.
On-boarding documentation	Covers the concerns of support functions, reduces iterations on non-core issues, saving time for the corporate program team and business units to focus energies on making the collaboration successful.
Curriculum and Mentorship activity map	Focuses on making a PoC successful – a clear activity map supports each start-up at a segment-of-1 without overwhelming the programme team.
Post-programme support	Ensures that successful PoCs deliver intended results at the integration and deployment stage. Further, it enables the corporate programme to provide continuous value to alumni (even if the initial PoC failed).
Ecosystem collaborations	Reduces set-up and operational expenses for the corporate programme while strengthening the value proposition for start-ups and improving the odds of success by collaborating with upstream and downstream partners in the ecosystem. It positions the programme as a key ecosystem contributor.
Growth strategy	Provides a vision and goal for the corporate programme team to continuously build capabilities and deliver results to become a critical function in the corporate strategy.
Marketing and communication strategy	Ensures integrated and unified messaging to all stakeholders – internally and externally – to create precise positioning, and hence, expectations, from the programme team.

Endnotes

[1]Kanbach, D and Stubner, S. 2016. Corporate Accelerators As Recent Form Of Startup Engagement: The What, The Why, And The How. *Journal of Applied Business Research.* 32.

[2]Cohen, S, Fehder, DC, Hochberg, YV and Murray, F. 2019. The design of startup accelerators. *Research Policy* 48(7): 1781–1797.

[3]Moschner, SL, Fink, AA, Kurpjuweit, S, Wagner, SM and Herstatt, C. 2019. Toward a better understanding of corporate accelerator models. *Business Horizons* 62(5), 637–647.

[4]Shankar, RK and Shepherd, DA. 2019. Accelerating strategic fit or venture emergence: Different paths adopted by corporate accelerators, *Journal of Business Venturing* 34(5):1-1.

[5]NASSCOM-Zinnov India Tech Startup Landscape Report, 2019.

[6]NetApp-Zinnov Report on B2B Tech Startup Landscape and The Role of Corporate Accelerators in India, 2019.

IN BRIEF

- Socially oriented innovations vary along three dimensions – what problem they are trying to solve (from market failure to marketplace exclusion), how they solve it (technology versus business model innovations) and why they want to solve it (social impact versus financial sustainability). Innovations that solve not only a social problem but also an industry problem are easier to scale.
- Assessment of the social impact of innovations should involve long-term tracking of appropriate breadth and depth indicators. Endorsing breadth indicators, such as number of beneficiaries impacted, alone may be short-sighted.
- Given the interconnected nature of social problems that social start-ups try to address, incubators can bolster their support to the start-ups by taking into account the beneficiary ecosystem.
- The policy guidelines and VC industry practices are still evolving and yet to mature. A worrying new development is the increasing prevalence of mainstream investment practices under the guise of impact investing.
- To facilitate capital availability for social start-ups, regulatory and policy frameworks must consider creating appropriate legal structures for social start-ups as well as for various categories of funders. Innovative funding mechanisms such as Social Stock Exchange must be seriously explored to ease capital constraints.

ANALYTICAL ARTICLE

5

Innovating for Social Impact

Sumelika Bhattacharyya, Simy Joy and Priya Nair Rajeev[1]

Bhattacharyya, S, Joy, S and Rajeev, PN. 2021. "Innovating for Social Impact". In *Shifting Orbits: Decoding the Trajectory of the Indian Start-up Ecosystem*, edited by Thillai Rajan A, Srivardhini K Jha, Joffi Thomas and Rohan Chinchwadkar, 46–59. Hyderabad: Universities Press (India) Private Limited.

Social Start-ups

Social start-ups – businesses that simultaneously pursue profit and social goals[2] – are a rapidly growing category among the start-ups that have sprung up in India in the last decade. Impact investments into social start-ups have grown almost 200 per cent, from $650 million in 2016 to $1,700 million in 2019.[3] By 2019, about 380 firms classified themselves as for-profit social start-ups and 66 venture funds self-identified as socially oriented impact investors. While start-ups, in general, look to impact consumer lives and solve a problem, what differentiates social start-ups is their primary aim of catering to underserved markets and addressing problems that speak mainly to social good rather than private or monopolistic gain. An ideal social start-up will not compromise their social mission for profits.

This unique goal of combining profits and social impact, while operating in challenging markets, makes the innovations of social start-ups different from those of mainstream start-ups. To better understand the difference, we spoke to the heads of nine leading organisations that provide funding and incubation support to social start-ups (Exhibit 5.2).[4] We also examined 13 social start-ups from agriculture, education, health and other sectors (Exhibits 5.4 and 5.5)[5]. We found three aspects that differentiate social start-ups from other start-ups – the kind of innovations pursued; the way the innovation's impact is evaluated; and the way the innovation is supported. We elaborate on the first two aspects in Part A and the third aspect in Part B of this article.

Exhibit 5.1: Social start-ups

CAN A START-UP MAKING PROBIOTIC SUPPLEMENTS BE DEEMED SOCIAL?

Aimed at the underprivileged section of society

Initially, when social innovation and entrepreneurship were beginning to be recognised as tools of social change, its pioneers, including incubators and funders, sought out those focussed exclusively on serving the underprivileged. In their assessment, a start-up manufacturing a probiotic supplement would be a 'social start-up' only if they aimed it to reduce the incidence of malnutrition.

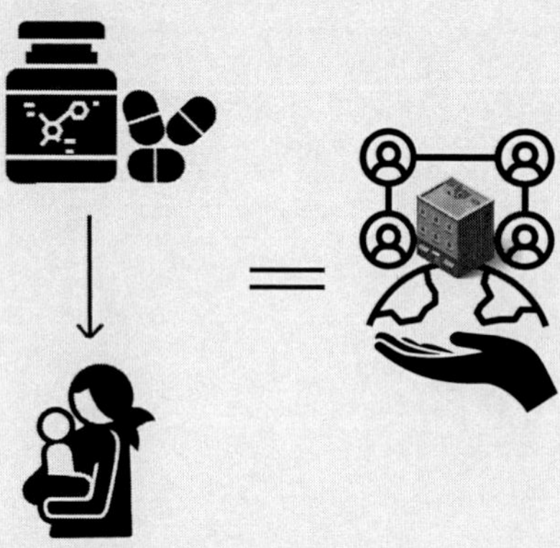

Offers broader social benefits

In recent years, with the entry of a wider range of players, what qualifies to be a social start-up has become open to interpretation. For instance, start-ups belonging to the healthcare, education or microfinance sectors that claim to offer broader societal benefits are often counted as social start-ups. By this token, probiotic supplements that promise better health outcomes for the urban health-conscious would also qualify as social.

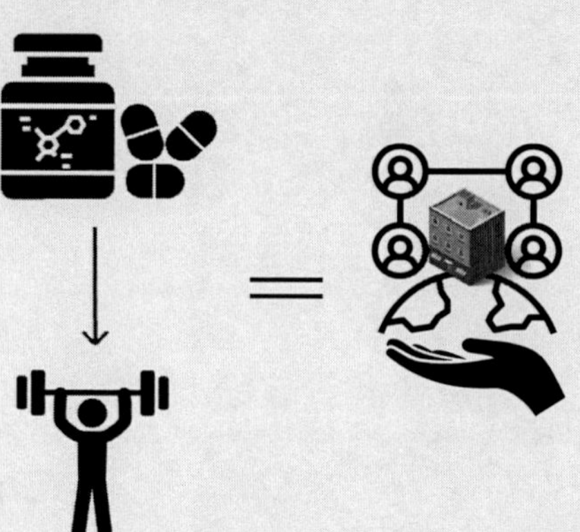

It remains to be seen whether such inclusions would depict social entrepreneurship as a tent that holds every other enterprise that is socially beneficial or as a dilution of purpose.

Exhibit 5.2: Interviewee details

Organisation	Interviewee	Designation
Acumen	Mahesh Yagnaraman	India Country Director
C4D Partners	Arvind Agarwal	Managing Partner
Nativelead	Sivarajah Ramanathan	Founder and CEO
RTBI	Jayalakshmi Umadikar	Senior Manager
Selco	Sarah Alexander	Senior Advisor
Social Alpha	Manoj Kumar	Founder and CEO
Upaya Social Ventures	Amit Antony Alex	India Country Director
Villgro Innovations Foundation	Srinivas Ramanujam	CEO
Yunus Social Business India	Suresh K Krishna	Founder, MD, CEO
	Priya Shah	Principal
	Sipika Nigam	Senior Portfolio Associate

Part A: Understanding the Characteristics of Innovations by Social Start-ups

Socially Oriented Innovations

Innovations of start-ups are commonly classified using a product versus business model innovation typology. Nevertheless, socially oriented innovations encompass aspects beyond this. Since the industry still lacks more nuanced and standardised frameworks to capture these aspects, most incubators and VCs have had to rely on their own parameters while classifying and evaluating innovations.

In our analysis of the interviews, we found these parameters to coalesce around three dimensions (Exhibit 5.3):

- What problem they solve – From market failure to market exclusion
- How they solve it – From technology to business model innovations as core value proposition
- Why they solve it – From social impact to financial sustainability

Social start-ups varied in where they positioned themselves on the continuum with respect to each dimension, akin to adjusting levels on a sound equalizer's parameters. Further, some (not all) of the incubators and VCs were seen to show preferences for start-ups at certain positions.

Exhibit 5.4: Market failure and market exclusion

In economic theory, market failure refers to a situation where the pursuit of self-interest by individual actors or firms results in societally inefficient outcomes, such that public goods are not provided and externalities are not accounted for. Public goods (such as roads and welfare programmes) and positive externalities (such as research and development) are benefits for which it is infeasible to charge the consumer, and negative externalities (such as air pollution) are costs for which it is infeasible to charge the consumer or the producer.

Market exclusion, on the other hand, refers to mechanisms through which individuals and communities are prevented from accessing resources and opportunities provided by the market to the average citizen.

1. *What problem they solve: From 'market failure' to 'market exclusion'*

The innovations vary in the nature of the 'social problem' they set out to address. At one end are the problems resulting from *'market failure'* [6] and at the other, those from *'market exclusion'*.[7]

Exhibit 5.3: Dimensions of socially oriented innovation

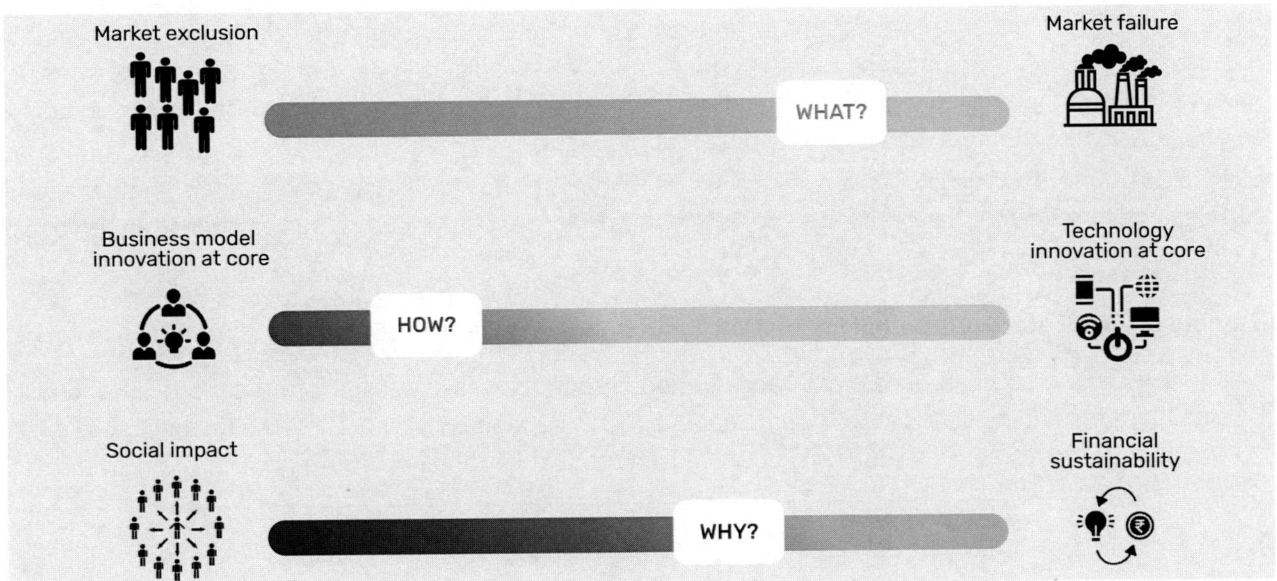

In practice, market failure denotes the situations where problems are left unaddressed as the market players find them too resource-intensive, making production risky or the project lacking in requisite returns in the short term. Traditionally, the government has been the key actor that has stepped in when the market has refused to provide funding for science and technology innovation and has set up high technology research institutes. As Manoj Kumar from Social Alpha observed: *"Now the government is not doing that. So, somebody has to do that. Slowly, private sector, non-profits will have to get into that space."* The start-ups, incubators and funders who take this perspective seek to solve grand societal challenges in line with sustainable development goals (SDGs) and often tend to promote deep science product innovations that support their objectives. Incubators and funders like Social Alpha support innovations that address SDGs, such as environment, healthcare and education, irrespective of the segments of the population they serve.

Marketplace exclusion, in practice, translates to the needs of specific segments of the population being un(der)served, owing to poverty that places them at the Base-of-the-Pyramid (BoP) and other sources of social exclusion such as physical or mental disabilities, non-binary gender, scheduled caste and tribe status, and so on. The start-ups, incubators and investors seeking to address this problem aim to extend market activities to the marginalised and un(der)served and enable their upliftment and empowerment. Among the incubators and investors we interviewed, six espoused this perspective. They supported only those start-ups that cater exclusively to or to a sizeable number among the marginalised populations (say, earning less than $3 per day). Two of these six go further and insist on specific types of impact for the beneficiary groups, such as employment or livelihood generation.

Balancing both: While there are debates as to which of these problems a social start-up should concentrate more on, we find that many of the start-ups, incubators

Exhibit 5.5: Examples of market failure and exclusion

Examples of social start-ups addressing market failure

- Ameliorate Biotech Private developed a rapid diagnostic kit that simultaneously detects three mosquito-borne diseases – malaria, dengue and chikungunya – widely prevalent in India.
- CultYvate, introduced AI and IoT-based farm and crop irrigation solutions to optimise water usage, prevent diseases and pest infestations, and increase yield.

Examples of social start-ups addressing market exclusion

- Meghshala, a social enterprise, aims at improving the quality of teaching in the government schools catering to poorer students. The teachers of government schools often lack practical teaching skills and have limited resources to make lessons interesting and enjoyable. Meghshala provides resource support and an app that mentors teachers in refining their pedagogy.
- Mirakle Couriers has developed a business model that generates livelihood opportunities for deaf people. It has been able to create a stable and efficient workforce in an industry badly affected by employee turnover and quality issues.

Example of social start-ups balancing market failure and exclusion

- Kamal Kisan, which produces small farm equipment, addresses the issue of precarious livelihoods of small farmers and aids the cause of sustainable agriculture in the process. They use technology to design and manufacture small farm equipment, enhancing productivity and improving small farmers' livelihoods.

and funders, in reality, would fall somewhere in between, albeit closer to one end than the other. Similarly, incubators, such as RTBI (Rural Technology and Business Incubator), while focussing exclusively on technology innovations that solve some of the grand challenges, insist that they are aimed at underserved rural populations.

The nature of market exclusion problems and failure, however, differs with the context. While health and environment are common public goods pursued across countries, nutrition and tropical disease prevention are more important in a developing country such as India than in a developed country such as Sweden. Domains like culture and recreation may be culturally more salient in a country like Spain than in India.[8] Market exclusion problems may also be viewed differently, like elderly care in Singapore or homelessness in Germany. Although market failure and exclusion capture a broad range of societal problems, the perspectives and solutions to them are based on the locally grounded experiences of incubators and founders.

2. *How they solve it: From technology to business model innovations as a core value proposition*

Irrespective of where the start-ups fall in the spectrum of market failure to exclusion, the solutions can originate as technology or business model innovation. Start-ups may offer a product that requires significant technological innovation, such as a medical device or a learning platform. This places technological product innovation at the core of their value proposition. While they may need to innovate their business model to suit their product offering, that is not their core value proposition. The case is the opposite for start-ups with business model innovation as their core value proposition. Given the nature of communication and technology today, all companies need some technology to enable the offering of their services – even if it is an app to take their services to the market. Here, technology acts as an enabler for its value proposition.

In practice, most take the middle ground. Technology and business model innovations are seen as two complementary aspects of the same solution, and what matters is an innovative and robust integration of technology (at the core or as an enabler) and the business model. Technology needs to be embedded in the right business model to be effective because business models help create and capture economic and social value. A business model strategises how a business identifies stakeholder needs, develops a process of addressing the needs, takes it to the stakeholder, monetises value and generates impact. Technology is often the secret sauce in one or many of these sub-parts of the business model and tends to be deployed differently depending on the start-up's nature (see Exhibit 5.6 for examples).

Many social start-up founders feel pressured to rope in technology and present their solutions as tech-based solutions, since the recent trends in the start-up ecosystems favour 'tech'. Most incubators and investors agree that technology is an inevitable enabler for scaling up in a large market like India. However, many are beginning to be wary of any and every applicant that attaches the 'tech' label to their name to be in vogue. While incubators and funders such as Social Alpha and RTBI actively seek out technology-based social start-ups, others such as C4D prefer to fund those who come up with sound business model innovations.

Historically, founders from a technology background have tended to create their solutions around technology. It is not surprising that Sneha Priya, winner of national and

Exhibit 5.6: Examples of different innovations as core value propositions

Examples for technology (product) innovation as core value proposition	Examples for business model innovations enabled by technology
• Innaumation Medical Devices, which creates cost-effective voice-boxes • CultYvate smart irrigators • Aarna Biomedical Products (silicone breast prosthesis)	• PotHole Raja, an app to report potholes • Meghshala, upskilling teachers and democratising access to resources • EasyGov, an app to provide citizens easy and convenient access to government schemes and services

Exhibit 5.7: Social ventures considered: Technology innovation in the value proposition

Tech product innovation as core to the value proposition	Tech innovation as enabling service-based value proposition
CultYvate (AI & IoT)	
Kamal Kisan	UzhavarBumi (App)
Innaumation Medical Devices	Meghshala (App)
Ameliorate Biotech	SP Robotics (Learning platform)
Aarna Biomedical Products	EasyGov (App)
Revy Environmental Solutions	PotHole Raja (App)

international competitions in robotics, felt that robots, AI, VR and other technologies were the best way to boost the creativity and imagination of new-age learners, and therefore made it the backbone of SP Robotics, which helps students build their STEM skills. The starting point for many founders from a non-technology background was business model innovation. It is the search for a solution that takes them to technology. While setting up Meghshala, 65-year-old Jyothi Thyagarajan, a teacher with 30 years of experience, discovered that technology could be a useful tool to empower and upskill well-crafted teaching kits, mentoring and guidance, turning them into master teachers.

Nevertheless, it needs to be borne in mind that the ability of these technology and business model innovations to generate real social returns depends on the extent to which the intended beneficiaries are involved in developing them. Beneficiary participation can be sought either at the innovation or the implementation stage. For instance, developing employment generating business models such as connecting rural–urban micro-entrepreneurs would require an understanding of the beneficiary lifestyle and preferences for technology adoption right from the early design stage. In contrast, innovations involving MedTech or AI may be developed in the labs first and then taken to beneficiaries for trials closer to the implementation stage. Lab- or boardroom-developed models may have to undergo more significant tweaking on the field than those developed in consultation with beneficiaries from the early stages if they are to create genuine social value. This brings us to the third dimension.

3. Why they solve it: From social impact to financial sustainability

A key dimension in which social start-ups differ from other start-ups is why they want to solve a problem. Social returns for their beneficiaries rather than financial returns for themselves are what drive most social start-ups. However, the paradox is that without the latter, they may not ensure the sustainability of the former. Balancing both is tricky, as focus on one tends to dilute focus on the other.

The tension between both becomes especially salient when the start-ups try to scale. Scaling is considered essential from both social impact (as it widens the social value capture by greater numbers of beneficiaries) and financial returns (as it enhances financial sustainability by more significant market value capture). Though desired from both perspectives, scaling is not as straightforward as it sounds, even in proven solutions developed with beneficiary participation. The diversity of the Indian population often poses a problem for firms while scaling. Solutions that worked well for, say northern Karnataka, may not even apply to southern Karnataka, leave alone other states. As language, regulations and lifestyles are varied, on-the-ground implementation of solutions requires continuous innovation, if not in technology, then business model–wise. This stretches the start-ups financially and adversely affects their viability.

Most of our interviewees believed that overemphasis on social returns would not help them in becoming financially sustainable. According to some, what helps the latter is having a solution that solves an industry problem and a social problem. C4D's Arvind Agarwal articulates this: *"If you are just solving a societal problem, eventually you will die while scaling because you will need to compete with everybody else in the sector. So, unless you are solving a pain point of the sector along with solving a pain point of the society, you will not be successful."* While generating and capturing market value in this manner would make the bottom-line more robust, the challenge would be in coming up with solutions that can simultaneously capture social and market value. In the absence of such solutions, they may have to look for alternative avenues for revenue (for example, non-beneficiary customers). At times, the founders themselves loathe to scale up through diversifying their target consumers to include privileged sections, such that income generated there can sustain their offerings for the underprivileged classes. This often dissipates the focus on the beneficiaries and results in what is known as 'mission drift', that is, compromising social goals for financial goals.[9] Thus, how to strike a balance between social impact and financial sustainability becomes a key decision point for founders.

Exhibit 5.8: Example of an innovation addressing a social and an industry problem simultaneously

The success of Mirakle Couriers can be attributed to the fact that not only have they developed a business model that provides employment to deaf people, but that in doing so they have also been able to create a stable and efficient workforce in an industry badly affected by employee turnover and quality issues.

(E)valuating Social Innovations

While innovation in social start-ups is driven by the imperative to create social impact, assessing the impact that they have been able to bring about remains a still-evolving area.

Impact assessment can inform a social start-up (and the stakeholders) of their effectiveness. A few of them do showcase 'impact' through various numerical indicators.

The debate is on as to whether these measures indeed indicate impact or just the reach or outcomes.

Exhibit 5.9: Examples of impact indicators for social start-ups

- Within a short span of two years, Uzhavar Bumi Agro Products Pvt Ltd has grown to serve 4,500 customers daily, benefitting around 600 dairy farmers and employing over 70 people as factory workers and delivery agents. More than 30 women's self-help groups have been empowered through the start-up.
- Meghshala has covered over 2,500 schools and benefitted students through 4,500 lessons in English and regional languages in three states. Their app has been downloaded 14,000 times by teachers seeking teaching resources and guidance.
- SP Robotics has established its presence in 23 Indian cities that host 81 learning centres, reaching over 100,000 students.
- Having served customers including Mahindra & Mahindra, The Aditya Birla Group, Victory Art Foundation, JSW Group, Indian Hotels Company, Godrej & Boyce and Essel Propack in the past, Mirakle Couriers now has Amazon as their exclusive customer. It has bagged awards such as the National Award for the Empowerment of People with Disabilities (2010).

While standard criteria are difficult to define, the general sense is that measurement of impact depends on the target beneficiary, sector and problem being addressed. Also, impact indicates tangible long-term durable improvements to quality of life, which are hard to measure within the short period post the product or service innovation hitting the market. Although there is a shared feeling that the focus should be on the quality rather than the quantity of change brought to people's lives, the question is: will an ecosystem that is used to financial performance indicators that are short-term in nature appreciate it? The following two quotes put forth this issue succinctly:

"From an impact point of view, working with 20 farmers over a period of 10 years would be more significant than working with 2,000 farmers for one crop. But prima facie,

2,000 sounds better than 20. The emphasis, when it is investor-driven, is always going to be on scale."

—Amit Antony Alex, Upaya SV

"A lot of people do say, well, why don't you just give me the number of households or just give me the number of lights that you've sold. I do not think that is the point. The point is that it is not about that light, but about how the person paid for it such that it became an asset for that person."

—Sarah Alexander, Selco Foundation

All the incubators and investors we interviewed said that the first gate that start-ups applying to them have to pass was impact. While some used impact criteria in terms of a particular population (say 50 per cent BoP customers), others specified it as critical themes of societal challenges that need to be addressed. Only after the impact avenue was confirmed were these start-ups evaluated based on their business models, potential scalability and sustainability through profit generation. Post selection, organisations like Villgro, C4D and YSB used their instruments for tracking ongoing impact. For most incubators working with BoP beneficiaries, impact involved measuring the breadth (how many customers and beneficiaries) and the depth (quantum of increase in indicators such as income, learning curve, quality of life, and so on). Baseline, midline and end-line surveys were conducted annually or semi-annually for several years to track on-the-ground impact.

Implications

Thus, although social start-ups are a promising category that will contribute to economic growth and social development, more targeted approaches may be needed to enable them to fulfil their potential.

For start-ups

While working on their proposals, it may be helpful to think along the three dimensions – what problem they are trying to solve (market failure versus exclusion), how they are trying to solve it (technology versus business model innovation), and why they want to solve it (social impact versus financial sustainability) – and to develop clarity as to where they want to position themselves along the continuum on each of these dimensions. While approaching incubators and funders, start-ups need to bear in mind that some of them may have specific preferences. The chances of receiving support are enhanced by approaching those incubators and fund managers whose orientations are aligned with the start-ups'. Start-ups then need to ensure that the technological innovations they have in mind are appropriate for solving the problem they have chosen to address. They need to do a thorough job of integrating technology with the business model. It might also help start-ups to consider how their solution to a social problem can also solve an industry problem. This would improve their chances of scaling up.

For incubators or VCs

Using the 'what–how–why' framework in evaluating social start-ups may help in quickly identifying those who are better aligned with your vision and strategic objectives. Start-ups may need support and guidance in balancing the breadth and depth of social impact. Endorsing breadth indicators alone may be short-sighted.

Part B: Understanding the Dynamics of Supporting Social Innovations: Exploring the Incubation and Funding Landscape

Of late, there has been a rapid rise in the incubation and funding support extended to social start-ups. Though this has mainstreamed social start-ups to some extent, the approaches taken to support them are varied and still evolving. Lessons are yet emerging as to what kind of support activities yield better outcomes.

1. Incubation support: Firm-level and ecosystem approaches

We found that most incubators typically take a firm-level focus in supporting start-ups, while a few work with an ecosystem focus.

Those with firm-level focus concentrate on individual start-ups and seek to guide and assist them in their activities from product development to marketing through financial and business support. Some of the incubators such as YSB, Upaya and Acumen support innovative firms by forming networks with each other or other potential investors, and those such as RTBI and

Nativelead also provide additional mentoring and pilot study support through their networks. Social Alpha has scaled up the network-based approach to supporting innovation by partnering with various stakeholders of the ecosystem including government universities that provide wet labs, investors and local NGO partners who facilitate ground-level pilot studies, and the government is the primary customer of the innovations. The focus here is still on individual start-ups.

Those who have adopted an ecosystem focus promote a system perspective. For instance, Selco Foundation, while focussing on sustainable energy solutions for BoP persons, seek to bundle financial and social innovation together with technological innovation. They upskill customers and facilitate financial instruments for them. Moreover, they look to act as an enabler to bring together all the stakeholders of the sustainable energy ecosystem and create holistic solutions for different aspects of implementing energy technology in rural India. This includes creating markets for micro-entrepreneurs and conducting risk analysis of potential problems that implementing a particular solution might lead to.

"If we're going into a community to solve a problem, then we need to be thinking holistically. For example, when putting a solar water pump in a region, Selco will automatically think of what's the groundwater level here? How long will the farmer use this for? So that one doesn't create a water problem because now one has a solar water pump."

—Sarah Alexander, Selco Foundation

There has been no comparative research on if and how either approach differs in generating outcomes such as social impact, revenues and firm viability. However, given the intertwined nature of social problems that may not fit the industry and sectoral boundaries, and the need for cross-industry or sector collaboration of stakeholders to meaningfully solve them, it may help to have an ecosystem view while extending firm-level support.

2. Funding support: Policy-level and ecosystem-level challenges

Providing funding to social start-ups remains a complex issue, thanks to the lingering inadequacies of the regulatory framework and the investment ecosystem's current mindset. While this is to be expected in the early stages of evolution in any sector, going forward might prove to be unnecessarily tricky without concerted efforts from the policymakers and key stakeholders to resolve them.

Policy landscape

Despite their proliferation, in India, neither social start-ups nor those who fund social start-ups are recognised by distinct legal structures that differentiate them from their mainstream counterparts and allow for effectively pursuing social impact. Social start-ups in countries such as the US have benefitted from the newly introduced legal structures that confer legitimacy to them and enable flow of funds in ways that accommodate the intrinsic tensions they try to balance.

Exhibit 5.10: SEBI regulations for social venture funds

In India, SEBI (2012, 2020) regulations[10] provide the guidelines under which social start-ups operate, and they do not offer much wriggle room for them to secure appropriate kinds of funding. For instance, categorised under alternative investment funds (AIFs), SEBI definitions of social venture funds (SVF) and social ventures (SV) is a much more restricted version of the nomenclature used in the market. As per SEBI regulations, for-profit ventures cannot be designated as social ventures (unless they are Section 8 companies which cannot issue dividends to investors) and social venture funds have to invest 75 per cent of their investible funds in social ventures. Moreover, firms classifying themselves as social ventures can only promise muted returns to investors. This creates a difficulty in raising capital, especially as regulations do not allow Indian philanthropic capital (including CSR) to be invested in for-profit ventures through venture funds. Neither can foreign funds be used as grants to for-profit ventures, under FCRA regulations[11] (even though AIF regulations allow it). Restrictions exist in disbursing foreign capital through debt instruments as well.[12]

The current policy framework governing social start-ups amounts to the fact that ventures that see themselves as social cannot get registered as legal social ventures if they want to work for a profit. Thus, most such entities in India are so due to informal self-categorisations. The majority of start-ups we examined were set up as private limited companies (Exhibit 5.11). This means that the same regulations and taxes applied to commercial, for-profit businesses and to social businesses, and they had to compete on an equal footing for investor funding.

Similarly, VCs also have to manoeuvre through the regulatory frameworks. For example, to invest in for-profit social businesses, many of the socially oriented venture funds register as non-profit entities. These entities' funding arm often acts as category II debt funds to enable both offshore and domestic risk investments. Funds with foreign sources can be invested in debt funding only subject to restrictive clauses. The key instruments they use are equity shares and compulsorily convertible preference shares (CCPS). Among the funds we interviewed, different funds had different structures in place to fund social start-ups. To cite two examples, Acumen functions as a non-profit foundation which desists from promising a double-digit financial return to investors (that is, it promises highly muted returns). YSB, on the other hand, is an NBFC[13] which provides debt funding. Many impact funds also receive foreign capital from international development funds such as DFID (UK), DOM (the Netherlands) and foreign philanthropic foundations.

Investment ecosystem

More investors have now come forward to fund social start-ups; however, the underlying mindset still largely reflects those of mainstream financial markets. Social start-ups find many of their expectations unrealistic. Unlike their mainstream counterparts, the critical customers for most social start-ups are the BoP population (at times, with per capita income of less than $3 a day) and/or the government (whose payment processing takes a long time), and therefore profits are not made quickly. Incubation periods are long, with 7–10 years of gestation before an early investor can exit. Also, the norms applied in the valuation of start-ups do not include provisions for attaching a premium to the social impact they generate. Loans and debt fund interest also run into double-digit percentages (10–25 per cent). Engaging with commercial investors, who look for quick and high returns, often poses a risk of mission drift. Those who want to stay true to their mission find it challenging to identify investors with matching philosophies to fund scaling up activities. Involvement with investors who focus on short-term, easy-to-count metrics of impact may also be problematic as that may not bring long-term benefits. Thus, despite the increasing number of investors, securing appropriate funding remains a big challenge for social start-ups. Many cross the start-up stage holding on to a combination of grants and private equity in addition to bootstrapping (Exhibit 5.11).

The investment ecosystem currently shows an overwhelming presence of 'impact investors' who seek to pump commercial capital into social start-ups. Many social business entrepreneurs now raise money from commercial LPs with the promise of double-digit percentage IRRs. Among sectors, while microfinance has become well-established and positively mainstream, agriculture, education and healthcare are the 'flavour of the season' among commercial investors, with a huge impetus from the COVID-19 pandemic (Exhibit 5.12).

However, this is viewed with a fair amount of scepticism, as it has left the term 'impact' open to interpretation, enabling any start-up to call themselves a social start-up and any investor an impact investor. Sipika of YSB observes: *"Impact investing has become very mainstream today. Many well-established, domestic and international fund houses, banking arms, family offices, have started impact investment funds, thereby bringing focus and attention to it. Nevertheless, there is a difference in how impact-oriented each of them are between the various impact funds. Because the definition of 'impact' is not in place, many funds consider themselves impact funds. Their theory maybe, 'the company that we are investing in is indirectly able to create so much employment; hence they are creating impact.' Going by that definition, any work done in India will result in some kind of impact. We make it very clear that the entrepreneur or the enterprise we invest in should create a direct impact in the life of the otherwise excluded beneficiaries."*

A differentiation that is becoming more meaningful in this context is impact investment versus patient capital. Mahesh Yagnaraman of Acumen says: "*We never use the word 'impact' ever. We say that we use 'patient capital' to invest in solutions which can solve the problems of the*

Exhibit 5.11: Social ventures considered: Funding patterns

	Name (Year of founding)	Founders	Nature of incorporation	Funding sources		
				Grants	Equity	Debt
1	Aarna Biomedical Products (2017)	Dr Pawan Mehrotra	Private Limited Company	👍	👍	–
2	Ameliorate Biotech Private Limited (2015)	Dr Rashbehari Tunga Dr Binita Shrivastava Tunga	Private Limited Company	👍	👍	–
3	Bare Necessities (2019)	Sahar Mansoor	Private Limited Company	–	👍	–
4	CultYvate (2016)	Mallesh Tigali, M Bhavana Mallesh Arun Kumar	Private Limited Company	👍	👍	–
5	EasyGov (2015)	Amit Shukla, Prabha Shukla	Private Limited Company	–	👍	–
6.	Innaumation Medical Devices (2017)	Dr Vishal Rao, Shashank Mahesh	Private Limited Company	👍	👍	–
7	Kamal Kisan (2013)	Devi Murthy	Private Limited Company	👍	👍	–
8	Meghashala (2013)	Jyoti Thyagarajan Shridhar Ranganathan	Not for Profit Trust	👍	👍	–
9	Mirakle Couriers (2009)	Dhruv Lakra	Private Limited Company	–	👍	–
10	PotHole Raja (2016)	Prathaap B	Public–Private Partnership	–	–	–
11	Revy Environmental Solutions (2017)	Dr Vanita Prasad	Private Limited Company	👍	–	👍
12	SP Robotic Works (2012)	Sneha Priya Pranavan S	Private Limited Company	–	👍	–
13	UzhavarBumi (2017)	Vetrivel Palani Paneerselvam	Private Limited Company	–	👍	–

poor. That is so as most of the products and solutions are ones which typically take time to become adapted for implementation among the targeted population." This takes a more extended period than the 1–5 years that typical investors aim to exit in.

The industry experts interviewed feel that policy changes, including a stock exchange for social businesses or a different approach to social enterprises and their financing, might be more pertinent.

"Many of these places which are creating social impact, valuations won't grow that fast. Because this is not like making some map and getting customers while making a loss. So, in that sense, real social enterprise as I see them would fall into the bracket of MSMEs. I believe that social

Exhibit 5.12: Number of deals and investment amount by industry: January 2016–December 2020

Industry	FY16		FY17		FY18		FY19		FY20	
	No. of Deals	Amount ($M)	No. of Deals	Amount ($M)	No. of Deals	Amount ($M)	No. of Deals	Amount ($M)	No. of Deals	Amount ($M)
Agri-business	10	22.4	9	102.38	10	47.97	11	93.12	9	6.07
BFSI	28	659.35	34	848.95	42	874.13	29	893.66	15	253.23
Education	10	19.65	13	21.13	15	55.74	8	18.52	8	47.87
Healthcare and Life Sciences	5	4.43	12	22.43	10	38.39	5	34.86	3	62.13
IT and ITES	43	199.89	42	111.31	55	20914	63	565.52	40	416.70
Others	19	41.97	17	105.93	22	175.45	13	153.86	18	242.49
Total	115	947.53	127	1212.13	154	1400.82	129	1759.54	93	1118.49

enterprises should stop thinking of themselves as start-ups and getting fascinated by the VC start-up model. They should focus on being more like MSMEs, focused on banks and other kinds of capital. They should not just run after equity capital. But frankly, it is a question of structure and transaction costs, which are then going to get higher."

—Srinivas Ramanujam, Villgro

Implications

For Incubators or VCs

Given the interconnected nature of the social problems that the start-ups try to address, it helps to maintain an ecosystem outlook while evaluating the solutions' appropriateness and extending help for their further development. Since the innovative solutions that the social start-ups pioneer is of cross-sectoral and inter-disciplinary nature, it will be of immense value to create extensive networks of diverse actors who can aid them in various aspects of solution development and implementation. In the absence of policy guidelines and VC industry practices that allow for different valuation norms for social start-ups, the interested parties may have to come together to initiate discussions on new norms and shared practices. In the absence of tailored norms and practices, genuine social start-ups are unlikely to survive.

For Policymakers

Comprehensive regulations, which pay attention to the unique characteristics and challenges of social start-ups, are a pressing need to ensure the survival of social start-ups. An essential requirement may be appropriate legal structures for social start-ups that accommodate their social and profit goals and resource requirements to pursue these twin purposes. Innovative funding mechanisms such as Social Stock Exchange must be seriously explored to ease this sector's struggles.

Endnotes

[1]The three authors contributed equally to this article.
Author acknowledgements: We profusely thank Nagaraja Prakasam, angel investor and mentor in residence, NSRCEL, IIM Bangalore, for helping us access all the interviewees. We also extend our heartfelt gratitude to all the interviewees who generously supported us with their time and thoughts. Finally, we would like to thank Ms. Akhila E and Mr. Biswa Prakash Jena for support with tables and interview transcription.

[2]Battilana, J and Dorado, S. 2010. Building sustainable hybrid organisations: The case of commercial microfinance organisations. *Academy of Management Journal* 53(6): 1419–1440.

[3]*Source:* Venture Intelligence

[4]Disclaimer: The choice of these 9 is based solely on access. It is a coincidence that these also happen to be well-known and reputed for their social orientation.

[5]Disclaimer: The choice of the 13 social start-ups was based on availability of online resources about them. They are intended to be only examples and not exemplars.

[6]https://www.econlib.org/library/Topics/College/marketfailures.html

[7]https://gtr.ukri.org/projects?ref=ES%2FL001101%2F1

[8]Mair, J. 2020. "Social Entrepreneurship: Research as Disciplined Exploration". In *The Nonprofit Sector: A Research Handbook,* edited by WW Powell and P Bromley, 333–357. Stanford: Stanford University Press.

[9]Ebrahim, A, Battilana, J and Mair, J. 2014. The governance of social enterprises: Mission drift and accountability challenges in hybrid organisations. *Research in Organisational Behavior* 34: 81–100.

[10]https://www.sebi.gov.in/legal/regulations/jun-2018/sebi-alternative-investment-funds-regulations-2012-last-amended-on-may-10-2019-_34621.html

[11]The Foreign Contribution Regulation Act, 2010, https://fcraonline.nic.in/home/PDF_Doc/FC-RegulationAct-2010-C.pdf

[12]For more details, please see report by Nishith Desai Associates and Thomson Reuters, available here: http://www.trust.org/contentAsset/raw-data/ac41fcc1-d161-4b62-b64b-fc92e310397f/file

[13]Non-banking financial company

Section II

INCUBATION

IN BRIEF

- The number of incubators in India grew 15 times between 2000 and 2020.
- Non-metro cities, which account for more than 60 per cent of incubators in India, are gearing up to become future start-up capitals.
- The highest density of incubators in the south and west of India and within academic institutions highlights the common assumptions around start-ups as entities founded by young graduates commercialising technology developed in labs.
- There has been vigorous incubation policy activism in India between 2008 and 2020. Most of the current policies and schemes recognise technology commercialisation as the primary goal of incubators.
- To remain effective, incubators must define their performance measures around the goals of building founders, start-ups, ecosystems as well as themselves as organisations.
- In the past, many services of incubators, such as co-working spaces, were disaggregated and commercialised.
  In a post-COVID-19 world, incubators must explore novel offerings to remain effective and impactful.

6

The Past, Present and Future of Start-up Incubation in India

Supriya Sharma, Neharika Vohra
and Shailaja Shukla

Sharma, S, Vohra, N and Shukla, S. 2021. "The Past, Present and Future of Start-up Incubation in India". In *Shifting Orbits: Decoding the Trajectory of the Indian Start-up Ecosystem*, edited by Thillai Rajan A, Srivardhini K Jha, Joffi Thomas and Rohan Chinchwadkar, 62–73. Hyderabad: Universities Press (India) Private Limited.

Prolific, expansive and promising – these are some common adjectives used to describe India's start-up ecosystem. Incubators are a prominent part of and contributor to this ecosystem. In 2017, NASSCOM found over 140 incubators in India and placed the country third in the world for the number of incubators, behind USA and China.[1] By October 2020, this number had multiplied. While the number of incubators is believed to be much higher, we have listed and verified over 326 incubators in India. This translates roughly to one incubator per 150 start-ups in India.[2]

As the start-up ecosystem is emerging from COVID-19, we pause to reflect upon the future pathways for incubation. We examine the history and current landscape of incubation in India. We analyse the incubation policy landscape to highlight gaps and opportunities for sharper regulatory or schematic interventions. Finally, we critically examine the design and operation of incubators. We conclude with suggestions and questions for incubators to consider, so as to remain relevant and impactful.

The Past and Present of Incubation

Incubation in India can be analysed in three ways – temporal or growth of incubators over time and the evolution of the policy landscape; spatial or geographic spread of incubators; and affiliation and focus of incubators.

Temporal – Incubators' Growth and Evolution of the Policy Landscape

Until 2000, India had just about 20 incubators. In a decade, this number had increased four times, with over 60 incubators being founded between 2000 and 2010. The growth curve became steeper in the next decade (2010–2020), with over 200 incubators being established. We listed 326 incubators by October 2020.

We predominantly find incubators housed within academic institutions (such as IITs, IIMs, universities) or as part of industry bodies and organisations (such as NASSCOM) and research agencies (such as C-CAMP). The steep rise in incubators – over 15 times in the last two decades – can be largely attributed to the growth in incubators affiliated to academic institutions (Exhibit 6.1). The jump during 2015–2019 in academic institution–based incubators could also be a result of the push from the central government towards evangelising entrepreneurship and making India "a nation of job-creators".[3]

Setting up incubators within academic institutions is often seen as creating infrastructure to support and inspire young graduates to start up. Most successful founders stress upon starting up after a few years of working with other organisations. Family businesses also adopt an informal apprenticeship so as to ensure that the incoming generations learn the ropes before being inducted formally. Incubators based in academic institutions may be better placed at creating apprenticeship opportunities for young graduates to train them for entrepreneurship.[5] Additionally, the incubators may also consider creating programmes and support structures for alumni who may wish to venture out after a few years in the industry.

The institutionalisation of incubation policies in India dates back to 1955, with the setting up of the National Small Industries Corporation (NSIC) by the Ministry of Micro, Small and Medium Enterprises (MoMSME). While NSIC focussed on evangelising small businesses, technology entrepreneurship received a significant boost with the setting up of the National Science and Technology Development Board (NSTEDB) by the Department of Science and Technology (DST) in 1982. The Incubation Policy of the MoMSME and Technology Incubation and Development of Entrepreneurs (TIDE) scheme by the Ministry of Electronics and Information Technology (MeitY) followed the setting up of NSTEDB; both these initiatives adopted 'commercialisation of

Exhibit 6.1: Growth in incubators in India[4]

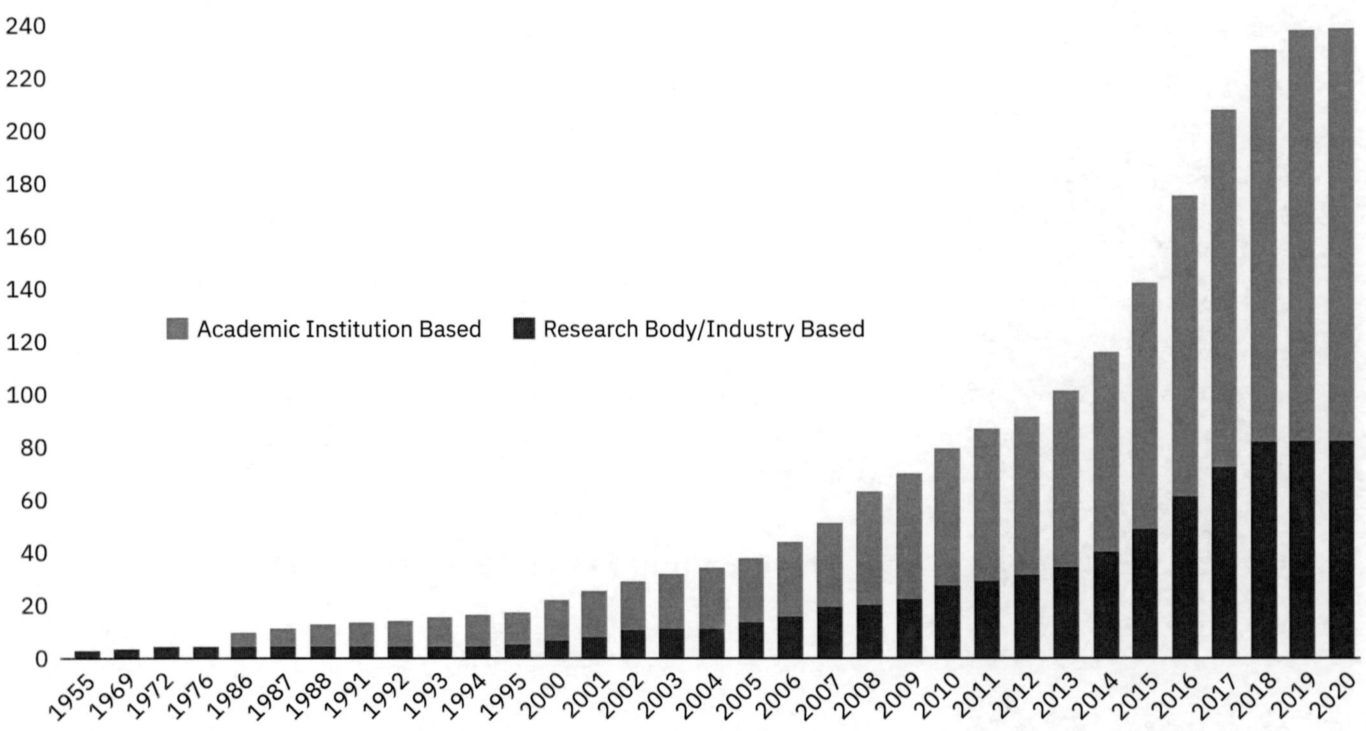

Exhibit 6.2: Evolution in incubation policies of the central government

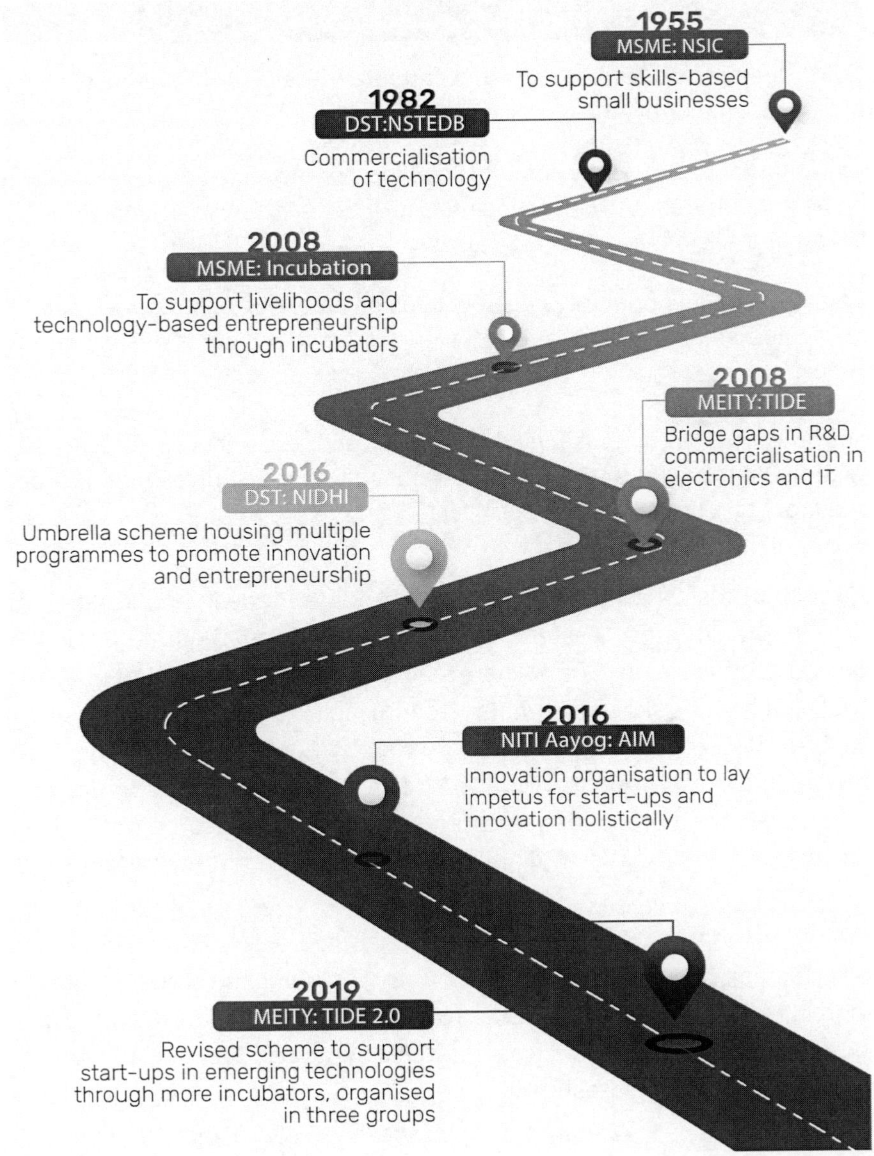

Source: Adapted from Sharma and Vohra (2020)[6]

research and technology entrepreneurship' as the goal for incubation (Exhibit 6.2).

Two of the most recent incubation policy interventions – NITI Aayog's Atal Innovation Mission (AIM; through Atal Incubation Centres) and the revised scheme from 2008, TIDE 2.0, from the Ministry of Electronics and Information Technology (MeitY) – present a somewhat novel approach of incubation. By virtue of being the implementing body of the Startup India Initiative, AIM takes a more holistic view of entrepreneurship as against the entrepreneurship-as-technology-commercialisation stance of the older policies and schemes. The mandates of incubators affiliated to AIM encapsulate a variety of goals including training entrepreneurs and building start-up business models.[7]

MeitY's recent scheme, TIDE 2.0, recognises the differences among incubators and classifies them into three levels: G1, G2, G3, which are organised into a funnel. G3 incubators are expected to undertake entrepreneurship evangelising activities in unexplored regions; this group primarily includes recently established incubators in academic institutions. G2 incubation centres are expected to undertake entrepreneurship training and acceleration programmes at scale. In addition, G2 incubators are also expected to mentor G3 centres. Finally, G1 centres are more matured incubators that are mandated with capacity building and post-investment support to start-ups. These centres are also expected to supervise and mentor G2 and G3 incubators.[8] This acknowledgement of the differences between incubators and structuring them as a system holds promise. Such a systemic view will help in consolidation of efforts, knowledge sharing and breaking silos between incubators, thereby unlocking significant value for the whole ecosystem.

The schemes have varied expectations from their supported incubators. Amongst the incubation schemes currently in force, we compare the four most prominent ones. Exhibit 6.3 highlights how the incubation schemes of MoMSME and DST underscore the commercialisation of technology for their supported incubators, while AIM's Atal Innovation Incubators (AIC) are expected to enable start-ups to survive and scale by providing them the necessary inputs.

The period between 2008 and 2020 witnessed vigorous incubation policy activism in India. In this time, new policies and schemes were launched in addition to existing ones being fine-tuned. It is important to

Exhibit 6.3: Objectives of incubators

Ministry	Primary incubation objective
Ministry of Micro, Small and Medium Enterprises[9]	Promote speedy commercialisation of technology developed in the host institute, predominantly in the agriculture sector.
NSTEDB, Department of Science and Technology[10]	Provide a platform for speedy commercialisation of technologies developed by the host institution or by any academic, technical, R&D institution or individual in areas of national importance.
TIDE 2.0, Ministry of Electronics and Information Technology (MeitY Startup Hub)	Support ICT start-ups primarily engaged in using emerging technologies such as IoT, AI, blockchain, robotics, and so on, in pre-identified areas of societal relevance.
Atal Innovation Mission, NITI Aayog (Atal Innovation Mission)	Provide start-ups with necessary guidance, tech support, infrastructure, access to investors, networking, and facilitating a host of other resources that may be required for start-ups to survive and scale.

note that this was also a period of sharp growth in the number of start-ups being founded.[11] The growth in the number of start-ups between 2005 and 2008 may have created a 'pull effect', that is, motivated incubation policy interventions. However, towards the late 2010s, this expanded incubation ecosystem may have, in turn, stoked the growth in new start-ups being founded. In other words, this was a 'push effect' of incubators on start-ups.

It is important to note that the widest reaching schemes and policies (such as those by NSTEDB, MeitY) are oriented towards technology commercialisation. While this may impel more technologies developed in labs reaching the market, it may limit other forms of starting up, such as innovative adaptation of existing technology to novel problems (such as blockchain for medical teleconsultation) or exploiting market asymmetries with limited play of technology (such as web aggregators for insurance). Furthermore, technology commercialisation as an objective may be more suited to incubators established within technical, science or medical institutions. Policymakers must consider incubators in non-engineering schools and make relevant adjustments to the schemes.

Spatial – Geographic Spread of Incubators in India

The growth in the number of incubators comes predominantly from the southern states (Tamil Nadu, Karnataka, Telangana, Andhra Pradesh and Kerala) and the western states (Maharashtra, Gujarat, Rajasthan and Goa). There can be several reasons driving this skewed regional growth, including blossoming business activity. As an after-effect of COVID-19, incubation may move to virtual platforms as well. Hence, the location of incubation centres may perhaps also be determined by the availability of affordable and quality talent and infrastructure.

At present we find incubators across the geographic landscape of the country, including the regions that have even remained physically or socio-politically difficult to reach (such as the states of Assam, Manipur, and Jammu and Kashmir).

We find a disproportionately higher presence of incubators in the southern and western regions. Tamil Nadu (46), Maharashtra (38) and Karnataka (34) have the most number of incubators (Exhibits 6.4 and 6.5). The National Capital Region (NCR) has the highest physical density, with one incubator every 138 sq. km.

While the high number of incubators in Maharashtra and NCR can be linked to these being centres of economic activity, in Tamil Nadu, the high density of incubators is linked to that of academic institutions. Eighty-four per cent of incubators (about 39 in number) in Tamil Nadu have been hosted by academic institutions. As expected, this high density of academic institution–based incubators matches the concentration of higher education institutions in the state.[12]

Exhibit 6.4: Regional growth in incubators in India

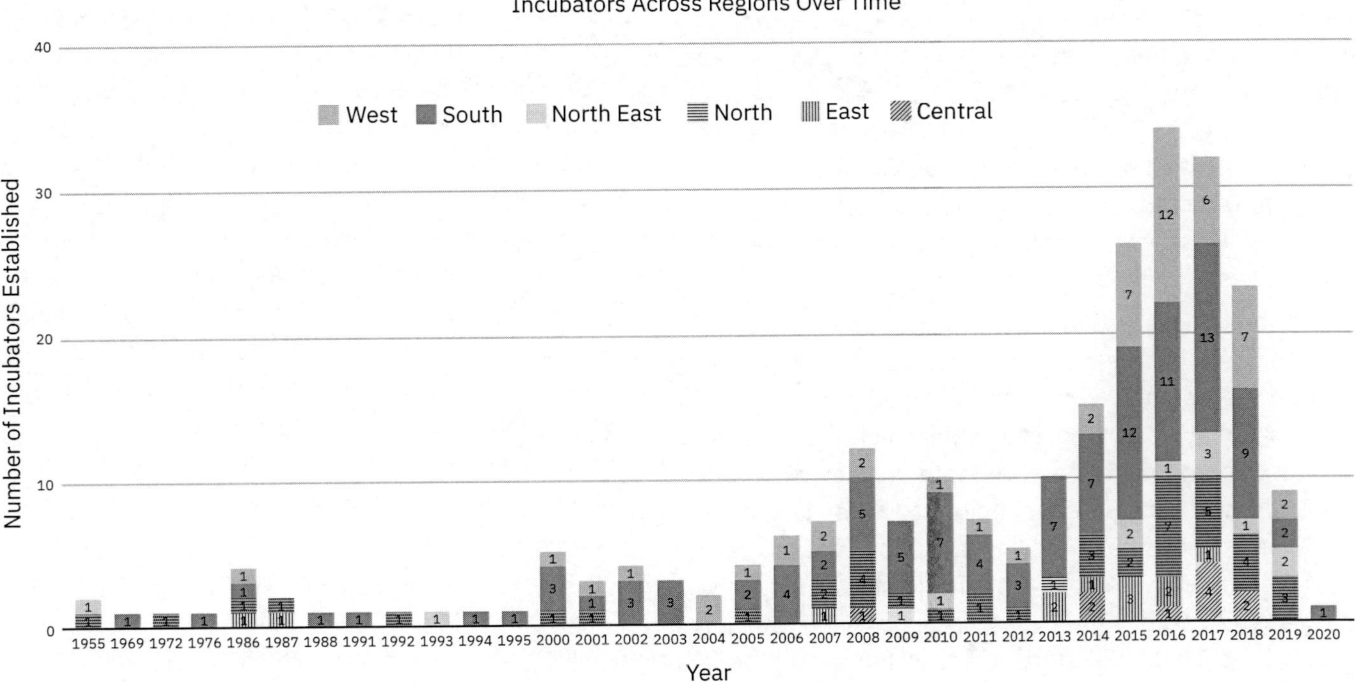

Exhibit 6.5: Geographic spread of incubators

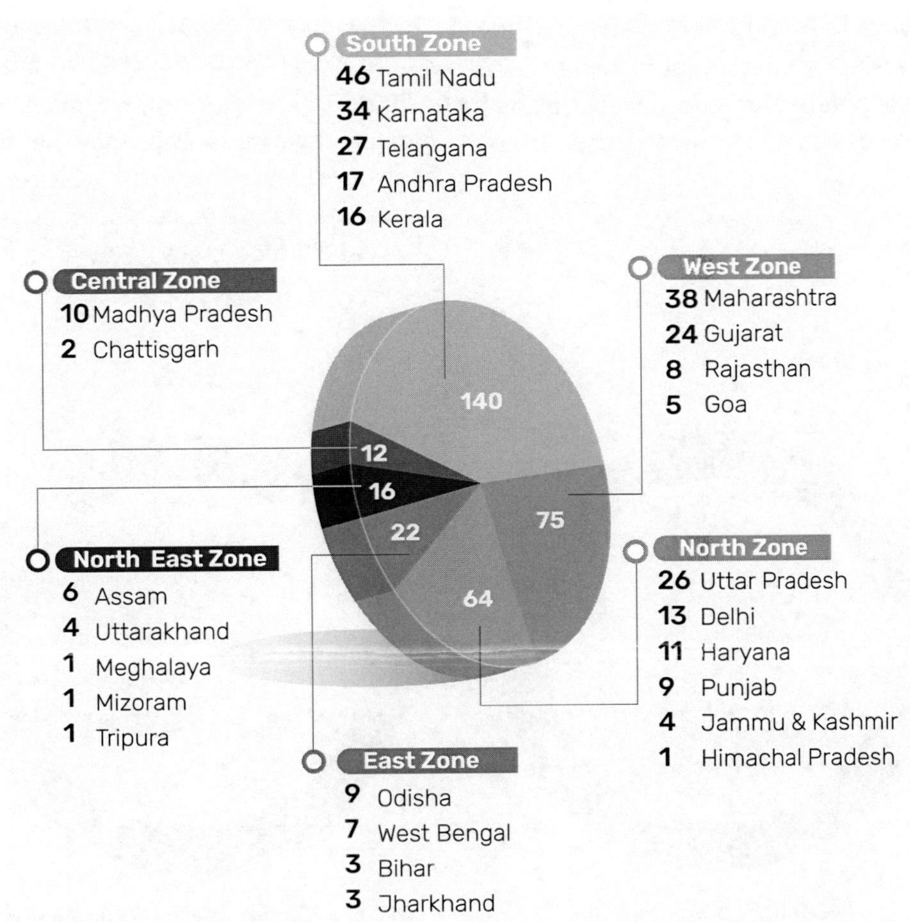

If we were to zoom in further from the states into the locations of incubators, we would find some promising trends. Over 60 per cent of the 326 incubators are located in non-metro cities;[13] of these, over 70 per cent (about 160 incubators) are located in cities and towns that are not state capitals (Exhibit 6.6). This trend foretells a more balanced future for the start-up ecosystem in India. To reiterate, the location of incubators in smaller towns may also be impacted by a movement towards virtual incubation.

Incubators are also found in smaller cities and towns with populations of less than 6,00,000, such as Bagalkot, Karnal, Koovapally, Ajmer and Berhampur. Most of these incubators are housed within higher education institutions, and it is imperative for them to expand their remit of activities beyond technology commercialisation. Many of these smaller towns and non-metros have a thriving ecosystem of family businesses. While business communities in these cities may be thriving in limited pockets, the start-up ecosystem would be in its infantile stages. Incubation centres set up in these cities and towns must consider engaging with the local family business ecosystems to create market linkages, investment and other support mechanisms for the incubated start-ups. The incubators could then become the germination bed, not just for start-ups, but also for the entire start-up ecosystems in the respective towns, cities and regions.

Affiliations and Focus Areas

Almost half the incubators in our dataset are affiliated to DST. Other ministries and departments that have active incubator programmes include AIM: Atal Innovation Mission; DARE: Department of Agricultural Research and Education; DBT: Department of Biotechnology; DoS: Department of Space; DSIR: Department of Scientific and Industrial Research; MDoNER: Ministry of Development of North Eastern Region; MeitY: Ministry of Electronics and Information Technology; MoE: Ministry of Education; MoAFW: Ministry of Agriculture and Farmers' Welfare; MoD: Ministry of Defense; MoFPI: Ministry of Food Processing Industries; MoSDE: Ministry of Skill Development and Entrepreneurship; MoT: Ministry of Tourism; MoMSME: Ministry of Micro, Small and Medium Enterprises.

The affiliation of incubators over a period of time indicates a pattern related to their age – some of the oldest incubators have been affiliated predominantly with either DST or MoMSME. In the last 10 years, MeitY and AIM have scouted and onboarded incubators with fervour, under their schemes (TIDE, launched in 2008 by MeitY and the Startup India Initiative, launched in 2016, being operationalised by AIM).

More often than not, an incubator is affiliated to multiple agencies. This may be due to reasons of financial sustainability or a quest for the incubator to better use its available resources (such as talent and physical infrastructure). However, this multiplicity of

Exhibit 6.6: Locations of incubators

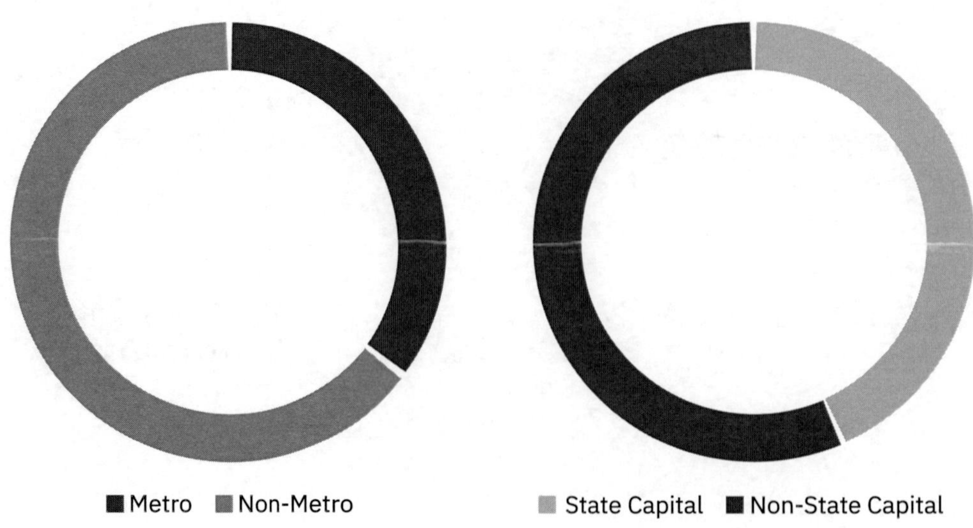

affiliation may also add to the pressure on the incubator to deliver upon the mandates of all the schemes as well as report progress to multiple agencies.

The Future of Incubation: Challenges and Questions to Reflect Upon

Do incubators create entrepreneurs, enterprises or ecosystems?

What do incubators do? Many scholars have debated and are continuing to do so about defining the function of an incubator. Several have attempted to resolve this by proposing typologies and classifications that are more accepting of the differences between incubators and their goals and processes. The most common and widely applied primary functions of an incubator – infrastructure, business support and mediation (networking) – revolve around the fundamental needs of a young enterprise.[14] Broadly, incubators enable nascent enterprises to overcome their liabilities of newness and smallness.[15] We believe that incubators legitimise start-ups by sharing their brand with the incubated ventures and entrepreneurs. By doing this, they enable the start-ups to obtain access to various resources (such as funding, talent, and so on) from the ecosystem.

Amongst all the functions of an incubator, the most difficult one is that of supporting the person behind the enterprise; this often goes unmentioned as any incubator's stated goal. It is critical to support the person (the entrepreneur) to deal with internal and business-related struggles (many of which continue even after the enterprise graduates from an incubator). Many incubators often undertake business and attitudinal training for entrepreneurs.[16] However, attitudinal training may be insufficient in preparing the entrepreneur to navigate the technical, adaptive and personal challenges that are often characteristic of start-up life. The development of strong cognitive and emotional abilities needed by entrepreneurs[17] must be taken up by incubators on a sustained basis.

The current trend of disaggregation of incubation into 'services' such as co-working spaces and accelerators throws up an existential dilemma for incubators. As physical entities, incubators are different from co-working spaces and accelerators. The latter are primarily concerned with providing good physical infrastructure and, to some extent, curated networking. The high-intensity, short-duration form of accelerators may perhaps not be suited to sustainably build entrepreneurial skills and aptitudes. In contrast, an incubator as a model has affordances for capacity building for an entrepreneur, enterprise and perhaps an ecosystem too. A question for each incubator to answer is – what are we building? This reflective question may help incubator managers identify the most aligned policies and schemes to seek affiliation under and, therefore, design their operations more effectively.

What are valid measures of incubators' performance?

The popular saying – what gets measured, gets done – needs to be thoroughly applied to incubation in India. Research suggests that the performance of incubators that focus on commercialisation of technology must also be measured on their management policies and the impact of value-added services made available to the tenant enterprises.[18]

Given the evolution in the Indian start-up ecosystem, the role and forms of incubators, and the proliferation of disaggregated alternatives such as co-working spaces and accelerators, there is a need for incubators to identify and adopt more relevant measures of performance. What would be valid metrics to assess the impact of an incubator on diverse objectives such as building entrepreneurs vis-a-vis enterprises? There are four predominant focus areas for incubators: ecosystems, start-ups, entrepreneurs and internal processes. To make the performance assessment less onerous and more thorough, incubators must identify relevant metrics under each of these pillars. Exhibit 6.7 presents some of the aspects or goals on which incubators' performance can be measured under the respective focus areas.

At present, incubators' performance measurement is also linked to their affiliations. The supporting agencies may define the focus areas for the incubators, which could be specific sectors (for example, MoAFW supports incubators to focus on agriculture) or technologies (for example, MeitY supports incubators to help start-ups using emerging technologies such as IoT and blockchain) or perhaps even regions (for example, incubators supported by state governments may be mandated to help start-ups and develop ecosystems within the respective states).

Exhibit 6.7: Suggested performance measures for different focus areas of an incubator

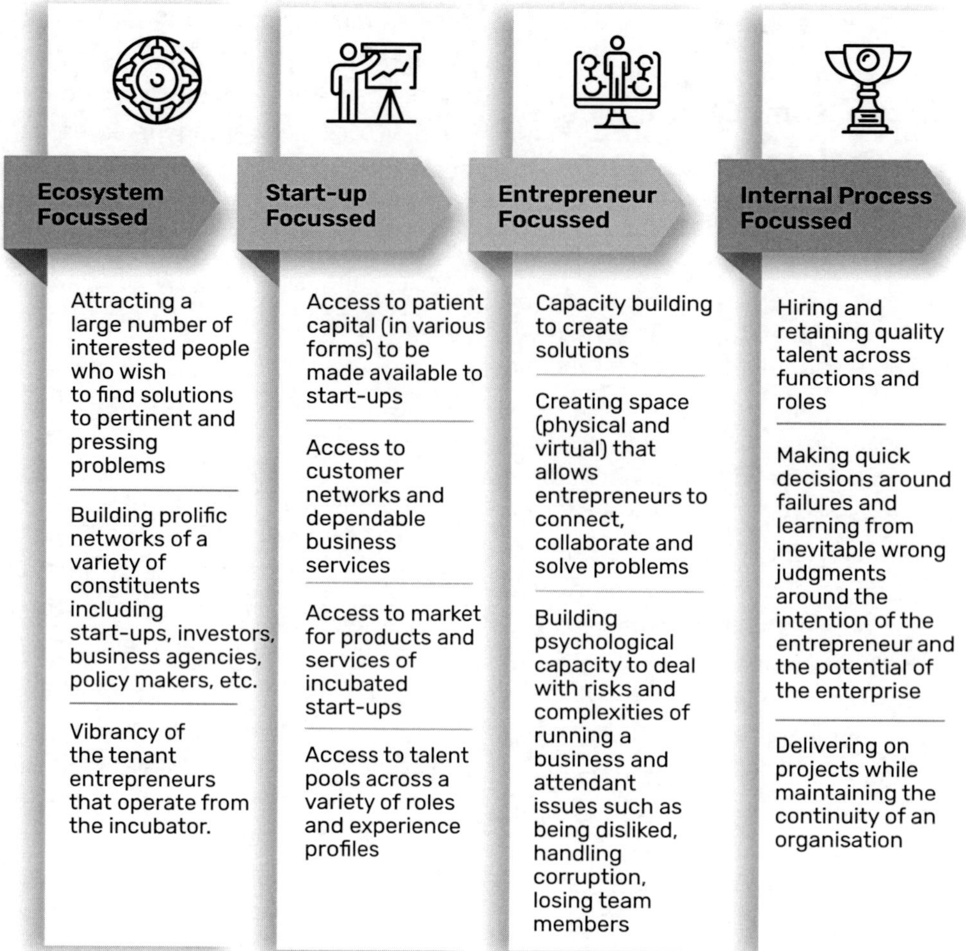

Multiple affiliations may entail variety in the performance measures that incubators need to track. Misalignment in the goals of the supporting schemes may unleash inefficiencies, on account of designing and implementing initiatives as well as reporting of impact and performance to multiple agencies in a variety of formats. This may even lead to vision dilution for the incubator. Thus, it is important for incubators to identify affiliating agencies with care, so as to align all their functions more efficiently. Policymakers may want to consider adopting performance measurement systems that are not loaded only on metric, but instead aim at gauging the performance of the incubator more comprehensively, such as by the four-pillar model suggested below.

How might incubators become well-functioning and effective organisations?

An aspect of incubators that often gets missed, both in research and in practice, is that it is an organisation. As a result, issues related to talent management, organisation structure, strategy and identity are often not explored. Delivering on ambitious goals such as making India a nation of job creators would need incubators to build themselves as effective organisations as well.

The diverse functions of the incubator would require a variety of roles, including liaising with various agencies and sourcing funds for start-ups; scouting for and selecting the start-ups to support; curating and maintaining the physical infrastructure; engaging with the community for access to expensive, hard-to-find resources; nurturing and managing relationships with start-ups and taking informed decisions about the length of their tenancy; maintaining books of accounts; and time-bound reporting to supporting agencies, among others. Given the scale of operations, an incubator must also dwell upon structuring these roles so as to remain agile and effective.[19] However, not much attention has been paid towards equipping incubators to build themselves as effective organisations.

Incubators need to explicitly manage the expectations of the growth and development of its employees to attract and retain good talent. While attracting and selecting motivated and talented people and designing a relevant organisational structure may be critical to managing incubator personnel, the incubators' ability to pay for the high-quality talent would mainly ensure continuity of personnel within the incubator. Also, the possibility of upward mobility is often not clear or stated, which may lead to a higher churn rate. To overcome high attrition and retain quality talent, it is important for incubators to craft career growth paths for their employees. It is also critical for incubators to not remain project organisations so that there is greater continuity in the operations of the organisation as well as the talent.

How can incubators remain steadfast in their mission?

Often, incubation support and start-up policies (and funds) may not reasonably factor in the cost of running incubators. In the case of incubators housed within academic institutions, the host institution provides the space at no or nominal cost. In some cases, we also find faculty of the institute deputed as incubator managers. However, the cost of the personnel may not be provided for by the host institutions. Incubators, thus, necessarily depend on the funding received from the affiliating agencies for their financial sustenance. To some extent, excessive dependence on government support may lead to mission drift for incubators.[20]

Some incubators in India have tried to fund the cost of their personnel in a variety of ways, including by setting up investment funds, raising grants from multilateral agencies and providing consultancy services. We believe that while some of these solutions ensure that the personnel are competitively paid and thus retained, taking on such projects leads to mission dilution of the incubator. The attention to actual incubation of start-ups may be much lower than required. Thus, as they mature, incubators must pay close attention to their structure so as to ensure that they continue to remain steadfast in their mission to support and incubate fledgling start-ups, while growing as an organisation. The case of CIIE.CO (Exhibit 6.8) serves as a reference for growing incubators.

Incubators can be permanent physical spaces, with the people occupying its space changing frequently. As is true in any frequently changing occupancy establishment (such as hotel rooms and hostel rooms), the cost of maintenance is high and the need to focus attention on the occupants' well-being is primary. If we hope to succeed in handholding entrepreneurs and nurturing fledgling enterprises, the policies of the state have to realistically provide for the support of the personnel and the maintenance of the premises.

Conclusion

Incubators in India are typically involved in the full spectrum of incubation functions, ranging from evangelising entrepreneurship, providing initial capital in the form of grants, a physical space (at no or low cost) and an environment where everyone has the same purpose. To be able to persist in their mission and deliver impact on scale, incubators need to sharpen their focus and configure their functioning and services around it.

The policies of the government around start-ups and incubators need to make allowances for the human-resource needs and high maintenance costs of the incubator. This is particularly necessary to train and equip entrepreneurs so as to make them immune to the shocks that they may encounter as they scale operations.

Post COVID-19, incubators have the challenge of creating virtual locations that mimic the physical environments. However, they need to clearly delineate what cannot be replaced physically and what can be. Incubation is not just a platform. In the changing world order, incubators must revisit their thinking about start-ups, incubation and their own organisations, pause to align themselves better and then power on to their missions.

Exhibit 6.8: CIIE.CO: A model for a scaled-up incubator

CIIE.CO, as it is known today, was set up as an academic centre (called the Centre for Innovation Incubation and Entrepreneurship) at the Indian Institute of Management Ahmedabad in 2002. In 2008, as the Indian start-up ecosystem began to open up, a not-for-profit entity called CIIE Initiatives was registered.

Between 2008 and 2020, CIIE Initiatives designed and undertook a variety of interventions to fill the multiple, emerging gaps in the Indian entrepreneurship ecosystem. In 2008, it launched India's first accelerator programme – iAccelerator – to support ICT start-ups. In the same year, it published the book *Stay Hungry Stay Foolish* to inspire more youngsters towards the entrepreneurial path. To evangelise entrepreneurship at scale, between 2010 and 2018, it ran a large-scale training and acceleration programme called The Power of Ideas. Aiming to fill a variety of gaps in acceleration, it offered accelerators in difficult sectors, including water, food and agri businesses, green energy, healthcare and mobility, among others.

In 2013, CIIE Initiatives laid the foundation for catalysing entrepreneurship in unexplored regions with the setting up of its incubation arm, Start-up Oasis, in Jaipur. In 2017, a virtual incubation programme – Innocuity – was started to reach and equip entrepreneurs across regions.

Realising a critical gap in funding available to start-ups in the clean technology space, CIIE.CO instituted a public–private–academia partnership to set up a fund – INFUSE Ventures. To catalyse innovation-driven start-ups at scale, in 2015 it launched a $100 million fund – the Bharat Innovation Fund. Realising the limited funding and support available to start-ups in the domain of livelihoods and financial inclusion, it instituted the Bharat Inclusion Seed Fund in 2018. These funds were in addition to the seed investments made by CIIE.CO.

Recognising the growth of incubators and the lack of trained personnel in incubation in 2013, extensive training of incubators was undertaken and a Handbook for Not-for-Profit Incubator Managers was published. In 2016, a research function, which went on to publish research and learning resources relevant to the Indian start-up ecosystem, was set up.

By the end of 2019, CIIE.CO had its interventions spread across the continuum of training and incubation, acceleration, seed and pre-series A investing and research.

Over its journey, CIIE.CO has inspired over 1 million with its publications, accelerated over 1,000 start-ups and invested in over 150 start-ups. It has received profitable exits from about 30 of these investments.

Endnotes

[1]NASSCOM. 2017. *Incubator/Accelerators Driving Growth Of Indian Start-Up Ecosystem – 2017*. Retrieved November 1, 2020 from https://nasscom.in/knowledge-centre/publications/incubators-accelerators-driving-growth-indian-start-ecosystem-2017 Accessed on May 24, 2021

[2]Assuming 53,000 start-ups in India (Tracxn 2019b).

[3]PTI. 2015. 'Start up; Stand up India' initiative to create more jobs: PM Narendra Modi on Independence Day. *Financial Express*. Retrieved November 1, 2020 from https://www.financialexpress.com/economy/start-up-stand-up-india-initiative-to-create-more-jobs-pm-narendra-modi-on-independence-day/119788/

[4]Based on founding year data of 250 incubators.

[5]Davey, T, Hannon, P and Penaluna, A. 2016. Entrepreneurship education and the role of universities in entrepreneurship: Introduction to the special issue. *Industry and Higher Education* 30(3): 171–182.

[6]Sharma, S and Vohra, N. 2020. Incubation in India: A multilevel analysis. *IIM Ahmedabad Working Paper* WP 2020-03-01. Retrieved October 30, 2020 from https://web.iima.ac.in/assets/snippets/workingpaperpdf/16280815672020-03-01.pdf

[7]Atal Innovation Mission. (n.d.) *Atal Incubation Centres*. Retrieved October 30, 2020 from https://aim.gov.in/atal-incubation-centres.php

[8]MeitY Startup Hub. 2019. *Technology Incubation and Development of Entrepreneurs (TIDE) 2.0*. Retrieved October 30, 2020 from https://meitystartuphub.in/incubators/schemes/tide-2-0

[9]ASPIRE. 2018. *A Scheme for Promotion of Innovation, Rural Industries and Entrepreneurship (ASPIRE)*. Retrieved June 10, 2019 from https://aspire.msme.gov.in/ASPIRE/AFHome.aspx
Accessed on May 24, 2021

[10]NSTEDB. 2016. *Guidelines and proforma for submission of proposal, 2016*. Retrieved June 20, 2019 from www.nstedb.com

[11]Tracxn. 2020. *Geo - India Tech.* Retrieved January 5, 2021 from https://tracxn.com/a/s/practicearea/563098e2e4b0a21c87b2c9b2/t/companiescovered/t/all/card#%7Csort%3Drelevance%7Corder%3DDEFAULT

[12]Department of Higher Education. 2018. *All India Survey of Higher Education 2017–18*. Retrieved October 30, 2020 from https://epsiindia.org/wp-content/uploads/2019/02/AISHE-2017-18.pdf

[13]Bengaluru, Chennai, Ghaziabad, Greater Noida, Gurugram, Hyderabad, Kolkata, Mumbai, Navi Mumbai, New Delhi, Noida are considered as metros.

[14]Bergek, A and Norrman, C. 2008. Incubator best practice: A framework. *Technovation* 28(1–2): 20–28.

[15]Mireftekhari, S. 2017. Business incubator, a solution for start-up's challenges. A qualitative look at business incubator's support for start-ups to overcome the liability of newness and smallness (Master's thesis). *Center for Entrepreneurship, The Faculty of Mathematics and Natural Sciences, University of Oslo*. Retrieved June 20, 2019 from https://www.duo.uio.no/bitstream/handle/10852/57517/1/Master-Thesis---Pedram-Mireftekhari.pdf

[16]Aernoudt, R. 2004. Incubators: Tool for entrepreneurship? *Small Business Economics* 23(2): 127–135.

[17]Rhee, KS and White, RJ. 2007. The emotional intelligence of entrepreneurs. *Journal of Small Business & Entrepreneurship 20*(4): 409–425. Shaver, KG and Scott, LR. 1992. Person, process, choice: The psychology of new venture creation. *Entrepreneurship Theory and Practice* 16(2): 23–46.

[18]Mian, SA. 1997. Assessing and managing the university technology business incubator: An integrative framework. *Journal of Business Venturing* 12(4): 251–285.

[19]Holbeche, L. 2015. *The Agile Organization: How to build an innovative, sustainable and resilient business.* Kogan Page Publishers.

[20]Tamasy, C. 2007. Rethinking technology-oriented business incubators: Developing a robust policy instrument for entrepreneurship, innovation, and regional development? *Growth and Change* 38(3): 460–473.

IN BRIEF

- **Founders:** MedTech offers rich opportunities for start-up ventures, driven by market pull and technology push. However, the entrepreneurial journey in this domain is long, hard and expensive. Founders need to understand the full pathway, recognise the challenges (valleys of death) and ensure that adequate resources are available or accessible.
- **Policymakers:** Lack of medical-grade pilot manufacturing and device testing facilities (prerequisite for human clinical trials) hampers the market entry of indigenous medical devices. The facilities need to be world-class (in terms of equipment, operators and quality system), and offered at subsidised rates for MedTech start-up companies.
- **Incubators:** Affordable office space and access to investors are essential but insufficient to ensure the success of MedTech start-ups. Dedicated mentors with first-hand experience in medicine, engineering and management are required as 'running partners' for the entrepreneurs to successfully define, develop, deliver and deploy the products.

7

Technology Incubation and Start-up Creation: Lessons from BETIC, IIT Bombay

Bhallamudi Ravi

Ravi, B. 2021. "Technology Incubation and Start-up Creation: Lessons from BETIC, IIT Bombay". In *Shifting Orbits: Decoding the Trajectory of the Indian Start-up Ecosystem*, edited by Thillai Rajan A, Srivardhini K Jha, Joffi Thomas and Rohan Chinchwadkar, 74–83. Hyderabad: Universities Press (India) Private Limited.

Introduction

India is among the top three nations globally in terms of the number of start-ups.[1] A number of these start-ups are technology-led ventures focussing on healthcare. This sector is growing rapidly, driven by innovation, as evinced by the large number of patents filed.[2] Most Indian technology start-ups, however, face challenges while traversing the technology readiness levels from concept to commercialisation, and face the prospect of stiff competition from global brands who dominate 80 per cent of the local market. In this context, we present a case study of the Biomedical Engineering and Technology Innovation Centre (BETIC) at IIT Bombay along with satellite centres and cells in a dozen partner institutes.

In the last five years, different teams from these centres have developed a range of innovative devices for screening, diagnosis, surgery and rehabilitation, which has led to the creation and incubation of 16 start-ups. Most of the founders have been engineering graduates and first-generation entrepreneurs hailing from small towns; and often had master's or doctoral degrees. They had all won highly competitive seed grants, which had provided the necessary funding to kick-start the ventures. A close study of these start-ups has revealed several critical insights regarding their journey, as well as challenges and enabling factors.

Medical Technology Start-Ups

India has recently broken into the top 50 nations in the Global Innovation Index. In terms of 'ease of doing business', it has jumped to the 63rd position among 190 nations, up from 130 five years back. Twenty per cent of India's start-ups have been in technology-led ventures in the automotive, agriculture, biotech, consumer electronics, defence, energy, environment, education, e-commerce, finance, gaming, healthcare and logistics sectors.[3]

Among the various sectors, healthcare has emerged as one of the most attractive for start-ups owing to the large market size, innovation potential, increased funding from various agencies and social impact through affordable healthcare. The sector has become the biggest employer in both the USA and Europe and is also witnessing the highest number of patent filing, pointing to continued growth in the future.

Medical devices, equipment and software, collectively referred to as 'MedTech,' represent a large and critical segment of the healthcare sector. The global MedTech market size is valued at over $500 billion, dominated by 6,500 American companies and 27,000 European companies.[4] The Indian medical device market too is growing rapidly and is estimated to exceed $7 billion annually.[5] The majority of the medical device requirements so far have been primarily met by imports from the USA, Germany and other countries. Their prohibitive cost, coupled with the unique requirements of the Indian population, represents a great opportunity for local companies. It is, therefore, not surprising that a significant number of start-ups in incubation centres across the country now belong to the MedTech sector. In the last 10 years, nearly 500 of these have been funded by the Biotechnology Industry Research Assistance Council (BIRAC), under the Department of Biotechnology of the Ministry of Science & Technology, New Delhi. More than 50 products have reached the market so far, which is considerable given the long gestation period and intensive funding requirements of products in this sector.[6]

A typical MedTech start-up venture begins by identifying and defining an unmet clinical need based on domain immersion and market research. It then proceeds through the stages, or technology readiness levels (TRLs),[7] of ideation, proof of concept, functional prototyping, laboratory testing, field testing (initial and detailed), mass production and market launch. Traversing all these technology readiness levels (Exhibit 7.1) requires considerable expertise and resources. In general, 90 per cent of all start-ups are reported to fail within five years of incorporation.[8] Indian start-ups, particularly MedTech ones, face additional challenges in terms of relevant resources – especially for detailed field testing (TRL-7) and initiating production (TRL-8) – not being easily available to local innovators when compared to their counterparts in global innovation hotspots such as Silicon Valley, Singapore, South Korea and Shenzhen. This delays the start-ups' progress and limits their success upon reaching the market.

Today, we are in urgent need of successful models of pre-incubation that enable start-ups to quickly traverse the technology readiness levels. This is critical in the healthcare sector for the indigenous development of affordable solutions. BETIC has addressed this need by evolving a unique model of technology innovation and start-up pre-incubation.

BETIC Ecosystem and Start-Ups

BETIC was established at IIT Bombay in 2014 to foster the local ecosystem by connecting doctors, researchers, entrepreneurs and investors. A hub-and-spoke model was adopted, with two satellite centres established at College of Engineering, Pune (COEP) and Visvesvaraya National Institute of Technology (VNIT), Nagpur. All three centres were supported by the RG Science & Technology Commission, Government of Maharashtra. The centres established basic facilities for product engineering and rapid prototyping (plastic, metal and electronics), and approached local vendors for functional prototyping and testing. They also tied up with local business incubators including Society for Innovation and Entrepreneurship in IITB, Bhau Institute of Innovation, Entrepreneurship and Leadership in COEP and Centre for Innovation at VNIT, as well as other well-known incubators such as Venture Centre in Pune (Exhibit 7.4). BETIC essentially acted as an incubator for technology development and product innovation, as well as a business pre-incubator for start-ups looking to commercialise innovations.

Exhibit 7.1: Technology readiness levels

TRL	Stage	Description of activities
TRL-1	Need Definition	Domain immersion, market research, unmet need identification, relevant scientific research, product specifications
TRL-2	Ideation (Concept)	Basic device design, competitor analysis, patent landscaping, freedom to operate ensured
TRL-3	Proof of Concept	Individual components developed and their functionality demonstrated at laboratory or breadboard level
TRL-4	Functional Prototype	Prototype fabrication in functional materials, module integration, demonstration of full system performance and efficacy
TRL-5	Laboratory Testing	Testing as per relevant national and global standards to establish product performance and safety
TRL-6	Initial Field Testing	Regulatory approvals, pilot field study with limited number of volunteers to establish product performance and safety
TRL-7	Detailed Field Testing	Pilot batch manufacturing with quality management system, field studies with many volunteers to establish value proposition
TRL-8	Start of Production	Manufacturing licence obtained from government agency, mass production planning, commercial batch manufacturing
TRL-9	Market Launch	Commercial launch of the new product, revenue generation, scaling up of operations

To rapidly traverse the medical technology readiness levels, a systematic innovation process was developed, applied and refined.[9] It comprises four stages: *defining* a clinical problem, in which doctors play a critical role; *developing* an innovative solution through translational researchers; *delivering* a tested product by entrepreneurs; and *deploying* it in clinical practice supported by other stakeholders. Each stage is divided into four steps (Exhibit 7.2). The process, which received ISO 13485 certification in 2018, has been employed to develop many novel medical devices. Most of them are low-risk devices for screening, diagnosis and monitoring of patients. One such example is the smart stethoscope that proved very useful for screening camps, telemedicine and remote auscultation (Exhibit 7.3). Moderate-risk products such as surgical instruments and assistive devices, as well as a few high-risk devices such as orthopaedic implants, have also been taken up. The BETIC process has provided a clear roadmap to the innovation teams, allowing them to plan suitable activities in advance or in parallel, significantly reducing the overall lead time from concept to market.

To create a continuous stream of products and start-ups, BETIC also established a pipeline for identifying, training, supporting and networking the innovators. It began from the Medical Device Hackathon (MEDHA) to identify potential innovators, conducted over weekends at multiple partner institutes during the summer. Each hackathon had 40 participants who form 10 teams of four participants from medical, design, mechanical and electronics backgrounds. Each team was guided by a dedicated mentor. Those interested in medical device innovation and entrepreneurship were further trained in an intensive one-week boot-camp to equip them with the necessary skill set and mindset. This was conducted at either IIT Bombay or a satellite centre in September. The innovators who were committed to pursuing medical device innovation full-time were supported through fellowships, funds and facilities. Senior mentors at BETIC connected the innovators to expert clinicians, technology gurus and industry partners for clinical feedback, product fine-tuning, pilot batch manufacturing and safety testing.

At the end of one year or more (depending on product complexity), the innovators exhibited their devices

Exhibit 7.2: The BETIC process for medical device innovation

DEFINE (unmet clinical need)	
Team building	Build multi-disciplinary team with clinical and engineering backgrounds
Clinical immersion	Observe clinical procedures and devices for diagnosis and treatment
Problem definition	Clearly define the unmet clinical need and functional requirements
Concept and feasibility	Evolve multiple ideas, evaluate (problem–solution fit), check feasibility
DEVELOP (innovative solution)	
Detailed design	Product configuration, components, materials, quality requirements
Virtual prototyping	Solid modelling, engineering analysis (simulation), design optimisation
Rapid prototyping	3D printing (plastics), laser cutting, PCB fabrication, product assembly
Functional prototyping	Component manufacturing using industrial equipment and processes
DELIVER (certified product)	
Pilot manufacturing	Medical-grade manufacturing, clean room assembly, ISO 13485 system
Pre-clinical testing	Testing in accredited labs for electrical, mechanical, biological safety
Human clinical trials	Pivot and pivotal trials on volunteers after Institutional Ethics Committee and Central Drugs Standard Control Organization (CDSCO) approvals
Device certification	Product dossier and clinical trials data submission to CDSCO
DEPLOY (product in market)	
IPR (patent filing)	Patent filing with detailed specifications and claims, Patent Cooperation Treaty application
Business model	Commercialisation pathway, product positioning, pricing, funding
Mass production	Manufacturing licence, equipment, human resources, production
Distribution	Marketing, distribution partners, channels, sales, revenue generation

Exhibit 7.3: Smart stethoscope: proof of concept (left) and deployment (right)

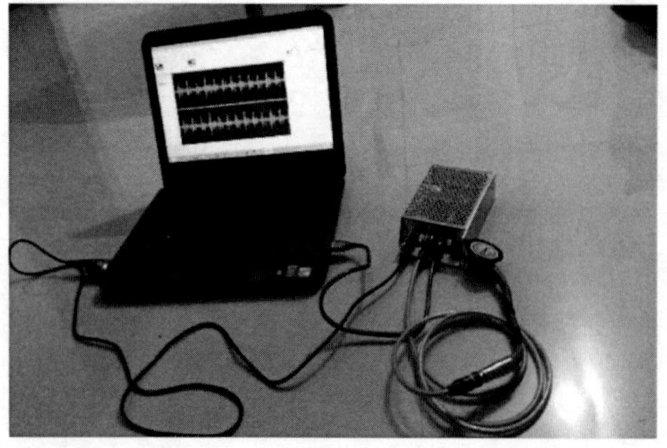

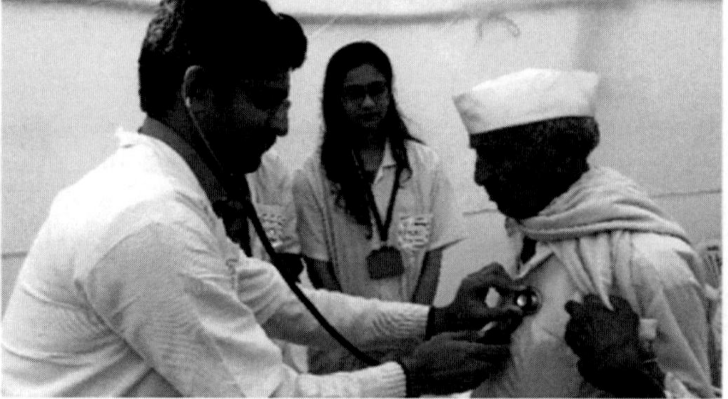

to expert clinicians, industry professionals and other stakeholders. This was the acid test that determined the further course of action. Many innovators decided to incubate a start-up, others decided to further refine the product and a few also decided to license their technology to an interested industry partner. The intellectual property right (patent filing) and technology know-how of a start-up documented in a comprehensive dossier facilitates regulatory approvals and knowledge transfer to industry partners. This is facilitated by patent attorneys and regulatory experts who guide the innovators accordingly.

The BETIC process and pipeline have been adopted by several engineering colleges and medical institutes across Maharashtra (Exhibit 7.4), making it one of the largest such networks in the country. The medical partner institutes identify and curate clinical problems that can be taken up, provide clinical feedback during device development, plan and conduct clinical trials, and promote the device.

Exhibit 7.4: BETIC centres and cells in partner institutes

Type of centre	Institute
BETIC Main Centre	Indian Institute of Technology Bombay, Mumbai
BETIC Satellite Centres	Visvesvaraya National Institute of Technology, Nagpur
	Government College of Engineering, Pune
BETIC Cells (Engineering)	KJ Somaiya College of Engineering, Vidyavihar
	MIT Art, Design & Technology University, Pune
	Symbiosis International University, Pune
	GH Raisoni College of Engineering, Nagpur
BETIC Cells (Medical)	Haffkine Institute for Training, Research and Testing, Mumbai
	Grant Medical College and Sir JJ Group of Hospitals, Mumbai
	CHMS, MGM Institute of Health Sciences, Navi Mumbai
	BJ Medical College and Sassoon General Hospital, Pune
	Datta Meghe Institute of Medical Sciences, Wardha
	BKL Walawalkar Rural Hospital & Medical College, Dervan

Exhibit 7.5: BETIC start-ups and their products

Company name	Year Estb.	Product
Algosurg	2016	Orthopedic surgery simulation
Ayu Devices	2017	Digital smart stethoscope
Medi Asha Technologies	2018	Fracture splint (instant aid)
Nu Ossa Mediquip	2018	3D-printed temporal bone
Pacify medical	2018	Skin spray gun to heal burns
Ayati Devices	2019	Potable neuropathy screener
Aumeesh Tech	2019	Knee-ankle-foot orthosis
Atmen Technovention	2019	Endotracheal tube monitoring device
OKO Icare Solutions	2019	Digital glaucoma screening device
Precisurge	2019	Surgical osteotomy guide
Prosthocentric	2019	Jaw relation recorder
Care Form Labs	2020	Menstrual cup
Denovo Bioinnovations	2020	Automatic suturing device
Lucid Implants	2020	Craniomaxillofacial implants
MedGyor	2020	Affordable isolation room
Aur Innovations	2020	Flexible plastic dental burr

Between 2016 and 2020, BETIC teams had organised 10 hackathons and 5 training camps, where about 700 students and professionals developed nearly 200 proofs of concept of different medical devices. About 40 full-time fellows, 30 post-graduate (PG) students (master's and PhD) and 30 undergraduate (UG) students and interns joined various BETIC centres to further develop their ideas into commercially viable products. They filed close to 60 patents and exhibited their devices at 25 events in various locations across the country. Five technologies were licensed to local companies; 16 of these teams decided to further take their products to the market by incubating their own start-up companies (Exhibit 7.5).

BETIC Experience and Learning

BETIC innovators embarked on their entrepreneurship journey despite being young and lacking business experience. They were mainly driven by a strong desire to see their products reach the end-users and create social impact. Many of them left well-paying jobs or ignored such offers, much to the chagrin of their families. However, passion alone is not enough. Start-ups need seed funds to cover salaries, product development, testing, manufacturing, marketing and other costs. One of the best sources for funding MedTech start-ups is the Biotechnology Ignition Grant (BIG) of ₹5 million from BIRAC, New Delhi. The competition is tough – only about 60 out of over 800 teams who apply every six months get the grant after multiple rounds of scrutiny and presentations. Another such prestigious award is the India Innovation Growth Programme (IIGP) of the Department of Science & Technology (DST), New Delhi.

During the last five years, 16 start-ups associated with BETIC had applied for BIG and IIGP. All of them had won BIG, while three had won both the awards. They also obtained technology licences from their institutes for the patents of their respective innovations.[10] There has been a smooth transition from BETIC to the business incubators, and the entrepreneurs have continued to get help from the mentors, especially in the areas of design for manufacturability and pre-clinical testing for biological, electrical and mechanical safety. Several start-ups have reached human clinical trials; a few have set up manufacturing lines and started marketing and selling their products across the country. The successful journey of the start-ups across the TRLs has been enabled by 16 elements of the BETIC ecosystem,[11] which can be clustered into four groups: team structure, innovation culture, infrastructure and standard procedures. The details are given in Exhibit 7.6.

To identify the most critical elements of the ecosystem, we carried out a structured survey of the start-ups in two stages. The first stage required the start-up founders to fill out a form about their background (family, education, professional experience, exposure to MedTech, and so on) and their start-up company (employees, product, value proposition, funding, and so on). The second stage involved a virtual meeting to explain the ecosystem elements and obtain their feedback on the relative importance of the elements, and their contribution to project cost saving, lead time reduction and product quality assurance.

Fifteen start-up founders participated in the survey. In terms of their background, it was found that more than half of them had master's degree in engineering (8 out of 15 founders); three had doctoral and three had medical degrees; and one was a high school graduate. Only three of them were from an IIT. All of them were from small towns; none from metro cities. Only three founders had family members engaged in business ventures, though two-thirds (10 out of 15 founders) had some prior experience in industry. Only four founders had prior familiarity with the MedTech domain; all others were exposed to this domain during medical device hackathons or training camps organised by BETIC.

Of the 15 entrepreneurs, 10 had started marketing their products, and five were in intermediate stages (one each at TRLs 2, 3, 4, 6 and 7). Those with PhD degrees had translated their own thesis research work into marketable products. Others chose their devices based on interactions with clinicians during the medical device hackathons and on subsequent visits to hospitals. The backgrounds indicated the possible importance of higher degrees for MedTech ventures, coupled with a deep interest to utilise the research skills and industry experience in product innovation.

The interviews with the entrepreneurs revealed several key insights. They were asked to rank the relative importance of the four groups of ecosystem elements, as well as the individual elements on a scale of 1 (very low) to 5 (very high).The results showed that 'team structure' and 'innovation culture' were the most important groups (average score of 3.0 and 2.9, respectively), compared to 'infrastructure' and 'standard procedures'.

The weighted scores of individual elements were calculated by multiplying the score of the ecosystem element with the score of the group to which it belonged. In this regard, the two elements 'inter-disciplinary team' and 'experienced mentors' emerged

Exhibit 7.6: BETIC ecosystem elements

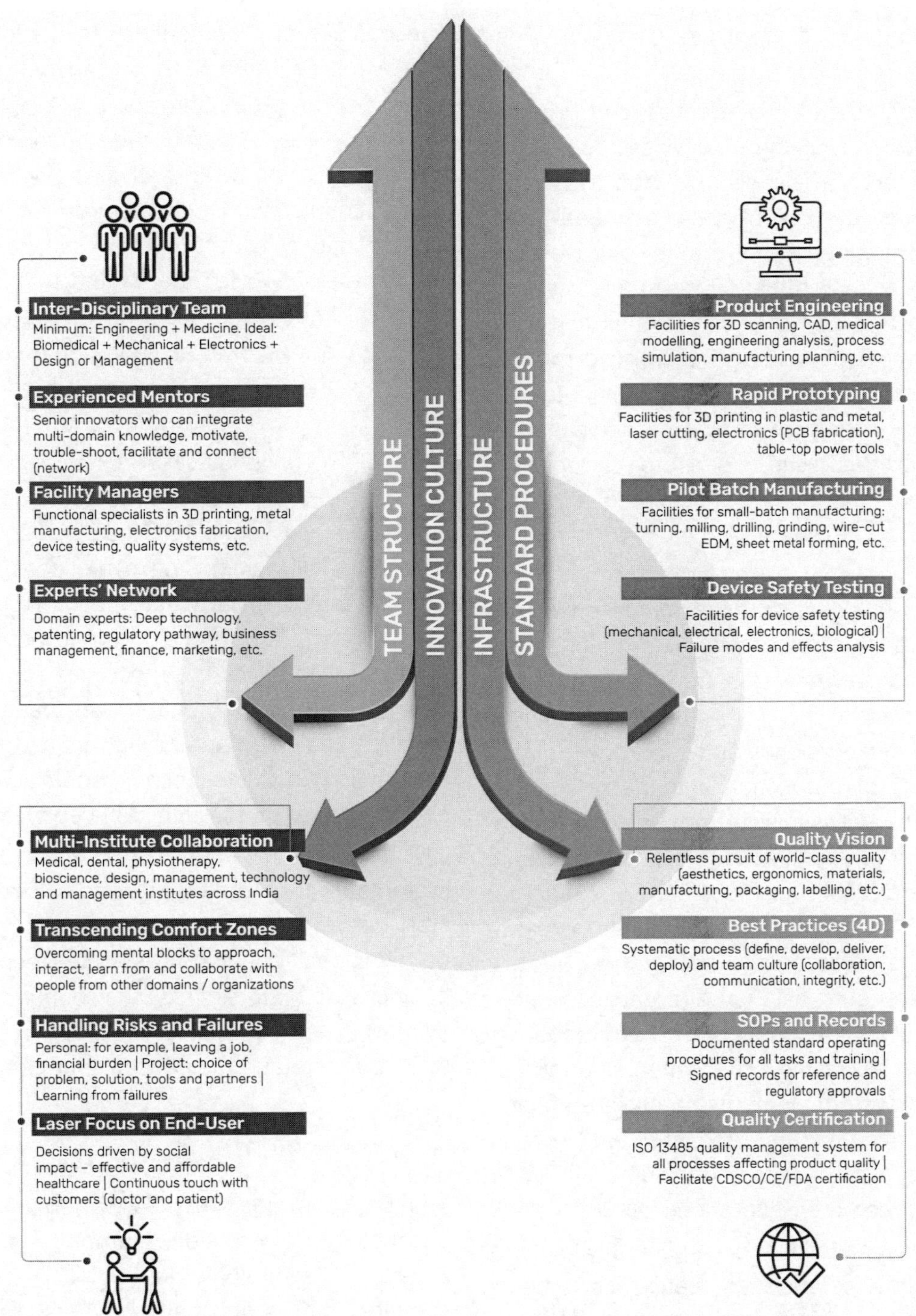

as the most important, with weighted scores of 8.9 and 8.5, respectively. This was followed by 'multi-institute collaboration' and 'learning from failures', both with a score of 7.6. These highlight the importance of inter-disciplinary and multi-institution collaborative culture for medical device innovation.

The critical role of mentors cannot be emphasised enough. They are essential for ensuring a culture of collaboration among team members and associates with different backgrounds and belonging to different organisations. The mentors act like 'running partners', continuously guiding the innovators and motivating them to keep going despite failures on the way. Indeed, failures are analysed to gain new insights and to improve the best practices. The mentors meet the innovators every week, and if needed, are accessible even at odd hours.

On the other hand, pilot manufacturing of products – to produce the initial batch of devices required for lab testing and clinical trials – showed up as a major bottleneck. Among all the ecosystem elements, 'pilot batch manufacturing' received the lowest weighted score of 4.0, less than half that for team and mentors. This was due to the lack of such facilities at BETIC, and the difficulty of outsourcing the work to multiple vendors, which led to high costs, erratic schedules and unreliable quality. Clearly, setting up medical-grade manufacturing facilities at subsidised rates can go a long way in smoothening the journey of MedTech innovators and increase the success rate of their products in the market.

The impact of the ecosystem elements on project cost savings, lead time reduction and product quality assurance showed an increasing trend from TRL-1 to TRL-9 across the start-ups. This reflected the higher challenges faced in later stages of the journey (detailed field testing, start of production and market launch) that required stronger support from the ecosystem. The ratings for standard practices related to quality management were higher for those start-ups who had reached higher TRLs. This could be attributed to increasing recognition of quality assurance as a critical success factor by entrepreneurs as they approached market launch and faced competition from other companies. Among various stages of the entrepreneurship journey, the impact of ecosystem elements on all three factors (project cost savings, lead time reduction and product quality assurance) was found to be the highest in TRL-8, that is, the start of commercial production.

The project cost and lead time are generally lower for low-risk medical devices, such as screening instruments, compared to high-risk devices such as implants. Start-ups involved in high-risk medical devices gave higher rating to the role of 'visiting experts' (medical, manufacturing, regulatory, and so on). Start-ups involved in complex devices with mechanical and electronic components gave higher scores to 'product engineering' facilities, compared to those involved in less complex products. This shows the need for higher level of engineering skills in developing high-tech medical products.

Summary

The positive environment for technology-based start-ups in India is empowering many young engineers to explore entrepreneurship and self-employment instead of seeking jobs in established companies. Healthcare has emerged as an attractive sector due to the large market coupled with technology drivers and government support along with the potential for social impact. MedTech start-up founders need to have the required technical knowledge acquired through higher degrees (master's or doctoral) as seen in the study of 15 start-ups from the BETIC network reported here. However, most of them were first-generation entrepreneurs and faced many challenges in their journey.

The study of the BETIC start-ups shows that a conducive ecosystem is critical for speeding up their journey, while minimising overall costs and ensuring product quality. In particular, the role of inter-disciplinary teams mentored by senior innovators and domain experts came up as the most important factor. On the other hand, the lack of medical-grade manufacturing facilities has been hampering progress. Such facilities are required in all MedTech hotspots across the country, and can be set up through public–private partnerships.

While the above conclusions are drawn based on a systematic study, the sample size is small, and limited to start-ups from the BETIC network alone. The study could be expanded to include other MedTech start-ups from business incubators across the country. The study could also be extended to cover start-ups in other sectors as well to understand their specific requirements.

Acknowledgements

The BETIC project was supported by RG Science & Technology Commission, Mumbai and Department of Science & Technology, New Delhi. The heads of BETIC satellite centres and cells in various engineering and medical institutes are to be thanked for their commitment and cooperation in creating the innovation ecosystem. The study of the start-ups was led by Dr. Nishant Tikekar in his role as a quality consultant, supported by Dr. Rupesh Ghyar, Senior Executive Officer of BETIC. The excellent cooperation from the start-ups in sharing their company data and feedback about the ecosystem elements without hesitation is deeply acknowledged.

Endnotes

[1]PTI. 2019. NASSCOM: Over 1,300 start-ups added in 2019, over 8,900 tech-start-ups in India now *The Economic Times*, (November 5, 2019), retrieved from https://economictimes.indiatimes.com/small-biz/startups/newsbuzz/over-1300-startups-added-in-2019-over-8900-tech-startups-in-india-now-nasscom/articleshow/71925791.cms

[2]See Chapter 2 of this report.

[3]*The Economic Times*, 2019. See endnote 1.

[4]Fortune Business Insights Report.2020.*Medical Device Market Size, Share and Industry Analysis by Type, End User and Regional Forecast: 2019–2025*.

[5]PTI. 2018. Medical technology sector may hit $9.6 bn in 2022: Report by PWC,*The Economic Times* (October 1, 2018).

[6]BIRAC. 2020. *Annual Report*, accessed at https://birac.nic.in/webcontent/1612825200_Birac_Annual_Report_English.pdf

[7]Originally put forth by NASA, the TRLs have been adapted by the DBT, GoI for various biotechnology sectors, including medical devices. https://birac.nic.in/webcontent/birac_trl_doc5_medical_devices_and_diagnosis_12_09_2018.pdf

[8]IBM Institute for Business Value. 2016. *Entrepreneurial India*, Executive Report.

[9]Ravi, B. 2018. *The Essence of Medical Device Innovation*, The Write Place (Crossword), Mumbai.

[10]Kawdikar, T, Harshe, S, Pritesh, C, Pallavi, G, Patel, AA, Rajendra, US, Ghyar, R and Ravi, B. *A device to detect tracheostomy tube blockage*, Indian patent filed, 201621012390, 2016, licensed to Atmen Technovention Pvt. Ltd.

Ghyar, R, Ravi, B and Bhansali, H. *An automated needle holder and suturing device*, Indian patent filed, 1051/MUM/2015, 2015, licensed to Denovo Bioinnovations Pvt. Ltd.

Karade, V, Tapadia, R, Shetty, V and Ravi, B. *Modular femoral patient specific jig for total knee arthroplasty*, Indian patent filed, 2574/MUM/2012, 2012, licensed to Algosurg Pvt Ltd.

Mawale, M and Kuthe, AM. *Rapid prototyping assisted fabrication of a device for detecting glaucoma*, Indian patent filed, 201721031952, 2017, licensed to OKO Icare Solutions Pvt Ltd.

Dahake, S, Kuthe, AM and Mawale, M. *Customized implant and customized osteotomy guide in ablative tumour surgery for accurate mandibular reconstruction*, Indian patent filed, 201721033416, 2017, licensed to Precisurge Pvt Ltd.

Sapkal, P and Kuthe, AM. *3D-plotted scaffolds to heal small size bone defects*, Indian patent filed, 201721035919A, 2017, licensed to Lucid Implants Pvt Ltd.

Mawale, M and Kuthe, AM. *Device for detecting glaucoma*, Indian patent filed, 2123/MUM/ 2015, licensed to OKO Icare Solutions Pvt Ltd.

Poyarekar, S, Mahale, C, Panse, N, Phulwer, R, Anasane, S and Ahuja, BB. *Epidermal suspension spray device*, Indian patent filed, 201821011504, 2018, licensed to Pacify Medical Pvt Ltd.

Bhagat, A, Salvi, S, Sanas, M, Anasane, S, Sonawane, BU, Mulay, AV and Ahuja, BB. *Device to monitor and detect obstruction in an endotracheal tube*, Indian patent filed, 201821011502, 2018, licensed to Atmen Technovention Pvt Ltd.

Sanas, M, Ahuja, BB andMulay, AV. *An orthopaedic plaster splint*, Indian patent filed, 1464/MUM/2015, licensed to MediAsha Technologies Pvt Ltd.

Karma, A, Ghyar, R and Ravi, *B. Stance controlled knee ankle foot orthosis for weak knee patients*, Indian patent filed, 201921005973, 2019, licensed to Aumeesh Tech Pvt Ltd.

Joseph, D. *A portable sterile enclosure for surgical procedures*, Indian patent filed, 201821030523, 2018, licensed to MedGyor Pvt Ltd.

Pakhare, C, Gupte, Y, Kathpal, N, Ghyar, R, Ravi, B and Mullerpatan,R. *Device for screening of diabetic foot*, Indian patent filed, 201821005692, 15 Feb 2018, licensed to Ayati Devices Pvt Ltd.

Pandey, T Adarsha, K, Ghyar, R, Ravi, B and Konar, BN. *A novel device for conventional auscultation, electronic recording, transmitting wireless information and simultaneous hearing by multiple users*, Indian patent filed, 201621029618, 2016, licensed to Ayu Devices Pvt Ltd.

[11]Ravi, B. *2020*. "Medical Device Innovation: Idea to Impact". In *Engineering for the Future*, Institution of Engineers (India).

IN BRIEF

- Virtual incubators have the advantage of reach and cost over conventional incubators.
- Virtual incubation helps early-to-mid-stage ventures that focus on technology products and solutions and is sector-agonistic.
- The pandemic expedited the global shift towards virtual incubation.
- NASSCOM's 10,000 Start-ups programme is one of the largest virtual business incubation programmes in the country, creating the right environment for start-ups to scale. By 2020, it had impacted 6500+ start-ups and supported close to 400 start-ups every year.
- The use of technology to deliver incubation virtually reduces the opportunity to build the strong engagement and trust that comes with in-person interactions. The programme has overcome this challenge by assigning experienced regional entrepreneurs and dedicated full-time resources to the start-ups.

CASE STUDY

8

Virtual Incubation: Helping Indian Start-ups Grow and Scale

Kritika Murugesan

Murugesan, K. 2021. "Virtual Incubation: Helping Indian Start-ups Grow and Scale". In *Shifting Orbits: Decoding the Trajectory of the Indian Start-up Ecosystem*, edited by Thillai Rajan A, Srivardhini K Jha, Joffi Thomas and Rohan Chinchwadkar, 84–93. Hyderabad: Universities Press (India) Private Limited.

Start-ups play an integral role in the economic and social development of a country. It has been estimated that in 2019, start-ups in India generated 60,000 direct jobs and 130,000–180,000 indirect jobs.[1] In the last decade, we have witnessed start-ups driving and disrupting technology innovation that has been at the core of our business and day-to-day lives. Over the last decade, start-ups have defined the advent of social media, e-commerce and FinTech, and today they continue to dominate emerging technologies such as artificial intelligence (AI), Software as a Service (SaaS) and HealthTech.

The increasing number of start-ups has resulted in a greater demand for quality incubators that can offer them funding, networking, idea validation, market access and mentoring opportunities at price levels that they can afford. As the third largest start-up ecosystem in the world, India has more than 520 incubators and accelerators and 12,500 tech start-ups.[2]

In 2013, the National Association of Software and Services Companies (NASSCOM), the largest industry body for the tech industry in India, launched 10,000 Start-ups, India's first tech entrepreneurship programme. This case study explores the virtual incubation concept and briefly touches upon how the pandemic brought the required push for virtual incubation. Subsequently, the case study examines the objectives and evolution of NASSCOM's virtual incubation programme and its impact on the Indian start-up ecosystem. Four caselets of start-ups that have been incubated by the 10,000 Start-ups virtual incubation programme and their impact are discussed, followed by policy imperatives.

Virtual Incubation

The idea of virtual incubation was first propounded in 2000[3] as a means to facilitate start-up success and business network formation, creating a 'virtual value chain'. Virtual incubation was further defined as an incubator that provides knowledge brokering using digital and information technology channels to develop innovative start-ups.[4] Virtual incubators differ from conventional incubators in terms of market reach and interaction richness (Exhibit 8.1).[5]

Virtual business incubation (VBI) finds application in several instances such as remote places where the target group is dispersed, ICT-based businesses or those with high virtual content, early-stage start-ups and those that do not require a physical office space. Specifically, the major differences between conventional and virtual incubation are across the following parameters: definition, incubator development, incubator configuration and incubatee development (Exhibit 18.2).[6]

Exhibit 8.1: Virtual versus conventional incubators

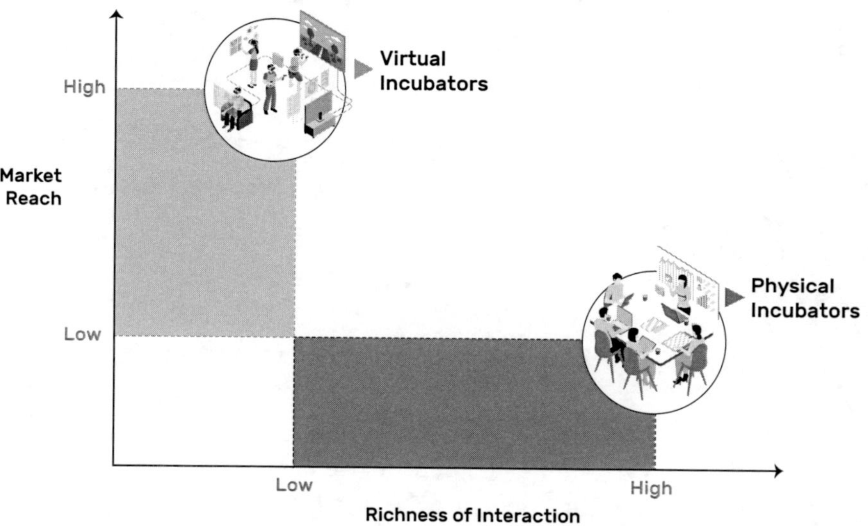

Exhibit 8.2: Conventional versus virtual incubation

Dimensions	Conventional	Virtual
Definition	A dynamic community where selected incubatees can locate their firms. This includes procedures, culture, working environment, learning experience and working costs, which incubatees can hardly obtain by themselves. [9, 10]	A programme that provides incubation services electronically, with little or no face-to-face interaction.[11]
Incubator development	A programme where several start-ups develop alongside each other, traditionally sharing office space. Challenges in such a set-up are the absence of capital, human resources and management capabilities.	Offers online access to a network of entrepreneurs, investors and advisors, as well as support to help match other entrepreneurial needs to professional advice.
Incubator configuration	Models fitted to the requirements of the selected incubatees.	Business models depend on the variety of start-ups rather than a particular geographical focus.
Incubatee development	Includes providing technological facilities and advice, initial growth funds, network and linkages, co-working spaces, lab facilities, mentoring and advisory support.	Offers a greater advisory network to their incubatees, better matching supply and demand of management and technical talent.

Pandemic: Impetus to Virtual Incubation

The pandemic and the nation-wide lockdown in 2020 severely impacted start-ups with limited cash; survival and sustainability became critical for the entrepreneurs. It expedited and made more urgent the global shift towards an innovation economy. Physical business incubators pivoted to virtual programming to continue to serve the entrepreneurs. Due to the lockdown, incubation too went virtual, with start-ups, incubators, mentors and investors staying connected online, with mentoring and workshops.[7] Start-ups had to learn to develop products, connect with their customers and raise funds under the constraints of the pandemic.[8]

NASSCOM's 10,000 Start-ups programme has emerged as one of the largest VBI programmes that helps start-ups to scale and connect with a widespread network of evaluators and mentors, who are investors, accelerators and industry veterans.

The following section discusses the 10,000 Start-ups programme briefly, along with its evolution and benefits.

10,000 Start-ups Virtual Incubation Programme

Objectives

10,000 Start-ups would help technology ventures to achieve growth and global scale by providing incubation, funding, market access and several other resources.

The programme focusses on early-stage technology products and solutions start-ups and is sector-agonistic. As of December 2020, the 10,000 Start-ups programme had the largest pan-India presence and had impacted more than 6,500 ventures.

The programme has been playing an active role in evangelising and building the tech start-up community. It collaborates with key stakeholders, such as governments, academia, other incubators and accelerators, and corporations to bring the entire ecosystem together.

The VBI programme started with offering a *Warehouse Incubation Programme* to support technology start-ups across India. Six state governments provided 10,000 Start-ups an annual grant to lead and manage incubation centres in key start-up hubs, including Bengaluru, Chennai, Gurgaon, Kolkata, Mumbai and Noida (National Capital Region). This also provided start-ups in nearby Tier 2 and 3 cities access to infrastructure and resources needed to scale their businesses at highly subsidised costs. The state grants are being received since the programme began in 2013.

Warehouse vs Virtual Incubation Programme

The warehouse, as defined by NASSCOM, is a *"co-working facility that can be leased by start-ups for one year at a nominal cost. It consists of plug-and-play facilities with high-speed internet connections of up to 10 Mbps, and basic utilities like electricity and water"*.

Exhibit 8.3 lays out the major differences between the two programmes.

Exhibit 8.3: Differences between Warehouse Programme and Virtual Incubation Programme

Warehouse Programme	Virtual Incubation Programme
Provides affordable co-working space and mentoring to start-ups	Leverages digital technologies for mentoring start-ups in virtual mode
Localised reach: 10 warehouses incorporated since its inception in 2013	Wider reach: Over 2,400 start-ups across India have been incubated by the 10,000 Start-ups Virtual Incubation Programme
Cost of space allotted, shared use of equipment and other infrastructure	No attached costs
Involves personalised face-to-face interactions, mentoring and pitching	Needs to overcome challenges of trust owing to non-physical interactions

The Delivery Model

NASSCOM's virtual incubation programme has adopted the FAME (Funding, Acceleration, Mentoring and Enterprise connect) model (Exhibit 8.4) to support technology start-ups across India. This model focusses on the primary aspects that are required by any start-up to move from idea to building a venture and eventually creating a scalable business.

Funding: Raising money from investors such as angels, venture capitalists (VCs), government funds and corporations.

Acceleration: All resources such as industry events, networking, idea validation, IP, government programmes and knowledge-sharing that help the start-up to move to the next stage.

Mentoring: Receiving guidance and insights from mentors, including investors, seasoned entrepreneurs, innovators and industry experts on various facets to grow one's start-up. This will include pitching, go-to-market strategy, product management, financing and talent.

Enterprise Connect: NASSCOM has over 2,800 member companies, including both Indian and multinational organisations. 10,000 Start-ups leverages this vast network for collaboration opportunities between start-ups and corporations.

Evolution of the 10,000 Start-ups Virtual Incubation Programme

In 2015, the 10,000 Start-ups programme increased evangelising and promoting start-ups in Tier 2 and Tier 3 cities. The presence in the key geographies had helped in covering reasonable ground in the major start-up hubs and their neighbouring cities. There were deliberations about opening more warehouses beyond the metros, though this came at high set-up costs such as premises, infrastructure and staff. The other challenge with setting up incubators in smaller cities was limited or no access to resources such as mentors, networks, investors, corporate decision-making and R&D centres, which are concentrated in Tier 1 cities.

The virtual programme was also envisaged to continue to engage with those start-ups that have finished their tenure at the NASSCOM Warehouse and those that have moved to their own offices due to growth in team size. In an attempt to satisfy requirements from

Exhibit 8.4: FAME delivery model

Mentoring
Receiving guidance and insights from industry experts and mentors

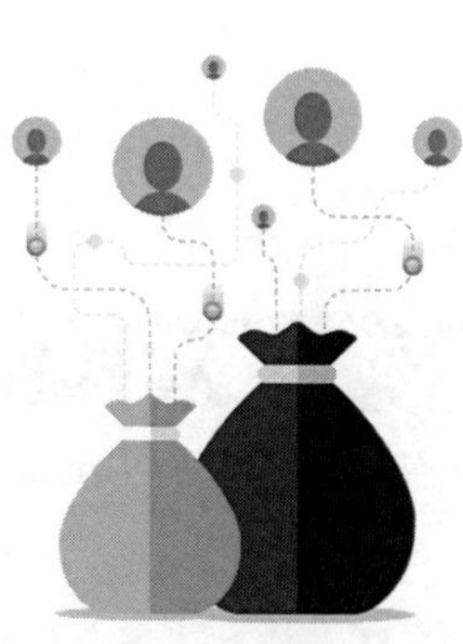

Funding
Raising money from investors such as angels, VCs and corporates

Enterprise Connect
NASSCOM has 2800+ member companies. Start-ups can leverage this vast network for collaboration opportunities

Acceleration
All resources that help the start-ups to move to the next growth stage

multiple perspectives, NASSCOM leveraged the growth of digitalisation in the form of higher internet penetration across India, better networks and availability of smarter online collaborative tools and launched the 10,000 Start-ups Virtual Incubation Programme.

Selection Process for 10,000 Start-ups Virtual Incubation Programme

A selection committee that includes investors, corporate leaders and experienced entrepreneurs screens the applicants. The evaluators score the start-up applications on various criteria, including innovation, founders' profile, product or technology offering, quality of pitch and opportunity size. Every month, the Virtual Incubation Programme receives close to 100 applications and has an acceptance rate of 57 per cent.

The rigorous and detailed selection process ensures that start-ups which make it to the programme have an idea that can be scaled up even if it may need some changes at the time of induction and that the founders are passionate and committed to building a successful business.

Impact of the Virtual Incubation Programme

Since its inception, more than 2,400 start-ups across India have been incubated by the 10,000 Start-ups Virtual Incubation Programme. Participation from start-ups from Tier 2 and Tier 3 cities increased from 15 per cent to 25 per cent over five years.

The pre-COVID growth and success of the virtual incubation programme serendipitously prepared 10,000 Start-ups for the global COVID-19 pandemic, which began in early 2020. 10,000 Start-ups was quickly able to move its warehouse start-ups to the existing virtual incubation programme and continue to support them. During April–November 2020, the 10,000 Start-ups had seen a 90 per cent increase in the number of start-ups inducted to the virtual incubation programme compared with the same time period in 2019, and a 35 per cent increase in start-ups from Tier 2 and Tier 3 cities joining the programme. It has covered start-ups from over 40 cities.

From April to November 2020, the programme was able to deliver the following through the virtual incubation programme:

Exhibit 8.5: Benefits of virtual incubation

Investor connect
Pitch session with investors

Global capital access programmes
Helps connect the investor community from across the globe with Indian start-ups

Innovation challenges
Hurdles faced in new-age verticals and emerging technologies

Mentor connect
Over 250+ mentors sharing experiential knowledge and one-to-one guidance

Tech WE programme

A customised programme for women entrepreneurs in technology

Enterprise connect
NIPP is India's largest industry-backed open innovation platform with 40+ corporations as partners

Start-up Kit
Tech support by leading technology service providers such as AWS, Zip Bizz and others

Government programmes
10,000 Start-ups collaborates with governments

Knowledge series
Regular meet-ups are organised to exchange knowledge

Legal and operations support
Offers resources for legal support for valuations, contracts, agreements and much more

NASSCOM Start-up hub
All-in-one online platform for 4,200+ start-ups

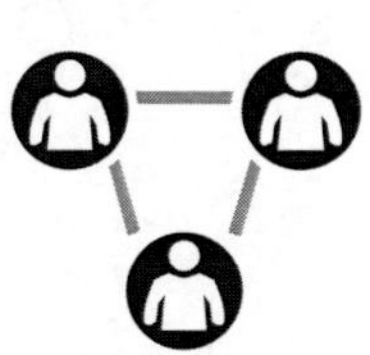

- 47+ start-ups pitched at 7 sessions – 170+ meetings
- 50+ start-up solutions identified in various verticals
- 40 PoCs, 1000+ start-ups recommended for 180+ use-cases, 281 start-ups connected for further discussions, 12 pitch sessions for 80 start-ups
- Virtual Investor Connect – 100+ start-ups, 40+ investors, 90+ one-on-one sessions

Benefits of Virtual Incubation

The virtual incubation programme has several benefits (Exhibit 8.5). For one, it connects start-ups with investors in different countries. 10,000 Start-ups has executed programmes with Japan, the US and Canada, and more such initiatives were being planned with Singapore, the European Union and Korea. It offers enterprise connects, access to more than 250 mentors, a customised programme for women entrepreneurs in technology, and innovation challenges on verticals such as mobility, blockchain and FinTech.

Overcoming the Challenge of Building Trust and Engagement in a Virtual Environment

Delivering the incubation programme virtually means forgoing the strong engagement and trust that come with in-person interactions. 10,000 Start-ups has overcome this challenge by assigning a Regional Lead to every start-up that joins the virtual incubation programme, based on its geographic location. The Regional Leads are experienced entrepreneurs and are full-time resources of 10,000 Start-ups. They provide support in the form of one-on-one mentoring on varied topics such as funding, marketing, idea validation, market access, pitching, enterprise and government connect, talent management and audits. Exhibits 8.6–8.9 provide examples of start-ups that participated in NASSCOM's Virtual Incubation Programme.

Exhibit 8.6: Caselet 1: CustomFit.ai

About	Support required	Outcomes and impact
Start-up Name: CustomFit.ai **Region:** Bengaluru **Incubated** in April 2019 as BlackBuckle.io CustomFit.ai is a purpose-built B2B website personalisation platform designed for B2B marketers. It converts website traffic into leads by dynamically changing website content and CTAs as per visitor characteristics such as company size, industry, source, the product they are currently using and based on their past behaviours and interests. It helps businesses to understand what their users want and need, when they need it and how businesses can help them find exactly what they are looking for. This 'no-code' platform can be easily integrated with any of the existing platforms used by businesses.	Building an emerging AI start-up, the CustomFit.ai founders felt a need for focussed mentorship and connect with corporate decision-makers.	The programme has helped CustomFit.ai: ▪ Develop its go-to-market strategy. ▪ Find engagement opportunities with mentors. ▪ Receive ₹1 million worth of credits through its Start-up Kit. ▪ Market access – the founders were able to pitch to senior leaders of five Fortune 500 companies; they are also in touch with multiple investors. ▪ Upon completion of the virtual incubation phase, the start-up also joined the incubation programme at the 10,000 Start-ups Bengaluru warehouse. **https://www.CustomFit.ai Milestones** ▪ Raised a pre-seed round from Java Capital. Upsparks, FirstCheque and LetsVenture. ▪ Winners of *Unicorn Battle*, India Chapter. ▪ Winners of South Asia division of 3551 Optics Valley Global Entrepreneurship Competition.

Exhibit 8.7: Caselet 2: 13TABS

About	Support required	Outcomes and impact
Start-up Name: 13TABS **Region:** Dhanbad, Jharkhand With 571 websites created every minute, it becomes difficult for a user to search for the relevant option under one single page, but explaining a search is equally troublesome. 13TABS gives individuals the result they want and, with 13 categories, it is always easier to switch to the relevant tab rather than scrolling down and loading the next result page. 13TABS does not capture or save any user information on the computer or on the web. They crawl over 3000 GB of text data and perform 20,000 searches per month.	Coming from a Tier 2 city, 13TABS found limited scope in terms of growth of network, mentorship and operational cost efficiencies.	The start-up was incubated by NASSCOM's 10,000 Start-ups in September 2019. Since then, it has connected with several entrepreneurs and industry veterans. ▪ Over the course of the incubation period, the start-up has saved operational costs of up to ₹0.5 million through the Start-up Kit offered by 10,000 Start-ups. ▪ It received access to more than 20 expert sessions. ▪ It connected with three mentors in the business and technology domains.

Exhibit 8.8: Caselet 3: ellow.ai

About	Support required	Outcomes and impact
Start-up Name: ellow.io **Location:** Kochi, Kerala ellow.io is a talent marketplace that connects pre-vetted remote engineers from handpicked development houses and top-quality freelancers using AI and ML.	In its developmental stage, ellow.io was looking to acquire more customers. It wanted to expand its market access to IT services companies.	▪ Enterprise Connect: With its vast network of software and tech service companies, NASSCOM was able to provide a connection to various organisations that needed developers. They were connected to about 10 IT services companies for product pitches. ▪ Since joining the NASSCOM Start-up Hub, ellow.io has been able to connect and network with various founders and investors. ▪ The company has saved approximately ₹0.35 million through the complimentary AWS offerings on the Start-up Kit.

Policy Imperatives

NASSCOM's 10,000 Start-ups Virtual Incubation Programme offers several learnings for other incubators and many advantages for budding entrepreneurs. However, a few policy initiatives are needed to successfully implement more such programmes at the national level:

1. Coordinated investments are needed in ICT infrastructure at local, national and more so at regional levels by governments to encourage start-ups in smaller towns.
2. Privacy and data security have to be ensured in the digital programmes.
3. There is a need to develop user-centric policies and programmes, and availability of smarter online collaborative tools.

Exhibit 8.9: Caselet 4: Genrobotics

About	Support required	Outcomes and impact
Start-up Name: Genrobotics **Region:** Thiruvananthapuram, Kerala Genrobotics' innovations combine AI and robotics to address social issues. Its latest G2 model has the capability of performing multifarious tasks like handling logistics in combat military operations, at construction sites or performing roles for firefighting and rescue missions. The start-up has also developed Bandicoot, the world's first robotic scavenger, which has transformed manholes into roboholes and has been adopted in more than 10 states. The product has been making a positive impact on thousands of manual scavengers. The company recently announced the G-Gaiter, an affordable robotic gait training platform for rehabilitation of paraplegic patients.	Established in a Tier 2 city, the start-up was looking for increased market access, nation-wide as well as globally.	▪ Genrobotics could connect with a large number of mentors, opening up many growth opportunities. ▪ They have connected with various founders and investors through the NASSCOM Start-up Hub. ▪ The start-up was selected to pitch at the NASSCOM Global VC Connect 2020: Japan session. **Genrobotics Milestones** ▪ Won the National Award for the best campus-initiated start-up from Startup India. ▪ Received the Young Change Maker Award from the Vice-President of India for the innovative solution, Bandicoot Robot. ▪ Raised pre-Series A funding from Unicorn India Ventures, Anand Mahindra and SEA Fund as new investors.

4. Training programmes can be introduced to improve networking skills and expertise of entrepreneurs to make the best use of online incubation such that these incubators become potential one-stop platforms for entrepreneurs to connect with global mentors.
5. Governments should encourage and facilitate investments in virtual incubators and incubation programmes, especially for students in schools and colleges, to enable entrepreneurship at a young age.

Considering the reach of the virtual incubation programme and the benefits it has been able to provide, virtual incubators will continue with a contactless and digital operating model across geographical boundaries. With policy interventions towards robust telecommunications and digital infrastructure, especially in remote areas, virtual incubation is expected play a vital role for nurturing more start-ups and contributing to India's stature as a leading start-up nation.

Endnotes

[1]*The Economic Times*. 2019. Over 1,300 start-ups added in 2019, over 8,900 tech-start-ups in India now: NASSCOM, Retrieved on January 20, 2021 from https://economictimes.indiatimes.com/small-biz/startups/newsbuzz/over-1300-startups-added-in-2019-over-8900-tech-startups-in-india-now-nasscom/articleshow/71925791.cms?from=mdr

[2]StartupIndia.com

[3]Nowak, MJ and Grantham, CE. 2000. The virtual incubator: Managing human capital in the software industry. *Research Policy* 29(2): 125–134.

[4]Mian, S, Lamine, W and Fayolle, A. 2016. Technology Business Incubation: An overview of the state of knowledge. *Technovation* 50: 1–12.

[5]Von Zedtwitz, M and Grimaldi, R. 2006. Are service profiles incubator-specific? Results from an empirical investigation in Italy. *The Journal of Technology Transfer* 31(4): 459–468.

[6]Hackett, SM and Dilts, DM. 2004. A systematic review of business incubation research. *The Journal of Technology Transfer* 29(1): 55–82.

[7]Daily Hunt. 2020. Top 5 incubators for start-ups gone virtual to fight the pandemic in India, Retrieved from https://m.dailyhunt.in/news/india/english/news+patrolling-epaper-newspatr/top+5+incubators+for+startups+gone+virtual+to+fight+the+pandemic+in+india-newsid-n206165556

[8]*Business Today*. 2021. From launch to growth: Why incubators need to re-strategize in post-covid world, Retrieved from https://www.businesstoday.in/opinion/columns/from-launch-to-growth-why-incubators-need-to-re-stragetise-in-post-covid-world/story/430888.html

[9]Hackett, SM and Dilts, DM. 2004b. A Real Options-Driven Theory of Business Incubation. *The Journal of Technology Transfer* 29 (1): 41–54.

[10]Bergek, A and Norrman, C. 2008. Incubator Best practice: A framework. *Technovation* 28 (1/2): 20–28.

[11]Colbert, C, Adkins, S, Wolfe, C and LaPan, K. 2010. *Best Practices in Action*. Athens, Ohio: NBIA Publications.

IN BRIEF

- Despite high levels of self-employment in India, entrepreneurs who formally set up start-ups have been low. A major reason has been the lack of access to entrepreneurial ecosystems.
- Atal Innovation Mission is a programme of the Indian government that provides a suitable environment for entrepreneurs to convert their ideas into start-ups and provides a platform for coordination between various stakeholders such as government agencies, industry and research institutes.
- Atal Incubation Centres (AICs), created as a part of the Atal Innovation Mission, differ from other incubation programmes in the diversity of sectors supported. While most of the 100-odd incubators have a strong sectoral focus, the sectors covered by AICs range from cyber security to manufacturing.
- The goal of AICs has been to take the success ratio of start-ups to 80 per cent from a failure ratio of 80 per cent. In order to achieve the same, the programme management of AICs has a strong focus on data collection and analysis, enabling the incubators to understand the factors contributing to the success and failure of start-ups.
- Capacity building of incubators plays a critical role in ensuring the quality of support that start-ups receive from them. Therefore, AICs have various components such as special capacity building programmes, awareness programmes, networking to better mentor start-ups, and so on.

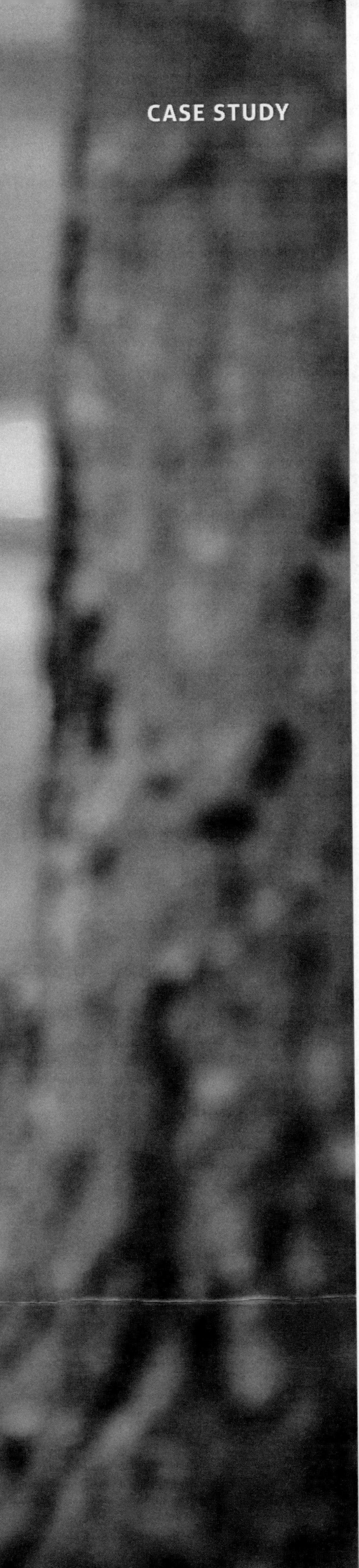

9

Building Synergies for Ensuring Venture Success: The Case of Atal Incubation Centres

Abha Rishi, Ajith Chandran and Rahul Singh

Rishi, A, Chandran, A and Singh, R. 2021. "Building Synergies for Ensuring Venture Success: The Case of Atal Incubation Ccentres". In *Shifting Orbits: Decoding the Trajectory of the Indian Start-up Ecosystem*, edited by Thillai Rajan A, Srivardhini K Jha, Joffi Thomas and Rohan Chinchwadkar, 94–106. Hyderabad: Universities Press (India) Private Limited.

Channelling India's Entrepreneurial Spirit

India has always had a vibrant and energetic entrepreneurial environment. The levels of self-employment in India (which includes entrepreneurs and small business owners) have remained substantially above the global average for the past three decades (Exhibit 9.1). However, the number of entrepreneurs who have set up successful start-ups or formal organisations is rather low.[1] Much of the entrepreneurship often happens in the informal sectors, where there is limited scope for growth and expansion. For example, despite the recent exponential growth in the number of limited liability companies registered in India, the density of new companies (number of new companies per 1,000 people in the working age range)[2] remains substantially lower than the global median (Exhibit 9.2).[3]

The fundamental aim of the Atal Innovation Mission (AIM) is to enable entrepreneurs to set up successful start-ups by creating a suitable environment for them to incubate their ideas and convert them into viable business ventures. AIM aspires to develop a start-up environment by coordinating and creating synergies among various stakeholders (such as government agencies, universities, research institutions, MSME [micro, small and medium enterprises] and the industry) to bolster entrepreneurship and innovation in India.

Exhibit 9.1: Self-employed population as a proportion of the employed workforce[4]

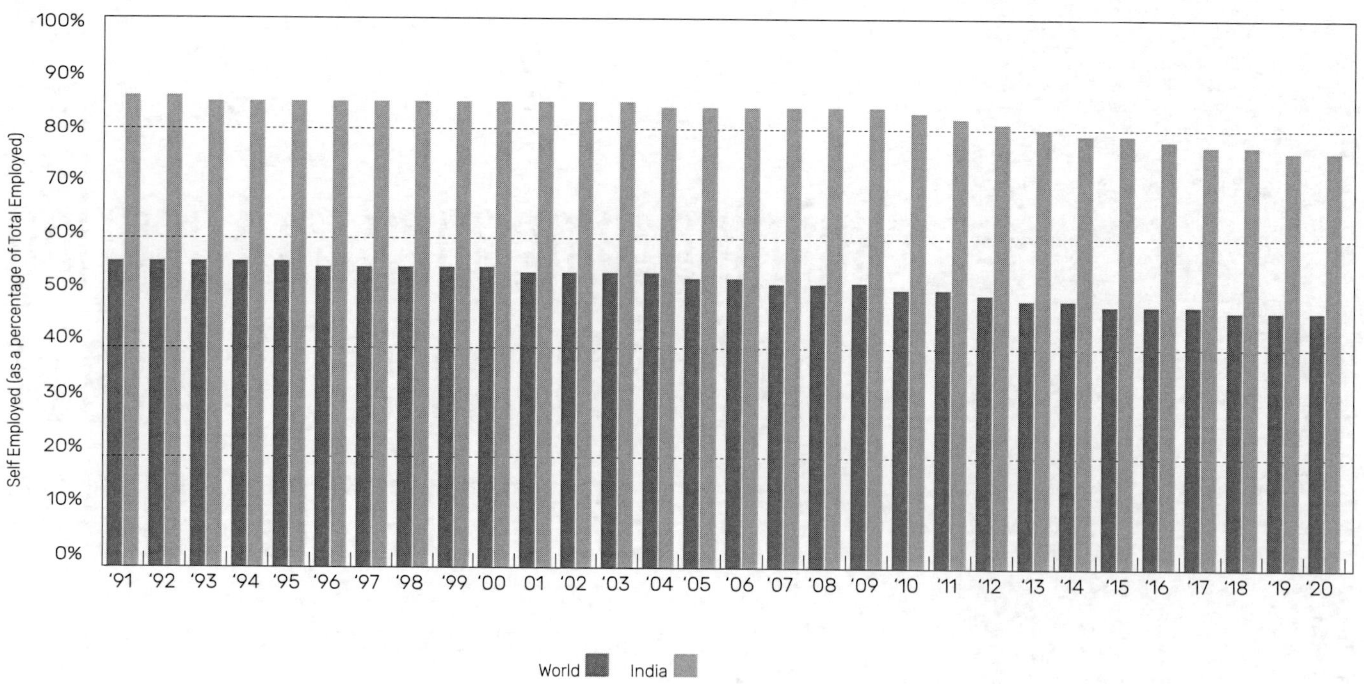

Source: World Bank DataBank, based on modelled estimates of International Labour Organization

Exhibit 9.2: Number of new limited liability companies registered and density of new companies[5]

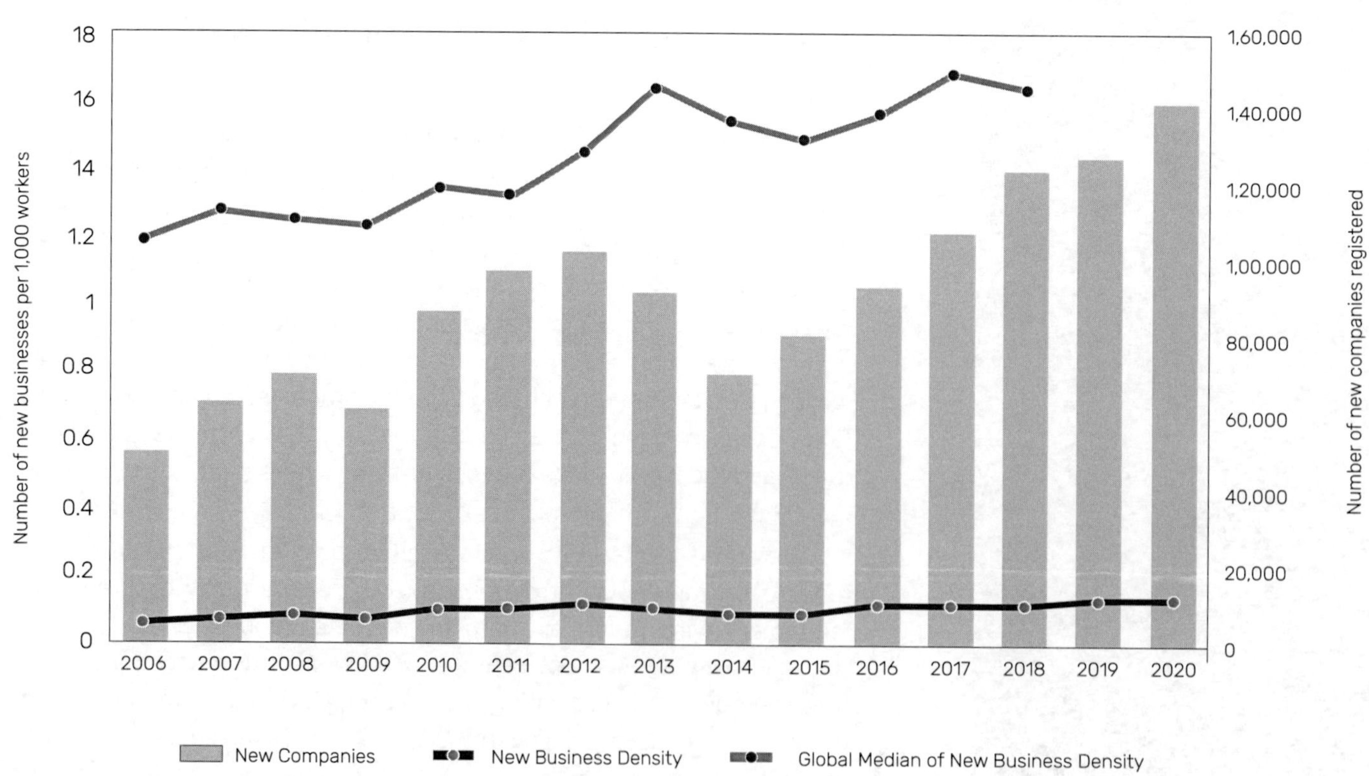

Source: World Bank's Ease of Doing Business Initiative, Ministry of Corporate Affairs, and World Bank DataBank

To turn AIM's vision into reality, one of the major steps taken is the establishment of new incubation centres called Atal Incubation Centres (AICs) across leading educational and research institutes in India (see Exhibit 9.3 for an introduction to incubation centres). Most AICs have a sectoral focus such as manufacturing, transport, agriculture, Internet of Things (IoT) and cyber security. AICs provide budding start-up founders with access to sectoral experts, seed capital, opportunities for partnerships with industry, mentorship, and the necessary physical infrastructure.

Exhibit 9.3: What are incubation centres?

Incubation centres are entities that provide support and create a congenial environment for innovation and entrepreneurship. Such centres are responsible for providing budding start-ups with the necessary business and technical support, mentorship, access to networks and funding. Incubation centres also provide resources like office space and support, which individually might be expensive, but which work out economically on a collective basis.

In the last decade, the idea of business incubators has taken root in India and in many other parts of the world, especially in developing nations. Since early 2000, many Indian institutions, notably the IITs (Indian Institute of Technology), IIMs (Indian Institute of Management) and several private organisations have been offering business incubation facilities. India has the third highest number of incubators after China (2,400 incubators) and the United States of America (1,500 incubators).[6]

Most incubators are run by universities and educational institutions. There are also privately held incubators, which are run by corporate entities and multinationals such as Airbus, Boeing, Rolls-Royce, Microsoft and Google. Corporate incubators typically encourage and incubate start-ups in their area of expertise. Some of the Indian corporates running such programmes are Yes Bank and JioGenNext.[7]

The Indian Incubator and Accelerator Landscape and the Role of AIM

In order to better appreciate the role of AICs in the Indian start-up ecosystem, it is important to understand the Indian incubator and accelerator landscape. In India, incubators are generally sector-agnostic while accelerators are more inclined towards having an industry focus. This focus has led to significant corporate or private funding and support to target accelerators. On the other hand, public and academic support is more skewed towards incubators (Exhibit 9.4).

Exhibit 9.4: Percentage of incubator and accelerator programmes by sector[8]

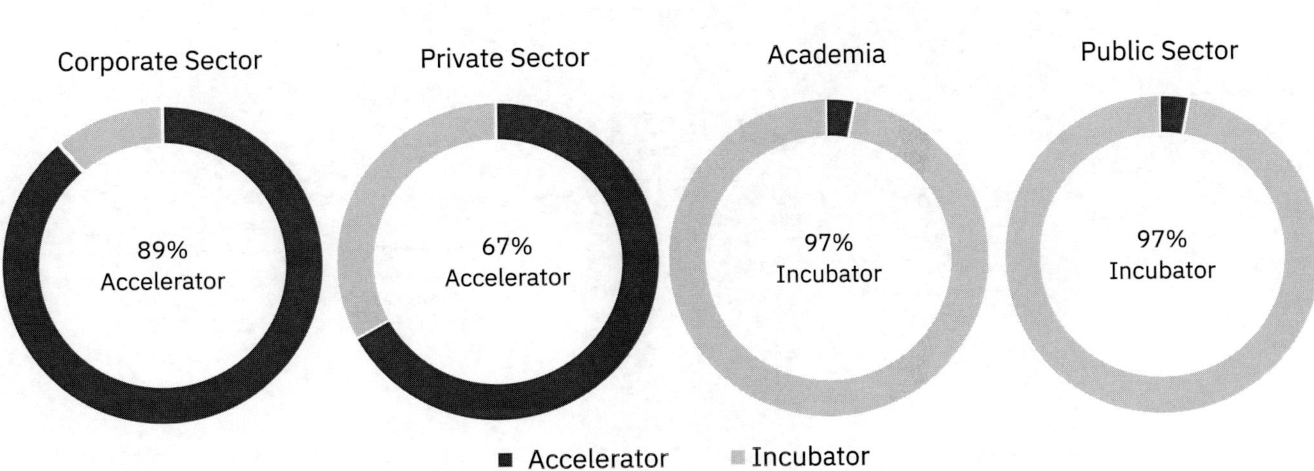

Source: NASSCOM

While both work in tandem, accelerator support has been typically short term (15 weeks to 6 months), helping cohorts of start-ups with their new venture processes, whereas incubator support is most often long term and continuous.[9]

Types of Incubators

Academic incubators (or university business incubators [UBIs]) focus on propelling student entrepreneurs through alumni support, and typically have extended gestation periods (from 6 months to 3 years).

Academic institutions are the first stage of economic and social creation labs, as they produce the two core components of value creation – talent and technological innovation. Drawing on the talent in students and professors, UBIs primarily support the development and commercialisation of ideas from research outcomes. Universities in the West have been more proactive in creating economic value from research outcomes, by taking forward the practices and findings from research and applying it for practical use by developing valuable products and services.

The UBI ecosystem develops a space to ideate and produce social or commercial solutions to the problems and challenges faced by society. UBIs achieve this by fostering engagement between the academic community (professors, students and researchers), industry, government and social entities.[10] The core pillars of the UBI ecosystem are illustrated in Exhibit 9.5.

The corporate incubators, on the other hand, focus more on co-creation or co-innovation and client-specific solutions and are better equipped to provide investor connect and business mentorship to the start-ups. Incubation programmes enable corporations to shift a part of their R&D burden onto the incubated start-ups in a diversified manner, while cutting their direct costs and strengthening their balance sheets. The indirect promotion of products (promoting through start-ups instead of the corporation itself) has also proven to be a viable sales and marketing technique, helping corporates garner loyal customers. Apart from pure financial returns, the corporate entities seek to capitalise on the economic benefits of incorporating innovative technologies to their existing product offerings and processes.[11] From the perspective of start-ups, corporate incubators provide access to market insights that help them read and target

Exhibit 9.5: The four pillars of university business incubators (UBIs)

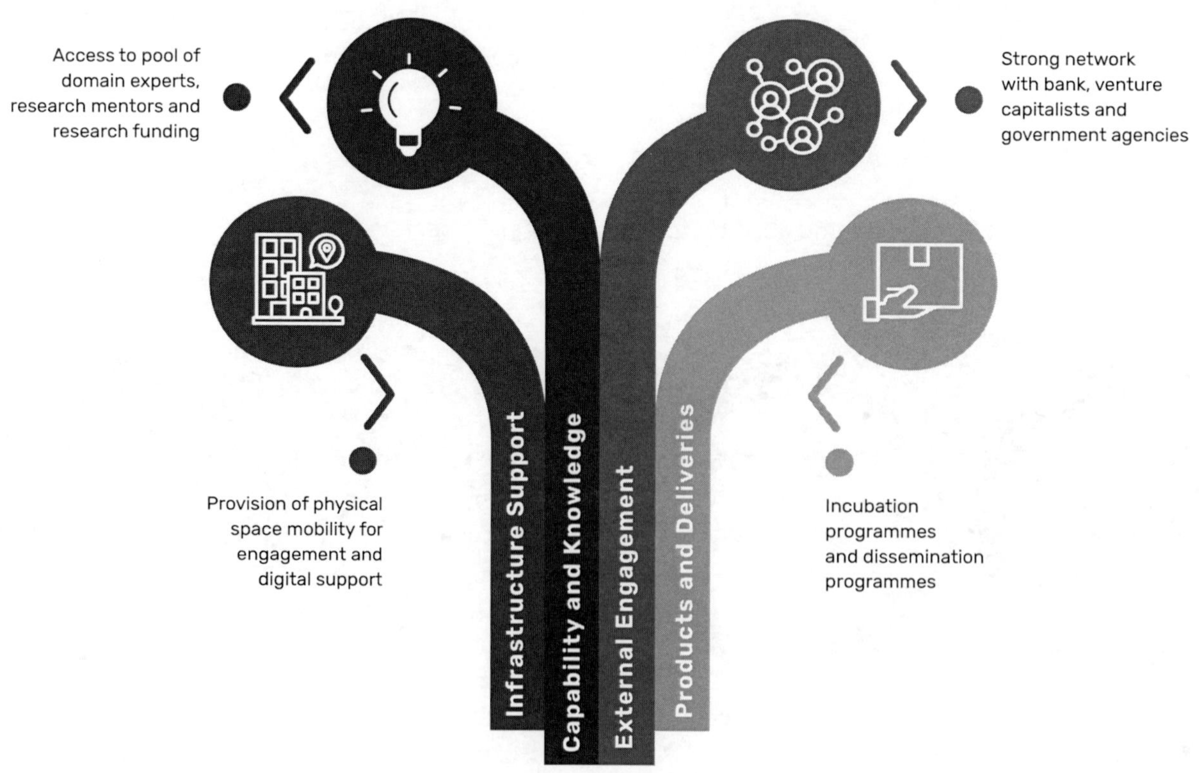

the market accurately, coupled with seed capital and mentorship. The model has been very successful across industries. Exhibit 9.6 describes the distribution of active corporate incubator programmes across industries.

Private sector boutique incubators are typically seed funds that focus on identifying disruptive start-ups at an early stage. The private sector incubators mentor and groom seed-stage start-ups to a point where the start-up can secure funding from large VC investors. The incubators typically exit, with the profits from the increase in valuation of the start-ups between seed stage and growth or VC stage.

Types of Accelerators

As in the case of incubators, it is possible to distinguish between the different types of accelerators. Government accelerator programmes such as the National Science and Technology Entrepreneurship Development Board's (NSTEDB) NIDHI[12] initiative have sponsored several accelerator centres in different cities in India. The government primarily partners with academic and non-academic research institutions to provide technology start-ups with the necessary seed capital, coupled with access to relevant research and business networks.[13] The focus in the case of government-backed accelerators has been typically on socially relevant technological innovation such as healthcare or urban mobility.[14]

Corporate accelerators, on the other hand, focus more on technological innovations that are related to their area of business. Corporate accelerators use their programmes as 'experimental playgrounds' to quickly experiment with emergent and potentially disruptive technologies related to their field of business.[15]

Classical private sector boutique accelerators such as Y Combinator are typically sector-agnostic and primarily focus on start-ups with the greatest market potential. They provide an intense learning environment, where start-ups receive targeted mentorship to improve their ability to raise funds from venture capitalists and to streamline their product offerings to gain higher levels of customer traction.[16] Financial returns are often the primary motivator for such accelerators.

Exhibit 9.6: Distribution of active corporate incubation programmes[33]

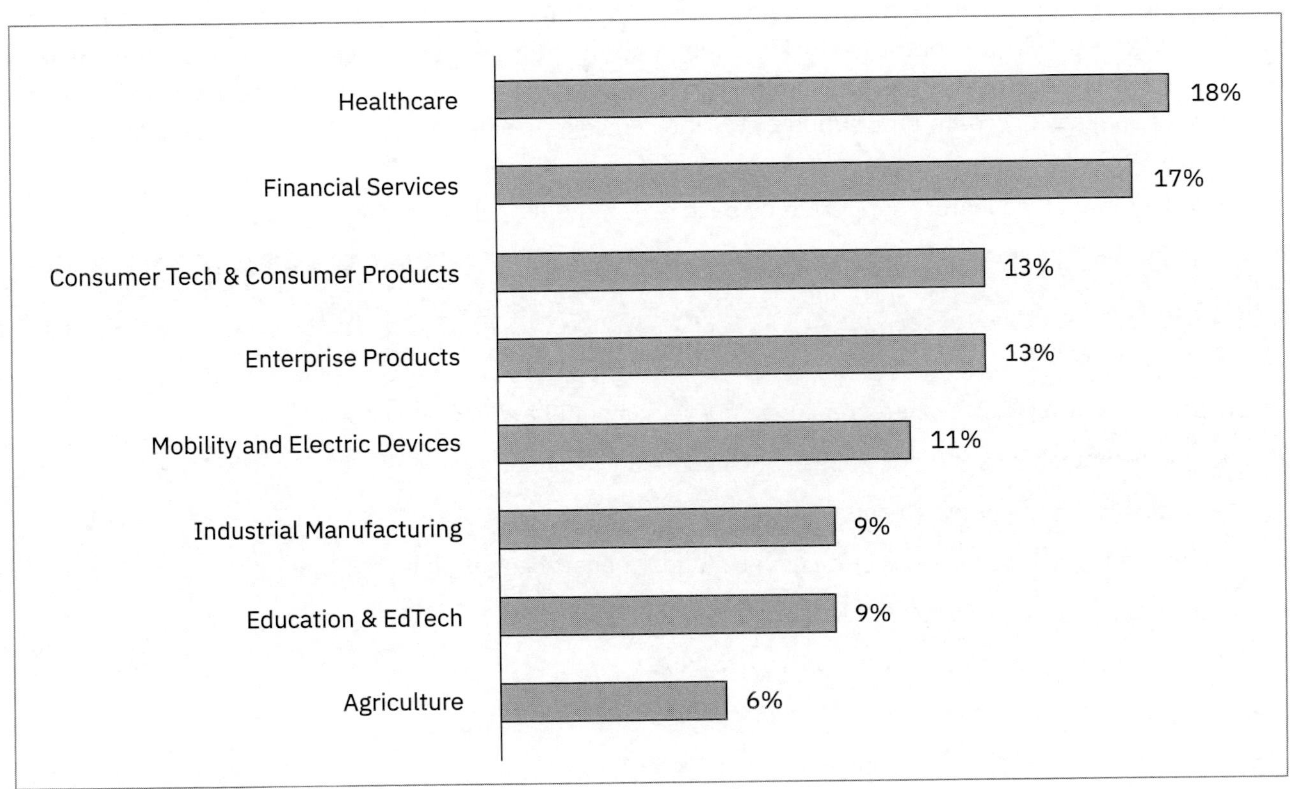

Source: NASSCOM

Diversity of the Ecosystem and the Vision of AIM

The rich diversity of incubators and accelerators is vital to the proliferation of innovation in India since they cater to various segments of the market. For example, academic incubators are well equipped to cater to translational research ventures and emergent technology ventures, given their strong technical know-how. On the other hand, corporate incubators are well versed with the needs and demands of the market, and would be able to support ventures with unique product offerings catering to underserved segments of the market. A number of government agencies including the Technology Development Board (TDB), NSTEDB, Biotechnology Industry Research Assistance Council (BIRAC) and Ministry of Micro, Small and Medium Enterprises (MoMSME) have supported incubators serving start-ups in their respective fields of expertise. For example, BIRAC provides funding and mentorship to operational start-ups in the biotech and life sciences sector, through their partners in several biotechnology research institutions.[17] Exhibit 9.7 summarises the number of incubators supported by different government agencies.

Given that most agencies focus on supporting incubators and start-ups in their specific fields, AIM is unique in that it provides support to a wide variety of incubators across different sectors and fields. AIM provides holistic government support to the entrepreneurial ecosystem in its entirety, with an aim to fully leverage India's demographic dividend. The objective of AIM has been to provide access to the entrepreneurial ecosystem for the youth in educational institutions and corporate entities. The vision led by NITI Aayog succinctly summarises the motivation for AIM, *"to develop a holistic environment of start-up and innovation ecosystem with important stakeholders engaged in creating knowledge and manpower for the larger pool of the country"*.[18]

The mission seeks to nurture the development and proliferation of incubators across India by providing academic and corporate institutions with the right support to set up greenfield incubation projects across sectors. This enables the strong growth of diverse incubators who can provide entrepreneurs with targeted support and mentorship, creating a vibrant and specialised ecosystem for supporting entrepreneurship and innovation.

Atal Innovation Mission – The Nuts and Bolts

To implement the aforementioned vision of AIM, the mission had five essential programmes.[19] The programmes were targeted to work with institutions across several levels, including schools, universities, research institutions, MSMEs (micro, small and medium

Exhibit 9.7: Number of incubators supported by each government agency (allowing for overlaps)

Government agency	Total number of incubators
Atal Innovation Mission (AIM)	102
National Science and Technology Entrepreneurship Development Board (NSTEDB)	128
Technology Development Board (under Ministry of Science and Technology)	36
Department of Agricultural Research and Education (DARE)	8
Biotechnology Industry Research Assistance Council (under Department of Biotechnology)	50
Space Technology Incubation Centre (under Department of Space)	3
Ministry of Micro, Small and Medium Enterprises (MoMSME)	207
Ministry of Electronics and Information Technology (MeitY)	27
Innovations for Defence Excellence (under Ministry of Defence)	9

Source: Compiled from the websites of the government agencies

enterprises) and industry. Exhibit 9.8 summarises the five programmes.

In May 2016, NITI Aayog came up with detailed guidelines for setting up incubation centres across India, named Atal Incubation Centres (AICs).[20] As of January 2021, there were 102 incubation centres identified and supported under this scheme, across 23 states.[21] The AICs have been hosted at both academic institutions (such as universities and higher education institutions) and at non-academic institutions (such as private limited companies and foundations). As of January 2021, 68 of the 102 centres were ready to establish incubator programmes with a cohort size of 50 start-ups, in four-year cycles.[22]

AIC's Journey

A total of 3,658 entities applied for a grant of ₹100 million ($1.48 million) to host AICs in May 2016. The entities comprised about 1,300 private institutions, 425 academic institutions, 1,050 corporate entities and 900 smaller groups, including individuals. Of this, 19 entities were shortlisted after a rigorous three-round selection process. This consisted of stringent verification of the documents submitted, a field visit to the incubator premises and an in-depth discussion of the implementation of an action and sustainability plan over the five-year period of the grant. Thirteen of the 19 shortlisted entities were greenfield[23] incubators designated as AICs. The other six were existing incubators, designated as Established Incubation Centres (EICs), which had the mandate to mentor the newly established AICs. In May 2018, the second cohort call received 2,676 applications, of which 72 institutions were shortlisted for receiving the grants. To date, AIM has supported over 1,700 start-ups, including over 500 women-led start-ups.[24]

Atal Incubation Centres – The Differentiating Factors

With 40,000 recognised start-ups providing over 420,000 jobs, spread across 586 districts in a total of 29 states and UTs, India has transformed into the third-largest start-up ecosystem in the world (in terms of the number of start-up cluster cities),[25] after the United States and United Kingdom.[26] In 2020, India had 38 cities that were ranked in the top 1,000 cities for start-ups.[27]

The targeted objective of AICs has been to create systems where start-ups can succeed. The goal has been to take the success ratio to 80 per cent from a failure ratio of 80 per cent. In order to achieve this target, AICs have a special focus on data collection and its analysis. This has enabled the incubators to understand the factors

Exhibit 9.8: The five programmes under the Atal Innovation Mission

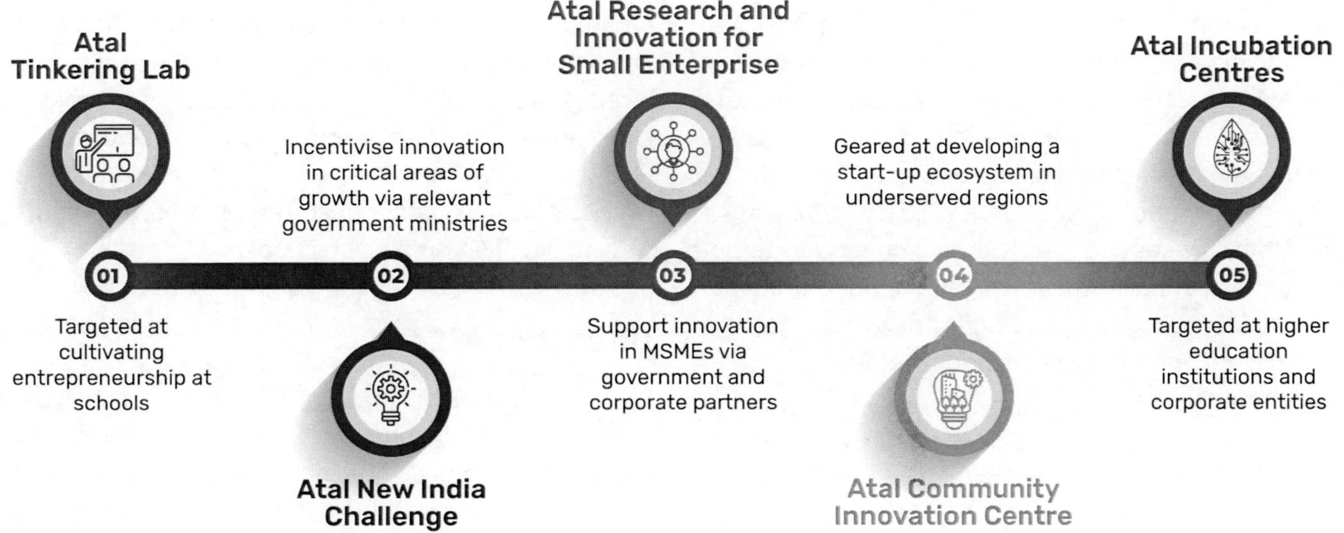

Source: NITI Aayog, AIM Brochure

Exhibit 9.9: Top 10 countries based on the number of cities ranked in the top 1,000 cities for start-ups[28]

Country	Number of cities
USA	383
UK	50
India	38
Germany	31
Brazil	29
Italy	29
Canada	29
China	24
Spain	23
Netherlands	21

Source: StartupBlink

contributing to the success and failure of start-ups, and provided start-ups with a well-informed perspective of the market and its requirements.

To ensure seamless collection of data, AIC has implemented processes that allow data on a set of metrics to be captured from the incubators almost on a real-time basis. This data is recorded on a monthly basis and the metrics include the number of start-ups incubated (virtually or physically), the number of women-led start-ups incubated, the number of events conducted, the number of training and workshops conducted, the mentors onboarded, the IP (intellectual property) created or filed for, and the number of jobs created by the start-ups. Such key performance indicators (KPIs) have enabled the management team to identify successful strategies of well-performing incubators that could be recreated by the other incubators participating in the programme.

Apart from the KPIs, the incubators' success has also been determined by their agility and ability to create partnerships and network with VC funds in order to provide their cohorts with access to global markets and funds. To further empower the incubation centres to embed themselves in the global start-up ecosystem, AIM actively assisted incubation centres in getting access to international partnerships and funding.

In addition, AIM has been conducting special capacity building programmes, awareness programmes and networking to improve the capabilities and skills of incubators to better mentor start-ups. Special programmes like iCrest[29] have been created to help incubators chart their path forward. These programmes leverage on learning from the best practices across the globe in order to shorten the learning curve of AICs. Such additional support mechanisms coupled with the well-established institutional structures have helped the AICs to positively impact start-ups.

Impact of AICs

Most AIC incubators have a limited operational track record (only 11 incubators have been operational for three years or more). Though the jury is still out on the impact and success of the AIC model, we highlight four cases that showcase the impact of AICs on social and technical entrepreneurship (Exhibits 9.10 and 9.11, respectively). Exhibit 9.12 presents the case of AIC-BIMTECH and its impact.

Exhibit 9.10: AIC's impact on social entrepreneurship

AIC Banasthali Vidyapith	AIC-SMUTBI
In three years, AIC Banasthali Vidyapith in Rajasthan has become one of India's leading women-centric business incubators. By 2020, it had supported 73 women start-ups, of which 28 have raised over ₹250 million in funding and created over 1,100 jobs. AIC Banasthali has partnered with over 25 national and international organisations to create a world-class ecosystem for women start-ups in India. The start-ups have received over 35 awards, including international achievements such as the 2020 DIANA Award, the Forbes 30 under 30 in the social category, and the AABI Asia Torch Bearer Award.	AIC-SMUTBI, Sikkim, was the first Atal Incubation Centre in Sikkim and northeast India. It became operational on September 7, 2018. In 2.5 years, it incubated 38 start-ups and created 127 jobs. It conducted 57 events, workshops and training to enhance the start-up founders and their teams' skill sets. The start-ups have won several awards at national and regional level such as NERES 1.0, 2019 E-mobility Summit, and so on. The incubator also partnered with 34 organisations that enabled the start-ups to leverage about ₹34 million in its offerings through the incubator. By the end of 2020, the start-ups had raised aggregate funding of ₹40.7 million. The presence of AIC-SMUTBI has changed the landscape of start-ups and entrepreneurship in Sikkim and northeast India, from the "beginners" position in 2019 to "emerging state" in 2020 in the Startup India state-wise ranking.

Exhibit 9.11: AIC's impact on tech entrepreneurship

AIC-BIMTECH	AIC-CCMB
AIC-BIMTECH, based in Uttar Pradesh, began its operations on January 20, 2018. It onboarded 92 start-ups, created 360 jobs and conducted 113 events and 169 training workshops in three years. It also partnered with 77 organisations, both national and international, which has helped the incubator offer the incubatees ₹82.7 million worth of partner benefits when they were onboarded. AIC-BIMTECH has helped 11 of its start-ups to raise funds to the tune of ₹92.9 million. Start-ups like TruckSuvidha, LQI and Energinee Innovation have won regional and national awards too. In total, the start-ups incubated by AIC-BIMTECH have won a total of 14 awards till January 2021.	AIC-CCMB, Telangana, was established at CSIR-Centre for Cellular and Molecular Biology, Hyderabad, with a vision of catalysing homegrown enterprises in the life sciences by addressing the most pressing issues in healthcare, food and animal health. Since its inception in August 2017, AIC-CCMB has incubated 41 start-ups with 11 successful graduations by building an empowering ecosystem of mentors and partners, along with world-class research facilities. The start-ups have created more than 150 jobs, raised more than ₹200 million in funding and won numerous awards. Taking a leadership role in making India "Atmanirbhar" in COVID-19 diagnostics, AIC-CCMB has promoted indigenous product development through validation services, quality control and scale-up support for start-ups and MSMEs.

Exhibit 9.12: AIC-BIMTECH: Social dimension

The incubator also had its social impact directly on the underprivileged. AIC-BIMTECH has been involved in a project, Project Uthan, run in conjunction with the BIMTECH Foundation. Dr Abha Rishi commented on the same, *"Project Uthan is for the inmates of 11 prisons across Uttar Pradesh state, wherein the main idea is to educate and skill the men and women prison inmates so that recidivism is reduced. Women, especially, have no recourse to a dignified life of labour and either resort to prostitution or revert to crime to earn a livelihood. By educating and skilling them through various workshops conducted in the libraries, these women can be brought back into the mainstream. The prison project gives female and male inmates equal opportunities to access the libraries and attend workshops, but the focus has been on helping the women inmates create microenterprises"*.

BIMTECH also ran programmes in collaboration with organisations like Goldman Sachs and United Nations Global Compact Network India (UNGCNI), which promoted innovation and entrepreneurship. 10,000 Women, a global initiative by Goldman Sachs, fostered economic growth by providing first-generation women entrepreneurs without higher formal education with business and management training, mentoring and networking, and access to capital. The Young SDG Innovators Programme (YSIP) by UNGCNI was a 10-month accelerator programme for young talent within member organisations to collaborate and accelerate business innovation towards sustainable development goals (SDGs), to develop and drive innovative solutions through new technologies, initiatives and business models and deliver on their company's sustainability objectives.

The Challenges and Prospects

Despite the massive impetus provided to incubators across various segments, global rankings tend to indicate that much more effort would be required to make India a global leader for start-ups. A UBI benchmark study for 2019–2020 ranked 364 university-based incubators from 82 countries based on 21 KPIs. The only Indian mention was the Kerala Startup Mission under the World Top Public Business Accelerators.[30] Despite many successes in India's incubation and accelerator initiative, this ranking suggests that more work is required to compete at the global level.[31]

Further, there is a need to develop a strong network of high-impact innovation hubs around the country. For example, Mumbai was the only Indian city to feature in the Global Start-up Ecosystem Report 2020[32] that ranked the top 100 start-up ecosystems in the world. To ensure that the other cities also become successful, it is critical to recognise the essential dimensions that influence the agenda of start-up ecosystems, like the clustering of technology hubs (such as Silicon Valley, Bengaluru, Boston), financial hubs (such as New York, Mumbai, London) and market hubs (such as Beijing, Jakarta, Mumbai and Delhi).

India, which is at an early stage in the development of innovation hubs, has the potential to become a global epicentre for innovation, with the right policies and initiatives. At the global level, India has been witnessing the formation of significant clusters around Mumbai, Bengaluru, Chennai, Hyderabad and Delhi. At the national level, clusters around Jaipur, Ahmedabad, Cochin and Pune have also emerged as strong contenders with the potential to become start-up hubs. However, the incubation ecosystem would need to be strengthened to ensure success. Increased participation by and coordination among research institutions, industry and start-ups would lead to the formation of innovation triangles that can significantly strengthen the innovation ecosystem.

Some progress has already been made by academia on this front. Specifically, academic regulators such as the University Grants Commission and AICTE have been focussing on incubator and accelerator friendly policies to incentivise the formation of innovation triangles. They have begun to support developing clusters with policy support and according quick approval to institutions with higher efforts on innovation, entrepreneurship and incubation.

How Can the Incubators Succeed?

With a large pool of talented professors, researchers, students and associated industry professionals, the Indian academic institutions' network is the largest and potentially the most influential stakeholder of the start-up ecosystem. Our analysis and interactions with experts and policymakers on critical factors such as performance, funding, market reach and talent led to two key insights that can help incubators succeed in creating a congenial ecosystem for innovation and entrepreneurship.

Firstly, incubators need to focus more on ensuring the success of their cohorts by identifying approaches to improve financial viability and market reach, instead of merely providing physical infrastructure. This would require incubators to partner with a number of stakeholders, including the industry, academia and research institutions.

Secondly, it is essential to design a framework that can be used for benchmarking the parametric impact of incubator and accelerator programmes. A list of success metrics for evaluating and quantifying the value created by incubators and accelerators in India should be created for different categories. Startup India incorporates such categories in their awards. These metrics should significantly reduce failure and help track the outcomes of the incubators and the incubatees.

As India aspires to be a leading economy, the broad-level observations indicate the need for a transformational shift, and it requires relevant inputs from multi-stakeholders, primarily policymakers, academic institutions and industry, without which India cannot aspire to achieve the future goals it has created for itself. Attaining the goal requires systems and mechanisms to convert the current demographic dividend into high-quality technical human resources capable of cutting-edge research, innovation and deep tech entrepreneurship.

Endnotes

[1]See Chapter 2 (pp.28 to 38) of Department of Economic Affairs, Ministry of Finance, Government of India. 2020. *Economic Survey 2019–20 (Volume 1)*. Oxford University Press, New Delhi.

[2]The working age range is defined as ages between and including 15 and 64.

[3]This aspect is also discussed in the Economic Survey of India 2019–20, retrievable at: https://www.indiabudget.gov.in/budget2020-21/economicsurvey/doc/echapter.pdf

[4]World Bank DataBank (https://databank.worldbank.org/home.aspx). The indicator's code is 'SL.EMP.SELF.ZS'.

[5]The data from new companies registered and density for 2006–2018 comes from the World Bank's 'Doing Business' database (https://www.doingbusiness.org/en/data/exploretopics/entrepreneurship).

The data for new companies registered from 2019 to 2020 comes from the Ministry of Corporate Affairs' monthly master list (http://www.mca.gov.in/MinistryV2/incorporatedorclosedduringthemonth.html). The data for working age population for 2019 comes from the World Bank (Indicator-'SP.POP.1564.TO'). We use linear interpolation (assuming the same growth rate as between 2018 and 2019) to extrapolate the working age population for 2020.

[6]Inc42. 2019. Indian Incubators incubating a growing economy one step at a time, Retrieved from https://inc42.com/resources/indian-incubators-incubating-a-growing-economy-one-step-at-a-time/
Accessed on May 24, 2021

[7]Ibid.

[8]Ibid.

[9]Cohen, S. 2013. What Do Accelerators Do? Insights from Incubators and Angels. ***Innovations Technology Governance Globalization*** 8(3): 19–25. 10.1162/INOV_a_00184

[10]Hassan, NA. 2020. University business incubators as a tool for accelerating entrepreneurship: theoretical perspective. ***Review of Economics and Political Science*** (ahead of print). https://doi.org/10.1108/REPS-10-2019-0142

[11]Ibid.

[12]NIDHI is an acronym for National Initiative for Developing and Harnessing Innovations.

[13]Sourced from the official website: http://www.nstedb.com/new-programmes.htm

[14]National Initiative for Developing and Harnessing Innovation (NIDHI). 2016. ***NIDHI-Accelerator: Guidelines and Proforma for Submission of Proposals.*** Department of Science and Technology (DST), Ministry of Science and Technology, Government of India. Website: http://www.nstedb.com/New_Programmes/2018/NIDHIAccelerator.pdf

[15]Deloitte Digital. 2015. Design principles for building a successful corporate accelerator. Website: https://www2.deloitte.com/content/dam/Deloitte/de/Documents/technology/Corporate_Accelerator_EN.pdf

[16]Hathaway, I. 2016. What Startup Accelerators Really Do. Retrieved from *Harvard Business Review*, Entrepreneurship website: https://hbr.org/2016/03/what-startup-accelerators-really-do
Accessed on May 24, 2021

[17]Sourced from the official website: https://birac.nic.in/seedFund.php

[18]NITI Aayog (Government of India). 2020. *Atal Innovation Mission - Leading Innovation in India*. Government of India. https://aim.gov.in/AIM_Brochure.pdf

[19]Ibid.

[20]NITI Aayog (Government of India). 2016. *Guidelines for setting up of Incubation Centres under Atal Innovation Mission - 'Atal Incubation Centres'*. Government of India. https://niti.gov.in/writereaddata/files/Guidelines%20to%20setup%20AIC%20May%202016.pdf

[21]Ramanan, R. 2020. Atal Innovation Mission – Its Importance To Our Nation. *Business World* (March 30, 2020), retrieved January 24, 2021 from http://www.businessworld.in/article/Atal-Innovation-Mission-Its-Importance-To-Our-Nation/30-03-2020-187644/

[22]Atal Innovation Mission. 2020. *Atal Innovation Mission*. Retrieved December 2020 from https://aim.gov.in/overview.php

[23]Greenfield refers to establishing a completely new incubation centre, instead of scaling up existing incubators.

[24]Interview with Mr. Ramanan Ramanathan – Mission Director, AIM.

[25]India ranks third in the number of cities featured in the ranking of top 1,000 cities for start-ups by StartupBlink.

[26]StartupBlink. 2021. *Startup Ecosystem Rankings 2020*. Website: https://report.startupblink.com/

[27]Ibid.

[28]Ibid.

[29]AIM iCRESt (incubator capabilities enhancement for a robust ecosystem for high performing start-ups) is an AIM initiative in partnership with Bill & Melinda Gates Foundation and implemented by Wadhwani Foundation. It is a structured capacity building programme for incubators and a training programme for all AIM incubators as well as the start-ups supported by them.

[30]It is possible that some incubators and accelerators in India are missing from the ranking because they did not participate in the study or were not considered for ranking by the authors of the study.

[31]Meyer, H and Sowah, J. 2019. UBI World Rankings of Business Incubators and Accelerators 2019–2020. *UBI Global*. 10.13140/RG.2.2.16066.53441

[32]The Global Start-up Ecosystem Report. 2020. *Startup Genome and Global Entrepreneurship Network*. https://startupgenome.com/report/gser2020

[33]NASSCOM. 2020. *NASSCOM Start-up Catalysts-Incubators and Accelerators 2020*. https://nasscom.in/knowledge-center/publications/start-catalysts-%E2%80%93-incubators-accelerators

IN BRIEF

- Start-up founders can gain most from incubators whose expertise matches that of their offering, intended market segment and vision. Self-reflection and knowledge of incubators is crucial.
- Incubation is more than a provision of physical infrastructure and business services. The vision and identity of an incubator manifests in its strategy and value proposition, which in turn, helps in attracting suitable start-ups. Universities can leverage their existing resources and strengths to differentiate their incubators and offer unique value propositions, thus requiring low investment capital.
- It is important to build networks with other incubators, industry experts, domain experts and investors to provide optimum support to start-ups.
- Government support has been pivotal thus far in bringing the concept of incubation into the mainstream discourse and enabling universities across India to set up incubators. The next thrust towards innovation through incubation will come from developing successful models of incubation as pertinent to the Indian ecosystem.
- Financing may be momentarily targeted at enhancing the quality rather than the quantity of incubators at this stage so that exemplar models can be developed and scaled in a few years.

10

Nurturing the Next Gen: University Incubation in India

Rohan Chinchwadkar

Chinchwadkar, R. 2021. "Nurturing the Next Gen: University Incubation in India". In *Shifting Orbits: Decoding the Trajectory of the Indian Start-up Ecosystem*, edited by Thillai Rajan A, Srivardhini K Jha, Joffi Thomas and Rohan Chinchwadkar, 108–115. Hyderabad: Universities Press (India) Private Limited.

Business incubators are set up to nurture early-stage entrepreneurs and start-up firms. The first business incubators were formed in the US in the 1950s and became widespread worldwide in the 1980s. Researchers point to how incubators have evolved in terms of the services they provide – what started out as providing space with built-in infrastructure has evolved to offering specialised coaching and business services (HR, legal, strategy) with clear exit timelines. Many incubators now opt to invest in their incubated companies. Some key parameters on how incubators differ are: stakeholders and region, value proposition to start-ups and funding activities. Some incubators may be specific to certain sectors or stages of selected companies.

We conducted a roundtable discussion moderated by Rohan Chinchwadkar with the heads of leading academic incubators of India to understand the dynamics of incubating in the current start-up ecosystem. The panellists were Poyni Bhatt, Tamaswati Ghosh, Rajiv Sawhney, Jayalakshmi Umadikar and Kunal Upadhyay. This chapter is an excerpt from that discussion.

Key Features of Different Academic Incubators

Rohan: What would be some of the features or practices of your incubator that you think differentiates it from others?

Kunal: We stopped calling ourselves an incubator long back. We think of ourselves as more than just a physical infrastructure provider. We call ourselves an entrepreneurship centre. For us, incubation is a process of de-risking enterprises and helping them overcome the proverbial valley

Exhibit 10.1: The distinction between incubator and accelerator

Incubator

vs

Accelerator

The definitions of incubator and accelerator are not very stringent globally. Depending on the sector and geography, they can last from a few months to a few years. What is common in the set of definitions, however, is the notion that incubators are longer term, less time-bound support for start-ups, especially the early-stage ones, to develop their products and businesses. If part of a university or government, they often come without equity stake costs. On the other hand, accelerators are shorter, fixed-term, cohort-based support programmes from which start-ups 'graduate'. They are suitable for more mature start-ups that have their product and business model but need support to refine and rapidly scale up. Often competitive to get into, these programmes frequently come with the promise of some funds in return for equity.

of death.[1] We find that most start-ups fail not because the product was bad but because it was not a good fit for the problem it was intended to solve. Therefore, our focus is on helping start-ups achieve the product–market fit[2] through two ways. First, we provide capital to run their experiments, and second, equally importantly, we help in getting the product–market fit by enabling product validation through connecting them to appropriate stakeholders, who are primarily the end customers. We have a collection of services set up around this goal, be it research, venture funds, government cooperation or accelerator programmes.

Rajiv: For us too, the principle is similar. Physical support is a low priority. We try to be the sounding board that can help start-ups ask the right questions and answer them. We try and see how we can navigate their journey, how we can try and open doors for them. I would also like to add here that though we are in an academic institution, we are open to all. In fact, the number of Indian Institute of Management (IIM) Bangalore alumni who participate in any of our programmes would be less than 5 per cent.

Poyni: While there is overlap with what Kunal and Rajiv mentioned, one of our differentiators comes from our strength that being part of an Indian Institute of Technology (IIT) gives. We are able to provide core engineering and technology support to companies. Second, we are able to leverage some basic funds, such as government grants, to create pipelines of companies. Third, we have some very-early-stage companies to whom we provide considerable handholding and mentoring support. We help them not only to understand their product–market fit but also to connect them to industry mentors and external stakeholders like consumers and manufacturers. We have tried to create our own ecosystem and mentors. In a nutshell, we provide the three Ms – money, mentors and marketing – while engaging with very-early-stage to even mature start-ups in our acceleration programme. We focus on various stages – from starting up to scaling up.

Tamaswati: Like incubators at other IITs, deep tech is indeed our forte and key differentiator. However, the wide impact and value created by our start-ups bring out certain unique features and value propositions from the IIT Madras Incubation Cell (IITMIC). First, we have a very strong participation from IITM's faculty members (over 10 per cent of institute faculty are co-founders in our start-ups), and this underlines our ability to translate cutting edge innovations to market requirements. We have also been open to innovators and entrepreneurs beyond IITM, as reflected in our portfolio with diverse founder backgrounds. Our focus has been on enabling entrepreneurs to create sustainable and scalable enterprises with deep tech innovation and impact as key drivers: many at the forefront of national efforts in sectors including energy, water, e-mobility, maritime, IoT, space, data sciences, manufacturing, nanoscience and non-destructive evaluation. Second, over the years, we have created a thriving ecosystem consisting of pipelines within IITM; a global mentor network comprising of alumni, industry, tech leaders and serial entrepreneurs; an investor and partner network among angels, VCs, CSR funds and banks; managers of central start-up schemes (such as Oil & Gas) and agencies; and a vast network of business support service providers. This helps us support our start-ups over a longer time period, with a flexible or 'exit when you want' approach. It helps us in steering them through the very challenging initial years of the slow-starting deep tech space where other sources of support or funders are more cautious to move in. The third differentiating factor is that the IITM incubation and start-up hub is located within IITM Research Park (largest such innovation hub in the country), housing R&D centres of national and multinational corporates and research centres of IITM from across diverse domains. This provides start-ups with a dynamic environment where tech innovation and commercialisation converge and flourish.

Exhibit 10.2: What are research parks?

University Research Parks, also known as Science Parks or Technology Parks, are real estate spaces where different stakeholders come together to foster innovation and research translation especially in the deep science sectors. The first such entity to be set up was the Stanford Research Park. Since then, the concept has evolved to entail what is called the "triple helix model." The three helices comprise the local governments, industry and academia, which work together to contribute to the regional and national knowledge economy. Scholars have recently proposed adding a fourth helix – users of innovation – to facilitate the development of socially impactful innovations. In practice, members of the helices are co-located and often share office infrastructure, utility infrastructure and social networks. These diverse social networks have been found to be crucial in fostering innovation.

Evaluating Start-ups for Incubation

Rohan: What are the selection criteria you look at while evaluating applicant start-ups? How does it differ from those being used by angel investors and venture capitalists (VCs)?

Kunal: Since we wear many hats, we receive applicants from a pre-idea stage to a Series B[3] stage. This determines both the criteria we look at and the way we differ from angel investors and VCs. Different stages of a start-up have different risk profiles. When we get a pre-idea application, we mainly look at the individual's or team's profile and passion. In the next Stage, we look at the market they are targeting in terms of growth potential. We might provide a small amount of capital at this stage to help them access the right stakeholders for developing the product. The next stage involves exploring whether or not the team's product has real customers, and helping them achieve the product–market fit. From a funding standpoint, we may be putting in a small investment of around ₹250K to ₹500K. The more mature the start-up is, the more the data points exist to investigate the product–market fit in terms of customer segments, market focus, competition, global demand and even operational issues such as risks and addition of senior members to the team. Thus, how we view start-ups changes across stages.

Poyni: We too have similar criteria. Most of us will have similar criteria till Series A and B. In our case, we do not commit to funding upfront. Where we differ from mainstream investors is that we also engage with start-ups which have a wild or disruptive idea or have a social strategic mission. These are perceived as very high risk by mainstream investors or promise extremely low returns. For example, we have incubated a start-up that in the late 2000s had gotten rejected by almost a 100 VCs. Today they have almost ₹10 billion in revenue. Other examples include innovative medical or defence sector start-ups. Or in the social impact sector, we have incubated start-ups with innovative products, such as low-cost wheelchairs, which have gone on to expand in 15–20 odd countries. We are able to leverage government grants to fund such early stage or non-mainstream sectors like deep science and social impact projects, which would be considered high risk, low return or long horizon by mainstream investors.

Rajiv: Just to add to what Poyni said, at the early stage, resilience, resolve and motivation is something we try and see in the individual or team. It is important to understand where they are coming from – do they have it in them for the roller-coaster ride that is entrepreneurship?

Rohan: Jaya, can you elaborate a bit on social start-ups?

Jaya: In Rural Technologies Business Incubator (RTBI) and IITMIC, we have several start-ups trying to make a social impact and work in sectors that are critical to the country. All these entrepreneurs come in with a certain passion and vision. Especially when it comes to start-ups for which making a social impact is of far more value, we need to help them understand that profitability and being cash positive is important even when they are developing their ventures. We stay continuously engaged with them to help them to stay on track, grow their ventures and also accomplish what it is they hold so dear in terms of the vision. For us, the success of the start-up is to understand how true they have stayed to that vision and not necessarily how much investment they have raised. Which is why, when they come to us, even if we feel that they need little bit more work to be incubation-ready, we stay in touch and try to help them. Through our engagement with them or through conversations with our senior start-ups, with our mentors, we kind of try to give them a glimpse of what the typical start-up journey is like and what it takes to scale.

Funding Incubatees

Rohan: How do you decide which start-ups should get funding? What percentage of your incubatees do you fund?

Poyni: For us, funding is not by default and start-ups have to apply. We have an investment committee, comprising a few board members and investors from our community, which takes the decision. In this case, the exit[4] potential is a major criterion in terms of whether we will be able to get returns if the venture exits in 5–7 years. Around 40 per cent of our start-ups get funding. The amount of funding, though, is small right now. We also invest in ventures which may not receive the next round of mainstream funding but carry disruptive ideas or social impact that really convinces us. To be honest, it is impact rather than exit that we consider in such cases.

Rajiv: We have a process through which about one in eight to ten ventures ends up receiving financial support from us. We too have an investment committee comprising a diverse set of people with backgrounds ranging from VC to PE[5] to finance to industry and academia. We ask the start-ups to apply for funds and decide on where our finite funds would be best invested.

Tamaswati: We currently provide seed funding to incubated start-ups as a combination of grants, soft loans and convertible debt, which is governed by an Investment Committee (comprising mostly investors as members). Start-ups need to apply, and funding is not by default. ₹0.5–1 million is given as an initial grant for prototype and product development, and up to ₹4.5 million is disbursed as soft loan, for early market traction and revenue with an option to convert to equity. We also enable grant funding from PSU[6] and Industry CSR[7] (up to ₹10 million) following the required due diligence, and more recently working capital loans (up to ₹2 million) from banks. Around 47 per cent of our start-ups have been supported so far. We also connect and facilitate regular interaction between start-ups and angel investors and VCs from our extended network.

Kunal: Our engagement with start-ups is along a continuum across different stages of the company. We mainly have two verticals of engaging with start-ups: local incubation and accelerator. On an annual basis, we engage with close to 200 very-early-stage start-ups across these two business units. Of these 200, we would be providing funding support to about 50–75. Again, for this we run early-stage and later programmes. Early-stage programmes such as “That’s the Power of Idea”, “India Innovation Growth Programme” and others work through the provision of grants in the range of ₹0.5–4 million for prototype or product development.[8] The grant capital source is typically the government, be it the centre or state, and their mandate is to facilitate grants without taking equity. For slightly later stage programmes, we have created seed funds, raised CSR-linked funds and embarked on a bunch of other initiatives. For example, on the inclusion and social impact side, we are partnering with a host of donors such as Gates Foundation, Dell Foundation, Omidyar Network and JP Morgan. As part of this, we provide up to ₹5–6 million, not only as grants but also as equity-linked investments wherein we would take a stake of anywhere between 2 per cent and 5 per cent. Finally, at an even later stage, we would possibly be backing around 10–15 companies on an annual basis through our own funds or commercial seed funds.

Rohan: What kind of funding instruments do you use?

Tamaswati: For early-stage start-ups, we give small grants for prototype and product development. We usually give larger seed support at a later stage through soft loans, which in some cases is convertible to equity.

Kunal: It is similar for us. For very early stages, it is a grant. For ventures somewhere in between, the funds either take the form of convertible[9] or equity. Our experience has been that typically, for investments up to ₹5 million, we would not take more than 5–7 per cent equity or would stay put as convertible. At a later stage, when we are putting in much bigger cheques of the order of around $2 million, we may end up taking anywhere between 10–20 per cent stake in the company based on how the round construct is.

Current Incubator Challenges

Rohan: What are the challenges you face as an incubator manager in the current ecosystem?

Kunal: The fundamental challenge for me is how to scale up the throughput of our incubators. How do we increase research translation from our labs and convert them to real high-end deep science and deep tech companies? That is the challenge we are grappling with. Between IIT Bombay and IIT Madras, we have hundreds of great companies, but how do we take them to the next level? Being an IIT Madras alumnus, I have a soft corner for it but even objectively, the work that IIT Madras has done in the context is phenomenal. The research translation output has been pioneering, not only the IITM Incubation Centre and Research Park, but even beyond those in a bunch of other centres at IIT Madras. Much more of that needs to happen and many more researchers, scientists and students need to be commercialising deep tech and deep science innovation beyond Artificial Intelligence. In my mind, that is the biggest challenge that the country faces today. And without mincing words, I would say that capital is critical.

Poyni: Be it in technological or management institutes, I believe the challenge for incubators is to stay relevant and offer meaningful value propositions as the larger ecosystem evolves. With maturity of the system, investors and start-ups are getting closer. Start-ups may not be motivated to come to incubation centres and incur extra cost in terms of equity and other fees. In that case, only deep science start-ups requiring long gestation periods will opt for incubation. If incubators do not want to be reduced to a co-working space, they have to evolve. I do believe CIIE.CO has done a remarkable job in that evolution. They have enhanced their core strength of management knowledge by building a mentorship network and establishing funds. At our end, we are engaging with several investors who refer pre-incubation stage companies to us. Once we bring the companies to a certain maturity, the investors are willing to fund the ventures. We are continuously looking for ways to evolve keeping the larger ecosystem in mind.

Tamaswati: We have grown at break-neck pace over the last seven years since launch, digesting prior experiences at the Incubation Cell; spearheading policies at both state and national levels; setting up business support services and partnerships; engaging with government, industry, angel and VC investors, and CSR bodies; and indeed, overseeing the mushrooming of the start-up ecosystem at IITM and Research Park. IITMIC's main focus, going forward, is to set an agenda and charter the course for the coming years. We wish to stabilise our growth and make it sustainable, while also emerging as a national hub for deep tech start-ups. We envision becoming an aspirational force for young entrepreneurs across the country, as 'the place to be' to build global brands from Indian technological innovations and eventually expanding our presence in the ASEAN and African region. On the other hand, we are looking at partnerships for start-ups to receive stronger support for scale-up efforts, whether through industrial support or high-impact funds. We are exploring alternative routes for transfer and translation of academic innovations and are engaging more with the industry and government for this. We also wish to develop ways to replicate our model nationally and in the wider region, and engaging more strongly with other colleges and universities is a key step in this process. All of this requires upskilling our existing workforce, while also acquiring much more talent as well as access to funds to fuel this growth. However, these are positive challenges to have and we look forward to this next and exciting phase of our activities!

COVID-19 and Virtual Incubation

Rohan: How has the Covid pandemic impacted your incubators? Has there been a push towards virtual incubation?

Poyni: How Covid has impacted us is closely associated with the value proposition that we offer. The fundamental value proposition and motivation for any institute to host an incubator is to leverage the internal strength of that organisation. Being an engineering and science-based incubator, a key investment or resource value addition of ours is the physical infrastructure we provide in terms of laboratories and equipment. Due to Covid, we have to think about how to continue with active physical infrastructure support while engaging in an increasingly remote manner. We have been interacting with start-ups virtually, especially when focussing on intangibles like product–market fit, but I am not sure we will completely switch to a virtual model as we are also investing significantly in our lab infrastructure, given the pipeline and the interest from potential incubatees both inside and outside the campus.

Tamaswati: Although the impact of the pandemic has been brutal on the start-up landscape in the country, it has also been an opportunity to change for many: work with strained resources, innovate, reimagine businesses and pivot to quickly respond to new market behaviours. We too had to quickly shift gears. Interactions were more virtual and hence access to help and mentors was not bound to any office hours. Our support was more to help start-ups deal with their immediate challenges, including providing short-term loans to many struggling with cash flow. It was heartening to see the resilience of the start-ups during the Q1–Q2 period, with no stoppage of business activities. Q3 saw businesses bouncing back, revenues picking up, operations gradually reaching pre-Covid levels. Some of our start-ups continued to attract investments, with most closing rounds towards Q3 of the year. With respect to incubation activities, we did see a decrease in the pipeline. However, we have not shifted away from our original approach to incubation. Being a deep tech incubator, we truly believe in the benefits of physical incubation whereby start-ups can fully leverage the different strengths of the ecosystem, including access to specialised labs and the infrastructure and the peer network.

Kunal: The entire start-up landscape has gone through or will go through a significant shift because of Covid. Many businesses that had not achieved product–market fit many not be able to do so anymore because the market will change. They might have to go back to the table and rethink their fundamental offering. So, in my mind as an incubator manager, the biggest challenge that we face is the uncertainty brought about by Covid. However, our conviction in focussing on the strong basics of technology and product–market fit was validated. The work has dropped a bit in terms of investments, especially in terms of commercial investments, because we have to be cautious in reserving money for follow-on investments. As regards virtual incubation, even traditionally, a large chunk of our work has been virtual in nature. The big change has been that the 20–25 per cent of physical element that used to exist has come down to nil. However, we have used this as an opportunity to democratise the whole process and scale up our regional offerings in Rajasthan and Gujarat across the country – be it workshops or start-up engagement.

Rohan: This has been a fantastic conversation. On behalf of the iVEIN team, I would like to thank all of you for taking the time to be here and sharing wonderful insights in a frank way. We wish you the best of luck and success for your journey ahead.

Panellists

Poyni Bhatt is CEO of Society for Innovation & Entrepreneurship (SINE), IIT Bombay. She has been part of the founding team of SINE, the technology business incubator at IIT Bombay, and has been managing the incubator since 2004. She has been involved in 140+ start-ups incubated at SINE. Poyni actively contributes to the entrepreneurial ecosystem and is also a member of the boards of several incubators in India.

Kunal Upadhyay is Co-founder and Managing Partner, Bharat Innovation Fund, CIIE. Kunal co-founded CIIE. CO – The Innovation Continuum – providing investment, insights and incubation support for start-ups. He has experience in setting up and leading venture funds (Bharat Innovation Fund, Bharat Inclusion Seed Fund and Infuse Ventures) and accelerator funds (CIIE Initiatives, iAccelerator, Bharat Inclusion Initiative, Power of Ideas). He was listed in the Economic Times 40 under Forty in 2018.

Rajiv Sawhney is COO of NSRCEL, IIM Bangalore. Prior to joining NSRCEL in 2016, Rajesh garnered diverse industry experience with about 15 years in the telecom industry. He was part of the Telecom Startup team at Hutchison Telecom that led one of the biggest business growths India has seen and has built shareholder value of $18.8 billion for Hutchison Whampoa.

Tamaswati Ghosh is CEO of IIT Madras Incubation Cell. A graduate of Queen's University, Canada (BSc Honors Biochemistry and BA Mathematics) and Imperial College London, UK (PhD Molecular Biophysics), Tamaswati has served as the CEO of IITM Incubation Cell since its inception in 2013, and in 2016, took up the additional role of CEO, IITM's RTBI. Living across four continents of the world has contributed to her unique worldview and ability to steer work in diverse teams.

Jayalakshmi Umadikar is Head of Corporate Connect, Academic Liaison & Social Start-ups Portfolio, IIT Madras Incubation Cell. Jaya has over 25 years of varied technology experience, from teaching and research to software development. Of this, she has over six years of personal entrepreneurial experience, as a partner in a technology start-up venture in Israel. She has been associated with the IIT Madras incubation ecosystem for over eight years. She is currently helping the IITM Incubation Cell strengthen its support system to start-ups so that they can grow and scale-up more successfully.

Endnotes

[1]Valley of death indicates the period in the life of a start-up during which it experiences negative net cash flows, that is, the start-up spends more than it earns. Start-ups have to rely on external financing to survive the valley of death.

[2]Product–market fit means being in a good market with a product that can satisfy that market.

[3]A start-up usually raises money from VCs in different rounds at periodic intervals of time. Series B financing is the second round of funding that a start-up raises from VCs and is usually at a higher valuation than the first round or Series A. Before Series A, start-ups may raise money from sources like incubators, grants, angel investors, seed funds and early-stage VCs who provide seed and pre-Series A funding.

[4]Exit is an important stage in start-up financing when the investor sells the stake in the start-up, either partially or completely, in order to realise returns from the investment.

[5]Private equity

[6]Public sector undertaking

[7]Corporate social responsibility

[8]See Innovation section roundtable chapter for definitions

[9]Convertible note is a commonly used financial instrument to invest in start-ups. It is a form of debt that is designed to convert into equity, under pre-determined conditions such as a future round of financing.

Section III

FUNDING

IN BRIEF

- In the past decade (2011–2020), venture funding to start-ups and the number of start-ups that have been venture funded have seen remarkable growth, with a CAGR of 76 per cent and 49 per cent, respectively.
- The funding rounds at the base of the start-up pyramid have been shrinking since 2016, with a drop of close to 29 per cent in the number of angel rounds.
- The trends in terms of spatial distribution of venture investments show a high level of persistence, with Bangalore, Delhi and Mumbai securing 91 per cent of all VC investments (on average) throughout the decade.
- Start-ups in the Retail, FinTech and TravelTech sectors have accounted for more than half (close to 57 per cent) of the total funding received by all start-ups.
- Despite the milestones achieved, only 11 per cent of start-ups succeed in receiving external funding. Moreover, funding in India is excessively skewed to late-stage start-ups – about 70 per cent of the total funding has been in Series C and beyond, as opposed to the global benchmark of 48 per cent.

ANALYTICAL ARTICLE

11

Venture Financing in India: The Seven Trends that Defined the Decadal Trajectory

Akshay Natteri Mangadu, Neha Singh and Thillai Rajan A

Mangadu, AN, Singh, N and Thillai Rajan A. 2021. "Venture Financing in India: The Seven Trends that Defined the Decadal Trajectory". In *Shifting Orbits: Decoding the Trajectory of the Indian Start-up Ecosystem*, edited by Thillai Rajan A, Srivardhini K Jha, Joffi Thomas and Rohan Chinchwadkar, 118–132. Hyderabad: Universities Press (India) Private Limited.

The Rise of Venture Capital Investing in India

India houses the world's third largest start-up ecosystem,[1] with over 70,000 start-ups, of which 21 are Unicorns[2] (valued at over $1 billion). The emergence of a young and technically skilled crop of entrepreneurs, along with the rise of an economically empowered middle class, have put India at the forefront of the start-up revolution.[3] Venture capital (VC) is an important source of financing that has been fuelling this surge in start-ups in India, with over 850 funds[4] providing over $175 billion in funding since 1990.[5]

Several key stakeholders, including the government and large overseas institutional investors, have identified VC funds as an ideal vehicle to invest and grow the start-up environment in India.[6] For example, in 2016, the central government of India, as a part of its 'Startup India, Stand Up India' initiative had announced a corpus of ₹100 billion to be invested in leading venture funds in the Indian start-up ecosystem.[7] Further, several state governments, including those of Bihar, Gujarat, Karnataka, Kerala, Rajasthan, Tamil Nadu and Uttar Pradesh, have established their own corpuses (that is, fund of funds)[8] to be invested in start-ups through venture funds.[9] Venture financing has therefore become the investment vehicle of choice for private and public players to enable the formalisation and future growth of the Indian start-up economy.

In this chapter, we identify the key trends that have characterised the growth of the Indian VC industry in the last decade and discuss the contours that the industry needs to evolve to in the coming years.

Overall Trends in Venture Financing

Broadly speaking, the growth rate of VC funding in India has been among the top three globally since 2011. The compound annual growth rate (CAGR) in the real[10] amount of funding received between 2011 and 2020 was a staggering 76 per cent. In this period, about 10,000 companies were funded, with each firm receiving an average of ₹605 million.[11] The number of start-ups funded in 2020 was four times that in 2011 – a significant growth, despite the COVID-19 pandemic affecting the investments in 2020. Exhibit 11.1 summarises the marked increase in venture financing in India during the decade ending 2020. We identify three prominent trends in venture financing and explore the factors driving these changes.

1. The funding rounds at the base of the start-up pyramid have been shrinking

While the amount of funding received has grown through the years, the number of companies funded each year peaked at 1,531 in 2016, after which there has been a steady fall, with a 9 per cent annual decline on average between 2016 and 2020 (Exhibit 11.2). The reduction in the number of funding rounds has been driven by the reduction in the angel funding rounds. Specifically, the number of angel rounds dropped by 29 per cent on average annually between 2016 and 2020. However, it is well known among industry observers that the number of angel investors, angel networks and total quantity of angel investments have increased during this period (see Chapter 12 for further insights on the growth in angel networks and investors). Our results indicate that though the size of the average funding round has increased, the number of funding rounds has decreased. Angel-funded companies form the deal pipeline for subsequent VC investors. Therefore, the reduction in

Exhibit 11.1: Trends in the number of companies funded and total funding amount (2011–2020)

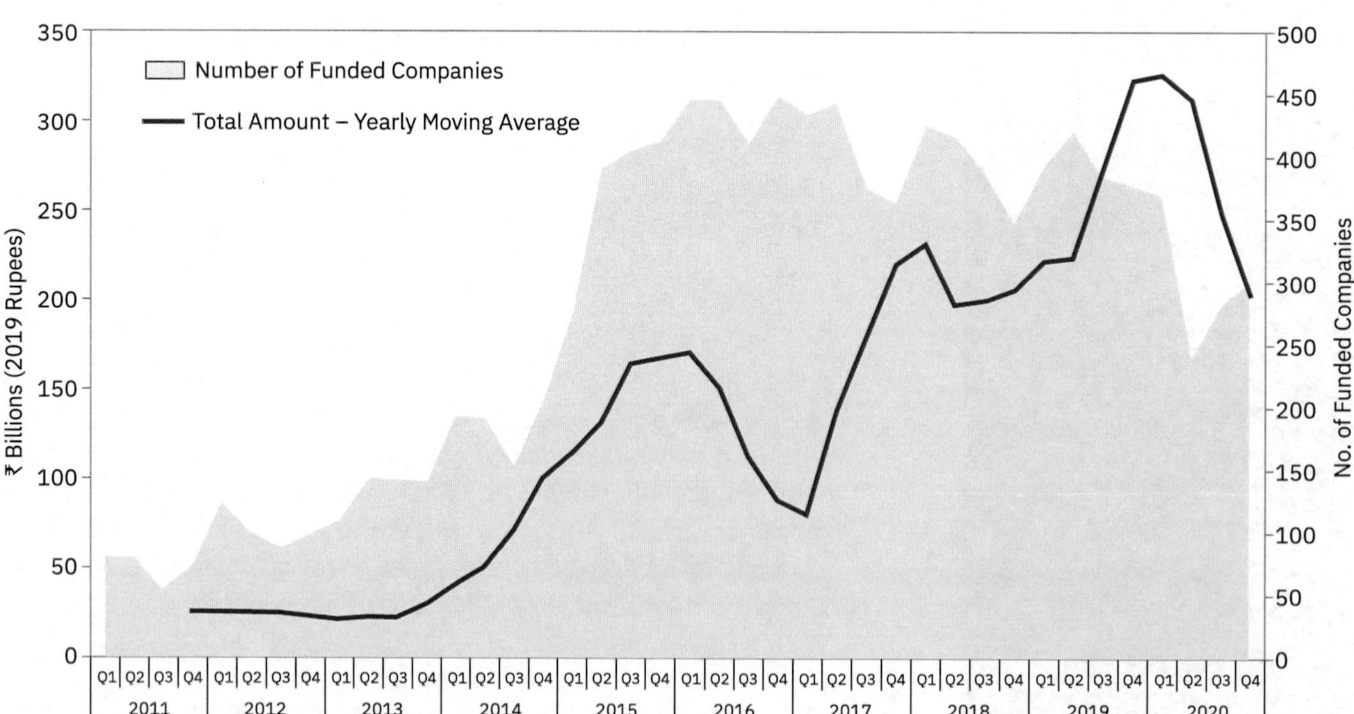

Source: Tracxn database (accessed March 1, 2021)

the number of angel rounds could impact the long-term growth of the industry.

Interestingly, the period 2016–20 was characterised by robust growth in the number of incubators. Between 2014 and 2019, over 217 incubators entered the Indian market,[12] rapidly increasing the incubation support capacity for start-ups.[13] While the increasing capacity for incubation has been a welcome development for early-stage start-ups, they cannot fully compensate for the reduction in funding rounds, since the main focus of incubators has been to provide non–funding-related support. Funding support, even when available, did not exceed ₹5 million in most cases. The components of a vibrant start-up ecosystem should not only measure the number of start-ups formed or total VC funding, but also specifically consider the start-ups that have been funded at the base of the pyramid. As they say, the extent of growth of the pyramid is dependent as much on the base that can support this growth. The growth in the number of incubators was supposed to have the catalytic effect of more companies receiving angel funding. However, it seems to have resulted in the opposite, namely, crowding out of the number of companies that have been receiving angel investment. The reasons for the reduction in angel rounds need to be identified and appropriate policy support measures need to be taken to reverse this trend for the long-term growth of the start-up sector in India.

2. Increase in the average size of funding rounds, rather than in the number of funding rounds, has been the main driver of growth in VC funding

Between 2011 and 2016, the average quarterly growth of the size of a funding round was 10 per cent. However, post 2016, the growth rate in the size of the funding rounds was 31 per cent (Exhibit 11.3). This growth was seen across all investment stages and was most pronounced for Series C+ investments followed by angel and seed-stage investments (Exhibit 11.4). The pronounced impact of this trend is that a decreasing number of start-ups have been successful in attracting a larger share of funding. Investors seem to be keen to increase the size of their bets rather than the number of horses they are willing to bet on.

Exhibit 11.2: Trends in the number of rounds conducted each year (2011–2020)

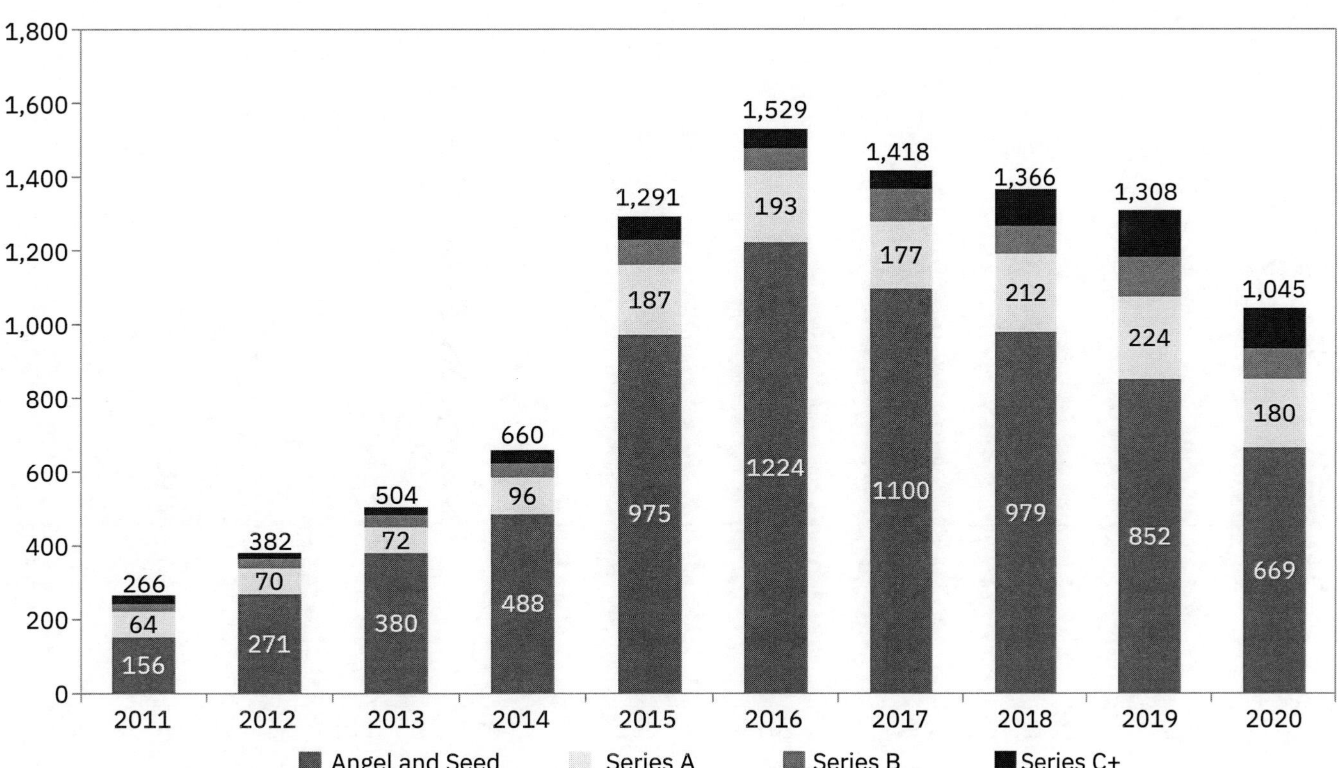

Source: Tracxn database (accessed March 1, 2021)

Exhibit 11.3: Average funding per company (2011–2020)

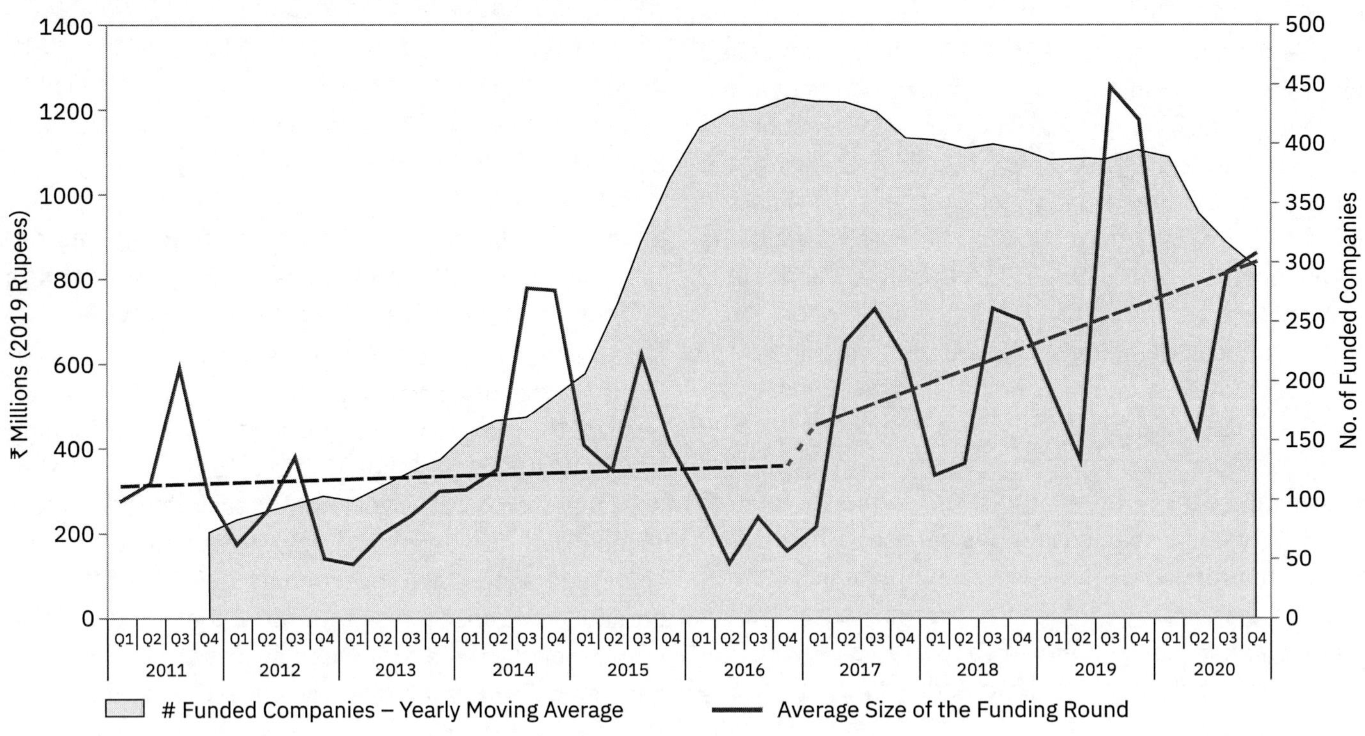

Source: Tracxn database (accessed March 1, 2021)

Exhibit 11.4: Annual real year-on-year growth rate in the average amount of funding per round, by stage of investment (2011–2020)

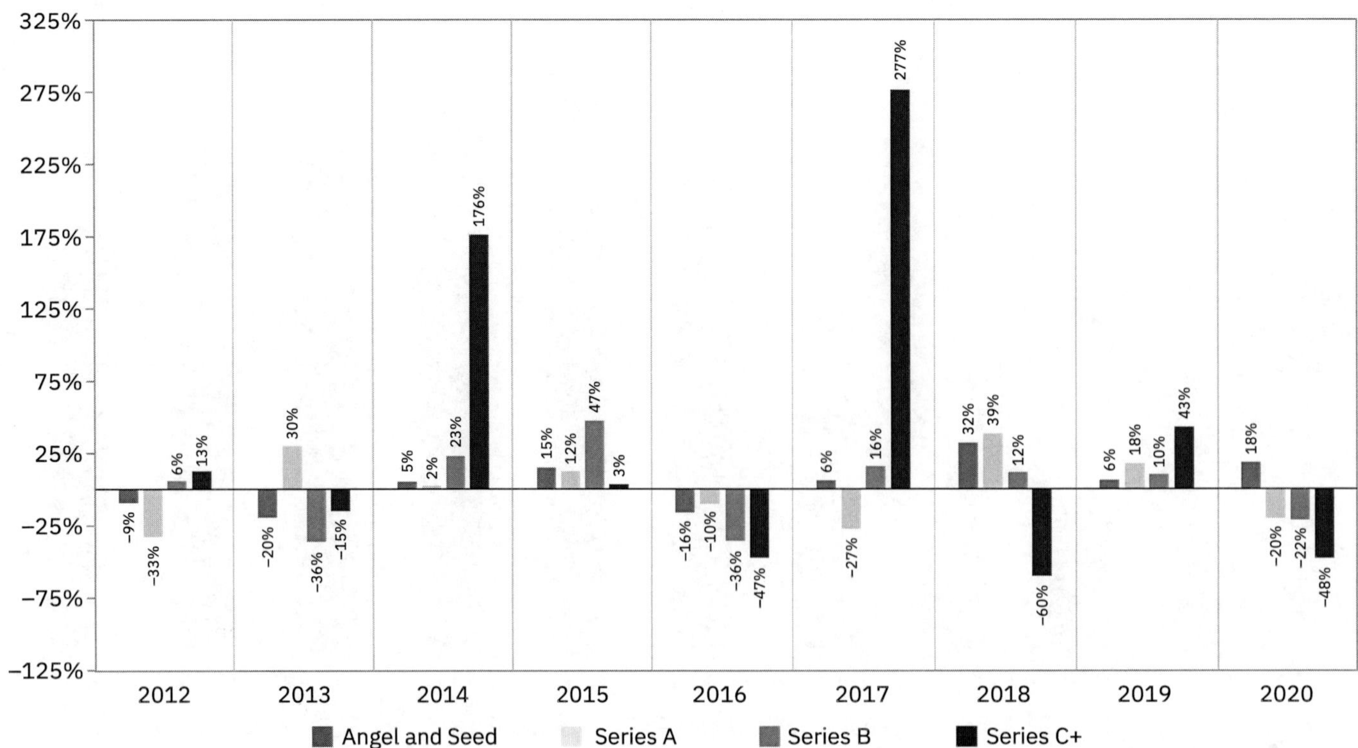

Source: Tracxn database (accessed March 1, 2021)

Exhibit 11.5: Cumulative distribution of total amount of funding and number of rounds (2011–2020)

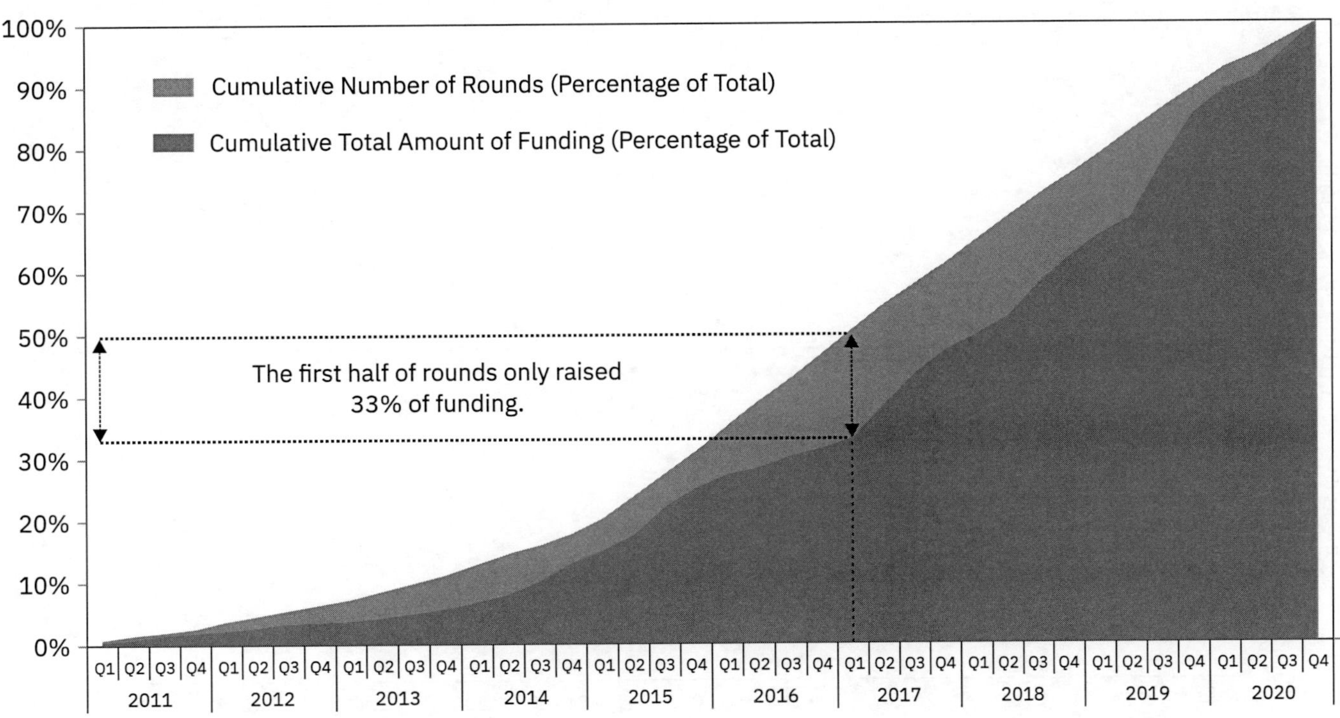

Source: Tracxn database (accessed March 1, 2021)

The scale of this change is evident in Exhibit 11.5. We observe that the first 50 per cent of funding rounds (before 2017) raised only 33 per cent of funding, whereas the second half of the rounds funded raised the remaining 67 per cent of funding, highlighting the gap between the amount of funding received and the number of rounds funded. The reasons behind this trend could be several. Firstly, from the demand side, the average capital needed for the start-up to achieve 'escape velocity' could have increased in recent years. Investors are therefore allocating more capital to their investee companies. Secondly, from the supply side, the fee structure in the VC industry is based on the quantum of total capital invested and does not necessarily depend on the number of companies invested. Investing more per company can optimise the effort–benefit ratio.

3. VC funding is highly correlated with the underlying economy, rather than the stock market

The overall trends in the amount of VC funding received over the years is well correlated with economic metrics and market indices such as gross value added (GVA) and Sensex. VC funding is also correlated with the dollar-to-rupee exchange rate, meaning a depreciation in the rupee *potentially* attracts more funding. This is a plausible outcome, given that a large amount of capital to VC funds and investments in India has come from overseas. While a weak stock market leads to a reduction in VC investments since investors could potentially limit investing in alternative assets because of wealth loss as a result of falling stock prices, a bull run in the stock market need not lead to a growth in VC funding, as the COVID-19 pandemic situation indicates. Thus, it is felt that VC funding correlates more to the underlying economy rather than the stock markets. The worsened economic situation did not adversely affect the stock market, while the amount invested in start-ups did witness a sharp downturn. In a time of economic uncertainty, investors tend to preserve their capital, and hence, avoid inherently risky investment options such as start-ups. For the start-up founder, this result has strong implications. The fund-raising window can close quickly when the economic conditions turn adverse. It is therefore important to make haste during fund raising or be well capitalised to tide over periods of economic uncertainty.

Exhibit 11.6: Correlation of amount of VC funding with macroeconomic indicators (2011–2020)[14]

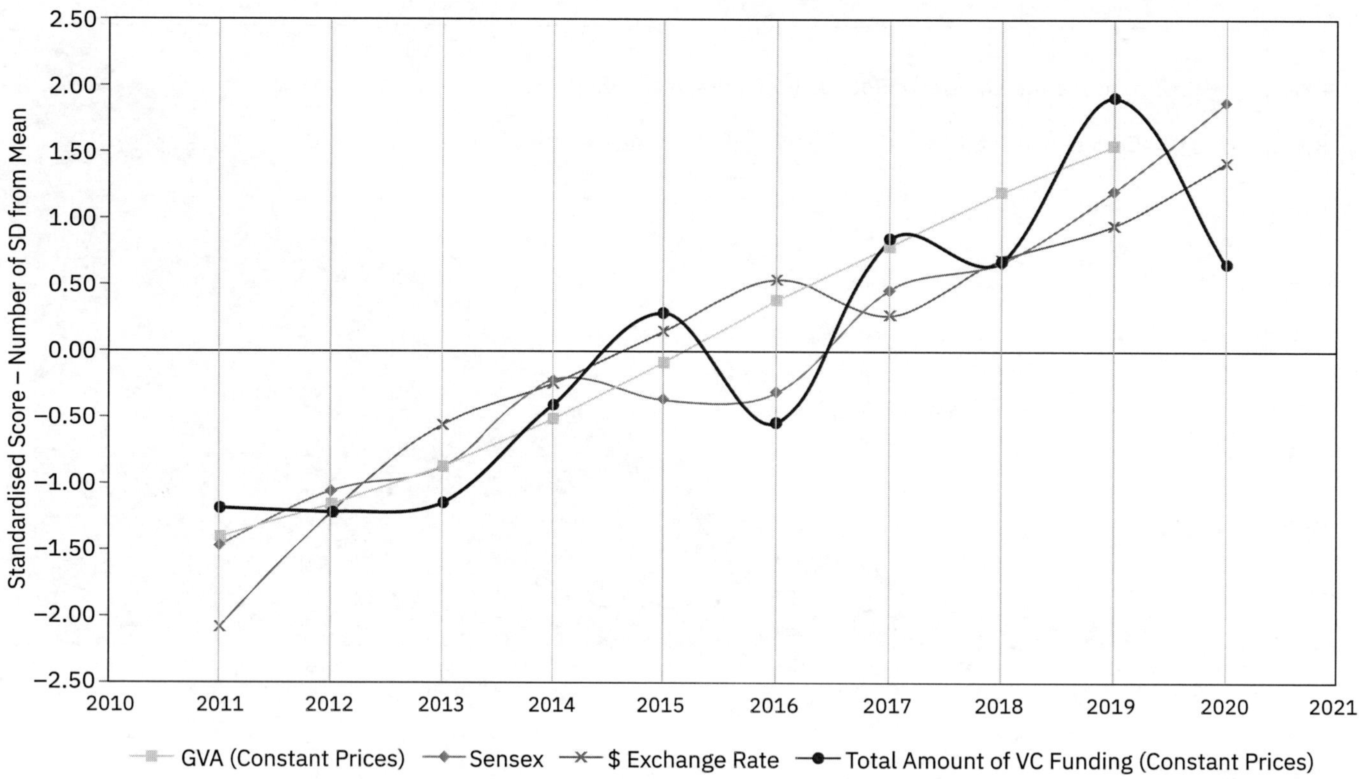

Source: Tracxn database (accessed March 1, 2021), BSE's Sensex data and World Bank's DataBank

Spatial Distribution of VC Funding

Over the past decade, India has seen extraordinary growth in 'start-up hubs', specifically in Tier 1 cities. Several factors have enabled certain cities to become start-up hubs, including access to funding, political leadership, business environment, policy and regulatory framework, access to a vibrant and productive talent pool, access to a broad client base and access to cheap and affordable office space. Additionally, the growth in the number of incubators and angel investors in Tier 1 cities in India has also led to a proliferation of start-ups in these cities.

4. The golden triangle of start-up hubs – Bangalore, Mumbai and Delhi

Start-ups based in three metropolitan cities, namely, Bangalore, Mumbai and Delhi, have accounted for the lion's share of VC funding in India. Between 2011 and 2020, on an average, 91 per cent of the total yearly VC funding went to start-ups in these three cities. Exhibit 11.7 presents the trend in the proportion of total VC funding received by the three hubs, over the years. The VC funding landscape has seen little change over the past decade, with Bangalore, Delhi and Mumbai consistently dominating. Exhibit 11.8 presents the distribution of active start-ups across nine prominent cities in India (based on the number of start-ups), and the distribution of amount of funding received across the cities. We see the domination of Bangalore, Delhi and Mumbai in both aspects. Specifically, despite having only 21 per cent of the active start-ups, Bangalore-based companies received a mammoth 42 per cent of all funding. On the other hand, though cities like Chennai, Hyderabad and Pune individually account for 7–8 per cent of start-ups, the start-ups in these cities received only 1–3 per cent of the funding. This could be due to the stage of the start-ups in the different cities. Bangalore (being one of the earliest cities where the start-up ecosystem blossomed) has more mature start-ups that are raising later-stage rounds with larger targets, while the start-ups in other cities are relatively new, raising early-stage funding. Further, there has been strong anecdotal evidence that early-round investors nudge the start-ups in other

Exhibit 11.7: Per cent of total venture funding received by start-ups in different cities (2011–2020)[15]

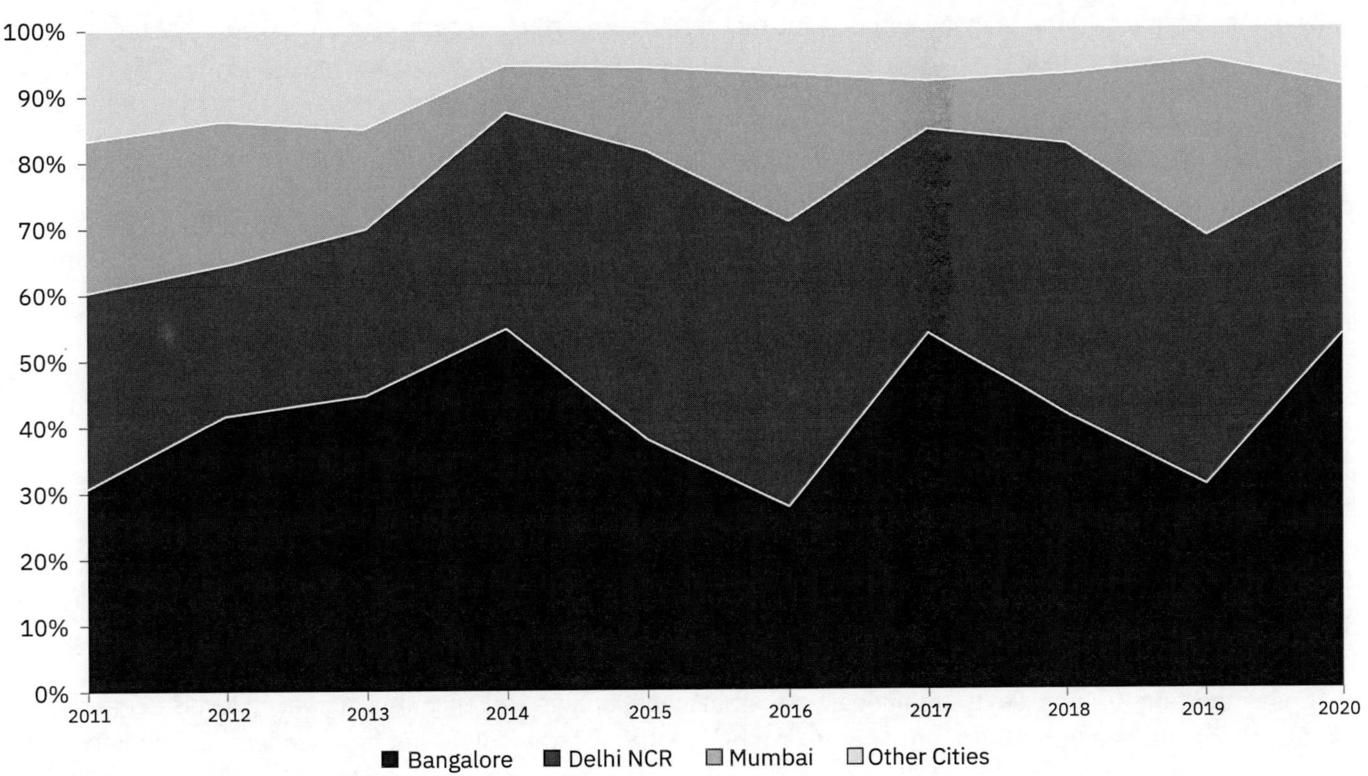

Source: Tracxn database (accessed March 1, 2021)

Exhibit 11.8: Distribution of active companies and the aggregate amount of funding for start-ups in prominent Indian cities (2011–2020)

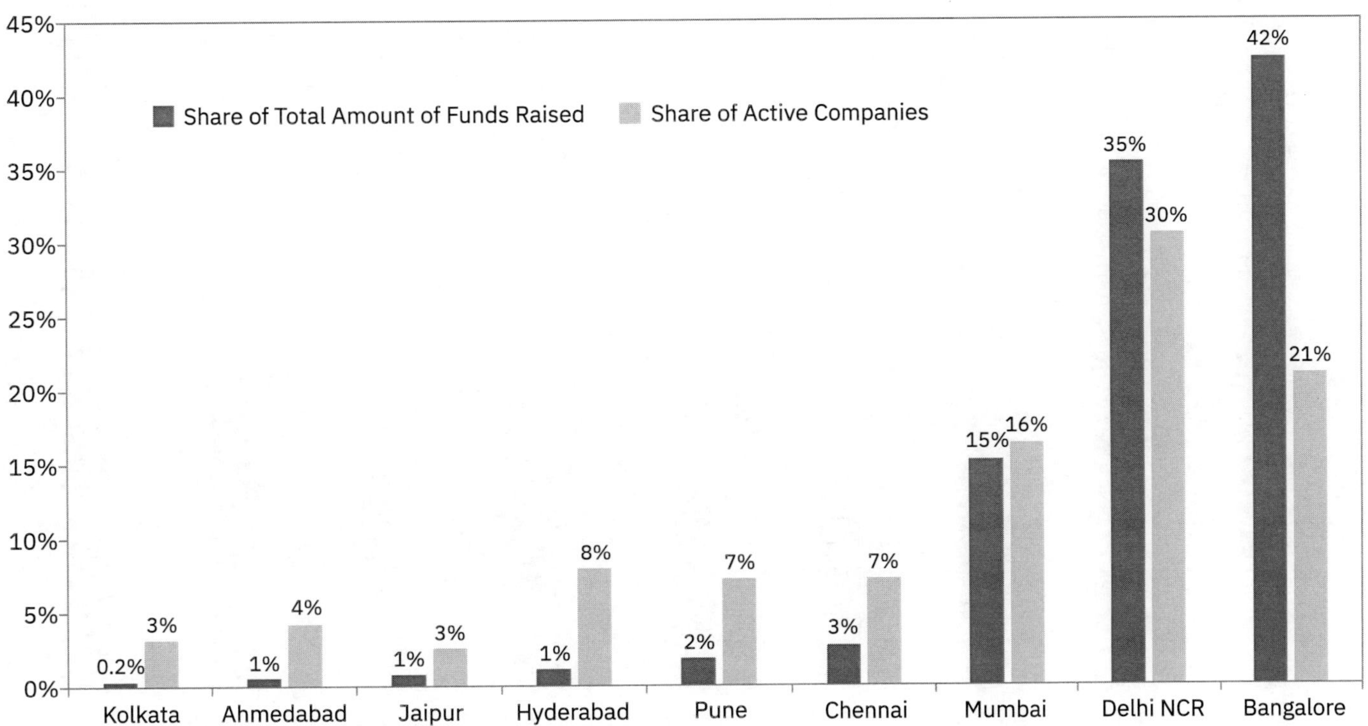

Source: Tracxn database (accessed March 1, 2021)

locations to migrate to these three cities (Bangalore, Delhi, Mumbai) at their later stages in order to attract a wider group of investors, talent and traction.

5. The potential future start-up hubs – Jaipur, Ahmedabad and Pune

The cumulative VC funding for start-ups in Jaipur, Ahmedabad, Bangalore and Pune posted significant growth rates in the past decade. The CAGR[16] for Jaipur in the past decade was the highest, at 189 per cent, followed by Ahmedabad at 86 per cent. These high rates could also be attributed to the low prevailing base in these cities. Bangalore, despite being the largest start-up hub, had the third highest CAGR of 61.1 per cent, followed by Pune in fourth place with 60.6 per cent, closely followed by Delhi and Chennai at 59 per cent and 49 per cent, respectively. Kolkata recorded the lowest growth rate among the nine cities, at 21 per cent. Exhibit 11.9 summarises the CAGRs for the various cities.

It is important to note that traditional industrial hubs such as the textile hub of Coimbatore–Tiruppur, the leather manufacturing hub of Kanpur–Lucknow, the heavy electricals hub of Vadodara or the chemical manufacturing hub of Durgapur–Asansol have not become start-up hubs as well.[17] Given that the majority of start-ups are in the technology and services space, cities with well-established infrastructure and talent pool in such sectors have taken the lead.

The phenomenal success of Bangalore, in particular, has been attributed to the symbiotic relationships between academia, industry and government, forming a 'triple helix', which is supported and bolstered by investors, human capital (mentors, skilled employees and nurturers) and robust markets.[18] The initial success of technology start-ups from Bangalore and the entrepreneurial wealth created therein has also been a very important reason for Bangalore becoming a leading start-up hub. It is therefore important for future hubs to not just be well-funded, but to also be well-staffed and guided. As they say, nothing succeeds like success. Nurturing potential start-ups that can become initial successes can seed the growth of the ecosystem. Policies that enable and encourge increased levels of interaction and partnership among academia, industry and government are of paramount importance in ensuring the development of robust start-up ecosystems.

Exhibit 11.9: CAGR of amount of funding received (inflation adjusted) (2011–2020)

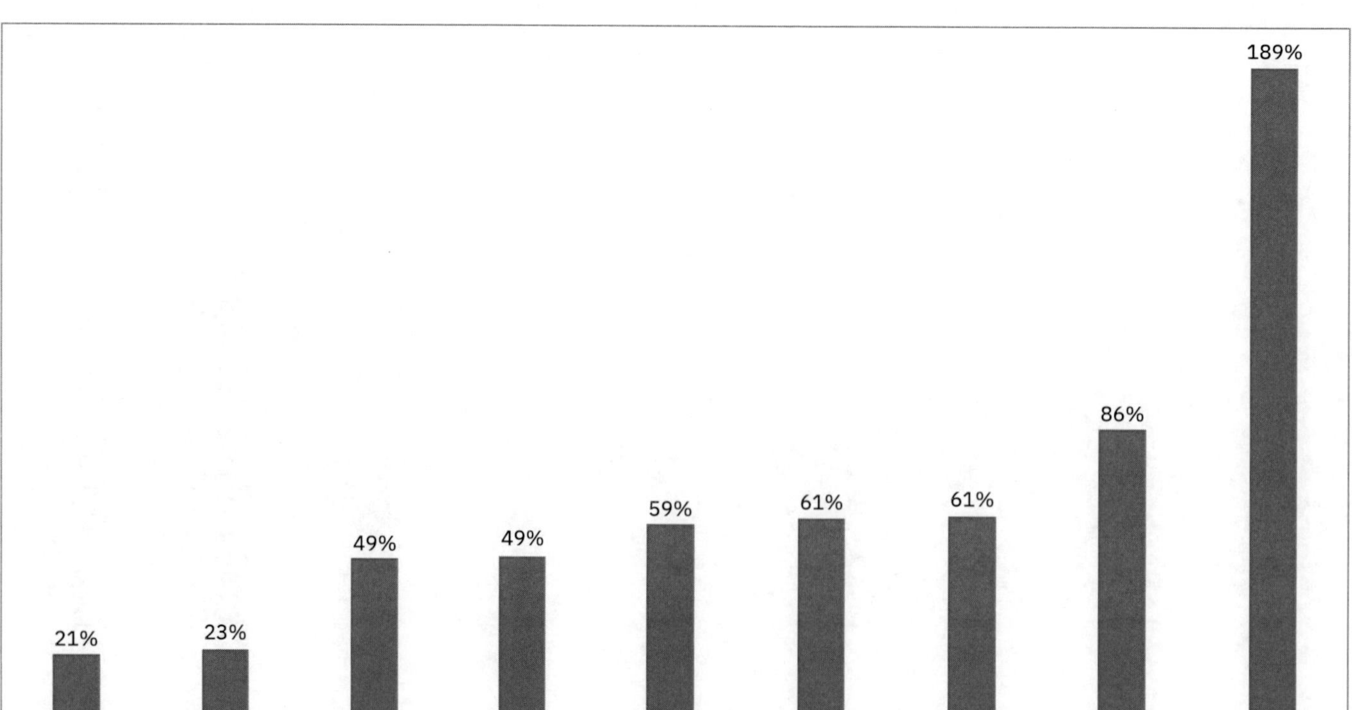

Source: Tracxn database (accessed March 1, 2021)

Exhibit 11.10: Total amount of funding received and total number of rounds, by sector (2011–2020)

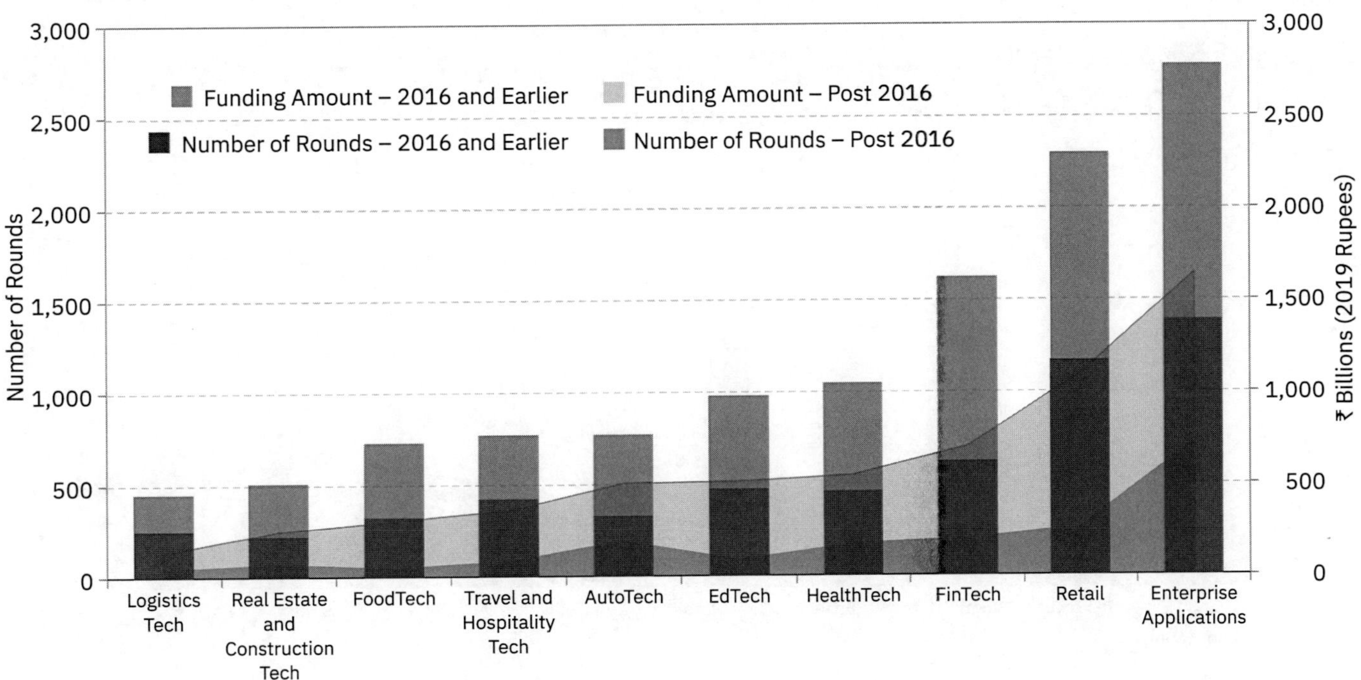

Source: Tracxn database (accessed March 1, 2021)

Sectoral Trends

6. The largest sectors in terms of VC funding are Retail, FinTech and TravelTech; Logistics and FoodTech are rising stars

Retail, FinTech, and Travel and Hospitality start-ups have received the largest amount of VC funding. The three sectors, put together, attracted 57 per cent of all VC funding between 2011 and 2020 (inflation adjusted). In all the three sectors, more than half the funding was received post 2016. Exhibit 11.10 presents the total amount of funding (after accounting for inflation), received by each sector between 2011 and 2020.

In terms of the number of rounds of funding raised, there have been more rounds for Enterprise Applications, followed by Retail and FinTech. These funding trends suggest the following: Firstly, except in one or two cases, the trends have persisted throughout the decade. There has not been much variation in the trend between the first half of the decade and the second half. Secondly, even within technology investments, much of the VC funding has been channelised to select sectors. These sectors reflect the growth and return opportunities for the investors. For example, VC capital flow to Retail start-ups is about seven times more than that to HealthTech. The capital flow in Retail probably also reflects the potential that is attributed to demographic dividend. On the other hand, entrepreneurs venturing in those sectors that attract lower levels of VC investment should also look at other options for raising capital for their companies.

An increase in the average amount of funding raised per round for a sector often indicates the VC investors' expectation for increased growth in the coming years for the start-ups in that sector. It is a good proxy to measure the confidence of investors in the success of start-ups in a given sector. Using this as a yardstick, we identify the upcoming start-up sectors in India.

Travel and Hospitality, Logistics and FoodTech have seen the largest growth in terms of the average funding raised per round. Treebo, Zoomcar, Grab, Zomato and cure.fit are some of the leading ventures that have received significant funding. Exhibit 11.11 presents the leading sectors in terms of average amount of funding raised per round. Unfortunately, the COVID-19 pandemic put paid to the growth of some of these sectors, specifically Travel and Hospitality. It remains to be seen whether the mojo can return to some of these

Exhibit 11.11: Average amount of funding raised per rounds by sector (2011 –2020)

Average Amount Raised per Round – ₹ Millions (2019)

Sector	2016 and Earlier	Post 2016
Enterprise Applications	138	224
HealthTech	158	291
Real Estate and Construction Tech	194	302
EdTech	102	500
Retail	621	815
FinTech	422	822
AutoTech	518	850
FoodTech	271	1,033
Logistics Tech	348	1,311
Travel and Hospitality Tech	477	1,429

– – - Average 2016 and Earlier ····· Average Post 2016

Source: Tracxn database (accessed March 1, 2021)

sectors, since consumer preferences and behaviour that could have altered because of the pandemic and the accompanying lockdown could persist for longer duration.

Further, to understand the sectors that have grown the most in terms of overall funding received, we compute the CAGR for the cumulative amount of funding received (adjusted for inflation) and the number of rounds of funding. In terms of overall growth between 2011 and 2020, FoodTech, Real Estate and LogisticsTech were the leaders. Exhibit 11.12 lists the CAGRs for each of the sectors. It can be seen that funding growth is faster than the number of rounds, which reiterates the observation made earlier that higher amounts of capital are flowing to fewer ventures. The implication for entrepreneurs is that investors prefer to invest in entrepreneurs who think big, and a very ambitious business plan with significant investment requirements is more likely to be viewed favourably rather than plans with more modest requirements.

Stage of the Venture

The life cycle of a venture consists of several stages, such as pre-seed, seed, early stage, venture stage, growth stage, late stage, and so on. Though there are no strict definitions for these stages, it is well understood that these stages are an indication of the maturity and size of the venture. While start-ups raise capital to meet their financial needs at different stages of the venture, the source and the nature of funding differs across these stages. While pre-seed and seed-stage funding is provided by angel investors, late-stage funding is provided by private equity (PE) firms. Given the risk of start-up failure at different stages, it is but natural that there would be more pre-seed and seed-stage start-ups, and only a few of them would be able to successfully reach the late stage. Our final observation for this article pertains to investment flow in different stages of the start-up life cycle.

7. The start-up life cycle between seed and late stage has been characterised by a significant chasm in funding

The vast majority of start-ups in India, almost 89 per cent, do not receive any external funding. Of those that receive seed funding, only 27 per cent succeed in securing early-stage funding (stages prior to and including Series C). On the other hand, 48 per cent of the start-ups that received seed funding in the US succeed

Exhibit 11.12: Compound annual growth rate – total amount of funding (adjusted for inflation) and number of rounds, by sector (2011–2020)

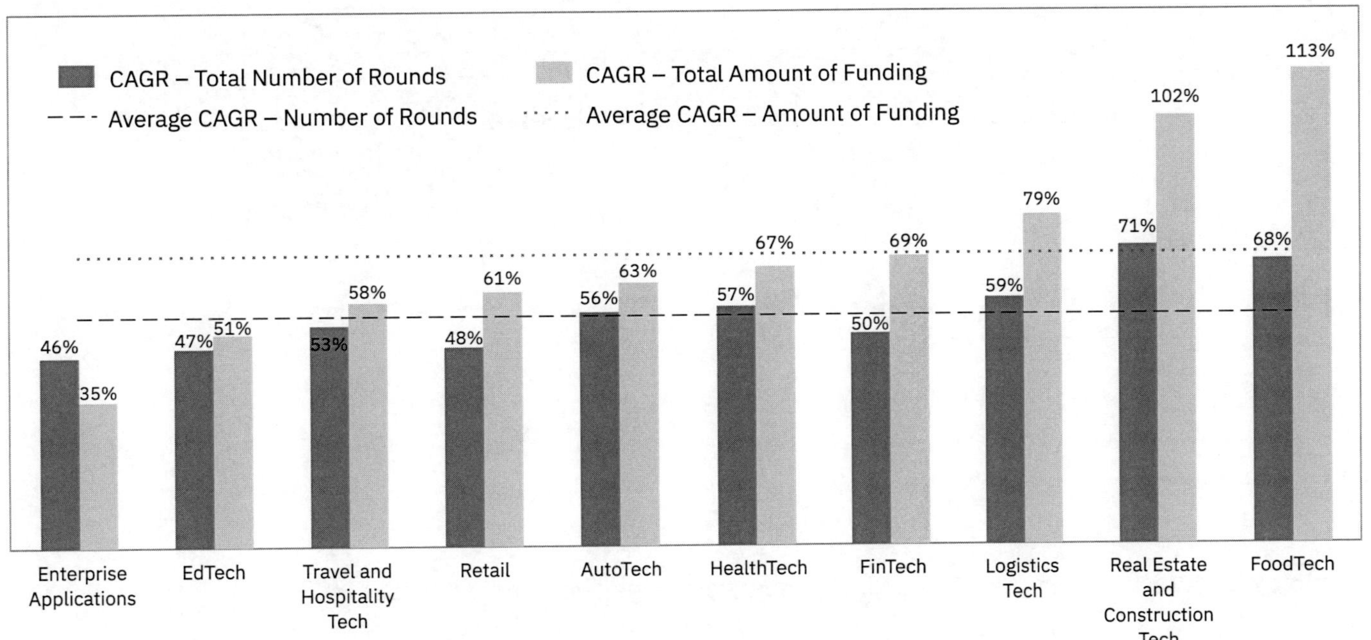

Source: Tracxn database (accessed March 1, 2021)

in securing early-stage funding (that is, the odds are 1.7 times better in the US for entrepreneurs for securing early-stage funding).[19] The low frequency of start-ups receiving early-stage funding does lead to higher start-up mortality, and a potential bottleneck withholding the expansion of the start-up economy in India. Exhibit 11.13 depicts a comparison of 'funding funnel' for start-ups in India and the US, illustrating the number of companies that secure early-stage and late-stage funding for every 100 start-ups that received seed funding.

Much of the start-up funding in India, namely, close to 70 per cent, has been in 'Series C and above' funding, with only 25 per cent of the total funding going towards Series A and Series B investments. On the other hand, globally, only 48 per cent of the funding has been directed toward 'Series C and above', and close to 45 per cent directed to Series A and Series B investments.[20]

In addition, the number of funding rounds raised by early-stage start-ups (Series A and Series B) has also been significantly lower than the global level. Series A and B rounds contribute to only 21 per cent of the Indian funding rounds, while globally, they contribute to 45 per cent.

In essence, the Indian start-up funding environment is characterised by a deeper chasm between the seed and late stages. The lower percentage of early-stage funding has been captured by a higher percentage of growth and late-stage funding, indicating a great missing middle, as far as early-stage funding is concerned. For entrepreneurs, this can be a serious bottleneck and would have an adverse impact on start-up survival. Greater thrust is therefore needed in setting up mechanisms for early-stage funding to stabilise and sustain the start-up growth in the country.

Looking Forward

The coming decade is crucial for India to sustain its position as one of the largest start-up ecosystems in the world. The availability of adequate venture funding is a critical ingredient for the growth of the start-up economy. While the past decade has witnessed significant progress in the development of venture capital funding in the country, certain critical directional changes are needed to benefit from the overall progress achieved so far.

A vibrant and robust start-up ecosystem requires a sturdy foundation. The recent slide in the number of angel funding rounds is a worrying trend that could severely affect the very foundation of the Indian start-up ecosystem. Without a wide base of start-ups being

Exhibit 11.13: The funding funnel – the number of start-ups that received early-stage and late-stage funding for every 100 seed-funded start-ups

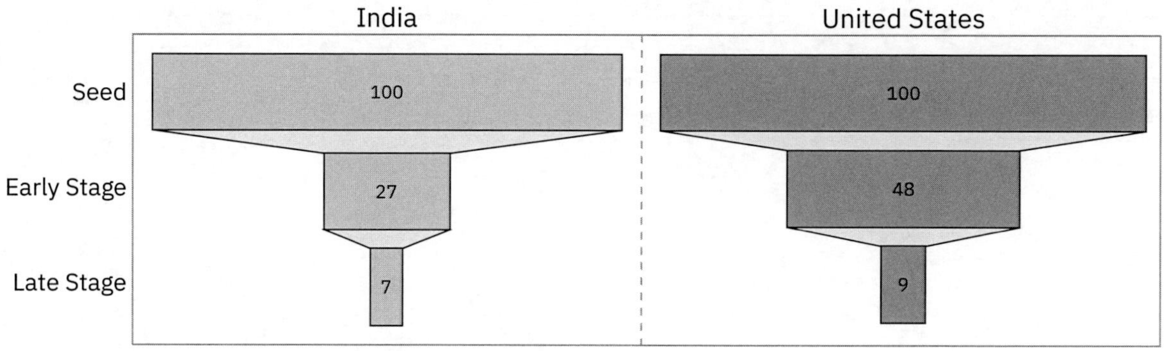

Source: Tracxn database (for India) (accessed March 1, 2021), CB Insights 2018 (for USA)

Exhibit 11.14: Distribution of amount of investment across stage of funding (2011–2020)[21]

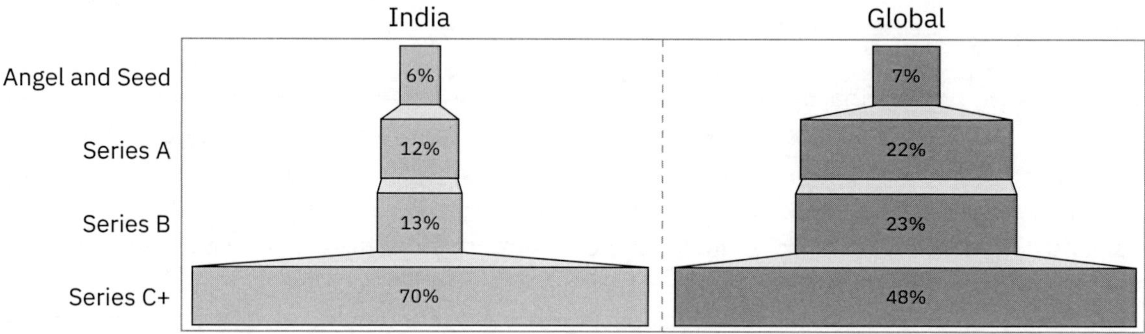

Source: Tracxn database (for India) (accessed March 1, 2021), KPMG Venture Pulse 2017 (Q4) and 2020 (Q4) (for global data)

Exhibit 11.15: Distribution of number of funding rounds across stages of funding (2011–2020)

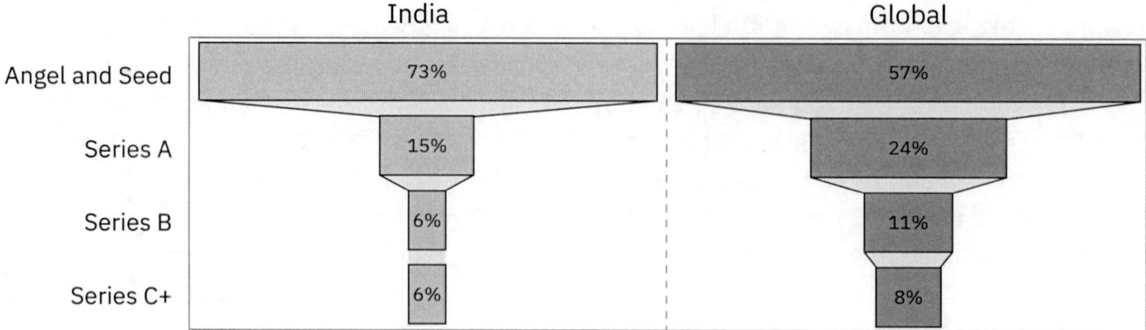

Source: Tracxn database (for India) (accessed March 1, 2021), KPMG Venture Pulse 2017 (Q4) and 2020 (Q4) (for global data)

supported at the angel stage, VC investors would be left with fewer options to diversify their portfolios in the future. It is therefore extremely crucial to arrest the decline in the number of angel funding rounds.

Moreover, it is important to ensure that the increase in funding is driven by a commensurate increase in the number of funding rounds. Increase in the size of funding rounds would result in the concentration of funding in a few start-ups and could adversely affect the deal pipeline.

The start-up ecosystem has not fully tapped into India's vast diversity of talent and industry. The promotion of new start-up hubs across India (specifically in Tier 2 cities) would democratise start-up creation and would aid in unlocking the latent potential among Indian entrepreneurs.

Apart from increasing the geographic spread, it is also important to have sectoral diversity. Start-ups in key sectors of the Indian economy, such as manufacturing, agriculture and small trade, have been in the rain shadow region of venture capital funding. Special impetus should be created to ensure that entrepreneurs in these sectors also have access to the necessary capital for their growth and sustenance.

While the overall growth of the Indian start-up ecosystem has been impressive, the odds for start-ups to secure early-stage funding still fall short of global benchmarks. Therefore, it is important to ensure that promising start-ups can cross the valley of death by increasing the availability of early-stage funding. A strong base of seed and early-stage start-ups, supported by angel investors and VCs with adequate capital, coupled with increased geographic and sectoral diversity, would ensure the sustained growth of India's start-up ecosystem.

Endnotes

[1]NASSCOM. 2019. **The Indian Tech Start-up Ecosystem – Leading Tech in the 20s**. Retrieved from *NASSCOM*, NASSCOM Product Conclave website: https://nasscom.in/sites/default/files/media_pdf/pr-indian_start_up percent20_ecosystem.pdf
Accessed on May 29, 2021

[2]Press Trust of India. 2020. **21 Indian startups are 'unicorns' valued over $1 bn, just a tenth of China's: Study**. Retrieved from *The Economic Times*, website: https://economictimes.indiatimes.com/small-biz/startups/newsbuzz/21-indian-startups-are-unicorns-valued-over-1-bn-just-a-tenth-of-chinas-study/articleshow/77348001.cms

[3]David, D, Gopalan, S and Ramachandran, S. 2020. ***The Startup Environment and Funding Activity in India.*** Tokyo: Asian Development Bank.

[4]Sabarinathan, G, Muralidhar, A and Shetty, A. 2018. Venture Capital and Private Equity Investing in India – An Exploratory Study. ***IIMB Working Paper,*** 542.

[5]Original estimate from Annamalai, TR and Bandyopadhyay, S. 2014. The landscape of Institutional LPs investing in India. In: TR Annamalai, ***India Venture Capital and Private Equity Report 2014 – The Fuel for Wealth Creation,*** 66–80. Chennai: Indian Institute of Technology, Madras. The estimate has been updated using the Tracxn dataset.

[6]Sabarinathan, G, Muralidhar, A and Shetty, A. 2018. Venture Capital and Private Equity Investing in India – An Exploratory Study. ***IIMB Working Paper,*** 542.

[7]Department for Promotion of Industry and Internal Trade. 2018. ***Venture Funding Support***. Retrieved from *Department for Promotion of Industry and Internal Trade, Startup India, Stand Up India* website: https://www.startupindia.gov.in/content/sih/en/compendium_of_good_practices/angel_and_venture_funding.html

[8]See Exhibit 13.3 in Chapter 13 for an introduction to the concept of 'fund of funds'.

[9]Department for Promotion of Industry and Internal Trade. 2018. ***Venture Funding Support***. Retrieved from *Department for Promotion of Industry and Internal Trade, Startup India, Stand Up India* website: https://www.startupindia.gov.in/content/sih/en/compendium_of_good_practices/angel_and_venture_funding.html

[10]A note on methodology: To adjust for inflation, we used the urban Consumer Price Index (CPI-U) published by the Reserve Bank of India in the Database on Indian Economy (https://dbie.rbi.org.in/DBIE/dbie.rbi?site=home). We used 2019 as the base year to inflate the numbers. Before adjusting for inflation, we converted the numbers from $ to ₹ using the noon buying rates in New York City for cable transfers payable in foreign currencies.

Source for Exchange Rate: Board of Governors of the Federal Reserve System (US), India / US Foreign Exchange Rate [EXINUS], retrieved from FRED, Federal Reserve Bank of St. Louis (March 1, 2021): https://fred.stlouisfed.org/series/EXINUS

[11]This estimate is reported in 2020 rupees, corrected for inflation using CPI-U.

[12]NASSCOM. 2019. **The Indian Tech Start-up Ecosystem – Leading Tech in the 20s.** Retrieved from *NASSCOM*, NASSCOM Product Conclave website: https://nasscom.in/sites/default/files/media_pdf/pr-indian_start_up percent20_ecosystem.pdf

[13]While this number might vary with the statistics indicated by the authors in Chapter 6, both of them point to a strong growth in the number of incubators in the country.

[14]We used the Sensex closing levels at the end of the calendar year to derive the Sensex time series (https://www.bseindia.com/Indices/IndexArchiveData.html). We used gross value added (GVA) data reported in the World Bank's DataBank (https://data.worldbank.org/ - ID: NY.GDP.FCST.KN). The exchange rates are from FRED, see footnote 10. We standardised the data by mean-centring it and dividing by the standard deviation.

[15]Other cities include Ahmedabad, Chennai, Hyderabad, Jaipur, Kolkata and Pune.

[16]All CAGR estimates are for the growth in the total amount of funding (inflation adjusted).

[17]Invest India (Government of India) and JLL. 2020. *Great Places for Manufacturing in India*. Accessible at: https://static.investindia.gov.in/s3fs-public/2020-06/Invest%20India_%20Full%20Report_Lighter10%20June.pdf

[18]Bala Subrahmanya, MH. 2018. Comparing the Entrepreneurial Ecosystems for Technology Startups in Bangalore and Hyderabad, India. *Technology Innovation Management Review* 7 (7): 47–62.

[19]CB Insights. 2018. *The Venture Capital Funnel*. Retrieved from CBInsights, Research website: https://www.cbinsights.com/research/venture-capital-funnel-2/. To establish a comparison between Tracxn data and the study, we considered 'early stage' to be between the second and fourth rounds in the study. We considered the fifth round and onwards as 'late stage'.

[20]We constructed a time series of the annual aggregate amount of investment, and the number of rounds, by each stage from the *KPMG Venture Pulse* reports for 2017 (Q4) and 2020 (Q4).

Source: KPMG Private Enterprise. 2021. *Venture Pulse Q4 2020 – Global analysis of venture funding*. Retrieved from KPMG website: https://assets.kpmg/content/dam/kpmg/xx/pdf/2021/01/venture-pulse-q4-2020-report-global.pdf - Page 12. (and) KPMG Enterprise. 2018. *Venture Pulse Q4 2017 – Global analysis of venture funding*. Retrieved from KPMG website: https://assets.kpmg/content/dam/kpmg/xx/pdf/2018/01/venture-pulse-report-q4-17.pdf - Page 13.
Accessed on May 29, 2021

We accounted for inflation in the Global time series using CPI-U released by the US Bureau of Labor Statistics. See footnote 21 for further details.

[21]To adjust the Indian data for inflation, we used the urban Consumer Price Index (CPI-U), reported by the RBI, as in footnote 10. For the Global data, we used the CPI-U for the US reported by the US Bureau of Labor Statistics. Source: US Bureau of Labor Statistics, Consumer Price Index for All Urban Consumers Price Index: All Items in US City Average [CPIAUCSL], retrieved from FRED, Federal Reserve Bank of St. Louis (March 6, 2021): https://fred.stlouisfed.org/series/CPIAUCSL

IN BRIEF

- Successful entrepreneurs have taken to angel investing in a significant way, resulting in robust growth in the number of the angel investors and the number of investments.
- Newer approaches to angel investing such as angel funds and the formation of specialised social capital–based angel networks have provided founders with a wide array of choices from which to raise capital.
- Angel investors have backed many of the popular start-ups that were founded in the current decade.
- Several state governments have implemented measures to create an enabling environment to channelise investments or create avenues that makes it easier for start-ups to get angel investments.
- The existing policy regime lacks clear incentives for angel investors. Fiscal concessions to angel investors, both during investment and at exit, would help to draw more capital inflow to start-ups.
- Creating and maintaining a list of registered angel investors would expedite the introduction of the e-verification procedure to validate the legitimacy of investments made in start-ups.

ANALYTICAL ARTICLE

12

The Wood and the Trees: The Angel Investing Landscape in India

Thillai Rajan A and Akshay Natteri Mangadu

Thillai Rajan A and Mangadu, AN. 2021. "The Wood and the Trees: The Angel Investing Landscape in India". In *Shifting Orbits: Decoding the Trajectory of the Indian Start-up Ecosystem*, edited by Thillai Rajan A, Srivardhini K Jha, Joffi Thomas and Rohan Chinchwadkar, 134–152. Hyderabad: Universities Press (India) Private Limited.

Angel Investors: The First Port of Call

For start-up founders who have exhausted their personal funding sources (self, family and friends) as well as other soft sources such as incubation grants, the first port of call to raise significant capital would usually be angel investors.[2] While numerous definitions of angel investors exist, a generally accepted characterisation is that angel investors are individuals who invest their personal wealth in start-ups. Since start-ups are inherently risky, those investing in such risky enterprises should not be averse to writing off their investment. Only high-net-worth individuals (HNI's) can afford to do that and, therefore, angel investors are all essentially individuals having significant investible capital. The converse is not true, that is, all high-net-worth individuals are not angel investors.

Exhibit 12.1: Typical profile and portfolio of angel investors

Angel investors are typically very successful entrepreneurs or business leaders, who are interested in supporting impactful business ideas and innovations. For example, about 55 per cent of angel investors in the US have either been the founder or a CEO of a start-up in the past.[3] Angel investing provides investors the opportunity to be involved in bringing the latest innovations to the market, without the responsibility of being a part of the implementation.

Angel investors typically invest a small portion (ranging from 10 per cent to 20 per cent) of their wealth in promising start-ups. Apart from providing financial capital, angel investors also provide advice and guidance to the entrepreneurs in making crucial business decisions. Despite the high risk of failure, experienced angel investors manage to make sizable returns. Some seasoned investors state that the returns from angel investments are higher than what is obtained from conventional assets such as listed equity (over 14 per cent in annualised returns).[4]

The roundtable discussion featured in Chapter 13 provides detailed insights from leading angel investors on their motivations for angel investing, best practices and their returns on investments.

Angel investors help entrepreneurs in three different ways, apart from providing capital. Firstly, entrepreneurs look to angel investors for mentorship and guidance as many investors would have had vast experience in building and running successful businesses. Secondly, founders seek to leverage the connections and networks of angel investors to scale their businesses. The connections can provide them entry into new markets or provide them access to additional capital from leading venture capital (VC) firms. Finally, angel investors add a certain 'brand value' to the venture. Raising capital from angel investors with high reputation improves the credibility of the venture in the eyes of the market and can greatly improve the trust factor with clients and other stakeholders. Hence, angel investing, unlike conventional assets, also requires 'soft' inputs from the investors such as mentoring and brand value.

This chapter highlights the trends in angel investing in India since the early 2000s. The evolving role of the government in promoting angel investing has also been discussed. Finally, we benchmark India's position in the global angel investing arena.

QUICK STATS

3.5 Average age of the start-up at the time of receiving angel investment (in years)

4 India's global rank by the number of angel investments made

5.9 Percentage of angel deals in start-ups in Tier 2 and Tier 3 cities

6.2 Percentage of women angel investors

8.5 Percentage of start-ups that are successful in getting early-stage funding from angel investors

45 Number of active angel networks in 2020

48 Average age of angel investors (in years)

73% CAGR (compound annual growth rate) of the number of angel investors between 2008 and 2020

96% Ratio of angel investors in Tier 1 cities (Ahmedabad, Bengaluru, Chennai, New Delhi, Hyderabad, Kolkata, Mumbai, Pune)

4,200+ Number of active angel investors in the country[1]

Trends in Angel Investing – The Exponential Growth Story

The concept of angel investing, in its modern sense, took root in India during the mid-2000s. The formation of angel networks such as the Indian Angel Network (IAN) (established in 2006), Mumbai Angels (established in 2006) and Chennai Angels (established in 2007) were important milestones during the early years of angel investing in India.[5] These angel networks brought together investors from different backgrounds under one roof, enabling them to invest in a diverse portfolio of start-ups by leveraging their collective expertise and capital. The networks also offered various advantages to the entrepreneurs as compared to individual angel investors (see Chapter 13, the roundtable article on angel investors for more discussion).

Angel investing in India has grown exponentially since 2006, with the number of angel investment deals growing from just 21 in 2006 to 387 in 2019. Exhibit 12.2 shows the trend in the number of angel deals in India since 2006.[6] Between 2011 and 2019, the number of angel deals in India grew at a remarkable rate of 38 per cent[7] annually.[8] Angel deals comprise investments made by individual angel investors, angel networks and other vehicles such as angel funds.

Individual Angel Investments

Investments made by individual angel investors account for more than two-thirds of the total angel deal. Investment by individual angel investors does not mean that there would be only a single angel investor in the round. Usually, there are many investors in the round, but they are not part of any common platform.

The community of angel investors in India comprises a vibrant and diverse set of individuals, ranging from established industrialists and business leaders such as Ratan Tata (former Chairman of the Tata Group) and Mohandas Pai (former CFO and Director of Infosys) to young entrepreneurs who have built successful enterprises in the recent past, including Girish Mathrubootham (founder of Freshworks) and Kunal Shah (founder of Freecharge and CRED). The angel investor community in India, according to recent estimates, comprises over 4,200 active angel investors and has grown at a CAGR of 73 per cent between 2008 and 2020.[9] Indian angel investors have backed start-ups that have become household names such as OLA, Oyo, Paytm,

Exhibit 12.2: Number of angel investment deals in India, 2006–2020

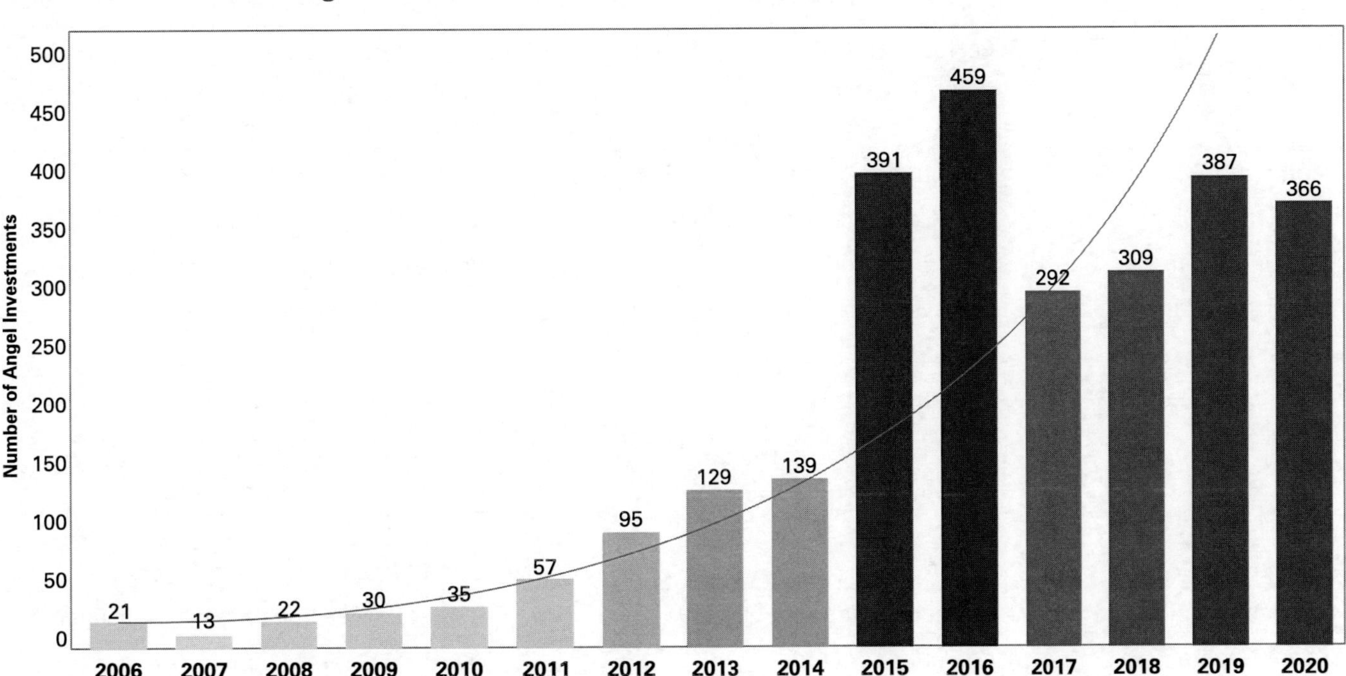

Source: The data for 2006 to 2008 is from Sabarinathan, G. (2014), data for 2009 and 2012 is from Sabarinathan, G. (2019), data for 2013–2020 (as of December 20, 2020) is from Crunchbase.

Razorpay and Unacademy, to cite a few (Exhibit 12.3). This underlines the important contribution of Indian angel investors in supporting and financing ventures in their most risky phase. It can also be seen that active angel investors have been predominantly successful entrepreneurs, indicating that entrepreneurs have a disposition to invest a portion of their wealth on other entrepreneurs, as a way of giving back to the system. This results in a virtuous cycle, namely, successful entrepreneurs leading to more angel funding. Many of the new-age Unicorns could not have been created from traditional bank and equity funding.

Exhibit 12.3: Leading angel investors in India

Angel investor	Primary job title	Some key investments
Alok Mittal	Co-founder & CEO, Indifi	Drivezy, myUpchar, YAP
Amit Gupta	Co-founder & CEO, Yulu	Applicate, Razorpay, Wooplr
Anand Chandrasekaran	Director, Platform & Product Partnerships, Facebook	EduRev, Interview Mocha, Khatabook
Ankur Mittal	Co-founder, Inflection Point Ventures	Milkbasket, Oga, Touch
Anupam Mittal	Founder & CEO, Shaadi.com	Interactive Avenues, Little Eye Labs, Ola
Aprameya Radhakrishna	Co-founder & CEO, Koo	m.paani, Unacademy, Vogo
Arihant Patni	Managing Director, Nirvana Venture Advisors	DocTalk, The Math Company, Yulu
Binny Bansal	Co-founder & Executive Chairman, xto10x Technologies	Acko, Mobikon, Rupeek
Girish Mathrubootham	Founder & CEO, Freshworks	FactorDaily, Interview Mocha, Josh Talks
Jitendra Gupta	Founder & CEO, Jupiter	MitronTV, OPEN, YAP
Kris Gopalakrishnan	Chairman, Axilor Ventures	Freshworld, Furlenco, Jetsynthesys
Kunal Bahl	Co-founder & CEO, Snapdeal	Ola, Razorpay, Urban Company
Kunal Shah	Founder & CEO, CRED	Dil Mil, Mobile Premier League (MPL), Unacademy
Mohandas Pai	Co-Founder & Chairman, Aarin Capital	Velvetcase, Vyom, Zoomcar
Nandan Nilekani	Non-Executive Chairman, Infosys	Ninjacart, ShopX, Tracxn
Phanindra Sama	Director, T Works	Betaout, RheoTV, Unacademy
Rajan Anandan	Managing Director, Sequoia Capital	Let's Venture, POPxo, Tax Spanner
Rajesh Sawhney	Founder, GSF Accelerator	Gingr, Gogobus, Loan simple
Ramkanth Sharma	Co-Founder, Livspace	AirMeet, Niki, Shop101
Ratan Tata	Chairman Emeritus, Tata Sons	Ola, Snapdeal, Your Story
Rohit Bansal	Co-founder, Snapdeal	Let's Venture, Razor pay, Urban Company
Sachin Bansal	CEO, Navi	Inshorts, Ola, Unacademy
Sandeep Tandon	Partner, Whiteboard Capital	Bharat Bazaar, Shaadi Saga, Unacademy
Sanjay Mehta	Co-Founder, 100X.VC	Oyo, Wow! Momo, Zippr
Vijay Shekhar Sharma	Founder & CEO, Paytm	Milaap, Innov8, Treebo Hotels

Source: Crunchbase and publicly available profiles of the investors (as of October 2020).

Angel Networks

An 'angel network' is a group of angel investors, who collectively identify and co-invest in start-ups. Typically, these networks comprise a like-minded group of investors with diverse backgrounds and expertise. Angel networks leverage the collective wisdom of the members to identify promising investment opportunities. Chapter 13 has more insights on the benefits of angel networks.

The rise in the number of incubators and accelerators[10] has enabled start-ups to receive sizable investments at the very early stages of growth. Hence, at the angel stage, the capital requirements have substantially risen, going beyond the capacity of what individual angel investors can make in a single investment. Therefore, angel investors have started to collectively invest in start-ups, by pooling their capital through angel networks and consortiums. Angel networks enable angel investors to provide the necessary funds to start-ups, which the members of the network might not be able to fulfil individually. Many angel networks have a secretariat, which does a round of pre-screening of the deals before presenting to their member community. The diligence in an angel network is, therefore, higher than that of individual angel investments.

Consistent with the growth in individual angel investors, angel networks have also grown significantly in India. About 69 per cent of the currently active angel groups in India were formed between 2012 and 2020. Exhibit 12.4 tracks the trend in the number of angel groups in India by the year of formation.[11] More often than not, many angel investors are members in more than one angel network. Being part of multiple networks ensures that investors get to see a comprehensive deal flow in the market. Angel networks account for the second highest number of angel deals after individual angel investments.

Angel networks have begun to make a significant impact and have been instrumental in the success of recent start-ups such as Chai Kings and Codemojo. Some of the leading angel networks operating in India are listed in Exhibit 12.5. In Exhibit 12.6, we present the number of deals made by six large Indian angel networks in each year since 2012.[12] The consistent investment activity across the years by the six large angel networks is an indication of the vibrant angel investing ecosystem in India. Since geographical proximity is one of the

Exhibit 12.4: Number of active angel groups by year of formation

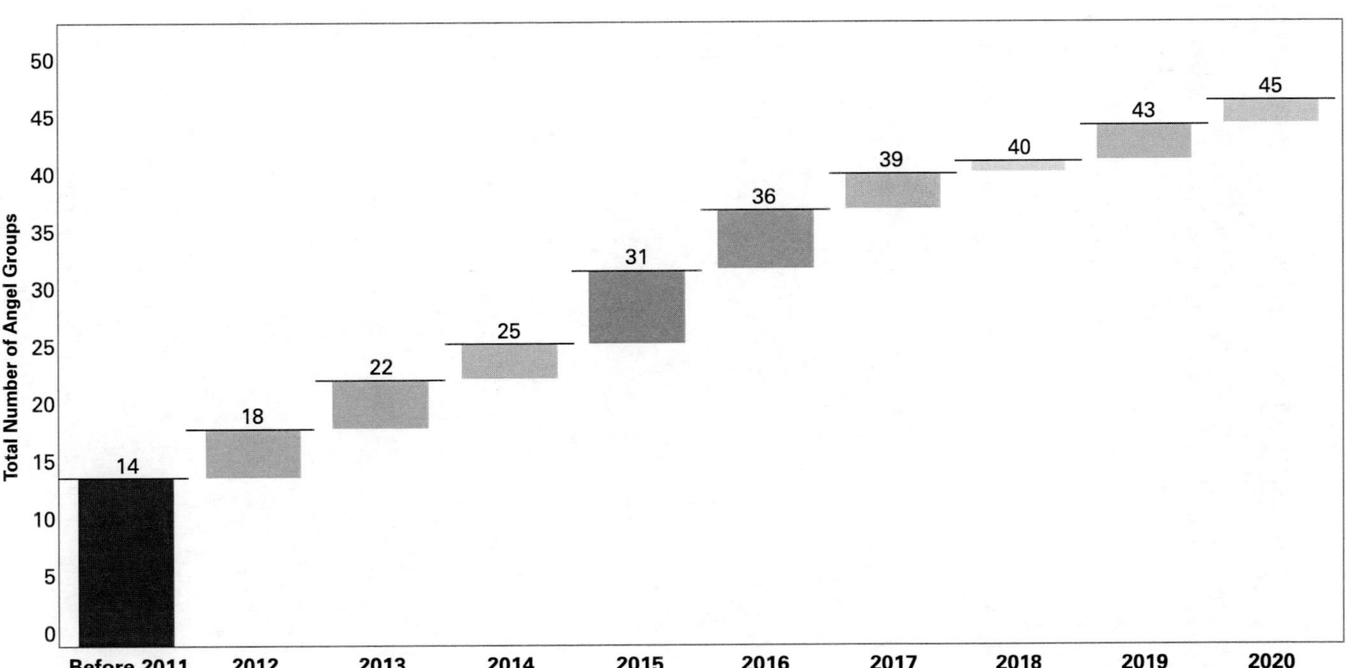

Source: Crunchbase (accessed October 7, 2020). Five angel networks were dropped from this analysis as their founding date was not known.

Exhibit 12.5: Leading angel networks in India

Name of the Angel Network	Total number of investments[14]	Year of formation	Headquarters	Number of members[15]	Some key investments
Indian Angel Network	206	2006	Delhi	393	ExtraaEdge, Freshworld, MinionLabs
Mumbai Angels	188	2006	Mumbai	Over 300	Crimson Healthcare, EdHusk, Trukky
The Chennai Angels	55	2007	Chennai	101	Chai Kings, Nanoclean, Trulymadly.com
ah! Ventures	59	2009	Mumbai	Over 3,200	Corefactors, Loanadda, MiStay
Hyderabad Angels	43	2010	Hyderabad	60	Chai Kings, StanPlus, ZineOne
Stanford Angels India	16	2010	Bengaluru	NA [16]	Betaout, GyanDhan, MoneyTor
Artha India Ventures	85	2012	Mumbai	NA	Baby Chakra, Book my Cab, Oyo
Lead Angels Network	40	2013	Mumbai	Over 150	Driveu, Kaarva, PlanetSpark
50k Ventures	17	2014	Hyderabad	NA	Book My Bai, NicheAI, Scholr
Capier Investments	10	2015	Bengaluru	NA	Ambee, Doxper, Parentlane
Keiretsu Forum India	201	2015–17	Bangalore, Chennai, Delhi NCR, Mumbai	292	Planys, DeTect, 6Degree, Virohan, Origa Leasing
Venture Catalysts	139	2016	Mumbai	1,100 [17]	BluSmart, Peppermint, Rooter
JITO Angel Network	35	2017	Mumbai	200	BluSmart, Netambit, Toch
Native Angel Network	9	2017	Chennai	242	Happy Hens, Pepperlearn, SP Robotic Works
Inflection Point Ventures	35	2018	Gurgaon	Over 350	Milkbasket, Trulymadly.com, Wellcure
Yatra Angel Network	4	2018	Mumbai	30	Riskcovry, YAP, Zimyo
100X.VC	14	2019	Mumbai	NA	Data Sutram, Foodmonk, Knorish

Source: The data on the number of investments is the highest number published in Crunchbase, PitchBook and the networks' official websites or obtained directly from the angel network. The number of members data is from the networks' official websites, direct correspondence, or published newspaper articles. The sources were accessed in October 2020.

important factors in angel investments, the initial angel networks were city-based networks (such as Mumbai Angels, Chennai Angels, and so on). However, in recent times, angel networks have moved beyond city-centric networks to focus on other aspects such as community, specific domain or industry, start-up stage, and so on.

With increasing segmentation of the start-up sector, innovative models of angel networks have also emerged. While the traditional angel networks are open for membership to qualified investors, networks have emerged whose membership is restricted to a closed group. A prominent example of the latter is 100XVC (whose members[13] include Sanjay Mehta, Ninad Karpe and Shashank Randev). Being a closed group of investors, they fall between angel networks and VC firms. Similarly, there are angel groups that fall between family offices and angel networks. Artha India Ventures is an example where members of the Damani family came together as a group of angel investors to invest in early-stage start-ups. Naturally, the beneficiaries from the growth in diverse angel investment models have been the entrepreneurs themselves as nuanced funding options became available to meet the niche needs of different ventures.

Angel Funds

Apart from investing individually or through angel groups, investors in India also have the option of investing in 'angel funds'. The idea of an angel fund is to pool in capital from individual angels and institutional investors, which is then invested in start-ups at the seed and early stages. The investors of these funds come from a wide variety of fields and geographical locations. This helps investors build a wider portfolio (with greater potential for diversification) and greatly reduces the search costs for start-ups. Angel groups such as the Indian Angel Network (IAN) and platforms such as Let's Venture have started their own angel funds. IAN's angel fund raised ₹3.75 billion,[18] while Let's Venture's angel fund has raised ₹2.38 billion.[19] These funds are registered with the Securities and Exchange Board of India (SEBI) as alternative investment funds (AIF).

The considerable costs and regulatory requirements associated with starting an angel fund render it a non-option for small consortiums of angel investors seeking to pool their funds to invest in start-ups. Platforms like Angel List provide a solution to this by enabling investors to use their platform to start small quasi-

Exhibit 12.6: Number of deals by six leading angel networks in each year, 2012–2020

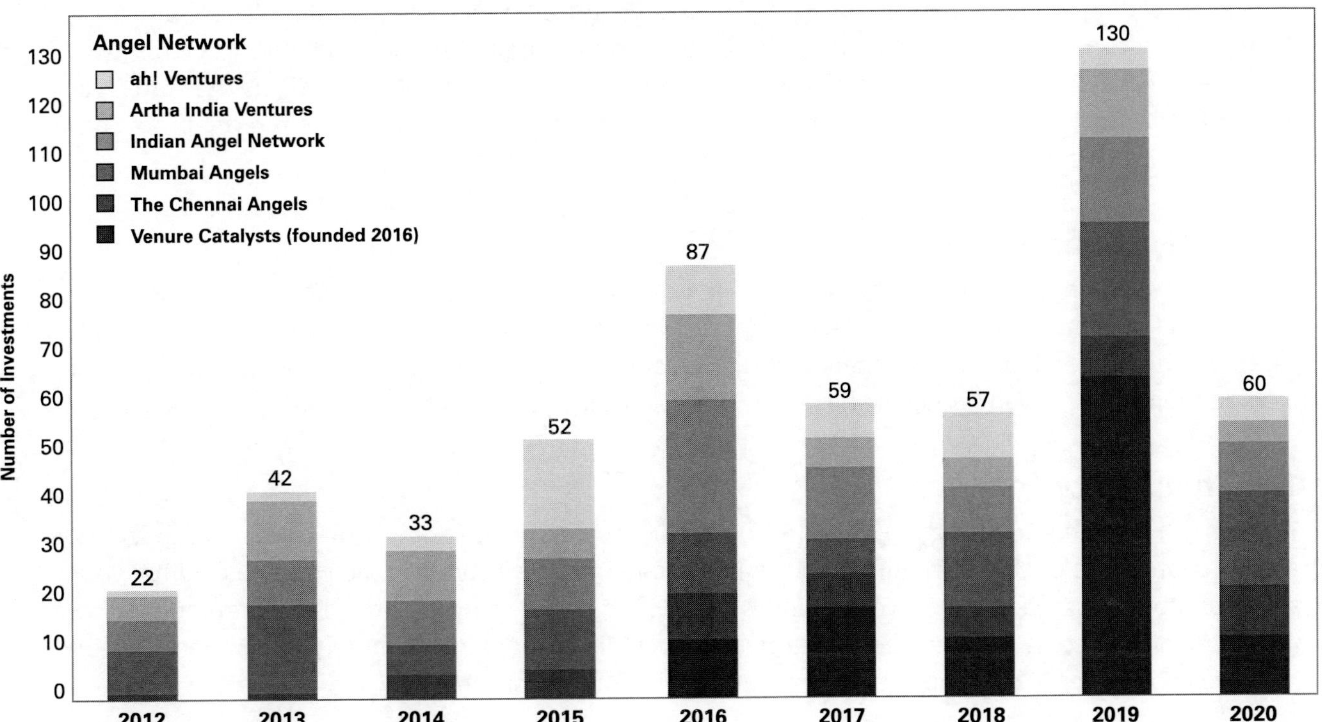

Source: Crunchbase (as of October 7, 2020).

angel funds.[20] Using the platform, investors can pool capital (between ₹ 20 million and ₹ 80 million) from co-investors, which they can then invest in a variety of start-ups. The fund functions just like a typical venture fund. The platform charges a fee in return for providing all the necessary back-office support needed for the fund.[21] Alumni of premier management institutions such as Indian Institute of Management (IIM) Kozhikode and IIM Indore have used the platform to start 'alumni funds', where alumni pool in their capital (through the platform) to co-invest in promising start-ups.[22] This innovation lets investors solely focus on selecting the right investments, while the platform's team handles compliance requirements, reporting requirements and the overall management of the fund.

Innovative methods of angel investing have also emerged in recent years, which involve the use of social capital and the personal brand value of the angels. Some examples are presented in Exhibit 12.7.

Challenges in Securing Angel Investment

Despite the incredible growth in angel investing over the past two decades, the demand for angel investments far exceeds supply. Start-ups face severe competition in securing funding, with many failing to raise their targeted amounts. Just over 8.5 per cent of the start-ups founded are successful in getting early-stage funding from angel investors.[24] Central and state governments have tried to bridge this gap and have implemented several initiatives to bring investors closer to Indian entrepreneurs.

Governmental Initiatives in Promoting Angel Investments

The central and state governments have pitched several initiatives to bolster the growth of start-ups in India.[25]

Exhibit 12.7: Innovations in angel investing[23] – putting social capital to good use

Leveraging Celebrity Brand Value

Instead of providing capital, celebrity angel investors trade their endorsement services for equity in start-ups. Leading actors including Deepika Padukone, Priyanka Chopra Jonas, Shahid Kapoor and Suniel Shetty have recently invested in start-ups such as Bumble, Epigamia, Furlenco and Purplle. Celebrity angel investors see such investments as a win–win situation for both parties involved as the start-ups gain from the reach and popularity that such celebrity endorsements provide, while the celebrities have an opportunity to earn sizable future returns from the success of their firms.

The Native Connect

Native lead is an angel group specifically aimed at bringing together successful entrepreneurs from small towns to mentor and invest in the next crop of founders from their native towns. Mentors would be able to understand the specific challenges and obstacles that founders face and would be able to provide them with relevant guidance based on their own experiences in tackling these challenges.

The Community Connect

The Jain International Trade Organization (JITO) has founded an incubation centre in Mumbai to support and incubate ideas of entrepreneurs from the Jain community, by leveraging their established network of successful business leaders in the community. Further, their angel network provides entrepreneurs from all communities access to prominent mentors and investors in the Jain community. Their angel network has invested in over 29 start-ups across several sectors in the past three years.

The 'Startup India' initiative of the central government in 2015[26] was an important milestone as it signalled the government's strong intent to promote start-ups and entrepreneurship in India.[27] Several state governments had also formulated their own initiatives for start-ups, such as the 'Kerala Startup Mission', 'Maharashtra State Innovation Society' and 'iStart Initiative' of Rajasthan to name a few. Exhibit 12.8 captures highlights of the policies implemented by various state governments.[28] It can be seen that rather than directly investing in start-ups, many state governments have been keen on creating an enabling environment to channelise investments or create avenues that make it easier for start-ups to get angel investments. A clear message for the entrepreneurs is that while they may expect non-financial support from the governments, funding has to come from private sources.

Changes in Regulations Governing Angel Investments

The central government has taken various measures to reform and streamline the regulatory framework.

Exhibit 12.8: Government initiatives to promote angel investing in India[29]

State	Policy initiative
Andhra Pradesh	The state signed a Memorandum of Understanding (MoU) with Indian Angel Network (IAN) in 2018 to support start-ups registered in the state in securing funding from IAN.
Bihar[30]	Under the Bihar Startup Policy 2017, the government provides a success fee (set at 2 per cent of the investments raised) to start-ups that have successfully raised funds from angel investors registered with the state. The state also matches angel investments with loans and financial assistance, on a case-by-case basis.
Chhattisgarh	The state government started an angel fund in 2018 to co-invest in the state's start-ups along with angel groups and funds.
Goa	In 2018, the state government tied up with the Mumbai Angels group to organise capacity building seminars for aspiring angel investors in the state and to also guide the state in developing a robust angel investing ecosystem.
Karnataka	Starting in 2015, the state provides free access to state-sponsored events and pitching sessions for angel investors registered with its start-up portal.[31] In some cases, the state also provides the angels with an opportunity to judge its pitching sessions and gives them a chance to participate as speakers or mentors in its seminars. The state also provides matching funds to angel-backed start-ups in emerging technology sectors.
Madhya Pradesh	Starting from 2018, the state government provides a list of registered angel investors on its start-up portal. The state is working on improving the platform to enable investors to be in closer touch with entrepreneurs from Madhya Pradesh.[32]
Odisha	In 2018, the state government reached out to leading angel groups such as the Indian Angel Network and TiE Silicon Valley to support start-ups in their state. They also conducted information sessions to promote angel investing in their state.
Other States	States such as Kerala,[33] Maharashtra,[34] Rajasthan and Uttar Pradesh have conducted large-scale events to promote start-ups in their state among high-net-worth individuals (HNIs) and seasoned angel investors. Gujarat has provided free space for angels interested in conducting pitching events and seminars in their state.

Angel investing in India was long crippled by stringent regulations governing the funding and sale of companies. One such regulation was the 'angel tax' (see Exhibit 13.2 in Chapter 13), which deemed investments made over the fair market value of a start-up (or any unlisted firm) as taxable income for the start-up. This was a severe burden on angel investors, as a substantial part of their investment would be taxed away and not available for the start-up. Further the requirement of a three-year 'lock-in' period on investments, the stringent requirements to move for an initial public offering (IPO), and the large capital gains tax liability associated with profitable exits[35] had made exits convoluted and less profitable for angels.[36] The regulatory burden made angel investing an unattractive option to most investors. In 2011, even before the introduction of the angel tax,[37] angel investing only accounted for 7 per cent of early-stage funding.[38] This is extremely low when compared to the US, where angel investing accounted for 75 per cent of the early-stage funding.[39]

Taking due notice of the impact of such regulations, the government sought to streamline the regulatory framework to ease the compliance and tax burden on investors. Between 2016 and 2019, the central government made several reforms to reduce taxation of angel investors and start-ups. During this period, the stringent requirements enforced by SEBI for starting angel funds were also relaxed. Exhibit 12.9 summarises the major reforms carried out in recent years.

Exhibit 12.9: Regulations governing angel investments[40]

Area of reform	Year	Regulatory change
Capital Gains Taxation	2016	Angel investors who had invested in registered angel funds were exempt from long-term capital gains tax on the gains realised from the funds (Section 54EE of the Income Tax Act, 1961 (IT Act)).[41] Capital gains arising from the sale of residential houses and plots were exempt from capital gains tax if the taxable amount was invested in registered start-ups (Section 54GB of the IT Act).[42] The only additional condition was that the investor must hold at least 25 per cent of the share capital in the start-up.[43]
Angel Funds	2016[44]	The maximum number of investors permitted in an angel fund was increased to 200 from 49 investors. The minimum investment requirement in a start-up for angel funds was reduced to ₹2.5 million from ₹5 million. The lock-in period for angel fund investments was reduced from 3 years to 1 year. Indian angel funds were permitted to invest up to 25 per cent of their corpus in foreign start-ups.
	2018[45]	The investment ceiling for an angel investor in a start-up was increased to ₹100 million from ₹50 million. The minimum corpus requirement for angel funds was halved from ₹100 million to ₹50 million.
Start-up Firm Taxation	2019	Start-ups registered under the Department for Promotion of Industry and Internal Trade (DPIIT) were given tax exemptions on investments over the fair market value of the firm.[46] The verification of the identity of the investors and their source of funds would be done through a digital verification system and would not require any scrutiny from the Income Tax Department. This simplifies and expedites the verification process, making it convenient to investors.[47]

Despite the reforms, industry experts have been concerned by certain problems that still linger. Apoorva Ranjan Sharma, co-founder of Venture Catalysts, had raised three specific concerns.[48] The first issue pertained to the registration of start-ups with the DPIIT. To be exempt from the angel tax, a start-up must be recognised by the DPIIT (Department for Promotion of Industry and Internal Trade). Commentators opine that some start-ups find the documentation process required for registering with the DPIIT to be a major challenge, specifically when the start-up is from the smaller towns and villages of the country.[49]

Secondly, start-ups that invest capital raised in immovable assets or shares and securities are not exempt from angel tax. This is a major obstacle for start-ups. Typically, start-ups invest capital earmarked for future expansion projects or commitments in debt mutual funds[50] till the capital would be needed. This ensures that the capital grows and earns some interest till the time it would be required by the start-up. The angel tax regulation impedes such approaches to managing capital, as the start-up would have to forfeit 30 per cent of the capital as angel tax to the government in order to invest in debt mutual funds, which would defeat the purpose of such investments.[51]

Lastly, while angel funds are exempt from long-term capital gains tax, capital gains from the sale of equity held directly by angel investors is still subject to taxation. Capital gains from investments in start-ups is taxed at the same rate as unlisted equity, 28.5 per cent. This is more than double that for capital gains from listed equity investments, which is taxed at only 11.9 per cent.[52] The high level of capital gains tax on direct equity investments in start-ups (or unlisted entities in general) remains a cause of concern to investors. Leading investors claim that this is a major reason for the relocation of start-ups to foreign countries.[53] Given that start-ups play a crucial role in furthering innovation and entrepreneurship,[54] investments in start-ups must be encouraged by at least setting the capital gains tax at the same rate as for listed equites. Despite the progress that has been made in streamlining the regulatory

Exhibit 12.10: Share of angel investment deals across 10 countries and regions

	2013	2014	2015	2016	2017	2018	2019	2020
United States	57%	57%	52%	49%	48%	48%	47%	45%
European Union	15%	15%	15%	17%	18%	17%	17%	17%
United Kingdom	10%	11%	11%	12%	13%	13%	12%	14%
India	4%	3%	7%	8%	5%	6%	7%	8%
Canada	5%	5%	5%	5%	6%	4%	4%	3%
Singapore	2%	2%	3%	3%	3%	3%	3%	4%
Japan	2%	2%	2%	2%	3%	4%	4%	4%
Israel	2%	2%	2%	2%	2%	2%	2%	2%
Australia	2%	1%	2%	2%	2%	2%	1%	2%
Brazil	1%	1%	1%	1%	1%	1%	1%	1%
Total Number of Deals	3,589	4,588	5,879	5,756	5,590	5,492	5,281	4,579

Source: Crunchbase (as of December 21, 2020).

framework of angel investments, several areas still require attention.

Comparison of Angel Investments in India to Global Trends

Benchmarking helps to avoid delusions of grandeur. Though the Indian angel ecosystem has grown significantly in the last decade, assessing the relative scale and growth vis-a-vis other prominent angel investing economies would give a better indication of the relative standing of angel investments in India. We have benchmarked angel investments in India to nine other top destinations for angel investments: Australia, Brazil, Canada, European Union,[55] Israel, Japan, Singapore, United Kingdom and United States.[56]

The percentage share of deals made by Indian angels was only four per cent of the total number of deals made across the 10 countries in 2013. The share however doubled to eight per cent in 2020, making India an emerging hub of angel investing activity in the world. The increase in the share of angel investments in India can be attributed to: (i) successful young tech entrepreneurs[57] becoming angel investors to support the next generation of entrepreneurs; (ii) the increased intensity of government initiatives and reforms; and (iii) the secular increase in wealth in the economy leading to professionals and top echelons in management making angel investments. Globally, the biggest market for angel investments has been the US. However, because of the faster growth in other countries, the share of deals funded in the US has been steadily decreasing from 57 per cent in 2013 to just 45 per cent in 2020. This is an indication that angel investing activity in the rest of the world is rapidly catching up with the United States.

In terms of the share of angel investors and groups, India ranks fourth among the countries studied (Exhibit 12.11).[58] Comparison of the intensity of investing activity of top angel investors (based on the number of investments) in the US and India is given in Exhibit 12.12.[59] The total number of investments made by the top 10 individual investors in the US is about 4.6 times the number of investments made by their Indian counterparts. This clearly illustrates that fact that India is still at a relatively early stage in the development of the angel investing ecosystem and has tremendous scope for growth.

Exhibit 12.11: Share of angel investors and groups among 10 countries and regions

	Share of angel investors	Share of angel groups
United States	59%	51%
European Union	14%	18%
United Kingdom	9%	7%
India	7%	4%
Canada	3%	3%
China	2%	9%
Australia	2%	1%
Japan	2%	0.3%
Israel	1%	2%
Brazil	1%	2%
Singapore	1%	1%

Source: Crunchbase (as of October 7, 2020).

Exhibit 12.12: Comparing the number of investments made by the top 10 angel investors in India and USA

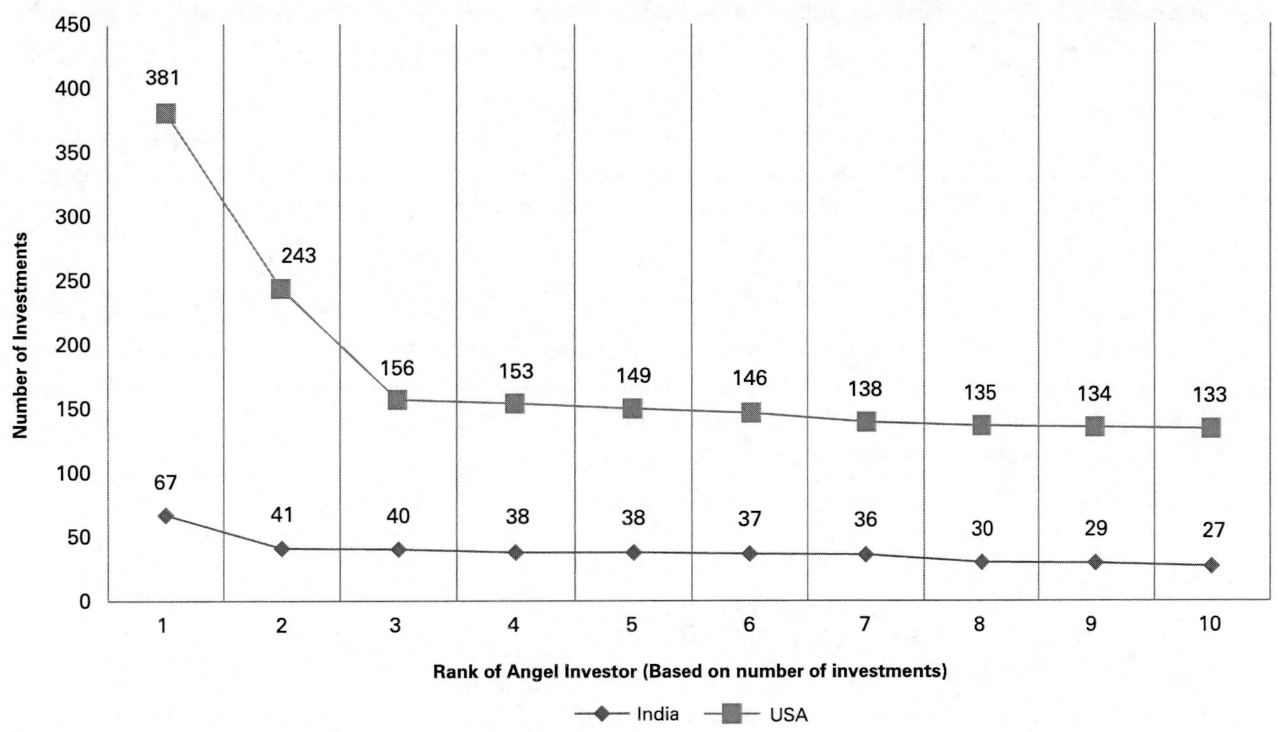

Source: Crunchbase (as of October 7, 2020).

Despite the impressive performance over the past decade, India still lags behind major start-up hubs such as Australia, Israel, Singapore, UK and US in terms of the provision of tax incentives for angel investors (Exhibit 12.13). Given that the odds of securing funds are very low for Indian entrepreneurs, the government could aim at making angel investing an attractive option by providing strong tax incentives and by reducing the compliance burden on investors. The reduction of tax rates, by providing tax credits or deductions (as in the case of countries mentioned in Exhibit 12.13), would attract a more diverse group of investors to angel investing. This would increase the overall availability of funds for entrepreneurs and would greatly improve their odds of being funded.

Unlike the examples mentioned in Exhibit 12.13, angel investors who directly invest in Indian start-ups neither get tax credits or deductions during the time of investment nor do they get capital gains tax exemption on the gains made from profitable exits. Worse still, the capital gains tax on start-ups is double that for listed equities. The prevailing policy paradigm has been to disincentivise the practice of using start-ups as a channel to legitimise tainted capital. Be that as it may, it is time to incentivise those legitimate investors who assume significant risk when investing in ventures. In the absence of appropriate fiscal incentives such as tax credits on investments made in start-ups and tax rate concessions on gains from successful exits (as in the case of leading start-up hubs), angel investment flow in the country is likely to be modest. Such positive inducements would also go a long way in signalling the intention of the government to attract and legitimise angel investments.

Further, the government should expedite the implementation of the proposed digital verification process[68] to verify investors and their source of funds.[69] This would ensure that start-ups are not needlessly scrutinised about the investments raised from angel investors. The e-verification process could be extended to form a register of certified angel investors. This would enable the start-up founders to quickly identify legitimate angel investors and would help the

Exhibit 12.13: Incentives for angel investors in leading start-up hubs

Country	Tax exemptions provided for angel investors
Australia[60]	Angel investors investing in early-stage start-ups are eligible to deduct 20 per cent of the total investment amount from their taxable liability. For example, if an eligible investor[61] were to invest AU $100,000 in an early-stage start-up, then the investor is eligible to reduce tax liability by AU $20,000 for the tax year in which the investment is made. The maximum amount of deduction is capped at AU $200,000 for a given tax year. Further, there is no capital gains tax for gains on shares in early-stage start-ups that are held continuously for at least 12 months and less than 10 years.
Israel[62]	Under 'Angel's Law', angel investors who provide seed capital for high-tech Israeli start-ups can deduct up to ₪ 5 million from their taxable income over a period of three years, commencing from the time the investment is made. Investors can enjoy this exemption only if they maintain the ownership of their shares over the three-year period. For example, if an investor were to invest ₪ 1 million in an early-stage, R&D-intensive start-up, then the investor can reduce taxable income by a total of ₪ 1 million over the next three years.
Singapore[63]	Under the 'Angel Investors Tax Deduction Scheme', angel investors who invest in start-ups and hold the investment for two years can claim a tax deduction of 50 per cent of the investment made after the two-year holding period. For example, if an approved investor[64] were to invest SG$100,000 in a start-up in January 2020 and hold on to the investment till January 2022, then the investor is eligible to reduce the taxable income by SG$50,000 for 2022. The maximum deduction that can be claimed is capped at SG$500,000.
United Kingdom[65]	Under the Seed Enterprise Investment Scheme, the UK government provides tax credits worth 50 per cent of the investment amount in seed-stage start-ups. The exemptions are capped at £100,000. The tax reliefs can be claimed for three years from the year of investment, provided the investor holds on to the shares. For example, if an eligible investor[66] were to invest £200,000 in a seed-stage start-up, then the investor would get a tax credit of £100,000. Hence, if their tax liability was £220,000 for the year in which the investment was made, it would reduce to £120,000. Further, 50 per cent of the investment made is exempt from capital gains tax. The capital gains exemption is capped at £50,000.
United States[67]	Thirty-one US states allow investors to claim tax credits worth a stipulated proportion of the total investment amount in seed-stage start-ups. The eligibility criteria, proportion of investment amount that is provided as tax credits, and the maximum cap for tax exemptions vary from state to state. For example, consider a hypothetical state that provides tax credits worth 20 per cent of the investment amount in seed-stage start-ups. If an investor invests $100,000 in seed-stage start-ups, then they can reduce their state tax liability by 20 per cent of $100,000, which is $20,000. Hence, if they had a state tax liability of $60,000, they can use this tax credit to reduce it to $40,000.

government seamlessly process requests from investors for tax deductions or exemptions.

Summary

Without a doubt, the angel investing ecosystem in India has seen phenomenal growth since the beginning of the previous decade. There have been a number of innovations in the area such as the formation of angel funds and the advent of specialised angel networks that leverage social capital. Further, investors have also used unconventional approaches to invest in start-ups. Celebrities, for example, are trading brand endorsements (instead of hard capital) in return for equity in start-ups. Start-up founders hence have a wide array of choices and opportunities to raise capital. Founders should be open to consider bespoke approaches for raising capital and must efficiently leverage their social capital in order to reach the right group of investors.

The regulations governing angel investing have seen several changes and revisions since the launch of the Startup India Initiative in 2015. Despite the major reforms in the past five years, angel investors still require considerable support from the government, specifically with regard to taxation. For example, the capital gains tax regime for investments in start-ups is not very attractive. This is a serious concern that is turning many investors away from angel investing. Further, unlike other leading economies, angel investors have neither any tax deductions or credits during the time of investment nor an attractive capital gains tax regime to benefit from at the time of exit.

The e-verification process to scrutinise investments received by start-ups would need to be expedited to ensure start-ups are not subjected to needless scrutiny. Creating and maintaining a register of verified angel investors after scrutinising the professional and financial background of the investors may be the first step needed to implement fiscal incentives. This would reduce the burden on start-up founders to verify the legitimacy of their investors and would enable the government to seamlessly process requests for tax concessions and deductions. Implementation of taxation and procedural reforms would help us to leapfrog even higher in the list of leading angel investment economies. For capital-starved start-ups in India, such policy incentives can be one of the biggest gifts from the government.

Endnotes

[1]Source: YNOS Venture Engine, www.ynos.in

[2]Increasingly, the line between angel investors and pre-seed funds are blurring. As round sizes are getting larger, angel investors are co-investing with venture funds. Venture capital companies have set up pre–seed stage funding schemes that make investments which are similar to angel investments in terms of quantum. For example, K-Start and the Surge Program have been set up by Kalaari Capital and Sequoia, two well-known VC companies in India, to make very early stage investments.

[3]Huang, L, Wu, A , Lee, MJ, Bao, J, Hudson, M and Bolle, E. 2017. *The American Angel: The First In-Depth Report on the Demographics and Investing Activity of Individual American Angel Investors* (pdf) *Report*, Overland Park, Kansas.

[4]Based on the roundtable discussion presented in the next chapter.

[5]Thillai Rajan, A and Jain, A. 2012. *India Venture Capital and Private Equity Report 2012*. Chennai: Indian Institute of Technology, Madras.

[6]Data for 2020 only considers those investments that were announced till December 20, 2020.

[7]Annual average growth rate.

[8]The data for 2006 to 2008 is from Sabarinathan, G. 2014. Understanding angel investing in India: an exploratory study based on publicly available data. *IIMB Working Paper*, 448.

The data for 2009 to 2012 is from Sabarinathan, G. 2019. Angel Investments in India–Trends, Prospects and Issues. *IIMB Management Review* 31(2): 200–214.

The data for 2013 to 2020 is from Crunchbase (https://crunchbase.com/). The database was accessed on December 20, 2020.

[9]The 2006 data is from Trends in the Sands of Time. In *Inspiration and Momentum for the Gladiators: A study and analysis of the start-ups*. *India Venture Capital and Private Equity Report 2016* by Thillai Rajan A. 51–76.

The 2020 data is from YNOS Venture Engine, www.ynos.in (accessed December 2020).

[10]Trends in the Sands of Time. In *Inspiration and Momentum for the Gladiators: A study and analysis of the start-ups*. *India Venture Capital and Private Equity Report 2016* by Thillai Rajan A. 51–76. Chennai: Indian Institute of Technology, Madras.

[11]Data from Crunchbase (https://www.crunchbase.com/). Five angel groups had to be dropped from the analysis as data on their year of formation was not available. The database was accessed on October 7, 2020.

[12]Data from Crunchbase (https://www.crunchbase.com/), accessed on October 7, 2020.

[13]Though we refer to them as members, they are officially called 'partners' in line with the VC terminology.

[14]We take the highest number published between Crunchbase (https://www.crunchbase.com/) and PitchBook (https://www.pitchbook.com/). For Yatra Angel Network and Native Angel Network, we use the data from their own website, as the networks are relatively new. The two databases were accessed on October 7, 2020.

[15]With the exception of Venture Catalysts, data for the number of members comes from the websites of the respective angel networks or from their response to our data request.

[16]Not Available is abbreviated as NA.

[17]Dash, S. 2020. This Indian investment firm wants to bring on board angel investors from India's smaller cities. *Business Insider India* (24 August, 2020). Website: https://www.businessinsider.in/business/startups/news/this-indian-investment-firm-wants-to-bring-on-board-angel-investors-from-indias-smaller-cities/articleshow/77715629.cms

[18]Saxsena, R. 2019. IAN marks final close of ₹375 crore maiden venture capital fund. *Mint* (6 November, 2019). Retrievable from: https://www.livemint.com/companies/start-ups/ian-marks-final-close-of-375-crore-maiden-venture-capital-fund-11573060999310.html

[19]Gooptu, B. 2020. Angel funds need approval from all before investing. *The Economic Times* (29 September, 2020). Retrievable from: https://economictimes.indiatimes.com/small-biz/startups/newsbuzz/angel-funds-need-approval-from-all-before-investing/articleshow/78376565.cms

[20]The official website for the product is https://angel.co/india/angel-funds.

[21]Peermohamed, A. 2019. Silicon Valley-based AngelList launches angel fund in India. *The Economic Times* (8 November, 2019). Retrievable from: https://economictimes.indiatimes.com/small-biz/startups/newsbuzz/silicon-valley-based-angellist-launches-angel-fund-in-india/articleshow/71964472.cms

[22]Ibid.

[23]Information on celebrity investments is from Findlay, S. 2019. Bollywood stars tap India's start-ups for brand boost. *The Financial Times* (26 July, 2019). Website: https://www.ft.com/content/63a2b5d2-ac7a-11e9-8030-530adfa879c2. Information about NativeLead is from their official website (http://nativelead.org/). Details about JITO Angel Network were provided by the network to the iVEIN consortium.

[24]Thillai Rajan A and Danak, A. 2016. The Gladiatorial Arena of Start-ups. In *Inspiration and Momentum for the Gladiators: A study and analysis of the start-ups*. India Venture Capital and Private Equity Report 2016 by Thillai Rajan A. 77–92. Indian Institute of Technology Madras, Chennai.

[25]Thillai Rajan A. 2017. Government Policy and Support for Start-ups - A Phase of High Momentum. In *India Venture Capital and Private Equity Report 2016* by Thillai Rajan A. 1–16. Indian Institute of Technology Madras, Chennai.

[26]The Prime Minister of India announced this initiative during the Independence Day speech on August 15, 2015. Accessible at: https://www.pmindia.gov.in/en/news_updates/english-rendering-of-pms-address-to-the-nation-from-the-ramparts-of-the-red-fort-on-the-69th-independence-day/

[27]Ibid.

[28]Based on Department of Industrial Policy and Promotion. 2018. *States' Startup Ranking 2018*. New Delhi. (and) Department of Industrial Policy and Promotion. 2020. *States' Startup Ranking 2019*. New Delhi.

[29]Primarily based on the 2018 and 2019 *States' Startup Ranking* reports published by the Department of Industrial Policy and Promotion.

[30]Department for Promotion of Industry and Industrial Trade. 2018. *Awareness and Outreach*. Retrieved from *The Government of India, Department of Commerce and Industry* website: https://www.startupindia.gov.in/content/sih/en/compendium_of_good_practices/awarenessAndOutreach.html

The 2017 Bihar Start-up Policy is accessible at: http://udyog.bihar.gov.in/NewPolicy/Bihar-Startup-Policy-2017.pdf

[31]Government of Karnataka. 2015. Karnataka Startup Policy 2015–2020. Bengaluru. Accessible at: https://startup.karnataka.gov.in/docs/Startup_Policy_Karnataka.pdf

[32]Government of Madhya Pradesh. 2019. Madhya Pradesh Startup Policy 2019. Accessible at: https://www.startupindia.gov.in/content/dam/invest-india/Templates/

public/state_startup_policies/Madhya_Pradesh%20 Incubation%20&%20Startup%20Policy%202016.pdf

[33]Department of Industrial Policy and Promotion. 2020. *States' Startup Ranking 2019*. New Delhi.

[34]Ibid.

[35]Capital gains from investments made in start-ups is taxed at the same rate as gains from investments made in unlisted companies (28.5%).

[36]The Planning Commission of India (2012). *Creating a Vibrant Entrepreneurial Ecosystem in India*. New Delhi.

[37]Income Tax Department, Circular Number 3/2012, Dated 12-06-2012. Accessible at: *https://incometaxindia.gov.in/Communications/Circular/910110000000000801.htm*

[38]NITI Aayog. 2015. *Report of the Expert Committee on Innovation and Entrepreneurship*. New Delhi.

[39]Ibid.

[40]Primarily based on Department of Industrial Policy and Promotion. 2018. *States' Startup Ranking 2018*. New Delhi.

[41]Section 32, Finance Act of 2016 – Accessible at https://www.incometaxindia.gov.in/_layouts/15/dit/mobile/viewer.aspx?path=https://www.incometaxindia.gov.in/acts/finance%20acts/2016/102120000000058864.htm&k=54EE.

The official copy of the whole act is accessible at https://www.cbic.gov.in/resources/htdocs-cbec/fin-act2016.pdf

[42]Section 33, Finance Act of 2016 – Accessible at https://www.cbic.gov.in/resources/htdocs-cbec/fin-act2016.pdf (Amendment to Section 54GB of the Income Tax Act)

[43]Another amendment was made to Section 54GB in 2019, which reduced the minimum holding requirement from 50% to 25%. The amendment was a part of the Finance Acts of 2019 (No.2) – Section 20. Accessible at https://www.incometaxindia.gov.in/_layouts/15/dit/mobile/viewer.aspx?path=https://www.incometaxindia.gov.in/acts/finance%20acts/2019_2/102120000000074123.htm&k=54GB

The official copy of the whole act is accessible at https://www.cbic.gov.in/resources//htdocs-cbec/Finance_Bill-2019.pdf

[44]SEBI Board Meeting Press Release – PR No. 161/2016. Accessible at: https://www.sebi.gov.in/sebi_data/docfiles/35234_t.html

[45]SEBI Board Memorandum (April 2018). Accessible at: https://www.sebi.gov.in/sebi_data/meetingfiles/apr-2018/1524117274041_1.pdf

[46]Section 21, Finance Acts of 2019 (No.2) - Amendment of Section 56 (2) (viib) of the Income Tax Act of 1961. Accessible at: https://www.incometaxindia.gov.in/_layouts/15/dit/mobile/viewer.aspx?path=https://www.incometaxindia.gov.in/acts/finance%20acts/2019_2/102120000000074124.htm&k=56

Notification G.S.R 127(E) - Accessible at https://www.startupindia.gov.in/content/dam/invest-india/Templates/public/198117.pdf

[47]Bora, S. 2019. Budget 2019: Government removes the sting of angel tax, entrepreneurs & investors rejoice. *The Economic Times* (5 July, 2019). Retrievable from: https://economictimes.indiatimes.com/small-biz/startups/newsbuzz/budget-2019-government-removes-the-sting-of-angel-tax-entrepreneurs-investors-rejoice/articleshow/70091664.cms?utm_source=contentofinterest&utm_medium=text&utm_campaign=cppst

[48]Sharma, AR. 2020. Budget 2020: Startups seek more changes to the provisions of Angel Tax. *The Economic Times* (31 January, 2020). Retrievable from: https://economictimes.indiatimes.com/small-biz/startups/newsbuzz/budget-2020-startups-seek-more-changes-to-the-provisions-of-angel-tax/articleshow/73802466.cms?from=mdr

[49]Ibid.

[50]Ibid.

[51]Ibid.

[52]Ibid.

[53]Pai, M and Krishnan, S. 2020. Abolish LTCG tax, incentivise investors. Retrieved from *The Financial Express* (24 August, 2020) website: https://www.financialexpress.com/opinion/abolish-ltcg-tax-incentivise-investors/2063250/

[54]KPMG. 2015. Why are big businesses looking to start-ups for innovation? Retrieved from *KPMG, Australia* website: https://assets.kpmg/content/dam/kpmg/pdf/2015/02/big-business-start-ups-innovation.pdf

[55]We consider all the current (as of October 2020) member countries in the European Union as one country in this analysis.

[56]Data from Crunchbase (https://www.crunchbase.com/), accessed on December 21, 2020.

[57]Prominent investors include Anupam Mittal, Binny Bansal, Kunal Bahl, Kunal Shah, Rohit Bansal and Vijay Shekhar Sharma.

[58]Data from Crunchbase (https://www.crunchbase.com/). Accessed on October 7, 2020

[59]Ibid.

[60]Australian Taxation Office. 2020. *Tax incentives for early stage investors*. Retrieved from Australian Government, Australian Taxation Office website: https://www.ato.gov.au/Business/Tax-incentives-for-innovation/In-detail/Tax-incentives-for-early-stage-investors/
Accessed on May 29, 2021

[61]In order to be eligible, firstly, the angel investor must not have any prior affiliation with the start-up. Secondly, the investor must not receive more than 30% of the distribution of income or voting rights as a consequence of the deal. Finally, the deal must not be under any employee share scheme where shares are sold at a discounted price to current or former employees.

[62]Harris, L. 2014. *Your taxes: Angel Law amendment proposals*. Retrieved from *The Jerusalem Post* website: https://www.jpost.com/business/commentary/your-taxes-angel-law-amendment-proposals-375536
Accessed on May 29, 2021

[63]Inland Revenue Authority of Singapore. 2020. *Angel Investors Tax Deduction Scheme (AITD)*. Retrieved from Government of Singapore, Inland Revenue Authority of Singapore website: https://www.iras.gov.sg/irashome/Schemes/Individuals/Angel-Investors-Tax-Deduction-Scheme--AITD-/

[64]Angel investors would need to apply and get approved by 'Enterprise Singapore' (a government agency), before they can claim deductions.

[65]HM Revenue & Customs. 2019. *Tax relief for investors using venture capital schemes*. Retrieved from Government of the United Kingdom, HM Revenue & Customs website: https://www.gov.uk/guidance/venture-capital-schemes-tax-relief-for-investors
Accessed on May 29, 2021

[66]In order to be eligible, firstly, the investor must not have any prior familial ties with any of the start-up founders. Secondly, the investor must not be an employee of the company. Finally, the investor must not have over a 30% share in the firms equity, right to assets and voting rights.

[67]Denes, M, Wang, X and Xu, T. 2019. *Financing Entrepreneurship: Tax Incentives for Early-Stage Investors*. Retrievable at: http://jhfinance.web.unc.edu/files/2019/12/2020_Denes_Wang_Xu__Financing_Entrepreneurship_Tax_Incentives_for_Early_Stage_Investors.pdf

[68]The e-verification of angel investments was announced by the Union Minister for Finance in the 2019 budget speech. See https://www.indiabudget.gov.in/doc/bspeech/bs201920.pdf

[69]Mohammed, S. 2019. Start-ups welcome e-verification of angel investments. Retrieved from *The Hindu,* Hyderabad Edition (05 July, 2019) website: https://www.thehindu.com/news/cities/Hyderabad/start-ups-welcome-e-verification-of-angel-investments/article28299010.ece

IN BRIEF

- Understanding the non-financial motivations of an angel investor is critical when pitching an investment proposal.
- Since the number of proposals received by angel investors has grown significantly in recent years, the investment proposal from the founders should be of very high quality to attract investor attention.
- Raising capital through an angel network helps to raise a higher quantum of funding.
- Start-ups should develop the ability to take advantage of the opportunities in adverse business environments through business model innovation.
- Exit opportunities are important for growth in venture investments. Leveraging existing institutions such as SME (small and medium enterprise) exchanges to facilitate exits for investors can significantly increase investment flow.
- Reforms such as tax deductions for venture investments, withdrawal of provisions pertaining to tax on angel investments and withdrawal of cases pertaining to angel tax would bolster investor confidence.

ROUNDTABLE

13

More than a Century of Angel Investments: A Perspective

N Ramakrishnan

Ramakrishnan, N. 2021. "More than a Century of Angel Investments: A Perspective". In *Shifting Orbits: Decoding the Trajectory of the Indian Start-up Ecosystem*, edited by Thillai Rajan A, Srivardhini K Jha, Joffi Thomas and Rohan Chinchwadkar, 154–165. Hyderabad: Universities Press (India) Private Limited.

Why this Roundtable?

A journey of a thousand miles starts with a single step. For an entrepreneur, very often the first port of call for capital in their entrepreneurial voyage is the angel investor. Angel investing in India has witnessed exponential growth in recent years. The number of angel investment rounds has grown at an average annual rate of 22 per cent between 2011 and 2020.[1] India has also witnessed the formation of several angel networks and has seen a rapid increase in the number of angel investors. With over 4,200 active angel investors[2] and over 45 angel networks, India has grown to be a prominent angel investing hub in the world.[3] Despite the increase in the number of investors, entrepreneurs still find it difficult to raise capital from angel investors. One of the prominent reasons for the poor rates of funding has been the prevailing information asymmetry in seed-stage investing. Entrepreneurs are not fully aware of the motivations of angel investors, their investment rationale and expectations.

In this roundtable conversation, we bring together prominent angel investors, Padma Chandrasekaran, Naganand Doraswamy, Naru R Narayanan, Aprameya Radhakrishna and Rajesh Sawhney, who have cumulatively made over 100 investments, to share their perspectives on angel investing in India. These perspectives provide insights on the investor mindset that would help both entrepreneurs and policymakers.

What Motivates Angel Investors?

***Ramakrishnan (Ramki):* In a recent tweet,[4] a venture capitalist (VC), who, when asked by four friends whether they should become angel investors, replied with an emphatic 'No'. His reasons were access, influence and diversification. The VC argued that angels don't have access, they would not be able to influence the decision-making, and diversification of their portfolio should not be the reason for them to become angel investors. With so much going against the grain, what is the motivation for angel investments?**

Rajesh: If VC investments are risky, angel investments are riskier. Because of their very nature, angel investments cannot have the same level of extensive due diligence and risk assessment that are typically associated with VC investments. To take my own example, I make 10 to 15 investments every year, of which only 20 per cent to 30 per cent are successful. In angel investing, one high yielding investment among 20 could well compensate for the losses incurred and provide a substantial overall return.

Moreover, the three factors mentioned in the tweet need to be cultivated over time. For example, it takes time to build networks that are of any value. When I debuted in angel investing, I had access to a strong VC network, but it was not helpful. On the contrary, the network of young entrepreneurs that I had developed as a result of my investment activity over the years has been the most helpful. As they say, Rome cannot be built in a day. I would therefore encourage investors who have the time, monetary resources and passion for angel investing to invest 10 per cent to 15 per cent of their portfolio in this asset class. They must, however, take gradual incremental steps, while patiently building their networks and diversifying their investments. I primarily spent my first five years building networks, learning from my mistakes and understanding angel investing. Post this period, I have been reaping the benefits of the initial efforts. The returns on my initial investments are flowing in, my networks are primed, and the deal flow has been exceptionally smooth. In fact, from a financial standpoint, angel investment has been one of my best performing asset classes. In the learning phase, it is important to avoid over-analysing a failure. We need to write-off the failure quickly, acknowledge the fact that the entrepreneur has worked hard against all odds, and help the entrepreneur in making a smooth transition out of the venture. Over-intellectualising failures would invariably lead to making judgements about the entrepreneur's character, which often leads to wrong conclusions, as it is a very complicated problem for the human mind to solve.

Despite the risks involved, my primary motivation to become an angel investor was to keep myself involved with the latest innovations and to learn from young smart technology entrepreneurs. I have enjoyed the journey and this kind of learning could not have been obtained by any other means.

Aprameya: Fundamentally, it boils down to the objective of angel investing. If it were financial returns, it is important to understand that angel investing is not a game of fantasy but a game of probability. Angel investing happens at so early a stage in the life of a start-up, where a multitude of factors will affect its success. It is therefore extremely hard to be able to control the success of every investment. The factors mentioned in the tweet can only increase the odds of making the right investment, but do not guarantee success. For example, for an investor without any access and influence, the odds of making the right investment might be one in a thousand. However, if the investor were to gain access to networks and information, the odds might improve to one in a hundred. One can consider debuting in angel investing as long as one is aware of the odds of success and has an appetite for the risks involved. Aspiring angel investors should be cognizant of the fact that they would start with very poor odds of success, and that over a period of time, their odds would gradually improve, as they gain more access to the ecosystem and understand the factors involved.

If the motivation was non-financial and was more for societal signalling, then it is a different ball game. The risks involved do not matter at all, since it is about the 'snob value' one derives from claiming to invest in start-ups.

Personally, my motivation to invest is to be a part of future creations. Angel investing is a great way to get involved with a kaleidoscope of creations and innovations, without necessarily being involved with the execution. It would be impossible to achieve this as an individual if one were to be fully responsible for building and managing the ventures. Another reason for angel investing is to ensure that good entrepreneurs have access to the necessary capital. My experience as an entrepreneur has taught me the importance of access to capital. When we started 'TaxiForSure',[5] we had to struggle to attract the necessary capital, as the angel investing ecosystem was very nascent at that time. If only we had had access to the quantum of capital that is typically available today, we would have been able to achieve much more than what we did.

Padma: The tweet appears to be advice for aspiring angel investors who are looking to debut in angel investing in the context of the current economic contraction caused due to the outbreak of the COVID-19 pandemic. Seasoned investors are well aware of the fickle nature of angel investing. We realized the importance of access and networks even when angel investing was very nascent in India, and we did not expect others to come and help us in getting those. We formed partnerships with other like-minded investors to seed the formation of networks and in building the ecosystem. The Chennai Angels network is an example.[6] As a result of our ground experience, we now have healthy access to start-ups and understand the ecosystem well. Nevertheless, angel investing requires one to handle initial failures and learn from them. The financial and reputational risks involved are high. For example, I may be investing a couple of million in a venture, but should have the willpower to walk away from it without any tears, should it unfortunately fail.

Despite the risks involved, my motivation for angel investing stems from the opportunity it provides of being at the vanguard of potentially successful companies that can change the face of India. Being at the cutting edge of business and product innovation is an exhilarating experience and the amount of learning that I get is vast.

Naganand: The decision to start angel investing must depend on what one can bring to the table. It is not just a question of monetary resources, but also about providing the entrepreneurs with the necessary time, inputs and contacts. In my opinion, one can start angel investing if one has the time, money and relevant expertise for the venture. If they do not have the time or relevant expertise, it is important to co-invest in consortiums that provide it.

When I make an investment, I enter with my eyes open, knowing that the probability for the investment to be written off is non-trivial. No one can be sure about the success of their product – the market humbles us every time. Further, it is impossible to expect rigid timelines for exiting the venture and reaping returns. It is the ability to work with an exciting team in an exciting market that motivates me, more than the financial returns. There is never a dull moment in angel investing.

Naru: Angel investing gives me an opportunity to reinvent myself and be involved in all the action. Further, it provides me an opportunity to lend my 50 years of professional experience, both in large companies as well as start-ups, to entrepreneurs, whenever they desire it. From a financial standpoint, I am optimistic about my investments and am content if it yields even a little more than what I earn from the stock market.

Identifying Promising Ventures

***Ramki:* A common thread in the responses has been that angel investing carries significant risks and that one must be prepared to write-off one's investments. With such high risks involved, how do you identify potential investments? What is your strategy for evaluating investment proposals?**

Aprameya: The entrepreneur and the market are the two key aspects that I evaluate in the business proposal. When evaluating the entrepreneur, I look for passion and agility. The entrepreneur must stay true to solving the customer's problems and must be responsive to the evolving needs of the customer. When evaluating the market, I look for how deep the pain point is, how many people it affects (which gives us a sense of the potential size of the target market segment) and how well the solution addresses the pain point.

Padma: My first requirement is for the venture to have a proof of concept and some pilot customers. I agree with Aprameya that it is important to identify the right entrepreneur and market. Persistence is a quality that I value very highly when evaluating entrepreneurs. I might be willing to work with a persistent entrepreneur again even if their prior venture had not been successful. However, it is important to differentiate between persistence and stubbornness. While stubbornness is sticking with the same outlook and approach irrespective of the evolving circumstances, persistence is about the unwavering pursuit of success, where the entrepreneur adapts to the evolving circumstances to achieve the objectives. For sure, persistence is a hard quality to gauge, but I try to infer it from my interactions with the entrepreneur and from their background. As far as the market is concerned, I would only invest in ventures that are in relatively uncontested markets. The scope for success is close to none when investing in a late entrant, especially when the market already has several well-funded start-ups.

***Ramki*: A steady development in recent years in the investment landscape has been the formation of angel networks.[7] Does investing as a part of an angel network, rather than as an individual angel investor, increase the chances of identifying the right investments? Is there a group-think advantage?**

Rajesh: Yes, I would agree that networks help in increasing the chances of identifying the right investments. Apart from that, there are two other advantages that make investing as a network a better option. Firstly, angel networks enable angels to easily meet the large capital requirements of start-ups. The average amount required often ranges between ₹10 million and ₹50 million, which in most cases is only possible for a consortium of angels to raise. The second advantage is the mentoring and guidance that a like-minded group of angels with diverse backgrounds and expertise can provide to the start-up. The expertise would come in handy when taking tough decisions during the start-up's journey, such as identifying the CEO or when strategising an exit.

Naru: I have greatly benefitted from making investments along with networks. Networks give investors an opportunity to listen to a range of opinions and arguments, which greatly helps the decision-making process. Specifically, the opportunity to discuss with a talented group of investors brings a greater degree of maturity to one's outlook of the decision-making process.

Padma: The wisdom of the crowd, to put it succinctly, is the most salient feature of investing as a network.

Aprameya: There are significant challenges to investing as a network, which also need to be mentioned at this point. To be successful, networks need to take decisions with agility, which often proves to be a challenge. There is a need for cohesion among the members to ensure that decisions are made swiftly.

***Ramki:* Apart from gauging the entrepreneur and the market, would you also decide on an exit timeline and strategy prior to investing?**

Naganand: Given that there are a plethora of factors that influence the exit from ventures, it is extremely hard to enforce strict exit timelines. On average, it takes more than five years for a profitable exit.

Rajesh: The highest yielding exit strategy would be through the initial public offering (IPO). On average, it would take around 15 years for a start-up to reach the IPO stage in India, while it only takes 10 years in the United States. Hence, Indian angel investors must expect a longer exit duration. As far as my portfolio is concerned, my exits have primarily been through buyouts or secondary exits. In the case of buyouts, there is very little an angel investor can do, since the deals are primarily negotiated between the founder and the VCs.

Secondary exits typically happen at various stages of VC investment. Specifically, during the Series C stage, there is tremendous pressure to streamline the capitalisation table and to consolidate equity by easing out smaller investors (see Exhibit 13.1 for an introduction to capitalisation tables). My recommendation, based on my personal experience, would be to hold on to potential investments for a longer period and avoid early secondary exits.

Value Addition by Investors

***Ramki:* Apart from capital, many entrepreneurs also expect the investors to contribute to their portfolio companies in terms of their expertise and connections. What should be the ideal role for the investor in their portfolio companies?**

Naganand: It is important to ensure that the entrepreneurs run the company. The angel investors should ideally just serve as mentor–partners. An ideal angel investor must allocate time to the founders when requested, patiently attempt to fully appreciate the founders' problems, and provide relevant inputs to address their problems. It is counter-productive to be extremely intrusive and to get involved in the day-to-day functioning of the firm. Having said that, it is important to ensure that there are quarterly or monthly meetings –

Exhibit 13.1: The capitalisation table

The capitalisation table lists all the shareholders of a company, along with details about the number of shares they hold, the amount of money they had invested to procure those shares, and the type of shares they own.

Let us look at the capitalisation table for a hypothetical early-stage tech start-up called 'Unnamed Tech Solutions' (UTS). The company was founded by a tech entrepreneur who had invested the initial capital of ₹100,000 from personal finances. The founder owns 50 shares in the firm. In the first round of financing, the founder issued 50 more shares to a group of five angel investors at a price of ₹10,000 per share. UTS issued preferential shares instead of common shares to the angel investors. The capitalisation table[10] for this start-up is presented below.

Capitalisation Table for Unnamed Tech Solutions (UTS)

	UTS valuation			
	Total amount raised	Value per share	Number of shares	% of total shares
Series X				
Pre-money valuation	₹100,000	₹2,000	50	50%
Fresh equity raised	₹500,000	₹10,000	50	50%
Post-money valuation	₹600,000	₹6,000	100	100%

	UTS capitilisation table			
	Capital invested	Number of common shares	Number of preferential shares	Ownership shares
Series X				
Founder	₹100,000	50	0	50%
Angel investor A	₹200,000	0	20	20%
Angel investor B	₹100,000	0	10	10%
Angel investor C	₹50,000	0	5	5%
Angel investor D	₹70,000	0	7	7%
Angel investor E	₹80,000	0	8	8%
Total	**₹600,000**	**50**	**50**	**100%**

Types of Shares

Shares are broadly classified into two types: common and preferential. Common shareholders have voting rights and can influence the decision-making process. On the other hand, preferential shareholders do not have voting rights, but are given additional privileges that partly insulate them from the risks of failure. For example, during liquidation, preferential stock owners are often given the first priority to recover their investments from the company's net assets (assets remaining after all liabilities are settled).

such discipline is greatly beneficial to both the investors and the founders.

Aprameya: Entrepreneurs tend to have varying preferences when it comes to the frequency of sending progress updates to investors. It is important to note that the frequency has little correlation with the success of the firm. It is therefore important to ensure that investors adapt to the entrepreneur's preference and personality. If investors fail to adapt, it would needlessly encroach on the entrepreneur's freedom and might prove to be counter-productive.

Padma: I believe it is important to trust the entrepreneur and to be available when they need advice or mentorship. One needs to learn that influence on the start-up founder must be earned and not demanded.

The Trajectory of Angel Investing in India

***Ramki:* Naturally, a segment as dynamic as angel investing would have morphed significantly over the years. What has been the nature of such changes? And more importantly, what are the implications of these changes for start-up founders?**

Naru: The most important trend is the increase in the number of investment proposals and the improvement in the quality of proposals. My experience with 'The Chennai Angels' network has given me a first-hand experience of the change in the angel investing landscape. Around 2012, The Chennai Angels would only received two to three proposals a month. However, in 2020, the number of proposals received has increased to around eight to ten a week.

Likewise, the quality of proposals has also drastically improved. In the early years, we had to nurture some entrepreneurs for a few months, in order to aid them in developing a meaningful business plan that might interest investors. However, in recent years, this has completely changed. Many of the proposals received have well-developed business plans, which provide investors with a clear value proposition and growth trajectory. In fact, proposals without such well-developed plans, which used to be entertained 10 years ago, are instantly rejected in recent years. This clearly illustrates the phenomenal improvement in the quality of proposals.

Rajesh: The degree of VC participation in early-stage start-ups has also significantly risen in the recent past. VCs have started writing smaller cheques for early-stage companies, which has increased the competition for angel investors. Angel investors are now forced to compete with prominent VCs for equity in promising start-ups. Hence, angel investors who collaborate with VCs have been very successful. However, only angel investors who enjoy certain brand equity and reputation would be able to co-invest with VCs.

The Impact of COVID-19

***Ramki:* How has the COVID-19 pandemic and the countrywide lockdown affected the investing landscape and the existing investment portfolio? In what ways do the start-ups have to restructure themselves to be resilient in a pandemic?**

Padma: The impact of COVID-19 has been heterogenous. Companies that require or thrive on physical presence have been impacted significantly. On the other hand, companies that predominantly operate in the digital space, such as EdTech, have prospered during the crisis.

Firms have also been using varying strategies to weather the storm. Some firms, typically the mature and established start-ups, have sought additional funding by raising bridge rounds to overcome the shortfall in revenue and to stay afloat. Others, that expect the continuation of lockdowns and social distancing measures for some more time, are attempting to seize the opportunity by migrating to a purely digital product offering.

Rajesh: My portfolio has performed exceptionally well during 2020. Most notably, eight companies in my portfolio have successfully raised capital in 'up-rounds'[8] during this year. I have not faced any retardation in terms of deal flow and have invested in six companies since the outbreak of COVID-19. Further, I have had two successful exits in 2020, in the months of March and August.

Having said that, there were four to five companies in my portfolio that faced severe challenges due to the pandemic. These firms can be classified into two categories. The first were those that were facing a cash deficit and were on the verge of running out of funds. The second were in sectors that were directly affected by the suspension of regular economic activity, such as the food sector. However, start-ups that were accelerating prior to the pandemic in my portfolio have continued to accelerate at a more pronounced rate even during the pandemic.

Naru: At The Chennai Angels, the start-up selection process had to be moved to virtual platforms due to the lockdown and social distancing measures. This has increased the overall efficiency of the process, reduced response times, and has attracted greater participation from members. For example, prior to the pandemic, the network required start-ups to make physical presentations to the members. The logistical challenges involved in attending physical meetings meant that only 15 to 18 members (on average) took part in a presentation. However, the shift to virtual presentations post COVID-19 has enabled 40 to 50 investors to participate in a presentation with great ease.

Aprameya: Unfortunately, a higher number of companies have suffered due to the pandemic than those that have thrived. In specific, the micro-transit sector has been severely affected. Apart from the social distancing and lockdown measures, the prevailing fear among commuters to share a vehicle with others has also been a major detriment to the sector.

While it is important to adapt to the changing customer preferences during the pandemic, it is also crucial to work towards preparing for the post–COVID-19 market. Hence, start-ups are fine-tuning their strategies based on their outlook for the evolution of consumer behaviour post COVID-19. From an angel investor's perspective, it would be profitable to invest in start-ups that cater to market preferences and behaviours that initially emerged during the pandemic but would continue to remain even after COVID-19.

Naganand: COVID-19 has had a debilitating impact on humanity, having claimed the lives and livelihoods of many. Start-ups have not been immune to the disruptions caused by the pandemic, specifically those in the hospitality, mobility and travel sectors.

However, from a business perspective, the pandemic has created opportunities that would have otherwise been unimaginable. For example, if not for the pandemic, it would have been impossible to witness a situation where companies had to ensure the smooth functioning of their businesses despite all their employees working remotely. The challenges that arose from the crisis have resulted in significant acceleration of digital transformation across all sectors including education, health and enterprise applications.

As for start-ups in sectors that were severely affected, the crisis provides an opportunity to re-evaluate and improve their business models. As they say, every crisis presents an opportunity.

Government Policies and Angel Investing

***Ramki:* Given the increasing importance of start-ups in policies, what should be the role of the government to strengthen the ecosystem for angel investments?**

Naru: As discussed earlier, the exit timelines are much longer in India, primarily due to the convoluted nature of exits. I have two policy suggestions that would greatly simplify exits and incentivise angel investing. Firstly, the government must focus on aggressively developing the Micro, Small and Medium Enterprises (MSME) market, to facilitate smoother exits. Currently, the MSME markets are far from being viable exit options. Secondly, there needs to be major reform in the taxation code. The government must introduce complete tax deductibility for investments made in start-ups for a specified number of years, in order to incentivise investments by boosting profitability.

Rajesh: Often, there is a large chasm between the espoused policy and the actual implementation of the policy. For example, while the government promised serious reform on the issue of angel taxes, the ground reality is very different (see Exhibit 13.2 for an introduction to angel taxes). Rather than withdrawing the pending angel tax–related cases,[9] the government only suspended them. Hence, the sword of angel tax liability still hangs over the start-ups.

Further, a number of companies are getting incorporated outside India. This is extremely detrimental to India's start-up ecosystem. The government must act swiftly to incentivise companies to incorporate in India and must provide further incentives to angel investors.

Exhibit 13.2: The angel tax

To understand how the angel tax works, let us consider a hypothetical early-stage tech start-up called 'Unnamed Tech Solutions' (UTS), that is actively raising capital for its growth and expansion. The company was founded by a tech entrepreneur who had invested the initial capital for the firm from personal finances. The founder owns 50 shares. The founder is seeking to issue 50 more shares to angel investors at a price of ₹10,000 per share (₹500,000 in total).

What is a good price?

To check if ₹10,000 is a good price for a share, the investors value the firm based on its future profit potential and see if the price truly captures its value.

The software that UTS is developing has great potential and is projected to generate ₹1 million in future profits valued at today's money, after adjusting for inflation and time value. Apart from the potential profits, the company currently owns assets worth ₹100,000 and does not have any liabilities. The angel investors hence value UTS at,

$$\frac{\text{Projected profits + Assest − Liabilities}}{\text{Total number of shares}} = \frac{₹1{,}000{,}000 + ₹100{,}000 - ₹0}{100} = ₹11{,}000 \text{ per share}$$

Given that the perceived value of the share to investors exceeds the price, the angel investors decide to invest ₹500,000 for 50 shares in UTS.

Fair market value and angel tax

The tax authorities, however, value the company only based on its net assets. The government does not include the projected profits, as it is just a subjective estimation by angel investors. Hence, to the government, the value of UTS is,

$$\frac{\text{Assest − Liabilities}}{\text{Total number of shares}} = \frac{₹100{,}000 - ₹0}{100} = ₹1{,}000 \text{ per share}$$

The government hence deems the fair price of 50 shares to be ₹50,000. The government considers the capital raised in excess of the fair value, which is ₹450,000 (₹500,000 – ₹50,000), as taxable income. UTS is therefore sent a notice to pay 30 per cent of the excess capital (liability of ₹135,000) as tax to the government. This tax liability is referred to as angel tax.

Legal action against angel tax defaulters

Cases were filed against start-ups that failed to pay this liability. In 2019, the government suspended these cases, but did not withdraw them.

Therefore, for UTS, while the demand for payment of angel tax amounting to ₹135,000 is currently suspended, investors are concerned that there is a possibility for the government to reopen the cases and legally sanction UTS to pay the tax liability.[11]

Naganand: The government has made a number of crucial policy reforms for VC investing, including the introduction of 'fund of funds' and the policies governing alternative investment funds (AIFs) (see Exhibit 13.3 for an introduction to fund of funds). However, there has not been any significant reform specific to angel investors. There is significant scope for policy changes which can lead to a growth in angel investments. For example, reforms that enable angel networks or a consortium of angel investors to be listed as one entity in the capitalisation table, instead of listing each member is one such reform. This would greatly help in seamlessly

Exhibit 13.3: Fund of funds

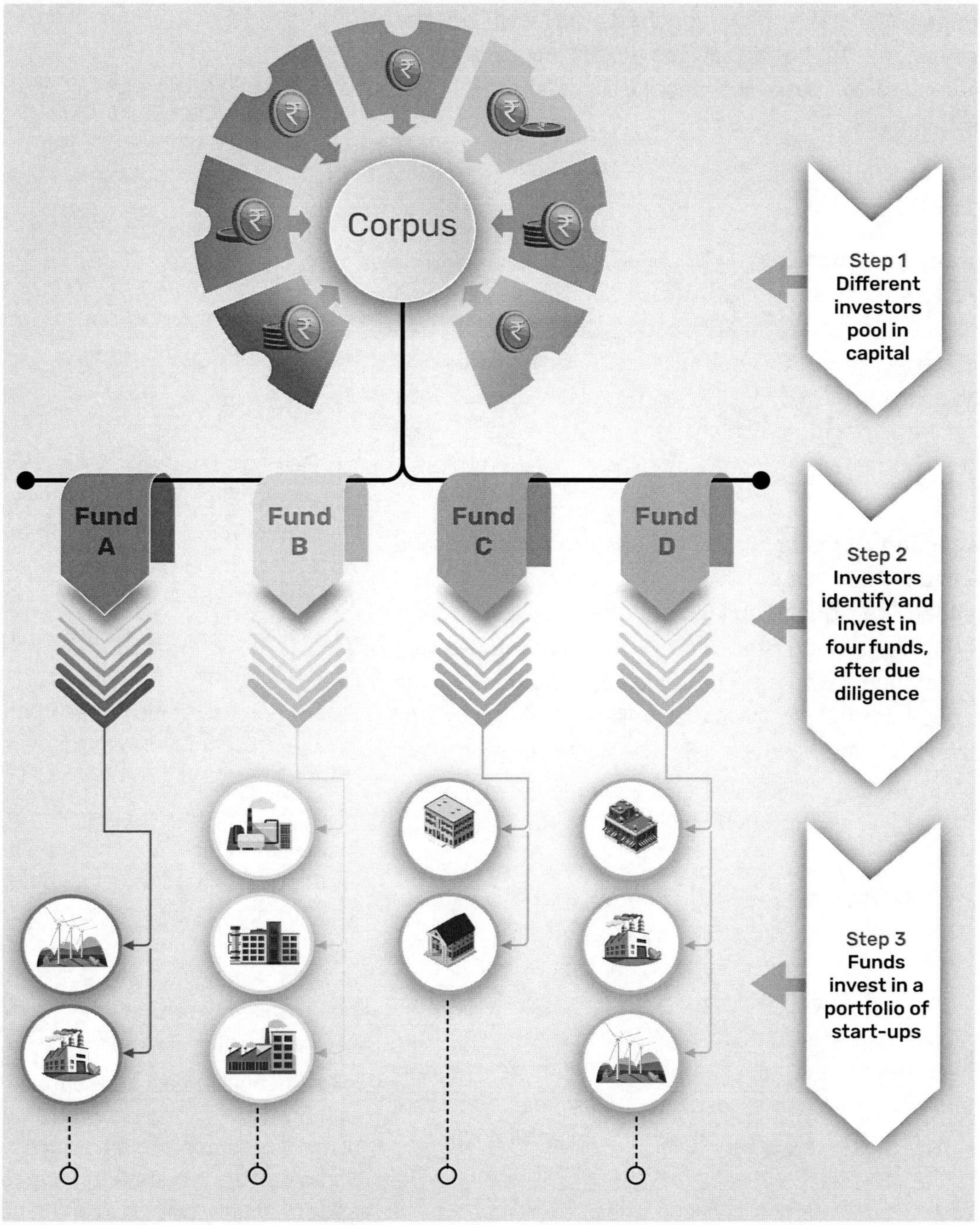

To explore the idea behind fund of funds (FoF), let us consider a hypothetical market where there are 10 VC funds and multiple start-ups seeking investment. A group of investors in this market has come together and created a corpus to invest in start-ups. Under the FoF investment strategy, the investors would evaluate the performance of the 10 VC funds and shortlist a certain number of funds in which to invest. Each of those VC funds would then invest the capital received in multiple start-ups. The choice of start-ups of each VC fund would vary depending on the fund manager's sector of expertise and risk appetite. This ensures that the overall portfolio of the investors is well diversified and balanced in terms of risk.

The biggest advantage of the FoF strategy is that it delegates the burden of identifying promising start-ups to the VC funds, and hence, eases the burden on the investors. They would only need to evaluate the performance of the funds and fund managers, instead of evaluating the start-ups. Most notably, the central and state governments have used this strategy extensively in the recent past to co-invest in budding Indian start-ups.

raising venture and growth funding from VC and Private Equity (PE) investors.

Ramki: **We have now reached the end of the discussion. On behalf of the iVEIN consortium, I would like to thank the speakers for sharing their perspectives.**

The Panellists

Aprameya Radhakrishna is one of India's leading angel investors and has invested in over 20 promising start-ups since 2015. Prior to angel investing, Aprameya founded and ran 'TaxiForSure', a successful taxi aggregator, which was acquired by OLA in 2016. He is an alumnus of Indian Institute of Management Ahmedabad, and National Institute of Technology Karnataka, Surathkal.

Naganand Doraswamy is a serial entrepreneur turned investor. After exiting his most recent start-up, he founded Ideaspring Capital to fund and actively support product innovation start-ups. He enjoys working with entrepreneurs who have the vision and passion to build products for the global markets. Naganand is very well networked and respected in the start-up ecosystem and he actively participates in various organisations focussing on Entrepreneurship and Innovation.

Naru R Narayanan is a graduate from the early batches of IIM Calcutta in 1969. He has largely been in FMCG, as in Coca Cola Export Corporation, Nestle, and a brief stint in Rediffusion Advertising before a becoming an entrepreneur. He founded Gum India Ltd and ventured into confectionery, followed by automatic dosa vending under the brand name Dosa King. He is a past President of TiE Chennai, and an active member of The Chennai Angels. He has made over 20 angel investments till 2020.

Padma Chandrasekaran is an angel investor actively seeking opportunities to invest in promising young start-ups. She has worked in senior and executive-level positions for 18 years in the for-profit and 8 years in the non-profit and research sectors in India and abroad. She was a founding member of Sify Ltd. and part of the team that took it public on NASDAQ in 1999. She subsequently founded, ran and then successfully sold a web services software technology company. Her current angel investment interests include biotech, health and clean energy.

Rajesh Sawhney is a serial entrepreneur and business builder who has set up multiple successful businesses over the last two decades. Rajesh is the founder of GSF, India's leading multi-city tech start-up accelerator. Rajesh has made 80 angel investments as an active and engaged angel investor, which include Viki, Little Eye Labs, Mobstac, Pokkt, Silverpush, Hackerearth, Docsapp, Whatfix and Daily Rounds.

Endnotes

[1]From Traxcn database (https://tracxn.com/).

[2]From YNOS Venture Engine (www.ynos.in). The Discover platform of YNOS lists the active number of angel investors investing in Indian start-ups. As of February 10, 2021, that number exceeded 4,200.

[3]The number of networks is from Crunchbase (https://www.crunchbase.com/).

[4]The tweet was by Mr. Rithesh Banglani on August 21, 2020. Retrievable from: https://twitter.com/banglani/status/1296705547043876864

[5]TaxiForSure was an aggregator of car rentals and taxis that ensured that customers are guaranteed a reliable and safe taxi ride. It was founded in 2011 by Aprameya Radhakrishna and Raghunandan G. It was acquired by OLA (one of their primary competitors) in 2016. During the five years between 2011 and 2016, the company raised close to $44 million from leading VCs including Blume Ventures, Accel and Helion Venture Partners.

[6]The Chennai Angels was founded in 2007 and is one of India's early angel network groups. The network has over 100 members and has invested in over 55 start-ups. Some notable investments include Chai Kings, NanoClean and TrulyMadly.com. Two of the panellists, Padma Chandrasekaran and Narayanan R, are members of the network and have been closely associated since its early years.

[7]The previous chapter on the changing landscape of angel investing in India provides a detailed description of the evolution of angel networks over the years. The chapter also looks at trends in the investing activities of leading networks over the years.

[8]A new funding round for a start-up is termed an up-round if the valuation of the firm (price per share) had increased since the previous round.

[9]The government had filed cases against more than 2,000 start-ups demanding the payment of taxes on funding received in excess of the start-up's fair valuation. See: Bora, S. 2019. Budget 2019: Government removes the sting of angel tax, entrepreneurs and investors rejoice. *The Economic Times.* Retrievable from: https://economictimes.indiatimes.com/small-biz/startups/newsbuzz/budget-2019-government-removes-the-sting-of-angel-tax-entrepreneurs-investors-rejoice/articleshow/70091664.cms?frm=mailtofriend&intenttarget=no

[10]The sample capitalisation table is based on the template prepared by the Corporate Finance Institute. See: Corporate Finance Institute. 2020. Capitalization Table - Guide, Example, Download a Cap Table. Retrieved from *The Corporate Finance Institute,* Resources website: https://corporatefinanceinstitute.com/resources/knowledge/valuation/cap-table-guide-template/

[11]Raghavan, P. 2019. **Angel tax breather: Startups, investors divided over clarity**. Retrieved from *The Indian Express* (July 9, 2019) website: https://indianexpress.com/article/business/startups/angel-tax-breather-startups-investors-divided-over-clarity-5821657/
Accessed on May 30, 2021

IN BRIEF

- An increasing number of high-net-worth individuals (HNIs) are setting up family offices to make investments in start-ups. The estimated investment by Indian HNIs and family offices directly in unlisted equity is around ₹10.5 trillion and in private and venture capital (VC) funds has been over ₹1 trillion.[1]
- The percentage allocation to investment in start-ups by Indian family offices has been one-tenth to one-twentieth of that of family offices in US and Europe. This indicates significant growth potential in the contribution of family offices for investment in start-ups.
- Established family offices that are experienced in investing in alternative investments and unlisted equity tend to prefer investing directly in start-ups, enabling them to have a more active association with the leadership of the ventures. On the other hand, nascent family offices typically seek a passive role, and hence, tend to invest as limited partners (LPs) in VC funds.
- Family offices typically bring their expertise of running a business to the ventures they invest in and prefer to have an active relationship with the founders. Hence, direct investments by family offices are likely to be in those start-ups that are associated with their primary business segments.
- Family offices form an interesting continuum between individual angel investors and institutional venture funds. They have the flexibility of angel investors (quicker decision-making, longer duration) while bringing in some of the strengths of institutional funding (larger funding, active involvement in the portfolio companies).

ANALYTICAL ARTICLE

14

Family Offices as a Source of Start-up Funding

N Ramakrishnan

Ramakrishnan, N. 2021. "Family Offices as a Source of Start-up Funding". In *Shifting Orbits: Decoding the Trajectory of the Indian Start-up Ecosystem*, edited by Thillai Rajan A, Srivardhini K Jha, Joffi Thomas and Rohan Chinchwadkar, 166–176. Hyderabad: Universities Press (India) Private Limited.

The Emergence of Indian Family Offices

Unlike those in the West, family offices in India are recent entrants into supporting start-ups, either through direct investments in ventures or as limited partners in funds. The country has a rich entrepreneurial history and there are any number of family businesses that have survived through generations, yet *"family offices remain a fairly new entity."*[2]

Simply put, a family office is a private office that manages the wealth of a business family. This can be an extension of the main business or structured as a separate entity with its own team, called a single-family office (SFO). Or, there are separate entities that manage the wealth of multiple families, called multi-family office. Those families that require greater control over their finances and business prefer to set up single-family offices, while multi-family offices deal with issues such as investments and asset management.[3] Some leading family offices in India are listed in Exhibit 14.1.

The family office gets the money to invest from the returns that are generated by the main operating business, including the dividend that is paid out regularly. Entrepreneurs who have sold their ventures have also set up family offices or holding companies that will invest in start-ups or in helping them start a second innings.

Exhibit 14.1: Family offices and proprietary funds

Name of the Family Office	Principal investor
Ajay Pramal SFO	Piramal Group
Burman Family Holdings	Burmans of Dabur group
Sharrp Ventures	Harsh Mariwala family
JSW Venture Fund	Sajjan Jindal
Lodha Group's Startup Investment Fund	MP Lodha
Pratithi Investment Trust	Kris Gopalakrishnan
Raay Global Investments	Amit Patni
Innovations Investment Management	SD Shibulal
Raintree Family Office	Dandekar family
YouWeCan Ventures	Yuvraj Singh
Soma Capital	Aneel Ranadive
PremjiInvest	Azim Premji
Aarin Capital	Dr Ranjan Pai and TV Mohandas Pai
Artha India Ventures	K Damani Group
Catamaran Ventures	NR Narayana Murthy
RNT Associates	Ratan Tata
Unilazer Ventures	Ronnie Screwvala
Info Edge	Naukri.com
Rainmatter	Zerodha
CESC Ventures	RP Sanjiv Goenka Group
SAR Group Family Office	SAR group
Hero Enterprises	Sunil Kant Munjal
Anand Mahindra family office	Anand Mahindra, Chairman, M&M

Source: Venture Intelligence and media articles[4]

The starting point for family offices is the population of wealthy individuals in the economy. Wealthy individuals or HNIs are those having investible assets of $1 million or more.[5] In 2018, there were an estimated 256,000 HNIs in India, which increased by about three per cent to 263,000 in 2019.[6] Exhibit 14.2 presents a global comparison of the number of HNIs in 2019. The number of HNIs for every million population in India is the lowest, indicating that the proportion of wealthy individuals in India is relatively low as compared to other economies. HNIs see family offices as vehicles to reinvest the capital into various asset classes, including start-ups, venture capital firms and growth capital enterprises.[7] Only a proportion of HNIs would set up formal family offices to manage their wealth. Setting up a family office involves engaging professionals to manage the investment activity. Only those HNIs who have a corpus that can yield returns to take care of the administrative overheads of such professional expertise would go ahead with the creation of family offices. The process of setting up family offices is an indication of the higher degree of institutionalisation of investment activities of the HNI.

While traditional asset classes such as gold, real estate, equities and mutual funds continue to form the bulk of the avenues for investment, alternative avenues such as investing in start-ups, unlisted equity, venture capital and private equity funds have been getting the attention of investors in recent years. Globally, family offices have been investing in start-ups for quite some time and in India, they are now expected to fuel the next phase of start-up growth.[12] Alternative investments, as investing in private markets is generally referred to, are now an important asset class for HNIs to invest their surplus capital. *"From traditional investments like real estate and commodities, Indian investors have progressed towards more sophisticated asset classes like venture capital, private equity, structured products and high yield debt."*[13]

An option for start-up financing, which is often overlooked, is the family office.[14] They are an important source of capital for small and medium businesses. Due to their very nature, access to family office capital most often is through referrals. Ventures seeking to tap them for funds must therefore be aligned with the family office's investment thesis. Many invest in companies that are directly or indirectly related to their core business.[15]

Exhibit 14.2: Number of high-net-worth individuals (HNIs) and the number of billionaires in 2019

	Number of HNI[8]	Number of US$ billionaires[9]	Percentage of HNI who are billionaires	Number of HNI per million population[10]
United States	5,909	607	10%	18.0
Japan	3,387	32	1%	26.8
Germany	1,466	114	8%	17.6
China	1,317	324	25%	0.9
France	702	41	6%	10.5
United Kingdom	591	54	9%	8.8
Switzerland	438	33	8%	51.1
Canada	392	45	11%	10.4
Italy	298	35	12%	4.9
Netherlands	287	11[11]	4%	16.6
Australia	284	36	13%	11.2
India	263	106	40%	0.2

Source: Capgemini Research – World Wealth Report 2020, Forbes and World Bank

Indian family offices are looking at new asset classes, and alternative investments are catching their attention. Alternative investments in India grew a little over 20 per cent from FY 2018 to reach ₹1.49 trillion in FY 2019.[16] Individual wealth in unlisted equity is growing at a healthy pace, while that in alternate assets – read private and venture capital funds – has grown at a much higher rate (Exhibit 14.3). This diversification into alternative

Exhibit 14.3: Average allocation of wealth of individuals in India – FY 2018 and FY 2019[17]

	Asset classification	Average wealth allocation – FY 2018	Average wealth allocation – FY 2019	Year-on-year growth percentage
Financial Assets	Direct Equity	12.48%	12.12%	7%
	Fixed Deposits and Bonds	10.73%	10.65%	9%
	Insurance	8.50%	8.58%	11%
	Current, Savings, and NRI Deposits	11.08%	11.19%	11%
	Cash	4.49%	4.77%	17%
	Pension and Provident Funds	5.21%	5.55%	17%
	Mutual Funds	2.98%	3.20%	18%
	Unlisted Equity	2.44%	2.45%	10%
	Small Savings	1.93%	2.01%	14%
	Alternative Investments[18]	0.32%	0.35%	20%
	International Assets	0.07%	0.08%	25%
Physical Assets	Precious Metals, Gems and Jewellery	22.06%	21.73%	8%
	Real Estate	17.73%	17.33%	7%
	Total Amount in All Assets	₹392 Trillion	₹430 Trillion	9.6%

Source: Karvy Wealth Report 2019

Exhibit 14.4: Top Indian family office investments in start-ups

Investors	Company	Sector	Amount ($ Million)[19]	Date
Kris Gopalakrishnan, Epiq Capital, Unilever Ventures, InnoVen Capital, Ascent Capital, Accel India, Chiratae Ventures, Temasek, Others	CureFit	Wellness	111	March 2020
Poonawalla Family Office, Kris Gopalakrishnan, Others	JetSynthesys	Consumer App	40	July 2020
Techpro Ventures, RPG Ventures, Eduardo Saverin, Rise Capital, Lionrock Capital, IIFL VC, Others	Hopscotch	E-Commerce - Baby Care Products	25	September 2020
Sharrp Ventures, Fireside Ventures, Stellaris Venture Partners, Sequoia Capital India	Mamaearth	Personal Care	18	January 2020
Narotam Sekhsaria Family Office, Omnivore Partners, FMO, Sequoia Capital India, Others	DeHaat	Marketplace - Agri Business	12	March 2020

Source: Venture Intelligence (as of October 2020)

assets has been driven by the next generation of the business families who want to play an active role in nurturing innovation and entrepreneurship. However, Indian family offices contribute just about one per cent of the investment that has gone into start-ups, while this figure is 10–20 per cent in the US and Europe.

Several leading family offices have successfully identified and invested in disruptive and innovative start-ups in the recent past. Exhibit 14.5 provides a list of a few leading family offices in India, along with a sample of their key investments. The impressive investments

Exhibit 14.5: Key investments of a few leading family offices in India

Family office	Principal partners	Year founded	No. of start-up investments[20]	Key investments
Aarin Capital	TV Mohandas Pai (Former CFO, Infosys) and Dr. Ranjan Pai	2011	42	Impact Analytics, PharmEasy, Vyome Therapeutics
Artha Ventures India	Anirudh Damani, Ashok Kumar Damani	2013	85	Agnikul Cosmos, Jadooz, Oyo
Catamaran Ventures	Narayana Murthy (Former Chairman, Infosys)	2010	35	Acko, Coverfox Insurance, Paper Boat
Narotam Sekhsaria Family Office	Narotam Sekhsaria (Chairman, ACC Cements)	NA	2	Centa, DeHaat
Pratithi Investment Trust	Kris Gopalakrishnan (Former Vice Chairman, Infosys)	NA	5	cure.fit, HungerBox, Myelin Foundry
PremjiInvest	Azim Premji (Former Chairman, Wipro)	2006	31	Anaplan, Innovium, Iora Health
RNT Associates	Ratan Tata (Chairman Emeritus, Tata Group)	2009	14	Altaeros Energies, CarDekho, Crayon Data
Sharrp Ventures	Harsh Mariwala (Founder, Marico)	2014	21	Kapiva Ayurveda, Leap, Nykaa.com
Techpro Ventures	Atul Nishar (Founder, Aptech and Hexaware)	2014	7+[21]	Acko, BigBasket, Nykaa.com

Source: Official sources, Crunchbase and PitchBook

made by the family offices establish their ability to identify and support impactful start-ups.

Of the total funds raised by start-ups, including from VCs and Private Equity (PE) investors, direct investment from the family office falls well below one per cent (Exhibit 14.6). However, it is possible that family offices could be investing in start-ups as a limited partner (LP) in various funds. When investment is made directly as an individual or as a family office, the investment is more likely in an early-stage start-up (seed or Series A funding). If the family offices participate as a LP in a fund, then investment is most likely to happen in growth or late-stage start-ups.

Investment Strategy of Family Offices

The allocation to unlisted equity by different family offices depends on their state of maturity.[24] Those that have been operating for more than five years, allocate 10–15 per cent of their wealth for investing in unlisted companies, whereas in the case of younger family offices, this is likely to be in single-digit percentages. In general, the actual investment is likely to be lower than the allocation target.

One example of a family office investing in start-ups is that of Raay Global Investments. This has been the single-family office of Amit Patni of Patni Computers, which was sold to I-Gate Corporation in May 2011 for $1.5 billion. It has a two-fold strategy. Raay Global invests directly in start-ups and also has a fund that invests in the technology and mobile sector. Raay Global has been investing in start-ups since 2012, focussing on sectors such as consumer goods, fintech and digital content. Their investment ticket size varies from ₹5 million to ₹150–210 million. Normally, Raay Global would look to hold a 15 per cent stake, apart from a board seat or an observer status.[25]

Family offices primarily focus on business fundamentals when evaluating investment proposals, apart from the usual parameters such as expected returns, associated risks, background of the start-up and the prospects for the broader industry. Given that much of the popular discussion is about valuations of start-ups and not profitability, family offices are keen to ensure that ventures are committed to bolstering the profitability of the business instead of merely focussing on their valuations. Seen from this perspective, the investment evaluation of start-ups by family offices is not very different from those of other investors.

The investment by family offices in start-ups can be classified into three categories. First, establishing a corporate venture capital style structure through which their investments are made. Second is the LP route, whereby they contribute to venture funds, which in turn invest in start-ups. Third is to directly invest in select start-ups (based on the advice of their wealth managers and advisors).[26]

The second category had been the predominant approach during the early years of the past decade. For example, in 2011–13, Blume Ventures raised its first fund of ₹1,200 million entirely from domestic investors. The investors comprised 50–60 families and

Exhibit 14.6: Investments made by Indian family offices compared to venture capital and private equity investments

Year	Indian family office		Overall VC and PE investment[22]		Family office investments as a percentage of VC and PE investments (by value)
	No. of deals	Amount $ million[23]	No. of deals	Amount $ million	
2016	101	127	890	13,464	0.94%
2017	73	108	858	23,920	0.45%
2018	75	188	980	36,329	0.51%
2019	90	240	1004	36,323	0.66%
2020	40	61	614	31,552	0.19%

Source: Venture Intelligence (as of October 2020)

an institution. The firm cast its net far and wide, and had marketed the fund to more than 500 families. Further, Indian families contributed to more than half of Blume's second fund of $60 million. Despite the marketing focus on institutional investors from Blume Ventures, families were keen to invest on their own. The firm also raised an Opportunities Fund of ₹2,750 million, of which ₹1,500 million was raised from Indian families. This example illustrates the extent of participation of families in VC funds during the early years of the past decade.

Family offices typically select the funds that they would like to invest based on their risks, returns, investment thesis and the fund duration. It is not uncommon for family offices to piggyback on VC firms to identify promising start-ups, in which they then co-invest along with the fund. This is specifically helpful to start-ups and VC funds when there is a shortfall in meeting the targeted amount to be raised, as the balance may not be large enough for another VC firm.

An increasing number of Indian families are recognising the potential of private investments. Indian families are now seeking to participate in wealth creation along with foreign investors, who have primarily led the investments in Indian start-ups thus far. Experts, therefore, predict a secular increase in the amount of investments made by family offices to the top 10–15 VC firms. Indian start-ups and funds can make the best use of this increased interest from family offices by providing smooth exits to their investors.

With family offices getting more experience in investing in start-ups, there has been an increased interest for directly investing in start-ups instead of going through the venture fund route. Sharrp Ventures is one such example. Sharrp Ventures, the family office of Harsh Mariwala (Founder and Chairman of Marico), has been investing in start-ups for the past five years. It has made about 20 investments, almost equally divided between direct investments and through VC funds. Almost 80 per cent of the Mariwala family's investments (in value) have been in listed equities and instruments, while the remaining 20 per cent was in unlisted equity. While the initial focus of the office was to invest in early-stage start-ups, the scope subsequently expanded to later-stage investments as well, providing the much-needed growth capital for a number of ventures. By the end of 2020, Sharrp Ventures had increased the proportion of their corpus that was directly invested in start-ups.[27] The objective of Sharrp Ventures for increasing the direct investments was to have greater level of interaction with the founders. Specifically, it provided an opportunity for Harsh Mariwala, an entrepreneur himself, to mentor and guide the founders. The preference for direct investment in start-ups has been fairly secular across family offices, with investment amounts typically ranging between ₹2 and ₹2.5 million. Admittedly, the investment ticket size for family offices has been closer to that of individual angels as compared to that of seed funds.

While making direct investments, a number of family offices have also formed a consortium to make investments, enabling them to leverage their collective wisdom instead of relying on VC firms. This has been due to the lack of consistent returns from VC funds and the high management fees charged.[28] About 20 families that have been active in the alternative investment space joined to form a consortium, with each office acting as their own investment manager for the deals they were leading.

While most family offices were sector agnostic, they preferred to invest in sectors that were adjacent to their primary area of business. For instance, Pawan Munjal of Hero MotoCorp may have a special interest in ventures in the mobility space, where the scope for contributing to the success of the start-up was higher.

Engagement with Start-ups

Experienced family offices typically bring their expertise of running a business to the ventures they invest in and prefer to have an active relationship with the founders. Raay Global Investments, for instance, helps founders across various aspects of business, from drafting the business model to de-cluttering the capitalisation table for future rounds of fund raising.

Such family offices tend to have monthly interactions with founders, specifically in the first three years of investing in the venture or until other investors are brought onboard. They show more involvement in their portfolio companies as compared to angel investors or nascent family offices, many of whom prefer to be passive investors. Such family offices also help entrepreneurs with the overall development of the organisation by contributing to the corporate governance guidelines.

The advantage with an established family office is that they are more flexible and nimble when compared to VC funds. They do their own due diligence, but it may not be as time-consuming as the diligence done by VC firms. This makes family offices more agile in making investment decisions. There have been instances where a family office had decided to invest in a prospective start-up within 45 days of the first meeting with the founder. In contrast, a VC fund could take up to six months to finalise their decision.

From a founder's perspective, the unique combination of agile decision-making along with vast industry connections differentiates experienced family offices from other investors. More importantly, when a venture is raising a large round, say, of $20 million, and the VC firm is not willing to commit more than $15–16 million, established family offices can be potential investors to bridge the gap.[29] With such family offices getting more sophisticated and professional, they have also relied on investing through structured products that have some characteristics of debt.[30]

On the other hand, nascent family offices tend to invest in VC funds and seek a more passive role until they develop a better understanding of the start-up landscape. With their increasing level of maturity and experience, we can expect a greater proportion of these family offices to switch to a more active approach to investing in start-ups.

To better illustrate the characteristics of experienced and nascent start-ups in relation to the other investors in the ecosystem, Exhibit 14.7 plots angel investors, VC funds, and family offices based on two key dimensions, namely, quantum of investment and level of involvement. As illustrated in the exhibit, experienced family offices serve as a bridge between angel investors and VC funds, and hence, complete the continuum between the two.

Return Expectations

It is fairly well known that returns from investing in individual start-ups widely vary. At the portfolio level, IRRs (internal rate of return) have ranged from 30 per cent in the best cases to zero in the worst. A proper start-up investment strategy must work on the basis of

Exhibit 14.7: Family offices in the start-up financing continuum

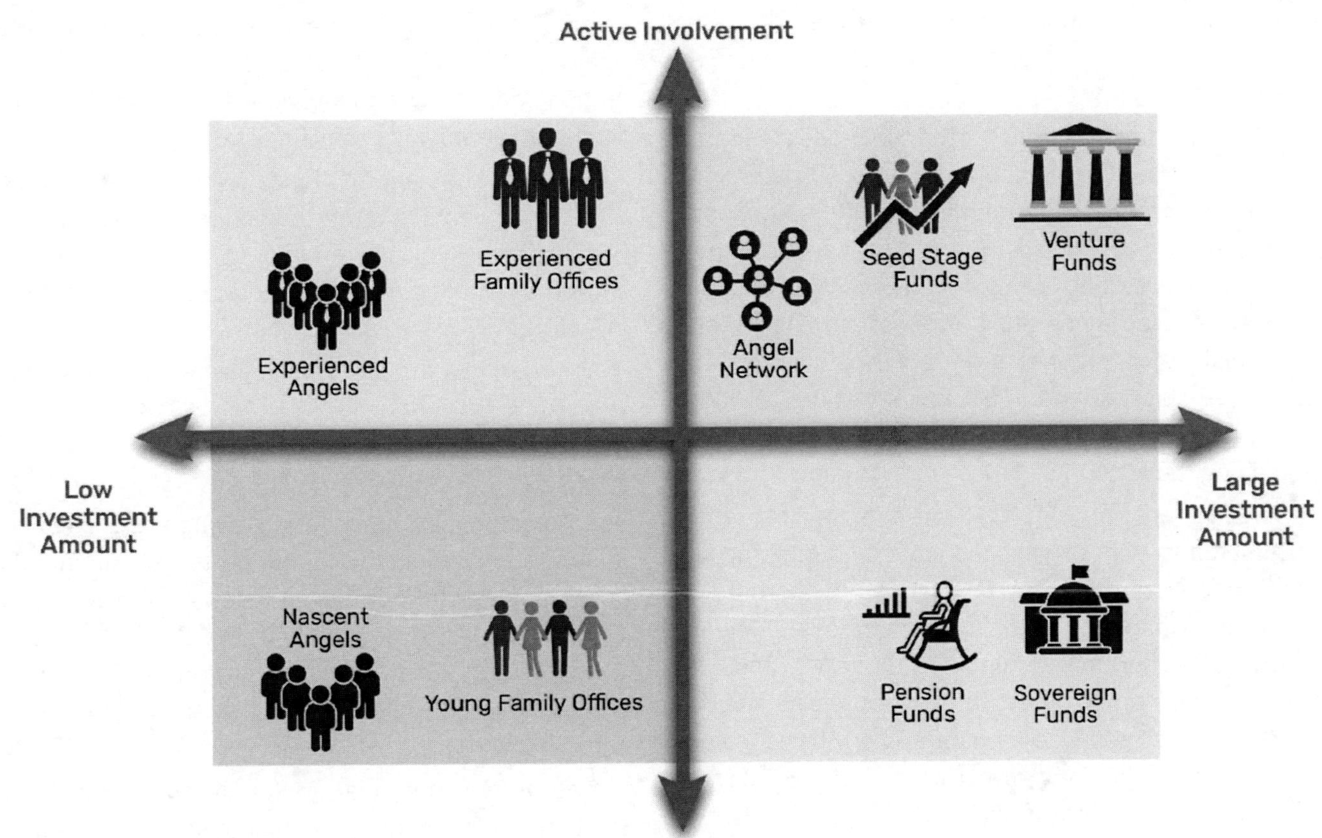

making investments in a diverse portfolio of ventures to ensure that the risk exposure is well diversified.[31] The investment duration associated with start-up portfolios are also longer than with other investments. The general experience is that a well-diversified portfolio of start-ups yields returns of around 15 per cent in the long run.

The return expectations from investing in start-ups for a family office (or, for that matter, for any investor) are higher than the average returns from investments in public markets, due to the higher degree of risk associated in investing with the start-up space. For example, if the return expectations from the listed equity market were 15–16 per cent, then the expectation for private markets could be 22–23 per cent.[32] Some families expect an IRR in the mid-20s, with the investment lock in duration not exceeding eight years.

Understanding the Construct of a Fund

Family offices considering investing in VC funds need to understand the construct and structure of a VC fund before making the investment decision. Family offices would have to consider the sectors that the VC fund would invest in, the stage of investment and the overall size of the fund's portfolio. Further, the family offices must also be convinced of the fund manager's investment strategy and team.

When Fireside Ventures started the process of raising its first fund in 2016, it counted family offices such as Premji Invest, Mariwala Family Office, RP-Sanjiv Goenka Family and Sunil Munjal's Hero Enterprise Investment Office as its investors. During the course of the fund raise, Fireside started generating interest among wealthy individuals who did not have a formal family office structure. This interest in VC funds can be attributed to the wealth advisors and fund managers who were managing the accounts of these individuals.

VC funds are very similar to investing in close-ended mutual funds, with very limited liquidity during the fund life. The private nature of the asset adds another level of risk as exits could be difficult to achieve at the end of fund life. Therefore, when investing in VC funds, it is important for family offices to fully appreciate the risks involved. The absence of guaranteed basic returns coupled with the long investment duration may not suit the risk appetite of all family offices. Further the complex nature of the management fees and profit-sharing incentives have to be considered as well.[33]

Updating the Investors

VC firms engage with the family offices as they do with any institutional investor, providing them periodic updates about the overall performance of the fund, along with detailed information about the health and prospects for each start-up in the fund's portfolio. The update is most often through a quarterly newsletter. The onset of the pandemic has induced a higher degree of uncertainty, due the increased volatility in the economic climate. Consequently, family offices are seeking more frequent updates.

Choosing their Areas of Interest

Most often, family offices prefer to invest in ventures or funds that are close to their area of expertise because they understand the business and also believe that they are better placed to help the venture. It is a matter of time before family offices understand that at the end of the day, venture investing is as much about diversification and risk management as it is about IRR and deal flow. Aligning with a good VC team will ensure smooth deal flow and provide a head start to family offices in identifying promising start-ups.

Unlike early-stage VC funds, which have a duration of 10 to 12 years, a family office fund is patient capital. Family offices typically tend not to have rigid investment windows, making them a more attractive option to investors.

Summary

While the entry of family offices to fund start-ups has been recent, they have been playing a significant role in supporting impactful ventures. Indian family offices have supported a number of leading start-ups such as Acko, Agnikul Cosmos, cure.fit, Big Basket, Nykaa and Vyome Therapeutics. Indian family offices are emerging as key sources of funding in the early-stage start-up ecosystem.

The growth potential for family offices investing in start-ups is very high. The percentage allocation to investment in start-ups by Indian family offices has only been one-tenth to one-twentieth of that of family offices in US and Europe. As the Indian family office landscape matures, the allocation of Indian family offices is likely to converge with their counterparts in the US and Europe over the coming years. Hence, India is at the cusp of a strong growth in investments in start-ups from family offices.

This potential presents a significant opportunity to both entrepreneurs and policymakers. In order to attract this emergent source of funding, entrepreneurs must convince family offices about the profitability of their business and must provide them with options for a smooth exit. From a policy angle, the government can consider providing appropriate fiscal incentives for the formation of family offices.

Apart from being yet another source of funding for start-ups, family offices are characterised by features that distinguish them from other investors in the start-up ecosystem. Specifically, family offices play a crucial role in completing the continuum between individual angel investors and institutional venture firms. They have the flexibility of angel investors (quicker decision making, longer duration) while bringing in some of the strengths of institutional funding (larger funding, active involvement in the portfolio companies).

Endnotes

[1]As of the 2018–2019 financial year. It is assumed that much of the investment in unlisted equity would be in start-ups. Source: Karvy Private Wealth. 2019. Karvy India Wealth Report 2019. Retrieved from *Karvy Private Wealth*, website: http://www.karvywealth.com/india-wealth-report.aspx

[2]Edelweiss Private Wealth Management & Campden Family Connect. 2018. The Family Wealth Report 2018: A roadmap for the Indian family office. Retrieved from *Edelweiss*, website: https://www.edelweissfin.com/wp-content/uploads/2020/03/RoadmapForTheIndianFamilyOffice-EPWM-Campden.pdf

[3]Botha, F. 2020. Emerging Forms of The Family Office. Retrieved from *Forbes* (February 12, 2020), website: https://www.forbes.com/sites/francoisbotha/2020/02/12/emerging-forms-of-the-family-office/?sh=4f6f0cd32fc4

[4]Gupta, A, Mukherjee, J and Chaudhary, D. 2018. Family offices: Designing the family's future. Retrieved from *Fortune India* (August 29, 2018), website: https://www.fortuneindia.com/macro/family-officesdesigning-the-familys-future/102339
Accessed on May 30, 2021

[5]Capgemini Research Institute. 2020. World Wealth Report 2020. Retrieved from *Capgemini Research, World Wealth Report*, website: https://worldwealthreport.com/resources/world-wealth-report-2020/

[6]Ibid.

[7]Edelweiss Private Wealth Management & Campden Family Connect. 2018. The Family Wealth Report 2018: A roadmap for the Indian family office. Retrieved from *Edelweiss*, website: https://www.edelweissfin.com/wp-content/uploads/2020/03/RoadmapForTheIndianFamilyOffice-EPWM-Campden.pdf

[8]Data comes from Figure 3 of *Capgemini Research Institute, 2020*. World Wealth Report 2020.

[9]Data comes from from Ponciano, J. 2020. The Countries with the Most Billionaires. Retrieved from Forbes, *Forbes* World's Billionaires List, website: https://www.forbes.com/sites/jonathanponciano/2020/04/08/the-countries-with-the-most-billionaires-in-2020/
Accessed on May 30, 2021

[10]The population data comes from the *World Bank Data Bank for 2019* (https://data.worldbank.org/, ID: SP.POP.TOTL). The number of HNIs reported in the first column is divided by the respective country's population in 2019 to arrive at the reported numbers.

[11]Data comes from *Forbes*, the data was retrieved on December 2 2020 (https://www.forbes.com/billionaires/).

[12]D'Souza, V. 2018. Are Family Offices Fueling Startup's Growth in India? Retrieved from *Entrepreneur Media Inc*. (December 27, 2018), website: https://www.entrepreneur.com/article/325376

[13]Karvy Private Wealth. 2019. Karvy India Wealth Report 2019. Retrieved from *Karvy Private Wealth*, website: http://www.karvywealth.com/india-wealth-report.aspx

[14]Staff of Entrepreneur Media, Inc. 2016. *Finance Your Business: Secure Funding to Start, Run, and Grow Your Business*. Irvine, CA: Entrepreneur Press.

[15]Ibid.

[16]Karvy Private Wealth. 2019. Karvy India Wealth Report 2019. Retrieved from *Karvy Private Wealth*, website: http://www.karvywealth.com/india-wealth-report.aspx

[17]The data is based on Tables 1, 4 and 5 of *Karvy Private Wealth*. 2019. India Wealth Report 2019.

[18]Alternative investments include venture capital fund investments and private equity investments along with

other funds and bonds such as real estate funds, hedge funds, infrastructure funds, sovereign gold bonds, and infrastructure investment trusts.

[19]Includes share of co-investors.

[20]The data is based on the highest number reported among three sources, the official website of the office, Crunchbase (https://www.crunchbase.com) and PitchBook (https://pitchbook.com/).

[21]The data was inferred from the LinkedIn profile of the office's Chief Investment Officer, Mr. Jagannadham Thunguntla (https://www.linkedin.com/in/jagannadhamt).

[22]The data may include approximation of values in co-investments.

[23]Investments in companies less than 10 years old.

[24]Telephone interview with Munish Randev, Founder & CEO, Cervin Family Office & Advisors, on October 9, 2020.

[25]Telephone interview with Benaifer Malandkar, Chief Investment Officer, Raay Global Investments Pvt Ltd, on December 16, 2020.

[26]Telephone interview with Ashish Fafadia, Partner, Blume Ventures, on September 26, 2020.

[27]Zoom interview with Rishabh Mariwala, Director, and Chaitanya Deshpande, Advisor, Sharrp Ventures, the Mariwala family office, on September 7, 2020.

[28]Dhanjal, SS. 2019. Family offices tie up to make direct PE, VC investments. Retrieved from *Mint* (August 29, 2019), website: https://www.livemint.com/companies/start-ups/family-offices-tie-up-to-make-direct-pe-vc-investments-1566757721516.html

[29]Zoom interview with Satyam Kumar, CEO and Co-founder, LoanTap Financial Technologies, on December 17, 2020.

[30]Ibid.

[31]Telephone interview with V Shankar, Director, Acsys Investments Pvt Ltd, on September 15, 2020.

[32]Telephone interview with Nitai Utkarsh, a senior family office executive, on September 15, 2020.

[33]Telephone interview with Kanwaljit Singh, Founder & Managing Partner, Fireside Ventures, on October 7, 2020.

IN BRIEF

- The scarcity of deep tech ventures in India is a current pain point that needs to be addressed with an increased focus on nurturing translational ventures.
- Nurturing translational ventures requires the participation of both research consortiums and the venture ecosystem, specifically those developing algorithms for Indian needs from scratch instead of leveraging existing models and technologies.
- Venture Capital firms (VCs) should assist in creating a network of Indian financial institutions, research labs in universities, university incubators, domain experts and government departments to identify, fund and nurture translational ventures.
- Indian limited partners (LPs) and family offices have come of age and can become an ideal source of funding for translational ventures, given the long gestation times of such ventures.
- For domains that are in a nascent stage in India, the initial investment should still be sought from overseas investors, given the maturity of the VC industry in US and Europe in funding translational ventures.

CASE STUDY

15

Venture Funding and Translational Research–based Ventures: AI, ML and Brain Science

N Dayasindhu and Krishnan Narayanan

Dayasindhu, N and Narayanan, K. 2021. "Venture Funding and Translational Research–based Ventures: The Case of AI, ML and Brain Science". In *Shifting Orbits: Decoding the Trajectory of the Indian Start-up Ecosystem*, edited by Thillai Rajan A, Srivardhini K Jha, Joffi Thomas and Rohan Chinchwadkar, 178–187. Hyderabad: Universities Press (India) Private Limited.

Translational Research – From Labs to Markets

Commercialisation of technology innovation plays an important role in the economic growth of a country and improves the quality of life of its citizens. Often, the 'lab to market' translation is fraught with difficulties and uncertainties. Let us take the example of vaccines. Only 1 in 10,000 candidate vaccines makes it to human clinical trials, and it takes an average of 10 years to progress from the pre-clinical stage to market development.[1] The year 2020 has shown us the importance of vaccine development. India's experience in developing the Rotavac vaccine helped us develop an indigenous vaccine against COVID-19 in a short time. Rotavac was a translational effort from teams at All India Institute of Medical Sciences (AIIMS), Christian Medical College (CMC) Vellore, the Department of Biotechnology and Bharat Biotech. Similarly, India's COVID-19 vaccine has been developed by Bharat Biotech and Indian Council of Medical Research (ICMR). Apart from biotech, artificial intelligence (AI), machine learning (ML) and brain science show good potential for translating research into ventures in the short to medium term.

Translating research outcomes to commercial products and outcomes needs significant additional funding over and above the funding from government and other grants for conducting the research itself. In many cases, government and grant funding support for commercialising research is very limited.[2] Conventional funding such as bank loans may not be available because of the uncertain nature of the technology and the consequent financial risk involved. Availability of risk capital such as venture funding is therefore critical for successful translational research–based ventures or translational ventures.

Exhibit 15.1: Fundamental research, translational research and translational ventures

Fundamental (or basic) research is the systematic study directed towards greater knowledge or understanding of the fundamental aspects of phenomena and is generally performed with an open mind without any thought of immediate practical applications. It results in an increased understanding of nature and its laws. For example, Willard Boyle and George Smith at Bell Labs conceived a design where a series of metal oxide semiconductor capacitors in a row, when connected under a suitable voltage, could be used to step a charge from one capacitor to the next.[3] This invention was called charge couple device or CCD.

Translational research is built on fundamental research to create new products and solutions that can have practical applications. For example, Fairchild Semiconductor took the CCD invention and developed a 100 x 100-pixel CCD device for the market. Kodak used Fairchild's CCD device to develop the world's first digital camera.[4]

An example of the same team converting its fundamental research into a product is the Backrub algorithm developed by graduate students Larry Page and Sergey Brin at Stanford University.[5] Backrub was the basis of the Google search engine. For this chapter, we define start-up ventures that result from translational research as translational research–based ventures or translational ventures.

Funding of translational ventures in AI, ML and brain science is akin to challenges in other similar translational research. The risks involved in financing translational research–based ventures do not make it feasible for commercial banks and other traditional forms of funding. Grant funding from governments, which plays an important role in providing the initial seed funding to ventures, can only go so far. For translational research–based ventures to fructify, larger amounts of funding – several times the magnitude of government grants – are needed. This can be provided only from private equity funding sources such as venture capital.

AI and ML are at the cusp of becoming major contributors to the Indian economy, with the potential addition of about $957 billion to India's GDP by 2035.[6] Brain science is likely to play an important role in India, given its population and the fact that the percentage of elderly population is likely to increase in the coming decades. India is expected to have the largest number of dementia patients in the world by 2050.[7] There are over four million dementia patients today in India and

Exhibit 15.2: Artificial intelligence, machine learning and brain science

AI is the study of intelligent agents that perceive their environment and take actions that maximize their chance of successfully achieving their goals. Colloquially, the term AI is applied when a machine mimics cognitive functions that humans associate with other humans, such as learning and problem solving. ML is a field of computer science that uses statistical techniques to give computer systems the ability to progressively improve performance on a specific task using historical data and without being explicitly programmed. ML is considered as a subset of the technologies that power AI. It provides AI the ability to automatically learn and improve from experience. AI and ML based solutions are transforming many industry sectors. While AI and ML have been making steady progress, there is another discipline on the horizon, viz., brain science, which that envisions a future beyond AI and ML. Brain science is a multi-disciplinary domain that helps us to unravel the biological basis of learning, memory, behaviour, perception and consciousness. Brain science is often slated as the 'ultimate challenge of the biological sciences' in the twenty-first century.

this number is likely to double by 2025.[8] India should harness the power of its fundamental research and translate them into products and solutions that can benefit citizens. This is not possible without a robust venture funding industry for translational ventures.

In this chapter, we establish the potential for these domains in the Indian context. Our observations are derived from 56 semi-structured, in-depth interviews of researchers[9] in the AI, ML and brain science domains.[10] Venture funding will play an important role in nurturing successful ventures in these domains.

The Potential of AI and ML – Propelling the Fourth Industrial Revolution

The fourth industrial revolution is expected to be powered by innovative cyber-physical systems that operate at the intersection of the physical and digital realms. AI and ML technologies have proven to be the cornerstone of cyber-physical technologies that are propelling the advancement of the revolution. AI and ML solutions are now emerging as new factors of production along with labour, capital and technology. They also have the potential to transform the Indian economy.[11] The Artificial Intelligence Task Force set up by the Ministry of Commerce and Industry identified 10 important domains of relevance to India including manufacturing, healthcare, fintech, agriculture, education, retail, accessibility, national security and public utility services.[12] Examples of solutions for select focus areas using Indian translational research in AI and ML technologies are presented in Exhibit 15.3.

While these solutions are globally relevant, there is a necessity to build these algorithms so that they are fine-tuned for Indian conditions and requirements. Interesting illustrative use cases that Indian AI and ML researchers are working on and which have the potential to translate into commercially viable ventures are:

- The development of a database on Indian road conditions to aid in the training of autonomous cars. A computer vision algorithm for autonomous vehicles with 80 per cent efficiency in Western conditions may only work at about 40 per cent efficiency on Indian roads. Hence, there is a need for curating databases on Indian road conditions which could be used for developing computer vision algorithms that perform better in India.
- Image recognition solutions that identify the condition of roads (such as potholes, water stagnation and pedestrian traffic).
- Character or text recognition algorithms, with a focus on Indian languages.
- Speech recognition in the context of multilingual speech, as in the case when Hindi and English are used in the same sentence.

Despite the progress seen in the AI and ML research ecosystems, India is still considerably behind global leaders like USA, China and Europe.

Brain Science – The Future of Technology

The brain science discipline is at a very nascent stage. Despite being in the early stages of research, it is evident that there is significant scope for translational

Exhibit 15.3: Examples of AI and ML solutions in focus areas

Focus area	Example solutions
Healthcare	Enhanced hospital productivity systems, accurate and efficient diagnosis systems and personalised health monitoring systems.
Financial services	Advanced risk modelling, improved fraud detection and automated report generation from unstructured text.
Information and Communication	Better search outcomes, improved information security and biometrics, crowd-sourcing platforms, complex text analytics, language processing and dialog systems.
Retail	e-Commerce applications like improving the correctness of an address, recommendation systems and advanced delivery route planning solutions.

research in the brain science domain, particularly in the healthcare sector.

In healthcare, the benefits of early translations are likely to be realised in diagnostics. Specifically, in areas such as the diagnosis and therapy of brain disorders like Alzheimer's disease, dementia, Parkinson's disease, autism, dyslexia and brain strokes.

Another promising translation area in healthcare is brain–machine interfaces (BMI) or brain–computer interfaces (BCI). BCI enables the translation of brain signals (arising from a thought) to commands that can control a mechanical equipment. For example, a BCI interface for someone who is speech challenged or a prosthetics solution for the differently abled.

Further, brain science has the potential to improve existing AI and ML solutions. For example, using brain science models of how decisions are made, we can better understand how consumers make choices, which can in turn be used to improve the suggestion algorithms for online retailers. The potential of this discipline to radically alter the technological paradigm has made it an important focus area for developed countries.

Venture Ecosystem and VC Funding for Translational Research

India has a vibrant and flourishing AI, ML and brain science research ecosystem. Interview responses from AI and ML researchers in India indicated that there are about 50–75 principal investigators (researchers experienced enough to independently lead a large research project) in the top Indian academic institutions, and several hundred principal researchers across all Indian universities. India ranks 10th globally in terms of number of PhDs in AI and ML disciplines, and 13th in terms of presentations in top AI and ML research conferences.[13] This growth trend is also reflected in the start-up ecosystem. India has seen an impressive growth in AI and ML–based start-up ventures. The sector attracted over $359 million funding in 2018–19, a five-fold increase from the previous year.[14]

With the rising prominence of the sector, venture capitalists (VCs) are beginning to collaborate and co-invest with academic incubators to help translational ventures. Many of the IITs, IISc and IIITs have developed strong academic incubator programs to provide translational research labs the necessary support to commercialise their ideas. Translational ventures in the AI and ML sectors are key beneficiaries of such incubation programs. For example, about 7 per cent of all companies incubated in IIT Madras have AI and ML as a core technology, some of which are listed in Exhibit 15.4.[15] Moreover, 40 per cent of the academic researchers we interviewed are working with start-up ventures or have start-up ventures getting incubated based on the work done in their labs.

Despite the impressive extent of interface between the start-up ecosystem and academia, academic researchers still desire better links between academic labs and key stakeholders in the funding ecosystem (such as VCs and angel investors).

As far as brain science is concerned, many of the national institutes of importance (including IISc, the IITs, NIMHANS and IISER Pune), research centres (such as NCBS and NBRC) and universities (like University of Hyderabad and University of Allahabad) have established research programs in brain science scattered across different departments. Fundamental research aimed at improving our understanding of the brain and its functions is the focus of Indian brain science researchers. Given that much of the focus is on fundamental research, we expect that it will take at least a few more years before we see increased traction in translational research in brain science.

The Catalytic Role of VC Funding

Venture funding beyond the standard grant funding is a crucial factor for technology-intensive translational ventures to proliferate. Many of these translational ventures are working on cutting edge technologies that may have longer incubation periods. This is especially true in the case of brain science, where some the technologies may require many years before a commercial prototype can be built. Research studies indicate that venture funding has a catalytic effect in nurturing start-up ventures (including translational ventures) to develop innovative solutions in different countries, including China[16] and the USA.[17]

Venture funding in China is significantly contributing to the regional economy as a whole by supporting innovation, creating jobs and generating wealth. It is important to include VCs as part of the translational research–based ecosystem to ensure that the ventures

Exhibit 15.4: A sample of translational research–based AI and ML start-up ventures incubated at IIT Madras Research Park

Start-up	Year founded	Description	Impact
Daksha Imaging[18]	2015	AI and ML solutions for video surveillance. The company specialises in image processing, pattern recognition and computer vision.	Provides small retail outlets and entrepreneurial organisations access to high-quality video surveillance, using low internet bandwidth at affordable rates.
Hyperverge[19]	2014	AI engines for identity verification in the finance and banking sectors.	The company uses advanced AI engines for digital KYC, deducing fraud check, data verification and credit scoring. The engines are specially designed to function in low bandwidth and on low-cost devices.
Ursugar[20]	2015	A clinical decision support system for diabetologists. The decision support system is powered by sophisticated AI and deep learning.	Helps doctors in providing personalised care to diabetic patients.
Zasti.ai[21]	2017	A proprietary deep learning algorithm for predictive and diagnostic solutions.	Can be employed for the diagnosis of diseases such as glaucoma and pancreatic cancer with high degree of accuracy.
Zmed[22]	2015	A medical IoT device that connects with crucial medical devices in a critical care unit (such as ventilators and syringe pumps). Data from IoT devices is analysed using advanced AI algorithms.	Assists medical professionals in determining patient decompensation, length of stay and mortality rates.

scale up and create a large impact. The US model of venture funding has transformed the innovation process in the US. An exemplar is Silicon Valley. VCs actively nurture networks of financial institutions, universities, large corporations, entrepreneurial companies and other organisations. The formation of these networks combined with free information flow among them has resulted in the reduction of many of the risks associated with technology-driven innovation and technology start-up formation.

The contribution of VCs to the Indian technology ecosystem is also noteworthy. Exhibit 15.5 indicates that Indian AI and ML ventures are indeed attracting VC funding. However, VC investment in translational ventures is still very limited. As of November 2020, only 23 per cent of all start-ups incubated at IIT Madras Research Park received VC or angel funding.[23]

Brain science, on the other hand, is still an emerging domain, and VC investment in brain science start-up ventures in the short term would be sparse.

Nurturing the Interface between Translational Research and the Start-up Ecosystem

About 90 per cent of the AI and ML researchers we interviewed had active collaborations with industry (including start-up ventures) or had collaborated with industry in the past in some capacity. Such a high percentage of collaboration is a reflection of the adoption of AI and ML solutions to solve real-world problems. In fact, India is at an inflection point of AI and ML driven ventures. It has been estimated that 18 per cent of all Indian start-ups leverage deep tech, of which 27 per cent leverage AI and ML. Between 2014 and 2019, the CAGR of AI and ML powered start-ups was about 65 per cent.[27]

Much of this growth in translational ventures in AI and ML could be attributed to a consortium of academic and commercial organisations that jointly undertake research (often referred to as the consortium

Exhibit 15.5: Leading VCs in Indian start-up ventures[24]

Venture capital	Year founded[25]	Total number of investments[26]	A sample of investments in ventures that leverage AI and ML
Axilor Ventures	2014	79	Datoin, Jubi.ai
Blume Venture	2011	210	Accio, Tricog Health
Exfinity Ventures	2013	36	CloudSEK, Mad Street Den, MoEngage
Kalaari Capital	2011	171	Edge Networks, Signzy, Embibe
Nu Ventures	2015	22	Coverfox Insurance, MuSigma
Pi Ventures	2016	20	SigTuple, SwitchOn, PyxisPM
Pravega Ventures	2016	18	Fyle, GreyAtom
SenseAI	2018	19	Artivatic.ai, CureSkin, Jovian.ml
StartupXseed Ventures	2015	12	Aibono, SmarterBiz Technologies
Unicorn India Ventures	2015	29	Fedo.ai, Finin
YourNest Venture Capital	2011	35	Dozee, Arya.ai

model). The blend of both academic and commercial organisations in a consortium nurtures translational research. These consortiums are usually embedded in a larger ecosystem that includes VCs. An example is The Robert Bosch Centre for Data Science and Artificial Intelligence (RBC-DSAI), at IIT Madras.[28] It is a multi-disciplinary AI research centre involving faculty from different departments and multiple partner organisations that both participate in and fund projects. Translational research in RBC-DSAI focuses on areas like manufacturing analytics, financial analytics, smart cities, systems biology and healtcare. NITI Aayog also favours the consortium model for nurturing AI and ML.

NITI Aayog has proposed a two-tier structure for the promotion of AI and ML based start-ups. The first tier focusses on the promotion of original research. As part of this, NITI Aayog proposes establishing Centres of Research Excellence in Artificial Intelligence (CORE), which aim to promote the creation of new knowledge in emergent technologies and the development of next-generation, technology-driven solutions in India.

The second tier focuses on translating cutting edge research to commercial ventures. To this end, NITI Aayog proposes establishing international centres called ICTAI (International Centres for Transformational Artificial Intelligence). These centres would facilitate, at a global scale, the development of marketable products from research prototypes or concepts by way of proactive coordination, communication and interfacing between academia and industry. ICTAIs will certainly help to accelerate translating research into start-up ventures.

The formation of ICTAIs also provides a unique opportunity for stakeholders in the VC ecosystem to collaborate with private sector partners and international partners to support the expansion and proliferation of translational ventures in India. Connecting the VC ecosystem with the ICTAIs will ensure that promising translational AI and ML ventures will continue to get funded once the grants from the academic incubators have been utilised. Collaborations between academic incubators and VC ecosystems can accelerate translating research into larger commercial ventures. Further, these commercial ventures can motivate the undergraduate, masters and PhD students to stay back in India for longer once they complete their educational programs. This is likely to start a positive spiral of funding, retaining the best of technical talent, resulting in economic benefits to India and wealth creation for VCs.

Compared to researchers in the AI and ML sectors, only 25 per cent of the brain science researchers we interviewed had active collaborations with industry or had collaborated with industry in the past in some capacity. Less than 25 per cent of the researchers felt that a start-up venture would be likely within the next two years. The main reasons for lower industry collaborations can be attributed to the fundamental nature of current brain science research in India, and the dearth of research projects in this sector.[29] This implies a lower probability for translating research into start-up ventures in the short term.

Indian VCs are, at best, merely aware of the potential of brain science in India. However, VCs based in the USA are ahead in terms of appreciating the potential of this domain. The animal trials of Elon Musk's Neuralink brain–machine interface and its application for starting human trials have enhanced interest in brain science among the VC community in the USA.[30] The interface can potentially help people with neurological conditions to control phones or computers with their mind. It can be used to help cope with conditions such as dementia, Parkinson's disease and spinal cord injuries.

As in the case of AI and ML, the consortium model might be an ideal approach for translating brain science research. A consortium approach to nucleate blue-sky projects has been successfully employed in initiatives like the Human Brain Project (Europe) and BRAIN Initiative (USA). In Germany, the Bernstein Network Computational Neuroscience was established through a central funding initiative of the German Federal Ministry of Education and Research in 2004. The network comprises six centres for computational neuroscience in four regions and 11 collaborations in the brain science space. India should consider setting up brain science consortiums that focus on specific objectives that are of national importance like preventing and managing dementia. Just as in the case of AI and ML, consortiums in brain science should also be networked with the VC ecosystem.

While it is important to get the VC ecosystem to interface with the translational research ecosystem, it is also important to orient academic researchers to the possibilities of translating research into ventures. At this point, brain science researchers may require more support to translate their research compared to what AI and ML researchers may require. This is where pan-institutional initiatives like the Gopalakrishnan Deshpande Centre for Innovation and Entrepreneurship can play an important role. They can help researchers translate their research into start-up ventures by helping them understand the market and funding landscape.[31]

Translational Ventures and VC Ecosystems should Converge

The number of deep tech ventures in India has not been very encouraging, which can only be addressed by increased focus on nurturing translational ventures, via consortiums of organisations from academia, industry and the funding ecosystem. For example, Indian deep tech ventures (having a predominantly information technology focus) received only 1.45 per cent of the total venture funding received during the first quarter of 2019.[32]

Translational ventures that are building India-specific algorithms would not be successful in getting funded unless the VC investors find them attractive. VCs may need to involve deep tech domain experts to assess the potential of the technology that a translational research generates. This requires working more closely with academic incubators. Given the VCs' sophistication in understanding the applications of AI and ML technologies, it should not be difficult for them to assess market potential and nurture translational ventures in the sector.

VCs must also proactively build a team of scouts who are both technology domain experts and are well connected with the academic incubators to build early sensing mechanisms to identify and nurture promising translational ventures. VCs will also have to play a boundary spanning role of creating a network of financial institutions, academic research labs, university incubators, domain experts and government departments to identify, fund and nurture translational ventures.

Finally, VCs may have to promote awareness about the potential for translational ventures among a growing base of Indian limited partners (LPs) and family offices. This will ensure that the Indian LPs and family offices understand the dynamics of investing in translational ventures. VCs also need to garner a greater degree of government backing, by promoting the creation of special fund of funds (or restructuring existing ones) to focus on translational ventures. These would provide robust support to translational ventures, enabling them to push the frontiers of technology and innovation.

Endnotes

[1]Aridi, A and Kapil, N. 2020. **The seven building blocks of a successful innovation agency**. Retrieved from *The World Bank*, World Bank Blogs website: https://blogs.worldbank.org/psd/seven-building-blocks-successful-innovation-agency
Accessed on May 30, 2021

[2]The Biotechnology Industry Research Assistance Council (BIRAC) is a non-profit public enterprise established by the Government of India's Department of Biotechnology (DBT) to enhance the interface between emerging biotechnology enterprises and academia. BIRAC seeks to help emerging enterprises by providing them access to risk capital for R&D projects and a bridge to the academia for technology transfer, intellectual property management and research guidance.

One of BIRAC's flagship projects is the Biotechnology Ignition Grant (BIG) scheme, which aims to help enterprises commercialise their translational research ideas and prototypes by providing them up to US$ 70,000 for a duration of 18 months. The scheme also enables start-ups to receive mentoring from leading scholars and stakeholders in the biotechnology ecosystem. See: https://www.birac.nic.in/big.php

[3]Smith, G. 2011. Willard Boyle (1924–2011). *Nature* 474 (7349): 37 –37.

[4]Marsh, A. 2020. **How the Digital Camera Transformed Our Concept of History**. Retrieved from *Institute of Electrical and Electronics Engineers, Spectrum* website: https://spectrum.ieee.org/tech-history/silicon-revolution/how-the-digital-camera-transformed-our-concept-of-history

[5]Brin, S and Page, L. 1998. The anatomy of a large-scale hypertextual web search engine. *Computer Networks and ISDN Systems* 30(1–7): 107–117.

[6]Accenture. 2017. ***Accelerating India's Economic Growth with Artificial Intelligence***. Retrieved from website: https://www.accenture.com/t20171220T030619Z__w__/in-en/_acnmedia/PDF-68/Accenture-ReWire-For-Growth-POV-19-12-Final.pdf

[7]Thacker, T. 2020. **Dealing with Dementia: A disease that affects memory, thinking and judgement**. Retrieved from *The Economic Times* (January 17, 2020), website: https://economictimes.indiatimes.com/magazines/panache/dealing-with-dementia-a-disease-that-affects-memory-thinking-and-judgement/articleshow/73339613.cms

[8]Ibid.

[9]Our interviewees were researchers affiliated to Indian public and private academic institutions, Indian government labs and industry labs of Indian companies and multinational companies in India. We also spoke to researchers affiliated with non-Indian universities and research labs who collaborated with Indian researchers.

[10]Yin, RK. 2009. *Case Study Research: Design and Methods (Fourth Edition)*. Thousand Oaks, CA: Sage.

[11]NITI Aayog. 2018. ***National Strategy for Artificial Intelligence,*** 26–46. Retrieved from NITI Aayog, website: http://www.niti.gov.in/writereaddata/files/document_publication/NationalStrategy-for-AI-Discussion-Paper.pdf

[12]Department for Promotion of Industry and Industrial Trade (2018). ***The Artificial Intelligence Task Force,*** 9–30. Retrieved from DIPP, website: https://dipp.gov.in/sites/default/files/Report_of_Task_Force_on_ArtificialIntelligence_20March2018_2.pdf

[13]Gagne, JF. 2018. ***Global AI Talent Pool Report 2018***. Retrieved from https://jfgagne.ai/talent/

[14]Narasimhan, TE. 2019. **PE/VC investments in AI space grows five-fold to $359 million in FY19**. Retrieved from *The Business Standard* website: https://www.business-standard.com/article/companies/pe-vc-investment-in-ai-space-grows-five-fold-to-359-million-in-fy19-119041400519_1.html

[15]Sourced from the official website: http://www.incubation.iitm.ac.in/home

[16]Cheng, C, Sun, Y, Su, Y and Yang, S. 2018. Venture capital, innovation, and growth: Evidence from Chinese metropolitan data. ***Applied Economic Letters 26*** (7): 549–553.

[17]Florida, RL and Kenney, M. 1988. Venture capital-financed innovation and technological change in the USA. ***Research Policy 17*** (3): 119–137.

[18]Sourced from the official website: https://www.linkedin.com/company/daksha/about/

[19]Sourced from the official website: https://hyperverge.co/

[20]Sourced from the website of the Healthcare Technology Innovation Centre (HTIC) at IITM: https://htic.iitm.ac.in/mti/project/mocero-health-solutions-pvt-ltd/

[21]Sourced from the website of HTIC at IITM: https://htic.iitm.ac.in/mti/project/zasti/

[22]Sourced from the website of HTIC at IITM: https://htic.iitm.ac.in/mti/project/zbliss-technologies-pvt-ltd/

[23]Sourced from the official website: http://www.incubation.iitm.ac.in/portfolio

[24]Sourced from the official website: https://indiaai.gov.in/investment-funds

[25]Data from Crunchbase (https://www.crunchbase.com/)

[26]We report the total number of investments made by the VC and do not restrict it to just AI/ML start-ups. The data is from Crunchbase (http://www.crunchbase.com/)

[27]NASSCOM & Zinnov. 2019. Indian Tech Start-up Ecosystem. Retrieved from *NASSCOM, 10,000 Start-ups Initiative*, website: http://10000startups.com/frontend/images/Indian-Tech-Start-up-Ecosystem-2019-report.pdf

[28]Sourced from the official website: http://rbc-dsai.iitm.ac.in/about

[29]There are a very few researchers in this discipline in India, specifically in top research institutions.

[30]BBC. 2020. Neuralink: Elon Musk unveils pig with chip in its brain. Retrieved from *BBC* (August 29, 2020), website: https://www.bbc.com/news/world-us-canada-53956683

[31]Ibid.

[32]Singh, S. 2019. Can Innovation Alone Buoy India's Deeptech Startup Ecosystem? Retrieved from *Inc42*, website: https://inc42.com/datalab/can-innovation-alone-fund-deeptech-startups/
Accessed on May 30, 2021

IN BRIEF

- Venture capital (VC) firms create impact in two ways: for the investors who provide capital as well as through the start-ups in which they invest.
- For the investors, VC firms help to channelise wealth from high-net-worth individuals (HNIs) and give an opportunity to acquire shareholding in high-growth companies, while also providing attractive returns.
- The impact and contribution of VC firms through start-ups has been in multiple levels. VC firms have funded start-ups that have provided technology-led, India-specific solutions such as e-commerce, FinTech, rural microfinancing, affordable healthcare solutions and cost-effective renewable energy solutions, while substantially contributing to the sustainable development goals.
- VC-funded start-ups have played a remarkable role in generating direct employment through start-ups as well as secondary employment by contributing to the development of sectors. A noteworthy aspect has been the job creation across the skill spectrum, from high-skilled technical jobs such as programmers and engineers to blue-collar jobs such as delivery partners.
- In instances, such as in AgriTech, where the impact on employment may not be significant, the start-ups have played an important role in augmenting incomes by increasing efficiency and improving productivity through technology innovations.
- The Unicorn status is an indication of the influence and potential the start-up has in the marketplace. The number of Unicorn start-ups from India is close to 50[1] and is expected to reach 100 soon, with more than 50 soonicorns (potential Unicorns) identified.[2] VC funding has played an important role in the creation of such Unicorns.
- The COVID-19 pandemic in 2020 created significant disruption to economic activity. Instead of waiting for the turbulent phase to pass, VC firms actively funded those start-ups that were able to address the opportunities that arose out of the crisis.

ANALYTICAL ARTICLE

16

Impact and Contribution of Venture Capital Funding

Akshay Natteri Mangadu and Thillai Rajan A

Mangadu, AN and Thillai Rajan A. 2021. "Impact and Contribution of Venture Capital Funding". In *Shifting Orbits: Decoding the Trajectory of the Indian Start-up Ecosystem*, edited by Thillai Rajan A, Srivardhini K Jha, Joffi Thomas and Rohan Chinchwadkar, 188–210. Hyderabad: Universities Press (India) Private Limited.

Start-ups – The Modern Engines of Economic Growth

Start-ups are constantly pushing the frontiers of technology and innovation, serving as the modern engines of economic growth. A key feature of start-ups is the emphasis and use of technology and innovation in delivering their products and services. Funding is a key requirement for many start-ups from the standpoint of building products and scaling businesses.[3] Investing in the technology sector, particularly in start-ups, requires good familiarity of the emerging technologies, and is characterised by very high rates of failure due to the uncertainty surrounding the development and commercialisation of the innovation.[4] This renders conventional financing options, such as loans from commercial banks, untenable. While government agencies provide a certain level of funding for commercialisation of innovation, much of the investment has to come from private equity (PE) sources. Venture capital (VC) firms and angel investors provide the much-needed funding for seeding and growth of start-ups.[5] Exhibit 16.1 provides a brief introduction to venture capital and the functioning of VC firms.

In this chapter, we share our view point on the contributions and impact of VC firms from two perspectives – direct and indirect. VCs make a direct impact on investors who invest in their funds as well as on the start-ups they invest in. The contribution of VCs (often referred

Exhibit 16.1: Venture capital, an introduction

Venture capital, in essence, is the source of risk capital for early-stage start-ups to take their innovations to market.[6] To understand the role of venture capital, it is important to recognise the two major obstacles that start-ups face in commercialising their idea. The first obstacle is capital, and the second is experience. The personal wealth of start-up founders and their families may not be adequate to meet the funding requirements of a fast growing organisation, namely, to increase production, expand their sales network and penetrate new markets. The high levels of risk involved, long commitment period, nascent stage of the business and the intangible nature of assets renders it impossible to secure loan-based funding from banks. Further, entrepreneurs often lack the commercial networks, marketing strategies and managerial experience to run large businesses.[7] VC firms enable start-ups to overcome these obstacles by providing the necessary risk capital, while supporting them in building commercial networks, and in strategising the venture's growth.

In order to raise the necessary corpus for investing in start-ups, VC firms raise capital from a diverse set of investors.[8] The investors often comprise high-net-worth individuals (HNIs) and institutional investors (such as corporate enterprises, pension funds, trusts or insurance companies).[9] The VC firms leverage their professional experience and technical know-how to identify promising start-ups. VC firms enable investors to delegate the due-diligence necessary for identifying potential start-ups to professional fund managers and help diversify their portfolio.

In the VC jargon, the investors in a fund are called LPs (Limited Partners), while the individuals managing the fund are called GPs (General Partners). The investors pay the VC firm an annual management fee, which is set at a fixed proportion of the funds committed (typically around 2 per cent).[10] Further, VC firms also take a fixed proportion of the gains realised from profitable exits (this is called *carry* and is often around 20 per cent).

The VC industry has been growing significantly in India, with 188 VC funds registered with the Securities and Exchanges Board of India (SEBI) as of December 2020.[11] An illustrative list of prominent Indian VC firms is shown in Exhibit 16.2. The assets under management underline the growing influence of VC firms in the start-up ecosystem.

to as the value addition function) to the start-ups that they invest in is well recognised.[12,13] In order to enhance the success of the start-ups that they invest in, VC firms provide inputs on a variety of areas such as recruitment of talent, raising follow-on funding, business strategy, access to business networks, and so on. However, in this chapter, we restrict our discussion to the direct impact of VC firms on its investors and the asset market in India.

The indirect impact of VC firms is far more significant. The impact created in the economy by the start-ups that the VC firms have invested in has been wide-ranging and powerful. For example, VC-backed start-ups have contributed to supporting India-centric solutions, increasing employment generation across skill levels and bolstering market competitiveness. VC-backed start-ups have also risen to the occasion during times of crisis to ensure the smooth continuance of the economy. VC-backed start-ups were at the forefront during the COVID-19 pandemic, providing businesses and consumers with seamless digital solutions. If not for these start-ups, key sectors such as education and banking would have faced stagnation, with legacy approaches adversely affecting millions. The second part of the chapter outlines the extent of the contribution of VC firms through their start-ups, on a few key dimensions.

Direct Impact on Investors and the Asset Market in India

Conduit to Acquire Shareholding in Fast Growing Early-Stage Technology Companies

Venture investments in India have made substantial progress in the past decade (Chapter 11 provides a detailed analysis about the decadal trajectory in venture

Exhibit 16.2: An illustrative list of leading venture capital firms in India

Name of the VC firm	No. of investments	Assets under management[14]	Year founded	City	Examples of investments	Sector
3one4 Capital	81	$263M	2016	Bengaluru	Aibono, Inc42, Mitron	Agnostic
Aavishkaar VC	69	$420M	2001	Mumbai	Agrostar, Ergos, Fabelio	Microfinance
Axilor Ventures	79	$26M	2014	Bengaluru	Vyapar, SigTuple, Mistay	Agnostic
Blume Ventures	210	$315M	2011	Mumbai	Jai Kisan, Printo, Sellapps	Technology
Chiratae Ventures (formerly IDG Ventures)	100	$850M	2006	Bengaluru	FirstCry, Flipkart, Myntra	Technology and Consumer
GenNext Ventures	72	NA	2013	Mumbai	Cab Dost, Conexstra, Easebuzz	Agnostic
India Quotient	92	$120.9M	2012	Mumbai	BharatAgri, Cityflo, Lendingkart	Agnostic
Kae Capital	81	$78M	2010	Mumbai	1mg, Healthkart, Zetwerk	Agnostic
Kalaari Capital	171	$650M	2011	Bengaluru	Dream11, MilkBasket, Snapdeal	Technology
Lightspeed India Partners	48	$590M	2004	New Delhi	Acceldata, BYJU'S, Oyo Rooms	Technology
Matrix Partners India	119	$836M	2006	Mumbai	Dailyhunt, Ola, Practo	Agnostic
Omnivore	66	$130M	2010	Mumbai	Aquaconnect, Intello Labs, Stellapps	Agriculture and Food
Orios Venture Partners	63	$200M	2008	Mumbai	Krishify, PharmEasy, Yumlane	Software and Technology
Saama Capital	62	$240M	2012	Bengaluru	Mezi, Naaptol, Veeba	Agnostic
Sequoia Capital India	395	$5.4B	2000	Bengaluru	CARS24, CRED, Freshworks	Agnostic
Smile Group	45	NA	1999	Gurugram	TrulyMadly, Tyroo, Yumlane	Internet Business

Source: Crunchbase (accessed January 2021), PitchBook, May 2021

financing). Venture investments into start-ups in India (as a proportion of the nation's GDP) have been in line with leading global start-up hubs such as the United States and have been substantially better than the overall global levels. The healthy levels of start-up market capitalisation prove that the Indian VC industry has created a positive mark in supporting Indian entrepreneurs and companies. For example, the annual revenue run rate of all active portfolio companies of Chiratae Ventures was about $1.1 billion in 2019, with a market capitalisation of $9.4 billion. This corresponds to about 0.3 per cent of the 2019 India GDP of $2.87 trillion. Extrapolating this to the combined contribution of all VC-funded companies in India (even after accounting for overlaps in investment by different VC firms) would help us to infer the magnitude of the contribution.

Further, unlike developed economies, India's GDP is projected to grow at around 6 per cent till 2025.[15] This growth in the economy is bound to attract a proportional increase in venture funding. India is hence at the cusp of a major increase in venture financing. Between 2012 and 2020, the estimated venture capital investment in India was $54.1 billion.[16] Much of this investment has been in technology companies,[17] indicating that VC firms have played an important role in providing capital for early-stage technology companies, when they are at the riskiest phase. For investors, VC firms act as a conduit to acquire positions in early-stage technology companies, which might not have been accessible otherwise.

Superior Returns

VC funds have emerged as a highly profitable asset class to investors and have consistently succeeded in providing profitable exits. Venture capital funds (excluding angel funds), small and medium enterprise (SME) funds, social venture funds and infrastructure funds have produced attractive returns, as evidenced by their realised IRR (presented in Exhibit 16.4).[19] These returns are arguably better than most traditional listed equity funds. Evidence obtained from multiple sources points to the growing consensus of superior returns provided by VC firms to its investors. For example, Cambridge Associates estimated that globally, venture capital outperformed S&P 500 by 420 bps during 2014–19.[20] Between 2000 and 2016, private market investments generated returns that were 500 bps higher relative to public markets.[21]

Exhibit 16.3: Venture investments as a proportion of GDP (2013–2019)[18]

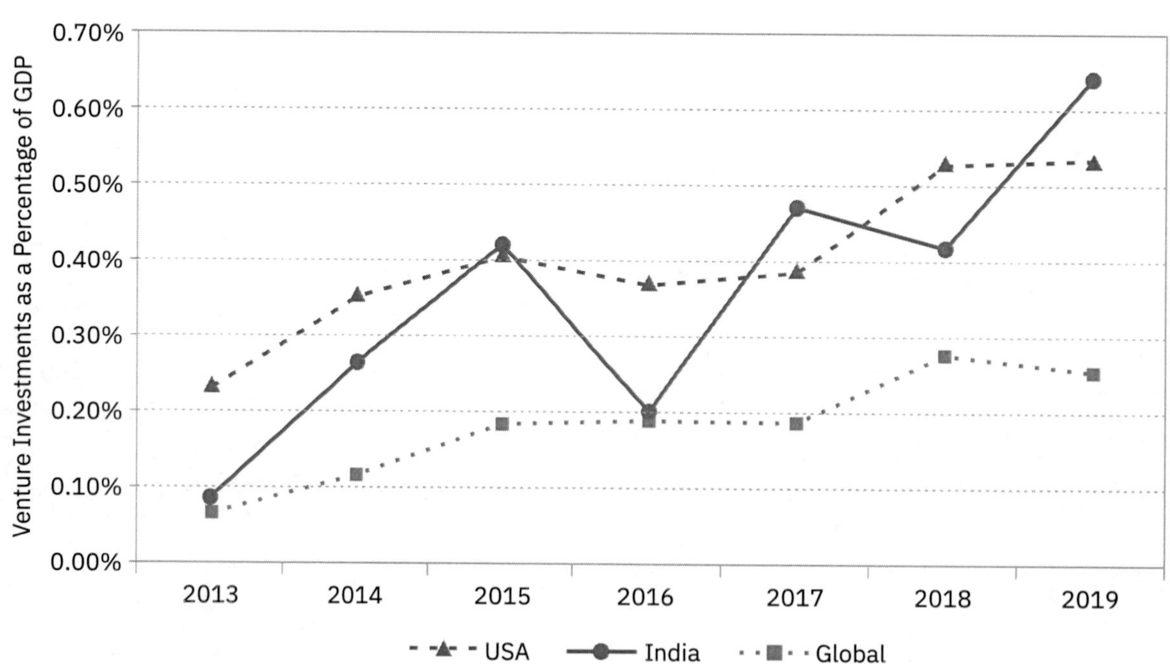

Source: The GDP estimates are from World Bank, the venture investment data for USA and Global are from KPMG Venture Pulse 2020 (Q4) and the venture investment data for India is from Tracxn.

Exhibit 16.4: Realised pooled internal rate of return[22] of Category I alternate investment funds (AIF)[23] (excluding angel funds) by vintage year[24]

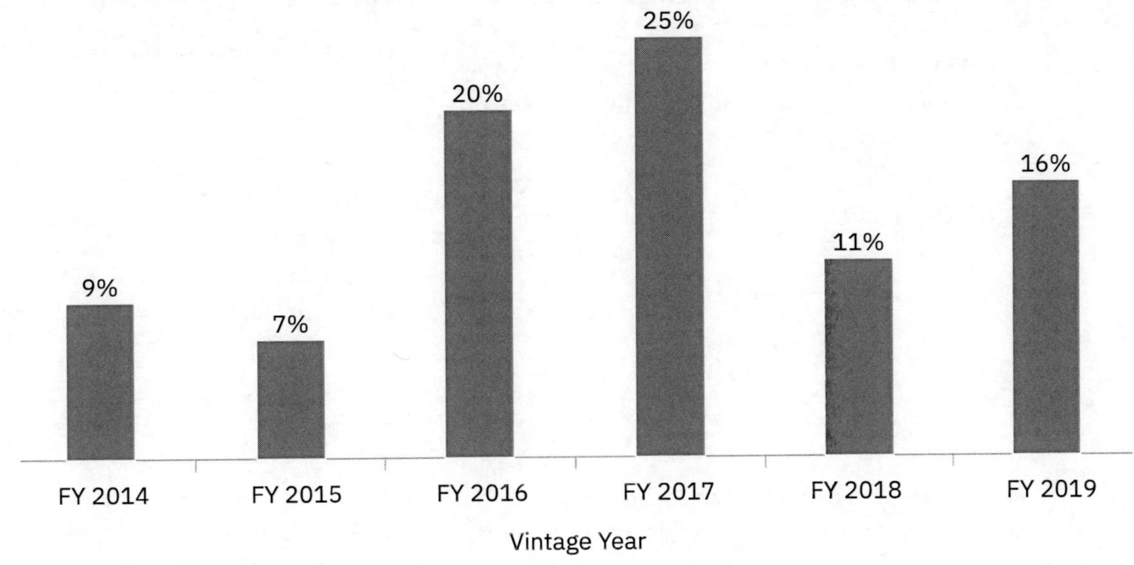

Source: CRISIL Category I AIF benchmarks (accessed April 2021)

Channelising Indian Wealth to Start-ups

On the back of sustained strong economic performance, wealth in India had increased fourfold between 2000 and 2019. By the end of 2019, the wealth in India was estimated at $12.6 trillion and the number of ultra High Net-worth Individuals (HNIs)[25] in the country was almost 6,000, making it the fifth highest globally.[26] The estimated wealth of ultra-HNIs in the country was $440 billion in 2019, and expected to increase to $707 billion by 2024. With the increase in personal wealth, professional wealth management and family offices are involved in the portfolio management of the wealth of the ultra-HNIs. In a typical portfolio, 20 per cent of the allocation is in alternative assets, which includes contributions to venture capital funds.

In 2019, 26 per cent of the total investment in India's start-ups came from domestic investments. With approximately $10 billion annual investment flowing into Indian start-ups, domestic investment in start-ups translates to $2.6 billion. Family offices and ultra-HNIs would account for a significant percentage in this investment. However, direct investment in start-ups by family offices during 2015–20 averaged only about 70 deals a year.[27] Therefore, it can be inferred that the majority of the investment made by family offices and ultra-HNIs has happened through contributions to venture funds. The VC firms have thus played an important role in channelising domestic capital to new innovative companies and organisations, which would lead to the economic progress of the nation. Without the professional expertise of the VC firms, many investors would have found investing in start-ups to be a very risky activity, which would have slowed down investment flow. Chapter 14 provides a detailed analysis of the potential for investments from Indian family offices in start-ups.

Indirect Contribution through the Invested Start-ups

Supporting India-centric Solutions

An important feature of India is the vast socio-economic diversity, which results in a multitude of market segments, each with their own set of problems and opportunities. One example of the 2*2 classification of the Indian market is by location (rural, semi-urban, urban or metropolitan)[28] and purchasing power (disposable income). Exhibit 16.5 provides a list of illustrative solutions in different sectors mapped under such a classification.

Exhibit 16.5: Examples of targeted solutions for various market segments

	High purchasing power	Low purchasing power
Rural	• **Agri-FinTech** solutions to provide crop insurance, flexible payment for agricultural input and easier access to banking channels. • **AgriTech** solutions focussed on using cutting-edge technologies (such as AI) to automate aspects of farming and increase productivity. • Solutions to enhance **supply chain integration with food processors**.	• **Financial inclusion** solutions that provide access to affordable credit. • **AgriTech** solutions for reducing farm input costs. • Solutions to provide access to **clean water and sanitation**. • Solutions to enhance **rural healthcare and education**.
Semi-Urban	• **Real estate and construction technology** solutions to accelerate the development of towns. • **RetailTech** solutions to improve the availability and variety of retail goods and commodities available in smaller towns. • **FinTech** solutions to digitise aspects of banking and reduce the dependence on physical branches. • **Enterprise applications** for small-scale businesses to manage finances, pay slips and inventory.	• **EdTech** solutions that provide courses in regional languages and courses that enhance vocational skills. • **Financial inclusion** solutions that provide easy access to business credit for setting up small businesses and shops. • **Healthcare solutions**, such as the development of affordable essential medical equipment.
Urban and Metropolitan	• **Taxi aggregators** that ensure availability of taxis during peak hours. • **Real estate** solutions for easy listing of apartments and homes for rent or sale. • **Travel and hospitality** solutions for seamlessly making travel arrangements.	• **Financial inclusion** solutions such as providing easy access to emergency credit for medical and personal emergencies. • **Job aggregators** for home services and other freelance services. • Solutions to provide access to **clean water and sanitation**, specifically in urban slums.

Naturally, a number of Indian start-ups have emerged, with the specific focus of solving problems that are endemic to India by developing indigenous technologies and innovations. Such start-ups have been able to solve existing challenges in new ways that have not been attempted before. Using technology innovation, start-ups are able to bring solutions to the market, which would not have been possible by traditional businesses.

Recognising the need to financially support such start-ups, the government's Technology Development Board (TDB) under the Department of Science and Technology (DST) has invested ₹3.1 billion in 13 VC funds to support indigenous start-ups at the forefront of technological innovation to address the needs of the Indian market.[29] The participation of a government agency led to a multiplier effect, with the VCs raising more capital from other sources.[30] Some of the active funds from the DST portfolio are mentioned in Exhibit 16.6.

Apart from the DST-supported funds, there are a number of funds that support start-ups in various sectors, including technology, education, healthcare and socio-economic inclusion (Exhibit 16.7).

Exhibit 16.6: Prominent VC funds that received TDB contribution[31]

Year of investment[32]	Venture capital firm	Fund	Total fund amount (₹ billion)[33]	Description	Examples of start-ups supported
2011–12	SEAF India Investment Advisors	SEAF Agribusiness Fund	1.25	SEAF's agribusiness fund aims to invest in SMEs[34] across 33 sub-sectors of India's agribusiness value chain.[35] The sectors include seeds, processing and warehousing.[36]	Abhay Cotex[37], Himadri Foods[38], Manisha Agri Biotech Limited[39]
2012–13	Blume Venture Advisors	Multi Sector Seed Capital Fund	1	Blume Venture's funds seek to identify and support start-ups that solve "uniquely Indian problems", across a multitude of sectors.[40]	Jai Kisan, Procol, Railyatri[41]
2012–13	IvyCap Venture Advisors	IvyCap Trust Fund - I	2	IvyCap's fund is focussed on supporting technically qualified entrepreneurs emerging from India's premier institutions such as IITs and IIMs. The fund primarily focusses on AgriTech, EnterpriseTech, FinTech, healthcare and emerging tech.[42]	Aujas, Fieldez, RML Farm Bee[43]
2013–14	CIIE, IIM Ahmedabad	Infuse Ventures	1.25[44]	This fund was formed jointly by BP Plc, International Finance Corporation (IFC), Ministry of New and Renewable Energy, Technology Development Board and IIM Ahmedabad.[45] The primary focus of the VC fund is to support early-stage start-ups in the sustainability and clean energy sector in India. The fund helped reduce over 85 million kilograms of CO_2 emissions.[46]	Altizon, Glowship, Tessol[47]

In the absence of VC funding, it would have been difficult for these start-ups to have attained the scale that made it possible to create the impact in different sectors of the economy. Exhibit 16.8 illustrates the impact created by some of these start-ups.

Exhibit 16.7: Examples of large India-centric VC funds

Sector	Year	Venture capital firm	Fund	Fund size (₹ billion)	Description	Examples of start-ups supported
Technology	2018	CIIE, Ahmedabad	Bharat Innovation Fund	6.7[48]	The fund seeks to support Indian ventures that produce globally competitive technological solutions. The fund aims to mentor and support start-ups that are at the frontlines of healthcare, agriculture, renewable energy and advanced technology solutions, which have the potential to dominate the global technology arena.[49]	Entropik Tech, Shifu, Zumutor Biologics[50]
Social Inclusion	2013[51]	SIDBI Venture Capital	Samridhi Fund	4.3[52]	The fund invests in ventures that aide in the development of 8 low-income Indian states (Bihar, Uttar Pradesh, Madhya Pradesh, Chhattisgarh, Jharkhand, Rajasthan and West Bengal). The fund invests in ventures that improve the availability of water, sanitation, affordable healthcare, education, infrastructure or access to financial services for the poor. The fund has provided over 1.5 million patients with access to healthcare, over 5.9 million citizens with access to financial services, and has benefitted over 29,000 farmers.[53]	Annapurna Finance, Gramco, Glocal Healthcare[54]
Financial Inclusion	2012	Aavishkaar VC and Goodwell Investments	Aavishkaar Goodwell India Microfinance Development Company II	1.68[55]	The company provides active support to commercial micro-finance organisations in India that aim to provide financial services such as housing loans and micro business loans to the poor.[56]	EPS, Intellecash, Swarna Pragati[57]
Agriculture and Rural Start-ups	2019	NABARD (The National Bank for Agriculture and Rural Development)	NabVentures	7[58]	The fund aims to invest in innovative tech start-ups in the agriculture, food and rural livelihoods sectors.[59]	Jai Kisan, Krishitantra, Unnati[60]
Healthcare	2020	Healthquad	Healthquad Fund 2	5.14[61]	The fund invests in start-ups that are disrupting India's healthcare sector with innovative solutions that improve the affordability, accessibility and quality of healthcare services.[62]	Medikabazaar, Regency Healthcare, Strand[63]
Education	2015	Michael & Susan Dell Foundation	India Educational Investment Fund	0.13[64]	The fund seeks to invest in start-ups that improve the quality of education and access to it for urban, low-income Indian families.[65]	ChipperSage,GuruG, Reportbee[66]

Exhibit 16.8: Impact of start-ups across various sectors

Start-up	Sector	Impact	VC investors
Caspian[67]	Social Sector Financing	Caspian Impact is a non-banking financial corporation that provides debt capital to social enterprises. They help social enterprises that aim to create an environmental and socio-economic impact while generating competitive returns. Caspian supports enterprises that focus on sectors such as food and agriculture, affordable healthcare and clean energy. The company has invested ₹20 billion in over 140 enterprises that are working to achieve over 13 of the United Nations' sustainable development goals (SDG).	SIDBI Ventures, Grayghost Ventures
CropIn[68]	AgriTech	CropIn leverages data and analytics to improve farm and soil management, resulting in better crop production. The company has helped over four million farmers in over 52 countries improve the sustainability and efficiency of their farm management. By 2020, they were supporting farm land area of 8 million acres, increasing at about 12 per cent every year.	Chiratae Ventures, Ankur Capital
Entropik Tech[69]	DeepTech	Entropik has developed multi-modal emotion recognition technologies that are powered by artificial intelligence. The technologies help brands understand their customers' emotional responses and product experience. For the development of these solutions, the company has used a panel of over 100 million testers and data of over 15 million unique human emotions.	CIIE - IIM Ahmedabad, Arthavida Ventures
Glocal Healthcare Systems[70]	Healthcare Access	Glocal focusses on providing advanced state-of-the-art medical facilities and infrastructure to the poorly served areas in India at an affordable price. The company has setup 12 hospitals and 241 digital dispensaries, and has successfully completed over 110,000 surgeries.	SIDBI Ventures, Sequoia Capital India
Jai Kisan[71]	Agricultural Financing	Jai Kisan provides affordable financing for agricultural equipment and inputs. The start-up has helped over 8,000 farmers across nine Indian states.	NabVentures, Blume Ventures
Khatabook[72]	MSME-specific Technology Solutions	Khatabook provides an Android application that enables small businesses and merchants to digitally record the credit they extend to their customers. The application has helped over 40 million businesses across 4,000 cities, handling over 200 million transactions every day.	Sequoia Capital India, Tencent

Continued . . .

Start-up	Sector	Impact	VC investors
Krishitantra[73]	AgriTech	Krishitantra provides advanced soil testing and soil health analysis solutions to farmers. Currently, there is only one lab available for every 150,000 farmers in India for soil testing. Krishitantra aims to democratise access to soil testing solutions to all farmers. The start-up works with farmer organisations and fertilizer companies to make soil testing solutions more accessible and affordable. The company has helped over 758 farmers.	NabVentures, Omnivore Partners
Rite Water[74]	Potable Water Supply	Rite Water focusses on providing potable water to the Indian rural population. They specifically work in regions where the natural sources of water (ground or surface) are contaminated by chemicals or pathogens. The company has set up over 1,500 purification plants, supplying potable water to over a million people.	SIDBI Ventures, Veolia
Swarna Pragati[75]	Rural Housing Finance	Swarna Pragati is focussed on creating access to affordable housing in rural India by providing housing loans at small and affordable monthly instalments. The company has a single-window clearance for its loans and does not require a stifling amount of paperwork. The company has over 64 branches in 101 districts, and has disbursed over 24,000 loans totalling over ₹3.2 billion.	Aavishkaar Venture Capital, Omidyar Network
Vayana Network[76]	MSME FinTech Solutions	Vayana is a B2B trade financial intermediary that democratises access to trade and finance for MSMEs. Vayana connects MSMEs to corporates and financial institutions that offer low-cost trade loans.[77] The start-up has facilitated over $5 billion in financing via over 1.7 million transactions across 20 countries. Vayana brings state-of-the-art FinTech and analytics solutions to the smallest of MSMEs, enabling them to improve their efficiency and thrive in the market.	Chiratae Ventures, Jungle Ventures

Furthering Social Development and Sustainability

Apart from the impact funds that focus on triple bottom lines, increasingly, mainstream VC funds have also recognised that it is not possible to build great businesses without contributing to society. VC firms are factoring the start-ups' contribution to social development in their assessment, because not only does it help in sustainability of the business but it also makes financial sense. Exhibit 16.9 illustrates the contribution of the Chiratae Ventures portfolio towards SDGs.

Augmenting Incomes and Empowering Job Creation

India is home to one of the world's youngest populations, with approximately 90 per cent of the population under the age of 60.[79] The demographic dividend is only an advantage to the Indian economy if there is adequate job generation. Start-ups, specifically those with VC backing, have been able to use this demographic dividend as an advantage and have been able to provide employment to various sections of the Indian workforce. The impact on job creation is at two levels. First, the jobs created by the start-ups directly. For example, VC-

Exhibit 16.9: Contributions of Chiratae Ventures portfolio companies towards SDGs

SDG goal	Impact of Chiratae's portfolio companies[78]
SDG 1 - No Poverty	FinTech companies such as EarlySalary, Vayana Network, Paisabazaar.com, PolicyBazaar.com and CreditMantri.com have provided 11.5 million people with over $140 billion in loans and insurance.
SDG 2 - Zero Hunger	Two AgriTech companies, CropIn and AgroStar, have helped over 1.3 million small land-holding farmers to improve the efficiency of their farm management.
SDG 3 - Good Health and Well-being	Ten HealthTech companies including Aether, Axio, HealthPlix, SigTuple, Ovo Health, WeInnovate, Onco.com, HealthifyMe, Firstcry, Lenskart and cure.fit have provided health services to over 31 million people.
SDG 4 - Quality Education	Two EdTech companies, Miko and Shifu, have helped over 195,000 young learners in India.
SDG 5 - Gender Equality	Thirteen portfolio companies cater to the needs of women and girls. Over 19 million women and girls have been served, with over 6,700 jobs created for women. Some examples include Nestaway, Ovo Health and Little Black Book.
SDG 7 - Affordable and Clean Energy	Two companies, Oye Rickshaw and Bounce, in the electric mobility space have assisted over 2.4 million electric vehicle rides.
SDG 8 - Decent Work and Economic Growth	Thirteen portfolio companies have helped over 183,000 MSMEs and nano-enterprises with access to technology, credit, insurance and market. Examples include Vayana Network, Peel-works, Go Mechanic, Bizongo, Locofast, WMall and Love Local.
SDG 9 - Industry, Innovation and Infrastructure	Forty-three portfolio companies are impacting over 50.5 million people and 290,000 businesses across various sectors, including infrastructure and logistics.
SDG 10 - Reduced Inequalities	Portfolio companies such as CropIn, AgroStar, Vayana Network and CreditMantri have helped over 5.6 million small land-holding farmers and lower income individuals.
SDG 11 - Sustainable Cities and Communities	Companies such as Pando, Blowhorn and Railofy in the mobility and public transportation sector have facilitated over 28 million rides or trips.
SDG 12 - Responsible Consumption and Production	Rentmojo, a consumer product rentals start-up in Chiratae's portfolio, has helped lower production rates to avoid over 14,000 tonnes in greenhouse gas emissions.
SDG 13 - Climate Action	Three companies in the logistics and mobility solutions space (Pando, Blowhorn and Bounce) have helped avoid 6.2 million tonnes in GHG emissions. KBCols Sciences extracts sustainable natural colours from microbes for use in paints, cosmetics, textiles, food, pharmaceuticals and plastics. The company's solution has the potential to reduce 47 kilograms of CO_2 emissions per garment, and also yield a 20 per cent reduction in water usage.

backed technology start-ups founded between 2009 and 2019 have cumulatively added over 430,000 direct jobs and over 2.6 million indirect jobs to the economy (as of 2019).[80] The CAGR for job creation by tech start-ups stands at an impressive 34 per cent between 2009 and 2019.[81] What has been noteworthy is that the job creation has been across the board, for both highly skilled individuals (such as engineers, AI scientists and computer programmers) as well as the less skilled (such as cab drivers, delivery partners and home care providers).[82] The most important contribution of VC-backed start-ups (specifically aggregators and retail apps) has been for many blue-collar workers in the urban and semi-urban areas, specifically from the lower quartiles of income distribution. Exhibit 16.10 lists some of the prominent start-ups along with the number of registered delivery partners, drivers or professionals associated with them. The second impact on job creation has been by way of facilitating sectoral growth, leading to tertiary employment. Let us take the case of Vayana, a start-up involved in providing trade financing for B2B MSMEs. They have financed over $5 billion and impacted more than 20,000 MSMEs.[83] These SMEs, as a result of such financing solutions that met their need, were able to grow faster, thereby generating more employment.

Many start-ups were able to increase the income of their users. A primary example has been in the case of agriculture. There are many start-ups that work on improving yield for farmers. While they may not have resulted in any significant employment creation, what these start-ups have assisted in is to enhance the income of the farmers by helping them with various crop and farm management tools. For example, AgriTech start-ups such as CropIn and AgroStar have helped over 1.3 million small land-holding farmers to improve the efficiency of their farm management, resulting in higher income for farmers.

Creating Global Companies: Scale and Disruption in the Marketplace

The liberalisation of the Indian economy in 1991 was one of the most important economic reforms in post-independence history. The dismantling of the "Permit Licence Raj"[91] enabled new entrepreneurs to enter the market and compete with existing manufacturers and service providers. The increase in the ease of doing business soon resulted in a vibrant entrepreneurial ecosystem,[92] propelling the nation's economy to stable and marked growth.[93] The success of the 1991 reforms indicate the role of an open and competitive economy for robust economic growth. Innovative start-ups that disrupt existing markets need to be well-funded and given the necessary support in terms of market access to effectively compete with existing giants while providing consumers with improved product and service offerings.

Venture capital provides much-needed funding for start-ups to thrive and grow. Entering new markets often entails massive investments, which start-ups would not be able to generate merely from their retained earnings.

Exhibit 16.10: Prominent start-ups and job generation

Start-up	Number of delivery partners/ drivers/professionals	Key VC investors[84]
Dunzo	Over 180,000[85]	Alteria Capital, Lightbox, Pivot Ventures
Flipkart	Over 650,000[86]	Manhattan Venture Partners, SoftBank, Tiger GlobalManagement
Ola	Over 2,500,000[87]	Accel, Falcon Edge Capital, SoftBank
Swiggy	Over 210,000[88]	Accel, Harmony Partners, SAIF Partners
Urban Company	Over 25,000[89]	Accel, Bessemer Venture Partners, Tiger Global
Zomato	Over 200,000[90]	Kora, Luxor Capital, Steadview Capital

Source: Various media articles and Crunchbase

Apart from capital, many start-ups also require guidance and mentorship in developing their businesses. VC firms address both these requirements: they not only provide capital, but they also actively add value to their portfolio companies by providing strategic inputs. By funding high-growth companies and actively adding value, VC firms have enabled the creation of global companies from India.

Instances of VC-backed start-ups that have grown to become formidable leaders by disrupting established markets is becoming more frequent. Exhibit 16.11 lists the start-ups that have disrupted well-established markets and which have become successful Unicorns (between $1 billion and $5 billion in valuation) and megacorns (over $5 billion in valuation).

Apart from catalysing the creation of global companies with large valuations, many of the VC-funded start-ups have been able to change the narrative in the market. The focus has shifted towards identifying with the problem more closely. For example, it is no longer agriculture, but AgriTech, with a focus on soil management, disease management, and so on. It is no longer just healthcare, but HealthTech, where start-ups use technology to address problems pertaining to affordable or accessible healthcare in rural areas. Extensive use of technology, directly focussing on the challenges and commercialising the opportunities that these challenges present have resulted in the start-ups bringing extremely innovative solutions that have disrupted the market, if not scale.

Agility: Backing Start-ups During COVID-19

The COVID-19 pandemic of 2020 has altered day-to-day life in innumerable ways. While governments, public agencies, corporations and civil society were all grappling with the challenges, start-ups quickly adapted to the challenges that arose due to lockdowns and social distancing measures, while fully utilising the opportunities they presented. What needs to be highlighted here is the support provided by VC firms to the start-ups responding to the COVID-19 challenges.

The rapid spread of the virus necessitated widespread lockdowns to curb its transmission. These lockdowns fundamentally altered how several social and economic activities were conducted. Many sectors were severely affected and faced an immediate requirement to switch to digital alternatives. This need presented start-ups in the EdTech, HealthTech, FinTech and EnterpriseTech sectors with an enormous opportunity to grow their businesses and to scale their product offerings for a broader customer base. While the chapters in the Industry Perspectives section provide detailed narratives on EdTech, HealthTech and FinTech, this section specifically highlights the responses by start-ups to the COVID-19 pandemic.

EdTech Sector – Enabling Remote Learning

During the lockdown, EdTech start-ups successfully expanded their customer base and provided remote learning solutions to the many students affected by the closure of schools. The number of users on EdTech platforms grew by a stupendous 122 per cent in 2020, from 2019. In absolute terms, the number of users rose from 45 million in 2019 to 100 million in 2020.[100] This success in attracting new customers, by providing timely remote learning solutions, was enabled by the large amounts of funding that EdTech start-ups were able to secure when the pandemic was raging. In 2020, Indian EdTech start-ups raised $1.7 billion, more than four times the funding raised in 2019.[101] BYJU'S, Unacademy and Vedantu together received the vast majority of the funding, close to $1.66 billion.[102] The EdTech sector could see further growth with the increased penetration of mobile telecommunication technologies. Experts believe that COVID-19 has served as a catalyst in changing the consumers' mindset to online learning and technology-based learning solutions.[103] Such solutions would be integrated with conventional pedagogical methods in the coming years, which would impact the quality and delivery of education.[104]

Enterprise Applications: Providing Cybersecurity and Digitisation Solutions

During the lockdown, work from home (WFH) went from being an occasional mode of working to the norm. Enterprise application start-ups were at the forefront of providing sustainable solutions to facilitate WFH. For example, start-ups played a key role in providing cybersecurity solutions for large companies that were transitioning from office-based digital systems to remote access systems.[105] A study by the Data Security Council

Exhibit 16.11: Prominent VC-backed Unicorns and megacorns[94]

Start-up	Valuation ($ billion)	Countries of operation	Sector	VC investors
Unicorns				
BillDesk	1.5	India	B2B Payments	Clearstone Venture Partners, SIDBI Venture Capital
Cars24	1	India	Auto Sales	Moore Strategic Ventures, Sequoia Capital India
Delhivery	1.6	India	Logistics	Nexus Ventures, SoftBank
Freshworks	3.5	India, United States	Customer Relationship Management Software	Accel, Sequoia Capital India
Lenskart	1.5	India, US, Singapore, UAE	Eyewear e-Commerce	Chiratae Ventures, Unilazer Ventures
Pine Labs	1.5	India, South-East Asia, Middle East	Payments	Madison India Capital, Sequoia Capital India
PolicyBazaar	1	India	Insurance Tech	Chiratae Ventures, SoftBank
Swiggy	3.6	India, Middle East[95]	FoodTech	Prosus Ventures, Samsung Ventures
Udaan	2.8	India	B2B e-Commerce	Footpath Ventures, Lightspeed India Ventures
Unacademy	2	India	EdTech	Blume Ventures, Sequoia Capital
Zomato	3.9	India, Middle East, Europe and North America[96]	FoodTech	Kora, Steadview Capital
Megacorns				
Byju's	11	India, US, UK, Australia[97]	EdTech	Aarin Capital, Lightspeed Ventures, Sequoia Capital
Flipkart	23	India	e-Commerce	Chiratae Ventures, SoftBank, Tencent
Ola Cabs	6.4	India, Australia, New Zealand, and UK[98]	Taxi Aggregator	Accel, Falcon Edge Capital
Oyo Rooms	10	Operates in over 80 countries[99]	Affordable Hotels	Lightspeed Venture, Sequoia Capital
PayTm	16	India, Canada	Payments	Investopad, K2 Global
Snapdeal	6.5	India	e-Commerce	Nexus Venture Partners, Softbank

Source: Venture Intelligence and Crunchbase

of India found that 76 per cent of all cybersecurity and technology solutions for leading companies were provided by start-ups in 2020.[106] Accops, Cyfirma, Ensurity, GAJSheild, InstaSafe, Securden and Wi-Jungle were some of the leading start-ups providing such security solutions. Companies such as Cyfirma and Secureden successfully raised capital, even during the pandemic.[107] A significant rise in funding in this sector is expected in the coming years to support these start-ups in serving their growing base of customers.[108]

Apart from cybersecurity solutions, start-ups that provide digitisation of business processes have also seen record growth. For example, Khatabook facilitated over 5 trillion transactions for over 8 million merchants in over 10,000 cities during the pandemic.[109] This enabled the start-up to attract $60 million in funding during the pandemic.[110]

FinTech: Digitising Payments and Transactions

FinTech start-ups, specifically in the digital payments sector, provided an effective solution for contactless transactions. The number of digital transactions in India grew by 38 per cent during the pandemic,[111] when compared to pre-COVID levels. Leading start-ups such as PhonePe and PayTM successfully grew their user base during this period. Further, online trading and investment platforms such as Groww and Zerodha were also able to achieve record growth.[112] For example, Zerodha increased their user base from two million users in 2019 to three million users by June 2020.[113] With the rise in popularity of digital payments and investment platforms, FinTech start-ups were able to double the amount of investments they received from pre-COVID levels.[114] FinTech start-ups raised $1.7 billion between January and June 2020.[115] Navi, Pine Labs and PaySense were some of the leading start-ups in terms of funds raised, attracting a total of $0.8 billion among them.[116]

HealthTech: Digital Consultations and AI-enabled Diagnostics

The increased demand on hospital resources and rise in the risk of hospital-acquired infections forced many patients with common ailments to switch to teleconsultations. Practo, a teleconsultations start-up, saw a 500 per cent increase in the number of online consultations during the lockdown, with about 44 per cent coming from non-metro cities.[117] Further, online fitness start-ups, AI-powered predictive diagnostics solutions and movement tracking start-ups grew their market base and provided much-needed solutions to the challenges posed by the pandemic.[118] The overall VC funding raised in this sector was $103 million as of June 2020,[119] while Practo successfully raised $32 million from AIA Group in August 2020.[120]

While the chutzpah of the Indian entrepreneurs played an important role in hyper-scaling in the aforementioned sectors, more often than not, they were accompanied on the journey by VC firms, who provided the fuel (both capital and value addition) to ride the crest of opportunities by being agile, resilient and consumer focussed, even in the most adverse of times.

Summary

The conventional yardstick of performance and impact of VC firms has been the returns generated for its investors. While the raison d'être for VC firms is to generate financial returns, we can understand the true impact and contribution of VC funds if we broaden our horizons beyond financial returns. The objective of this chapter has been to highlight additional perspectives on the impact that VC funds have created. First, we examined the role of VC firms for investors. VC firms help to channelise wealth from HNIs to innovative start-ups while also providing attractive returns.

Secondly, we looked at VC in relation to the role of technology in the modern economy. Technology companies are going to play a dominant role in the economy and wealth creation process. For example, in 2015, the market capitalisation of the top 15 technology companies in the US was about 15 per cent of the US GDP. By 2019, this had increased to 31 per cent. Technology upstarts play an equal, if not dominant, role in the wealth creation process and worldwide, it has been well recognised that VC firms play a very important role in the creation and growth of technology start-ups.

Third, we explored the disruptions that create new markets. Innovation is an important characteristic for businesses to survive in the marketplace. By funding innovative start-ups, VC firms play a very important role in bringing new products and services to consumers.

This has been possible by reacting quickly to change and capitalising on the opportunities when it arose. When COVID-19 presented an opportunity for digitisation and going online, VC firms quickly opened up the funding tap to support start-ups that were well-positioned to create an impact, both socially and financially.

The fourth viewpoint concerns speed and scale. It is not just that start-ups create a large impact, but that they are able to create it in a shorter time window. Whether it has been in reaching a certain valuation benchmark or creating employment in large numbers, start-ups have been able to significantly shrink the time it takes to reach the milestone. For a country like India that has a large unsatiated demand, it is not just the scale that matters, but also the speed. By providing a form of capital to start-ups that incentivizes speed and scale, VCs play a very important role in economic growth.

Finally, we looked at the gradual focus on the long term, which considers the relevance of long-term prosperity such as SDGs. What was once considered the sole prerogative of impact funds has now become a part of the thinking among mainstream VC firms. By funding firms that can address the opportunities arising from SDGs or by giving importance to social development as a part of their assessment criteria, VC firms play a noteworthy role in creating good corporate citizens.

The first-order impact of VC funding can be measured purely in terms of financial returns. However, the second-order impact, or the impact created by start-ups that the VC firms fund, is truly multi-dimensional. What this chapter has highlighted are but a few of the many. In sum, the sustained growth of the VC ecosystem would be a key requirement for the expansion of the Indian economy, as VC is the fuel that propels start-ups, the modern engines of growth.

Acknowledgements

The authors would like to gratefully acknowledge the helpful comments received from Sudhir Sethi and Subhrajit Chowdhury on the draft versions of this chapter.

Appendix: Websites for Start-ups Cited in this Chapter

Start-up	Website
1mg	https://www.1mg.com/
Abhay Cotex	https://abhaynutrition.com/
Acceldata	https://www.acceldata.io/
Accops	https://www.accops.com/
Aether	https://aetherbiomedical.com/
Agrostar	https://agrostar.in/shop
Aibono	https://www.aibono.com/
Altizon	https://altizon.com/
Annapurna Finance	https://annapurnafinance.in/
Aquaconnect	https://aquaconnect.blue/
Aujas	https://www.aujas.com/
Axio	https://axiobio.com/
BharatAgri	https://bharatagri.com/
BillDesk	https://www.billdesk.com/
Bizongo	https://www.bizongo.com/
Blowhorn	https://blowhorn.com/
Bounce	https://bounceshare.com/
Byju's	https://byjus.com/
Cab Dost	https://www.cabdost.com/
CARS24	https://www.cars24.com/
Caspian	https://www.caspian.in/
ChipperSage	https://www.thechippersage.com/
Cityflo	https://www.cityflo.com/
Conexstra	http://www.indonis.com/
CRED	https://cred.club/
CreditMantri.com	https://www.creditmantri.com/
CropIn	https://www.cropin.com/
Cure.fit	https://www.cure.fit/
Cyfirma	https://www.cyfirma.com/
Dailyhunt	https://m.dailyhunt.in//news/
Delhivery	https://www.delhivery.com/
Dream11	https://www.dream11.com/
Dunzo	https://www.dunzo.com/
EarlySalary	https://www.earlysalary.com/
Easebuzz	https://easebuzz.in/

Start-up	Website
Ensurity	https://www.ensurity.com/
Entropik Tech	https://entropiktech.com/
EPS	https://www.electronicpay.in/
Ergos	https://ergos.in/
Fabelio	https://fabelio.com/
Fieldez	https://www.fieldez.com/
FirstCry	https://www.firstcry.com/
Flipkart	https://www.flipkart.com/
Freshworks	https://www.freshworks.com/crm/
GAJSheild	https://gajshield.com/
Glocal Healthcare	https://www.ghspl.com/
Glowship	https://livguardsolar-dev-api.rpsapi.in/
Go Mechanic	https://gomechanic.in/
Gramco	https://www.gramco.in/
Groww	https://groww.in/
GuruG	https://guru-g.com/
Healthkart	https://www.healthkart.com/
HealthifyMe	https://www.healthifyme.com/in/
HealthPlix	https://healthplix.com/
Himadri Foods	https://www.himadrimasala.com/
Inc42	https://inc42.com/
InstaSafe	https://instasafe.com/
Intellecash	https://arohan.in/icash.php
Intello Labs	http://www.intellolabs.com/
Jai Kisan	https://www.jai-kisan.com/
KBCols Sciences	https://www.kbcolssciences.com/
Khatabook	https://khatabook.com/
Krishify	https://www.krishify.com/
Krishitantra	https://krishitantra.com/
Krishitantra	https://krishitantra.com/
Lendingkart	https://www.lendingkart.com/

Start-up	Website
Lenskart	https://www.lenskart.com/
Little Black Book	https://lbb.in/
Locofast	https://locofast.com/
Love Local	https://lovelocal.in/
Manisha Agri Biotech Limited	https://www.seaf.com/seaf-fund-invests-in-india-based-manisha-agri-biotech-limited/
Medikabazaar	https://www.medikabazaar.com/
Mezi	Sold to American Express
Miko	https://miko.ai/in
MilkBasket	https://www.milkbasket.com/
Mistay	https://www.mistay.in/
Mitron	https://web.mitron.tv/
Myntra	https://www.myntra.com/
Naaptol	https://www.naaptol.com/
Netaway	https://www.nestaway.com/
Ola	https://www.olacabs.com/
Onco.com	https://onco.com/
Ovo Health	https://www.ovohealth.com/
Oye Rickshaw	https://www.oyerickshaw.com/
Oyo Rooms	https://www.oyorooms.com/
Pando	https://www.pando.ai
PaySense	https://www.gopaysense.com/
PayTm	https://paytm.com/
Peelworks	https://www.peel-works.com/
PharmEasy	https://pharmeasy.in/
PhonePe	https://www.phonepe.com/
Pine Labs	https://www.pinelabs.com/
PolicyBazaar	https://www.policybazaar.com/
Practo	https://www.practo.com/
Printo	https://printo.in/
Procol	https://www.procol.in/
Railofy	https://railofy.com/
Railyatri	https://www.railyatri.in/
Regency Healthcare	https://regencyhealthcare.in/
Rentmojo	https://www.rentomojo.com/
Reportbee	https://www.reportbee.com/
RML Farm Bee	https://rmlagtech.com/

Start-up	Website
Rrite Water	https://www.ritewater.in/
Securden	https://www.securden.com/
Sellapps	https://sellapps.net/
Shifu	https://www.playshifu.com/
SigTuple	https://sigtuple.com/
SigTuple	https://sigtuple.com/
Snapdeal	https://www.snapdeal.com/
Snapdeal	https://www.snapdeal.com/
Stellapps	https://www.stellapps.com/
Strand	https://strandls.com/
Swarna Pragati	http://sphm.co.in
Swiggy	https://www.swiggy.com/
Tessol	https://www.tessol.in/
TrulyMadly	https://trulymadly.com/
Tyroo	https://www.tyroo.com/
Udaan	https://udaan.com/
Unacademy	https://unacademy.com/
Unnati	https://www.unnatiagri.com/index.php
Urban Company	https://www.urbancompany.com/
Vayana Network	https://vayana.com/
Vedantu	https://www.vedantu.com/
Veeba	https://veeba.in/
Vyapar	https://vyaparapp.in/
WeInnovate	http://www.weinnovatebiosolutions.com/
Wi-Jungle	https://www.wijungle.com/
Wmall	https://www.wmall.co.in/
Yumlane	https://www.yumlane.in/
Zerodha	https://zerodha.com/
Zetwerk	https://www.zetwerk.com/
Zomato	https://www.zomato.com/
Zumutor Biologics	https://www.zumutor.com/

Endnotes

[1]https://www.ventureintelligence.com/Indian-Unicorn-Tracker.php
Accessed on May 17, 2021

[2]Unicorns in India: 6 new unicorns in 4 days marks historic boom for India tech, https://www.livemint.com/companies/start-ups/unicorns-in-india-6-new-unicorns-in-4-days-marks-historic-boom-for-india-tech-11618190159349.html
Accessed on May 17, 2021

[3]Thillai Rajan A. 2018. "Pitching it Right: Raising Successive Funding Rounds". In *Howzat! Success and Impact of Start-ups* by Thillai Rajan A, 31–39. Chennai: IIT Madras.

[4]Chandrasekhar, KB & Committee. 2000. Report of K.B. Chandrasekhar Committee on Venture Capital. Retrieved from *SEBI*, website: https://www.sebi.gov.in/reports/reports/jan-2000/report-of-k-b-chandrasekhar-committee-on-venture-capital_21001.html

[5]Ibid.

[6]Zider, B. 1998. How Venture Capital Works. Retrieved from *Harvard Business Review*, website: https://hbr.org/1998/11/how-venture-capital-works

[7]Chandrasekhar, KB & Committee. 2000. Report of K.B. Chandrasekhar Committee on Venture Capital. Retrieved from *SEBI*, website: https://www.sebi.gov.in/reports/reports/jan-2000/report-of-k-b-chandrasekhar-committee-on-venture-capital_21001.html

[8]Zider, B. 1998. How Venture Capital Works. Retrieved from *Harvard Business Review*, website: https://hbr.org/1998/11/how-venture-capital-works

[9]Ibid.

[10]Mulcahy, D. 2014. Venture Capitalists Get Paid Well to Lose Money. Retrieved from *Harvard Business Review*, website: https://hbr.org/2014/08/venture-capitalists-get-paid-well-to-lose-money

[11]Sourced from SEBI's official website on January 5, 2021: https://www.sebi.gov.in/sebiweb/other/OtherAction.do?doRecognisedFpi=yes&intmId=21

[12]De Clercq, D, Fried, VH, Lehtonen, O and Sapienza, HJ. 2006. An entrepreneur's guide to the venture capital galaxy. *Academy of Management Perspectives* 20(3): 90–112.

[13]Pratch, L. 2005. Value-added investing: A framework for early stage venture capital firms. *Journal of Private Equity* 8(3): 13–29.

[14]Source: Crunchbase (https://www.crunchbase.com/)

[15]Source: International Monetary Fund (https://www.imf.org/en/Countries/IND)

[16]Published by Statista Research Department, March 30, 2021. Accessible at: https://www.statista.

com/statistics/1110119/india-total-venture-capital-investment/#:~:text=Total%20venture%20capital%20investment%20in%20India%20 2012%2D2020&text=In%202020%2C%20Indian%20companies%20attracted,the%20record%2Dbreaking%20 year%202019
Accessed on May 15, 2021

[17]We estimate that investment in technology companies would be about 70 per cent of the total investment.

[18]The GDP estimates are from World Bank (https://data.worldbank.org/indicator/NY.GDP.MKTP.CD), the venture investments data for USA and Global are from KPMG Venture Pulse 2020 (Q4) (https://home.kpmg/xx/en/home/campaigns/2021/01/venture-pulse-q4.html) and the venture investments data for India is from Tracxn (https://tracxn.com/).

[19]Source: CRISIL AIF benchmarks, accessible at: https://www.crisil.com/en/home/what-we-do/financial-products/alternate-investment-funds-benchmarks.html

[20]256 Network and Praxis Global Alliance. 2020. *Turning Ideas into Gold: Perspectives on Venture Capital for Indian Family Offices*. A report by 256 Network and Praxis Global Alliance.

[21]Based on the findings of Cambridge Associates and UBS Family Office Report 2019. Provided in *Turning Ideas into Gold: Perspectives on Venture Capital for Indian Family Offices*. A report by 256 Network and Praxis Global Alliance, 2020.

[22]Post expenses, pre-taxes and pre-carry.

[23]Category 1 alternate investment funds includes venture capital funds (excluding angel funds), SME funds, social venture fund and infrastructure funds.

[24]Vintage year is the year in which the fund made its first close. FY 2019, for example, represents the financial year from April 2018 to March 2019.

[25]UHNIs refers to individuals with net worth greater than $30 million.

[26]256 Network and Praxis Global Alliance. 2020. *Turning Ideas into Gold: Perspectives on Venture Capital for Indian Family Offices*. A report by 256 Network and Praxis Global Alliance.

[27]Ibid.

[28]Reserve Bank of India. 2016. Guidelines for Identifying Census Centres. Retrieved from *Reserve Bank of India*, website: https://rbidocs.rbi.org.in/rdocs/Content/PDFs/RBILIS130910.PDF

[29]Technology Development Board. 2020. List of TDB-contributed Venture Capital Funds. Retrieved from *Technology Development Board, Department of Science and Technology*, website: http://tdb.gov.in/wp-content/uploads/2017/02/VCFs.pdf

[30]Technology Development Board. 2020. Venture Capital Funds. Retrieved from *Technology Development Board, Department of Science and Technology*, website: http://tdb.gov.in/venture-capital-funds

[31]Technology Development Board. 2020. List of TDB contributed Venture Capital Funds. Retrieved from *Technology Development Board, Department of Science and Technology*, website: http://tdb.gov.in/wp-content/uploads/2017/02/VCFs.pdf

[32]Ibid. Represents the financial year starting April 1st of the previous year till March 31st of the following year.

[33]Technology Development Board. 2020. List of TDB contributed Venture Capital Funds. Retrieved from *Technology Development Board, Department of Science and Technology*, website: http://tdb.gov.in/wp-content/uploads/2017/02/VCFs.pdf

[34]Small and medium enterprises

[35]SEAF. 2020. SEAF India Agribusiness Fund. Retrieved from *SEAF*, website: https://www.seaf.com/investing/asia/seaf-india-agribusiness-fund/

[36]Ghosh, A. 2015. SIIA raising $150 million for its next agribusiness fund. Retrieved from *Mint* (16 September 2015), website: https://www.livemint.com/Companies/7Q6OOfCsyM9OPWjRZLjyhI/SIIA-raising-150-million-for-its-next-agribusiness-fund.html

[37]SEAF. 2016. SAF portfolio company Abhay Cotex enters Tanzania. Retrieved from *SEAF*, website: https://www.seaf.com/siaf-portfolio-company-abhay-cotex-enters-tanzania/

[38]SEAF. 2014. SEAF Invests in Leading Spice Processor/Supplier. Retrieved from *SEAF*, website: https://www.seaf.com/seaf-invests-in-leading-spice-processor-supplier/

[39]SEAF. 2013. SEAF Fund invests in India-based Manisha Agri Biotech Limited. Retrieved from *SEAF*, website: https://www.seaf.com/seaf-fund-invests-in-india-based-manisha-agri-biotech-limited/

[40]Sourced from official website: https://blume.vc/
[41]Sourced from official website: https://blume.vc/portfolio/

[42]Sourced from official website: http://www.ivycapventures.com/

[43]Sourced from official website: http://www.ivycapventures.com/#investing-philosophy

[44]Chathurvedula, S. 2016. Infuse Ventures to raise ₹1,000 crore to invest in multiple sectors. Retrieved from *Mint* (31 March 2016), website: https://www.livemint.com/Companies/JmeSfEdwc0pf0Ia3HI3q5O/Infuse-Ventures-to-raise-Rs1000-crore-clean-tech-fund.html

[45]Ibid.

[46]Infuse Ventures. 2018. Impact Report 2018. Retrieved from *Infuse Ventures*, website: https://www.infuseventures.in/images/impact-report-2018.pdf

[47]Sourced from official website: https://www.infuseventures.in/#infuse

[48]Kothiyal, K. 2018. Bharat Innovation Fund announces first close at $50 million. Retrieved from *Mint* (19 July 2018), website: https://www.livemint.com/Money/6yGGve5zMLCDsbsZRS1NdI/Bharat-Innovation-Fund-hits-first-close-of-100-million-vent.html

The original fund was closed at $100 million; we convert it to Indian rupees using the average exchange rate reported by the RBI for 2016–17. RBI Exchange Rates: https://www.rbi.org.in/scripts/PublicationsView.aspx?id=17923

[49]Sourced from official website: https://bharat.fund/innovation/

[50]Sourced from official website: https://bharat.fund/innovation/portfolio.html

[51]British High Commission New Delhi and DFID. 2013. UK awards first investments under the Samridhi fund. Retrieved from *Her Majesty's Government UK* (28 October 2013), website: https://www.gov.uk/government/news/uk-awards-first-investments-under-the-samridhi-fund

[52]Startup India. 2020. Samridhi Fund. Retrieved from *Government of India, Department for Promotion of Industry and Internal Trade*, website: https://www.startupindia.gov.in/content/sih/en/government-schemes/samridhi_fund.html

[53]Sourced from official website: https://www.samridhifund.com/legacy.php

[54]Ibid.

[55]Sourced from official website: https://www.goodwell.nl/fund/agimdc-ii/

The original fund was closed at $31 million; we convert it to Indian rupees using the average exchange rate reported by the RBI for 2012–13. RBI Exchange Rates: https://www.rbi.org.in/scripts/PublicationsView.aspx?id=17923

[56]Sourced from official website: https://www.goodwell.nl/fund/agimdc-ii/

[57]Ibid.

[58]NABARD. 2019. Nabard announces Rs 700-cr venture capital fund for agri, rural startups. Retrieved from *NABARD*, Media Room website: https://www.nabard.org/news-article.aspx?id=25&cid=552&NID=225

[59]Sourced from official website: https://www.nabventures.in/

[60]Ibid.

[61]Asian News International. 2020. Healthcare VC fund HealthQuad closes its second fund of ₹514 cr. Retrieved from *Mint* (13 July 2020), website: https://www.livemint.com/companies/news/healthcare-vc-fund-healthquad-closes-its-second-fund-of-rs-514-cr-11594644288745.html

[62]Sourced from official website: https://www.healthquad.in/

[63]Sourced from official website: https://www.healthquad.in/portfolio.html

[64]Press Trust of India. 2017. Dell Foundation-backed IEIF's investments cross Rs 13 crore. Retrieved from *Business Standard* (23 January 2017), website: https://www.business-standard.com/article/pti-stories/dell-foundation-backed-ieif-s-investments-cross-rs-13-crore-117012300230_1.html

[65]Ibid.

[66]Ibid.[67]Sourced from official website: https://www.caspian.in/

[68]Sourced from official website: https://www.cropin.com/

[69]Sourced from official website: https://entropiktech.com/

[70]Sourced from official website: https://ghspl.com/

[71]Sourced from official website: https://www.jai-kisan.com/

[72]Sourced from official website: https://khatabook.com/

[73]Sourced from official website: https://krishitantra.com/

[74]Sourced from official website: https://www.ritewater.in/

[75]Sourced from official website: http://sphm.co.in/

[76]Sourced from official website: https://vayana.com/

[77]Saxena, A. 2020. How Vayana Network aims to solve trade finance for India's SME sector amidst coronavirus. *YourStory*. Accessible at: https://yourstory.com/smbstory/vayana-network-solves-trade-finance-smes-coronavirus

[78]The portfolio companies and their profiles can be accessed at https://www.chiratae.com/portfolio/

[79]Balachander, P. 2020. Human Capital: Gaining from differential demographic dividend. Retrieved

from *Financial Express* (16 October 2020), web site: https://www.financialexpress.com/opinion/human-capital-gaining-from-differential-demographic-dividend/2106780/

[80]Indian Private Equity & Venture Capital Association & Zinnov. 2020. Creating Value for 1.3 Billion. Retrieved from *IVCA*, website: http://ivca.in/wp-content/uploads/2020/02/IVCA-Zinnov-Wealth-Creation-Report.-Creating-Value-for-1.3-Billion.pdf

[81]Ibid.

[82]Ibid.

[83]https://vayana.com/
Accessed on May 16, 2021

[84]Source: Crunchbase (https://crunchbase.com).

[85]Apurva, P. 2019. Dunzo introduces bicycle for delivery, welcomes new partners aboard. Retrieved from *YourStory* (21 August 2019), website: https://yourstory.com/2019/08/dunzo-bicycle-delivery-partners

[86]Indian Private Equity & Venture Capital Association & Zinnov. 2020. Creating Value for 1.3 Billion. Retrieved from *IVCA*, website: http://ivca.in/wp-content/uploads/2020/02/IVCA-Zinnov-Wealth-Creation-Report.-Creating-Value-for-1.3-Billion.pdf

[87]Ola Cabs. 2020. Ola announces plans to set up world's largest scooter factory in Tamil Nadu. Retrieved from *Ola Cabs* (14 December 2020), website: https://www.olacabs.com/media/in/press/ola-announces-plans-to-set-up-worlds-largest-scooter-factory-in-tamil-nadu-2

[88]Chaudhary, D. 2019. Swiggy eyes 100 mn customers using the app over 15 times a month in 10-15 years. Retrieved from *Mint* (18 October 2019), website: https://www.livemint.com/companies/start-ups/swiggy-eyes-100-mn-customers-using-the-app-over-15-times-a-month-in-10-15-years-11571422800906.html

[89]Urban Company. 2020. UrbanClap is now Urban Company. Retrieved from *Urban Company* (30 January 2020), website: https://www.urbancompany.com/blog/company-updates/urbanclap-is-now-urban-company

[90]Indo-Asian News Service. 2019. Chennai has highest Zomato female delivery partners. Retrieved from *The News Minute* (4 October 2019), website: https://www.thenewsminute.com/article/chennai-has-highest-zomato-female-delivery-partners-109969

[91]The phrase is attributed to C Rajagopalachari, former Chief Minister of the erstwhile state of Madras (Tamil Nadu). See Sanders, S. 1977. India: Ending the Permit-License Raj. *Asian Affairs* 5(2): 88–96. Retrieved January 5, 2021, from http://www.jstor.org/stable/30171608

[92]Anklesaria Aiyar, SS. 2016. Twenty-Five Years of Indian Economic Reform. In *CATO Institute - Policy Analysis* (803). Retrieved from https://www.cato.org/publications/policy-analysis/twenty-five-years-indian-economic-reform

[93]Kotwal, A, Ramaswami, B and Wadhwa, W. 2011. Economic Liberalization and Indian Economic Growth: What's the Evidence? *Journal of Economic Literature* 49(4): 1152–1199. Retrieved January 5, 2021, from http://www.jstor.org/stable/23071665

[94]From Venture Intelligence (https://www.ventureintelligence.com/Indian-Unicorn-Tracker.php) and Crunchbase (https://crunchbase.com)

[95]D'souza, V. 2018. Exclusive: India's Foodtech Unicorn Swiggy All Set to Test International Markets. *Entrepreneur India*. Accessible at: https://www.entrepreneur.com/article/318201

[96]Sourced from official website:https://www.zomato.com/directory

[97]Tanwar, S. 2019. Byju's hopes to replicate successful India model in US, UK, and Australia. *Business Standard*. Accessible at: https://www.business-standard.com/article/companies/byju-s-hopes-to-replicate-successful-india-model-in-us-uk-and-australia-119020300639_1.html

[98]Source: https://www.olacabs.com/about.html

[99]https://www.oyorooms.com/about?oyocorporate=

[100]TiE Delhi and Zinnov.2020. COVID-19 and the Antifragility of Indian Startup Ecosystem. Retrieved from: https://fastq.in/tie_delhi.aspx

[101]Meghani, V. 2020. Can EdTech keep up its momentum after Covid-19?. Retrieved from *Forbes India, UpFront* (2 November 2020), website: https://www.forbesindia.com/article/take-one-big-story-of-the-day/can-edtech-keep-up-its-momentum-after-covid19/63895/1

[102]Ibid.

[103]Ibid.

[104]Ibid.

[105]Majumdar, R and Guha, I. 2020. Cyber security firms gain currency. Retrieved from *Mint* (13 July 2020), website: https://www.livemint.com/companies/news/cybersecurity-firms-gain-currency-11594607145642.html

[106]Data Security Council of India. 2020.Security Use Cases & Solutions for Work from Home. Retrieved from *Data Security Council of India* (01 July 2020), website: https://

www.dsci.in/content/security-use-cases-solutions-work-home-0

[107]Majumdar, R and Guha, I. 2020. Cyber security firms gain currency. Retrieved from *Mint* (13 July 2020), website: https://www.livemint.com/companies/news/cybersecurity-firms-gain-currency-11594607145642.html

[108]Ibid.

[109]TiE Delhi and Zinnov. 2020. COVID-19 and the Antifragility of Indian Startup Ecosystem. Retrieved from: https://fastq.in/tie_delhi.aspx

[110]Goel, S. 2020. Innovation at knifepoint: Startups bid to survive Covid-19. Retrieved from *Deccan Herald* (18 October 2020), website: https://www.deccanherald.com/specials/insight/innovation-at-knifepoint-startups-bid-to-survive-covid-19-903466.html

[111]TiE Delhi and Zinnov. 2020.COVID-19 and the Antifragility of Indian Startup Ecosystem. Retrieved from: https://fastq.in/tie_delhi.aspx

[112]Ibid.

[113]Ibid.

[114]Press Trust of India. 2020. Domestic FinTech deals double to $1.7 billion during Jan-Jun: Report. Retrieved from *The Indian Express, Financial Express* (02 September 2020), website: https://www.financialexpress.com/industry/domestic-fintech-deals-double-to-1-7-billion-during-jan-jun-report/2073087/

[115]Ibid.

[116]Usmani, A and Kapoor, M. 2020. Startup Street: Covid-19 Fails to Dampen Fintech Investments in India. Retrieved from *Bloomberg Quint* (06 September 2020), website: https://www.bloombergquint.com/business/startup-street-covid-19-fails-to-dampen-fintech-investments-in-india#:~:text=Fintech%20Investments%20Remain%20Solid%20In%20India&text=Fintech%20investments%20till%20June%202020,annual%20Pulse%20of%20Fintech%20report

[117]TiE Delhi and Zinnov. 2020. COVID-19 and the Antifragility of Indian Startup Ecosystem. Retrieved from: https://fastq.in/tie_delhi.aspx

[118]Gupta, A. 2020. How healthtech startups are using cloud for innovation during COVID-19. Retrieved from *The New Indian Express, Express Health* (03 September 2020), website: https://www.expresshealthcare.in/news/how-healthtech-startups-are-using-cloud-for-innovation-during-covid-19/424486/

[119]Chakraberty, S. 2020. Post-Covid healthtech funding rebound is leaving India behind. Retrieved from *Mint* (28 June 2020), website: https://www.livemint.com/news/business-of-life/post-covid-healthtech-funding-rebound-is-leaving-india-behind-11593356352252.html

[120]Data from Crunchbase (https://www.crunchbase.com/).

17

Angel and Early-Stage Funding for Ventures[1]

Akshay Natteri Mangadu and Thillai Rajan A

Mangadu, AK and Thillai Rajan A. "Angel and Early-Stage Funding for Ventures". In *Shifting Orbits: Decoding the Trajectory of the Indian Start-up Ecosystem*, edited by Thillai Rajan A, Srivardhini K Jha, Joffi Thomas and Rohan Chinchwadkar, 212–221. Hyderabad: Universities Press (India) Private Limited.

The rise of a vibrant angel investing community in India has been one of the most notable features of the Indian start-up ecosystem in the past decade. In India's emergence as one of the largest start-up ecosystems globally, angel investors have played no small part. Most modern entrepreneurs in India are not from privileged backgrounds and do not have the ability to sustain their ventures on their own without external capital. Predominantly, the first stop for external funding has been angel investors. Most angel investors are busy professionals having multiple commitments and, unlike venture funds, they do not make information about their investment portfolio or preferences publicly available. Therefore, organised and accurate information on angel investors is very sparse. This chapter is a visual representation of key observations on angel investing trends in India based on data from the YNOS Technology Platform, India's largest platform for discovering and understanding angel investments.

#1: Will the twain ever meet? The trajectory of angel investors and incubators

Incubators and accelerators nurture ideas and technologies suitable for commercialisation till they reach a stage from where they would be able to attract capital and become sustainable. Tracking the quantum of venture investment in their portfolio of start-ups is a KPI (key

Exhibit 17.1: Proportion of angel-funded start-ups that have been incubated

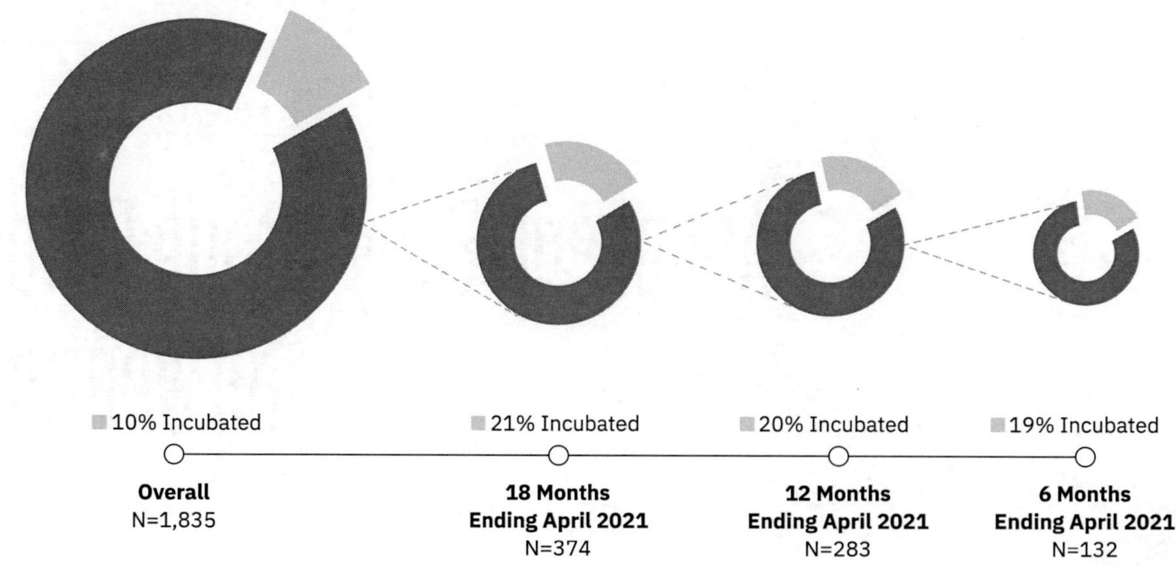

Source: YNOS Venture Engine

Exhibit 17.2: The intersection of angel-funded and incubated start-ups

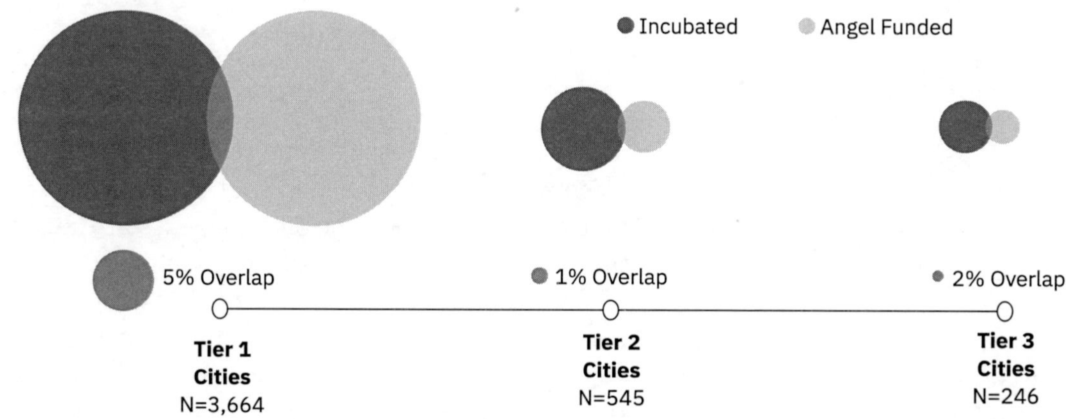

Source: YNOS Venture Engine

performance indicator) for many incubators. However, data shows that attracting funding in incubated start-ups has been more wishful thinking and is far from reality. Only a small proportion of the start-ups from incubators have been successful in getting angel-funded. The trend persists across time and geographies. Overall, only 6 per cent of angel-funded start-ups have been part of an incubator. Analysing by type of cities, it was found that the proportion[2] of companies that were both incubated and angel-funded ranged between just 3 per cent (in Tier 2 and Tier 3 cities) and 4 per cent (in Tier 1 cities).

Of course, the results raise more questions than it answers: Firstly, what is the primary role of incubators? Is it to help start-ups strengthen their business proposition and make them investible or is it to support those start-ups that would have been overlooked by investors and give them a lifeline? Secondly, has the functioning and selection of start-ups by incubators not been aligned with what the investors have been seeking? Instead of converging, the incubator and investor segments have been operating in more or less parallel trajectories. Thirdly, are the investors in India not yet ready to support translational ventures that incubators are mandated to support?

Seen any which way, these results are a cause for concern and is a wakeup call. With governments significantly investing in incubation programmes, it is important to create an institutional framework where two of the critical elements for early-stage start-ups complement each other rather than functioning in silos.

#2: In a world of single-horse carriages, investors are looking for chariots

Leading angel investors are particular about choosing the right entrepreneurs and the right market (investors have also articulated this during the roundtable discussion, see Chapter 13). Angel investors seek to support persistent and agile entrepreneurs, who have the capacity to foresee and adapt dynamically with the changing market. Given the competitive marketplace for businesses, a team of founders is expected to be more effective in navigating the uncertainties of early-stage ventures than a single founder. Having the right founding team is, therefore, an extremely important criterion that influences the odds of securing angel funding.

Upon analysing the probability of receiving angel funding and the size of the founding team, a clear trend emerges – angel investors prefer to invest in ventures that have a founding team rather than an individual founder. The proportion of start-ups with a single founder that were angel-funded stood at a sparse 2 per cent, while the same metric for three- and four-member teams stood at 14 per cent and 12 per cent, respectively (Exhibit 17.3). This is despite the fact that the vast majority of start-ups have only one founder.

While the data manifestly illustrates the angel investors' preference for optimum size of the founding teams, the reasons for this preference could be various. What are the unique advantages of having a founding team instead of a single founder? Is it the diversity in professional and creative backgrounds that teams bring? Are teams better at adapting to the changing market landscape and emergent business conditions? Are teams better at formulating and implementing innovative solutions? The laundry list of causal explanations for this trend is never-ending.

While the actual causal explanations for these results remain a puzzle, there is no denying the fact that larger teams (specifically teams with three or four founders) have a substantially higher chance of securing angel funding. Entrepreneurs desirous of getting angel funding should, therefore, form a strong founding team when embarking on a venture. Starting up as a single founder is very convenient for sure, but there stops the advantage.

#3: A glass ceiling for entry but not for success? Gender equity in the start-up ecosystem

Without a doubt, the proportion of women participating in various social and economic activities has increased over the years. However, as far as venturing is concerned, the proportion of start-ups having women founders has been only about 5 per cent. While it is important that policymakers formulate affirmative action policies that encourage women to pursue start-ups, the pattern of women-founded start-ups is equally instructive. First is the proportion of women-founded start-ups and the size of the founder teams. Exhibit 17.2 indicates that single-founder start-ups comprise the highest percentage. However, among the women-founded start-ups, the percentage of single-founder start-ups is the lowest.

Exhibit 17.3: Share of start-ups founded, proportion of start-ups that secured angel funding and the number of founders in the founding team

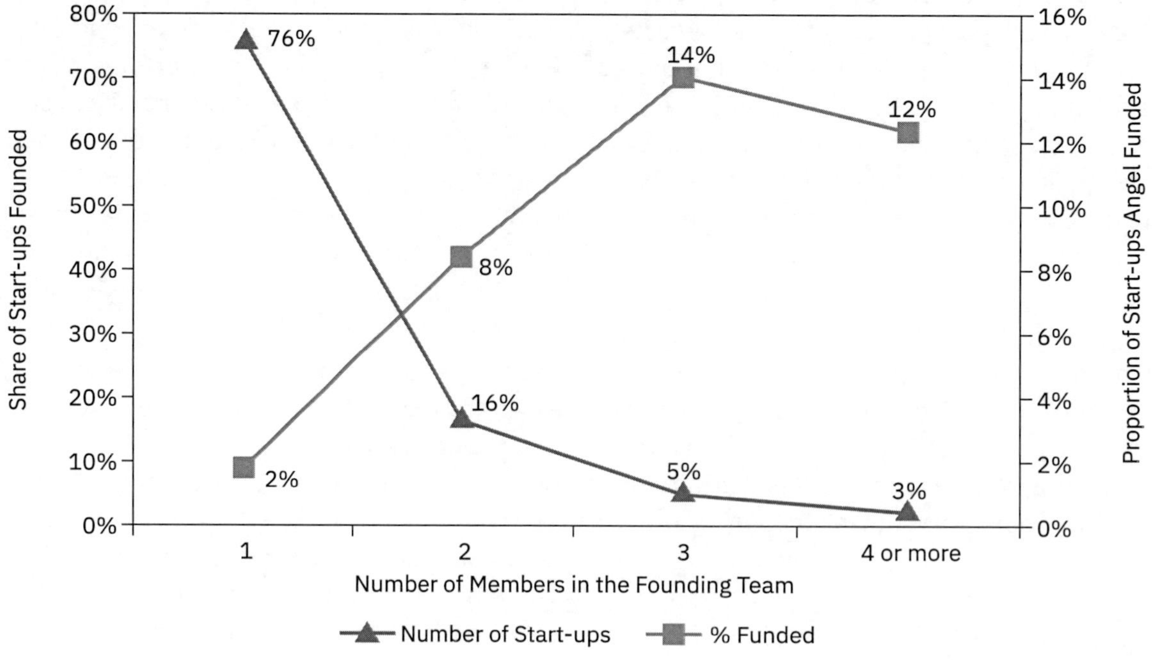

Source: YNOS Venture Engine

The percentage increases with an increase in the size of the founding team. This pattern is contrary to the overall pattern observed in the total start-up sample, where the percentage of start-ups shows a decreasing trend as the size of the founder team increases. This could indicate two things: Women are unable to found start-ups individually or they are fully aware of the advantages of having a team of founders and, therefore, of their own volition, join with other co-founders to start their venture. It can also be seen that as the size of the founding team increased, the percentage of women-founded start-ups that got funded also increased significantly.

Secondly, start-ups with women founders have been more successful than start-ups where the founders are all men, at securing angel funding, irrespective of the size of the founding team. This is evidenced by the fact that women-led, single-founder start-ups are nine times more prominently represented among the group of funded start-ups than in the overall group of start-ups.

To put this in perspective, among the single-founder start-ups started by men, only 2 per cent were successful in attracting angel funding. Whereas, among the single-founder start-ups started by women, the success rate in securing angel funding was a remarkable 24 per cent. This trend holds true for two-member start-ups as well (Exhibit 17.4).

For start-ups with three or more members, those with all-male founding teams were marginally more successful. However, it is important to note that the

Exhibit 17.4: Proportion of start-ups with women founders and the size of the founding team

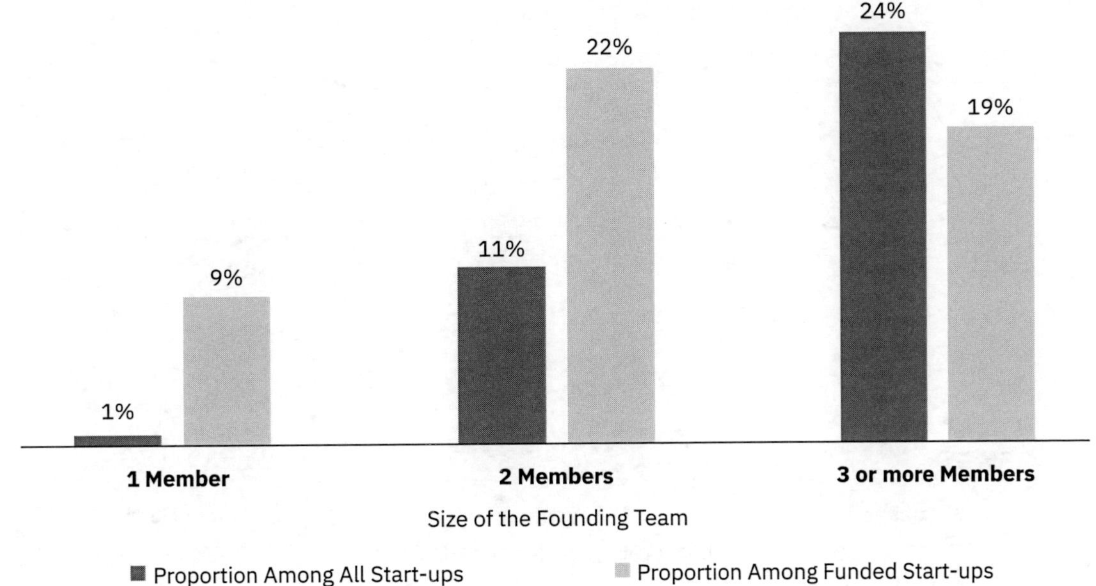

Source: YNOS Venture Engine

number of companies with three or more founding members is only 8 per cent of the total number of start-ups (Exhibit 17.5). Hence, this only mildly affects the overall gender ratio among funded start-ups. The overall gender ratio[3] among funded start-ups stands at 20 per cent, while the overall gender ratio among active start-ups is only four per cent.

The major takeaway is that while women-founded start-ups are rare, they are significantly more likely to be successful in getting funded. Multiple explanations are possible. The proportion of women pursuing start-ups may be fewer, but those start-ups are in areas that attract more investor interest. Alternatively, investors believe gender diversity among founders is expected to positively impact the start-ups and are therefore able to attract more investor interest.

#4: What helps in getting angel investment – the founders' education or their experience?

Start-ups need to innovate for survival. Technological and business innovation, coupled with a sound understanding of the market landscape, is crucial to ensuring the success of a start-up. Given the higher degree of uncertainty involved in investing in early-stage start-ups, the background of the start-up founders, namely, their education and experience, plays a very important role in investor decision-making.

Composite education[4] and experience[5] scores were calculated for the start-up founding teams. As evidenced in Exhibit 17.6, it is clear that founders with a strong educational and experiential background are more successful at securing angel funding. Education appears to be more sensitive than experience in increasing the probability of getting funded.

There are a number of possible explanations for the higher sensitivity of education over experience. One reason could be the high level of technological know-how required for a lot of emerging sectors such

Exhibit 17.5: Success rate in securing angel funding: Start-ups with all-male founders vis-a-vis start-ups with women founders

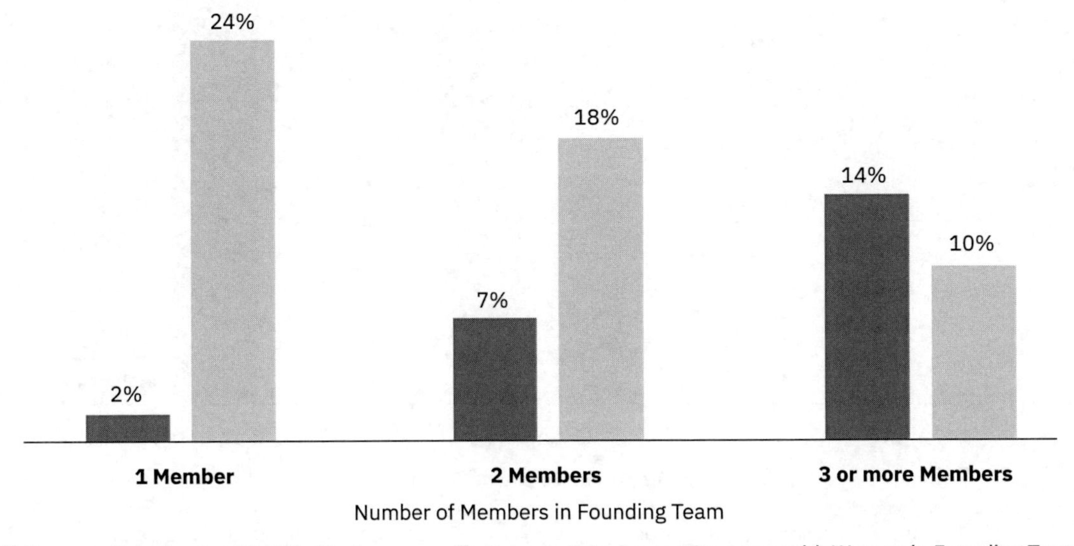

Source: YNOS Venture Engine

as FinTech, EdTech, LogisticsTech and AgriTech. Given that success for start-ups in these sectors is defined by their ability to disrupt established markets using technological innovation, it is important for founders to have a strong educational training which provides them with the technical knowledge required to build innovative tech solutions.

Another potential reason could be the alumni connect. Leading educational institutions such as the IITs and IIMs have a number of alumni programmes that bring together angel investors and founders from their institution. This provides a powerful platform for founders from these prestigious institutions to seek capital, which is not easily accessible to others.

#5: Incubators play an important role in democratising start-up creation

Angel funding plays an important role in supporting the start-ups in the initial years, and the education and experience of the founder team plays an important role in securing angel funding (Exhibit 17.6). However, for a variety of reasons, accessing angel capital remains limited to a privileged few. It is in this context that incubators play the very important role of democratising start-up creation. Exhibit 17.7 shows that the percentage of start-ups incubated has an inverse relationship with the education and experience score of the founder team. Incubators are thus extending incubation support to those founders who have entrepreneurial ambitions, but who would have otherwise been excluded from the start-up creation process.

There is, however, more scope for incubators to improve their reach. The exponential increase in the number of start-ups founded in recent years has resulted in a corresponding increase in the number of proposals that angel investors receive. Hence, several leading angel investors have the luxury of choosing the cream of the proposals with well-developed business plans, in-depth market analysis, clear value propositions

Exhibit 17.6: Probability of securing angel funding:[6] Education and experience of the founders

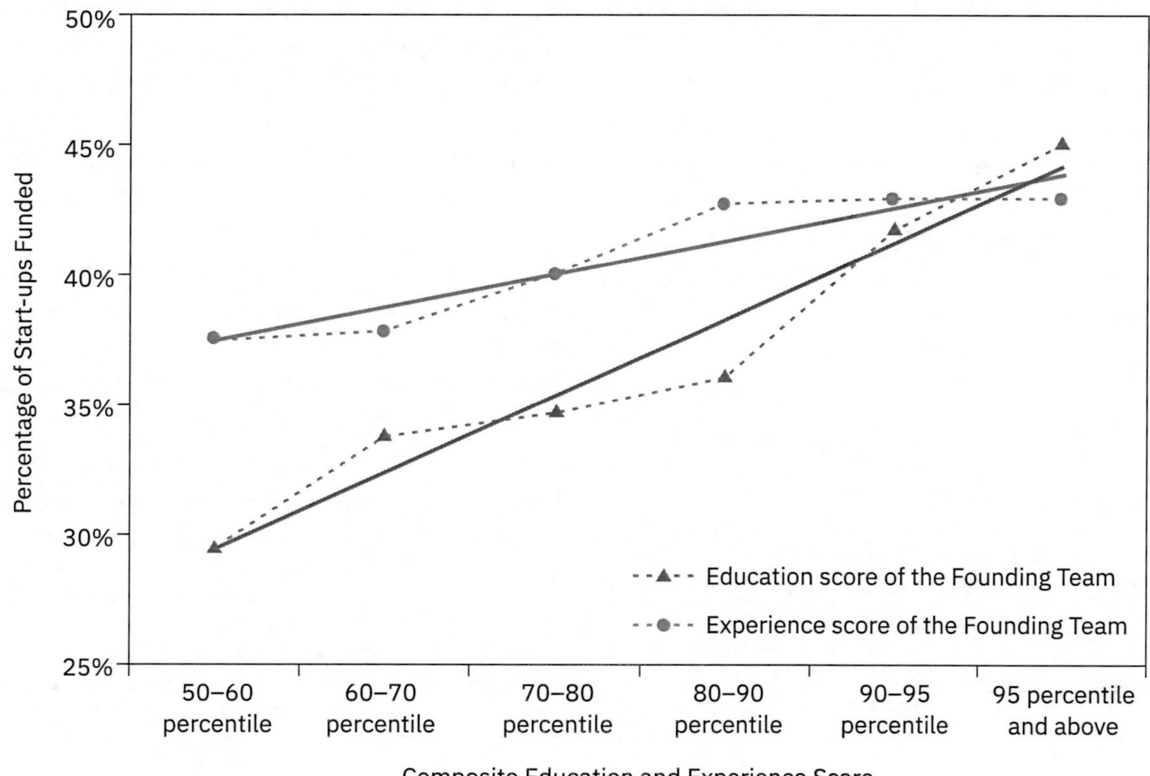

Source: YNOS Venture Engine

Exhibit 17.7: Probability of getting incubated:[7] Education and experience of the founders

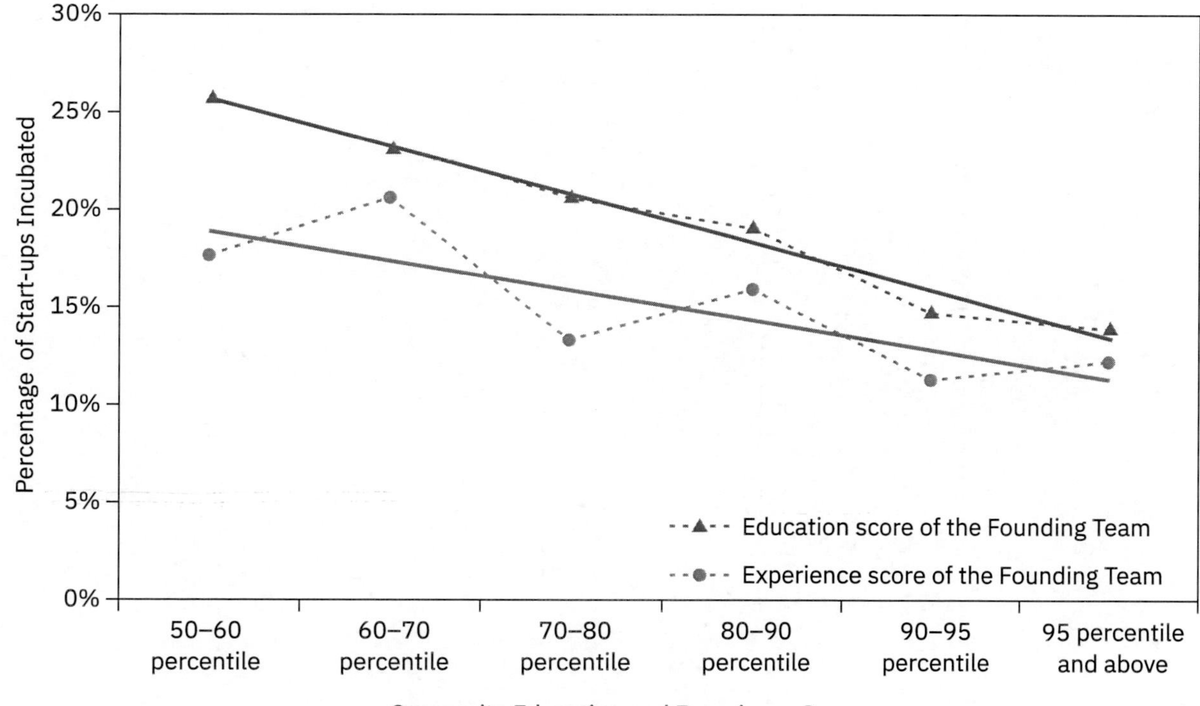

Source: YNOS Venture Engine

and formidable growth strategies. Hence, it is no longer sufficient to just have a good business idea, it is equally important to build a strong investment proposal around it (the roundtable discussion in Chapter 13 provides further insights).

It is, therefore, more important now than at any time in the past for incubators to help founders from modest educational and experiential backgrounds to develop strong investment proposals that would catch the eyes of angel investors.

#6: Heterogenous investors having more or less homogenous investment preferences. Why is that?

In matters pertaining to financial investments, the general trend is that age has an inverse relationship with risk appetite. Younger investors are willing to make more risky investments as compared to older investors, who, probably wizened by age and experience, may be more conservative. Does risk appetite change with age in the case of start-up investments? The answer is a resounding no (Exhibit 17.8). If we go with the grain, one would have expected younger investors to have a higher percentage of early-stage start-ups in their portfolio, where the risks involved are much higher, while the older investors would prefer to focus on mature start-ups with established track records. Far from this expectation, the age distribution of start-ups in the portfolio of various investor age groups is strikingly similar.

In fact, investors across age groups, tend to invest heavily in start-ups between the ages of one and three. What could be the reason for this?

Exhibit 17.8: Age distribution of start-ups in the portfolios of investors (segregated by investor age group)[8]

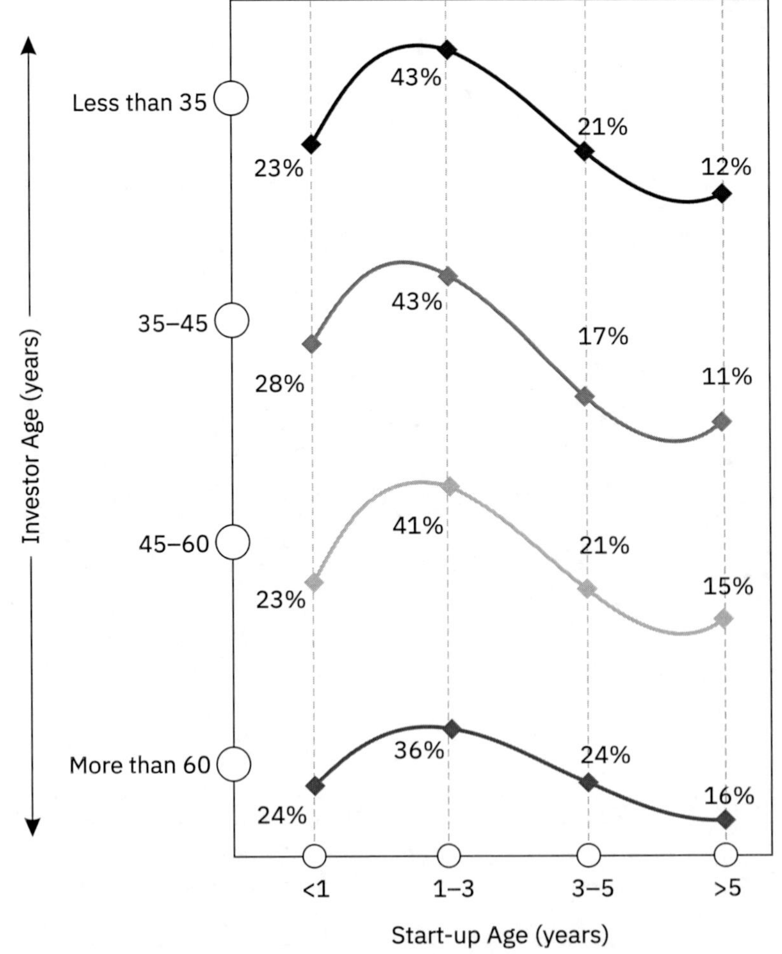

Source: YNOS Venture Engine

Angel investors often have much safer investment options at their disposal where they can earn sizable and near-guaranteed returns. In that case, what motivates investors to support start-ups? Angel investors are often motivated by the non-financial benefits of investing in start-ups, such as the opportunity to be instrumental in pushing the technological frontiers or the opportunity to work with young and budding entrepreneurs with the potential to shape the future (the roundtable in Chapter 13 has further insights into what motivates angel investors). Hence, financial risk does not influence their decision for investing in start-ups as much as it does for investment decisions in other assets. This shared passion to make an impact could potentially be the reason why the portfolio of start-ups (in terms of age) looks strikingly similar across investors from different generations.

Endnotes

[1]Data for all graphs is from YNOS Venture Engine (https://www.ynos.in).

[2]The overlap percentage is the number of start-ups that are both incubated and angel-funded expressed as a percentage of the total number of start-ups in the sample (i.e., Number of Angel-Funded Start-ups + Number of Incubated Start-ups – Number of Start-ups that are Incubated and Angel-Funded).

[3]Gender ratio is defined as the number of start-ups with at least one woman in the founding team expressed as a proportion of the start-ups with only men in the founding team.

[4]Education scores were calculated based on the number of years of study after school, the type of educational institutes where the founders studied and the subjects of their study.

[5]Experience scores were calculated based on the years of experience, the type of organisation they worked for, location of their work and the level at which they worked in the organisation.

[6]The probability of securing funding for start-ups whose founding team has an education (or experience) score in the ith percentile group is computed as (Number of Angel-Funded Start-ups in the ith Percentile Group) / (Total Number of Start-ups in the ith Percentile Group).

[7]The probability of getting incubated for start-ups whose founding team has an education (or experience) score in the ith percentile group is computed as (Number of Incubated Start-ups in the ith Percentile Group) / (Total Number of Start-ups in the ith Percentile Group).

[8]The numbers are rounded to the nearest integer; hence, the sum of the distribution proportions need not always sum to 100%. To compute the proportions, we use the following formula: (Number of Start-ups in Age Group i that are Funded by Angel Investors in Age Group j) / (Total Number of Start-ups Funded by Investors in Age Group j).

Section IV

INDUSTRY PERSPECTIVES

IN BRIEF

- **Emergence of a vibrant innovation ecosystem:** By the end of 2020, India was among the top four countries with a vibrant start-up ecosystem with 36 Unicorns.
- **Confluence of factors enabling growth:** A confluence of enabling factors of technology, talent, capital and supportive policy environment has led to the growth of the start-ups through the introduction phase (2006–2010), early growth phase (2011–2015) and accelerated growth phase (2016–2020). Venture capital investments of $19.85 billion went into 3,442 firms funding innovations during this period.
- **Accelerating innovation-led economic growth:** An enabling environment to further accelerate innovation-led growth requires continuous focus on key enabling factors: technology, talent, capital and policy support: (a) Technology – ensuring affordable digital technology access to the rural population, adoption of deep technologies across start-ups; (b) Talent – designing innovative mechanisms to attract and support talented entrepreneurs across sectors and regions; (c) Capital – accelerating investment flows by triggering investment–innovation–investor returns spirals in multiple sectors and (d) Policy Support – formulating proactive supportive policies with a 15-year and five-year planning horizons focussed on all-round development of the rural economy leveraging novel technologies; providing institutional support to exploit global market opportunities involving industry and academe.

ANALYTICAL ARTICLE

18

Driving Innovations, Leveraging Technology in a Turbulent Environment

Joffi Thomas and Dinesh Tiwari

Thomas, J and Tiwari, D. 2021. "Driving Innovations, Leveraging Technology in a Turbulent Environment". In *Shifting Orbits: Decoding the Trajectory of the Indian Start-up Ecosystem*, edited by Thillai Rajan A, Srivardhini K Jha, Joffi Thomas and Rohan Chinchwadkar, 224–239. Hyderabad: Universities Press (India) Private Limited.

Emergence of a Vibrant Indian Innovation Ecosystem

Disruptions brought about by technology advances, especially digitalisation, sustainability concerns and changes in globalisation perspectives have offered many new opportunities for business innovations, economic growth and the well-being of society at large. They have led to the growth of tech start-ups and ushered in developments in different spheres of life. At the same time, they are disrupting existing business models and incumbent businesses, especially in the last decade.

A new generation of entrepreneurs leveraging business opportunities offered by digital technologies in different markets has led to the creation of tech start-ups. Increasing penetration of personal computers, mobile connections, smartphones and internet connectivity combined with increased capital inflows have led to the explosive growth of tech start-ups in different sectors, namely, electronic retailing, financial services, logistics, software services, healthcare, education and agriculture, and opened up opportunities in many other sectors as well. Government initiatives to foster innovation by enabling the growth of the telecom

Exhibit 18.1: Number of Unicorns in major countries as an indication of start-up activity

Country	USA	China	UK	India	S. Korea	Germany
No. of Unicorns	233	227	24	21	11	10
New Unicorns	60	38	10	3	6	2
Years to Unicorn	6.5	5.5	8	7	11	7

Source: Hurun Research Institute, March 31, 2020

**March 2020 figures are taken for country comparisons; by December 2020, the number of Unicorns in India rose to 36, as reported by Venture Intelligence.*

industry over the last two decades, initiatives such as the implementation of Aadhaar, policies enabling digital payments and the growth of the engineering and higher education sectors have fuelled the use of digital technology and provided a conducive environment for tech start-ups to emerge.

Such start-ups leveraging the digital transformation have challenged existing business models, facilitating dis-intermediation, improving price discovery, reducing transaction costs and, thereby, lowering prices or enhancing customer value by offering superior solutions. While the initial impact was largely on start-up sectors such as e-commerce, financial services, mobility, travel and logistics, digital technologies are now being leveraged across different sectors, including healthcare, education and agriculture. The Indian start-up ecosystem with more than 9,000 start-ups[1] has emerged among the top four global ecosystems (Exhibit 18.1). India had 21 Unicorns collectively valued at $73.2 billion as on March 31, 2020, according to the Hurun Research report. Start-up ecosystems in Bangalore and Delhi were ranked among the top 50 in the world.

The rest of the chapter is organised in three sections. The first section explains the confluence of four key triggers contributing to the development of the innovation ecosystem; the second section analyses the emergence and growth of the innovation and start-up ecosystem over three phases from 2006 to 2020; and the concluding section discusses the way forward for driving innovation-led economic growth.

Growth of Indian Innovation Ecosystem: Key Enablers

In this section, we analyse the key enabling developments in the economy over the past few decades, which have contributed to the emergence and growth of tech start-ups and digital innovations in corporates. The key factors include (i) development of technical, managerial and entrepreneurial talent driven by growth in IT services export, (ii) exponential growth in internet, mobile and smartphone penetration, (iii) increased access to venture capital, angel funds and equity financing and (iv) government policy initiatives enabling the innovation ecosystem. The confluence of these enabling factors during the last decade has created a conducive environment for the formation of the innovation ecosystem in different consumer markets and business markets, represented in Exhibit 18.2.

Growth of IT Industry; Engineering and Management Institutes; Technical, Managerial and Entrepreneurial Talent Pool

The foundation for information technology–driven economic growth was laid in the 1980s and 1990s with the emergence of new tech companies like Infosys, HCL and the then corporates like TCS and Wipro developing information technology capabilities enabling the export of IT services to developed countries. The tech boom in the 1990s enabled by the growing access to personal computers to business and consumers, and the business opportunities offered by the Y2K concerns, led to the rapid growth of the Indian IT industry. It accelerated the growth of technical education institutions, including engineering colleges and management institutes, both in the public and in the private sectors, and contributed to the development of a large skilled resource pool. India developed into the technology back-office of the world in the last three decades, with the IT industry contributing to approximately 8 per cent of the country's GDP,

Exhibit 18.2: Confluence of factors contributing to the growth of the innovation ecosystem

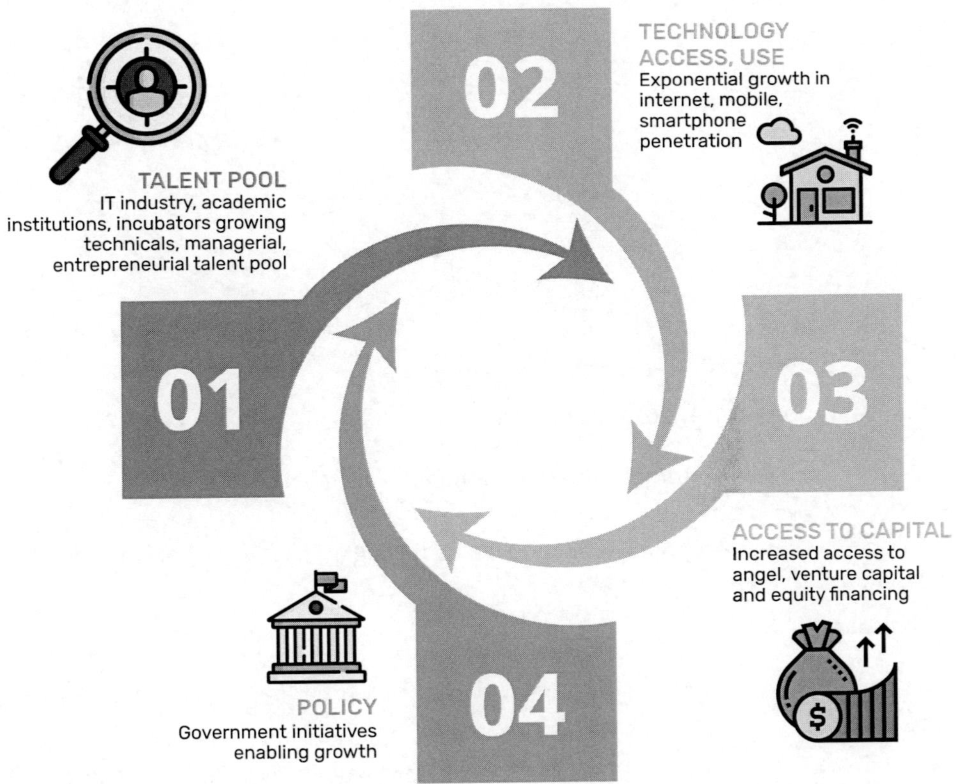

45 per cent of exports and generating direct employment for over 4 million and indirect employment to 10 million in 2017.[2]

The development of the IT industry and the emergence of many tech entrepreneurs in the 1990s and 2000 such as NR Narayana Murthy, Shiv Nadar and Kiran Majumdar Shaw also triggered interest in entrepreneurship. The significance of research and technology–led innovations was recognised at different levels of industry, government and academic institutes. It was also inspired by the explosive growth of new technology-based, innovation-led Silicon Valley firms. This led to the establishment of business incubators in leading academic institutes such as IISc (SID in 1991); IIM Bangalore (NSRCEL 2002); IIT Mumbai (SINE set up in 2004) and IIM Ahmedabad (CIIE 2007) to encourage entrepreneurship. This was followed by the setting up of industry incubators and accelerators, including Technopark TBI (later renamed Kerala Startup Mission) and Indian Angel Network incubator in 2006; NASSCOM 10,000 Start-ups 2013; Axilor Ventures 2014 and Venture Catalyst 2015. Later, most of the prominent academic institutes in the technology and management education domains set up their own incubators to identify and nurture entrepreneurship talent. By 2020, there were more than 335 active incubators and accelerators operating in the country.[3]

Exponential Growth in Mobile Connectivity, Internet and Smartphone Penetration

Mobile connectivity: The growth of mobile telecom services in India has resulted in reduction in mobile subscription costs (telecom ARPU lowest in the world),[4] adoption of smartphones and a continuous increase in internet penetration over the last two decades. By 2020, India emerged as the world's second largest telecommunications market, with a subscriber base of 1.16 billion and registered strong growth in the last decade. In 2019, India surpassed the US to become the second largest market in terms of the number of app downloads. The liberal and reformist policies of the government and strong consumer demand have been instrumental to the rapid growth in the Indian telecom sector. The government has enabled easy market access to telecom equipment and a fair and proactive regulatory

Exhibit 18.3: Technology penetration: Internet, smartphones and mobiles

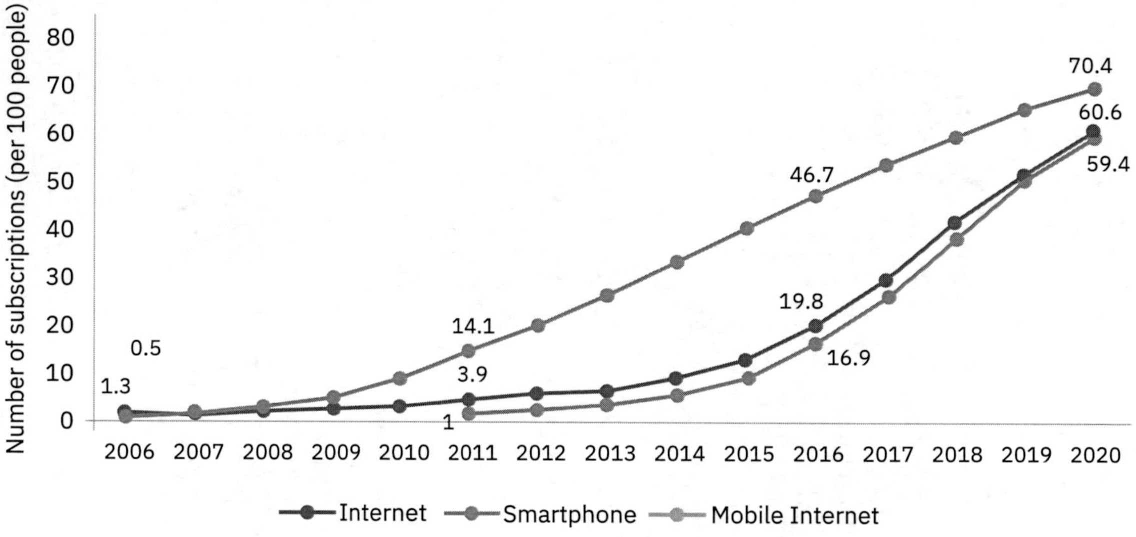

Smartphone: Household Penetration – Percentage of households having at least one item; Internet, Mobile Penetration – Percentage of the population

Source: Euromonitor International 2020[6]

framework that has ensured availability of telecom services to consumers at affordable prices.[5]

Internet connectivity: India ranks as the world's second largest market in terms of total internet users. The number of internet subscribers in the country increased at a CAGR of 21 per cent from FY 2016 to FY 2020 to reach 743 million in FY 2020. Over the next five years, rise in mobile phone penetration and decline in data costs will add 500 million new internet users in India, creating opportunities for new businesses. The increase in internet penetration has also started to make a material difference to the lives of a large section of the population. The trend in online travel bookings was fuelled by the Indian Railway Catering and Tourism Corporation (IRCTC) launching its e-booking services in 2002. Another factor that fuelled the growth of online booking in the country was the emergence of online travel aggregators (OTA) during the early 2000s, who initially focussed on airline bookings and later, with the entry of players like redBus, an internet platform enabling booking bus tickets, in 2006. These were among the early initiatives that popularised the possibilities of internet technologies to better the life of the average Indian.

Internet penetration enabling rural economy growth: Regional language–based social media and content sharing is bringing a new class of consumers. With the consolidation in the telecom industry and the entry of newer players like Reliance Jio in 2016, the price for internet data has come down significantly from ₹152 per GB in 2016 to ₹10 per GB in 2019. A large percentage of the new internet users in the country is consuming content in vernacular languages. Hindi is emerging as the most consumed language, with strong growth compared to other languages like English. Most of the new users largely consume video and audio content, enabled by the internet data penetration. Data consumption grew four times during 2016–19 (Exhibit 18.4).

Various state government initiatives, like the push towards digitisation of land records, will lead to clear land titles, thereby making borrowing from the formal sector easier for a large segment of the rural population.

The continuous reduction in internet access costs has led to a sharp increase in the sale of smartphones in the country, thereby enabling downloading of mobile apps and increasing digital adoption in the country.

Increased Access to Venture Capital and Equity Financing

Though venture capital (VC) has existed in India since the early 1990s, it was not till 2008–09 that VC investments in India began to scale up. Venture capital in India started

Exhibit 18.4: Falling cost of data and rise in data consumption

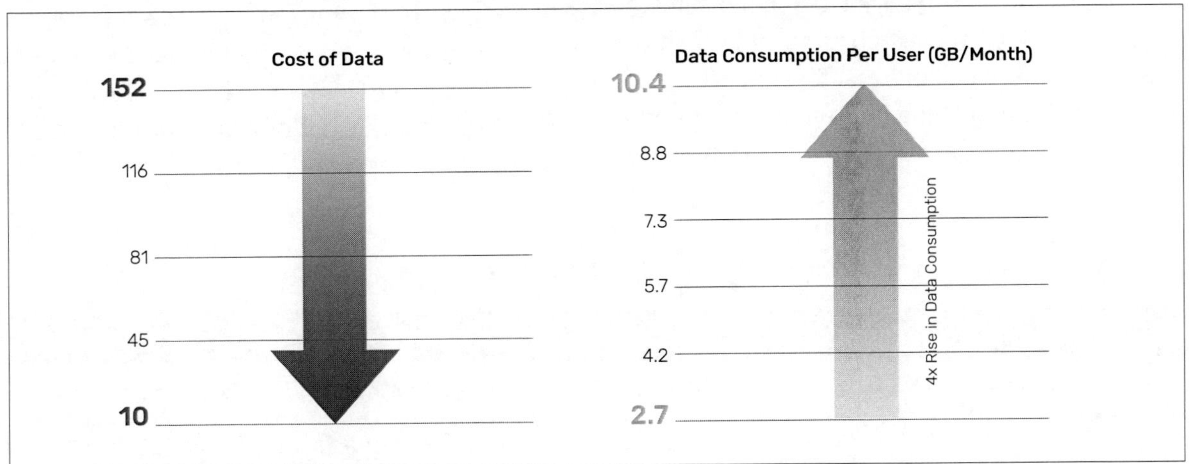

Source: Telecom Subscription Reports, 2020.[7]

in 1988 with the formation of Technology Development and Information Company of India Ltd. (TDICI), promoted by ICICI and UTI (now called ICICI Venture). Till 1995, VC was largely restricted to government-sponsored institutions. Post 1995, foreign venture funds started taking interest in Indian businesses, largely as a result of successful Indian technocrats in the US. In 1993, the Indian Venture Capital Association[8] was formally created to work with the government and regulators. The active institutional investors in the country numbered over 390 in 2020.[9]

The Indian VC industry has come of age, with several large-ticket investments and exits taking place. Marquee exits like the sale of Flipkart to Walmart have bolstered investor confidence. After the US and China, India has one of the most vibrant private equity and venture capital ecosystem.

Strong Regulatory Framework to Access Capital

The earliest regulations governing venture capital in India were the SEBI (Venture Capital Fund) Regulations, 1996. Since then, the regulatory framework has strengthened. The intent has been to build frameworks that protect investors and investee firms and to operate in an environment suitable for raising the risk capital necessary for promoting innovation through start-ups. In 2012, SEBI introduced new norms for investors in venture capital and private equity funds to be registered as AIFs (alternative investment funds) as a new class of pooled-in investment vehicles. SEBI has played a stellar role in encouraging the flow of capital to early-stage businesses. From VCF guidelines to AIFs, the regulator has ensured that the needs of the entrepreneurs are met, whilst protecting the interests of the investors. This has enabled India-based VC funds to develop a domestic investor base. In 2020, India-dedicated funds raised $5.4 billion from domestic and international investors.

Government Initiatives Enabling the Innovation Ecosystem

The government has a strong focus on digital transformation. The Startup India[10] programme is a flagship initiative of the government, intended to build a strong ecosystem for nurturing innovation and start-ups in the country that will drive sustainable economic growth and generate large-scale employment opportunities. Since its launch on January 16, 2016, the Startup India initiative has rolled out several programmes to support entrepreneurs, building a robust start-up ecosystem and transforming India into a country of job creators instead of job seekers. These programmes are managed by a dedicated Start-up India Team, which reports to the Department for Industrial Policy and Promotion (DPIIT).[11]

Apart from the Government of India, several state governments like Karnataka, Telangana, Kerala, Andhra and Maharashtra have implemented their own policies to encourage entrepreneurship with acceleration programmes and financial support. Apart from state government, individual ministries, including the Ministry of Electronics and Information Technology (MeitY) have also launched their own platforms to support early-stage businesses.[12] Some of the key initiatives taken by the government over the years are listed in Exhibit 18.5.

Development of IndiaStack

IndiaStack is a set of APIs that allows governments, businesses, start-ups and developers to utilise a unique digital infrastructure to solve India's hard problems towards presence-less, paperless, and cashless service delivery. Each API within the IndiaStack collection is owned by a separate entity, which owns the specification and the governance of that API. It creates a digital

Exhibit 18.5: Key government initiatives enabling innovation and entrepreneurship

Year	Government Programme	Aims and Target
2009	Invest India	Creation of an investment promotion and facilitation agency
2009	IndiaStack and UID	Digital push for cashless, paperless, scalable architecture to support the Aadhaar - Universal Identification Project
2013	SEBI Alternative Investment Fund Regulations	New norms for angel investors, who provide funding to companies in their initial stages
2014	Make in India	Flagship initiative of the Government of India (GoI) aimed at making the country a global 'design and manufacturing' destination
2015	Digital India	Flagship of GOI aimed at expanding e-governance to promote inclusive growth and transform India into a digitally empowered society and knowledge economy
2015	Skill India Initiative	A vocational training and certification programme aimed at giving 400 million youth the opportunity for a better livelihood by 2022
2016	Startup India initiative	Flagship initiative of GOI to catalyse the start-up culture and build an ecosystem for innovation and entrepreneurship
2016	Startup India Online Portal	367,171 registered steps, 26,374 recognised start-ups, 221 income tax exemptions, and 264 start-ups were funded by SIDBI FFS (as of December 31, 2019)
2016	Atal Incubation Centres (AIC) under Atal Innovation Mission (AIM)	31 AICs have been funded, with ₹1.4 billion (approximately $20.39 million) and ₹576.8 million ($8.12 million) disbursed
2016	SIDBI 'Fund of Funds (FFS) for Start-ups'	₹100 billion corpus (approximately $1.4 billion) contributing to the alternative investment funds (AIFs) for investing in start-ups
2016	Bharat Interface for Money (BHIM) and United Payment Interface	Mobile payment app developed by the National Payments Corporation on the United Payments Interface to allow seamless and verified payments
2019	Technology Incubation and Development of Entrepreneurs TIDE 2.0	MeitY-sponsored programme to promote socially relevant tech entrepreneurship through incubators engaged in supporting ICT start-ups using emerging technologies such as IoT, AI and blockchain)

Source: ADBI Working Paper Series[13]

infrastructure for presence-less (no need for physical authentication), paperless and cashless service delivery under five elements:

- e-KYC (know your customer)
- Aadhaar Payments Bridge System, which essentially turns an Aadhaar number into the person's financial address.
- eSign, a digital signature.
- Unified Payment Interface (UPI), which makes sending money as easy as sending an email or an SMS.
- A consent layer to share personal data (marksheets, health records, financial transactions) with a bank, insurer, employer or university for a limited time for a specific purpose.

IndiaStack can potentially make government services more efficient, and bring down leakages. It can give a boost to the start-up ecosystem by providing an open digital infrastructure, much like how building highways can boost the economy.

Growth of the Indian Innovation and Start-up Ecosystem

In this section, we analyse the emergence and growth of tech start-ups and the innovation ecosystem during 2006–2020 across three growth phases in five-year periods, with emphasis on the key milestones, investment flows and major innovation enablers (Exhibit 18.6).

1991–2006: Setting-up phase: A technology-driven innovation ecosystem fuelled by tech start-ups, especially in the last decade, owes its origin to the accelerated growth of the export-focussed IT services industry in the 1990s and the early 2000s. The confluence of policy initiatives directed towards liberalisation of the economy, facilitating the growth of technical and managerial institutions and the availability of talent, and enabling the growth of internet penetration and mobile usage resulted in the exponential growth of the IT industry contributing to 4.8 per cent of the GDP by 2006. Early applications bringing the benefits of digital technology to a larger population such as internet-enabled train ticket booking, online airline ticket booking and even bus booking (redBus) made the potential of the power of technology visible to many promising entrepreneurs who were professionals or students in technology and management institutes in the country. These developments set the stage for the exponential growth of the entrepreneurial ecosystem in the country, leading to the growth of tech start-ups and digital innovations.

2006–10: Introduction phase: This period can be regarded as the beginning of the innovation ecosystem in India. Inmobi, which later became the first Unicorn in the start-up tech ecosystem, was founded in 2007; Flipkart, which was valued at $16 billion in 2018, was also founded in the same year. With Zomato, Paytm, Snapdeal and OLA being founded in 2008, the seeds for the growth of e-commerce, FinTech and the logistics sector were planted in this period. Of the VC investments of $3.8 billion in this period, 25 FinTech firms received investments of $207 million, followed by e-commerce receiving $158 million investments in 18 firms. Government initiatives to attract investment under the "Invest India" programme and early policies towards leveraging technology in administration like the launch of UIDAI and IndiaStack set the stage for the

Exhibit 18.6: Tech start-up ecosystem: Growth phases

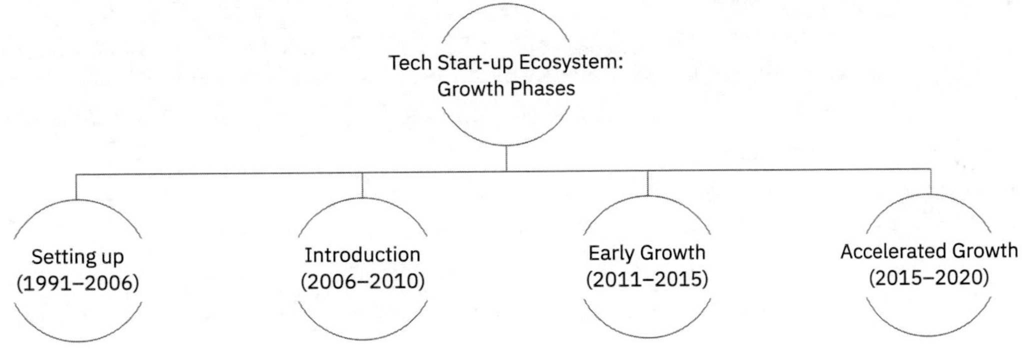

Exhibit 18.7: Setting-up phase (1991–2006): Enablers and outcomes

1991–2006: Setting-up Phase	**Enablers**
Setting the stage for tech start-ups' growth: ▪ IT Industry growth and availability of technical and managerial talent	▪ Policy: Liberalisation of the economy and the growth of the private sector ▪ Talent: Availability of technical talent enabled by growth of engineering institutes; development of managerial talent facilitated by management institutes; increased employment opportunities offered by growing IT industry ▪ Digital technology: Penetration of personal computers and networking through the decades; 2006 – internet subscribers at 15 million; 1995 – launch of mobile telephony across the country; 15 million users in 2006; Amazon reaching a turnover of over $10 billion in 2006 primarily from e-commerce operations, signalling opportunities for internet-based businesses **Outcomes** ▪ Exponential growth of the Indian IT sector: IT industry contributing to 4.8 per cent of GDP in 2006; Y2K contributing to sectoral growth ▪ Early adoption of internet and realisation of benefits by consumers ▪ 2002: Internet ticket booking launched by Indian Railways ▪ 2003: Launch of low-cost airlines; adoption of online ticket booking ▪ 2006: Early online bus ticket booking apps, like redBus, launched

development of multiple tech start-up sectors including FinTech, e-commerce and logistics. The number of internet users grew at a CAGR of 39 per cent to 31 million during this period. The telecom policies made mobile telephony increasingly accessible to the population, with the number of mobile users reaching 34 million by 2010. Sequoia, which entered the country in 2006, is the leading investor and has deployed the highest capital in the country, approximately $7 billion in 250 deals over 2014–2019 (India Venture Capital Report 2020). It is also widely observed that the 2008 global recession worked as a trigger, directing the flow of foreign capital to emerging markets. Many leading incubators like CIIE Ahmedabad were set up during this period.

2011–15: Early growth phase: Investments in 2006–10 gave birth to 8 Unicorns. The growth of these tech start-ups by young tech entrepreneurs did not fail to catch the imagination of many students and professionals and contribute their part in becoming entrepreneurs or early employees. Government and academic institutions

Exhibit 18.8: Introduction phase (2006–2010): Enablers and outcomes

2006–2010: Introduction Phase	**Enablers**
Early boost for e-commerce and FinTech sectors: ▪ Enabling technological environment ▪ Increasing consumer adoption of internet-enabled applications ▪ Access to capital	▪ Digital technology: 2008 – Launch of 3G; internet penetration CAGR 39 per cent; 31 million internet, 34 million mobile subscribers by 2010 ▪ Capital: Entry of global venture capital funds such as Sequoia (2006), Accel Partners and so on. ▪ Entrepreneurial talent: Setting up of incubators; 2004 – IIT Mumbai SINE; 2007 IIMA CIIE; 2007 Techno Park TBI Trivandrum (later renamed Kerala Startup Mission) ▪ Policy: Launch of government initiatives like Invest India; UIDAI, India **Outcomes** ▪ VC investments $3.9 billion in 675 firms ▪ Launch of start-up sectors: E-commerce, FinTech ▪ 2007: Flipkart, Inmobi founded; 2008: Zomato, Paytm, Snapdeal, 2010: OLA ▪ Sector: FinTech : $207 million in 42 firms; e-commerce: $158 million in 32 firms

Exhibit 18.9: Early growth phase (2011–2015): Enablers and outcomes

2011–2015: Early Growth Phase	**Enablers**
Growth in multiple sectors: Broad-based growth ▪ Scaling up of FinTech and e-commerce sectors ▪ Investment in LogisticsTech, HealthTech and EdTech	▪ Technology: Internet penetration CAGR 39 per cent; 161 million internet, 251 million mobile subscribers by 2015 ▪ Entrepreneurial and managerial talent: Increased emphasis on entrepreneurship: incubators and accelerators emerge across different cities and academic institutes (see Exhibit 18.5) ▪ Policy: Enabling government initiatives: 2012 – SEBI's alternative investment fund guidelines 2014 – Make in India; government regulations aid raising of domestic capital, increasing funding availability 2015 – Digital India; Skill India Initiative **Outcomes** ▪ VC investments in 1400 firms; $6.4 billion investments; 65 per cent growth over the first phase ▪ Start-up tech sector growth: — Strong growth in e-commerce, FinTech — Emergence of LogisticsTech sector; Delhivery founded 2011; 2014 – RIVIGO; 2015 – Blackbuck — 8 Unicorns emerged from the tech start-ups; e-commerce and e-marketplace firms driving the start-up tech sector — 2011: 1 – Inmobi (first Unicorn); 2012: 1 – Flipkart — 2013: 1 – Mu Sigma; 2014: 1 – Snapdeal — 2015: 4 – Ola, Paytm, Quickr, Zomato ▪ Sector investments: e-commerce: $1.2 billion in 212 firms; FinTech: $428 million in 87 firms; HealthTech: $207 million in 41 firms; Logistics: $113 million in 23 firms; EdTech: $181 million in 44 firms

did not fail to take notice and incubators and initiatives to promote the setting up of incubators in all major engineering colleges and management institutes were launched. The logistics tech firms Delhivery (2011) and Rivigo (2014), which grew to be counted among Unicorns, were founded during this period. The logistics and HealthTech sectors in particular got a boost during this period. Apart from FinTech and e-commerce, VC investments went into HealthTech, logistics and EdTech, similar to the quantum of investments that went to e-commerce and FinTech in the introduction phase. The investments in e-commerce and FinTech were $8.5 billion and $2.1 billion during this period while logistics, HealthTech and EdTech investments were $0.5 billion, $0.6 billion and $0.2 billion, respectively. The confluence of enabling factors pushed the growth of start-ups to a higher orbit; internet penetration grew at 39 per cent during this period; 161 million internet subscribers by 2015 ensured that digital technology crossed a threshold to make technology accessible to a significant section of the population. The promise of immense possibilities for the growth of the economy and the society at large pushed multiple stakeholders into action. Enabling policies like Digital India were launched during this period; incubators were set up in technology and management institutes across the country; alternative investment fund guidelines enabled capital inflow into new ventures; the enabling ecosystem accelerated the investments and growth of different start-up sectors.

2016–20: Accelerated growth phase: The period 2016–20 saw an acceleration in the growth of the innovation ecosystem in the country. From 27,000 start-ups in

2012 and 61,000 in 2016, the number increased to 80,000 start-ups across 20 industry sectors in 2020.[14] Approximately 8 per cent (6,400) of these start-ups were funded and 23 per cent were able to get post-seed funding. By the end of 2020, there were 37 Unicorns and a much bigger pipeline of soonicorns and minicorns. Exhibit 18.10 shows the early-stage and growth-stage funding and the number of firms that were funded over the 15-year period.

The sectors contributing more than one Unicorn were e-commerce (7), FinTech (5), Logistics (4), SaaS or Software (4) and EdTech (2), adding to 22 of 36 Unicorns. The four sectors with more than $4 billion investments over the 2006–20 period were e-commerce, FinTech, Logistics and HealthTech, with e-commerce drawing the highest investment of more than $25 billion during 2006–20. The FinTech and Logistics sectors benefitted from the growth of e-commerce and marketplace models.

Opportunities for investor exits made fresh capital available for reinvestments. At the same time, they had the spiralling effect of attracting more investors into the innovation ecosystem. Scaling up of start-ups to larger organisations with thousands of employees and high venture capital investments has gradually brought the niche start-up sector into competition with larger incumbents. These developments have also attracted top technological, managerial and entrepreneurial talent into the innovation and start-up ecosystem, further accelerating the growth of the start-up ecosystem.

The launch of Reliance Jio and their aggressive pricing in 2016 led to a fall in data connectivity prices and to the fast growth of internet penetration in the country. Internet penetration grew at a CAGR of 39 per cent in this period; by 2020, there were 848 million internet subscribers and 975 million mobile subscribers. The per GB data costs fell steeply, leading to four-times growth in data consumption during this period. Increasing accessibility and affordability of technology expanded the market for digital innovations in all aspects of human life; the increasing investments in HealthTech, EdTech and AgriTech in this period bear testimony to this fact.

Government initiatives like Digital India, demonetisation in 2016 and the implementation of

Exhibit 18.10: Total VC investments in early-stage, growth-stage funding and the number of firms funded

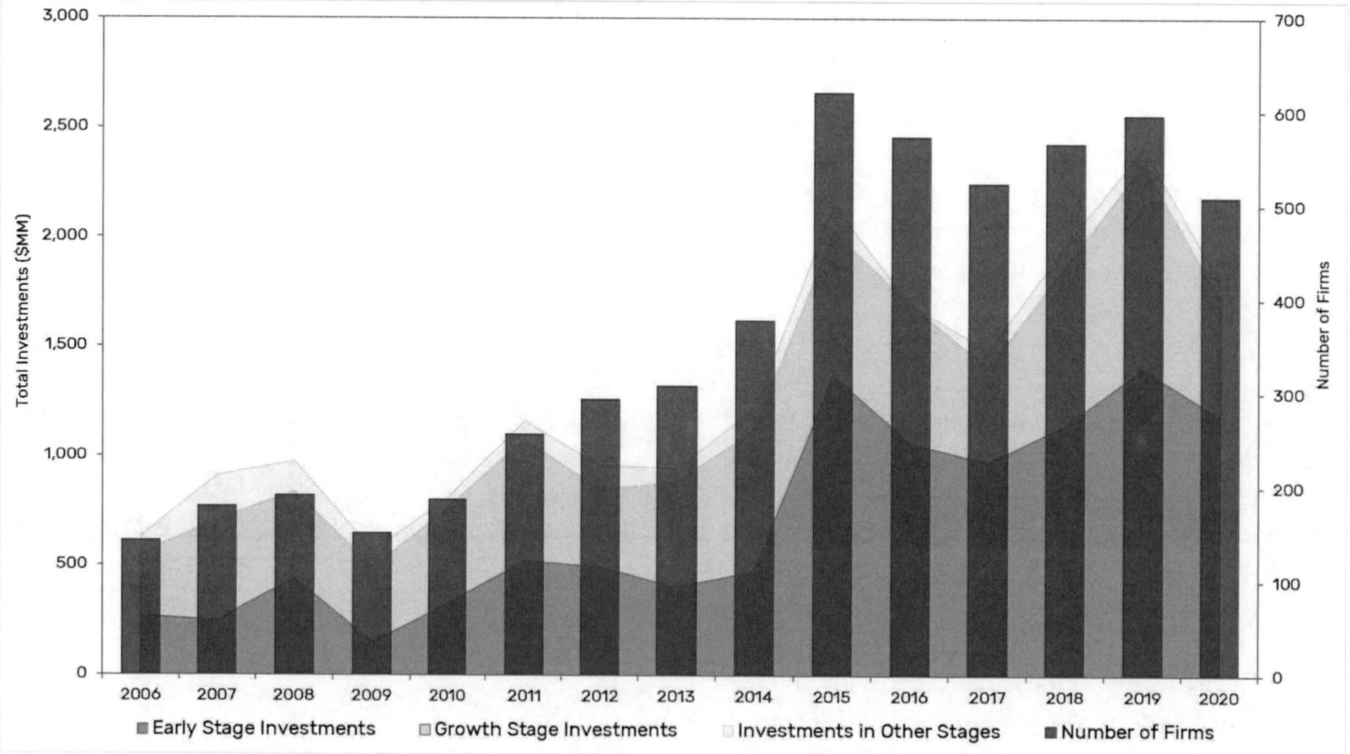

Source: Venture Intelligence

Exhibit 18.11: Accelerated growth phase (2016–2020): Enablers and outcomes

2016–2020: Accelerated Growth Phase	**Enablers**
Deepening and broadening of growth across and within start-up sectors. ▪ Indian start-up ecosystem ranked four based on number of Unicorns (37), after USA, China and UK ▪ Bangalore, Delhi and Mumbai among the top fifty global start-up ecosystems ▪ Investor interest fuelled by growing markets, investment return and exit opportunities ▪ Entrepreneurial talent attracted from big cities and small towns	▪ *Technology* — 2016: Launch of Jio; its fast growth with 406 million wireless subscribers by October 2020, aggressive pricing strategy resulting in competition, decrease in cost of data per GB and steep rise in data usage — Cost of data per GB from ₹152 in CY 2016 to ₹10 in CY 2019, data consumption per user has grown 4x times during this period — Internet penetration CAGR 39 per cent; 848 million internet, 974 million mobile subscribers (67 per cent of population) by 2020 ▪ *Capital* — Investor exits and increased access to capital: 2018: Walmart acquisition of Flipkart for $16 billion (77 per cent stake) increased global investor confidence in Indian start-ups; Softbank gained 60 per cent returns on its $2.5 billion investment; large exits by investors created a vibrant VC market and increased access to capital — Increase in the supply of technical and managerial talent: Larger pool of talent; increase in supply of technical, managerial talent and promotion of entrepreneurship across large cities and small towns ▪ *Policy* — 2016: Startup India Initiative; Startup India online portal; SIDBI Fund of Funds for start-ups, $100 billion contributing to the Alternative Investment Funds (AIF) for investing in start-ups — 2016: Demonetisation and 2017 GST implementation lead to greater formalisation of the economy, giving tech-enabled businesses a big boost — 2020: Ecological turbulence, pandemic and digital surge; tailwind for e-commerce, FinTech, EdTech, HealthTech, AgriTech sectors; headwind for travel, mobility segments **Outcomes** ▪ Growing sectors: E-commerce, FinTech; Emerging Sectors: HealthTech, LogisticsTech, EdTech; AgriTech ▪ $9.52 billion VC investments in 1908 firms; 48 per cent growth over the second phase ▪ Investments in sectors; E-commerce: $1.9 billion in 273 firms; FinTech: $1.57 investments in 241 firms; $483 million in 66 firms; HealthTech: $682 million in 139 firms; LogistichsTech: $451 million in 112 firms; AgriTech: $273 million in 65 firms ▪ Number of Unicorns: 36 (fourth highest, after USA, China, UK) — 2016: 2; Shopclues, Hike — 2018: 8; BYJU'S, PaytmMALL, Swiggy, PolicyBazaar, OYO Rooms, Udaan, Freshworks, Billdesk — 2019: 9; Delhivery, Dream11, Bigbasket, Rivigo, Druva Software, Icertis, CitiusTech, Ola Electric, Lenskart — 2020: 9; Pin Labs, Nykaa, Postman, Unacademy, Razorpay, Cars24, Zenoti, Dailyhunt, InmobiGlance

GST in 2017 accelerated the adoption and use of digital technology in different sectors. This period also saw marquee exits like Flipkart, earning returns to investors and attracting more investments and investors in the innovation space.

Driving Innovation-led Economic Growth: The Way Forward

Enabling Technology: Accelerating Digital Technology Adoption in Rural India; Leveraging Deep Tech in Different Sectors

Ensuring internet, mobile access to rural population: According to TRAI, the overall tele density in India is 86 per cent and averages 140 per cent in urban areas. The significant reduction in cost of data has led to a sharp increase in data consumption per user. Increased access to digital technology would open up rural demand and supply sources for businesses to offer increasingly affordable innovative services in the areas of healthcare, education, agriculture, retailing and financial services. Technology and tech entrepreneurs hold tremendous promise to transform the rural economy. It could help improve agricultural productivity, access to markets and earn higher returns for agricultural produce, enable skilling of rural youth to take up more attractive employment opportunities, addressing disguised employment, making quality education, healthcare, financial and other valuable services accessible and affordable to the population. Hence, it becomes imperative for governments to ensure data access to the rural population through innovative measures; a policy for setting up of public Wi-Fi systems in rural areas and waiving of the licence fee[15] are welcome moves in this direction.

Enabling development, adoption of deep tech to solve relevant problems: The NASSCOM–Zinnov study[16] reported that 18 per cent of all start-ups are now leveraging deep tech in their operations. Start-ups in FinTech, HealthTech, LogisticsTech and AgriTech are increasingly using deep technologies to offer superior value to their customers. It is important to accelerate the adoption of these technologies by offering necessary exposure to students in technology institutes. Centres enabling access to emerging technology in university incubators as well as industry incubators and accelerators could facilitate innovation leveraging these technologies. This in turn could attract new entrepreneurs leveraging these technologies as well as help existing start-ups to offer enhanced customer value.

Accelerating Investment Flows

Enabling investment exits; triggering investment–innovation–investor returns spirals in multiple sectors: Venture capital investors have continuously increased investment flows into the country especially in tech start-ups. The investment of $3.9 billion in 2006–10 grew by 65 per cent to $6.4 billion in the 2011–15 period and further by 48 per cent to $9.5 billion during 2016–20. Meanwhile, the exit data indicates that the Indian start-up ecosystem has been offering increased exit opportunities over these three growth phases, as indicated in Exhibit 18.12. This augurs well for further accelerating the growth of the sector by attracting increased investments into further scaling up the start-ups and meeting their shareholders' and other stakeholders' expectations.

The investor expectations of early-stage investments and late-stage investments are not exactly the same. The focus on attaining higher business sales, scale of operations and higher valuation of the firm in the early stages of the start-up has to shift to a focus on creating tangible value and generating return on capital

Exhibit 18.12: Number of investments – fully or partially exited

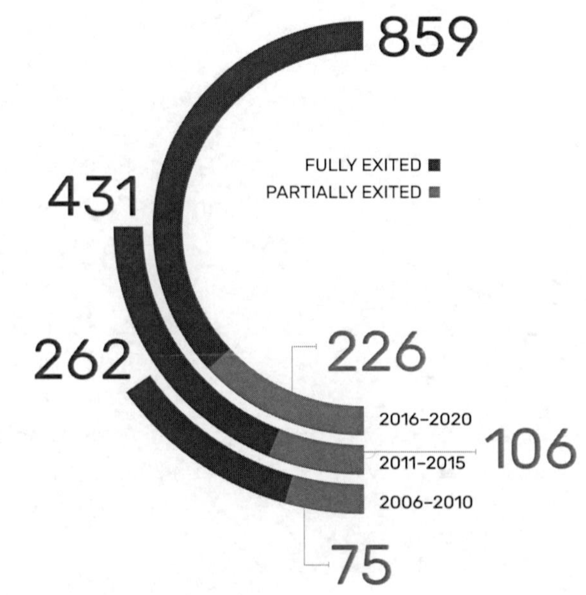

Source: Venture Intelligence

employed. Growth in profitability along with the higher scale of operations will open up many exit options for the venture capital investors in the firm. This will trigger the next cycle of investment, innovation, investor returns and sustain or further grow the start-up ecosystem. Increased corporate acquisitions of start-ups like the Walmart acquisition of Flipkart in 2018 ($16 billion for 77 per cent equity stake) offers a major exit route to generate returns and free capital for funding the next round of innovations. The transformation of disparate industries into a connected digital ecosystem is opening up more acquisition opportunities and exits for early-stage investors. Progressive policy interventions to sustain and accelerate investment flows are necessary for the growth of the ecosystem.

Attracting, Supporting Talented Entrepreneurs; Accelerating Innovation

Attracting top talent to the innovation ecosystem, improving incubation support: To keep the momentum of the start-up ecosystem, it is important to develop a supporting environment to attract quality talent. The educational background and experience of the early Unicorn start-ups is a case in point – most of them have been founded by entrepreneurs with strong technical and management backgrounds and work experience in leading corporates.

Once into the ecosystem, many of these talented prospective entrepreneurs may benefit from increased exposure to business realities as well as mentoring from seasoned professionals, entrepreneurs and experts in the technology domain and business. It is reported that only about 10 per cent of the prospective entrepreneurs end up getting access to capital to develop their ideas into a commercially feasible offering. However, entrepreneurs who fail in their early attempts have also become successful in their later attempts. High-quality mentoring and incubation support could improve their chance of success. While the number of incubators in the country is increasing, attention to quality is critical to sustain the growth. Benchmarking incubators with respect to the support facilities provided could enable incubators to continuously improve their quality of support. Academic institutes could be encouraged for their efforts in promoting use of advances in technologies to innovatively address industry issues.

The COVID-19 pandemic has made virtual incubation more acceptable than before. In virtual incubation support, all support other than the working space could be provided. Virtual incubation options could offer much higher reach to incubators to access prospective entrepreneurs without any location constraints. Industry associations could also play a more active role in encouraging the innovation ecosystem by setting up industry-focussed incubators as well as by providing mentoring support to incubators across the country.

Innovation thrust by corporates: digitilatisation, venturing, collaboration, acquisitions: Start-ups are increasingly posing stiff competition to existing companies by focussing on consumer-centric innovation. Established businesses are increasingly realising the need to innovate and adapt to maintain their market share and profitability impacted by increasing competition from new-age businesses and changing consumer expectations. Corporates are considering various alternatives to accelerate innovation and bring agility to their existing operations, including corporate venturing and acquiring start-ups that complement their business operations and goals. Many corporates have started to view their venturing as their R&D centres to experiment with newer business models and innovations. Examples of corporate venturing include Tata Innovation Fund, RP-SG Consumer Fund and Unilever Ventures. The NASSCOM–Zinnov 2019[17] study has reported more than 50 unique open innovation programmes in corporates in 2018.

Even in traditional businesses, there is an increasing tendency to hire a Chief Digital Officer, a role that did not exist even five years back. The launch of banking applications like SBI Yono and IRCTC train ticket booking services are examples of successful digitalisation corporate initiatives. Innovation initiatives in corporates augur well for the growth of the innovation ecosystem in various ways – supplying entrepreneurial, technological and managerial talent to the start-up ecosystem, collaborations enabling start-ups to find new markets or resources and providing exit options to start-ups through mergers and acquisitions. Industry associations need to facilitate active engagement of incumbent firms with start-up firms to explore mutually beneficial opportunities to enhance customer value and thereby shareholder value.

Ensuring Institutional Support: Institutional Interactions and Supportive Government Policies

One of the key drivers for the growth of the innovation ecosystem is the favourable policy environment created by successive governments. This is reflected in the improvement of the World Bank index of 'ease of doing business' of the country from 142 in 2014 to 63 in 2020.[18] In 2020, India was counted among the 10 economies improving the most across three or more areas measured by Doing Business in 2018–19.[19] This augurs well for attracting investors as well as removing bottlenecks for attracting talented entrepreneurs and for scaling-up businesses.

Developing the innovation ecosystem requires industry, academia and government to work together proactively to anticipate and create a favourable environment for innovation. Government initiatives to encourage incubators in academic institutions have enabled enhanced interaction between all the key partners and played a significant role in attracting technical, managerial and entrepreneurial talent to contribute in building the innovation ecosystem. These positive developments should further be taken forward to accelerate the growth of the innovation ecosystem. The triple helix strategic interactions proposed by Etzkowitz and Leydesdorff in 1995 – among universities engaging in basic research, industries producing commercial goods and governments that are regulating the market – is shown in Exhibit 18.13.[20]

Setting up science parks, tech parks or innovation labs by the collaborative efforts of government, academic community, industry association and corporates will encourage experimentation with emerging technologies and collaboration between the key entities to solve relevant business issues or social issues. Increased interaction between the three key institutions results in continuous improvement of the innovation ecosystem. In order to ensure success, it is imperative that this ecosystem is continuously facilitated and orchestrated proactively. *"Only things that can be measured can be improved";* while it is important to increase the investment in incubation and enhance the capacity, it is equally important to improve the effectiveness of these investments by improving the quality of these initiatives. This includes creating a competitive spirit, risk–reward mechanisms and continuous education to enhance quality.

Innovation ecosystem development needs persistent efforts over a long period of time. The analysis of ecosystem developments over the last 15 years, we feel, makes the case for a 15-year planning period for enabling the institutional changes. This has resulted in scaling

Exhibit 18.13: Triple helix strategic interactions in a developed country

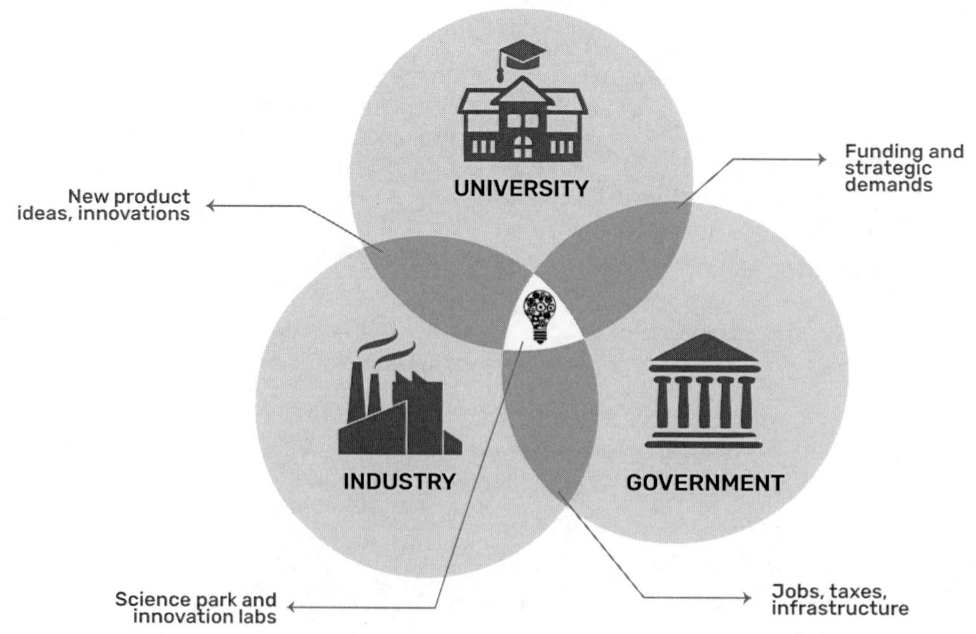

up of start-ups into large firms enabling investor exits, development of talent, technology and markets and has fuelled the next round of innovations. Initiatives directed towards leveraging digital technologies to impact the different sectors of the rural economy, implementing policy changes and creating institutional support to boost sectors (like HealthTech, EdTech and others) will surely benefit from such a long-term orientation. Policy interventions by the government to encourage interaction between key partners to develop necessary infrastructure will certainly accelerate innovation and economic growth.

Endnotes

[1]NASSCOM–Zinnov Start-up Report. 2019. Retrieved from https://nasscom.in/knowledge-center/publications/indian-tech-start-ecosystem-leading-tech-20s

[2]Statistia. 2021. IT industry in India - statistics and facts, retrieved from https://www.statista.com/topics/2256/it-industry-in-india/

[3]See endnote 1.

[4]The Hindu BusinessLine. 2020. Low ARPU levels, high debt pain points for operators, retrieved from https://www.thehindubusinessline.com/economy/low-arpu-levels-high-debt-pain-points-for-operators/article33419398.ece

[5]IBEF. 2021. Telecom Industry in India, retrieved from https://www.ibef.org/industry/telecommunications.aspx#:~:text=Revenue%20from%20the%20telecom%20equipment,CAGR%20of%2030%25%20by%202021

[6]Euromonitor. 2020. Retrieved from https://www.euromonitor.com/the-new-normal-future-of-consumer-mobility-urban-planning-and-construction/report

[7]HDSEC. 2020. Telecom Subscription Reports, 2020, Telecom Regulatory Authority.

[8]https://ivca.in/mission-vision/

[9]See endnote 1.

[10]Startup India 2016. Starting a start-up Revolution, retrieved from https://www.startupindia.gov.in/content/dam/invest-india/Templates/public/Action Plan.pdf

[11]https://www.startupindia.gov.in/content/sih/en/about-startup-india-initiative.html

[12]https://meitystartuphub.in/

[13]https://www.indiastack.org/about/

[14]ADBI Working Paper. 2020. The start-up environment and funding activity in India, retrieved from https://www.adb.org/sites/default/files/publication/612516/adbi-wp1145.pdf

[15]India Venture Capital Report 2020. Bain and Company.

[16]PM India 2020. Cabinet approves setting up of Public Wi-Fi Networks by Public Data Office Aggregators to provide public Wi-Fi service Through Public Data Offices without levy of any License Fee, Retrieved from https://www.pmindia.gov.in/en/news_updates/cabinet-approves-setting-up-of-public-wi-fi-networks-by-public-data-office-aggregators-to-provide-public-wi-fi-service-through-public-data-offices-without-levy-of-any-license-fee/

[17]See endnote 1.

[18]Ibid

[19]World Bank. 2020. Doing Business 2020, retrieved from http://documents1.worldbank.org/curated/en/688761571934946384/pdf/Doing-Business-2020-Comparing-Business-Regulation-in-190-Economies.pdf

[20]Etzkowitz, H and Leydesdorff, L. 1995. The Triple Helix–University-industry-government relations: A laboratory for knowledge based economic development. *EASST Review 14* (1): 14–19.

IN BRIEF

- Indian AgriTech investments have gathered momentum in the last five years. The pace of investments picked up from $18 million in 2015 to $363 million in 2020, at a CAGR of 83 per cent. NABVENTURES estimates that of the 1,100 agri start-ups in India, around 600 are AgriTech start-ups.
- The changing composition of food demand from grains towards pulses, fruits, vegetables and livestock products, growing awareness among consumers especially millennials regarding food safety, demand for sustainable foods along with demographic pressures are placing heavy demand on Indian agriculture, triggering multiple innovations which leverage digital technologies.
- In India, the peripheral AgriTech start-ups (e-commerce in agri produce) have raised the lion's share of VC funding. In order to tackle the more pressing problems of water stress, low yields, produce wastage, food safety, etc., the core AgriTech start-ups demand increased attention.
- Core AgriTech start-ups need to create horizontal platform–based solutions rather than standalone solutions in order to improve their scalability. Towards this end, the core AgriTech start-ups may be better off by forging partnerships with the peripheral AgriTech players in order to provide integrated or embedded solutions. Government support in the form of convertible grants and pilot programmes in multiple states could also give a boost to core AgriTech start-ups.

INDUSTRY PERSPECTIVE

19

AgriTech: Triggering Technology-Enabled Transformation

Rajesh Ranjan

Ranjan, R. 2021. "AgriTech: Triggering Technology-Enabled Transformation". In *Shifting Orbits: Decoding the Trajectory of the Indian Start-up Ecosystem*, edited by Thillai Rajan A, Srivardhini K Jha, Joffi Thomas and Rohan Chinchwadkar, 240–255. Hyderabad: Universities Press (India) Private Limited.

Overview

The United Nations projects that the world's population will grow by 2 billion between 2019 and 2050: from 7.7 billion to 9.7 billion. In India, the population is expected to grow by 270 million between 2019 and 2050: from 1.37 billion to 1.64 billion.[1]

Increasing income levels, evolving demographics, increasing urbanisation, lifestyle changes, increasing preferences for branded items, as well as a modernising retail sector are increasing the demand for processed food in terms of both quantity and quality. As per the Food and Agriculture Organization (FAO), food production needs to increase by 70 per cent from current levels to meet the food needs of the large population base using less energy and fewer agrichemicals while lowering the levels of GHGs (greenhouse gases) and coping with climate change. Significant investments need to be made in modernisation and rethinking of agriculture, food processing, logistics and retail in order to meet the increased demand for food.

Agriculture is a high-importance sector in the Indian economy. It contributes 16 per cent of India's GDP and employs 47 per cent of the workforce.[2] Over the years, the sector has been diversifying from grains towards pulses, fruit, vegetables and livestock products, largely driven by evolving demographics, urbanisation and changing demand patterns on the back of increasing incomes.

AgriTech in India has made inroads in conventional agriculture by solving some of the persistent problems plaguing the sector. The AgriTech start-ups are aiming to solve problems such as farmland degradation, low crop yield, overuse of agrichemicals, GHG emissions, labour shortage, opaque supply chains, distribution inefficiencies, food safety, food traceability, farming inefficiencies, unsustainable meat production, antibiotics in livestock and dairy products and adverse effects of climate change.

AgriTech

AgriTech encompasses products and services leveraging the use of new-age technologies (digital, AI or artificial intelligence, ML or machine learning, Internet of Things [IoT], computer vision, genetics, blockchain and automation) in agriculture and allied activities (livestock, etc.) to increase yields, improve decision-making, encourage novel farming, and enable digital distribution and alternate financing (Exhibit 19.1).

The main segments of AgriTech are presented in Exhibit 19.1. Food delivery (for example, Zomato, Swiggy) and processed food–related segments have not been included in AgriTech, but the m-commerce meat or seafood ordering start-ups (such as Licious, FreshToHome) have been included.

In this report, for analysis purposes, the AgriTech start-ups have been classified as core and peripheral.

Core AgriTech start-ups: The AgriTech start-ups that use new-age technologies such as AI, ML, computer vision, agri-biotechnology, blockchain and IoT for a large part of their business are classified as core AgriTech start-ups; examples include Satyukt, Krishitantra.

Peripheral AgriTech start-ups: The AgriTech start-ups that use digital interfaces for produce distribution, trading, aggregation, input selling and app-based agri-logistics are classified as peripheral AgriTech start-ups. They may use core agri technologies for a small part of their business. Examples include Ninjacart, FreshToHome and Licious.

Exhibit 19.1: Indian AgriTech landscape

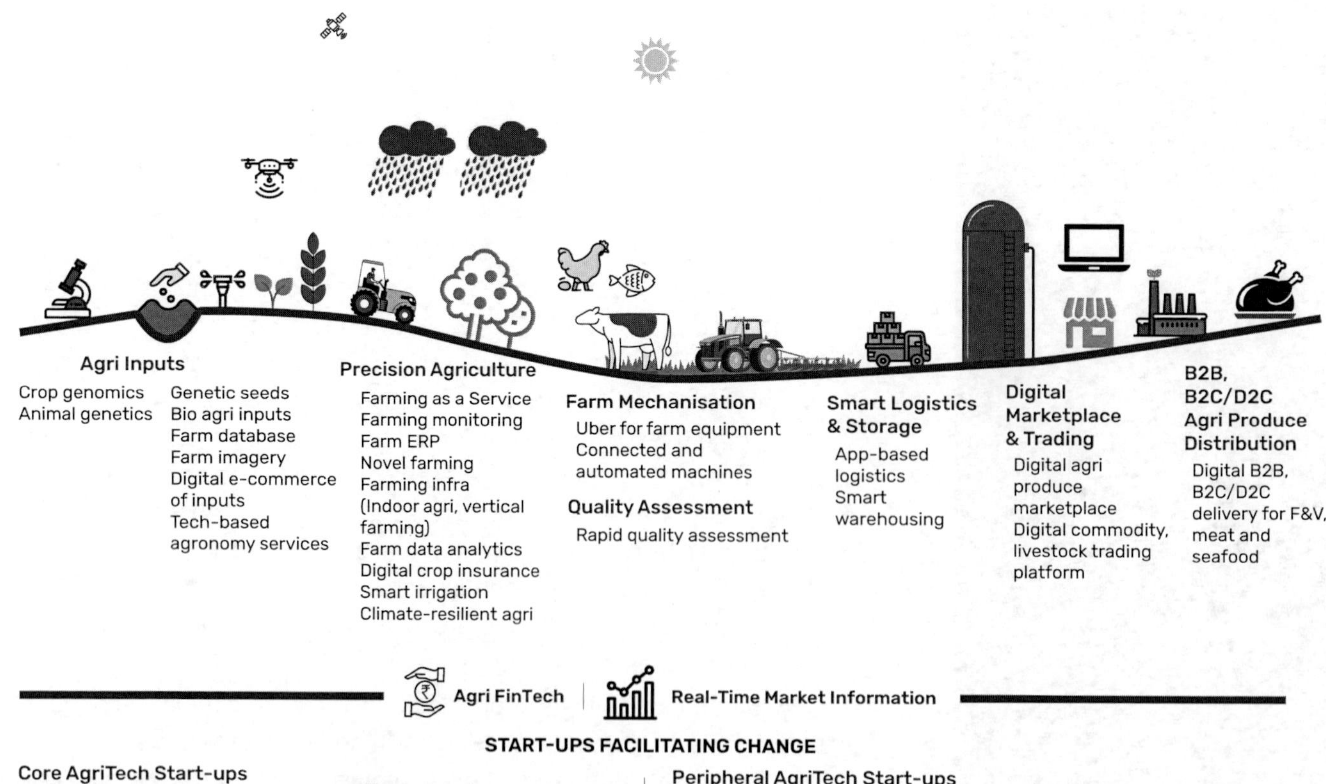

Source: NABVENTURES[3] Research. Select icons have been downloaded from Freepik.com.

Subsequent to the overview of the sector, this chapter is organised into three sections. The first section covers the evolution and growth of the AgriTech sector. The important elements of the AgriTech ecosystem, the need to focus on core AgriTech start-ups and the desired policy interventions are dealt with in the second section. The challenges and the way forward for enabling sector growth are discussed in the concluding section.

Evolution of the AgriTech Sector in India

The green revolution in cereal production (late 1960s to early 1980s) was succeeded by the white revolution in milk production (starting in the 1970s), the limited gene revolution in cotton production (early 2000s) and the more recent diversification of production towards pulses, fruit and vegetables as well as meat and meat products. This has been largely in response to evolving demand patterns driven by rising incomes, urbanisation and government encouragement.

The changing composition of food demand from grains towards pulses, fruit, vegetables and livestock products, growing awareness among consumers – especially millennials – regarding food safety, demand for sustainable foods along with demographic pressures have placed a heavy demand on Indian agriculture. AgriTech start-ups have emerged and evolved in response to the above demands and pressures using new-age technologies and digital platforms.

The Indian AgriTech sector has attracted around $888 million of VC investments from 2012 till 2020. Close to two-thirds of the investments have gone towards digital e-commerce models selling agri or meat produce. The other important segments that have attracted investments include e-commerce of agri inputs, agri-logistics and infra and farm management ERP (Exhibit 19.2).

The evolution of AgriTech in India can be divided into the following four phases (Exhibit 19.3):

Initial phase (2008–2011): In the early years of AgriTech, some of the conventional agribusiness seed

Exhibit 19.2: Composition of cumulative AgriTech investments (2012–2020)

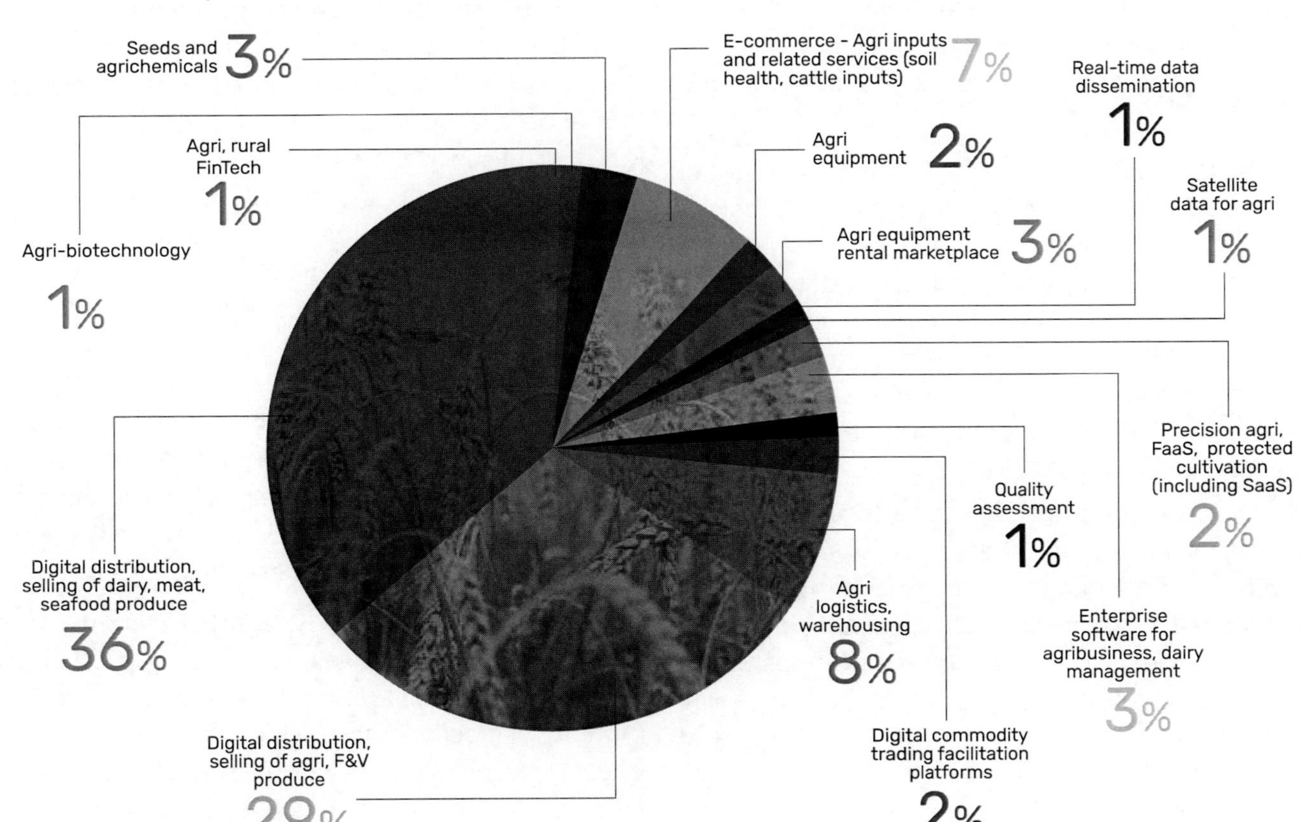

Source: NABVENTURES Research

Exhibit 19.3: Phases of evolution of the AgriTech sector

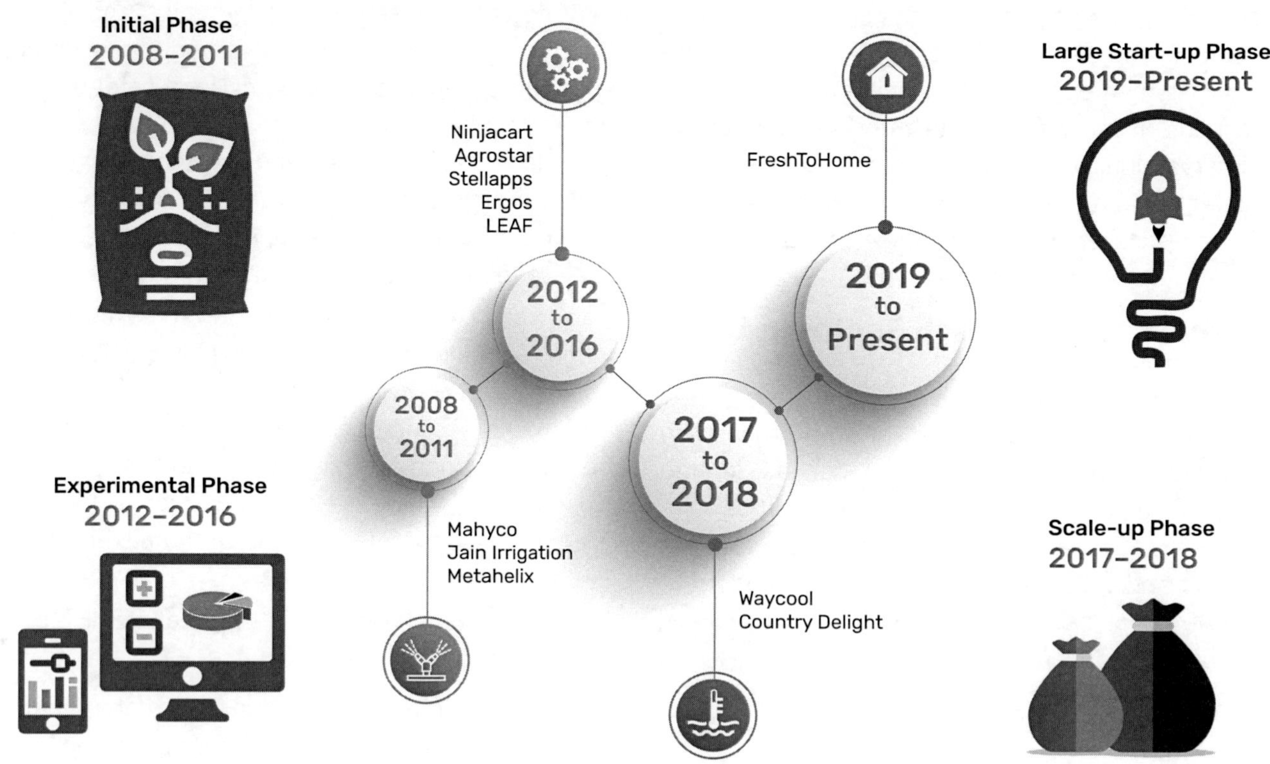

Source: Author

companies with limited AgriTech capabilities (Mahyco, Jain Irrigation and Metahelix) were funded by VC funds. These were mainly present in seeds and simple drip irrigation.

Experimental phase (2012–16): In this period, digital elements of AgriTech started coming to the fore with start-ups like RML, Stellapps, Cropin, Agrostar, Akshaykalpa, Ergos, EM3, Ninjacart, Licious and LEAF getting funding from VC funds. Some of these were pioneering start-ups in their segments. The AgriTech sector in India received a major boost post the announcement of the blockbuster acquisition of The Climate Corporation, a weather data company, by Monsanto in 2013.

A few of the start-ups were able to raise multiple rounds of funding, which gave lot of comfort and reassurance to the larger VC funds. Even though this phase started with core AgriTech and biotech start-ups, it soon gave rise to digital e-commerce start-ups, which in turn, set the stage for the launch of start-ups using IoT, AI, ML and computer vision. In this phase, deal values started becoming meaningful and the average deal value crossed $1 million. Angel, seed, pre-Series A and Series A deals dominated the landscape.

Scale-up phase (2017–18): This period was marked by scaling up of the pioneers on the back of higher funding support, as mid-to-late-stage deals began dominating the landscape in value terms. Agrostar, Licious and Ninjacart raised higher amounts as compared to the previous phase, and the average deal value crossed $5 million. Many start-ups in the peripheral AgriTech segments emerged (such as digital agriproduce distribution or dairy-produce–selling platforms like Waycool and Country Delight) while the core AgriTech start-ups gained more traction. The peripheral AgriTech start-ups tried to bring about behavioural changes in consumers. Farm mechanisation got a big boost as well. This phase saw funding participation from some of the large generalist VCs. Global liquidity continued to remain strong on the back of low interest rates globally.

Large start-ups phase (2019–present): The current phase has been marked by significant funding acceleration, albeit a small dip was witnessed during peak COVID-19 (April to October 2020). For the first time, single deal values crossed $100 million (Ninjacart in 2019 and FreshToHome in 2020). The B2B digital e-commerce model for agri produce was firmly established with quite a few start-ups reaching critical size, while the B2C, D2C digital e-commerce start-ups were not too far behind. The recent 'on hold' agri sector reforms (especially farm laws) have further added to the scale-up prospects of the peripheral AgriTech start-ups.

There is a general bullishness both at global and domestic level regarding AgriTech prospects that has resulted in high valuations. In the current COVID-19 period, many of the smaller core AgriTech start-ups that had raised funds in the past at high valuation are finding it difficult to raise future rounds. The large peripheral AgriTech start-ups have been able to raise funds as they are backed by large generalist VCs that have pursued a strategy of providing capital to see the start-ups through the COVID-19 phase for next 12–18 months. There was imminent fear of valuation correction during March–April 2020, but the $2 trillion quantitative easing by the Federal Reserve in the USA removed those fears.

The large peripheral start-ups with wafer-thin margins continue to remain vulnerable over the medium term from both valuation and exit standpoints if global interest rates start inching up over the medium term or if there is a major global liquidity shock in the future. Among other things, the relatively high valuations of customer-facing start-ups (peripheral) are driven by increased participation from generalist VCs with access to cheap global liquidity on the back of the prevailing close-to-zero interest rate environment in the developed world. More of the peripheral AgriTech start-ups in later stages have received funding from generalist VCs. The small generalist VCs and the agri-focussed specialist VCs, being much smaller in size, initially chose to focus on the seed or pre-Series A stages in core AgriTech start-ups but, of late, they have also started to focus more on peripheral AgriTech and, in some instances, on conventional asset-heavy start-ups. In the era of cheap global liquidity and large-size deal-making by the large generalist VCs, the smaller VC funds (including the agri-focussed specialist VCs) have been able to display high benchmarked valuations (but not exits) in a few AgriTech start-ups.

AgriTech Investments and Sector Growth: 2013–2020

It has been estimated that of the 1,100 agri start-ups in India, around 600 are AgriTech start-ups. The initial years of 2008 to 2012 saw a very small amount of seed investment in the nascent AgriTech sector. The cumulative investments from 2012 to 2020 is around $888 million.

The AgriTech investments (not including angel investments) from CY 2013 to 2020 are presented in Exhibit 19.4.

The AgriTech investments in India became significant only after 2014. The pace of investments picked up from $18 million in 2015 to reach $363 million in 2020 at a compound annual growth rate (CAGR) of 83 per cent (2015–20). In 2020, the investments reached $363 million compared with $300 million in 2019, an increase of 21 per cent as more of the pre-Series A, Series A and later-stage start-ups were funded mostly by existing investors and a few new investors. Similarly, the number of investment transactions steadily increased from a

Exhibit 19.4: Indian AgriTech investments (2013–2020) – value and number of investments

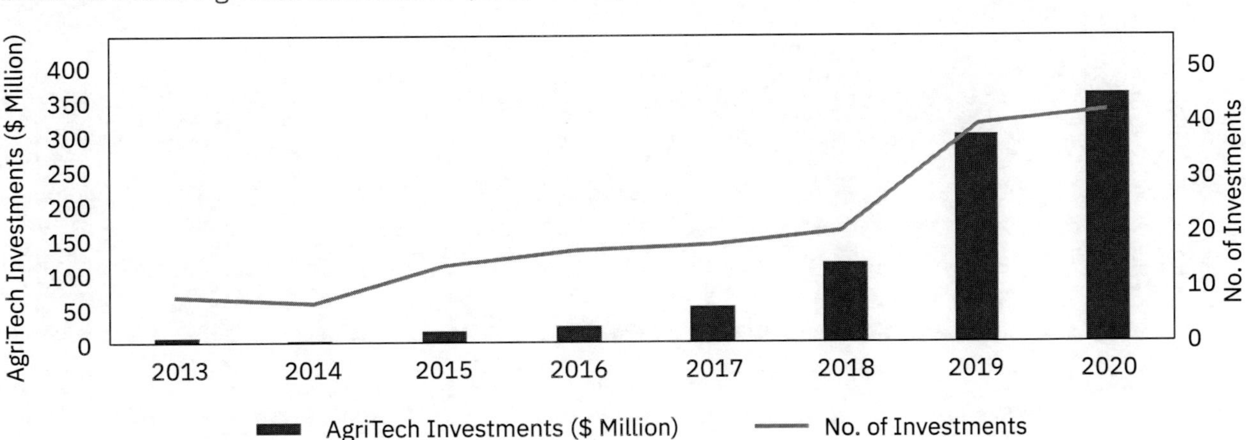

Source: NABVENTURES Research

small base to reach 20 in 2018. This almost doubled to 39 in 2019, marking the peak of the bull phase in AgriTech investing. Post the onset of COVID-19, the number of transactions declined briefly till August 2020 before resuming their upward movement during September–December 2020. In 2020, 42 deals (including two buyouts) were consummated, and this reflects the high resilience of the AgriTech sector during the COVID-19 pandemic.

Till 2015, seed, pre-Series A and small Series A rounds dominated and deal sizes were below $5 million (Exhibit 19.5). However, peripheral AgriTech start-ups like Farm Taaza (2016) and Agro star (2017) started the trend of larger rounds with a raise of $8 million and $7.2 million, respectively. The trend of large funding rounds for peripheral AgriTech start-ups gathered momentum in late 2018 and continues today. It is reported that Ninjacart raised close to $100 million, including a sliver of venture debt in April to June 2019, the first $100 million deal in AgriTech. Driven by the promise of hyper growth, large revenue potential (scale) and the potential to improve unit economics with scale, the peripheral AgriTech start-ups have seen higher and higher valuations with each round of capital raise. However, the core AgriTech start-ups have had less fanciful fund raises but have commanded high valuations even at smaller scales with extremely low revenues.

In 2020, while the deal values at seed stage fell marginally and the late-stage deal values barely increased, the pre-Series A and Series A deal values increased by 165 per cent.

In the initial years, more deals used to happen in the seed stages (Exhibit 19.6). The Series B and above deals (mid-to-late stage) picked up from 2016 and steadily increased till 2019 before witnessing a small dip in 2020. Pre-Series A and Series A deals were the mainstay during 2020 as these deals increased from 12 (2019) to 16 (2020).

Exhibit 19.7 paints a picture of sobering reality that only a few AgriTech start-ups have been getting new funding from VCs. Since 2012, close to 74 new AgriTech start-ups have been able to raise funds in seed and above stages from investors. The number of new AgriTech start-ups getting funded hovered in the range of 4 to 10 during 2013–2018 before moving to an all-time high of 16 in 2019. The number declined marginally to 15 in 2020. The increase in funding of new AgriTech start-ups in the last two years is because of the entry of new funds in the seed to pre-Series A stages. In FY 2020–21, NABVENTURES Fund, a new fund backed by NABARD, emerged as the largest investor (among agri FoodTech-focussed VCs) in terms of value of new deals in AgriTech.

It may be noted that certain AgriTech segments were not much sought after by the investors during 2020. These include agri equipment (including rentals), agri-biotechnology, real-time data dissemination, enterprise software and quality assessment. Since these are part of core AgriTech solutions, the start-ups in these areas may need to be incentivised through policy initiatives to design more robust and scalable business models with elements of peripheral AgriTech as well.

Exhibit 19.5: Round-wise AgriTech investments (2013–2020) in $ million

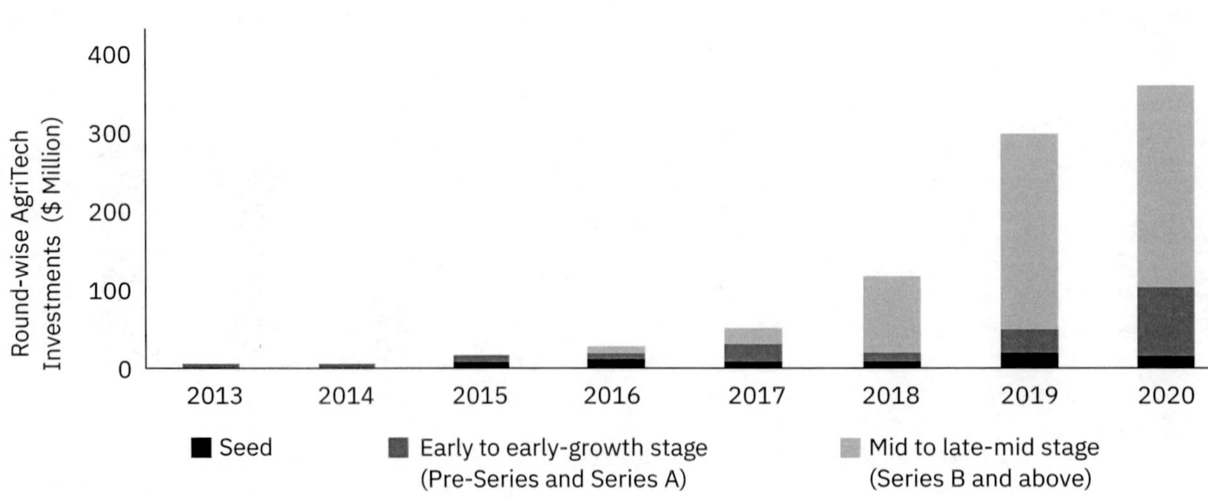

Source: NABVENTURES Research

Exhibit 19.6: Number of AgriTech deals (2013–Sep 2020)

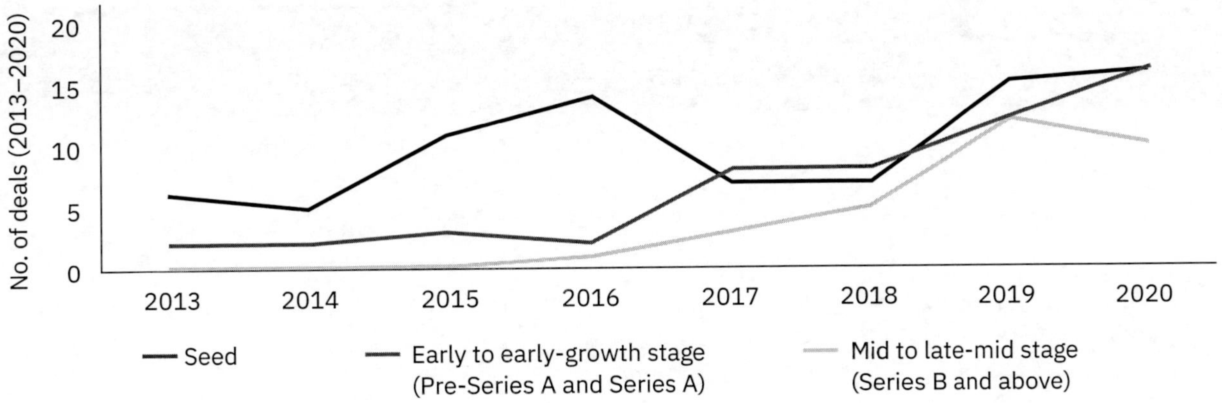

Source: VCCircle, Tracxn, NABVENTURES Research

Exhibit 19.7: Number of new AgriTech start-ups funded (2012–2020)

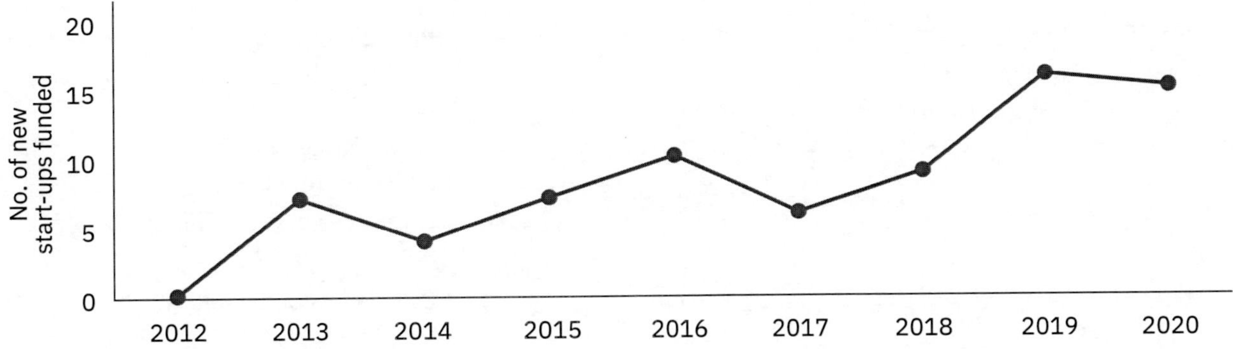

Source: NABVENTURES Research

Exit Prospects

It must be added that there have been very few successful mid-size exits, with practically no large-scale exits in the AgriTech start-up space as a lot of the AgriTech segments, barring customer-facing peripheral AgriTech, have yet to mature in terms of attaining significant scale. So far, the specialist VCs have had a dismal exit track record. It has been tough to find exits in AgriTech investing as the initial investments were mostly made in the seed stages and a large number of AgriTech start-ups have not been able to scale-up fast. The ones that have scaled up are more in the realm of peripheral AgriTech.

It is hoped that in the years to come, the sector will see increased consolidation through mergers among some of the large peripheral AgriTech start-ups, acquisition by strategic public and private companies and buyouts by large sovereign, buyout funds and agribusiness corporates. Some of the core AgriTech start-ups may be acquired if they are able to create strong IPs with a potential to serve a large customer base.

Value Creation and Business Models

AgriTech start-ups have emerged by successfully solving not only the pain points of Indian agriculture but also by solving the challenges in meeting the increased demand for proteins and processed food, food safety, consumer health and sustainable foods.

A few of the innovative solutions provided by the AgriTech start-ups are provided in Exhibit 19.8.

The AgriTech start-ups need to be supported not only with capital but also with guidance, scale-up support, management insights and talent retention. With increased usage of affordable technologies, the ability of start-ups to scale up profitably at a lower cost

Exhibit 19.8: Solutions provided by agri, food and rural start-ups

S. No.	Challenges	Sub-sector	Solutions	Nature of AgriTech solution
1.	Low yields, climate change	Agri-biotech	▪ Hybrid, gene-edited seeds ▪ Pest-resistant seeds ▪ Low water-consuming seeds ▪ Saline water–resistant seeds	Core
2.	Inefficient animal husbandry practices	ERP for agribusiness, dairy management Agri-biotech	▪ IoT-based animal monitoring ▪ Animal genetics	Core
3.	Soil degradation	Agri inputs	▪ Bio pesticides, bio fertilisers, biological plant growth regulators with no chemical residues	Core
4.	Rising input costs (including labour shortage)	Agri equipment Digital distribution of agri inputs	▪ Affordable equipment service providers with digital order booking capabilities ▪ Affordable digital farm monitoring services ▪ E-commerce platform for agri inputs	Core Peripheral
5.	High pressure on natural resources (water stress)	Precision agriculture	▪ Precision irrigation solutions ▪ Farming as a service ▪ Farm data analytics	Core
6.	Limited dissemination of real-time weather, farm-specific information ▪ Lack of hyper local weather conditions ▪ Lack of field-, village-specific yield forecasts ▪ Lack of local price information ▪ Lack of information about potential buyers of produce	Real-time data dissemination	▪ Affordable digital farm monitoring services (IoT enabled) ▪ Farm sensors, drones, satellite-based weather and field-specific information providers. Provide real-time actionable inputs based on AI-supported data analytics ▪ Digital market information services with predictive capabilities	Core
7.	Poor food quality on account of poor food safety practices ▪ Limited ability for food recalls	Quality assessment	▪ Digital traceability solutions using blockchain, RFID tags ▪ Instant spectrometers for monitoring food composition ▪ Digital image–based sorting solutions	Core

Continued . . .

S. No.	Challenges	Sub-sector	Solutions	Nature of AgriTech solution
8.	High food wastage due to low access to processing facilities, storage infrastructure	Agri equipment	▪ Affordable cold rooms ▪ Low-cost on-farm processing, sorting equipment	Core
9.	Poor, inadequate storage infrastructure	Storage and logistics	▪ Leased warehouses with IoT-based monitoring	Peripheral
10.	Weak market linkages including linkages to global value chains	Digital distribution of agri produce	▪ Tech-based farm produce aggregators with B2B, B2C distribution capabilities	Peripheral
11.	Limited access to credit	Agri, rural FinTech	▪ Digital lenders ▪ Farmer credit scoring solutions ▪ Digital 'ground-truthing' solutions on behalf of lenders ▪ Digital financial inclusion platforms for rural areas	Peripheral

Source: Author

as compared to the conventional players has increased tremendously.

Most of the core and peripheral AgriTech start-ups have not only created a huge impact on farmers' incomes by cutting down on middlemen but they have also made agriculture sustainable. A few of the AgriTech start-ups and their business models are presented in Exhibits 19.9 (a) and (b).

Exhibit 19.9 (a): AgriTech business models

Start-ups		What they do
Jai Kisan	Jai Kisan	Agri, rural FinTech
Satyukt	Satyukt	Satellite data analysis for agriculture
Krishitantra	KRISHITANTRA	Soil tech, rapid soil testing
Dehaat & Unnati	DeHaat | unnati	Tech-enabled agri input and output selling platforms with agronomy and credit services
Agnext, Intellolabs, Qzense	AGNEXT | INTELLO LABS | qZense	Digital rapid quality assessment of agri produce
FreshToHome, Licious, Tender Cuts	Fresh to Home | Licious | TENDER CUTS	M-commerce-based D2C ordering and delivery solutions for seafood, meat, chicken and poultry products
Ninjacart and Waycool	ninjacart | waycool	E-commerce, marketplace for agri produce

Exhibit 19.9 (b): AgriTech business models, a few examples

	Name	Solution	Business model
1.	Jai Kisan	Agri, rural FinTech	Jai Kisan is the category leading agri FinTech player with focus on equipment finance, invoice discounting and input finance. It has a digital bookkeeping ledger app for capturing transactions among stakeholders in the ecosystem.
2.	Satyukt	Satellite data analysis for agriculture	The only satellite data analytics start-up in India for measuring root zone soil moisture data at a depth of 1 metre in near-real-time, water stress measurement and other parameters.
3.	Krishitantra	Soil tech, rapid soil testing	Measures up to 15 parameters (macronutrients, micronutrients, microbial matter, etc.) in soil in 30 minutes using an automated device. Soil health data collected is provided to precision agriculture data companies.
4.	Dehaat, Unnati	Tech-enabled agri input and output selling platforms with agronomy and credit services	These start-ups ensure assured supply of quality inputs and agronomy services at affordable prices to farmers and help in providing market linkage for agri produce.
5.	Agnext, Intellolabs, Qzense	Digital rapid quality assessment of agri produce	The start-ups provide rapid quality assessment solutions using technology.
6.	FreshToHome, Licious, Tender Cuts	M-commerce or omnichannel-based D2C brands for seafood, meat, chicken	The start-ups focus on m-commerce or omnichannel-based D2C ordering and delivery solutions for seafood, meat, chicken and poultry products.
7.	Ninjacart, Waycool	E-commerce, marketplace for agri produce	The start-ups focus on direct sourcing of F&V from farmers and sell to B2B customers.

Source: Author

AgriTech Investments by VCs: Global Scenario

Global AgriTech investments by VCs have grown at an impressive CAGR of over 50 per cent per annum since 2010.[4] The aggregate deal value has jumped 5x since 2015. In the first nine months of 2020, $3.07 billion worth of AgriTech deals were consummated, even though the overall number of deals declined. It is estimated that global AgriTech deals by VCs reached $3.8 billion in CY 2020 (Exhibit 19.10).

Late-stage deals have started to dominate since 2012 and this reflects the maturity of AgriTech start-ups. In 2020, more than $3 billion of deals of the estimated total of $3.8 billion are estimated to have happened in the later stage. The median pre-money valuations across early- and later-stage rounds more than doubled between 2018 and 2019 and this queered the investment pitch for first-time specialist VCs in the sector, as the investments by first-time VCs declined in 2019.

Globally, more deals have happened in areas seeking efficiency in production (indoor agriculture), crop protection, inputs, sensors, quality and sustainability.

Exhibit 19.10: Global AgriTech investments by VCs ($ billion) – value and number of investments

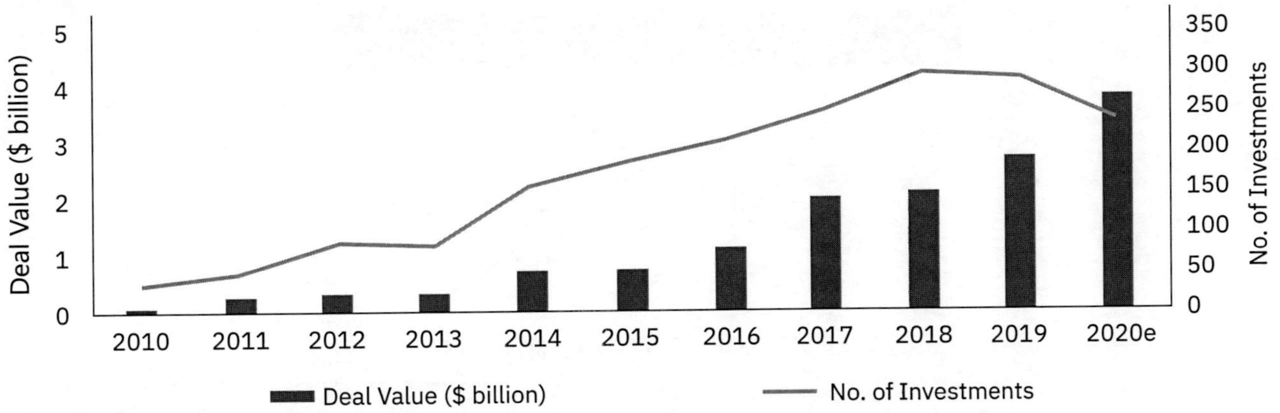

Source: Pitchbook

AgriTech Ecosystem Enablers

Agriculture is a state subject. Over the years, the Government of India (GOI) has been progressively reforming the sector. Various government bodies (NITI Aayog) and agri institutions such as NABARD have been supportive of the sector.

The entire agri-food ecosystem has been supported by the GOI and various state governments (Exhibit 19.11). The important AgriTech clusters are in Bengaluru, National Capital Region (NCR) and Pune.

The important elements of the AgriTech ecosystem are:

a) *Policymaking bodies*: The Ministry of Agriculture and Farmers' Welfare has been progressively reforming the agriculture sector in India and has been supportive of AgriTech start-ups. The AgriTech start-ups kept the supply chains active during the pandemic-induced lockdown. In a major reform promoting disintermediation in the sale of agri produce, the farmers have been allowed to sell their produce, from any place, although the Supreme Court has kept the new farm laws on hold for the moment. Earlier, the farmers had to depend on the APMC (Agricultural Produce Market Committee) markets and mandis to sell their produce and this practice had spawned multiple non–value-adding intermediaries and distorted the price discovery mechanism, which was reducing the farmers' income. Recently, the RBI included loans up to ₹500 million to agri start-ups as part of priority sector lending.[5] NABARD provides financial support to FPOs (Farmer Produce Organizations), agri lending institutions and provides grants as well to multiple agri start-ups. It has set up and supported a few incubation centres as well.

b) *R&D institutions*: The application of organised research and development (R&D) in agriculture is now more than a century old in India. It began with the strengthening of agricultural departments in the union and state governments, and the subsequent establishment of agricultural colleges in 1905 and of the Indian Council of Agricultural Research (ICAR) in 1929.[6] Since then, agricultural research has evolved from a few isolated government organisations to serve imperial interests into a well-coordinated and responsive system under ICAR. These include Indian Agricultural Research Institute, agri universities (Tamil Nadu Agricultural University, Pusa Agriculture University), and so on.

c) *Incubators, Accelerators*: The leading incubators include those run by agricultural universities, private sector (Indigram Labs) and public sector (Pusa Krishi Incubator).

d) *Venture funds*: Apart from generalist VC funds like Sequoia and Accel Partners, there are sector-specialist funds like NABVENTURES Fund and Omnivore Partners. In addition, the Indian AgriTech start-ups have been ably supported by impact funds like Gates Foundation, Omidyar Network and various family offices and angel networks.

e) *Lenders*: The generalist venture debt funds like Trifecta and Innoven have been supportive of the large AgriTech start-ups. NABKISAN, a NABARD-promoted non-banking financial company (NBFC), specialises

Exhibit 19.11: Agriculture ecosystem enablers

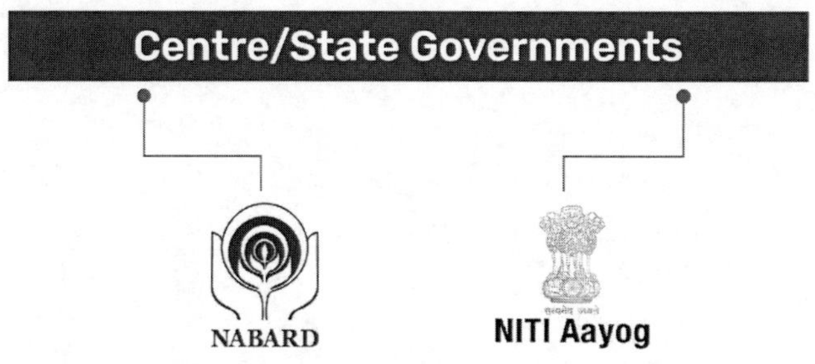

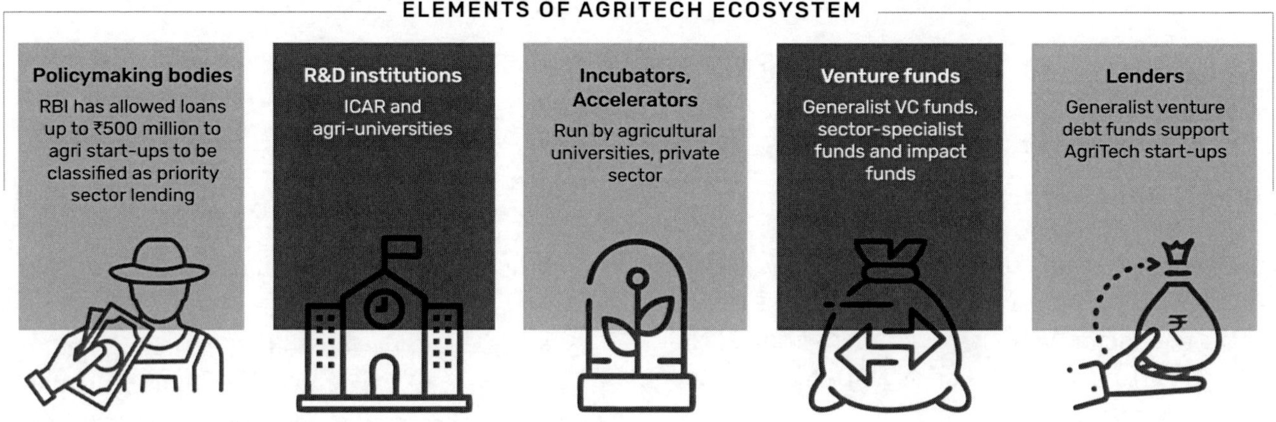

in lending to farmer producer organisations (FPOs), which in turn are clients of AgriTech start-ups.

However, despite the support and funding provided to AgriTech start-ups, it is estimated that they have been able to impact the lives of only 10 per cent of the farming population. There are no funders for frugal, social innovations, which impact the livelihoods of a large number of farmers. Only a few of these innovators have been able to tap the grants offered by public sector agencies (Department of Science and Technology (DST), Biotechnology Industry Research Assistance Council (BIRAC)).

Desired Policy Interventions

In India, peripheral AgriTech start-ups (e-commerce in agri produce) have raised the lion's share of VC funding. In order to tackle the more pressing problems of water stress, low yields, produce wastage and food safety, core AgriTech start-ups need to be supported as well. Less money should be spent on creation of incubation centre infrastructure and more on providing actual monetary and grant support to agri FoodTech start-ups.

Further, the domestic limited partnership (LP) ecosystem for AgriTech start-ups is limited to a handful of public sector financial institutions (FIs), banks like SIDBI Fund of Funds, NABARD, LIC and a few public sector banks. This small pool of LPs and contributors is not adequate to propel and promote a larger number of AgriTech start-ups needed in the core AgriTech areas. The possibility of channelising corporate funds through a centralised fund-of-funds for sectors of national importance, including core AgriTech, should be examined. Further, large FIs and banks should be allowed to contribute more than the current cap of 10 per cent of the fund's corpus. This cap may be revised to 25 per cent and the RBI as part of its review of prudential norms should consider revising the risk weights (currently at 150 per cent of the total exposure) for such contributions. The high risk weights make alternative investment fund (AIF) investments less attractive to bank treasuries. In order to balance the interests of both the government and the private sector, the government pools (fund-of-funds, PSU bank, FI treasury allocations to AIFs) should have the option to invest in the equity share capital of asset management companies and fund management entities. This is the prevalent practice in

China, where apart from making capital contributions, the fund-of-funds also takes equity stakes in fund management companies.

Challenges and The Way Forward

Challenges

The advent of new-age technologies has a huge potential to transform Indian agriculture in a big way. The AgriTech start-ups can play a major role in harnessing these new-age technologies to enhance farmers' incomes and improve the livelihoods of almost half of the Indian population.

There are more than 20 (out of 74) VC-backed AgriTech start-ups that have either shut down or are in a zombie mode. A large number of AgriTech start-ups fail or wither away in different stages of their growth; the reasons for their failure are listed in Exhibit 19.12.

India is a peculiar AgriTech market with a preponderance of 140+ million farmers of whom more than 80 per cent are smallholder farmers having small landholdings and are involved in subsistence agriculture.[7] The paying capacity of these farmers for various AgriTech services is on the lower side and, therefore, many of the start-ups in the first (except basic agri inputs) to middle part of the agriculture value chain ecosystem find it difficult to scale up rapidly. On the other hand, most VCs including the so-called 'impact' VCs, prefer rapidly scalable models. Due to the low paying capacity of farmers, AgriTech start-ups invariably pursue B2B models, which have their own challenges of low margins, working capital, etc.

Most of the AgriTech start-ups find it difficult to reach out to farmers who are geographically dispersed throughout India. This increases the customer acquisition cost significantly. AgriTech start-ups in different stages of growth require appropriate interventions for their survival and growth; the possible interventions in different stages are listed in Exhibit 19.13.

The Way Forward

Growth potential: AgriTech start-ups and technologies have the potential to transform Indian agriculture in a big way by solving some of the persistent problems. Both global and Indian AgriTech investments are on a major upswing. The pace of Indian AgriTech investments

Exhibit 19.12: Reasons for failure of AgriTech start-ups

S. No.	Stage	Reason
1.	Stage-agnostic reasons	▪ Lack of visionary founders and teams around them ▪ Poor understanding of nuances and economics of the specific agritech business model
2.	Idea, incubation, seed stage	▪ Poor product–market fit ▪ Chasing a narrow, addressable market ▪ Pursuit of 'me-too' models that lack differentiation ▪ Lack of proper guidance and mentorship ▪ Lack of funding from investors (angels, seed VCs)
3.	Series A stage	▪ Lack of deep innovation capabilities in an environment of rapid tech obsolescence ▪ Adverse per unit economics made worse by high customer acquisition costs ▪ Unsustainable burn rates, long path to profitability ▪ Lack of VC interest for next round ▪ Lack of robust handholding support by VC funds
4.	Post-Series A stage	▪ Ascent of a better model from competitor(s) ▪ Lack of venture debt, working capital

Source: Author

Exhibit 19.13: Recommendations for better outcomes in AgriTech start-ups

S. No.	Stage	Interventions for enabling growth
1.	Stage-agnostic	▪ Asset-light incubation, acceleration support for more agritech start-ups with proper monitoring of progress made by start-ups in terms of funds raised from third parties for funding next-stage growth within 6 months of graduation from incubation, acceleration centres ▪ Incubation, acceleration centres should be run by a person or team having start-up investing, entrepreneurial experience
2.	Idea, incubation, seed stage	▪ Better agritech-specific advisory from mentors ▪ Involvement of agritech mentors from other countries (USA, Israel, Netherlands) ▪ More exposure to investors ("what investors want") or ability to co-create solutions along with investors ▪ Creation of more seed funds with agritech as one of the core focus areas ▪ Creation of new funding vehicles and SPVs (rather than profit-oriented, so-called 'impact' VC funds which pursue collection of management fees, profit share and have a limited holding period of 4–5 years) for promoting true impact investments in agriculture ▪ Convertible grants[8] for deep tech agri start-ups
3.	Series A stage	▪ Raise funds from VCs who provide more than capital in the form of farmer–FPO connections, customer introductions, debt raising support (NABVENTURES Fund) ▪ Increased domestic institutional LP support for agritech funds along with option to buy stakes in the fund management companies ▪ The core agritech start-ups may be better off by partnering with peripheral agritech start-ups in order to provide integrated, embedded solutions
4.	Post-Series A stage	▪ Increased availability of working capital or venture debt

Source: Author

picked up from $18 million in 2015 to reach $363 million in 2020 at a CAGR of 83 per cent. Global AgriTech investments have grown at an impressive CAGR of 50 per cent since 2010.

Focus on core AgriTech: Core AgriTech start-ups are being overlooked by investors who prefer peripheral start-ups on account of better scalability. Core AgriTech start-ups need to create horizontal platform–based solutions rather than standalone solutions in order to improve their scalability. Towards, this end, the core AgriTech start-ups may be better off by partnering with peripheral AgriTech players in order to provide integrated or embedded solutions. Government support in the form of convertible grants and pilot programmes in multiple states is necessary for core AgriTech start-ups

Enabling enhanced access to capital: The number of AgriTech start-ups supported by funds continues to be low. More pre-seed, seed-stage funds, impact investment SPVs (not 'impact' VCs) and grants need to be made available for AgriTech start-ups in their formative years. Deepening of the domestic fund-of-funds pool and creation of more domestic LPs is required. Large FIs and banks should be allowed to contribute more than the current cap of 10 per cent of the fund's corpus. This cap may be revised to 25 per cent and the RBI as part of its review of prudential norms should consider revising the risk weights (currently at 150 per cent of the total exposure) for such contributions. Banks and FIs need to devise working capital support facilities for peripheral AgriTech start-ups.

Endnotes

[1]UN. 2020. The World Population Prospects 2019: Highlights, ***UN Department of Economic and Social Affairs***, Retrieved on December 23, 2020 from https://population.un.org/wpp/

[2]Periodic Labour Force Survey (PLFS) – ***Annual Report (July 2018 – June 2019)***.

[3]NABVENTURES Limited is the Investment Manager for NABVENTURES FUND, a fund focussed on AgriTech, FoodTech, agri rural FinTech, rural HealthTech and rural EdTech.

[4]www.pitchbook.com

[5]RBI Master Directions FIDD.CO.Plan.BC.5/04.09.01/2020-21 dated September 4, 2020.

[6]Pal, S. 2017. ***Agricultural R&D Policy in India***. ICAR-National Institute of Agricultural Economics and Policy Research.

[7]OECD, I. 2018. ***Agricultural policies in India***.

[8]Convertible grants convert to equity if the AgriTech start-up reaches a revenue or operational milestone. Necessary changes need to be made in the Negotiable Instruments Act to include convertible grants.

IN BRIEF

- **Strategic significance:** EdTech, with a market size of $2.8 billion in October 2020 and projected to grow to $10.4 billion by 2025, is strategically significant to the Indian economy, not only in terms of revenue and employment generated, but also in terms of nation building – making quality education and training available, accessible and affordable to both urban and rural populations. Indian EdTech has the potential to tap the global EdTech market, owing to its low-cost, high-talent ecosystem in content, delivery and technology.
- **Growth:** The entry of entrepreneurs with application of technology has resulted in the opening up and flow of global investments into the private sector, comprising supplementary education and private universities and colleges. With 250 million school-going children and 100 million working professionals, it is estimated that the number of paying users of EdTech will rise to 37 million by 2025.
- **Direction:** The New Education Policy (NEP) needs to focus on revolutionising the educational infrastructure by taking education online, where the same or better quality can be provided more effectively. The pandemic, which brought online learning to the forefront, making it on par with conventional learning for certain segments, has opened up the possibilities to different stakeholders more than ever before.

20

Indian EdTech: Revolutionising Learning

Arjun Mohan

Mohan, A. 2021. "Indian EdTech: Revolutionising Learning". In *Shifting Orbits: Decoding the Trajectory of the Indian Start-up Ecosystem*, edited by Thillai Rajan A, Srivardhini K Jha, Joffi Thomas and Rohan Chinchwadkar, 256–268. Hyderabad: Universities Press (India) Private Limited.

Overview

Education in India is undergoing a radical transformation leveraging digital technology. This has led to the emergence of a new business sector called EdTech, with a market size of $2.8 billion in October 2020.[1] Broadly, EdTech in India can be divided into the K12, test prep, higher education and institutional digitisation segments (Exhibit 20.1).

1. *K12*: Companies offering supplementary learning solutions to students in schools. This, the largest sector by revenue in EdTech, has BYJU'S (FY 2020 ₹2800 crores) leading the pack. The companies in this sector directly compete with tuition teachers and teach in two modes: synchronous or live mode and asynchronous or video mode.
2. *Test prep*: The coaching classes that train students for competitive exams like JEE, UPSC and NEET are slowly metamorphosing with the advent of technology. Though a very large market, EdTech takeover has been slow considering the high stakes of these exams. Models like live and hybrid are becoming popular in this sector, as against the asynchronous model. Aakash Institute, Allen Academy and Unacademy are the major players.
3. *Higher education*: The newest of the sectors to be revolutionised by technology. Due to the nature of the learner, this is also the sector where online learning is finding a lot of resonance by delivering outcomes, both from an individual's and from an organisation's

Exhibit 20.1: Pie chart of EdTech market (estimated share of each segment)

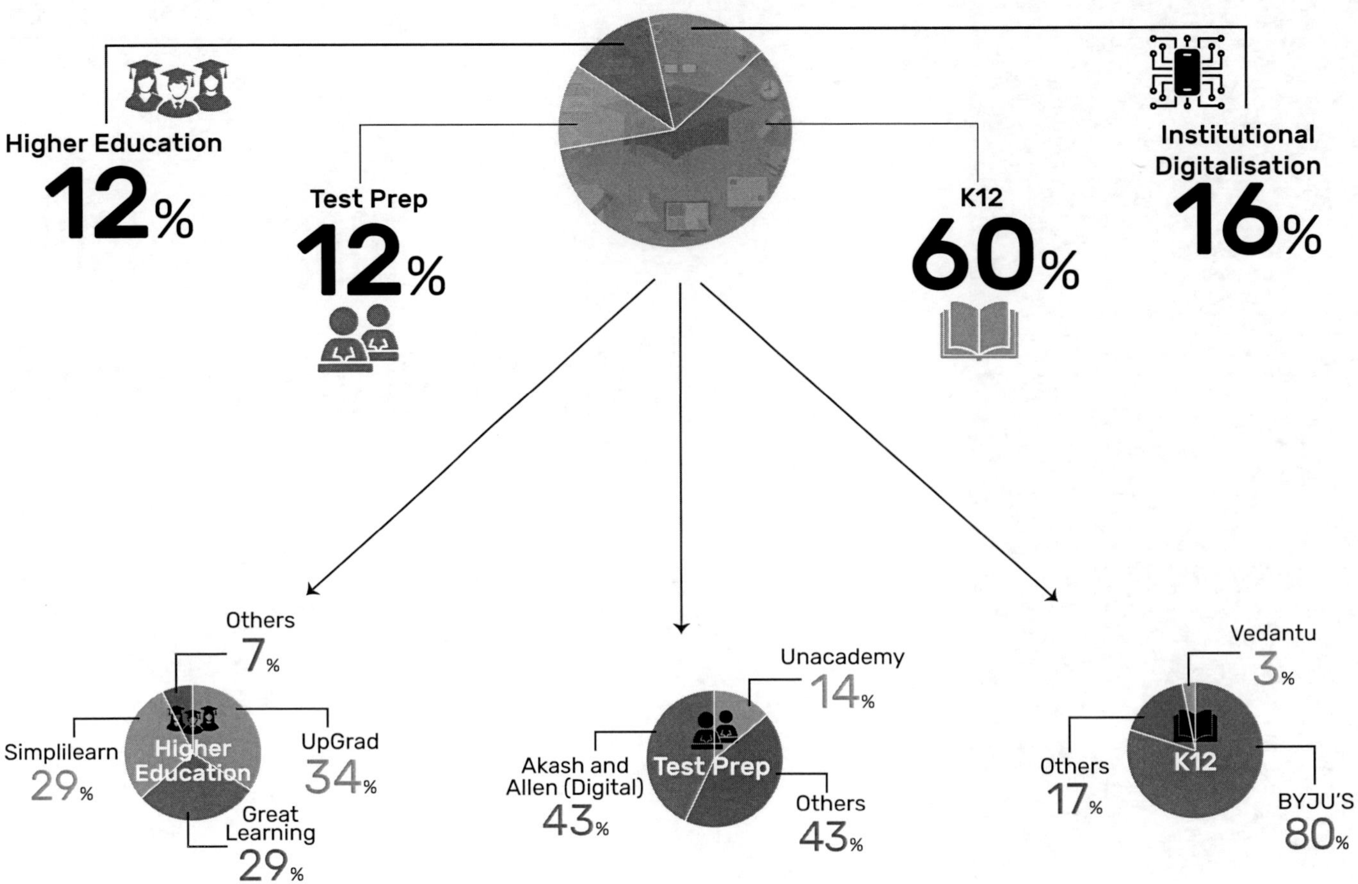

Source: Author

perspective. However, the traction is seen more for individuals, and hence, the segment is growing in the B2C mode. COVID-19 and the regulatory changes that occurred as part of the New Education Policy 2020 has helped propel this sector. Companies are focussed on providing online degrees, diplomas and certification courses to working professionals and students from some of the most aspirational university brands. Companies in this sector deliver value in two modes: while Udemy and Coursera deliver learning as massive open online course (MOOC) platforms, companies like upGrad deliver accreditation (online degrees) from top universities alongside services like mentoring and career support. Exhibit 20.2 displays the different models of EdTech start-ups in the higher education space.

Full-stack models (leading players such as upGrad and Simplilearn) with end-to-end delivery attract higher willingness to pay among customers. Although aggregators have the advantage of scale, with better control on outcomes and customer experience, full-stack players have an edge on customer stickiness and satisfaction. In the longer term, full-stack models serving both lifelong learning and higher education are best positioned to flourish.

4. *Institutional digitalisation*: The oldest EdTech sector focusses on digitalising schools, colleges and universities. What was largely a devices business is slowly transforming itself into an end-to-end SaaS (Software as a Service) business, complete with hardware, software and content. Next Education, Tata Interactive Systems and Extramarks are some players in the segment.

The EdTech market is expected to grow to $10.4 billion by 2025[3] (Exhibit 20.3). Anticipating this huge growth, investors pumped in $1.4 billion in the sector in 2020. With 250 million school-going children and 100 million working professionals, the industry estimates that the number of paying users in EdTech in India will

Exhibit 20.2: Models in online higher education

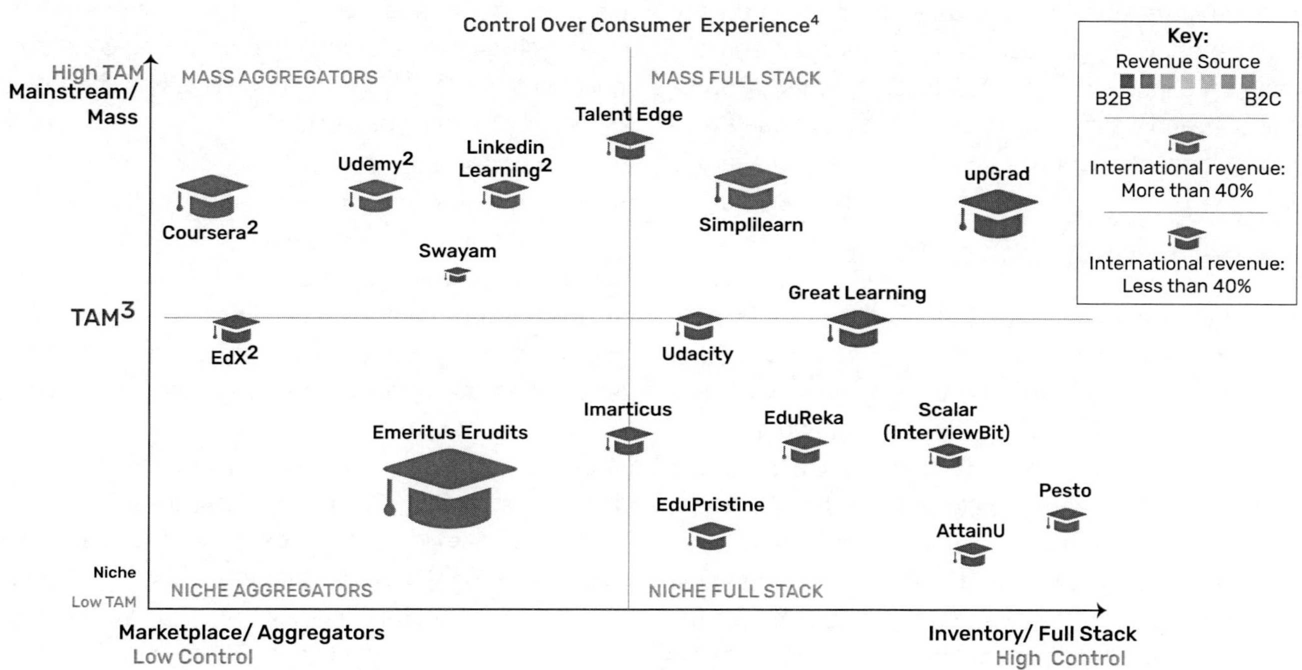

Note:
1. Selected companies have been included to substantiate the business models; basis RedSeer analysis.
2. For international players such as Coursera, Udemy, LinkedIn Learning, and EdX, only Indian revenues are considered while plotting their relative size on the chart.
3. Total addressable opportunity is determined by the type of offerings, that is, higher education and lifelong learning courses, types of subject focus and corresponding student base for the same in the markets where the EdTech player is present.
4. Involvement across the customer journey includes the extent of the platforms' control over content development, delivery, customer experience, assistance and the ability to influence outcomes.

Source: Redseer Report 2020[2]

Exhibit 20.3: Projected growth of EdTech market over years

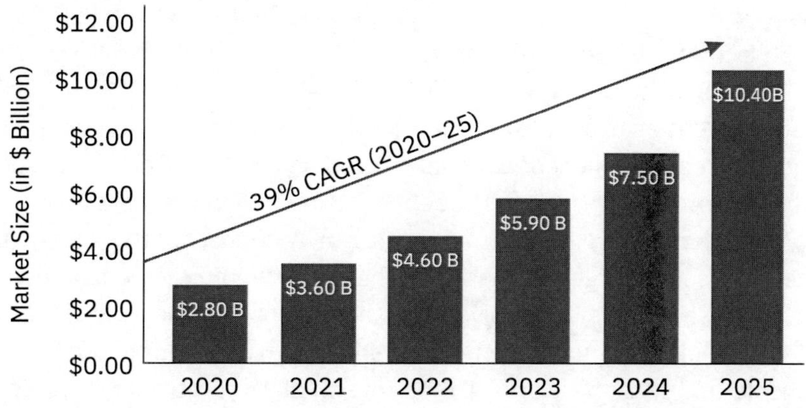

Source: Inc42Plus
(Note: The market size is calculated as the number of users' average ticket size of payment. Both the numbers are calculated using KPMG calculations for the same as the base).

rise to 37 million by 2025, thus becoming an important segment in the economy not only in terms of revenue and employment generated but also in terms of nation-building, making quality education and training available, accessible and affordable to both the urban and rural populations.

The chapter is organised into three sections. The emergence, evolution and growth of the EdTech sector is discussed in the first section. The role of both the public sector and the private sector in making quality education accessible and affordable to urban and rural populations leveraging technology is addressed in the second section. The recent developments, trends, challenges and way forward for the sector are dealt with in the concluding section.

Emergence of EdTech in India

Education in India has historically been state-controlled and kept out of commerce. Thanks to the law that prevented profit-making in education, the sector has been slow in growth and lacked competition. Over time, the quality deteriorated. At the same time, the high disparity between supply and demand for seats in good higher education universities resulted in these institutions conducting entrance examinations that were hard to crack. This led to the perception that the school system lacked the capability to make students smart. This belief was especially prevalent among the middle classes, which saw quality education as the only way to give their children a chance of the success that they themselves could not achieve. This resulted in the growth of a supplementary education system, with coaching centres training students for various competitive examinations, tuitions centres as add-ons to school learning and, most recently, learning apps that help them learn on the go.

The emergence of EdTech in the supplementary education segment in India is a classic example of growth propelled by market forces as against B2B, that is, catering to schools and colleges and other educational institutions where there is no motivation to invest due to lack of competition. When compared globally, this is the exact opposite of how EdTech emerged in markets like the US, where trust in the school system is pivotal. Parents in the US intuitively believe that they pay taxes to ensure quality in schools and it is the work of the government to do the same. This, along with abundant jobs, resulted in them not looking past schools. Hence, EdTech in the US emerged as a B2B business rather than a B2C business. Schools in the US, unlike in India, have huge budgets to spend on curriculum and delivery quality, and hence, businesses such as Google, Apple, Microsoft and, more recently, start-ups such as Clever and Blackboard have built huge businesses in the B2B space. Competition seems to be picking up between schools for students, and hence, adoption of EdTech tools in schools and educational institutions point to a trend showing the emergence of strong B2B play in India. Similarly, a B2C trend is slowly taking shape in the US through learning centres.

Though the approach of the government towards this sector has given rise to a B2C situation in India, certain government interventions and policies have helped the growth of some segments too. The advent of computerisation pushed higher education institutes to invest in computers and smart classrooms, which helped grow the hardware business and create companies like HCL. In recent years, the same push to use the latest hardware has gone into the school systems too. Another change that helped in the growth of EdTech is the decision to take government examinations like Bank PO online. This forced supplementary coaching institutes that were training for these exams to move online in a big way.

Evolution and Growth of the EdTech Sector

The application of digital technologies in EdTech started with Educomp in 1994[4] (Exhibit 20.4). The approach was B2B and Educomp went about installing its smart classroom solution in multiple schools. To accelerate the adoption of the technology by a moribund school network, Educomp resorted to large-scale financing, a move which went on to become their Achilles heel.

The next wave began with TutorVista in 2005, which took the B2C route and focussed on building a business by using Indian teachers to service the English-speaking North American and Western European markets. The business went on to become very successful and used service cost arbitrage to drive margins. Eventually, the business was sold to Pearson for ₹1,000 crores. It eventually crumbled under Pearson and was sold to BYJU'S in 2017.

The initial success of the TutorVista model and the growth in personal computing motivated entrepreneurs to foray into educational solutions for the Indian market. Edurite from TutorVista and Meritnation in 2009 launched video-based learning solutions for the Indian market. The videos were made in Flash and were largely a better version of the textbooks. The solutions were sold to students directly as supplementary products and

Exhibit 20.4: Evolution of the EdTech sector

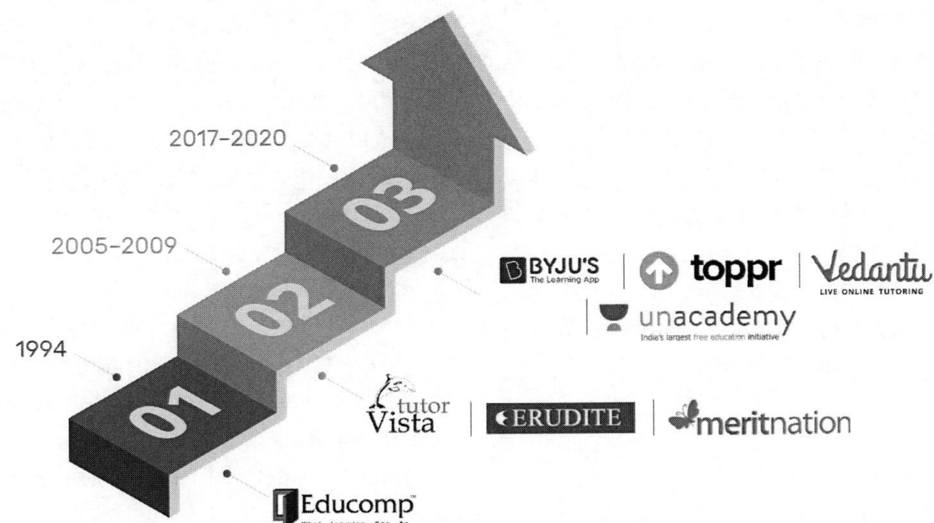

Source: Inc42, 2020

used the ingrained belief of the Indian middle class that schools lack the quality to build a business.

The smartphone revolution and the advent of apps for everything led to the next phase of Indian EdTech, wherein companies such as BYJU'S, Toppr, Vedantu and Unacademy launched hi-tech products that truly revolutionised the sector. Rather than giving a few videos, the focus now was on comprehensive learning with videos, live sessions, tests, doubt clearing, mentoring, etc. Of these, BYJU'S emerged as the winner with a disproportionate focus on sales and marketing, building a brand that became synonymous with online learning. The company grew from ₹600 million in revenue in FY 2015 to ₹2.8 billion in FY 2020 and owns approximately 85 per cent of the online K12 learning market.

The sector is currently entering a new phase, with online supplementary learning slowly integrating with offline supplementary players in test prep and formal education. Exhibits 20.5 and 20.6 illustrate the top

Exhibit 20.5: Prominent start-ups, segment, valuation and capital raised

Start-up	Segment	Valuation (in $ M)	Money raised (in $ M)
Think and Learn Pvt Ltd (BYJU'S)	K12	12000	2300
Unacademy	Test prep	2000	350
Vedantu	K12 and Test prep	800	200
Toppr	K12	150	100
upGrad	Higher Ed	NA	0
Simplilearn	Higher Ed	85	32
Eruditus	Higher Ed	700	200
Next Education	Platform (SAAS)	NA	0
Extramarks	Platform (Hardware)	NA	0
HCL	Platform (Hardware)	NA	–

Source: Inc42 Media Report Edtech 2020[5]

start-ups in EdTech, their valuation, the money they have raised and investments over five years.

These start-ups have evolved with various technological developments from 2G to 4G, broadband penetration, emergence of tablets, cheaper smart TVs, etc., innovating their offerings to give the best to the student population. Their survival and growth are a testimony to these innovations.

Exhibit 20.7 displays the top EdTech start-ups and their revenues and earnings before interest, taxes, depreciation and amortisation (EBITDA).

Business Models

Since education is a high-involvement purchase and these companies are not only selling their products but also selling the idea of learning online, all of them have resorted to a freemium model, where free users are acquired through digital or brand campaigns and subsequently converted to paid users through an assisted selling process.

The nature of this model makes it expensive to run, and hence, from day one, only companies which sold high ARPU (average revenue per user) have survived in the market. The majority of the cost goes into sales and marketing and the sustainability of the business is solely based on optimisation of sales and marketing over a period of time.

Most of the prospects or leads were generated online or digitally based on the logic that a consumer who accepts ideas online can be sold the concept of learning online. The idea was pioneered by TutorVista when it revolutionised SEO (search engine optimisation)-based lead generation by capturing the majority of K12 learning keywords on Google. The model worked well due to the right mix of organic and paid leads, plus the fact that they were always selling to the high-ARPU American markets. However, when the focus changed to India, these marketing models were ineffective, and hence, companies resorted to lead generation through mass channels, especially TV. The high spends on TV helped them build their brand, which in turn got them leads at lower cost. These large brand-building spends also helped grow the idea of learning online, building some of the largest brands in EdTech today. The advantages and disadvantages of some popular revenue models are displayed in Exhibit 20.8.

Global EdTech Industry: Opportunities for Indian Ventures

As mentioned earlier, EdTech in India emerged as a B2C market due to the large supplementary education market

Exhibit 20.6 : Total VC* investments in EdTech start-ups

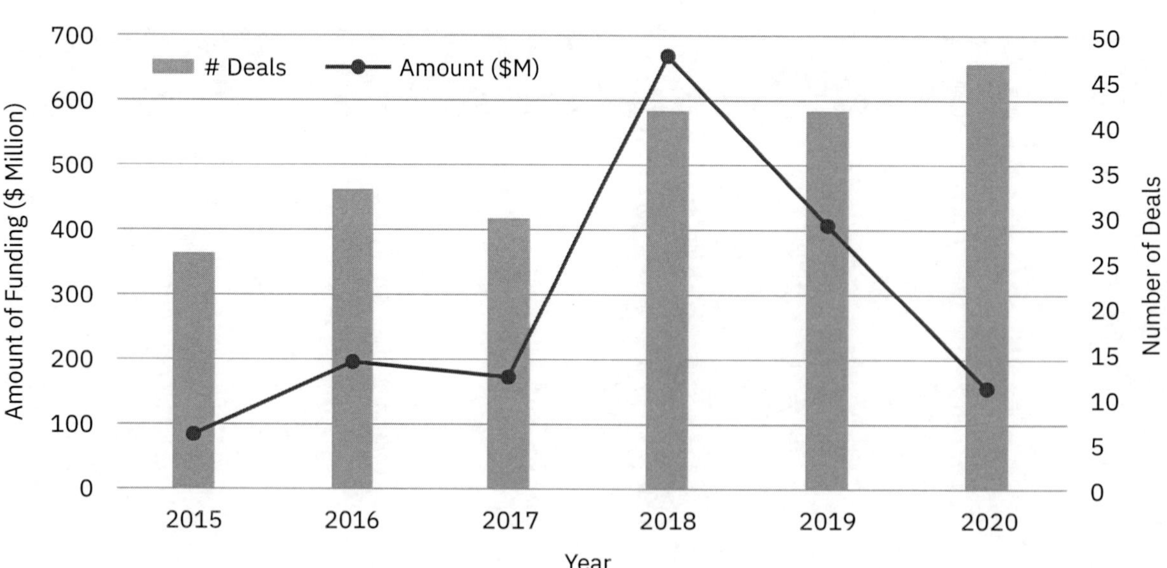

Source: Venture Intelligence[6]

*VC is defined as investments in companies less than 10 years old

Exhibit 20.7: Revenues for selected EdTech start-ups

SNo	Start-up	Total revenue (in $ M)	
		FY 2018	FY 2019
1	BYJU'S	70.6	193.3
2	Simplilearn	13.9	18.3
3	E1 Education initiatives	7.7	9.9
4	Toppr	3.7	8.7
5	Edureka	5.9	7.6
6	Collegeduniya	4.9	7.0
7	Imarctius Learning	5	6.8
8	Meritnation	4.7	5.1
9	I Nurture Education Solutions	3.1	4.3
10	Flintobox	2.5	4.0
11	CDUpristine	4.6	3.9
12	Unacademy	0.75	3.2
13	CollegeDekho	1.4	2.9
14	Jigsaw Academy	2.7	2.6
15	Avanti	1.3	2.5
16	Smartivity	1.4	2.5
17	Cuemath	1.1	2.3
18	Embibe	0.75	2.2
19	Onlinetyari	0.75	2.2
20	Testbook.com	1.1	2.0

Source: Registrar of companies, GoI[7]

that existed. Tuitions and coaching were the industry that technology revolutionised followed by skilling, while schools kept away from adoption. With COVID-19 forcing a lockdown, things are changing, with large-scale investment going towards smart classrooms and remote learning. However, time will tell if the teachers will adapt to these changes and if these transformations will stand the test of time.

At the same time, US and European EdTech developed in a completely different direction. The lack of supplementary markets and the complete dependence on schools for academics ensured that no B2C market developed, while a chunk of the technology investments went to schools. The focus has mostly been in deploying hardware to provide devices and internet access to every student. The Obama years saw a lot of investment in technology in classrooms, thus opening up huge opportunities to original equipment manufacture (OEM). Google, with its Chromebook and Google Classroom suite of products, was the biggest beneficiary of this move. Chromebooks revolutionised the school education system in the US and today every student in secondary school and above has access to a laptop that is used to carry out classwork and homework. US EdTech today is largely a school-focussed B2B business with an ecosystem of players creating apps and content. A small B2C market also exists as a replacement for learning centres, which are very popular in cities with large immigrant populations. EdTech is driving big changes in the US too. Big publications are struggling to adapt to the new-age digital era and losing revenue in a big way. College enrollments are also seeing a big dip, especially due to the huge cost involved in college education. Companies like Lambda School and 2U are trying to bring in an EdTech twist to the degree space, though not much has happened so far.

In China, EdTech followed a live model to grow, with some of the largest players in offline B2C business moving to online. Especially after COVID-19, EdTech players have captured a large market share, with 400 million+ students going online[9] (the growth of EdTech happened with offline players like TAL Education creating an online version of their services). Another pathway has been the craze for English learning, which helped create apps like VIPKid that focussed on English proficiency development. However, currently the market is quite developed, with multiple offerings of live and video learning, tech-enabled question banks, etc. Yuanfudao is the major player. All the big players utilise the craze for entrance examinations, which is big in China.

From a global perspective, India is currently very well placed to take advantage of the global EdTech phenomenon. India has a large pool of highly trained teachers available at low cost, technology manpower plus an equity as a country that is good in English, Mathematics and Coding. This has helped Indian EdTech go global and grow quickly in Western markets. This is seen especially with skill development. Quite a few higher education online players are leveraging this opportunity by targeting students across the globe with local university partnerships for each geography.

Exhibit 20.8: EdTech business models

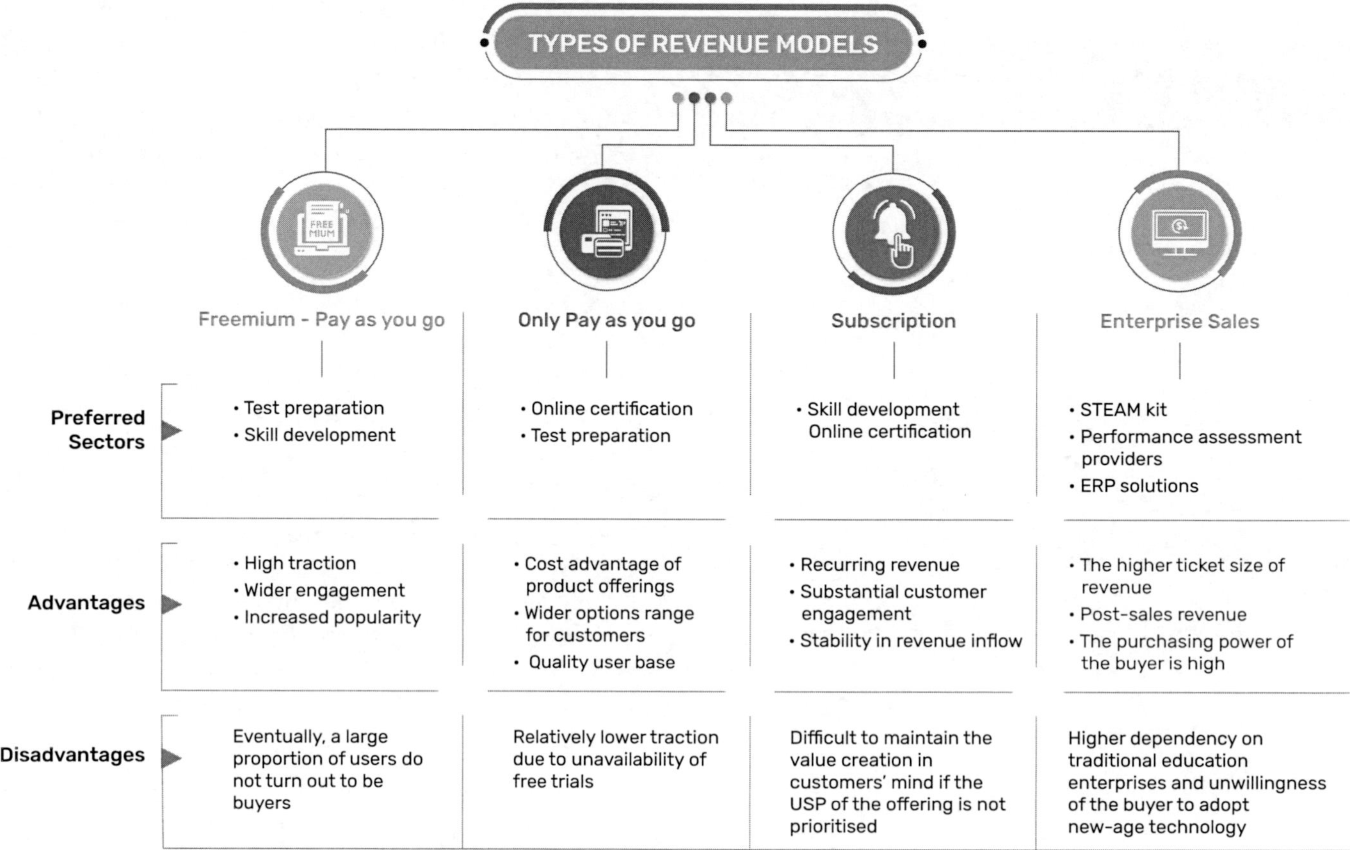

TYPES OF REVENUE MODELS

	Freemium - Pay as you go	Only Pay as you go	Subscription	Enterprise Sales
Preferred Sectors	• Test preparation • Skill development	• Online certification • Test preparation	• Skill development Online certification	• STEAM kit • Performance assessment providers • ERP solutions
Advantages	• High traction • Wider engagement • Increased popularity	• Cost advantage of product offerings • Wider options range for customers • Quality user base	• Recurring revenue • Substantial customer engagement • Stability in revenue inflow	• The higher ticket size of revenue • Post-sales revenue • The purchasing power of the buyer is high
Disadvantages	Eventually, a large proportion of users do not turn out to be buyers	Relatively lower traction due to unavailability of free trials	Difficult to maintain the value creation in customers' mind if the USP of the offering is not prioritised	Higher dependency on traditional education enterprises and unwillingness of the buyer to adopt new-age technology

Source: Goldman Sachs Global Investment Research 2020[8]

Role of the Government and Educational Reforms

Though the syllabus changes with every new government, serious reforms have bypassed education. In K12, effort has started slowly with implementing technology in education with smart classrooms. Sadly, on the ground, this mostly translates into giving a few projectors and systems to schools that then do not get used much. Since education is mostly bottom up, the top-down approach does not work in the sector. The lack of any major improvements vis-à-vis the supply–demand gap, making the top institutions tougher to get into (IITs, NITs), has resulted in the emergence of a very robust supplementary education sector covering competitive exams coaching, tuitions, EdTech, etc.

At the same time, in higher education, reforms giving freedom to operate to top institutions like IITs, IIMs, NITs, etc. helped propel the quality of learning to another level, making them more aspirational and tougher to get in. The same is true with the opening up of the university sector and allowing top private colleges to convert to deemed universities. If the quality of school-level teaching is the issue in K12, the supply–demand gap in educational infrastructure is the biggest issue in higher education. A major movement in the positive direction took place with the New Education Policy 2020,[10] which created a new category of degrees called online degrees that could be taken exclusively online from anywhere in the country. This could truly revolutionise higher education and GER in India, making college education both accessible and affordable to large segments of society.

Role of Private Sector

Along with private schools, which mushroomed due to quality issues in government schools, the private sector was involved in a big way in supplementary education and private universities and colleges. However, these sectors were always considered grey due to lack of transparency and something global investors kept away from. Everything changed when EdTech entrepreneurs entered the segment by deploying technology in a big way and finally proving scale. This has resulted in flow of capital to the education sector.

Recent Developments: COVID-19 Impact

COVID-19 changed the entire perception of EdTech in India. The sudden closure of schools made the EdTech apps the only resort for students to learn from home.

Immediately after lockdown, there was a growth of 500–600 per cent in traffic. However, the growth was mostly only to traffic since users were predominantly looking at free courses. The conversion cycles to paid went up due to the uncertainty in the economy. The sudden change in circumstances resulted in a large number of small players mushrooming and getting funded. However, the real advantage of COVID-19 finally went disproportionately to top players that ruled the market, like BYJU'S, Unacademy in school learning and upGrad in the working professional market. These players had solid products along with strong sales and marketing.

Fundamentally, COVID-19 brought online learning to the forefront and started making it acceptable in certain sectors and at the same level as conventional learning.

EdTech: The Way Forward

The EdTech sector has immense potential for expansion and can contribute to the economic growth of the country. It is important to ensure that the growth momentum the sector received due to the acceptance of "learning from home" possibilities to all geographies and age groups is retained and accelerated through relevant innovations. The challenges, emerging trends, global opportunities and way forward for the EdTech sector are discussed in this section.

Challenges

Like any other sunrise sector going through hyper growth, Indian EdTech also faces a plethora of challenges (Exhibit 20.9).

Need for innovations to make learning accessible and affordable: There are 250 million school-going children in India and another 100 million working professionals and degree audience. Making products that are relevant to this target audience (TG) and expanding the base in a big way is the biggest challenge facing Indian EdTech today. At the current price points and models, hardly 5 per cent of the base ends up adopting the products by paying. In a complex country like India, last-mile delivery will have to involve multiple innovations in pricing and delivery models to make it relevant to larger bases. Delivery in local languages and through various different form factors and internet speeds is another important flattening aspect.

Assessing learning outcomes: The topic of outcomes is another area where the jury is out on online learning. Especially in K12, since online learning is predominantly a supplementary affair, its efficacy towards getting outcomes or marks or ranks is still something that is not clear. Sooner or later, this is a question EdTech will have to answer. Only in higher education does this part appear to be moving in the right direction, since outcomes are more in the direction of job opportunities and professional confidence.

Need for innovations in reducing customer acquisition costs: The cost of acquiring a customer seems to be another big issue facing EdTech companies today. With increased competition, platforms like Google and Facebook have become expensive, and hence, the cost of acquiring a customer has gone up. The issue of increased number of impressions required to convert a customer also becomes a challenge, hence making the proposition loss-making.

Impending global competition: Especially at the higher end, the possibility of challenges from top international brands like Harvard going online is another interesting story that can unfold. The top educational institutions of the world today can go online and widely distribute their certifications, posing a challenge to smaller brands.

Emerging Trends and Innovation Avenues

One of the key developments in the sector is online becoming mainstream in higher education with organisations like upGrad taking top universities digital (Exhibit 20.10). With online degrees taking off, private

Exhibit 20.9: Challenges of EdTech

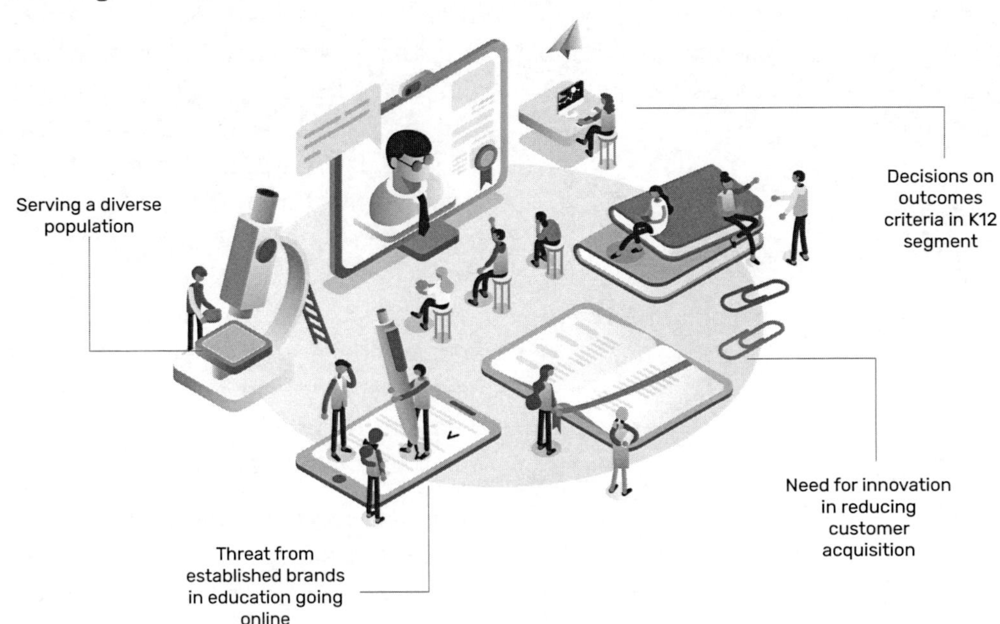

Source: Author

universities – Amity, Manipal, Narsee Monjee to name a few – have started offering Bachelors and Masters courses online. Similarly, an online school-integrated platform supporting home-schooling globally and solving the problem of one-on-one individual attention needs to be developed.

Large offline competitive examination players are going online out of necessity and top private schools are developing their own content. Slowly, content is getting commoditised with a large number of creators. This can move the baton of winners from start-ups that are creating content to start-ups with the best product in terms of technology and user engagement. For example, coding is fast emerging as a basic skill and is seen as something as important as mathematics and science by parents in metro areas. Companies like Whitehatjr have been riding this wave. Hybrid offerings with online and offline methods are picking up, bringing together two sectors – EdTech and competitive exam coaching. The Meritnation Aakash acquisition and all offline institutes going online due to COVID-19 has really given impetus to this model. Live video has become an inherent part of delivery. Companies like Vedantu have driven this business and BYJU'S has also joined the bandwagon with a live offering. Online learning centres have replaced the likes of Kumon. The worksheets and one-on-one attention can be solved much better through technology and India offers the best solution possible. Whitehatjr actually did something similar in coding; it will not be long before a player creates a platform. Further, as B2B in India is poised to grow and a large number of players will come up in this sector, it would not be surprising if Indian IT takes it up in a big way. TCS, which has always created platforms for assessment, may look at other segments of EdTech.

The Next Five Years

Indian EdTech is at the crossroads and the next five years can be really exciting. Based on the current picture, the sector has all the constituents to dominate EdTech the world over:

1. Access to high-quality English-speaking teachers in Mathematics, Coding and Science
2. Access to high-quality engineers who can develop the technology
3. Access to the above at a cost that is a fraction of what is available in Western nations

India can truly emerge as the EdTech destination that can propel and grow EdTech across the globe. In India also, there are huge changes taking place. The New Education Policy 2020 has laid a strong foundation to leverage technology in education. A few of the principles

Exhibit 20.10: Growth of the higher education market

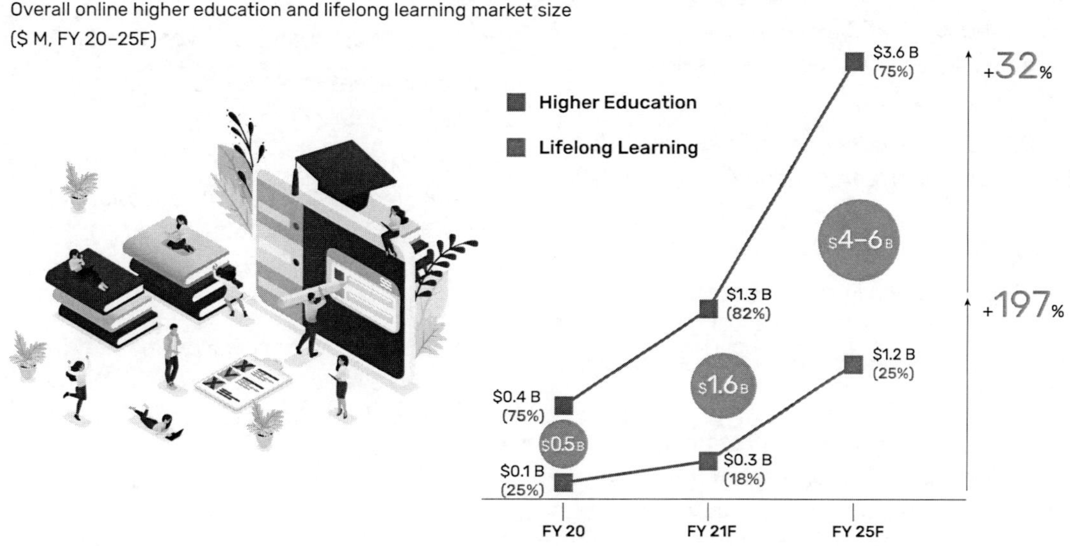

Note:
1. Includes sales by EdTech firms in India and B2C (direct to consumer) sales only; excludes revenue from international geographies by EdTech firms and any institutional and B2B sales.
2. $1 = ₹70

Source: RedSeer Report 2020

mentioned in the policy that will guide the nation's education system at large are:

- *Extensive use of technology in teaching and learning, removing language barriers, increasing access for Divyang students, and educational planning and management.*
- *Effective and sufficient infrastructure so that all students have access to safe and engaging school education at all levels.*
- *Special emphasis on socio-economically disadvantaged groups (SEDGs), the scope of school education will be broadened to facilitate multiple pathways to learning involving both formal and non-formal education modes. Open and Distance Learning (ODL) Programmes offered by the National Institute of Open Schooling (NIOS) and State Open Schools will be expanded and strengthened for meeting the learning needs of young people in India who are not able to attend a physical school.* (NEP, 2020)

Implemented well, it can truly revolutionise the education sector in India, solving our GER (gross enrollment ratio) problems and bringing us on par with Western nations. Currently, the two main reasons why youngsters, especially those from smaller towns, do not get a college education are access and affordability. On one side, they do not have access to top-quality education. On the other, the cost of such an education for them is unaffordable. The problem is more of an educational infrastructure issue than anything else. Intuitively, the solution is not about building more university buildings but taking things online where the same or better quality education can be provided easily. This is exactly what the government has formalised with NEP.

The promise of EdTech to improve the wellbeing of society at large is tremendous as education is an important element of the solution for many economic as well as social issues. Continuous effective intervention by multiple players in the ecosystem is vital to ensure that the power of EdTech is leveraged to make education available, accessible and affordable to different sections across the nation and the world at large.

Endnotes

[1]Inc42 Datalabs. 2020. *The Future of Edtech In India: Decoding The $10 Bn Market Opportunity*, Retrieved on January 5, 2021 from https://inc42.com/reports/the-future-of-edtech-in-india-decoding-the-10-bn-market-opportunity-report-2020/

[2]Redseer. 2020. ***Online Higher Education & Lifelong learning – 10x Growth Potential - A $5B Opportunity***, Retrieved on December 27, 2020 from https://redseer.com/reports/online-higher-education-lifelong-learning-10x-growth-potential-a-5b-opportunity/

[3]Inc42. 2020. ***The Future of Education: Indian Start-ups Chase $10 Bn Edtech Opportunity***, Retrieved on December 27, 2020 from https://inc42.com/datalab/the-future-of-education-indian-startups-chase-10-bn-edtech-market/

[4]Inc42. 2020. ***Welcome to the Future of Edtech; It's A Lot Like The Past!***, Retrieved on February 20, 2020 from https://inc42.com/features/welcome-to-the-future-of-edtech-its-a-lot-like-the-past/

[5]Inc42 Datalabs. 2020. ***The Future of Edtech In India: Decoding The $10 Bn Market Opportunity***, Retrieved on January 5, 2021 from https://inc42.com/reports/the-future-of-edtech-in-india-decoding-the-10-bn-market-opportunity-report

[6]Venture Intelligence Report 2020, Venture Intelligence, www.ventureintelligence.com

[7]Registrar of Companies, Government of India.

[8]Goldman Sachs Global Investment Research Report. 2021. ***The Future of Learning***.

[9]Dauxe Consulting. 2020. ***Eight Chinese EdTech start-ups leading the global educational technology industry***, Retrieved on January 16, 2021 from https://daxueconsulting.com/china-edtech-educational-technology-market/

[10]Ministry of Education, Government of India, ***NEP 2020***, Retrieved on January 27, 2021 from https://www.education.gov.in/sites/upload_files/mhrd/files/NEP_Final_English_0.pdf

IN BRIEF

- The Indian financial ecosystem has strong growth potential. The total Indian financial assets are 1.58 times GDP, compared to 3.14 and 6.73 times for emerging and advanced economies. Importantly, the growth rate of financial assets in India is 15.32 per cent for 2005–2019, compared to 14.72 per cent and 4.57 per cent for emerging and advanced economies, respectively.
- FinTech is expected to capture a large amount of potential value creation in the financial sector, as evidenced by VC investments. FinTech companies received 39.7 per cent of the VC funding in the financial sector in 2020. The amount of VC dollar invested in FinTech has grown at a rate of 35.6 per cent between 2006 and 2020, twice the rate of growth in the BFSI sector. Within FinTech, Payment is the dominant vertical, receiving 59 per cent of the cumulative 2006–2020 VC flow.
- Going forward, FinTech is expected to have more diversified growth due to regulatory initiatives and the enabling ecosystem. The non-bank Lending vertical is the potential future star, already accounting for 43 per cent of total FinTech funding rounds between 2015 and 2020. The creation of account aggregators and Open Credit Enhancement Network,[1] has paved the way for strong future growth of the vertical.

INDUSTRY
PERSPECTIVE

21

FinTech: The Leap Ahead

Qambar Abidi

Abidi, Q. 2021. "FinTech: The Leap Ahead". In *Shifting Orbits: Decoding the Trajectory of the Indian Start-up Ecosystem*, edited by Thillai Rajan A, Srivardhini K Jha, Joffi Thomas and Rohan Chinchwadkar, 270–291. Hyderabad: Universities Press (India) Private Limited.

Overview

Over the past two decades, technology-driven financial innovation has given rise to a few novel portmanteaus to characterise companies that directly provide or indirectly facilitate financial intermediation services. FinTech, WealthTech, InsurTech, PayTech and TechFin are a few such terms that have become common parlance in the world of financial and technology companies, market regulators and central banks. The umbrella term FinTech often refers to technology-enabled innovation by traditional financial intermediaries. At the same time, FinTech is also used to describe the new, technology-centred companies that are challengers to the incumbent financial intermediaries and which are disrupting the traditional financial services ecosystem. Although the rapid advancement in technology and development of business models for the digital economy has resulted in an unprecedented level of change in all industries and business sectors, the impact on the financial services industry has been of particular significance. Not least because of the special role the industry plays in the organisation of the modern economy.

In this chapter, we postulate that relative level and growth trend of financial assets in India, when compared with the emerging markets and advanced economies, provide a basis for a positive outlook for the Indian financial sector. Here, the region-wise total financial assets is taken as a simple proxy for assessing the size and growth potential of the financial ecosystem. We combine this understanding with a survey of the private equity (PE) and venture capital (VC) investment in the overall financial sector and FinTech companies in India for the past 15 years. The trends underline the increasing relevance of FinTech companies in India. Further, we find that the historical growth in VC investments in Indian FinTech has so far been led by Payment companies. The success of the Payment vertical is partly attributable to the UIDAI, the India stack project and regulatory interventions.

Meanwhile, Lending has witnessed accelerated growth in investments from 2015. At the same time, the Lending vertical relative to Payments has witnessed significantly fewer exits. It is, however, likely that the introduction of account aggregators, Open Credit Enhancement Network (OCEN) protocol[1] and implementation of regulatory sandboxes will pave the way for rapid growth in the Lending segment in years to come.

The chapter is organised as follows. The first section examines the growth potential of the Indian financial services sector and the rising share of FinTech within it. The second section details the FinTech ecosystem and analyses the evolution of FinTech in India across time and various sub-segments. Lastly, the third section discusses the growth trends in the FinTech sector and analyses the role of regulation therein.

FinTech: Foundations and Growth Potential

The Indian Financial Services Sector

As FinTech may be considered a sub-sector of the financial services industry or a use case of technology in the financial services industry, it is informative to examine the growth in the overall finance sector. Exhibit 21.1 presents the time series of total financial assets and GDP in current prices from 2005 to 2019 for a group of advanced economies,[2] emerging markets[3] and India.

The Financial Stability Board, funded by the Bank of International Settlement, recorded the value of total

Exhibit 21.1: Total financial assets and GDP in current prices (values in $ trillion)

Year	Advanced economies		Emerging markets		India	
	Total financial assets	GDP current prices	Total financial assets	GDP current prices	Total financial assets	GDP current prices
2005	164.11	31.63	10.22	5.45	0.53	0.50
2006	178.48	33.16	12.63	6.28	0.68	0.58
2007	200.56	34.66	15.90	7.51	0.85	0.68
2008	212.67	35.27	19.15	8.80	1.09	0.76
2009	210.22	34.31	22.56	9.32	1.27	0.88
2010	218.80	35.56	26.55	11.00	1.47	1.06
2011	228.79	36.65	31.69	12.97	1.73	1.22
2012	239.74	37.60	36.82	14.36	2.02	1.39
2013	247.91	38.58	42.58	15.72	2.29	1.57
2014	264.77	39.95	49.28	17.04	2.59	1.75
2015	269.97	41.38	56.83	18.12	2.88	1.93
2016	286.31	42.47	64.98	19.47	3.17	2.14
2017	299.53	44.06	70.92	21.42	3.58	2.35
2018	300.45	45.94	74.69	23.32	4.02	2.67
2019	320.83	47.63	80.23	25.49	4.52	2.85
CAGR (2005–2019)	4.57%	2.77%	14.72%	10.84%	15.32%	12.28%

Source: Financial Stability Board[4]

financial assets in the advanced economies at the end of 2019 to be 673.6 per cent of the annual GDP in current prices. However, the value of total financial assets in the emerging markets is a relatively modest 314.8 per cent of the aggregate GDP. In India, the same metric is at a significantly lower value of 158.4 per cent (Exhibit 21.2, Panel B). The value of the total financial assets indicates the size of the financial system in a region. Between 2005 and 2019, the total financial assets in advanced economies recorded a compound annual growth rate (CAGR) of 4.57 per cent. In that period, the total financial assets in the emerging markets and India recorded an impressive CAGR of 14.72 per cent and 15.32 per cent, respectively. Even adjusting for the GDP growth rate, we still observe a healthy CAGR in total financial assets of 1.76 per cent, 3.50 per cent and 2.71 per cent in the advanced economies, emerging markets and India, respectively. Notably, the recent year-on-year growth in financial assets for 2017–2019 has been considerably higher for India (Exhibit 21.2, Panel B). For India, the current lower levels of financial assets as a ratio of GDP, combined with a high growth rate of financial assets, underline the growth potential of the financial sector in the medium to long term.

Interestingly, the Indian financial assets managed by Other Financial Intermediaries[5] (OFI) have increased at a CAGR of 15.8 per cent between 2014 and 2019, while the financial assets managed by banks have increased at a CAGR of only 7.7 per cent (Exhibit 21.2, Panel C). The rapid rise in prominence of the non-banking financial intermediaries is another encouraging trend for the FinTech ecosystem.

The Indian FinTech Sector

Financial intermediaries provide brokerage and asset transformation services, with one of the primary functions being reduction of the cost of transaction between the counterparties by resolving pre-contract and post-contract informational asymmetry. Technology is especially adept at achieving this objective and it is of no surprise that it is the transaction and brokerage services that have witnessed the highest penetration by FinTech companies. The Medici India FinTech Report[6] identifies 2,174 total number of FinTech start-ups operational in India. Of this, 405 firms are identified as companies that provide digital payment services, 365 are digital lending companies, 486 firms belong to the

Exhibit 21.2: Growth in total financial assets

Panel A: Y-O-Y growth in total financial assets (%)

Panel A represents the year-on-year growth of total financial assets, while Panel B presents the annual trends in total financial assets as a percentage of GDP in current prices. Panel C presents the breakdown of the total financial assets in India into the constituents parts comprised of banks, central bank, public financial institutions, insurance corporations, pension funds, financial axillaries and other financial intermediaries.

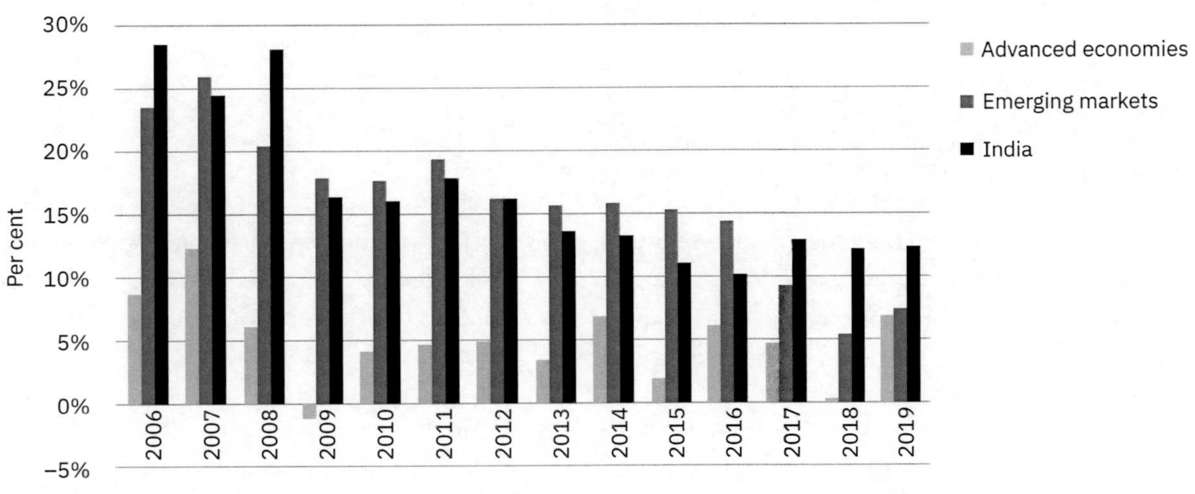

Exhibit 21.2 (contd.)

Panel B: Total financial assets as a percentage of GDP (current prices)

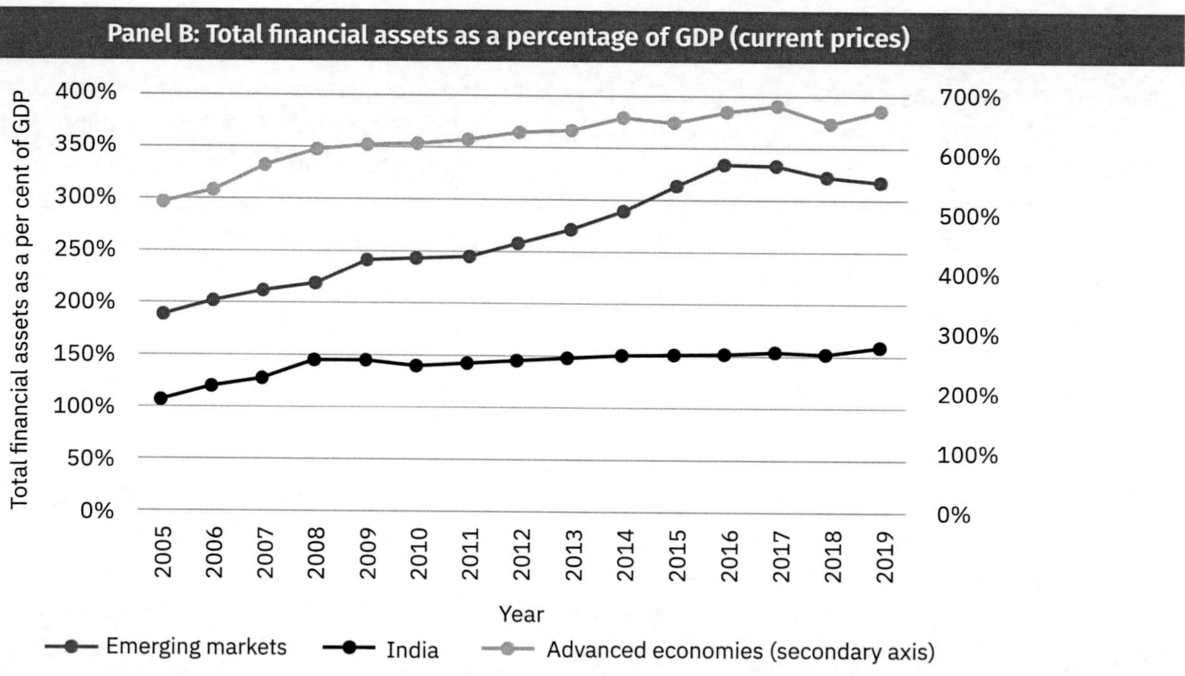

Panel C: Growth trend in value of financial assets across segments of financial economy in India ($ trillion)

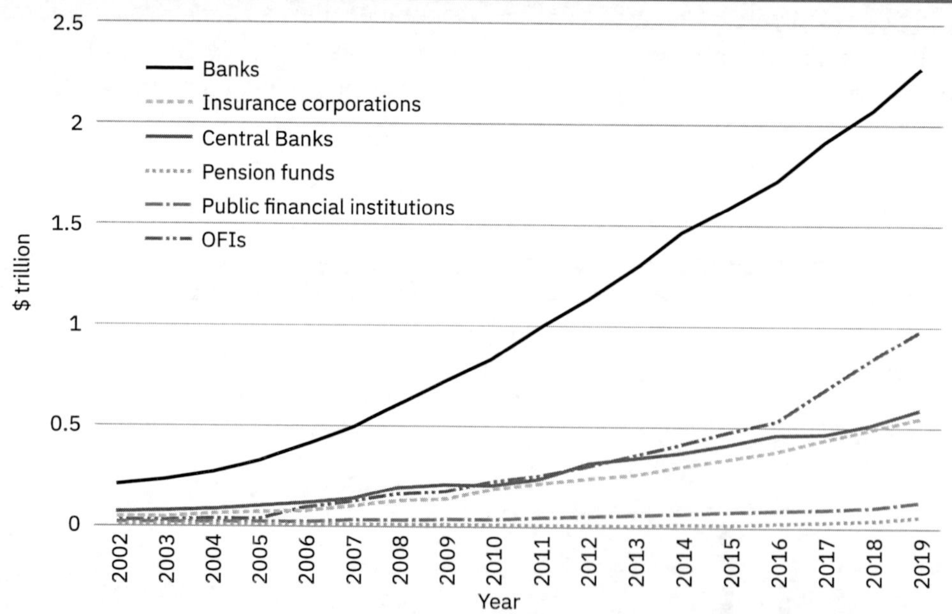

Source: Financial Stability Board

wealth management and personal finance segment, and 111 to the InsurTech segment.

However, it is more informative to examine the flow of institutional investment in the sector, which is indicative of capacity building with an informed outlook. The PE and VC investments in the Banking, Financial Services and Insurance (BFSI) sector underscore the growth potential of the sector in general and of the FinTech vertical in particular. According to the Venture Intelligence database, between the years 2006 and 2020,[7] the Indian BFSI sector attracted PE and VC funding of $35.56 billion across 1,398 funding rounds for 497 unique firms.[8] In the same period, 320 unique FinTech firms managed to raise more than $11.77 billion[9] from VC firms, across 759 investment rounds.[10] In the given period, the annual number of investment rounds in FinTech companies grew at an impressive CAGR of 20.8 per cent while the total annual value of the investment in USD grew at an impressive CAGR of 35.6 per cent. Meanwhile, the annual number of PE and VC investment rounds overall and in the BFSI sector grew at a relatively modest CAGR of 4.6 per cent and 14.3 per cent, respectively. Similarly, the value of the annual investments in USD grew at an annual rate of 17.8 per cent and 12 per cent for BFSI and for total Indian investments, respectively. Exhibit 21.3 presents the time series of the number of funding rounds and their dollar value for FinTech and BFSI companies.

As noted in Exhibit 21.3, the institutional investment in FinTech companies has grown at a robust pace over the past 15 years. However, an examination of investments in FinTech companies relative to the BFSI sector highlights interesting trends (Exhibit 21.4, Panel A). It is noteworthy that as of the end of 2020, the number of funding rounds in FinTech companies has risen at a steady rate to 71.8 per cent of the total number of funding rounds in the overall BFSI sector, from a modest 19.2 per cent proportion in the year 2010. The proportion of funding in dollar value terms is more volatile from 2015. It is, however, likely, given the recent funding trends, that FinTech firms set up in the past decade will attract increasing amounts of investment in successive funding rounds. Notably, a large number of FinTech start-ups that had already secured VC investments were incorporated in 2015–2017 (Exhibit 21.4, Panel B).

Unicorns and Other Top FinTech Companies

As start-ups mature, an important milestone is achieving a large valuation. Achieving Unicorn[11] status and the pace of reaching there contributes to the sustainability of the ecosystem. As at the end of 2020, the Venture

Exhibit 21.3: Time series of PE and VC investment in Indian BFSI and FinTech companies

Year	BFSI		FinTech		
	Number of funding rounds	Total funding ($ million)	Number of funding rounds	Total funding ($ million)	Maximum funding round value ($ million)
2006	19	312	6	15	7
2007	39	1,989	10	46	11
2008	36	597	10	62	20
2009	28	287	10	64	20
2010	52	718	10	22	8
2011	59	566	19	133	42
2012	59	712	21	115	40
2013	86	766	24	144	40
2014	80	1,006	34	269	60
2015	116	2,282	78	1,453	677
2016	124	2,604	79	628	300
2017	147	5,481	93	2,541	1400
2018	210	7,789	120	1,990	356
2019	201	6,822	143	2,850	1000
2020	142	3,633	102	1,442	136
Total	**1398**	**35,564**	**759**	**11,777**	**1400**
CAGR	14.3%	17.8%	20.8%	35.6%	

Source: Venture Intelligence

Exhibit 21.4: Annual trends for FinTech companies

Panel A: Investment in FinTech as a percentage of BFSI investments

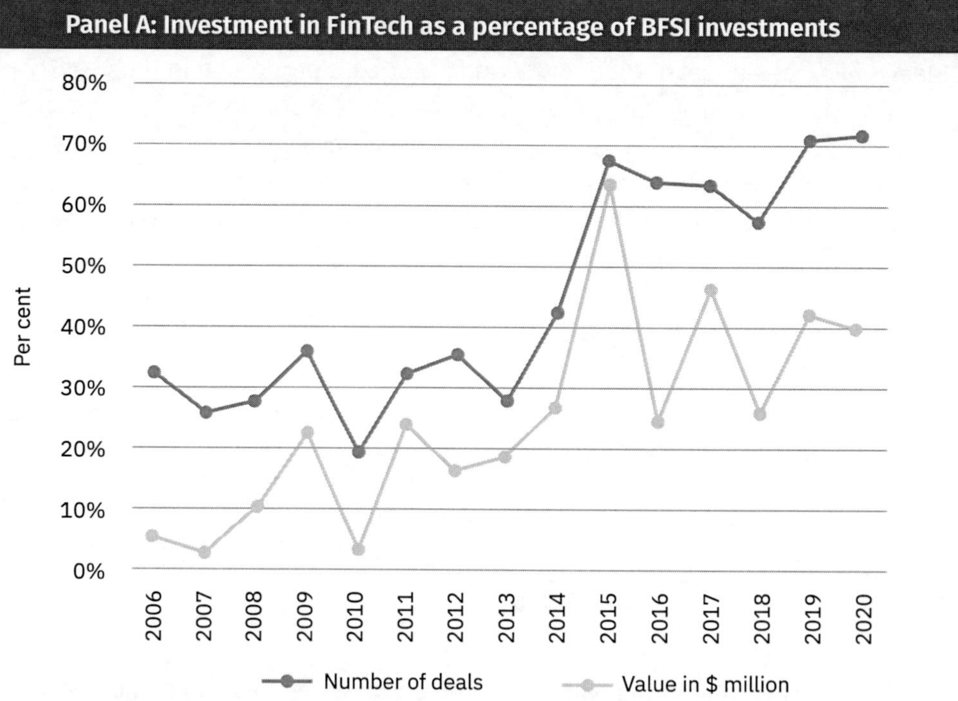

Panel B: The number of FinTech companies incorporated in a year (that secured institutional funding by end of 2020)

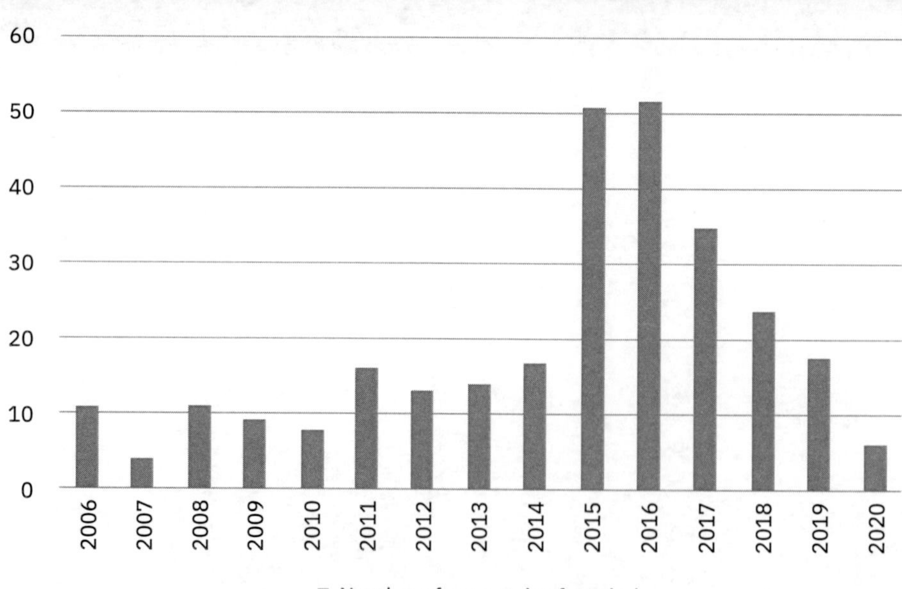

Source: Venture Intelligence

Intelligence database records 37 Unicorns in India, of which six belong to the FinTech vertical. The list of FinTech Unicorns is presented in Exhibit 21.5. The biggest Indian FinTech company by a long margin is PayTM, which achieved Unicorn status in 2015, 15 years after its inception. However, Digit, the latest entrant in the Unicorn club, took a mere five years since its inception. Interestingly, all the six companies in the list entered the Unicorn club after 2015.

Exhibit 21.6 presents the amount of VC investments these Unicorns have attracted so far, along with the

Exhibit 21.5: FinTech Unicorns

Company	Sector	Valuation ($ billion)	Year of realising Unicorn valuation	Year of founding
Digit	Insurtech	1.9	2021	2016
RazorPay	Payments	1	2020	2014
Pine Labs	Payments	1.5	2020	1998
BillDesk	Payments	1.5	2018	2000
PolicyBazaar	Insurtech	1	2018	2008
Paytm	Payments	16	2015	2000

Source: Venture Intelligence

Exhibit 21.6: Top Indian FinTech companies

Panel A: Top 10 Indian FinTech beneficiaries of institutional funds

S. No.	Company name and (FinTech vertical)	No. of institutional funding rounds (2006–2020)	Total institutional funding ($ million)	% of total institutional funding (2006–2020)
1	PayTM (Payments)	15	4,105.98	34.9%
2	PolicyBazaar (InsurTech)	10	649.57	5.5%
3	BillDesk (Payments)	5	523.90	4.4%
4	SBI Cards & Payment (Payments)	3	328.57	2.8%
5	Pine Labs (Payments)	6	243.00	2.1%
6	Cred (Payments)	3	226.07	1.9%
7	Digit (InsurTech)	4	213.06	1.8%
8	Acko (InsurTech)	6	207.44	1.8%
9	RazorPay (Payments)	6	206.50	1.8%
10	InCred Finance (Lenders)	3	180.63	1.5%

Panel B: Top 5 companies from FinTech verticals with highest cumulative investment value (2006–2020)

Banks		InsurTech		Investment Management		Lenders (non-bank)		Payments	
Name	Amt ($ M)	Name	Amt ($ M)	Name	Amt ($ M)	Name	Amt ($ M)	Name	Amt ($ M)
FINO	64.6	PolicyBazaar	649.5	Groww	59.4	InCred Finance	180.6	PayTM	4105.9
NiYO	49.2	Digit	213.0	IndWealth.	57.6	Lendingkart	158.7	BillDesk	523.9
Open F. T.	35.44	Acko	207.4	Scripbox	35.3	Aye Finance	123.5	SBI Cards and Payments	328.5
Jupiter Money	25.27	Turtlemint	64.4	Upstox	29.2	KrazyBee	119	Pine Labs	243
epiFi	13.21	Coverfox	51.9	Smallcase	23.6	Vistaar Finance	112.4	Cred	226.0

Source: Venture Intelligence

remaining top 10 beneficiaries of institutional funding in the FinTech vertical. Not surprisingly, the majority of institutional money into the FinTech vertical is cornered by a handful of companies. For the study period, nearly 60 per cent of cumulative VC funding amount was captured by the top 10 funded companies, with PayTM alone accounting for 35 per cent of the total. A closer examination of the top investments highlight the dominance of the Payment sector, followed by Lending and InsurTech.

The Evolution of the Indian FinTech Sector

In effect, the trend of financialisation of assets, the growth of VC inflows and attainment of Unicorn valuations

Exhibit 21.7: FinTech consumers adoption index

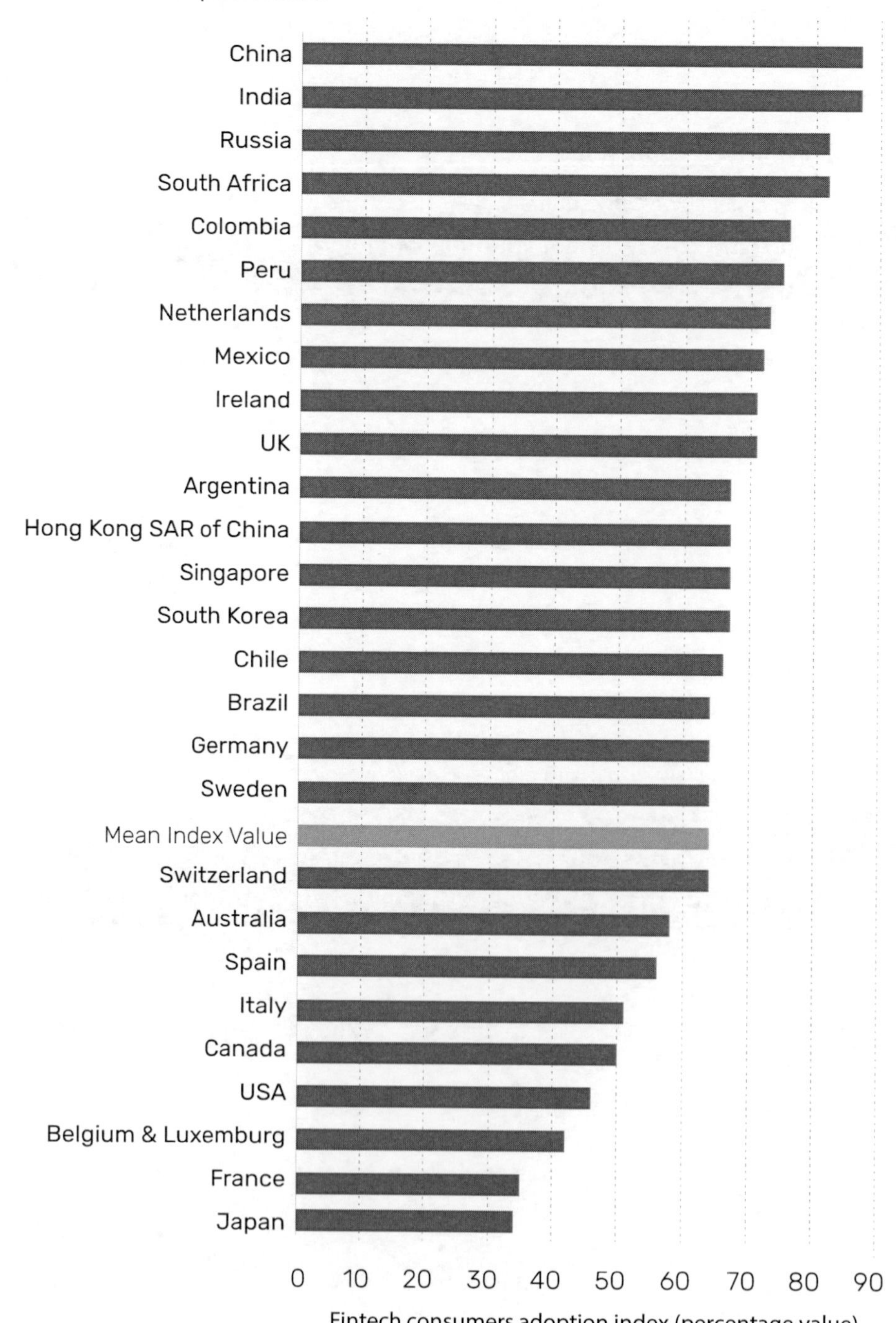

Source: Global FinTech Adoption Index 2019

indicates robust upside potential for the FinTech sector. Furthermore, FinTech adoption in India, as reported by the Global FinTech Adoption Index 2019,[12] is one of the highest globally, matched only by China (Exhibit 21.7).

However, to assess the realisability of the said potential and future viability of current trends, it is useful to examine the Indian FinTech ecosystem in some detail and identify the key drivers of historical and future growth. The FinTech tree developed by the staff at the Financial Stability Institute[13] provides a useful taxonomy of the FinTech environment (Exhibit 21.8).

The FinTech Ecosystem

FinTech ecosystem: Areas of application

The FinTech activity classification (Exhibit 21.8) is indicative of the primary areas of application. In this chapter, we have used a modified version, appropriate for the Indian FinTech environment. The FinTech verticals that we examine are Banks, Lenders (non-banking), Payments, Investment Management, Insurance and Others.[14] We have used the classification created by the Venture Intelligence database, where available, and have classified the remaining firms manually. However, the classification is not perfect. There are firms that operate in multiple categories and in the absence of transactional and financial data, the classification is, to a degree, subjective in nature. The following analysis has to be read with that caveat in mind.

FinTech ecosystem: Technology

Globally, the key technologies that are driving innovation in the financial sector and enabling the FinTech sector are artificial intelligence (AI) and machine learning (ML), application programming interface (API), cloud computing, distributed ledger technology (DLT), and biometric-based identification and authentication (biometrics).[15] As technology is permeable, what is more interesting in the Indian context is to examine

Exhibit 21.8: FinTech ecosystem

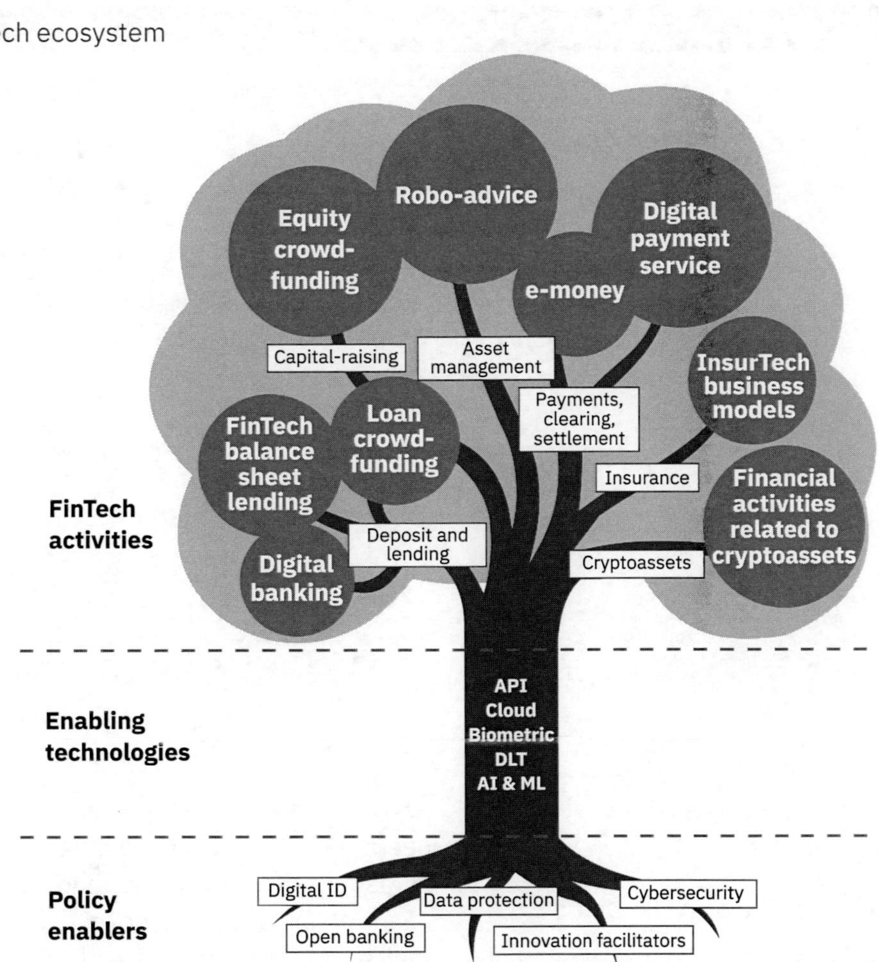

Source: Financial Stability Institute Insights[13]

Exhibit 21.9: Google Trends score for "FinTech" search string for 2006 to 2020

Panel A: Region – India

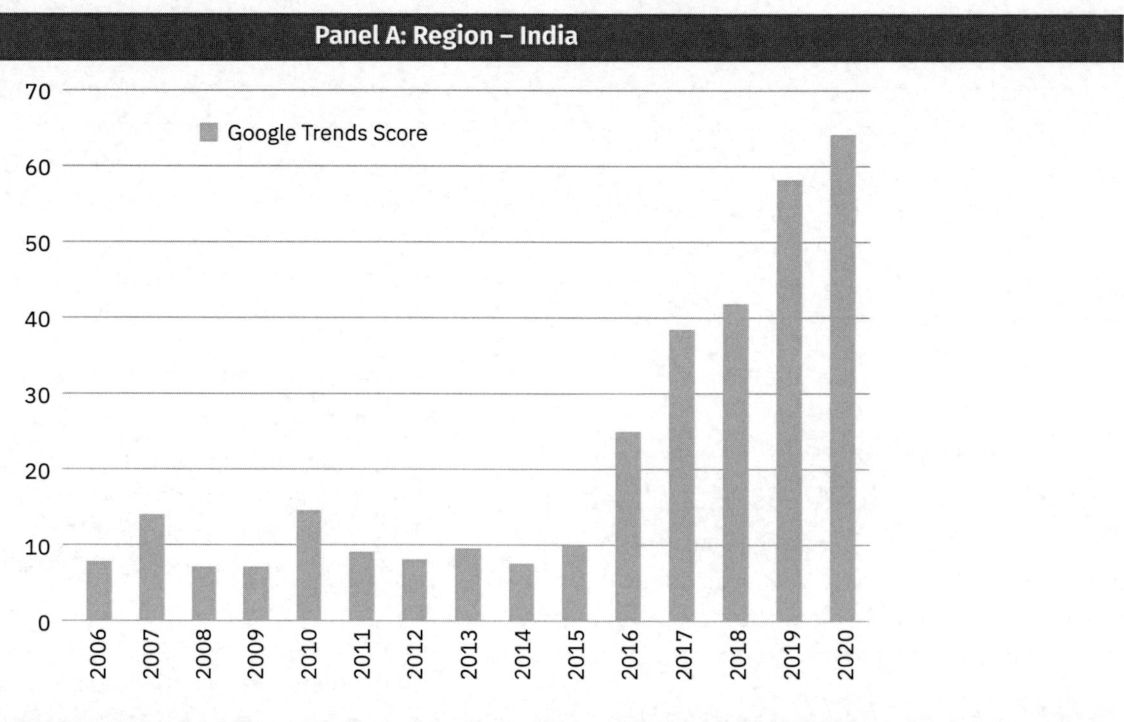

Panel B: Region – Worldwide

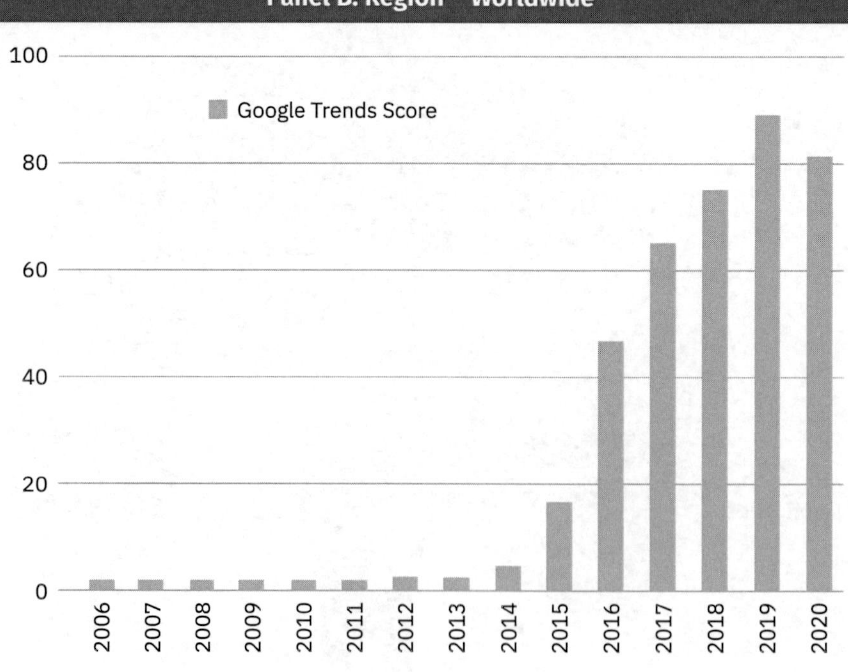

Source: Google Trends

the emphasis, and the change thereof, on a technology through regulatory interventions.

FinTech ecosystem: Regulation

As stated earlier, the size of financial assets in the Indian economy has lagged behind that of the advanced economies and even some of the emerging market peers (Exhibit 21.1). Lack of reliable identification infrastructure for citizens and relatively low level of financial inclusion in the country has contributed to that factor. The setting up of the Unique Identification Authority of India in 2009 was a policy response to

Exhibit 21.10: FinTech vertical classification

FinTech vertical	Percentage of number of funding rounds	Percentage of funding value ($ million)
Banks	2.77%	1.75%
Insurance	9.09%	11.00%
Investment management	9.62%	2.60%
Lenders (non-bank)	37.55%	20.26%
Payments	28.59%	59.02%
Others	12.38%	5.37%

Source: Venture Intelligence

several such infrastructural constraints. Alongside, the Payment and Settlement Systems Act, 2007 and the setting up of the National Payment Corporation of India in 2009 greatly facilitated the early growth of the Payments sector. In recent times, the Reserve Bank of India (RBI) and the market regulators have started to focus on the FinTech sector specifically, as a result of which we have started to witness faster and more broad-based growth.

Study of Indian FinTech

Our study sample goes back to 2006, but the examination of the data trends indicate that 2015 was a breakout year for the growth of the FinTech sector. Google Trends provides a simple and effective test for assessing the wide awareness of any keyword. Exhibit 21.9, which presents the results for "FinTech" search string for India and the Worldwide region, clearly demonstrates the rapid rise in the index score from 2015. For the Worldwide region, the average index for pre-2015 period is 2, while the post-2015 period has an average index score of 62. For the purpose of our analysis, we have divided our study period into two distinct phases: Phase 1 is from 2006 to 2014 and Phase 2 is from 2015 to 2020.

The data in Exhibit 21.3 informs us that the total number of funding rounds in Phase 1 was 144 at an average of 16 rounds per year, while Phase 2 witnessed 615 unique funding rounds at an average of about 102 rounds per year. Phase 1 attracted total institutional investment of $871.2 million at an average value of $5.9 million per round, while in Phase 2 the companies secured total institutional investment of $10,905.7 million at an average value of $18.7 million per round. Importantly, Phase 1 did not witness any FinTech Unicorns and all current Unicorns reached the valuation landmark in Phase 2.

Funding rounds in FinTech verticals

Exhibit 21.10 suggests an institutional preference for Payment companies in terms of money invested, although lending received a higher number of funding rounds. However, an examination of the annual trend presents interesting highlights. The advent of Phase 2 saw other sectors like non-bank lenders finding favour with investors; however, Payments continued to dominate the verticals in terms of the investment amount (Exhibit 21.11).

Exhibit 21.12 provides the sectoral break-up of the cumulative investment pie for Phase 1 and Phase 2 separately. A quick comparison shows us that the Lenders' share of the pie has seen the greatest gain from Phase 1 to Phase 2, increasing from 9 per cent to 21 per cent of the overall FinTech investment pool. Payments, riding on the likes of PayTM, continued to attract about 60 per cent of the total.

Stage of funding rounds

Further examination of the stage of the funding rounds across FinTech verticals and time presents no clear time series trend (Exhibit 20.13, Panel A). We do, however, observe that at an aggregate level, Phase 2 witnessed the increasing importance of non-bank lenders in terms of their share of the total early- and growth-stage VC funding rounds.

The total number of early-stage funding rounds increased from 75 in Phase 1 to 410 in Phase 2, an approximately five-fold increase (Panel B). The total number of growth-stage funding rounds increased from 49 in Phase 1 to 158 in Phase 2, an approximately

Exhibit 21.11: Investment trends for FinTech companies by sector

Panel A: Number of investment rounds (by year)

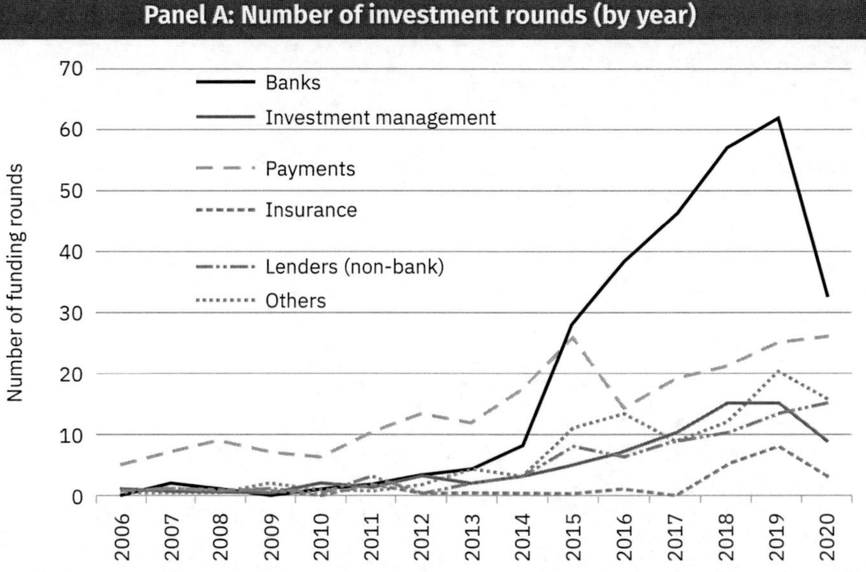

Panel B: Capital invested ($ million, annual)

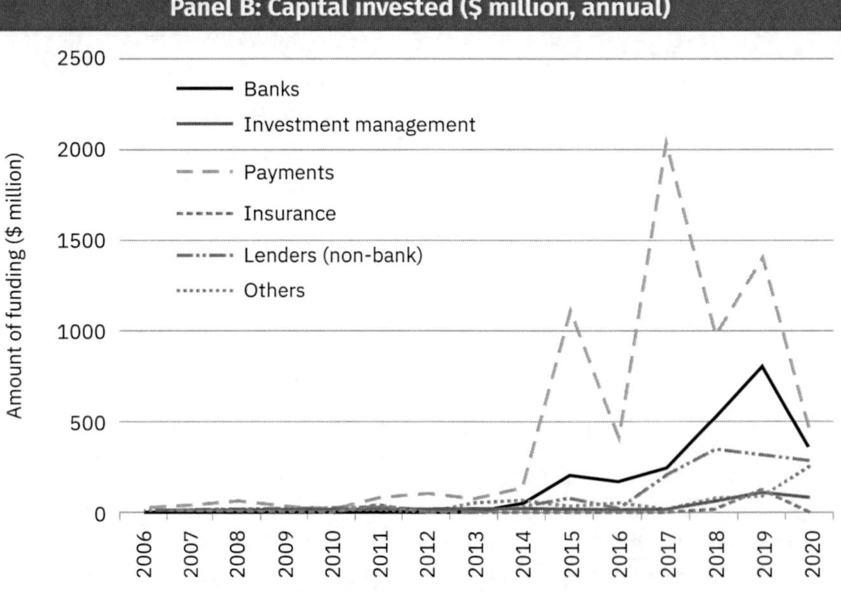

Source: Venture Intelligence

three-fold increase (Panel C). The total number of late-stage funding rounds went up from 20 in Phase 1 to 47 in Phase 2, an increase of about two-fold (Panel D).

For early stage, the proportion of Lenders increased from 15 per cent to 49 per cent while the proportion of Payments declined from 53 per cent to 15 per cent. In the growth stage too, Lenders witnessed an increase of 14 per cent to 34 per cent in proportion to the total funding rounds, for Phases 1 and 2, respectively. The proportion of Payments, meanwhile, went down from 66 per cent to 25 per cent. The share of the pie between Lender and Payment companies for late-stage funding remained relatively similar across the two phases of our analysis.

Exit status

VCs are financial intermediaries that require a high return on their investments, motivated by the high probability of failure of the start-up or early-stage companies they typically invest in. Therefore, an examination of "exit" events is particularly meaningful for the FinTech ecosystem. Between 60 per cent and 70 per cent of VC

Exhibit 21.12: Phase-wise investment in FinTech verticals

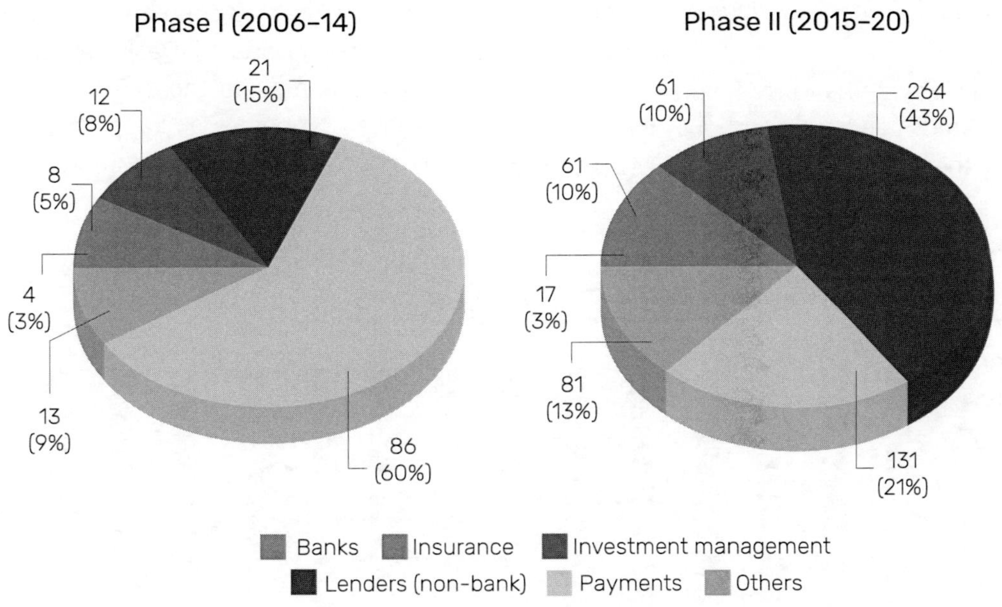

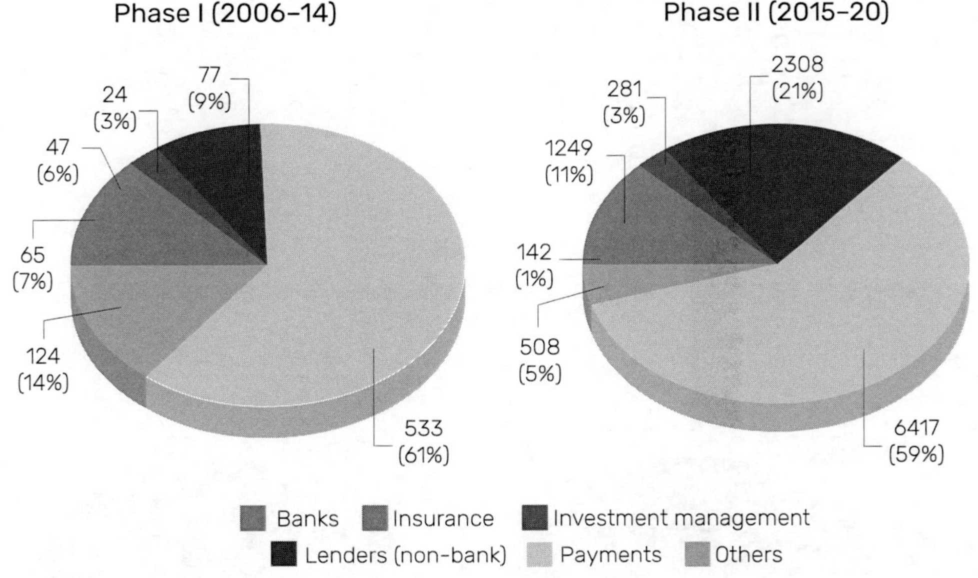

Source: Venture Intelligence

investors of funding rounds originating between 2006 and 2010 either partially or fully exited their positions. That proportion, as expected, went down gradually until only five deals from 120 deals in 2018 managed to have partial or full exit by the end of 2020 (Exhibit 21.14, Panel A).

Interestingly, Phase 1 funding into insurance companies witnessed 62.5 per cent partial or full exits, while Phase 2 saw 4.9 per cent partial or full exits. Similarly, Lenders and Payments Phase 2 funding rounds witnessed 6.4 per cent and 12.2 per cent partial or full exits. However, the interesting pattern that we observed is the relatively low proportion of exits for the Phase 1 funding rounds in Lending companies, where only 4.76 per cent of a total of 21 funding rounds secured an exit. On the other hand, 57 per cent of 86 Phase 1 funding rounds in Payment companies secured partial or full exits.

In effect, the Payments and Insurance verticals have demonstrated good exit options for VCs, as observed from the archival data above. The Lending vertical, however, seems to have faced demand-side constraints, and as a result, most of the VC investments in this vertical still have not got exits. It is noteworthy that the top invested companies in the Payment vertical such as PayTM and BillDesk are fairly popular, if not household names, in India. Similarly, the top invested Insurance companies such as Policy Bazaar and Acko enjoy good recall value in the consumer mind-space.

Exhibit 21.13: Stage of investment rounds

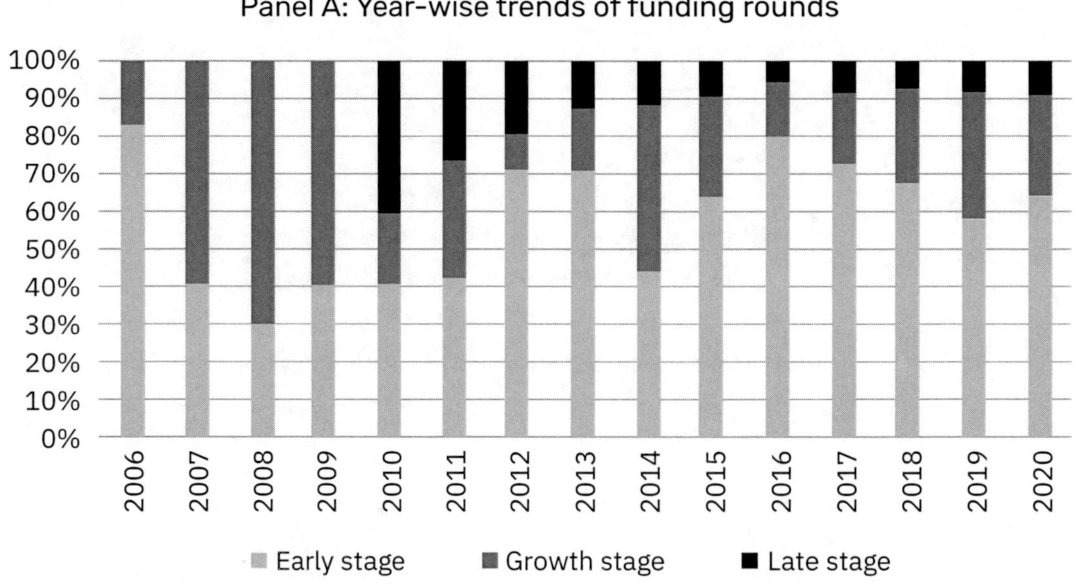

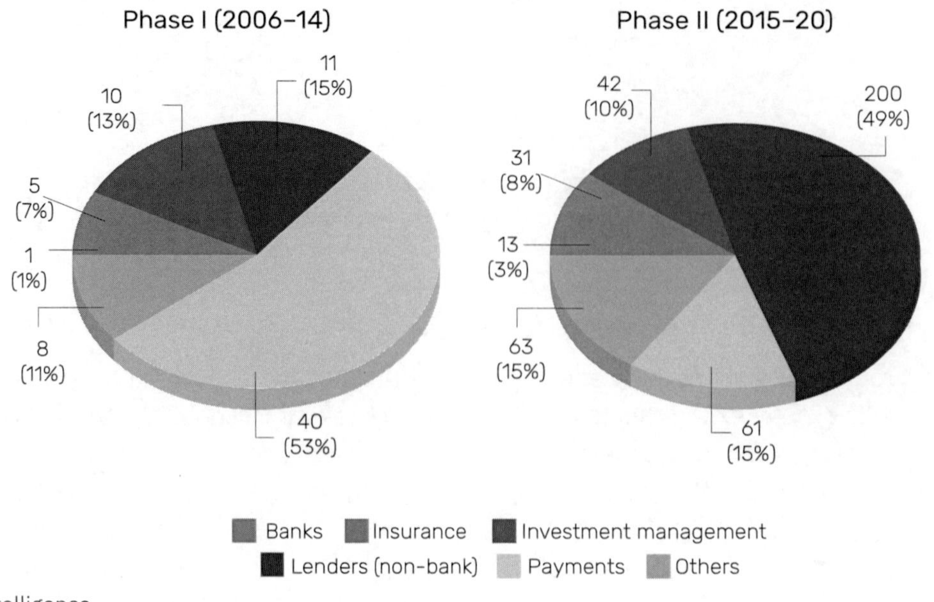

Source: Venture Intelligence

Exhibit 21.13: (Contd)

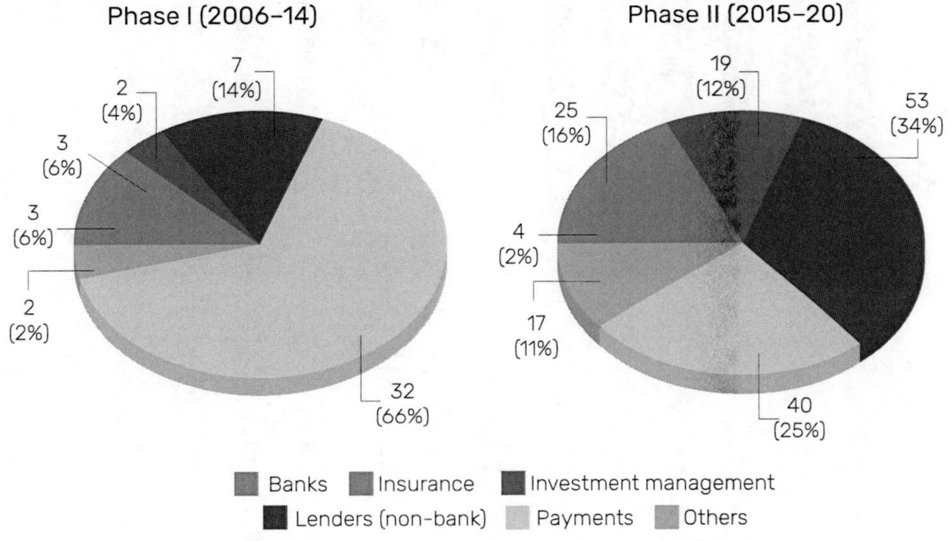

Panel D: Sectoral composition of total late-stage funding rounds

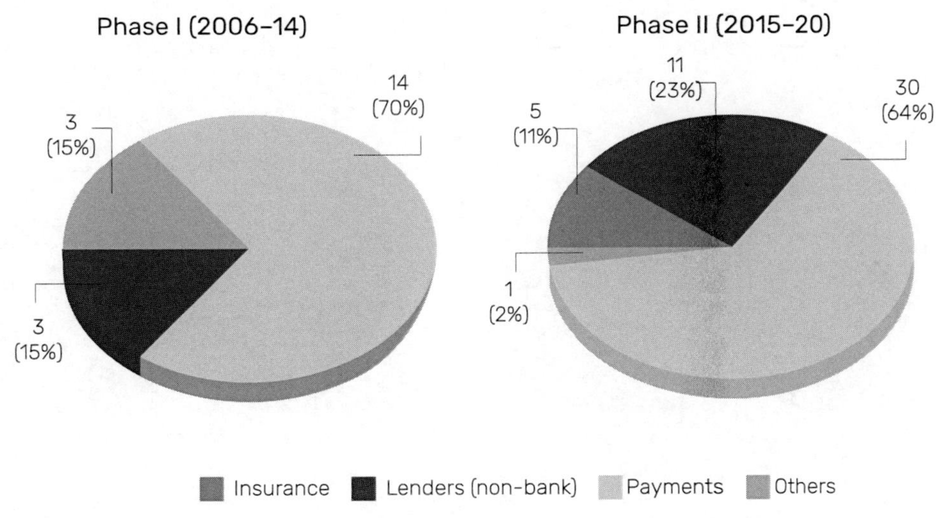

Source: Venture Intelligence

More importantly, the India stack has greatly enhanced the penetration of digital payment companies in India. FinTech Lending companies, however, have faced systemic issues pertaining to wider access to credit and transaction data history.

The COVID-19 Effect

An examination of the investment trends during COVID-19 allowed us to test the robustness of the FinTech ecosystem. We conducted a simple comparison of the VC investments in the year 2019 with the values in 2020. Starting from the end of the first quarter and till the end of third quarter of 2020, there was significant volatility in investment flow. The fourth quarter witnessed good recovery from the relative lows (Exhibit 21.15). The findings are in line with the findings of the Global COVID-19 FinTech Market Rapid Assessment study conducted by the World Bank Group and the World Economic Forum.[16] The study surveyed 1,385

Exhibit 21.14: Exit status

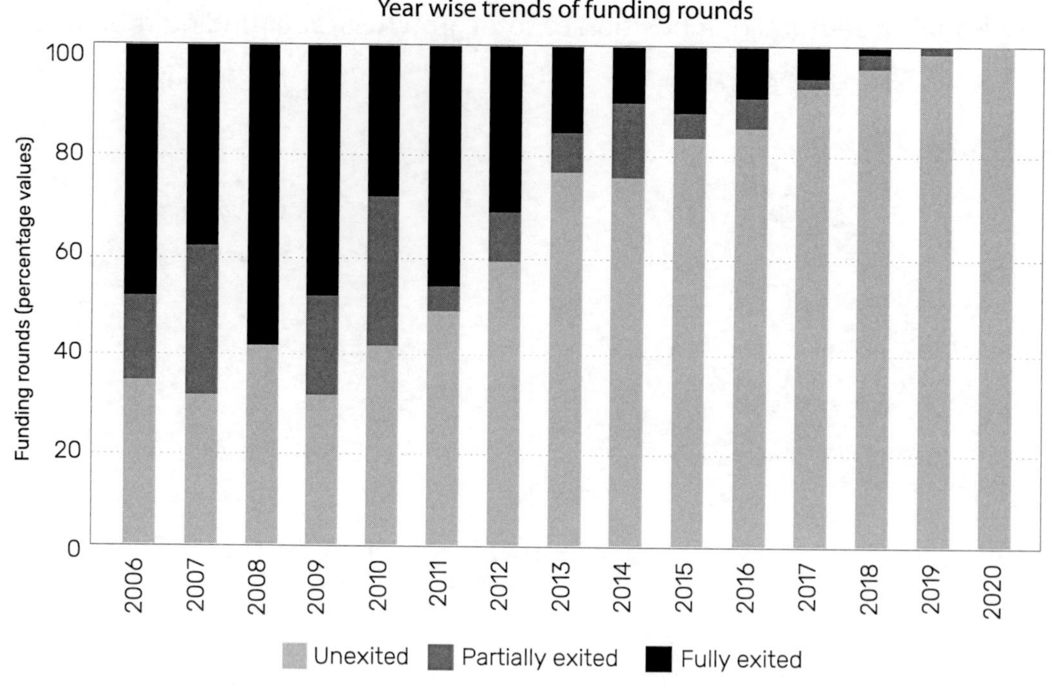

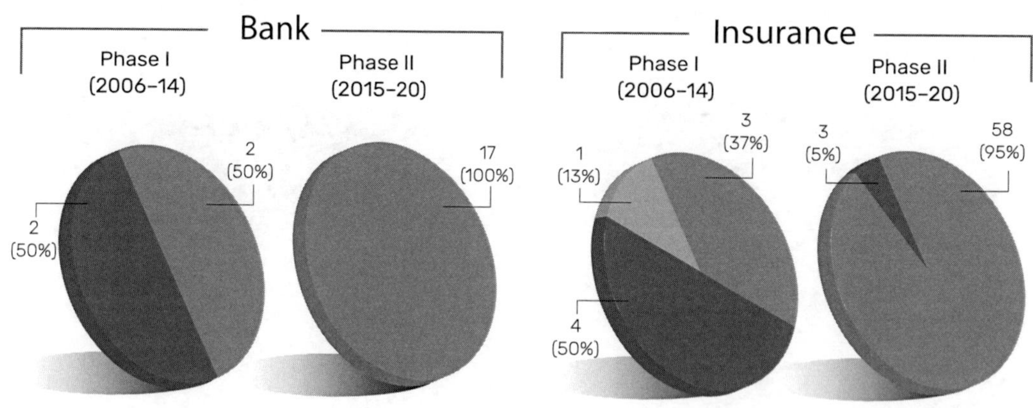

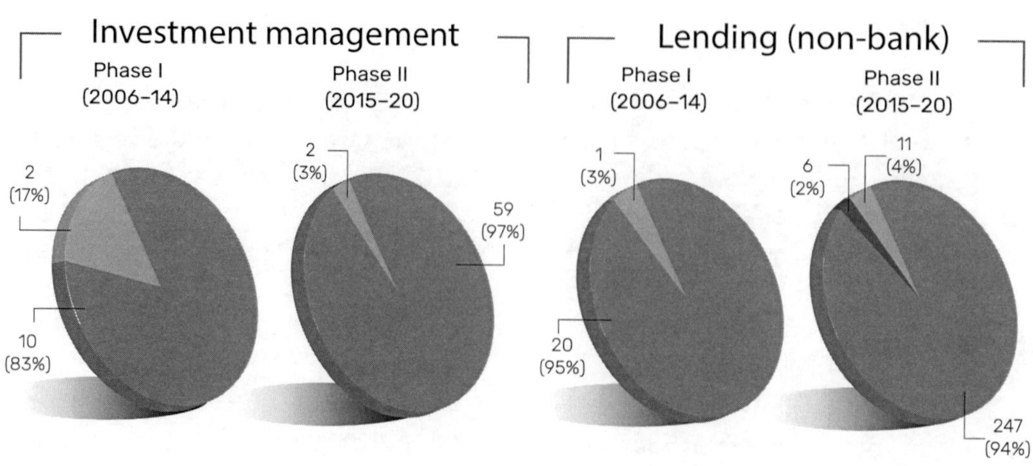

Exhibit 21.14: (Contd.)

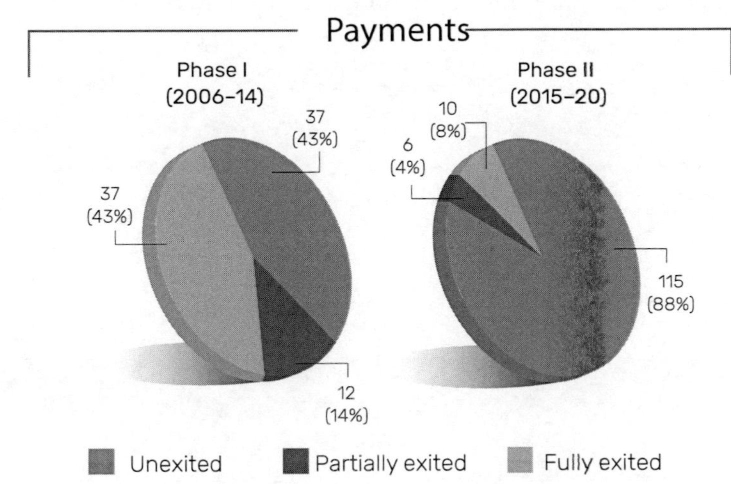

Source: Venture Intelligence

Exhibit 21.15: COVID-19 and FinTech investments

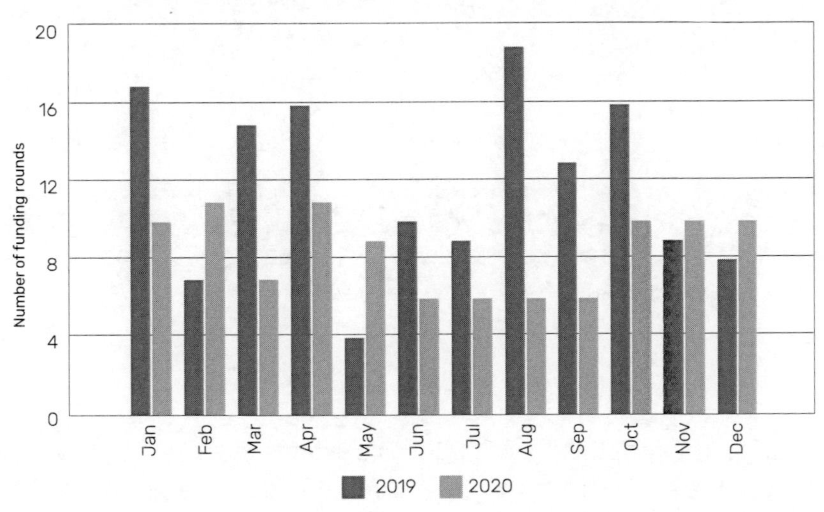

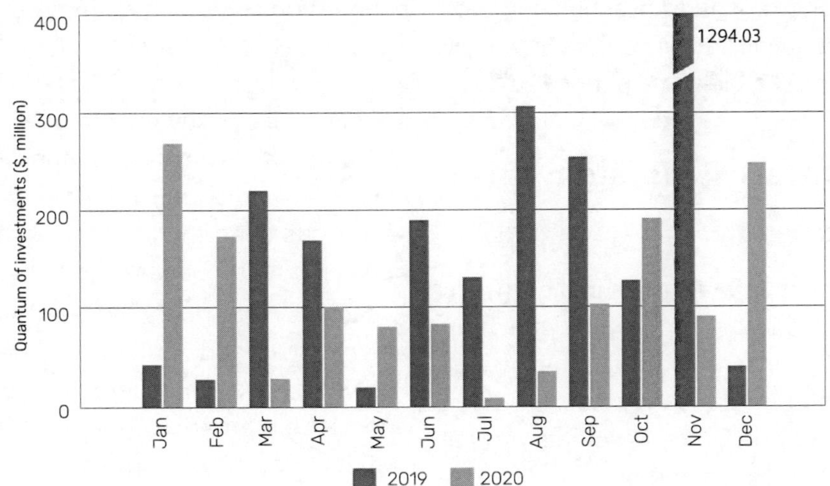

Source: Venture Intelligence

Exhibit 21.16: Select regulatory interventions in India

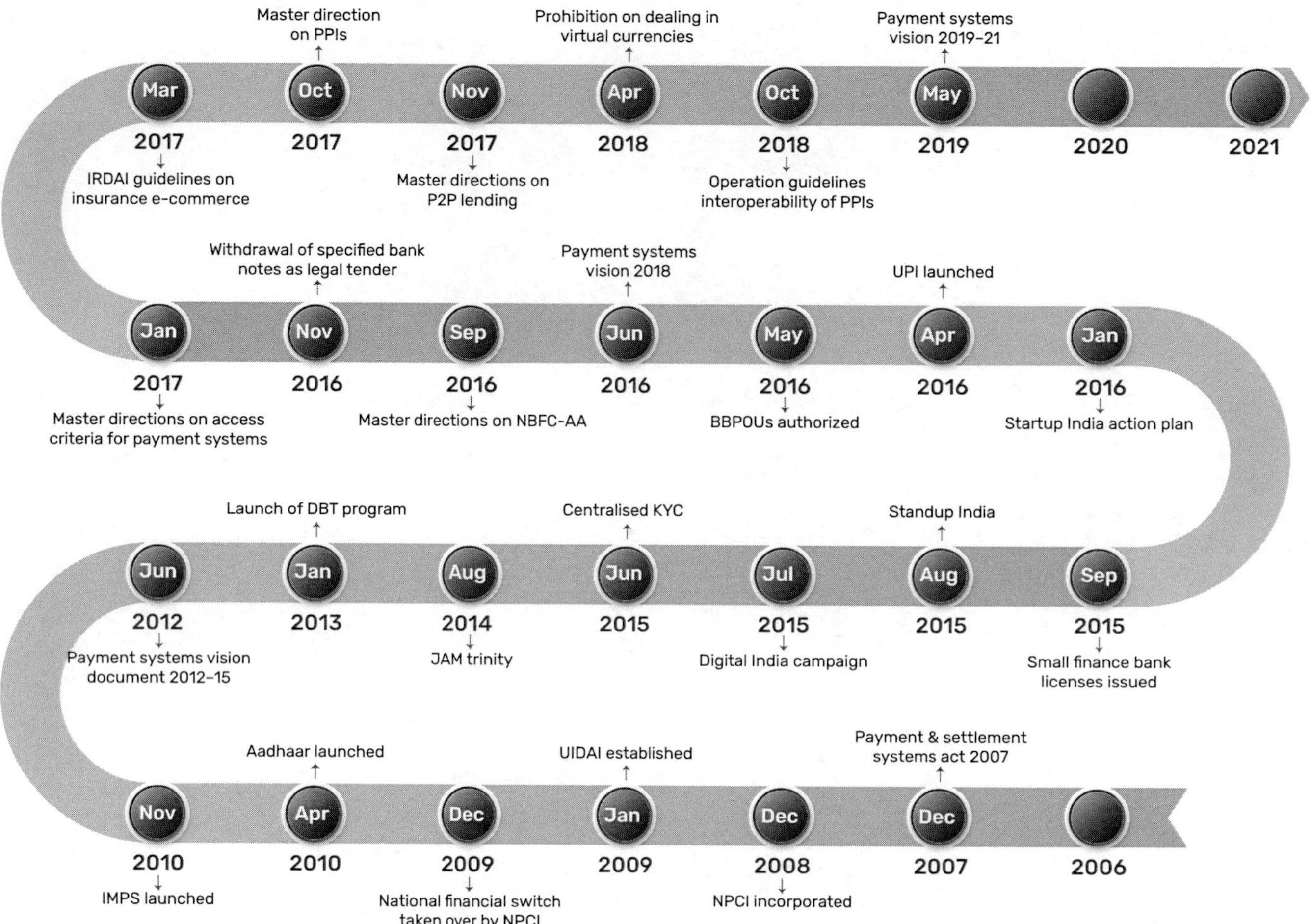

Source: Reserve Bank of India

FinTech firms operating in 169 jurisdictions, with 83 observations taken from India. The survey found that the FinTech firms faced "significant headwinds in operations and fundraising", despite 12 out of 13 FinTech verticals reporting a year-on-year growth in transaction numbers and volume of 13 per cent and 11 per cent, respectively Q1–Q2 2020, compared with the same period in 2019.

Summary: The FinTech Ecosystem and Growth Trends

In summary, the amount of VC investment in the FinTech sector until 2015 was modest and driven by growth in the Payments sector. However, since then, the pace of growth in the Lenders and Insurance verticals has been impressive, while the investors in the Payments vertical have enjoyed Unicorn valuations and robust exit options.

The extant literature recognises several factors that have contributed to the growth of FinTech companies in an economy. Under-developed traditional financial services ecosystem, rise of mobile usage, increase in internet penetration, rise of e-commerce, technology literate work force, under-serviced customer segments and high cost of delivery by traditional financial intermediaries are some of the key growth drivers. However, the most instrumental driving force in the widespread adoption of FinTech in India and the growth of investments in the sector has been the policy interventions by the central bank, market regulators and the government.

India is a member of a select group of countries that has payment and settlement laws. The RBI and Indian Banks' Association under the provisions of the Payment and Settlement Systems Act, 2007 constituted the National Payments Corporation of India in 2009 as the umbrella organisation for operating retail payments and settlement systems in India. In our analysis, the growth in the FinTech sector in the period between 2006 and 2014 (Phase 1) was driven by the Payments vertical. A big contributor to that phase of growth was the accommodative regulatory stance and the payment infrastructure created therein. The state-of-the-art payment infrastructure includes Immediate Payments Service, Unified Payments Interface, Bharat Bill Pay System and Aadhaar-enabled Payment System. The history of regulatory initiatives is mapped in Exhibit 21.16. The rise of the Payment vertical with the dual objective of financial inclusion was influenced by the setting up of the Unique Identification Authority of India (UIDAI) and National Payments Corporation of India in 2009, followed by Immediate Payment Service in 2011, linking of Jan Dhan, Aadhar and Mobile (JAM) in 2014, centralised Know Your Customer (KYC) in 2015, Unified Payment Interface in 2016, Bharat Bill Payment Operating Unit authorisation in 2016 and demonetisation in 2016.

Since 2015, the RBI and other financial market regulatory agencies have initiated substantive actions to respond to the emergence of FinTech specifically. The RBI in late 2015 approved the setting up of the Trade Receivables Discounting System (TReDs), an electronic platform for facilitating the financing and discounting of trade receivables of micro, small and medium enterprises (MSMEs) through multiple financiers. In 2016, the RBI approved the role of account aggregators to facilitate access to client data, without storage, provided that clients have given explicit consent. In 2018, the Working Group on FinTech and Digital Banking, constituted by the RBI, submitted its report. The RBI report acknowledges the risks inherent in platform-based FinTech. The report recommends risk assessment and impact on financial stability due to major FinTech innovations and calls for partnerships and engagements among regulators, existing industry players, clients and FinTech firms. The report underlines the importance of standalone data protection and privacy laws in the country. The report invites the adoption of digital channels to replace manual, time-consuming processes to empower customers and/or the workforce in the Insurance sector and recommends collaboration between Insurance and InsurTech firms. In our analysis, the growth in the FinTech sector in the 2015–2020 period (Phase 2) was more broad-based, partly due to these policy measures.

Importantly, the RBI report recommends a regulatory sandbox and innovation hub for developing FinTech innovations and testing of applications and APIs. One such recent initiative is the Open Credit Enablement Network (OCEN) protocol announced in 2020, with the objective of growing the MSME credit infrastructure. Sahay is the official app in OCEN, comparable to what BHIM was for payments. Within OCEN, the loan service provider will be responsible for handling the entire loan cycle flow while the actual loan provider may be a bank or non-banking financial company. Loan service providers access client data through account aggregators and would provide credit in a few simple steps (Exhibit 21.17). The framework allows flow-based lending where the businesses' operational data would become the collateral for loans. The OCEN infrastructure combined with the role of account aggregators promises strong growth potential for the Lending sector in the near future, and their role is likely to be similar to the role of UIDAI in the growth of the Payment sector.

Endnotes

[1]Open Credit Enhancement Network (OCEN) is the latest advancement in the India stack and is an open standards-based network, envisioned to accelerate access to affordable formal credit. Account aggregators will act as enablers in the OCEN framework, providing access to customer data and facilitating innovative ways to issue credit, such as credit based on cash flow and tax information–based underwriting process.

[2]Includes Belgium, France, Germany, Ireland, Italy, Luxembourg, Netherlands, Spain, Australia, Canada, Cayman Islands, Hong Kong, Japan, Korea, Singapore, Switzerland, United Kingdom, United States and the Euro area.

[3]Includes Argentina, Brazil, Chile, China, India, Indonesia, Mexico, Russia, Saudi Arabia, South Africa and Turkey.

[4]Financial Stability Board. 2020. *Global Monitoring Report on Non-Bank Financial Intermediation*. Interactive data, Time series view. Retrieved from https://data.fsb.org/dashboard/Time%20Series%20View

[5]Other financial intermediaries includes broker-dealers, central counterparties, captive financial institutions and money lenders, finance company, hedge funds, money market funds, other investment funds, real estate investment trust and funds, structured finance vehicles, trust companies and others.

Exhibit 21.17: Role of the account aggregator

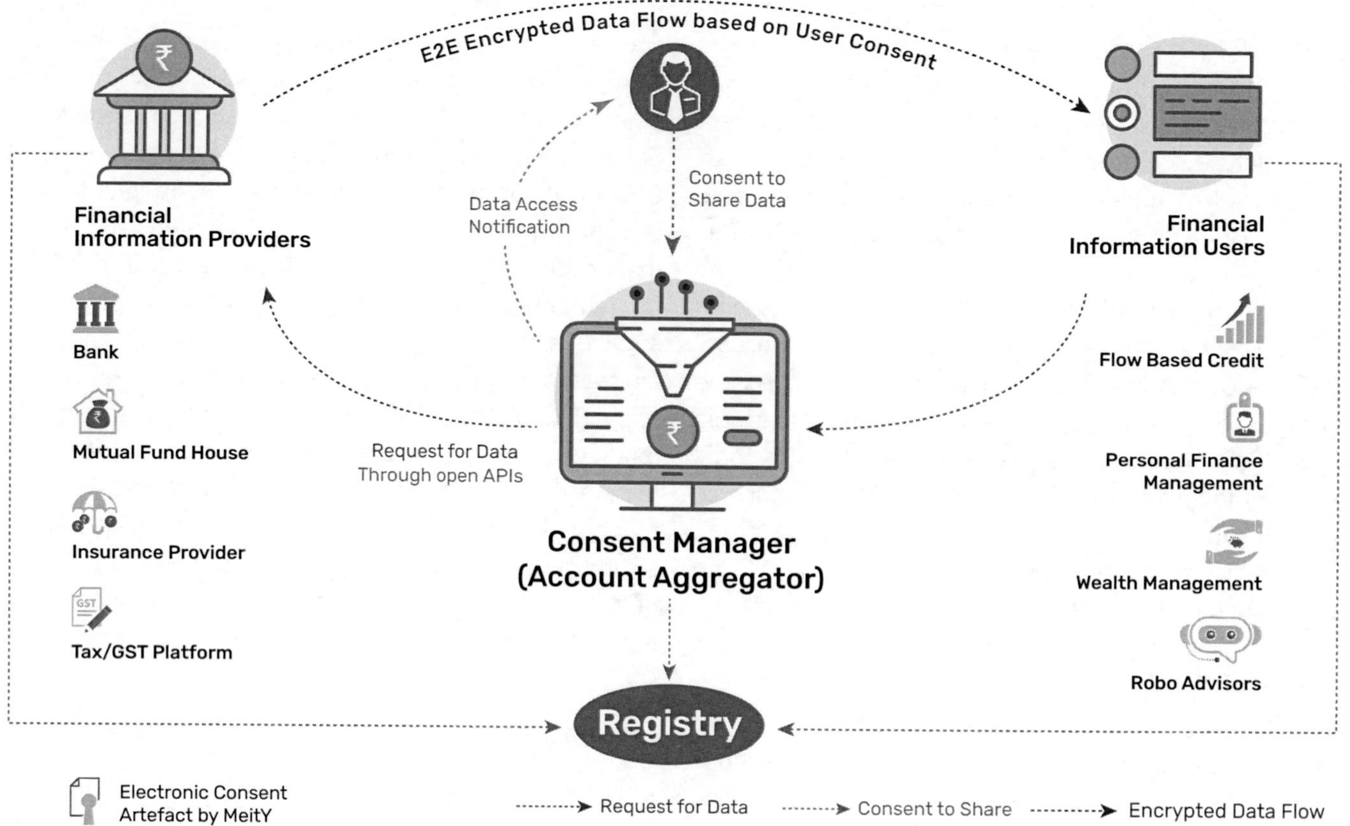

Source: Sahamati, https://sahamati.org.in

[6]Medici, India. 2020. *FinTech Report, Second Edition.* Retrieved from https://gomedici.com/research-categories/india-fintech-report-2020
(Report published in July 2020)

[7]Calendar year 2000 to 2020.

[8]The top 20 deals in the BFSI sector account for 32% of PE/VC funding which includes investments from Bain, KKR, Carlyle, Warbus Pincus, Blackstone and Goldman Sachs into traditional intermediaries such as Axis Bank, HDFC Bank, Insurance, ECL, NSE and Edelweiss Wealth.

[9]Of the 759 unique funding rounds, Venture Intelligence did not have data on the money raised for 57 rounds.

[10]In the given period, the overall PE/VC investment in Indian companies amounted to $240.38 billion across 10,022 investment rounds and 5,187 unique firms.

[11]Privately held start-up company, valued at over $1 billion.

[12]EY, Global FinTech Adoption Index. 2019. Retrieved from https://www.ey.com/en_in/ey-global-FinTech-adoptionindex

[13]Ehrentraud, J, Ocampo, DG, Garzoni, L. and Piccolo, M. 2020. Policy responses to fintech: a cross-country overview. *Bank for International Settlements, Financial Stability Institute.* Retrieved from https://www.bis.org/fsi/publ/insights23.htm

[14]As per the classification, Banks are primarily made up of neo banks and small finance banks. Lenders also include non-banking financial companies and crowd-funding companies. Payments also includes payment banks and firms that provide digital wallets. Investment Management include advisory firms for mutual funds and personal finance, trading and WealthTech firms. Lastly, Others include cryptocurrencies, PropTech, RegTech and technology enabler firms.

[15]APIs have also been extensively used by Payments, Lending and Deposit firms, as they may also enable controlled access to data and IT systems of related third

parties. On the IT infrastructure side, cloud computing enables conversion of capital expenditure to operating expenditure, thereby facilitating the survival and growth of several early-stage firms. AI and ML enable automation and facilitate decision-making and prediction amongst other uses and have found wide usage in risk management, portfolio construction, trading and robo-advisory. Lastly, DLT reduces the problems of information asymmetry and can potentially disintermediate several financial services companies.

[16]CCAF, World Bank and World Economic Forum. 2020. *The Global Covid-19 FinTech Market Rapid Assessment Report*, University of Cambridge, World Bank Group and the World Economic Forum. Retrieved from http://www3.weforum.org/docs/WEF_The_Global_Covid19_FinTech_Market_Rapid_Assessment_Study_2020.pdf

IN BRIEF

- Heightened capital investment and entrepreneurial activity in the HealthTech sector in the last decade, with over 3,000 start-ups including 21 soonicorns and 60 minicorns.
- The COVID-19 pandemic has been a disruptor, resulting in higher preference for out-of-hospital teleconsultations, crossing 1 million over eight months as reported by eSanjeevani telemedicine service in December 2020.
- Newer segments like chronic disease management, e-pharmacies and health data–based start-ups have emerged in recent times, broadening the HealthTech sector.
- The underserviced domestic market – one doctor per 1445 patients and 5 beds per 10,000 people compared to the WHO standard of one doctor for 1000 patients and 3 beds per 1000, as well as lack of adequate facilities, especially for the rural population – offers a valuable opportunity for the Indian HealthTech sector to create disruptive change leading to healthcare inclusion.
- Growth of $20 billion Chinese internet medical market with 620 million users, 100 internet medical platforms and 900 internet public hospital indicates the future growth possibilities in India.
- Indian HealthTech also has the opportunity to leverage its IT skill sets and low-cost high-quality service delivery capabilities to provide remote healthcare support services to global markets.

22

HealthTech: Shifting Gears

Sameer Wagle

Wagle, S. 2021. "HealthTech: Shifting Gears". In *Shifting Orbits: Decoding the Trajectory of the Indian Start-up Ecosystem*, edited by Thillai Rajan A, Srivardhini K Jha, Joffi Thomas and Rohan Chinchwadkar, 292–306. Hyderabad: Universities Press (India) Private Limited.

Overview

The World Health Organization (WHO) defines health technology as *"the application of organised knowledge and skills in the form of devices, medicines, vaccines, procedures and systems developed to solve a health problem and improve quality of lives"*.

While WHO's definition is broad, for the purpose of this report and to make it more relevant in the Indian context, we have considered a sharper definition of health technology as follows: *"Health technology (HealthTech) is any application of technology in the healthcare domain which helps in improving the scope, efficacy and efficiency of its ecosystem and operations"*.

The scope of Indian HealthTech is thus fairly diverse, incorporating areas such as patient acquisition and management, healthcare enterprise IT management, healthcare supply chain, medical devices, healthcare data analytics and healthcare IT outsourcing. The Indian HealthTech sector, which was estimated to be $5.2 billion in FY 2019 (excluding medical devices), is expected to grow to $21 billion by FY 2025.[1]

The Indian healthcare sector faces numerous challenges, namely, low public healthcare spending, shortage of human resources and inadequate infrastructure, low income levels and affordability and high out-of-pocket healthcare spending. For example, India has one doctor per 1,445 patients compared with the WHO norm of one doctor for 1,000 patients (Economic Survey 2019–2020). Likewise, the hospital bed to population ratio in India is only 5 per 10,000 people, much lower than international benchmarks.[2] This situation is aggravated by complications arising from the prevalence of a dual epidemic of both communicable and non-communicable diseases, inconsistent quality of healthcare delivery and fragmented healthcare supply chains. In this context, HealthTech, through its multiple sub-sectors, can play and is playing a transformative role by helping address and overcome these unique challenges.

This is taking place broadly on two fronts. In the domestic market, HealthTech can help address the huge healthcare infrastructure and manpower deficit by using technology to disproportionately leverage available resources and capabilities to increase access to healthcare services for a much larger population and geographical area and simultaneously significantly increase the efficiency and quality of services. The resultant improvement in healthcare outcomes will have a transformative impact on the economy, society and ultimately every Indian.

On the international front, India has the opportunity to leverage its unique combination of healthcare and IT skillsets and talent and low-cost high-quality service delivery capabilities to provide remote healthcare support services to global markets – ranging from healthcare IT outsourcing to knowledge processing outsourcing (KPOs) and remote diagnostic services. This can be a huge growth driver for the Indian economy with the potential to create a large number of jobs.

This chapter is organised into three sections: in the first section, the early growth of Indian HealthTech is dealt with. Recent developments in HealthTech with the arrival of mobile connectivity and the internet is covered in the second section. In the third section, government initiatives in setting up and enabling a policy environment for digitalisation are discussed; the emergence of the Chinese HealthTech industry, especially mobile medical platforms and internet hospitals, is also brought out to indicate the digitalisation possibilities in the Indian context. The chapter concludes by summarising the growth possibilities and details the next steps to be taken to make healthcare more accessible and affordable to realise its growth potential.

Early Growth of HealthTech in India

The HealthTech sub-sector in India is relatively nascent and has seen substantial growth only over the last decade. Specifically, the recent confluence of factors ranging from increase in smartphone penetration, low data costs to the COVID-19 pandemic has pushed HealthTech towards a higher growth trajectory, and this growth is only expected to accelerate over the next 10–15 years.

In India, historically the initial forays into HealthTech were on three fronts: healthcare enterprise IT, telemedicine and medical devices (Exhibit 22.1).

Healthcare Enterprise IT

The entry of the private sector into healthcare delivery led to increased focus on improving operational efficiencies, thus providing a fillip to investments into healthcare enterprise IT solutions and applications. In the first phase, this was in the form of basic IT applications where discrete offline processes (such as patient billing) were computerised. However, the bulk of the processes and activities was driven by paper records.

The next phase of evolution of healthcare enterprise IT was the automation of end-to-end systems across the healthcare enterprise, similar to ERP solutions. This was generally in the form of customised software solutions built for large hospitals either through in-house tech teams or through third-party vendors. With the maturing of the Indian healthcare industry and the onset of innovative healthcare delivery models (single speciality clinics), this subsequently progressed to the use of 'standard' healthcare IT products or solutions provided by specialised healthcare-focussed IT vendors, such as Instahealth, Attune, Palash and Akhil. The next phase in the healthcare enterprise IT space was the entry of cloud-based solutions and Software as a Solution (SaaS) applications where the solution is hosted on the cloud. Some examples of the companies in this space are iSmart and MedML.

One of the biggest constraints that the healthcare enterprise IT segment has faced is the resistance of the medical community to migrating from paper-based systems to one based on technology, especially on the patient-facing front. This barrier is slowly being reduced, thanks to the younger generation of medical practitioners and healthcare workers being more tech savvy and because of improvements in IT infrastructure.

Exhibit 22.1: Healthcare segments

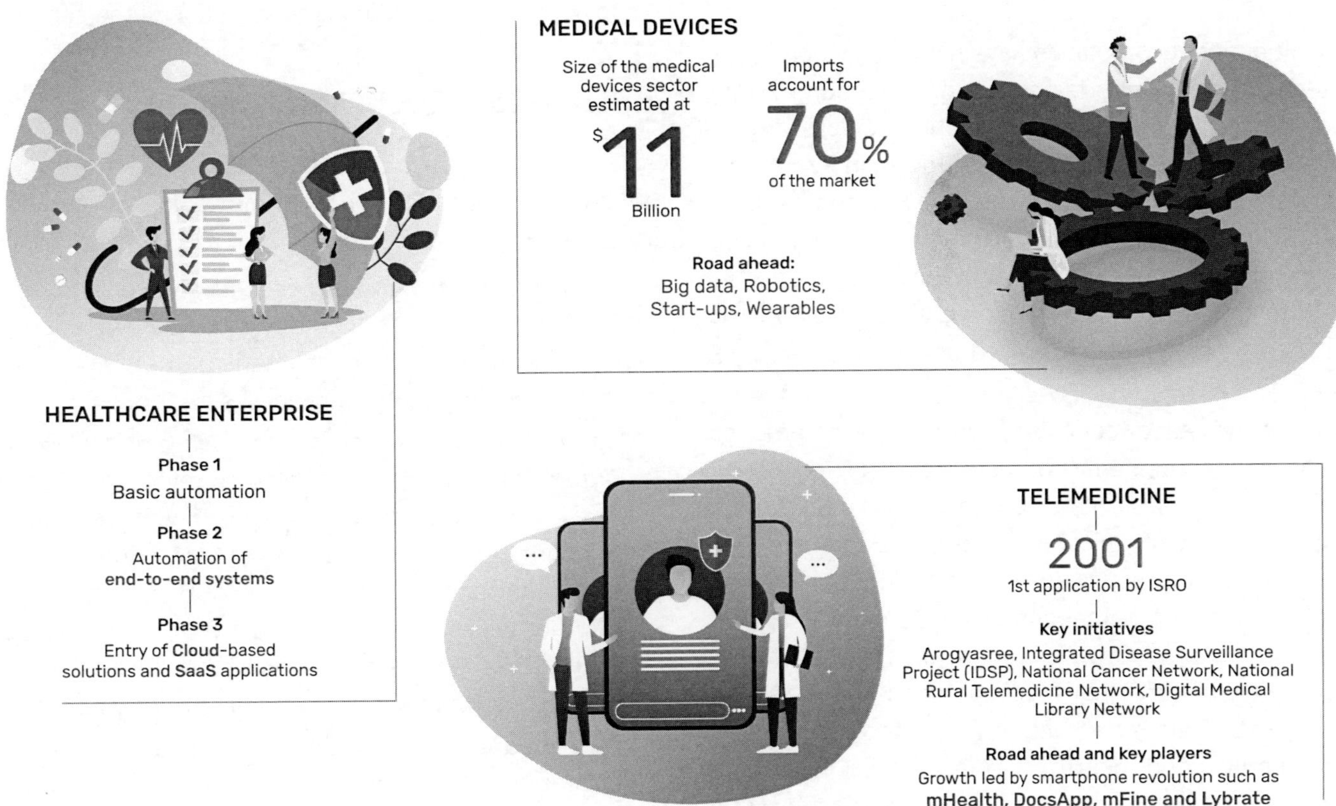

Source: Author

Telemedicine

In India, telemedicine was historically largely a government-owned or -driven initiative undertaken to provide healthcare access in rural areas where there is a dearth of healthcare professionals.

The Indian Space Research Organisation (ISRO) undertook the first large-scale telemedicine application in 2001 by linking Apollo Hospitals with its own rural hospital at Aragonda village (Andhra Pradesh). Subsequently, government steps like the roll-out of standardised telemedicine practice guidelines by the IT Ministry and establishment of a National Telemedicine Task Force by the Health Ministry in 2005 were key milestones in the evolution of telemedicine in the country.

The *Arogyasree* initiative by ICMR, Integrated Disease Surveillance Project (IDSP), National Cancer Network (ONCONET), National Rural Telemedicine Network and the Digital Medical Library Network were some of the key government initiatives in the field of telemedicine. In the private sector too, companies such as Neurosynaptic Communications, Prognosys Healthcare and Apollo Clinics played a key role in partnering with the government in their telemedicine initiatives.

The next phase of growth in telemedicine was driven by the telecom data and smartphone revolution, with companies such as mHealth, DocsApp, mFine and Lybrate moving beyond government-led models to target customers directly through both B2C and B2B2C models. Many of these companies have raised large amounts of private equity funding in recent times, accelerating the growth in this space.

However, telemedicine still faces challenges that include poor last-mile internet infrastructure, patient and doctor preference for physical consultations and reluctance to pay for online consultations. These need to be addressed to ensure that the full potential of telemedicine is realised.

Medical Devices

Medical devices are critical components in ensuring high quality of medical services. The current size of the medical devices sector in India is estimated at US$ 11 billion.[3]

Multinational companies have historically dominated this sector, with imports accounting for around 70 per cent of the market. The domestic medical devices players have been significantly sub-scale in size – while there are reportedly over 750–800 Indian companies in the medical devices sub-sector, only around 10 per cent of these would have individual revenues of more than ₹500 million. Historically, most Indian medical devices sector companies have focussed on "me-too" products competing largely on pricing.

The main reason for this is the preference amongst medical practitioners to use "established" MNC products because of their longer in-field track record, larger universe of clinical outcomes data, brand power, strong after-sale service and strong distribution network – all leading to a perception of higher quality. Limited availability of product development and R&D capabilities in India, lack of an established manufacturing ecosystem for medical devices and electronics, unfavourable policy environment and dearth of funding for early-stage medical devices are the other challenges faced by the Indian medical devices sector.

It is pertinent to note that many of these MNC devices are designed keeping the requirements of developed countries in mind, and hence, end up being "over-engineered" for the Indian context. Therefore, over-reliance on MNC medical devices by the Indian healthcare industry in general translates into higher investment outlays by healthcare delivery companies and doctors, ultimately leading to higher cost of healthcare services for patients. The ultimate loser as a result of this conundrum is the patient.

However, over the last decade, India has seen an improvement in this scenario, with significant growth in innovative "engineered for India" medical devices in areas ranging from ophthalmology to nephrology and oncology. Some prominent companies in this space include Forus Health, Perfint, Niramai and Tricog.

This trend has been driven by the advent of:

1. First-generation entrepreneurs with prior medical devices domain expertise
2. Sustained government initiatives to promote innovation in the medical devices space through grants and early-stage funding through organisations like BIRAC and CCAMP. More details of this are provided in the section on the evolution of the sector

Indian HealthTech: New Impetus

Over the last decade, a confluence of factors has moved the Indian HealthTech industry into a higher growth orbit. These factors include:

- *Rising health consciousness and spending power on healthcare:* With increasing health awareness, rising prosperity and consumerism, the market for HealthTech products and services has grown.
- *Smartphone penetration, internet usage and telecom data costs:* Thanks to the telecom revolution, India has transitioned from a country with very low telecom density and high usage costs to one with high smartphone ownership (> 400 million), high internet access (500 million active internet users) and one of the lowest data costs in the world. This is serving as a major enabler for HealthTech models.
- *Mainstreaming of consumer internet models:* The success of companies like Flipkart and Amazon has led to customer awareness and acceptance of business models with remote support and without proximate physical presence.
- *Growth in low-cost payment systems:* India has become a pioneer in low-cost mass payment systems riding on the JAM infrastructure (Jan Dhan accounts, mobile numbers and Aadhar cards) and UPI platform. This has made it possible for micro-payments to be made remotely, which is an important element in a geographically dispersed telemedicine model.
- *Maturing of early-stage investing ecosystem creating innovative HealthTech start-ups:* Government- and academia-driven incubators (DBT, BIRAC, CCAMP), which have been functional for the last couple of decades, have resulted in the creation and growth of innovative HealthTech and MedTech companies.

COVID-19: An Invisible Propeller

On top of all the above factors, the COVID-19 pandemic has emerged as a big disruptor, providing a strong fillip to the growth of HealthTech. Some of the key market trends created by COVID-19, which in turn are accelerating HealthTech adoption are:

Exhibit 22.2: HealthTech, new impetus

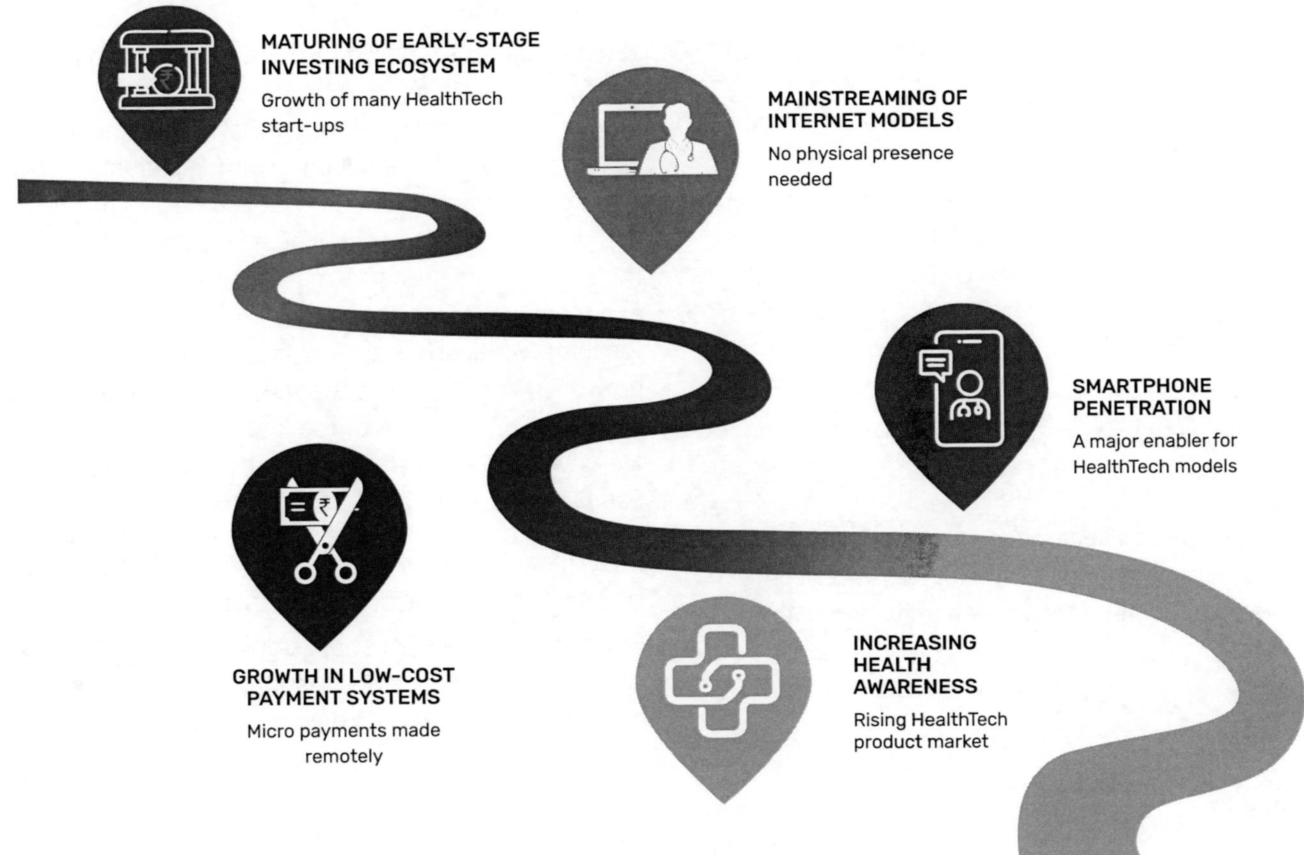

- *Formalisation of the sector:* After the COVID-19 pandemic, customers have demonstrated an increased preference for branded organised players because of perceived higher safety and better quality. The propensity and ability of organised players to adopt HealthTech is much higher.
- *Mindset change for both doctors and patients:* COVID-19 has resulted in both doctors and patients being forced to use and accept alternative healthcare delivery mechanisms. It is believed that this will result in a more permanent shift in mindset and more widespread adoption of HealthTech offerings like telemedicine.
- *Favourable regulatory environment:* Driven by COVID-19, the government accelerated the roll-out of new regulations facilitating the use of HealthTech; for example, the government roll-out of telemedicine regulations and e-pharmacies being allowed to operate as essential services during the lockdown. This has made the operating environment for HealthTech companies far more conducive.
- *Preference for out-of-hospital healthcare delivery:* There is now a visibly higher preference by consumers for lower risk, specialised environments for services that reduces the need for a visit to a hospital, where the risk of catching COVID-19 infection is higher.

This impact of COVID-19 is reflected in the initial post–COVID-19 trends for use of HealthTech:

- The Union Health Ministry's eSanjeevani telemedicine service crossed 1 million tele-consultations in a matter of eight months. The platform is currently used by patients in 550 districts, with the volume of consultations increasing to around 14,000 per day.[4]
- According to a recent FICCI-BCG (2020) survey,[5] 60–65 per cent of patients across metro and Tier 1 cities said they would continue to prefer the digital medium for accessing healthcare even in the post–COVID-19 world.
- Practo saw teleconsultations grow at over 100 per cent week-on-week in the first few months post COVID-19. Also, there has been an almost 50 per

cent increase in the number of doctors joining Practo.

- StepOne, a post–COVID-19 telemedicine initiative with over 7K volunteer doctors across 16 states, has completed more than 5 million calls across 10 states with over 30,000 daily calls.
- Investment bank UBS estimates[6] that the share of teleconsultations in the total OPD market (out of a total of 4.5–5.0 billion OPD visits per year) has grown to 2–3 per cent in FY 2021 from less than 0.5 per cent in the pre-COVID period.

Evolving Horizons: New Segments in HealthTech

As the HealthTech sector has evolved, new focus areas, business models and technologies have come into prominence. Some of these are highlighted below:

Advancement and Broadening of Telemedicine

Telemedicine has evolved from a focus on plain vanilla online consultation, which provided only the limited functionality of increasing access to healthcare, to a wider range of value addition, covering patient discovery and aggregation to chronic disease care management and preventive care and wellness. From a point solution, the offering has grown to managing end-to-end patient experience. This is the result of internet penetration reaching a critical mass, increased health awareness and growth in the number of patients with non-communicable diseases (NCD). Some of the key segments in this area along with specific start-up examples are presented in Exhibits 22.3 and 22.4.

Movement from Healthcare IT to Digitisation of Larger Healthcare Ecosystem

From a primary focus on implementing technology solutions within hospitals and clinics, healthcare IT has now moved towards digitising the larger healthcare

Exhibit 22.3: Telemedicine segment

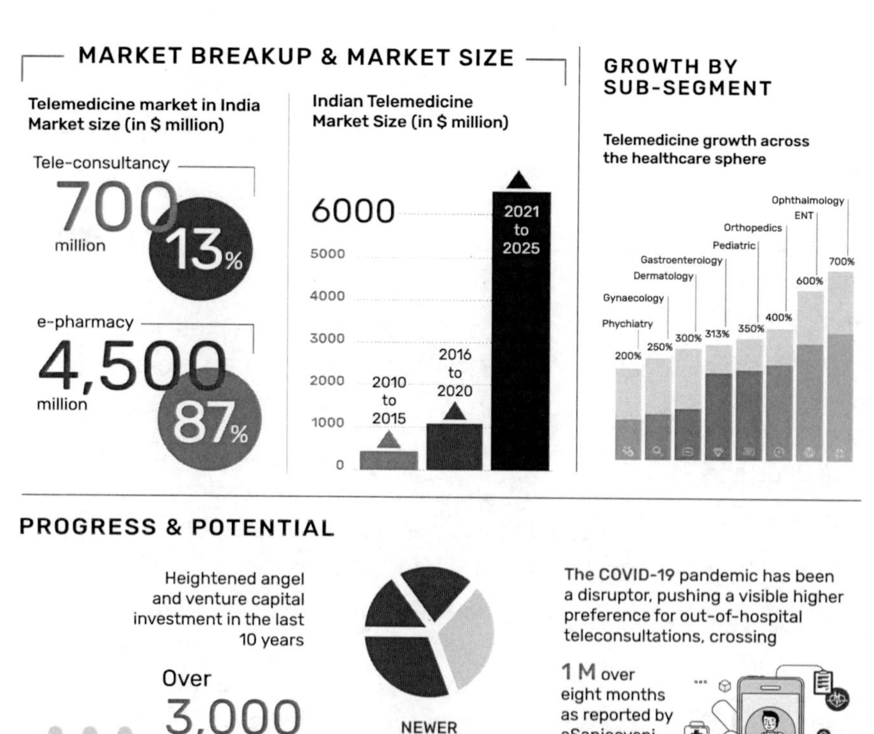

SOLUTION PROVIDER

AREA	ROLE
Online Patient Discovery	Source, aggregate and manage patient experience
Preventive Care / Wellness / Fitness	Helps patients in preventive care, wellness and fitness
Chronic Care Management	Handholding and managing chronic diseases
Home Healthcare	Using technology to provide high-quality homecare medical services
Patient Communities	Online Patient and Doctor communities

Source: Inc42, Statista, Practo[7], EY-IPA study[8]

Exhibit 22.4: Telemedicine segment-wise start-ups

Area	Role	Start-ups	Specific company example
Online Patient Discovery and Aggregation Platforms	Source, aggregate and manage patient experience across the treatment life cycle	Medfin Credihealth, Glamyo, Onco, Pristyn, Healthians	Glamyo is a technology-enabled asset-light healthcare platform utilising unused healthcare capacity to provide elective surgeries
Preventive Care, Wellness and Fitness	Helps patients in preventive care, wellness and fitness	Practo, Cure.fit, Healthifyme, GOQii	Healthifyme is a digital health and wellness platform that provides services such as calorie tracking, one-on-one nutrition, fitness coaching and diet and workout plans
Chronic Care Management	Handholding and managing chronic diseases	BeatO, Zyla	BeatO is an online platform to help diabetes patients manage the disease
Home Healthcare	Using technology to provide high-quality homecare medical services	Portea, Healthcare atHOME, Medwell, CallHealth	HealthCare atHOME provides personalised and professional home healthcare services to allow quick and convenient recovery within the comfort of one's home
Social Platforms, Patient Communities	Online patient and doctor communities	Healofy, Mylo, Curofy	Healofy is a pregnancy and parenting platform for Indian mothers

Source: Tracxn HealthTech – India and Global Report July 2020[9]

ecosystem. As mentioned earlier, the value chain in the healthcare sector is fragmented, with a high level of inefficiencies. This has provided the opportunity for start-ups to come up with innovative and disruptive solutions to address the pain points on both the supply chain end and customer-facing front (pharmacies, diagnostic labs and gyms).

In particular, e-pharmacies (Exhibit 22.5) have been the most high-profile sub-sector in this space, with companies raising huge amounts of VC funding and achieving significant scale addressing core issues like drug availability, identifying counterfeit drugs and lowering patient costs.

Medical Devices Moving to POC Devices

The next phase of growth for medical devices is likely to emerge from the movement towards point of care (POC) devices – devices simple enough to be used at the primary care level or in a remote or home setting with no lab infrastructure. These tests offer rapid results, allowing for timely initiation of appropriate therapy or facilitation of linkages to care and referral. Companies in this area include Forus Health, Renalyx and Tricog. For example, Forus Health has helped build one of the largest tele-ophthalmology platforms in Asia that has screened close to 1.5 million patients in Andhra Pradesh.

Data-led Business Models

With the availability of a large amount of healthcare data and increased processing capabilities, new start-ups have emerged leveraging data to improve the efficiency, scope and outcome of healthcare services. These include start-ups (Exhibit 22.6) using AI and analytics for faster, cheaper and more accurate diagnosis, companies using data IoT and data analytics to personalise disease management and medicine delivery and start-ups disrupting healthcare financing.

A total of 5,101 HealthTech start-ups were founded while there were 55 acquisitions in India in 2010–20. About 15 start-ups in HealthTech have a valuation of over $500 million.

HealthTech soonicorns (as per Tracxn report): cure.fit, Pharmeasy, 1mg, Innovacer, Netmeds.com, Practo,

Exhibit 22.5: Digitisation of healthcare ecosystem

Area	Role	Start-ups	Specific company example
Supply Chain Disruptors	Target and address the inefficiencies and fragmentation of the healthcare supply chain	Medikabazaar, Colmed, Pharmarack, Pinkblue Tarnea	Medikabazaar is an online B2B platform for doctors and hospitals
Digital Enablers	E-pharmacies, diagnostics aggregators, virtual labs and fitness aggregators	1mg, cure.fit Netmeds, Fitpass KlinicApp	1mg is an online pharmacy with a range of prescription and OTC medicines and lab tests
Electronic Health Records	Using tech to create EHR for hospitals and clinics	Healthplix, Medcords	Healthplix designs and develops software solutions for electronic medical records for personalised consultation based on a patient's medical history
Healthcare IT Outsourcing for Global Markets	Providing healthcare technology and KPO services to global customers	CitiusTech, Everise	CitiusTech is a specialist provider of healthcare technology services and solutions to some of the world's largest healthcare organisations

Source: Tracxn. 2020. HealthTech – India and Global Report.

Exhibit 22.6: Data-led business start-ups

Area	Role	Start-ups	Specific company example
AI and Data Analytics	Use of data analytics and artificial intelligence for diagnosis and treatment	Sigtuple, Qure.Ai, Forus Health, 5C Network	Forus Health has developed an AI-based platform for diagnosis of ocular and systemic diseases
Life Sciences Tech	Use of technology to help pharma and biotech companies to accelerate drug discovery and clinical trials	MedGenome, Axtria	MedGenome provides personalised medicine with unique genomic solutions in areas like immuno-oncology and diabetes
Digital Therapeutics	Use of digital technology for disease management and customised medicine delivery	Wellthy	Wellthy provides clinically validated digital therapies for chronic care patients
Healthcare Financing	Disrupting the healthcare financing value chain	Affordplan Impactguru, Ketto, Arogya Finance, Kenko	Impactguru is a crowdfunding platform focussed on funding medical expenses

Source: Tracxn. 2020. HealthTech – India and Global Report.

MedGenome, HealthKart, Medlife, Portea, Ascent Health & Wellness, Axtria, SastaSundar, SigTuple and Indegene.

Soonicorn is coined from the term "soon-to-be-Unicorn" and represents companies that are close to reaching the 'Unicorn' valuation of $1 billion.

Minicorn start-ups are those having a valuation of over $1 million and which seem to be on track to becoming Unicorns.

Exhibit 22.7: Health funding trend, India and global

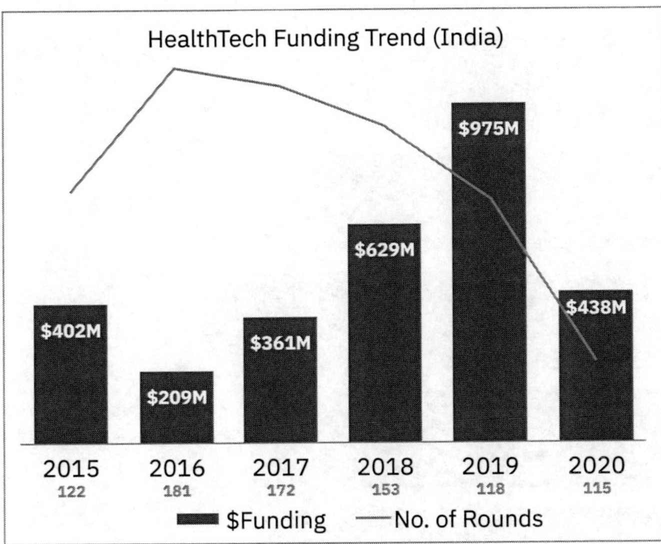

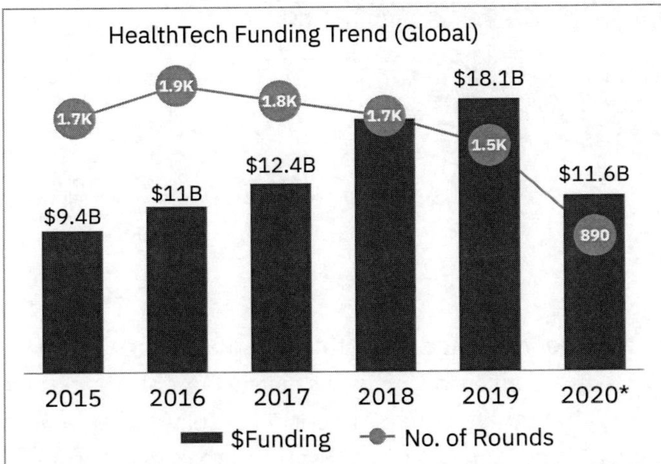

Source: Tracxn 2020 HealthTech India and Global Report. April 2021. Tracxn Feed Report

HealthTech Funding Trends: India and Global Data

Over the last six years, India has seen about $3 billion invested in the digital health opportunity, across 600+ start-ups. Leading up to 2020, the funding raised by Indian start-ups grew 4.7x over a period of three years. Globally, HealthTech companies have raised $78 billion in the same period, testifying to the huge growth potential of the sector.

Healthcare Policy Initiatives

The two key stakeholders in the Indian HealthTech sector are the public sector (government ministries and public health facilities) and the private sector (mainly start-ups). The government's role is primarily policy formulation and creating the infrastructure and governance structures for the sector while the private sector would complement this through innovations in technology applications and business models which leverage on the government-built infrastructure. The different categories of HealthTech players in the private sector and specific examples in each category have been described in the preceding sections. In this section, we focus on the role of the key players in the government sector.

Role of Government

The healthcare sector comes under the purview of the Ministry of Health & Family Welfare and digital health in particular is overseen by the National Digital Health Mission.

Over the last decade, the government has provided a strong push to the idea of digital health through policies and initiatives like National Health Policy (2017) and National Health Stack (2018). These have culminated in the ambitious National Digital Health Mission (NDHM) in 2019 under the National Health Authority (NHA) to create an Open Digital Health Ecosystem.

The idea behind the NDHM (Exhibit 22.8) is to build on the public digital infrastructure used by Ayushman Bharat PMJAY to provide end-to-end services and expand the reach of digital health to all residents, developing an open and inter-operable health management system that can be used by patients, healthcare providers, the government and the healthcare research community. Ayushman Bharat PMJAY is the largest health assurance scheme in the world that aims at providing a health cover of ₹5,00,000 per family per year for secondary and tertiary care hospitalisation to over 107 million poor and vulnerable families (approximately 500 million beneficiaries) that form the bottom 40 per cent of the Indian population.[10]

The key benefits expected from the NDHM are improvements in efficiency, effectiveness, quality, transparency and accountability of healthcare service delivery. This will come through easy and secure access to healthcare records, accurate information on healthcare facilities and service providers, empowerment of patients to access healthcare remotely through telemedicine and

Exhibit 22.8: NDHM stakeholders[11]

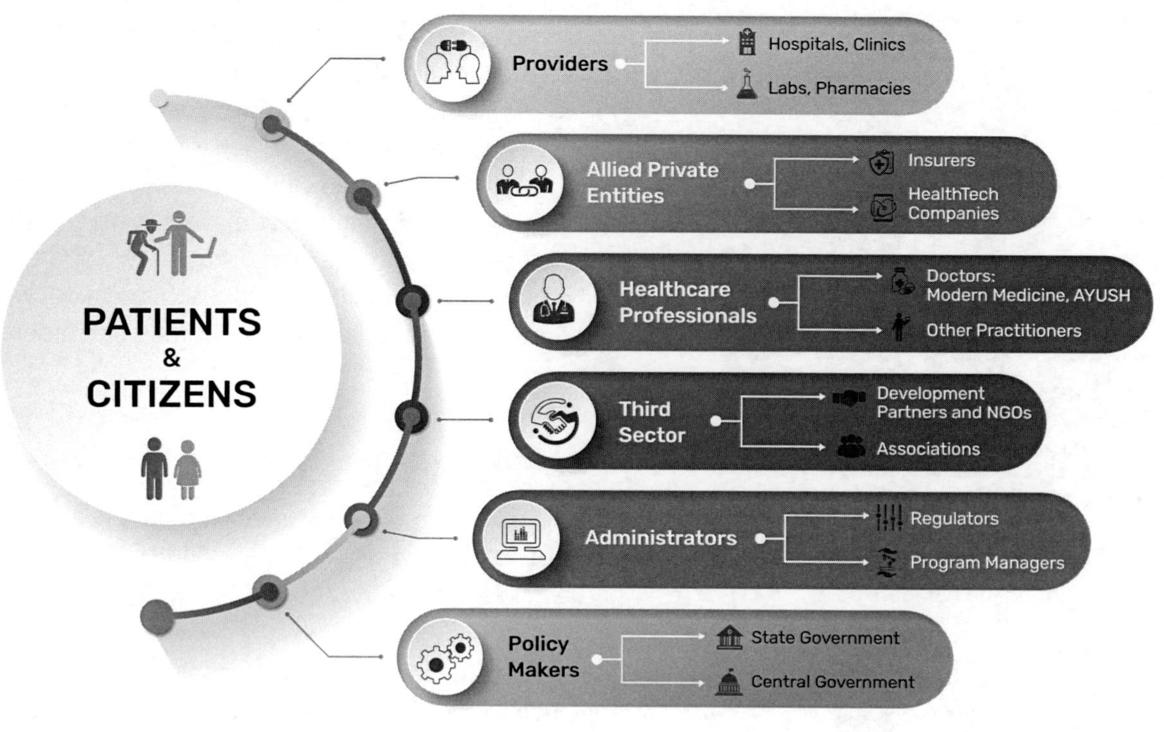

Source: https://ndhm.gov.in

e-pharmacy, faster reimbursement through digitisation of the insurance claims process and providing high-quality data to enable better and proactive public health decisions.

Architecture of NDHM

The envisaged basic building blocks of the NHDM include personalised health IDs, health registries (for doctors and hospitals), decentralised health records, coverage and claims platform, and open telemedicine and e-pharmacy network.

The building blocks are expected to be available as a collection of cloud-based services, with each part providing just one capability across multiple health services, accessible through simple open APIs, designed with built-in security and adequate authentication, authorisation and access protocols. Together, these will create a framework to enable better healthcare delivery and management.

It is envisaged that the NDHM will expand access to care services through a model that enables co-existence of public and private sector applications. A centralised, government-created, -operated and -managed engine will standardise and institutionalise the core back-end for digital healthcare services like telemedicine and e-pharmacy, and open the front-end to consumer apps, which will decouple and facilitate core engine and front-end app-side innovations.

Organisation of NDHM

The NDHM is being rolled out in three phases. The Phase 1 Pilot (with limited services) is ongoing in Union Territories, Phase 2 will take the pilot forward in additional states and expand the service bouquet and Phase 3 will target a nation-wide roll-out, operationalising and converging with all health schemes across India along with promotion, on-boarding and acceptance of NDHM across the country.

The NDHM is expected to have a significant impact on the HealthTech sector by enabling the development of the ecosystem required for the growth of the sector, through building the digital "commons" or digital public infrastructure for the HealthTech sector to ride on. This is similar to what has been seen in the FinTech space, where the development of the digital public infrastructure in the form of UPI and JAM triggered a huge growth in FinTech innovation and start-ups. The boost to the sector as announced in the 2020–21 budget by the government under the purview of PM Atmanirbhar Swasth Bharat Yojana to support over 17,000 rural and 11,000 urban wellness centres, will be an addition to the national health mission.[11]

The NDHM is also likely to facilitate the emergence of a new type of HealthTech start-up, which will better leverage the public digital health infrastructure. For example:

- Intermediaries in the digital infrastructure such as health facility verifiers, consent managers and health locker providers
- Cutting-edge patient solutions that challenge existing service delivery models, such as self-management applications and Clinical Decision Support Systems (CDSS)[12]

Competitive Landscape: Chinese HealthTech Industry

A good benchmark for the Indian HealthTech industry is China, where the growth demonstrated over the last 15 years provides glimpses of where the sector could reach in a comparable country like India. In 2019, China's internet medical market was estimated to be worth $20 billion, an increase of 36 per cent over 2018, and COVID-19 is only expected to further accelerate the growth of the market.[13]

The two key segments in the Chinese HealthTech system are mobile medical platforms (early entrants who used mobile-based platforms to address patient pain points) and internet hospitals (a unique Chinese "omni-channel" construct where physical hospitals launch their own internet service platforms).

According BCG-Tencent, China's internet medical care users today account for 620 million, and 70 per cent of China's mobile internet users and over 100 internet medical platforms compete in the same market, with some of the top apps reaching 1.1 billion cumulative user visits. China has close to 900 "Internet+" public hospitals, and more than 1 million doctors have provided consultation services on online platforms.

Some of the more prominent players in the Chinese HealthTech system are:

- **Alibaba Health**, which focusses on four main businesses: e-pharmacy, internet healthcare, tracking and digital health, and consumer healthcare. The company had revenues of $1.4 billion in FY 2020.
- **Ping An Good Doctor** with presence in four segments, namely, online medical service, consumer healthcare, health mall, health management and wellness interaction; with revenues of $750 million in 2019.
- **WeDoctor**, which follows a unique digital health community model, relying on the internet hospital to build a regional chronic disease management platform. Revenues of WeDoctor in 2020 are estimated to be over $450 million. WeDoctor is planning an IPO in Hongkong early next year.

Given the different economic and social situations, the China HealthTech growth story might not be fully replicable in the Indian context. However, the fact that the healthcare sector in both countries face similar challenges – unbalanced distribution of health resources, high out-of-pocket expenses and limited budget resources – leads one to believe that the Indian HealthTech industry would do well to draw inspiration and learn from the growth and success of its Chinese counterpart.

Prospects and Way Forward

Unlike its global peers that are only focussed on their own domestic markets, the Indian HealthTech sector is uniquely placed because of two complementary growth engines: the domestic and international markets will feed into each other to create a virtuous cycle leading to sustained growth.

Domestic Healthcare Sector: The Indian healthcare industry is expected to increase from $110 billion in 2016 to $372 billion in 2022.[14] This growth is expected to result in a significant demand for the latest HealthTech products and services. Moreover, close proximity to customers in the domestic market would facilitate faster innovation and better product–market fit.

Global Markets: Emerging trends in the global markets offer huge opportunities for Indian HealthTech companies. For example, medical devices companies would be a good fit for other emerging markets with similar demographic and economic conditions and looking for affordable high-quality medical devices. Likewise, companies focussed on SaaS and other outsourcing models can target healthcare enterprises in developed country markets.

Policy Interventions to Address Challenges in the HealthTech Sector

Notwithstanding the huge potential, the HealthTech sector faces a number of challenges, which need to be addressed to enable it to realise its full potential. Some of these are as follows:

Challenges of Rural India (Exhibit 22.9)

- *Improvement in last-mile IT and internet infrastructure:* India still faces the challenge of poor quality internet infrastructure outside cities. For example, as per government estimates, broadband penetration in rural India was a mere 33.9 per cent as of 30 September 2020.[15] Certain states like Bihar (21.69 per cent) and Uttar Pradesh (21.64 per cent) have even lower broadband penetration. Good-quality broadband infrastructure needs to be in place to enable rural India to really benefit from HealthTech services.
- *Availability of trained manpower:* Availability and training of healthcare human resources and empowering them to use technology will be a key factor in determining the success of HealthTech applications in the field, especially in rural and semi-urban India. It is estimated that though 70 per cent of the Indian population lives in villages, only 40 per cent of India's total healthcare workers work in rural India.[16]

  Close to 2000 primary healthcare centres (PHCs) in the country are without doctors and 50 per cent of the health and wellness centres do not have male health workers. Whilst HealthTech can help mitigate this deficit to some extent, it cannot provide a magic solution to the problem, and a sustained effort to increase manpower availability in rural areas is essential.
- One suggestion worth considering is to create a cadre of tech-savvy "tech assistants" who would help both the healthcare workers and patients to use technology at healthcare delivery points.
- *Availability of appropriate content:* Currently, a large chunk of the HealthTech service's interface with consumers is in English, which may act as a limiting factor for the growth of the industry in rural India. The availability of the 3Vs (vernacular, video and voice) content and services would play a major role

Exhibit 22.9: Challenges in HealthTech (Rural India)

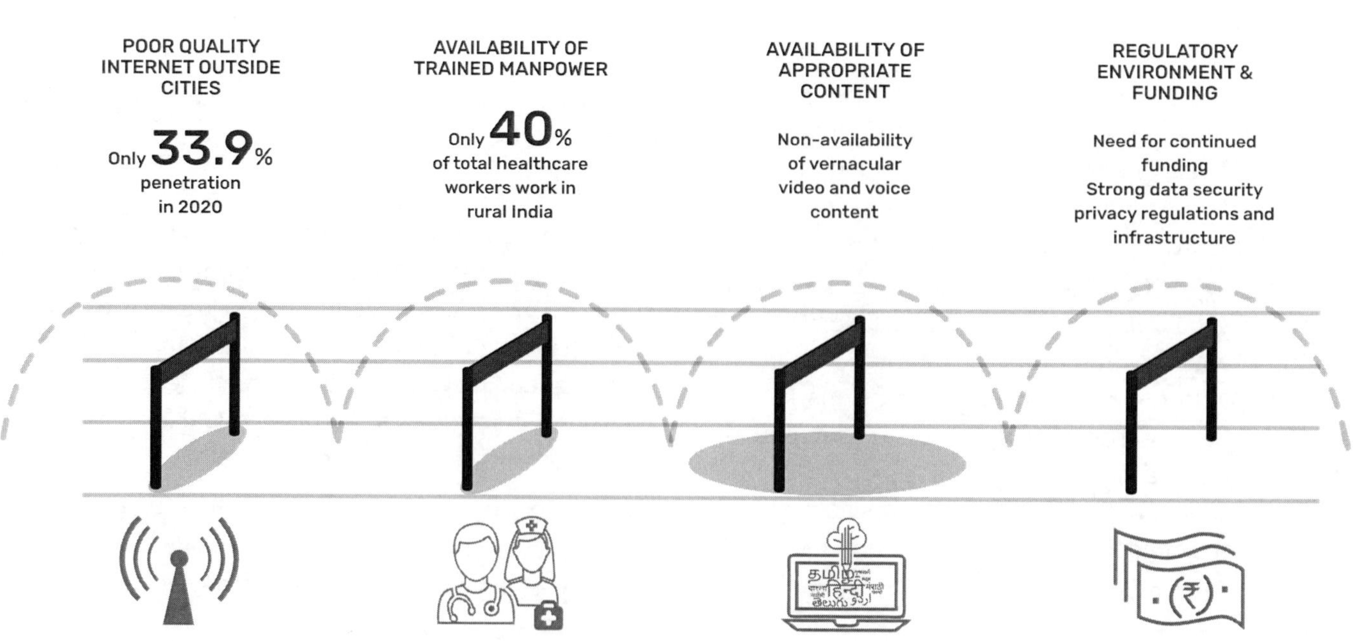

in the success of the models targeting Tier 2 and 3 towns and rural areas.

Regulatory environment and funding

- *Development of supportive regulatory environment:* A number of legacy regulations need to be modernised and upgraded in line with the current situation and the industry's needs. This includes strong data security and privacy regulations, and infrastructure needed to protect the interest of the patient.
- *Continued funding to provide for path to profitability:* Most companies in the HealthTech space, especially those in the customer-facing front, have faced challenges in monetisation, scaling-up revenues and achieving profitability because of high customer acquisition and retention costs and long gestation period. Thus, continued backing of such enterprises by patient investors with deep pockets will be required to enable the success of such models.

It is also important to make some key interventions in some of the government systems related to the healthcare sector:

- *Government procurement systems to be improved:* Given the huge amount of healthcare spending by the government, it can be the ideal reference or initial customer for HealthTech innovations coming out of India, a critical point in the growth journey of any start-up. Unfortunately, the government procurement systems are not appropriately designed for this (instead focussing purely on lowest price) and need to be re-engineered.
- *Promotion of PPP models in HealthTech platforms:* PPP models can combine the strengths of the public and private sectors and provide HealthTech solutions at scale. The government needs to promote such models more actively.
- *Funding ecosystem for high-risk healthcare IT innovation needs to be bolstered:* Most VC funding in India is focussed on companies with me-too service models, whereas innovative healthcare product companies do face a dearth of funding, especially in the early growth stage. There needs to be a stronger government attempt to promote risk investments into IP and product companies including in the HealthTech space.
- *Policy certainty and predictability:* Given that HealthTech companies operate in emerging areas with long time cycles, policy certainty and predictability are important to enable the companies to take a long-term growth approach. Policy flip-flops (e-pharmacy regulations) and movement towards populism (price caps for medical devices) should be avoided.

Summary

In the post–COVID-19 environment, the Indian healthcare sector is faced with a number of challenges, both legacy and new ones triggered by the pandemic. These range from poor infrastructure and dearth of trained manpower to budget constraints and prevalence of both communicable and non-communicable diseases. Use of technology in healthcare through innovative applications and business models offers the Indian healthcare sector a unique opportunity to overcome these challenges and leapfrog to the next stage.

After a tentative beginning in the form of government-led telemedicine models, the HealthTech sector has come a long way over the last few years. The confluence of multiple drivers has positioned the sector to grow exponentially over the next 10–15 years in the process transforming the healthcare ecosystem. This would be a game changer for the economy in general and the healthcare sector specifically, and dramatically improve the life and well-being of every citizen.

There are, however, a number of challenges faced by the sector, including last-mile internet infrastructure, trained manpower, outdated regulatory environment, funding availability and unsuitable government procurement systems. A technology-enabled, affordable and effective healthcare ecosystem is in the interest of the nation at large. Concerted efforts from multiple stakeholders in the innovation ecosystem will accelerate the growth of the sector.

Endnotes

[1]INC42 Datalabs. 2020. *Start-ups Watchlist: 6 Indian HealthTech Start-ups To Watch Out For In 2021*, Retrieved on January 18, 2021 from https://inc42.com/infocus/startup-watchlist-2021/startup-watchlist-6-indian-HealthTech-startups-to-watch-out-for-in-2021/

[2]Economic Survey 2019–2020.

[3]InvestIndia. 2020. *Fostering innovation for improved health*, Retrieved on January 22, 2021, from https://www.investindia.gov.in/sector/medical-devices

[4]Health ministry's telemedicine service eSanjeevani records 1 million teleconsultations, *Times of India*, accessed on 16, January 2021 from https://timesofindia.indiatimes.com/india/health-ministrys-telemedicine-service-esanjeevani-records-1-million-teleconsultations/articleshow/79721550.cms

[5]FICCI BCG. 2020. *Leapfrogging to a Digital Healthcare System, Re-imagining Healthcare for Every India*, Retrieved from https://web-assets.bcg.com/f6/3a/a701f7ab400494fe7aa600e96179/leapfrogging-to-a-digital-healthcare-system-bcg-ficci.pdf

[6]UBS Global Research. 2021. *India Healthcare, A new world of digital initiatives*, Retrieved on January 20, 2021.

[7]IANS. 2020. *Practo's telemedicine subscription plans record 250% growth in 6 months*, Retrieved on January 27, 2021 from https://www.business-standard.com/article/companies/practo-s-telemedicine-subscription-plans-record-250-growth-in-6-months-120120800867_1.html

[8]EY-IPA. September 2020, *Healthcare goes mobile: Evolution of teleconsultation and e-pharmacy in new normal*, retrieved from https://assets.ey.com/content/dam/ey-sites/ey-com/en_in/topics/health/2020/09/healthcare-goes-mobile-evolution-of-teleconsultation-and-e-pharmacy-in-new-normal.pdf

[9]Tracxn. 2020. *HealthTech – India and Global Report.* Retrieved on December 27, 2020 from https://tracxn.com/explore/HealthTech-Startups-in-India

[10]https://pmjay.gov.in/about/pmjay

[11]Budget 2021: Finance minister announces Rs 64,180 crore boost for healthcare sector, *Times of India*, February 1 2021, from https://timesofindia.indiatimes.com/business/india-business/budget-2021-finance-minister-announces-rs-64180-crore-boost-for-healthcare-sector/articleshow/80626049.cms

[12]FICCI-BCG Report and NDHM Strategy Overview. 2020. *Making India a Digital Health Nation Enabling Digital Healthcare for all*, retrieved from https://ndhm.gov.in/documents/ndhm_strategy_overview

[13]Jefferies Insights. 2020. *China's New Medical Era: Internet Healthcare On An Unprecedented Scale*, retrieved on December 28, 2020.

[14]IBEF. 2021. *Indian Healthcare Industry Analysis*, retrieved on January 15, 2021 from https://www.ibef.org/industry/healthcare-presentation

[15]TRAI. 2020. *The Indian Telecom Services Performance Indicators*, retrieved on January 30, 2021 from https://www.trai.gov.in/sites/default/files/QPIR_21012021_0.pdf

[16]WHO. 2020. *The Health Workforce in India*, retrieved from https://www.who.int/hrh/resources/16058health_workforce_India.pdf